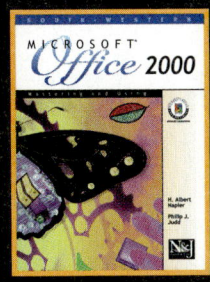

What's New in Office 2000

- ▶ Personalized menus and toolbars
- ▶ Multi-language support
- ▶ Web-based analysis tools
- ▶ Improved Office Assistant
- ▶ Online collaboration with NetMeeting and Web discussions from inside Office applications
- ▶ E-mail from inside Office applications
- ▶ Collect and Paste and Office Clipboard toolbar
- ▶ New Open and Save As dialog box features
- ▶ Saving directly to Web server
- ▶ Improved Clip Gallery format and new clips

Outlook

- ▶ Schedule resources for meetings
- ▶ Save calendars as HTML for Web publishing
- ▶ Create custom distribution lists from Contact Manager
- ▶ Track contact activity, including all related e-mails, tasks, appointments, and documents
- ▶ View Web pages in the Outlook window
- ▶ Create messages in HTML format with other Office applications
- ▶ Better integration with Internet Explorer 5
- ▶ Automatically filter junk e-mail

Word

- ▶ Web themes
- ▶ Web Page Preview
- ▶ Web Layout View (formerly Online Layout View)
- ▶ Print Layout View (formerly Page Layout View)
- ▶ 12-point default font size
- ▶ Nested tables
- ▶ Vertical and horizontal text alignment on Tables and Borders toolbar
- ▶ AutoFit table options on menu
- ▶ New tables properties dialog box
- ▶ Click and Type feature
- ▶ Web Page Wizard to create professional-looking Web pages and multipage Web sites

Excel

- ▶ See-through selection shading
- ▶ Euro currency symbol added to number formats
- ▶ Four-digit date formats
- ▶ List AutoFill automatically extends formatting of lists to new items
- ▶ PivotChart reports created from PivotTable reports
- ▶ Display units can be modified on charts
- ▶ Open and save HTML documents natively
- ▶ Create interactive PivotTables for the Web
- ▶ Create PivotTable reports directly on the worksheet
- ▶ Indented PivotTable report format
- ▶ PivotTable AutoFormat
- ▶ Row and column fields list arrow to hide or display items
- ▶ Digital signing of macros to ensure virus-free status
- ▶ Insert pictures directly from a scanner

PowerPoint

- ▶ Tri-Pane view
- ▶ Normal view
- ▶ AutoFit text
- ▶ Presentation Assistant—includes the StyleChecker, AutoClipArt
- ▶ Native tables
- ▶ Graphic and AutoNumbered bullets
- ▶ Tables and Borders toolbar
- ▶ Web Page Preview
- ▶ Present in Browser
- ▶ More AutoShapes
- ▶ Publish as HTML for the Internet
- ▶ Online Broadcast
- ▶ Send presentation as e-mail attachment
- ▶ Microsoft Script Editor

Access

- ▶ Switchboard
- ▶ Cascade Update and Cascade Delete
- ▶ Data Access Pages
- ▶ Macro builder
- ▶ Encrypting and decrypting a database
- ▶ Add-ins (Database Splitter, Analyzer)
- ▶ Convert database to prior Access version
- ▶ Improved Database window (Objects Bar)
- ▶ Conditional formatting
- ▶ Subdatasheets
- ▶ Drag-and-drop to Excel
- ▶ Hyperlink handling

Napier & Judd

In their over 48 years of combined experience, Al Napier and Phil Judd have developed a tested, realistic approach to mastering and using application software. As both academics and corporate trainers, Al and Phil have the unique ability to help students by teaching them the skills necessary to compete in today's complex business world.

H. Albert Napier, Ph.D. is the Director of the Center on the Management of Information Technology and Professor in the Jones Graduate School of Administration at Rice University. In addition, Al is a principal of Napier & Judd, Inc., a consulting company and corporate trainer in Houston, Texas, that has trained more than 90,000 people in computer applications.

Philip J. Judd is a former instructor in the Management Department and the Director of the Research and Instructional Computing Service at the University of Houston. Phil now dedicates himself to corporate training and consulting as a principal of Napier & Judd, Inc.

Philip J. Judd

H. Albert Napier, Ph.D.

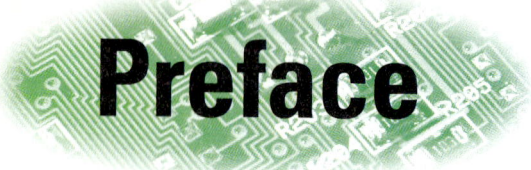Preface

At South-Western Educational Publishing, we believe that technology will change the way people teach and learn. Today there are millions of people using personal computers in their everyday lives—both as tools at work and for recreational activities. As a result, the personal computer has revolutionized the ways in which people interact with each other. The Napier & Judd series combines the following distinguishing features to allow people to do amazing things with their personal computers.

Distinguishing Features

All the textbooks in the *Mastering and Using* series share several key pedagogical features:

Case Project Approach. In their more than twenty years of business and corporate training and teaching experience, Napier and Judd have found that learners are more enthusiastic about learning a software application if they can see its real-world relevance. The textbook provides bountiful business-based profiles, exercises, and projects. It also emphasizes the skills most in demand by employers.

Comprehensive and Easy to Use. There is thorough coverage of new features. The narrative is clear and concise. Each unit or chapter thoroughly explains the concepts that underlie the skills and procedures. We explain not just the *how*, but the *why*.

Step-by-Step Instructions and Screen Illustrations. All examples in this text include step-by-step instructions that explain how to complete the specific task. Full-color screen illustrations are used extensively to provide the learner with a realistic picture of the software application feature.

Extensive Tips and Tricks. The author has placed informational boxes in the margin of the text. These boxes of information provide the learner with the following helpful tips:

► Quick Tip. Extra information provides shortcuts on how to perform common business-related functions.
► Caution Tip. This additional information explains how a mistake occurs and provides tips on how to avoid making similar mistakes in the future.
► Menu Tip. Additional explanation on how to use menu commands to perform application tasks.
► Mouse Tip. Further instructions on how to use the mouse to perform application tasks.
► Internet Tip. This information incorporates the power of the Internet to help learners use the Internet as they progress through the text.
► Design Tip. Hints for better presentation designs (found in only the PowerPoint book).

End-of-Chapter Materials. Each book in the *Mastering and Using* series places a heavy emphasis on providing learners with the opportunity to practice and reinforce the skills they are learning through extensive exercises. Each chapter has a summary, commands review, concepts review, skills review, and case projects so that the learner can master the material by doing. For more information on each of the end-of-chapter elements see page viii of the How to Use this Book section in this preface.

Appendixes. *Mastering and Using* series contains three appendixes to further help the learner prepare to be successful in the classroom or in the workplace. Appendix A teaches the learner to work with Windows 98. Appendix B teaches the learner how to use Windows Explorer; Appendix C illustrates how to format letters; how to insert a mailing notation; how to format envelopes (referencing the U.S. Postal Service documents); how to format interoffice memorandums; and how to key a formal outline. It also lists popular style guides and describes proofreader's marks.

Microsoft Office User Specialist (MOUS) Certification. The logo on the cover of this book indicates that these materials are officially certified by Microsoft Corporation. This certification is part of the MOUS program, which validates your skills as a knowledgeable user of Microsoft applications. Upon completing the lessons in the book, you will be prepared to take a test that could qualify you as either a core or expert user. To be certified, you will need to take an exam from a third-party testing company called an Authorization Certification Testing Center. Call **1-800-933-4493** to find the location of the testing center nearest you. Tests are conducted at different dates throughout the calendar year. To learn more about the entire line of training materials suitable for Microsoft Office certification, contact your South-Western Representative or call **1-800-824-5179.** Also visit our Web site at *www.swep.com.* To learn more about the MOUS program, you can visit Microsoft's Web site at *www.microsoft.com/train_cert/cert/.*

SCANS. In 1992, the U.S. Department of Labor and Education formed the Secretary's Commission on Achieving Necessary Skills, or SCANS, to study the kinds of competencies and skills that workers must have to succeed in today's marketplace. The results of the study were published in a document entitled *What Work Requires of Schools: A SCANS Report for America 2000.* The in-chapter and end-of-chapter exercises in this book are designed to meet the criteria outlined in the SCANS report and thus help prepare learners to be successful in today's workplace.

Instructional Support

All books in the *Mastering and Using* series are supplemented with the following items:

Instructor's Resource Package. This printed instructor's manual contains lesson plans with teaching materials and preparation suggestions, along with tips for implementing instruction and assessment ideas; a suggested syllabus for scheduling semester, block, and quarter classes; and SCANS workplace know how. The printed manual is packaged with an Electronic Instructor CD-ROM. The Electronic Instructor CD-ROM contains all the materials found in the printed manual as well as:

► Student lesson plans	► PowerPoint presentations
► Data files	► Portfolio assessment/worksheets
► Solutions files	► Learning styles strategies
► Test questions	► Career worksheets
► Transparencies	► Tech prep strategies

Testing Tools Package. Testing Tools is a powerful testing and assessment package that enables instructors to create and print tests from test banks designed specifically for South-Western Educational Publishing titles. In addition, instructors with access to a networked computer lab (LAN) or the Internet can administer, grade, and track tests online. Learners can also take online practice tests.

Course. Course is a template-based platform to deliver a Web-based syllabus. It allows instructors to create their own completely customized online syllabus, including lesson descriptions, dates, assignments, grades, and lesson links to other resources on the Web. To access this Web tool, an instructor must be a South-Western customer and contact sales support at 1-800-824-5179 for an access code. After the instructor has set up the online syllabus, students can access the Course.

Learner Support

Activity Workbooks. The workbook includes additional end-of-chapter exercises over and above those provided in the main text.

Data CD-ROM. To use this book, the learner must have the data CD-ROM (also referred to as the Data Disk). Data Files needed to complete exercises in the text are contained on this CD-ROM. These files can be copied to a hard drive or posted to a network drive.

How to Use This Book

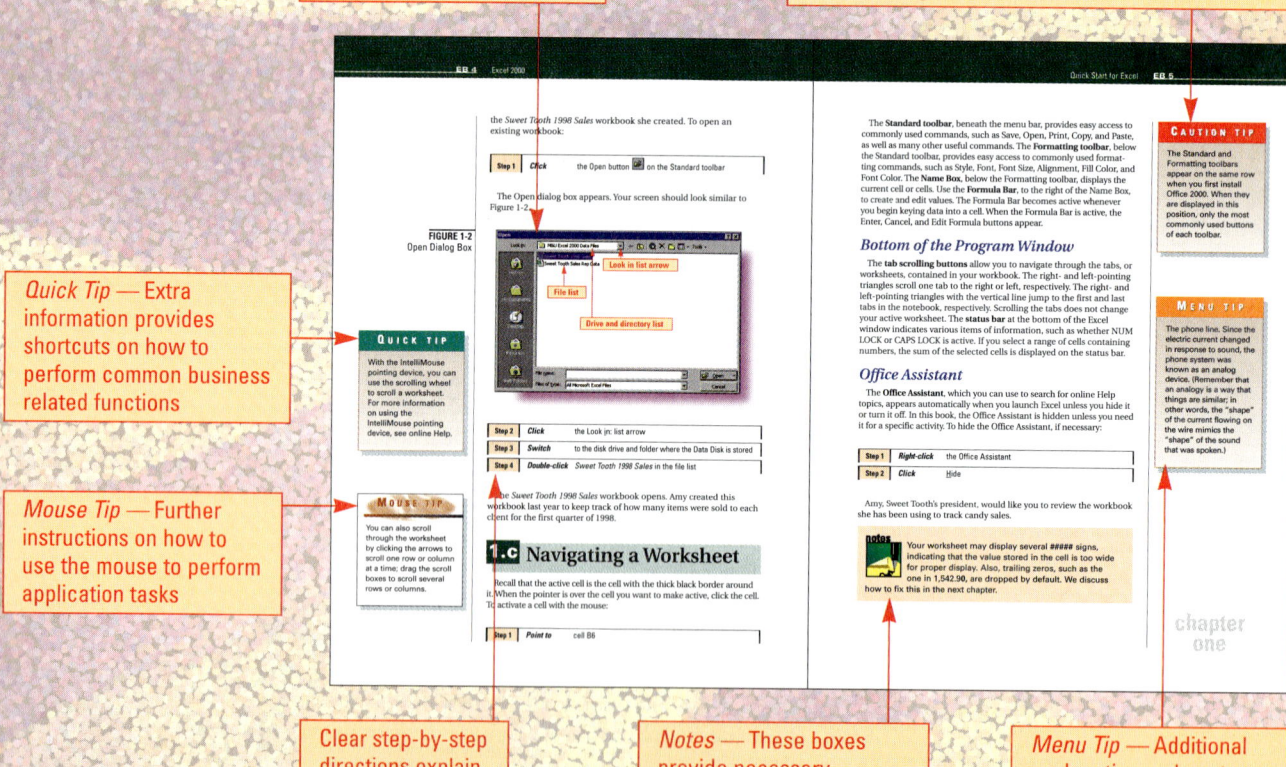

Learning Objectives — A quick reference of the major topics learned in the chapter

Case profile — Realistic scenarios that show the real world application of the material being covered

Chapter Overview — A concise summary of what will be learned in the chapter

Full color screen illustrations provide a realistic picture to the user

Caution Tip — This additional information explains how a mistake occurs and provides tips on how to avoid making similar mistakes in the future

Quick Tip — Extra information provides shortcuts on how to perform common business related functions

Mouse Tip — Further instructions on how to use the mouse to perform application tasks

Clear step-by-step directions explain how to complete the specific task

Notes — These boxes provide necessary information to assist you in completing the exercises

Menu Tip — Additional explanation on how to use menu commands to perform application tasks

End-of-Chapter Material

Concepts Review — Multiple choice and true or false questions help assess how well the reader has learned the chapter material

Summary — Reviews key topics discussed in the chapter

Commands Review — Provides a quick reference and reinforcement tool on multiple methods for performing actions discussed in the chapter

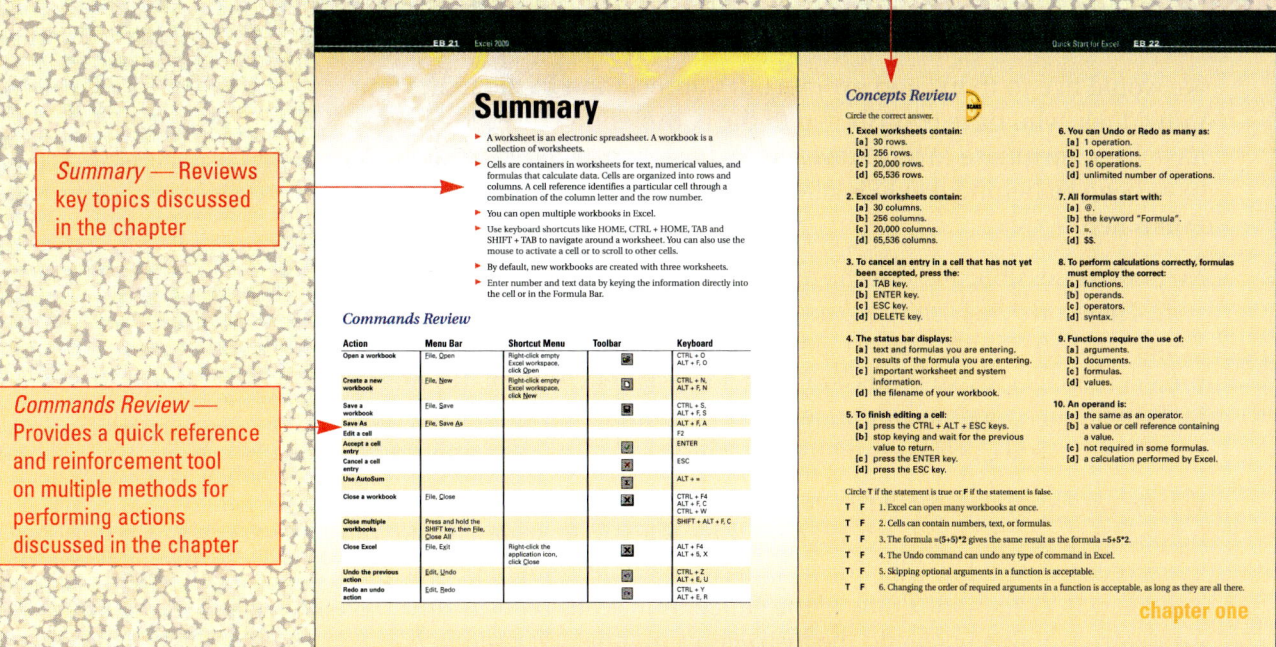

Skills Review — Hands-on exercises provide the ability to practice the skills just learned in the chapter

SCANS icon — Indicates that the exercise or project meets a SCANS competencies and prepares the learner to be successful in today's workplace

Case Projects — Asks the reader to synthesize the material they learned in the chapter and complete an office assignment

Internet Case Projects — Allow the reader to practice using the World Wide Web

MOUS Certification icon — indicates that the exercise or project meets Microsoft's certification objectives that prepare the learner for the MOUS exam

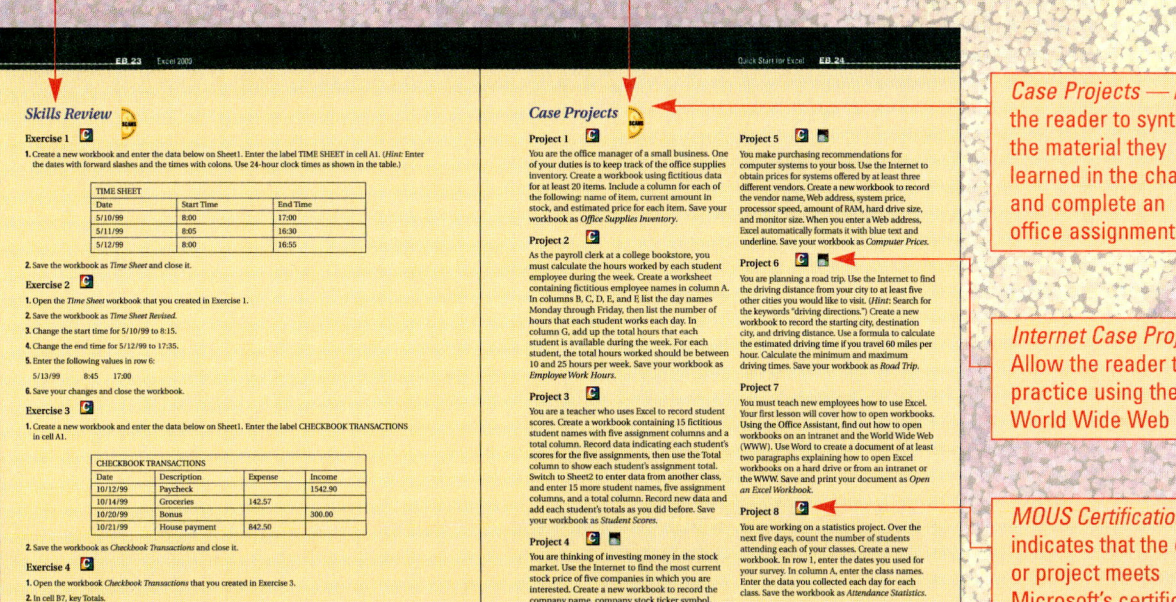

Acknowledgments

We would like to thank and express our appreciation to the many fine individuals who have contributed to the completion of this book. We have been fortunate to have reviewers whose constructive comments have been so helpful: Paul Fletcher, Lucinda Hawes, Kathy Koppy, and Ethan Bell.

No book is possible without the motivation and support of an editorial staff. Therefore, we wish to acknowledge with great appreciation the project team at South-Western Educational Publishing: Cheryl Beck, project manager; Mike Broussard, art and designer coordinator; Angela McDonald, production coordinator; Kathy Hampton, manufacturing coordinator, and Carol Volz, managing editor.

We are very appreciative of the personnel at Napier & Judd, Inc., who helped prepare this book. We acknowledge, with great appreciation, the assistance provided by Ollie Rivers and Nancy Onarheim in preparing and checking the many drafts of the Office unit, Word section, and Appendixes of this book and the instructor's manual. We gratefully acknowledge the work of Linda Sourek and Susan Lehner in writing the PowerPoint unit for this series, Benjamin Rand for the Outlook unit and Excel unit for this series, and Lisa Ruffolo for the Access unit for this series.

Contents

Napier and Judd   **v**

Preface   **vi**

OFFICE UNIT   OF 1

1 Getting Started with Microsoft Office 2000   **OF 2**
a. What Is Microsoft Office 2000   OF 3
b. Hardware and Software Requirements   OF 4
c. Identifying Common Office Elements   OF 4
d. Starting Office Applications   OF 7
e. Getting Help in Office Applications   OF 11
f. Closing Office Applications   OF 16

2 Working with Menus and Toolbars   **OF 20**
a. Working with Personalized Menus and Toolbars   OF 21
b. Viewing, Hiding, Docking, And Floating Toolbars   OF 25
c. Customizing the Menu Bar and Toolbars   OF 27
d. Viewing and Customizing the Office Shortcut Bar   OF 28

3 Working With Others Using Online Collaboration Tools   **OF 35**
a. Scheduling an Online Meeting   OF 36
b. Participating in Web Discussions   OF 42

4 Introduction to the Internet and the World Wide Web   **OF 50**
a. What Is the Internet?   OF 51
b. Connecting to the Internet   OF 52
c. Challenges to Using the Internet   OF 55
d. Using Internet Explorer   OF 56
e. Using Directories and Search Engines   OF 59

OUTLOOK UNIT   OL 1

1 Using Outlook 2000   **OL 1**
a. Identifying the Components of the Outlook Window   OL 2
b. Customizing Outlook   OL 4
c. Using Outlook as an E-mail Client   OL 6
d. Using the Outlook Calendar   OL 11
e. Using the Outlook Contact Manager   OL 16
f. Using the Outlook Task Manager   OL 18
g. Using the Outlook Journal   OL 22
h. Using the Outlook Notes Manager   OL 24
i. Using Advanced Outlook Features   OL 26

WORD UNIT — WB 1

1 Quick Start for Word — WB 2
a. Identifying the Components of the Word Window — WB 3
b. Composing a Simple Document — WB 6
c. Editing a Document — WB 7
d. Saving a Document — WB 8
e. Previewing and Printing a Document — WB 10
f. Closing a Document — WB 11
g. Locating and Opening an Existing Document — WB 11
h. Creating a New Document — WB 18
i. Closing Word — WB 19
j. Send a Word Document via E-mail — WB 19

2 Creating and Editing a Word Document — WB 28
a. Creating a Letter — WB 29
b. Selecting Text — WB 33
c. Cutting, Copying, Inserting, Moving, and Pasting Text — WB 36
d. Deleting Text — WB 40
e. Using the Undo, Redo, and Repeat Commands — WB 40
f. Using the Overtype Mode — WB 41
g. Switching Between Different Editing Views — WB 42

3 Using the Proofing Tools — WB 52
a. Using the Spelling and Grammar Features — WB 53
b. Using the Thesaurus — WB 56
c. Using AutoCorrect — WB 57
d. Using AutoText — WB 62
e. Inserting Dates with AutoComplete — WB 66

4 Formatting Text — WB 75
a. Formatting Characters as You Type — WB 76
b. Selecting and Changing Fonts and Font Sizes — WB 78
c. Applying Font Formats — WB 80
d. Applying Character Effects — WB 83
e. Applying Character Spacing and Animation Effects — WB 87
f. Duplicating Character Formats — WB 88
g. Changing the Case of Text — WB 90
h. Adding Bullets and Numbering — WB 91
i. Highlighting Text in a Document — WB 93
j. Inserting Symbols and Special Characters — WB 94

5 Using the Tabs Command — WB 104
a. Understanding Tabs — WB 105
b. Setting Left Tabs — WB 108
c. Setting Center Tabs — WB 110
d. Setting Decimal Tabs — WB 111
e. Setting Right Tabs — WB 112
f. Setting Tabs with Leaders — WB 114

6 Setting Spacing, Aligning Text, and Using Indentation Options — WB 123
a. Setting Character, Line, and Paragraph Spacing — WB 124
b. Aligning Text Vertically — WB 127
c. Aligning Text in Paragraphs — WB 129
d. Using Indentation Options — WB 131

7 Previewing and Printing a Document   **WB 144**
  a. Using Print Preview   WB 145
  b. Printing A Document   WB 150

8 Preparing and Printing Envelopes and Labels   **WB 159**
  a. Preparing and Printing Envelopes   WB 160
  b. Preparing and Printing Labels   WB 166

9 Working with Documents   **WI 1**
  a. Finding and Replacing Text   WI 2
  b. Inserting Page Breaks   WI 9
  c. Creating Sections with Different Formatting   WI 11
  d. Creating and Modifying Headers and Footers   WI 14
  e. Using Hyphenation   WI 19
  f. Setting Page Orientation   WI 23

10 Working with Columns and Drawing Objects   **WI 32**
  a. Creating and Using Newspaper-Style Columns   WI 33
  b. Using the Drawing Toolbar   WI 38

11 Using Tables to Organize Information   **WI 53**
  a. Creating and Formatting Tables   WI 54
  b. Revising Tables and Modifying Table Structure   WI 60
  c. Using Special Table Features   WI 67
  d. Switching Between Text and Tables   WI 77

12 Using Styles and Templates   **WI 91**
  a. Creating and Applying Styles   WI 92
  b. Editing Styles   WI 98
  c. Using Templates and Wizards to Create Documents   WI 101

13 Generating an Outline   **WI 114**
  a. Organizing a Document in Outline View   WI 115
  b. Modifying an Outline   WI 119
  c. Using Outline Numbered Formats to Create Outlines   WI 125

14 Creating Documents for the Internet or Intranet   **WI 137**
  a. Saving as a Web Page   WI 138
  b. Creating a Web Page   WI 140
  c. Testing and Publishing Web Pages   WI 151

EXCEL UNIT   **EB 1**

1 Quick Start for Excel   **EB 2**
  a. Exploring the Excel Components   EB 3
  b. Locating and Opening an Existing Workbook   EB 5
  c. Navigating a Worksheet   EB 6
  d. Entering Text, Dates, and Numbers   EB 7
  e. Selecting Cells   EB 9
  f. Editing Cell Content   EB 11
  g. Clearing Contents and Formatting of Cells   EB 13
  h. Using Undo and Redo   EB 13
  i. Entering Formulas and Functions   EB 14
  j. Saving Workbooks   EB 18
  k. Closing Workbooks and Exiting Excel   EB 20

2 Formatting Worksheets — **EB 28**
a. Merging Cells to Create a Worksheet Title — EB 29
b. Working with a Series to Add Labels — EB 30
c. Modifying the Size of Columns and Rows — EB 32
d. Changing Fonts and Font Styles — EB 33
e. Modifying the Alignment of Cell Contents — EB 35
f. Rotating Text and Changing Indents — EB 36
g. Applying Number Formats — EB 37
h. Applying Cell Borders and Shading — EB 40

3 Organizing Worksheets Effectively — **EB 52**
a. Performing Single and Multi-level Sorts — EB 53
b. Copying and Moving Data Using Drag and Drop — EB 54
c. Renaming a Worksheet — EB 56
d. Inserting, Moving, Copying, and Deleting Worksheets — EB 56
e. Copy and Move Data Using Cut, Copy, and Paste — EB 58
f. Inserting and Deleting Cells, Rows, and Columns — EB 61
g. Using Absolute, Relative, and Mixed References in Formulas — EB 62
h. Creating and Using Named Ranges — EB 65
i. Freezing and Unfreezing Rows and Columns — EB 67
j. Using Grouping and Outlines — EB 68
k. Checking Spelling in a Worksheet — EB 71

4 Previewing and Printing Worksheets — **EB 80**
a. Previewing and Modifying Page Setup Options — EB 81
b. Inserting and Removing Page Breaks — EB 88
c. Printing an Entire Workbook — EB 90

5 Creating Charts — **EB 98**
a. Using Chart Wizard to Create a Chart — EB 99
b. Formatting and Modifying a Chart — EB 102
c. Previewing and Printing Charts — EB 105
d. Working with Embedded Charts — EB 106

EX Integrating Excel with Office Applications and the Internet — **EX 1**
a. Integrating Excel with Word and PowerPoint — EX 2
b. Integrating Excel with Access — EX 9
c. Importing Data from Other Applications — EX 15
d. Sending a Workbook via E-mail — EX 16
e. Integrating Excel with the Internet — EX 20

PowerPoint Unit — PB 1

1 Quick Start for PowerPoint — **PB 2**
a. Starting PowerPoint — PB 3
b. Exploring the PowerPoint Window — PB 4
c. Navigating through a Presentation — PB 7
d. Navigating Among the PowerPoint Views — PB 7
e. Closing a Presentation — PB 11
f. Applying a Design Template — PB 11
g. Saving a Presentation — PB 14
h. Checking Spelling — PB 15
i. Changing the Presentation Design — PB 16
j. Printing a Presentation — PB 17
k. Exiting PowerPoint — PB 17

2 **Editing and Formatting Slides** **PB 25**
a. Opening a Presentation and Adding a Bullet Slide PB 26
b. Working with Second-Level Bullets PB 26
c. Using AutoCorrect PB 28
d. Working in Outline View PB 30
e. Moving a Slide in Outline View PB 32
f. Editing and Formatting Slides PB 32
g. Formatting the Slide Master PB 38
h. Printing an Individual Slide PB 41

3 **Using Clip Art and WordArt** **PB 49**
a. Using the Microsoft Clip Gallery PB 50
b. Editing Clip Art Images PB 54
c. Inserting Images from Another Source PB 59
d. Adding an Image to the Slide Master PB 59
e. Using the Clipboard Toolbar PB 61
f. Adding WordArt to a Slide PB 62

4 **Using Drawing Tools and AutoShapes** **PB 73**
a. Adding Shapes PB 74
b. Using the AutoShapes Tool PB 77
c. Editing and Formatting Shapes PB 77
d. Using the Format Painter PB 80
e. Working with Multiple Objects PB 80
f. Adding Text PB 84

PX **Integrating Word and Excel with PowerPoint** **PX 1**
a. Sending a PowerPoint Presentation to Word PX 2
b. Sending a Word Outline to a PowerPoint Presentation PX 7
c. Inserting Slides from a Word Outline PX 11
d. Inserting Slides from one PowerPoint Presentation to Another PX 12
e. Adding a Word Table to a PowerPoint Slide PX 14
f. Embedding an Excel Worksheet in a PowerPoint Slide PX 16
g. Linking an Excel Chart to a PowerPoint Slide PX 19

ACCESS UNIT — AB 1

1 **Introduction to Access** **AB 2**
a. Defining Access AB 3
b. Opening the Access Application AB 3
c. Viewing the Access Window AB 5
d. Getting Help AB 7
e. Identifying Access Objects AB 8
f. Exiting Access AB 17

2 **Designing and Creating a Database** **AB 24**
a. Planning a New Database AB 25
b. Creating a Database AB 26
c. Saving a Database AB 27
d. Creating a Table by Using the Table Wizard AB 29
e. Creating a Table in Design View AB 31
f. Modifying Tables Using Design View AB 40
g. Printing a Table AB 44

3 **Entering and Editing Data into Tables**   **AB 52**
  a. Entering Records Using a Datasheet   AB 53
  b. Navigating Through Records   AB 55
  c. Modifying Data in a Table   AB 55
  d. Adding Pictures to Records   AB 61

4 **Designing and Using Basic Forms**   **AB 70**
  a. Understanding Forms   AB 71
  b. Creating a Form with the Form Wizard   AB 71
  c. Creating a Custom Form   AB 77
  d. Modifying a Form Design   AB 80
  e. Using the Control Toolbox to Add and Modify Controls   AB 83
  f. Modifying Format Properties   AB 87
  g. Printing a Form   AB 90

AX **Integrating Access with Other Office Applications and the Internet**   **AX 1**
  a. Exporting Database Objects   AX 2
  b. Exporting Database Records to Excel   AX 9
  c. Using Excel Data with Access   AX 11
  d. Integrating Access with the Internet   AX 20

APPENDIX   AP 1

A **Working with Windows 98**   **AP 1**
  a. Reviewing the Windows 98 Desktop   AP 2
  b. Accessing Your Computer System Resources   AP 3
  c. Using Menu Commands and Toolbar Buttons   AP 5
  d. Using the Start Menu   AP 6
  e. Reviewing Dialog Box Options   AP 7
  f. Using Windows 98 Shortcuts   AP 8
  g. Understanding the Recycle Bin   AP 10
  h. Shutting Down Windows 98   AP 10

B **Managing Your Folders and Files Using Windows Explorer**   **AP 11**
  a. Opening Windows Explorer   AP 12
  b. Reviewing Windows Explorer Options   AP 13
  c. Creating a New Folder   AP 14
  d. Moving and Copying Folders and Files   AP 15
  e. Renaming Folders and Files   AP 15
  f. Creating Desktop Shortcuts   AP 16
  g. Deleting Folders and Files   AP 16

C **Formatting Tips for Business Documents**   **AP 17**
  a. Formatting Letters   AP 18
  b. Inserting Mailing Notations   AP 22
  c. Formatting Envelopes   AP 24
  d. Formatting Interoffice Memorandums   AP 26
  e. Formatting Formal Outlines   AP 28
  f. Using Proofreader's Marks   AP 30
  g. Using Style Guides   AP 31

Index   I 1

Microsoft
Office 2000

Office 2000

Getting Started with Microsoft Office 2000

Chapter Overview

Microsoft Office 2000 provides the ability to enter, record, analyze, display, and present any type of business information. In this chapter you learn about the capabilities of Microsoft Office 2000, including its computer hardware and software requirements and elements common to all its applications. You also learn how to open and close those applications and get help.

LEARNING OBJECTIVES

- ▶ Describe Microsoft Office 2000
- ▶ Determine hardware and software requirements
- ▶ Identify common Office elements
- ▶ Start Office applications
- ▶ Get help in Office applications
- ▶ Close Office applications

For more information on how to prepare for the MOUS certification exam, check out the MOUS certification grids located on the data CD-ROM under the MOUS correlation folder for each book.

chapter
one
1

1.a What Is Microsoft Office 2000?

Microsoft Office 2000 is a software suite (or package) that contains a combination of software applications you use to create text documents, analyze numbers, create presentations, manage large files of data, create Web pages, and create professional-looking marketing materials. Table 1-1 lists four editions of the Office 2000 suite and the software applications included in each.

Applications	Premium	Professional	Standard	Small Business
Word	X	X	X	X
Excel	X	X	X	X
PowerPoint	X	X	X	
Access	X	X		
Outlook	X	X	X	X
Publisher	X	X		X
FrontPage	X			

TABLE 1-1
Office 2000 Editions

The **Word 2000** software application provides you with word processing capabilities. **Word processing** is the preparation and production of text documents such as letters, memorandums, and reports. **Excel 2000** is software you use to analyze numbers with worksheets (sometimes called spreadsheets) and charts, as well as perform other tasks such as sorting data. A **worksheet** is a grid of columns and rows in which you enter labels and data. A **chart** is a visual or graphic representation of worksheet data. With Excel, you can create financial budgets, reports, and a variety of other forms.

PowerPoint 2000 software is used to create **presentations,** a collection of slides. A **slide** is the presentation output (actual 35mm slides, transparencies, computer screens, or printed pages) that contains text, charts, graphics, audio, and video. You can use PowerPoint slides to create a slide show on a computer attached to a projector, to broadcast a presentation over the Internet or company intranet, and to create handout materials for a presentation.

Access 2000 provides database management capabilities, enabling you to store and retrieve a large amount of data. A **database** is a collection of related information. A phone book or an address book are common examples of databases you use every day. Other databases include a price list, school registration information, or an inventory. You can query (or search) an Access database to answer specific questions about the stored data. For example, you can determine which customers in a particular state had sales in excess of a particular value during the month of June.

CAUTION TIP

This book assumes that you have little or no knowledge of Microsoft Office 2000, but that you have worked with personal computers and are familiar with Microsoft Windows 98 or Windows 95 operating systems.

QUICK TIP

Microsoft Office 2000 is often called Office and the individual applications are called Word, Excel, PowerPoint, Access, Outlook, Publisher, and so on.

chapter
one

MENU TIP

Publisher tutorials are a series of hyperlinked windows providing a brief introduction to a specific topic. Each window contains a series of hyperlink buttons at the bottom of the window you use to advance to the next tutorial page or return to the main tutorial menu. To review the online tutorials, open Publisher, click the <u>H</u>elp menu, and then click Publisher T<u>u</u>torials.

QUICK TIP

If you store your files and documents on diskette, make sure you have the proper type of diskette for your computer. A disk storage box is a good way to store and protect diskettes you are not using.

Outlook 2000 is a **personal information manager** that enables you to send and receive e-mail, as well as maintain a calendar, contacts list, journal, electronic notes, and an electronic "to do" list. **Publisher 2000** is desktop publishing software used to create publications, such as professional-looking marketing materials, newsletters, or brochures. Publisher wizards provide step-by-step instructions for creating a publication from an existing design; you also can design your own publication. The **FrontPage 2000** application is used to create and manage Web sites. **PhotoDraw 2000** is business graphics software that allows users to add custom graphics to marketing materials and Web pages.

A major advantage of using an Office suite is the ability to share data between applications. For example, you can include a portion of an Excel worksheet or chart in a Word document, use an outline created in a Word document as the starting point for a PowerPoint presentation, import an Excel worksheet into Access, merge names and addresses from an Outlook Address Book with a Word letter, or import a picture from PhotoDraw into a newsletter created in Publisher.

1.b Hardware and Software Requirements

You must install Office 2000 applications in Windows 95, Windows 98, or Windows NT Workstation 4.0 with Service Pack 3.0 installed. The applications will not run in the Windows 3.x or the Windows NT Workstation 3.5 environments.

Microsoft recommends that you install Office on a computer that has a Pentium processor, at least 32 MB of RAM, a CD-ROM drive, Super VGA, 256-color video, Microsoft Mouse, Microsoft IntelliMouse, or another pointing device, and at least a 28,800-baud modem. To access certain features you should have a multimedia computer, e-mail software, and a Web browser. For detailed information on installing Office, see the documentation that comes with the software.

1.c Identifying Common Office Elements

Office applications share many common elements, making it easier for you to work efficiently in any application. A **window** is a rectangular area on your screen in which you view a software application, such as Excel. All the Office application windows have a similar look and arrangement of shortcuts, menus, and toolbars. In addition, they share many features, such as a common dictionary to use for spell checking your work and identical menu commands, toolbar buttons, shortcut menus, and keyboard shortcuts that enable you to perform tasks such as copying data from one location to another. Figure 1-1 shows the common elements in the Office application windows.

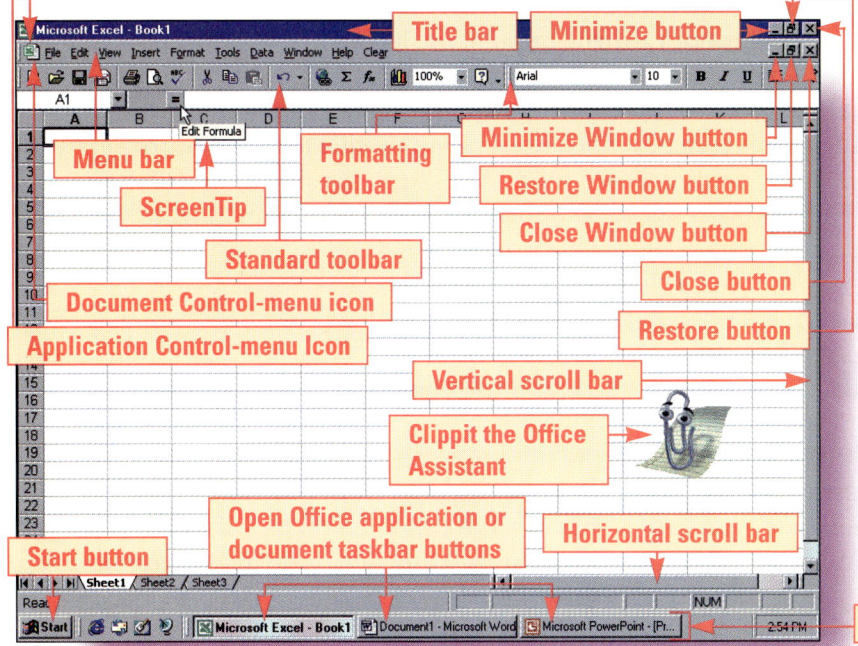

FIGURE 1-1
Common Elements in Office Application Windows

Title Bar

The application **title bar** at the top of the window includes the application Control-menu icon, the application name, the filename of the active document, and the Minimize, Restore (or Maximize), and Close buttons.

The **application Control-menu** icon, located in the left corner of the title bar, displays the Control menu. The Control menu commands manage the application window, and typically include commands such as: Restore, Move, Size, Minimize, Maximize, and Close. Commands that are currently available appear in a darker color. You can view the Control menu by clicking the Control-menu icon or by holding down the ALT key and then pressing the SPACEBAR key.

The **Minimize** button, near the right corner of the title bar reduces the application window to a taskbar button. The **Maximize** button, to the right of the Minimize button, enlarges the application window to fill the entire screen viewing area above the taskbar. If the window is already maximized, the Restore button appears in its place. The **Restore** button reduces the application window size. The **Close** button, located in the right corner of the title bar, closes the application and removes it from the computer's memory.

CAUTION TIP

In order to save hard disk space, Office installs many features and components as you need them. Shortcuts, toolbar buttons, and menu commands for these features appear in the application window or dialog boxes, indicating that the feature is available.

chapter
one

Menu Bar

The **menu bar** is a special toolbar located below the title bar and contains the menus for the application. A **menu** is list of commands. The menus common to Office applications are File, Edit, View, Insert, Format, Tools, Window, and Help. Each application may have additional menus.

The **document Control-menu** icon, located below the application Control-menu icon, contains the Restore, Move, Size, Minimize, Maximize, and Close menu commands for the document window. You can view the document Control menu by clicking the Control-menu icon or by holding down the ALT key and pressing the HYPHEN (-) key.

The **Minimize Window** button reduces the document window to a title-bar icon inside the document area. It appears on the menu bar below the Minimize button in Excel and PowerPoint. (Word documents open in their own application window and use the title bar Minimize button.)

The **Maximize Window** button enlarges the document window to cover the entire application display area and share the application title bar. It appears on the title-bar icon of a minimized Excel workbook or PowerPoint presentation. (Word documents open in their own application window and use the title bar Maximize button.) If the window is already maximized, the Restore Window button appears in its place.

The **Restore Window** button changes the document window to a smaller sized window inside the application window. It appears to the right of the Minimize Window button in Excel and PowerPoint. (Word documents open in their own application window and use the title bar Restore button.)

The **Close Window** button closes the document and removes it from the computer's memory. It appears to the right of the Restore Window or Maximize Window button. (In Word, the Close Window button appears only when one document is open. Otherwise, Word uses the title bar Close button.)

Default Toolbars

The **Standard** and **Formatting toolbars,** located on one row below the menu bar, contain a set of icons called buttons. The toolbar buttons represent commonly used commands and are mouse shortcuts used to perform tasks quickly. In addition to the Standard and Formatting toolbars, each application has several other toolbars available. You can customize toolbars by adding or removing buttons and commands.

When the mouse pointer rests on a toolbar button, a **ScreenTip** appears identifying the name of the button. ScreenTips, part of online Help, describe a toolbar button, dialog box option, or menu command.

Scroll Bars

The **vertical scroll bar,** on the right side of the document area, is used to view various parts of the document by moving, or scrolling, the document up or down. It includes scroll arrows and a scroll box. The **horizontal scroll bar**, near the bottom of the document area, is used to view various parts of the document by scrolling the document left or right. It includes scroll arrows and a scroll box.

Office Assistant

The **Office Assistant** is an animated graphic you can click to view online Help. The Office Assistant may also anticipate your needs and provide advice in a balloon-style dialog box when you begin certain tasks, such as writing a letter in Word.

Taskbar

The **taskbar,** located across the bottom of the Windows desktop, includes the Start button and buttons for each open Office document. The **Start button,** located in the left corner of the taskbar, displays the Start menu or list of tasks you can perform and applications you can use.

You can switch between documents, close documents and applications, and view other items, such as the system time and printer status, with buttons or icons on the taskbar. If you are using Windows 98, other toolbars—such as the Quick Launch toolbar—may also appear on the taskbar.

QUICK TIP

You can use the keyboard to access Office application features. This book lists all keys in uppercase letters, such as the TAB key. This book lists keystrokes as: Press the ENTER key. When you are to press one key and, while holding down that key, to press another key, this book lists the keystrokes as: Press the SHIFT + F7 keys.

1.d Starting Office Applications

You access the Office applications through the Windows desktop. When you turn on your computer, the Windows operating system software is automatically loaded into memory. Once the process is complete, your screen should look similar to Figure 1-2.

notes The desktop illustrations in this book assume you are using Windows 98 with default settings. Your desktop may not look identical to the illustrations in this book. For more information on using Windows 98 see Appendix A or information provided by your instructor.

chapter one

FIGURE 1-2
Default Windows 98
Desktop

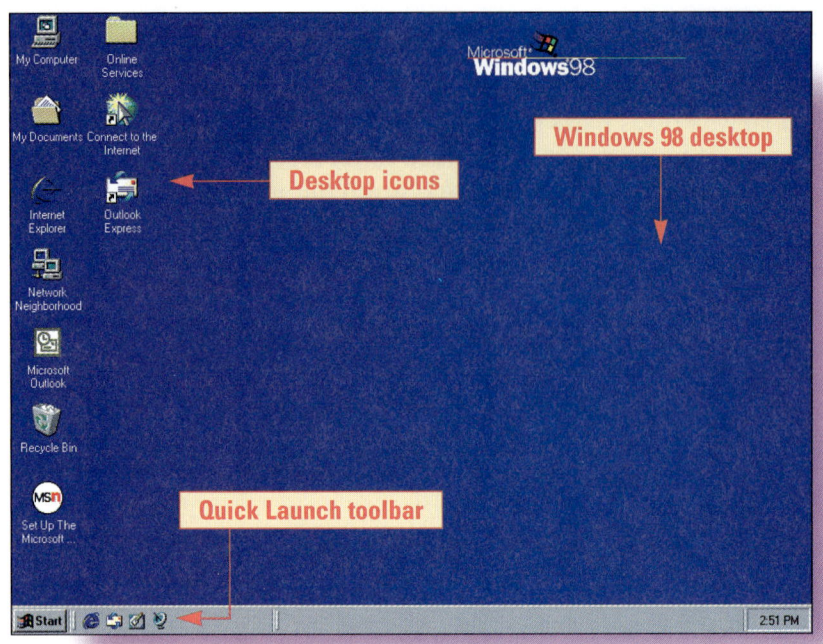

You begin by opening the Excel application. To use Start button to open Excel:

Step 1	*Click*	the Start button [Start] on the taskbar
Step 2	*Point to*	Programs
Step 3	*Click*	Microsoft Excel on the Programs menu

The Excel software is placed into the memory of your computer and the Excel window opens. Your screen should look similar to Figure 1-1.

You can open and work in more than one Office application at a time. When Office is installed, the Open Office Document command and the New Office Document command appear on the Start menu. You can use these commands to select the type of document on which you want to work rather than first selecting an Office application. To create a new Word document without first opening the application:

Step 1	*Click*	the Start button [Start] on the taskbar
Step 2	*Click*	New Office Document
Step 3	*Click*	the General tab, if necessary

The dialog box that opens should look similar to Figure 1-3.

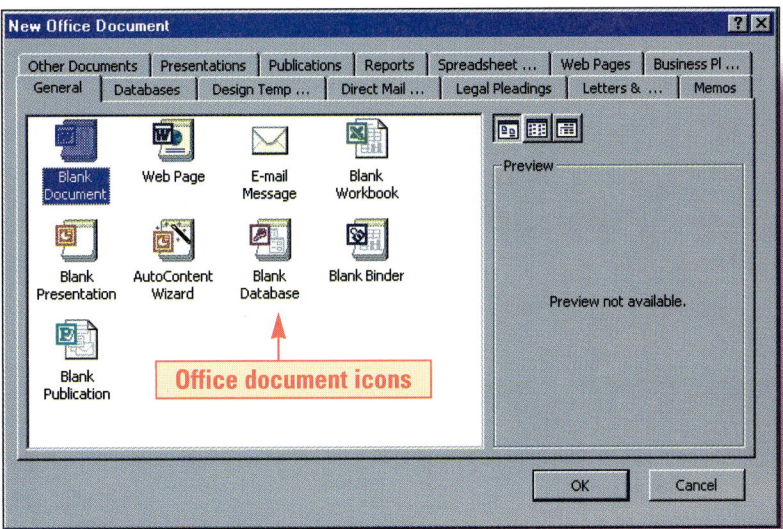

Office document icons

FIGURE 1-3
General Tab in
the New Office
Document Dialog Box

QUICK TIP

A **dialog box** is a window that contains options for performing specific tasks. The New Office Document dialog box contains **icons** (or pictures) for creating a blank Word document, Web page (in Word), e-mail message (using Outlook or Outlook Express), Excel workbook, PowerPoint presentation, Access database, or Publisher publication. The available icons depends on the Office applications you have installed.

To create a blank Word document:

| Step 1 | *Click* | the Blank Document icon to select it, if necessary |
| Step 2 | *Click* | OK |

The Word software loads into your computer's memory, the Word application opens with a blank document, and a taskbar button appears for the document. Your screen should look similar to Figure 1-4.

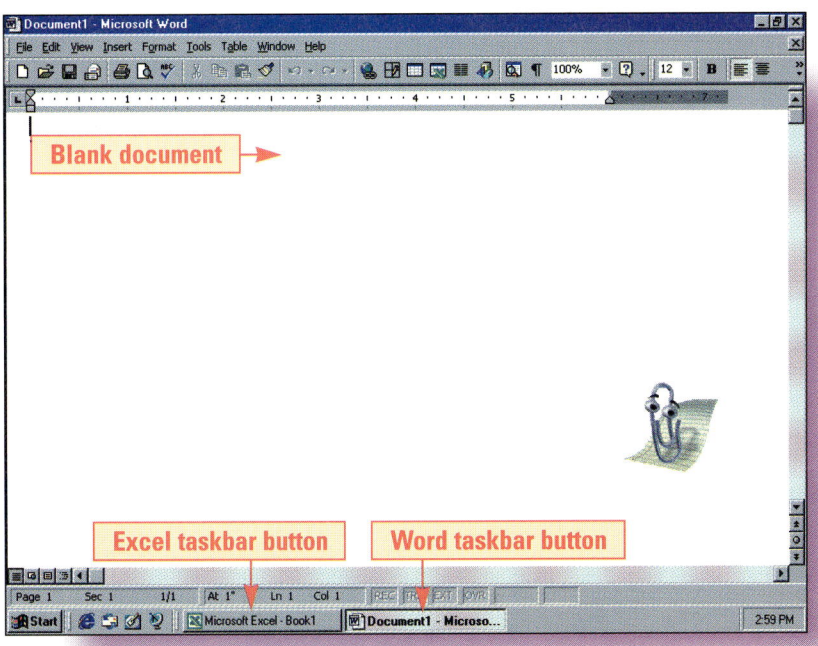

Blank document

Excel taskbar button   Word taskbar button

FIGURE 1-4
Word Application Window

chapter
one

Next you open a blank presentation. To open the PowerPoint application and a blank presentation:

Step 1	*Open*	the New Office Document dialog box using the Start menu
Step 2	*Double-click*	the Blank Presentation icon
Step 3	*Click*	OK in the New Slide dialog box to create a blank title slide, as shown in Figure 1-5

FIGURE 1-5
Blank PowerPoint
Presentation

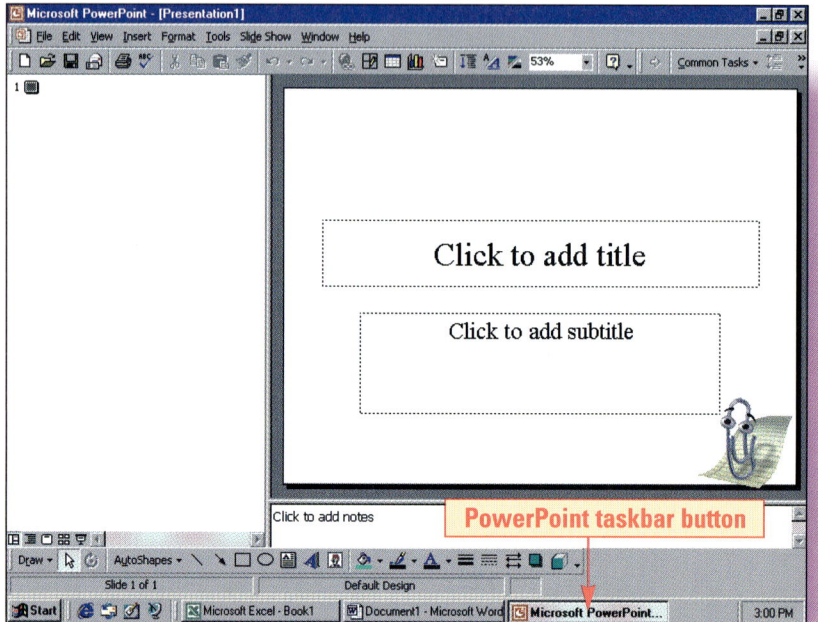

PowerPoint taskbar button

You can also open an Office application by opening an existing Office document from the Start menu. To open an existing Access database:

Step 1	*View*	the Start button 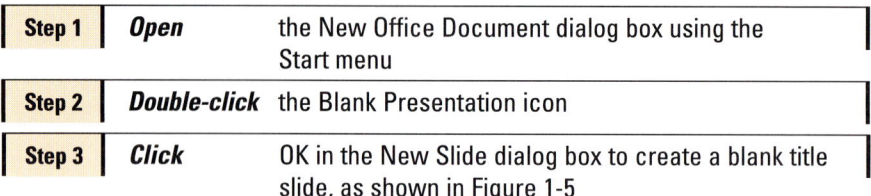 on the taskbar
Step 2	*Click*	Open Office Document
Step 3	*Click*	the Look in: list arrow in the Open Office Document dialog box
Step 4	*Switch*	to the disk drive and folder where the Data Files are stored
Step 5	*Double-click*	*International Sales* to open the Access application and database, as shown in Figure 1-6

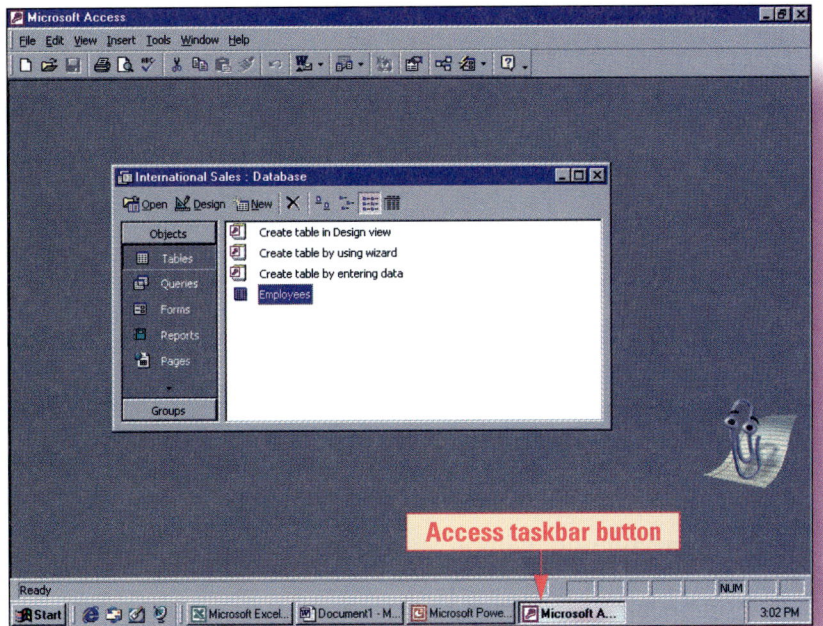

FIGURE 1-6
International Sales Database in Access Window

You can switch between open Office documents by clicking the appropriate taskbar button. To switch to the Excel workbook and then the Word document:

Step 1	*Click*	the Excel button on the taskbar
Step 2	*Observe*	that the Excel window and workbook are visible
Step 3	*Click*	the Word Document1 button on the taskbar
Step 4	*Observe*	that the Word window and document are visible

QUICK TIP

If multiple windows are open, the **active window** has a dark blue title bar. Inactive windows have a light gray title bar.

1.e Getting Help in Office Applications

There are several ways to get help in any Office application. You can display the Office Assistant, get context-sensitive help, or launch your Web browser and get Web-based help from Microsoft.

Using the Office Assistant

The **Office Assistant** is an interactive, animated graphic that appears in the Word, Excel, PowerPoint, and Publisher application windows. When you activate the Office Assistant, a balloon-style dialog box

chapter
one

opens containing options for searching online Help by topic. The Office Assistant may also automatically offer suggestions when you begin certain tasks. As you begin to key a personal letter to Aunt Isabel, the Office Assistant automatically asks if you want help writing the letter. To begin the letter:

Step 1	*Verify*	the Word document is the active window
Step 2	*Click*	the Microsoft Word Help button [?] on the Standard toolbar, if the Office Assistant is not visible
Step 3	*Key*	Dear Aunt Isabel: (including the colon)
Step 4	*Press*	the ENTER key

The Office Assistant and balloon appear. Your screen should look similar to Figure 1-7.

FIGURE 1-7
Office Assistant Balloon

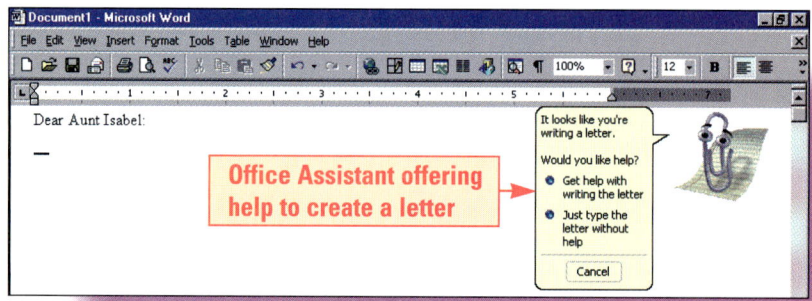

Office Assistant offering help to create a letter

The Office Assistant balloon contains three options you can click with the mouse. If you click the "Get help with writing the letter" option, the Letter Wizard dialog box opens. A **wizard** is a series of dialog boxes you can use to complete a task step-by-step. If you click the "Just type the letter without help" option or the Cancel option, the balloon closes.

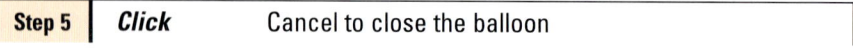

Step 5	*Click*	Cancel to close the balloon

If you prefer to use the Microsoft Help window to access online Help, you can choose to show or hide the Office Assistant or you can turn off the Office Assistant completely. To hide the Office Assistant:

Step 1	*Right-click*	the Office Assistant
Step 2	*Click*	<u>H</u>ide

You can activate the Office Assistant at any time to search online help for specific topics or to customize the Office Assistant. Custom options affect all Office applications. To review the Office Assistant customization options:

Step 1	*Click*	the Microsoft Word Help button 🔲 on the Standard toolbar
Step 2	*Click*	the Office Assistant to view the balloon, if necessary
Step 3	*Click*	Options in the Office Assistant balloon
Step 4	*Click*	the Options tab, if necessary

The dialog box that opens should look similar to Figure 1-8.

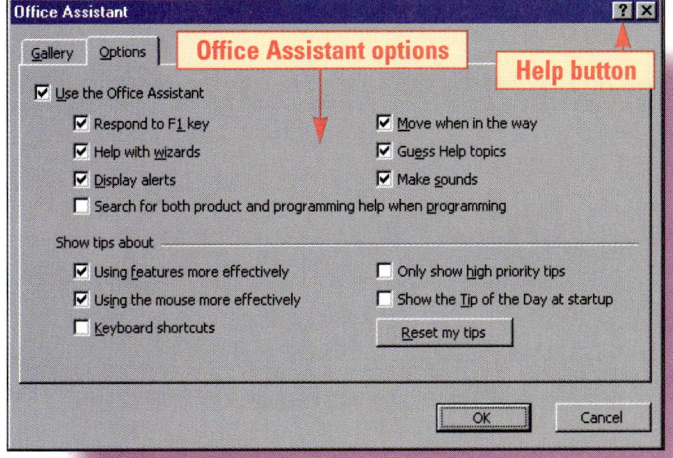

FIGURE 1-8
Options Tab in the Office Assistant Dialog Box

To learn about dialog box options, you can use the dialog box Help button or you can right-click an option. To view the ScreenTip help:

Step 1	*Drag*	the Office Assistant out of the way, if necessary
Step 2	*Right-click*	the Keyboard shortcuts option
Step 3	*Click*	What's This? to view a ScreenTip help message for this option
Step 4	*Press*	the ESC key to close the ScreenTip help message

The default Office Assistant image is Clippit. But you can select from a gallery of animated images. To view the Office Assistant image options:

| Step 1 | *Click* | the Gallery tab |

MENU TIP

You can hide the Office Assistant by clicking the Hide the Office Assistant command on the Help menu. You can redisplay the Office Assistant by clicking the Show the Office Assistant on the Help menu.

MOUSE TIP

You can drag the Office Assistant to a new location with the mouse pointer.

chapter
one

| Step 2 | *Click* | the <u>N</u>ext> and <<u>B</u>ack buttons to view different image options |
| Step 3 | *Click* | Cancel to close the dialog box without changing any options |

You can use the Office Assistant to search an application's online Help. Suppose you want to learn how to turn off the Office Assistant. To search online Help:

Step 1	*Click*	the Office Assistant to activate the balloon
Step 2	*Key*	turn off the Office Assistant in the text box
Step 3	*Press*	the ENTER key to view a list of help options in the balloon dialog box
Step 4	*Click*	the Hide, show, or turn off the Office Assistant option

The Microsoft Word Help window opens and contains information about how to manage the Office Assistant. Your screen should look similar to Figure 1-9.

FIGURE 1-9
Microsoft Word
Help Window

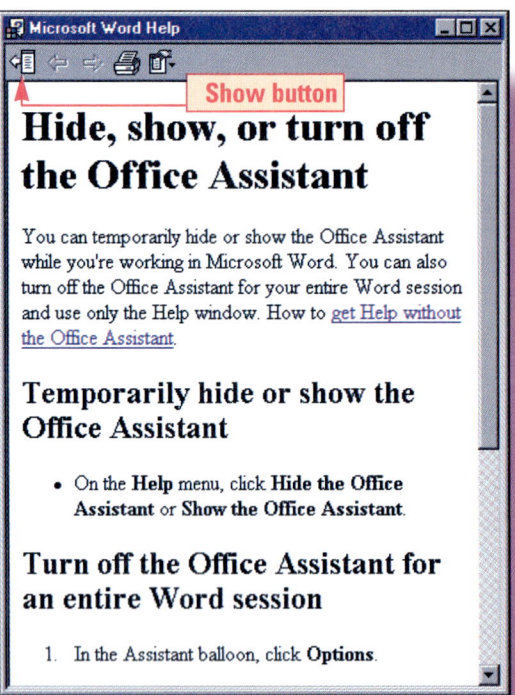

You can scroll the Help window to view all the information. You can click the Show button to view the <u>C</u>ontents, <u>A</u>nswer Wizard, and <u>I</u>ndex tabs that access other help topics. If you have Internet access, you can view a Microsoft Help Web page from inside the Help window. To view the additional tabs:

| Step 1 | *Click* | the Show button in the Help window, if necessary, to display the Contents, Answer Wizard, and Index tabs |
| Step 2 | *Click* | the Close button ☒ in the upper-right corner of the window |

Using the Help Menu

The Help menu provides commands you can use to view the Office Assistant or Help window, show or hide the Office Assistant, connect to the Microsoft Web site, get context-sensitive help for a menu command or toolbar button, detect and repair font and template files, and view licensing information for the Office application. To review the Help menu commands:

Step 1	*Click*	Help
Step 2	*Observe*	the menu commands
Step 3	*Click*	in the document area outside the menu to close the Help menu

Using What's This?

You can get context-sensitive help for a menu command or toolbar button using the What's This? command on the Help menu. This command changes the mouse pointer to a help pointer, a white mouse pointer with a large black question mark. When you click a toolbar button or menu command with the help pointer, a brief ScreenTip help message appears describing the command or toolbar button. To a ScreenTip help message for a toolbar button:

Step 1	*Press*	the SHIFT + F1 keys
Step 2	*Observe*	that the help mouse pointer with the attached question mark
Step 3	*Click*	the Save button 💾 on the Standard toolbar
Step 4	*Observe*	the ScreenTip help message describing the Save button
Step 5	*Press*	the ESC key to close the ScreenTip help message

> **QUICK TIP**
>
> You can press the ESC key to close a menu.

chapter
one

1.f Closing Office Applications

There are many ways to close the Access, Excel and PowerPoint applications (or the Word application with a single document open) and return to the Windows desktop. You can: (1) double-click the application Control-menu icon; (2) click the application Close button; (3) right-click the application taskbar button and then click the Close command on the shortcut menu; (4) press the ALT + F4 keys; or (5) click the Exit command on the File menu to close Office applications (no matter how many Word documents are open). To close the Excel application from the taskbar:

Step 1	*Right-click*	the Excel button on the taskbar
Step 2	*Click*	Close

You can close multiple applications at one time from the taskbar by selecting the application buttons using the CTRL key and then using the shortcut menu. To close the PowerPoint and Access applications:

Step 1	*Press & Hold*	the CTRL key
Step 2	*Click*	the PowerPoint button and then the Access button on the taskbar
Step 3	*Release*	the CTRL key and observe that both buttons are selected (pressed in)
Step 4	*Right-click*	the PowerPoint or Access button
Step 5	*Click*	Close

Both applications close, leaving only the Word document open. To close the Word document using the menu:

Step 1	*Verify*	that the Word application window is maximized
Step 2	*Click*	File
Step 3	*Click*	Exit
Step 4	*Click*	No in the Office Assistant balloon or confirmation dialog box to close Word without saving the document

Summary

- The Word application provides word processing capabilities for the preparation of text documents such as letters, memorandums, and reports.

- The Excel application provides the ability to analyze numbers in worksheets and for creating financial budgets, reports, charts, and forms.

- The PowerPoint application is used to create presentation slides and audience handouts.

- You can use Access databases to organize and retrieve collections of data.

- Publisher provides tools for creating marketing materials, such as newsletters, brochures, flyers, and Web pages.

- The Outlook application helps you send and receive e-mail, maintain a calendar, "to do" lists, organize the names and addresses of contacts, and perform other information management tasks.

- One major advantage of Office suite applications is the ability to integrate the applications by sharing information between them.

- Another advantage of using Office suite applications is that they share a number of common elements, such as window elements, shortcuts, toolbars, menu commands, and other features.

- You can start Office suite applications from the Programs submenu on the Start menu and from the Open Office Document or New Office Document commands on the Start menu.

- You can close Office applications by double-clicking the application Control Menu icon, clicking the application Close button on the title bar, right-clicking the application button on the taskbar, pressing the ALT + F4 keys, or clicking the Exit command on the File menu.

- You can get help in an Office application by clicking commands on the Help menu, pressing the F1 or SHIFT + F1 keys, or clicking the Microsoft Help button on the Standard toolbar.

chapter one

Concepts Review

Circle the correct answer.

1. ScreenTips do not provide:
   [a] the name of a button on a toolbar.
   [b] help for options in a dialog box.
   [c] context-sensitive help for menu commands or toolbar buttons.
   [d] access to the Office Assistant.

2. To manage a Web site, you can use:
   [a] Outlook.
   [b] FrontPage.
   [c] PhotoDraw.
   [d] Publisher.

3. The title bar contains the:
   [a] document Control-menu icon.
   [b] Close Window button.
   [c] Standard toolbar.
   [d] application and document name.

4. The Excel application is best used to:
   [a] prepare financial reports.
   [b] maintain a list of tasks to accomplish.
   [c] create newsletters, brochures, and flyers.
   [d] create custom graphics.

Circle **T** if the statement is true or **F** if the statement is false.
T   F   1. You use Publisher to create newsletters and brochures.
T   F   2. Excel is used to create presentation slides.
T   F   3. The default Office Assistant graphic is Clippit.
T   F   4. Access is used to create and format text.

Skills Review

Exercise 1

1. Identify each common element of Office application windows numbered in Figure 1-10.

FIGURE 1-10
Excel Application Window

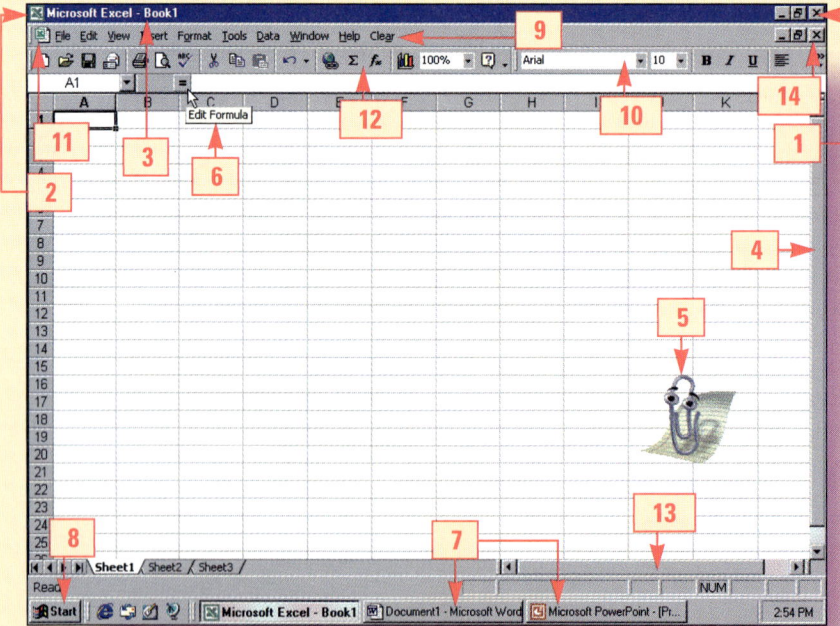

Exercise 2

1. Open the Word application using the Programs command on the Start menu.
2. Close the Word application using the taskbar.

Exercise 3

1. Open the Excel application and then the PowerPoint application using the <u>P</u>rograms command on the Start menu.
2. Open the Access application and the *International Sales* database using the Open Office Document command on the Start menu.
3. Switch to the PowerPoint application using the taskbar button and close it using the Close button on the title bar.
4. Close the PowerPoint and Access applications at the same time using the taskbar.

Exercise 4

1. Create a new, blank Word document using the New Office Document command on the Start menu.
2. Create a new, blank Excel workbook using the New Office Document command on the Start menu.
3. Switch to the Word document using the taskbar and close it using the title bar Close button.
4. Close the Excel workbook using the taskbar button.

Exercise 5

1. Open the Word application using the Start menu.
2. Show the Office Assistant, if necessary, with a command on the <u>H</u>elp menu.
3. Hide the Office Assistant with a shortcut menu.
4. Show the Office Assistant with the Microsoft Word Help button on the Standard toolbar.
5. Search online Help using the search phrase "type text." Open the Type text help page.
6. Click the underlined text <u>typing text</u> to view a help page of subtopics. Scroll and review the help page.
7. Close the Help window. Hide the Office Assistant with a shortcut menu.

Case Projects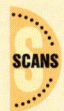

Project 1

You are the secretary to the marketing manager of High Risk Insurance, an insurance brokerage firm. The marketing manager wants to know how to open and close the Excel application. Write at least two paragraphs describing different ways to open and close Excel. With your instructor's permission, use your written description to show a classmate several ways to open and close Excel.

Project 2

You work in the administrative offices of Alma Public Relations, and the information management department just installed Office 2000 Professional on your computer. Your supervisor asks you to write down and describe some of the Office Assistant options. Open the <u>O</u>ptions tab in the Office Assistant dialog box. Review each option using the dialog box Help button or the What's This? command. Write at least three paragraphs describing five Office Assistant options.

Project 3

As the new office manager at Hot Wheels Messenger Service, you are learning to use the Word 2000 application and want to learn more about some of the buttons on the Word toolbars. Open Word and use the What's This? command on the <u>H</u>elp menu to review the ScreenTip help for five toolbar buttons. Write a brief paragraph for each button describing how it is used.

Project 4

As the acquisitions director for Osiris Books, an international antique book and map dealer, you use Publisher to create the company's catalogs and brochures. A co-worker, who is helping you with a new brochure, opened Publisher and did not know why the Catalog window appeared. She has asked you for an explanation. Open the Publisher application and review the Catalog window. Close the Catalog window leaving the Publisher window open. Use the Office Assistant to find out more about the Catalog by searching online Help using the keyword "catalog." Write your co-worker a short note explaining how the Catalog is used.

chapter one

Working with Menus and Toolbars

Chapter Overview

Office 2000 tries to make your work life easier by learning how you work. The personalized menus and toolbars in each application remember which commands and buttons you use, and add and remove them as needed. In this chapter, you learn how to work with the personalized menus and toolbars, how to customize the menu bar and toolbars, and how to view and customize the Office Shortcut Bar.

LEARNING OBJECTIVES

► **Work with personalized menus and toolbars**
► **View, hide, dock, and float toolbars**
► **Customize the menu bar and toolbars**
► **View and customize the Office Shortcut Bar**

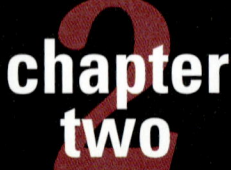

chapter
two

2.a Working with Personalized Menus and Toolbars

A **menu** is a list of commands you use to perform tasks in the Office applications. Some commands also have an associated image, or icon, shown to the left of a command. A **toolbar** contains a set of icons (the same icons you see on the menus) called **buttons** that you click with the mouse pointer to quickly execute a menu command.

When you first open Excel, Word, or PowerPoint, the menus on the menu bar initially show only a basic set of commands and the Standard and Formatting toolbars contain only a basic set of buttons. These short versions of the menus and toolbars are called **personalized menus and toolbars**. As you work, the commands and buttons you use most frequently are stored in the personalized settings. The first time you select a menu command or toolbar button that is not part of the basic set, it is added to your personalized settings and appears on the menu or toolbar. If you do not use a command for a while, it is removed from your personalized settings and no longer appears on the menu or toolbar. To view the personalized menus and toolbars in PowerPoint:

Step 1	*Click*	the Start button Start on the taskbar
Step 2	*Click*	the New Office Document command on the Start menu
Step 3	*Click*	the General tab in the New Office Document dialog box
Step 4	*Double-click*	the Blank Presentation icon
Step 5	*Click*	OK in the New Slide dialog box to create a blank title slide for the presentation
Step 6	*Click*	Tools on the menu bar
Step 7	*Observe*	the short personalized menu containing only the basic commands, as shown in Figure 2-1

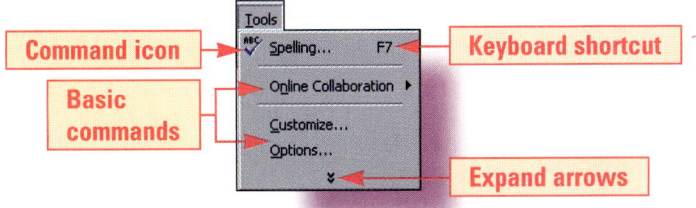

FIGURE 2-1
Personalized Tools Menu

chapter
two

If the command you want to use does not appear on the short personalized menu, you can expand the menu by pausing for a few seconds until the menu expands, clicking the expand arrows at the bottom of the menu, or double-clicking the menu name.

Step 8	*Pause*	until the menu automatically expands, as shown in Figure 2-2

FIGURE 2-2
Expanded Tools Menu

QUICK TIP

You can also use keyboard shortcuts to perform tasks in Office applications. Many of these keyboard shortcuts are shown on the menus to the right of the menu command.

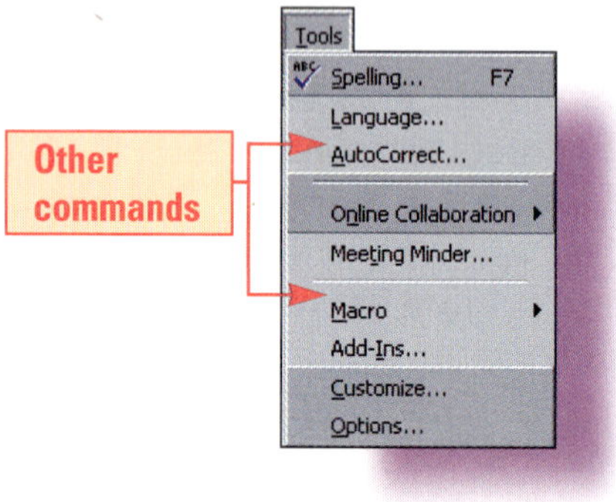

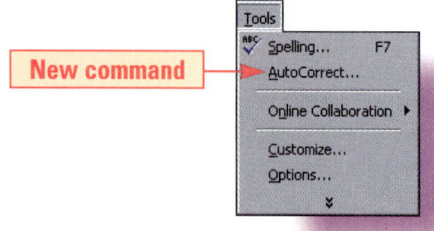

You move a menu command from the expanded menu to the personalized menu, simply by selecting it. To add the AutoCorrect command to the short personalized Tools menu:

Step 1	*Click*	AutoCorrect
Step 2	*Click*	Cancel in the AutoCorrect dialog box to cancel the dialog box
Step 3	*Click*	Tools on the menu bar
Step 4	*Observe*	the updated personalized Tools menu contains the AutoCorrect command, as shown in Figure 2-3

FIGURE 2-3
Updated Personalized Tools Menu

When you first open Word, Excel, or PowerPoint, the Standard and Formatting toolbars appear on one row below the title bar and some default buttons are hidden. You can resize a toolbar to view a hidden button by dragging its **move handle**, the gray vertical bar at the left edge of the toolbar, with the **move pointer,** a four-headed black arrow. To resize the Formatting toolbar:

Step 1	*Move*	the mouse pointer to the move handle on the Formatting toolbar
Step 2	*Observe*	that the mouse pointer becomes a move pointer
Step 3	*Drag*	the Formatting toolbar to the left until nine Formatting toolbar buttons are visible
Step 4	*Observe*	that you see fewer buttons on the Standard toolbar

The buttons that don't fit on the displayed area of a toolbar are collected in a More Buttons list. To view the remaining the Standard toolbar default buttons:

| Step 1 | *Click* | the More Buttons list arrow on the Standard toolbar |
| Step 2 | *Observe* | the default buttons that are not visible on the toolbar, as shown in Figure 2-4 |

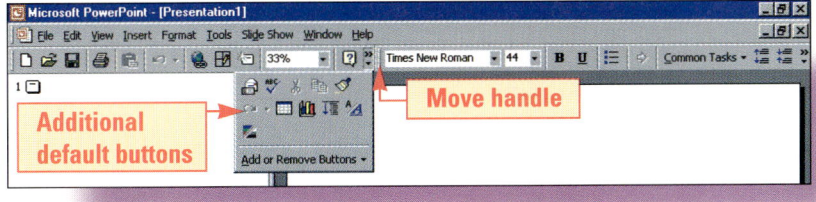

| Step 3 | *Press* | the ESC key to close the More Buttons list |

If you want to display one of the default buttons on a personalized toolbar, you can select it from the More Buttons list. To add the Format Painter button to the personalized Standard toolbar:

Step 1	*Click*	the More Buttons list arrow on the Standard toolbar
Step 2	*Click*	the Format Painter button 
Step 3	*Observe*	that the Format Painter button is turned on and added to the personalized Standard toolbar, as shown in Figure 2-5

FIGURE 2-4
More Buttons List

chapter
two

FIGURE 2-5
Updated Personalized
Standard Toolbar

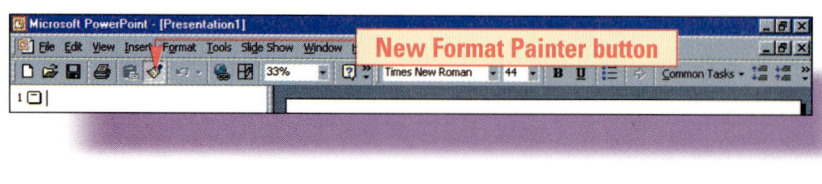

Step 4	*Click*	the Format Painter button on the Standard toolbar to turn it off

If you want to view all the menu commands instead of a short personalized menu and all the default toolbar buttons on the Standard and Formatting toolbars, you can change options in the Customize dialog box. To show all the toolbar buttons and menu commands:

Step 1	*Click*	Tools
Step 2	*Click*	Customize
Step 3	*Click*	the Options tab, if necessary

The dialog box that opens should be similar to Figure 2-6.

FIGURE 2-6
Options Tab in the
Customize Dialog Box

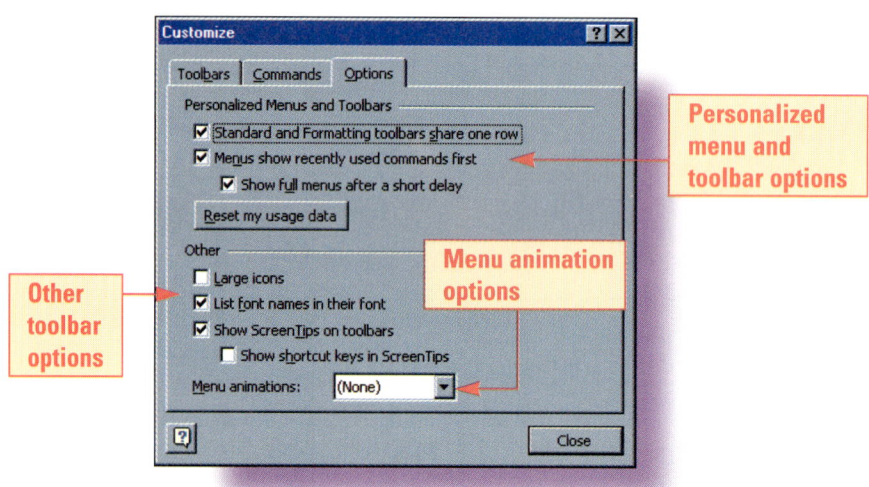

Step 4	*Click*	the Standard and Formatting toolbars share one row check box to remove the check mark and reposition the Formatting toolbar below the Standard toolbar
Step 5	*Click*	the Menus show recently used commands first check box to remove the check mark and show the entire set of commands for each menu
Step 6	*Click*	Close to close the dialog box

Step 7	*Observe*	the repositioned Standard and Formatting toolbars
Step 8	*Click*	Tools to view the entire set of Tools menu commands
Step 9	*Press*	the ESC key

You can return the menus and toolbars to their initial (or **default**) settings in the Customize dialog box. To reset the default menus and toolbars:

Step 1	*Open*	the Options tab in the Customize dialog box
Step 2	*Click*	the Standard and Formatting toolbars share one row check box to insert a check mark
Step 3	*Click*	the Menus show recently used commands first check box to insert a check mark
Step 4	*Click*	Reset my usage data
Step 5	*Click*	Yes to confirm you want to reset the menus and toolbars to their default settings
Step 6	*Close*	the Customize dialog box
Step 7	*Observe*	that the Tools menu and Standard toolbar are reset to their default settings

2.b Viewing, Hiding, Docking, and Floating Toolbars

Office applications have additional toolbars that you can view when you need them. You can also hide toolbars when you are not using them. You can view or hide toolbars by pointing to the Toolbars command on the View menu and clicking a toolbar name or by using a shortcut menu. A **shortcut menu** is a short list of frequently used menu commands. You view a shortcut menu by pointing to an item on the screen and clicking the right mouse button. This is called right-clicking the item. The commands on shortcut menus vary—depending on where you right-click—so that you view only the most frequently used commands for a particular task. An easy way to view or hide toolbars is with a shortcut menu. To view the shortcut menu for PowerPoint toolbars:

| Step 1 | *Right-click* | the menu bar, the Standard toolbar, or the Formatting toolbar |
| Step 2 | *Observe* | the shortcut menu and the check marks next to the names of currently visible toolbars, as shown in Figure 2-7 |

CAUTION TIP

When you choose the Menus show recently used commands first option, it affects all the Office applications, not just the open application.

Resetting the usage data to the initial settings does not change the location of toolbars and does not remove or add buttons to toolbars you have customized in the Customize dialog box.

chapter
two

FIGURE 2-7
Toolbars Shortcut Menu

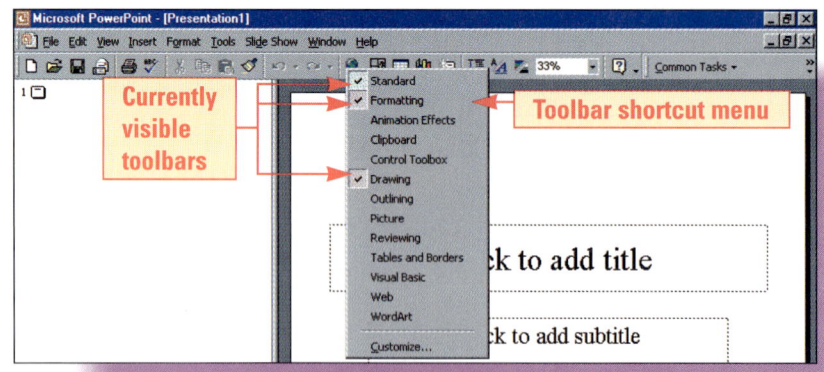

Step 3	*Click*	Tables and Borders in the shortcut menu
Step 4	*Observe*	that the Tables and Borders toolbar appears on your screen

The Tables and Borders toolbar, unless a previous user repositioned it, is visible in its own window near the middle of your screen. When a toolbar is visible in its own window it is called a **floating toolbar** and you can move and size it with the mouse pointer just like any window. When a toolbar appears fixed at the screen boundaries, it is called a **docked toolbar**. The menu bar and Standard and Formatting toolbars are examples of docked toolbars. In PowerPoint, the Drawing toolbar is docked above the status bar. You can dock a floating toolbar by dragging its title bar with the mouse pointer to a docking position below the title bar, above the status bar, or at the left and right boundaries of your screen. To dock the Tables and Borders toolbar below the Standard and Formatting toolbars:

Step 1	*Position*	the mouse pointer on the blue title bar in the Tables and Borders toolbar window
Step 2	*Drag*	the toolbar window slowly up until it docks below the Standard and Formatting toolbars

Similarly, you float a docked toolbar by dragging it away from its docked position toward the middle of the screen. To float the Tables and Borders toolbar:

Step 1	*Position*	the mouse pointer on the Tables and Borders toolbar move handle until it becomes a move pointer
Step 2	*Drag*	the Tables and Borders toolbar down toward the middle of the screen until it appears in its own window

When you finish using a toolbar, you can hide it with a shortcut menu. To hide the Tables and Borders toolbar:

Step 1	*Right-click*	the Tables and Borders toolbar
Step 2	*Click*	Tables and Borders to remove the check mark and hide the toolbar

2.c Customizing the Menu Bar and Toolbars

Recall that you can add a button to a personalized toolbar by clicking the More Buttons list arrow on the toolbar and then selecting a button from the list of default buttons not currently visible. You can also add and delete buttons and commands on the menu bar or other toolbars with options in the Customize dialog box. To customize the menu bar:

Step 1	*Right-click*	any toolbar (the menu bar, Standard toolbar, or Formatting toolbar)
Step 2	*Click*	Customize
Step 3	*Click*	the Commands tab, if necessary

The dialog box on your screen should look similar to Figure 2-8.

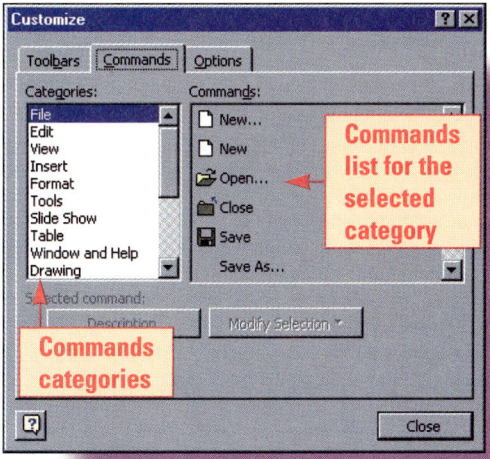

FIGURE 2-8
Commands Tab in the Customize Dialog Box

You add a button on the menu bar to route the active presentation to other users on the network via e-mail.

chapter
two

Step 4	*Verify*	that File is selected in the Categories: list
Step 5	*Click*	Routing Recipient in the Commands: list (scroll the list to view this command)
Step 6	*Click*	Description to view the ScreenTip
Step 7	*Press*	the ESC key to close the ScreenTip
Step 8	*Drag*	the Routing Recipient command to the right of Help on the menu bar
Step 9	*Click*	Close to close the dialog box and add the Routing Recipient button to the menu bar
Step 10	*Position*	the mouse pointer on the Routing Recipient icon to view the ScreenTip, as shown in Figure 2-9

FIGURE 2-9
Button Added to Menu Bar

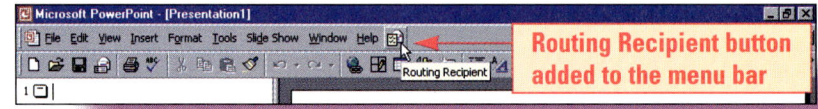

You can remove a button from a toolbar just as quickly. To remove the Routing Recipient button from the menu bar:

Step 1	*Open*	the Customize dialog box
Step 2	*Drag*	the Routing Recipient button from the menu bar into the dialog box
Step 3	*Close*	the dialog box
Step 4	*Close*	the PowerPoint application and return to the Windows desktop

2.d Viewing and Customizing the Office Shortcut Bar

The **Office Shortcut Bar** is a toolbar that you can open and position on your Windows desktop to provide shortcuts to Office applications and tasks. It can contain buttons for the New Office Document and Open Office Document commands on the Start menu, shortcut buttons to create various Outlook items like the New Task button, and buttons to open Office applications installed on your computer.

You can view and use the Office Shortcut Bar as needed or you can choose to have it open each time you start your computer. To view the Office Shortcut Bar:

Step 1	*Click*	the Start button ![Start] on the taskbar
Step 2	*Point to*	Programs
Step 3	*Point to*	Microsoft Office Tools
Step 4	*Click*	Microsoft Office Shortcut Bar
Step 5	*Click*	No in the Microsoft Office Shortcut Bar dialog box to not open the Office Shortcut Bar each time you start your computer

The Office Shortcut Bar may appear docked in the upper-right corner or along the right edge of your Windows desktop. Your screen may look similar to Figure 2-10.

| Step 6 | *Right-click* | the Office Shortcut Bar Control-menu icon |

The Office Shortcut Bar Control-menu contains commands you can use to customize or close the Office Shortcut Bar. If your Shortcut Bar does not already contain buttons to open the individual Office applications, you may want to customize it for the Office applications you use frequently. To open the Customize dialog box:

| Step 1 | *Click* | Customize |
| Step 2 | *Click* | the Buttons tab |

The dialog box on your screen should look similar to Figure 2-11.

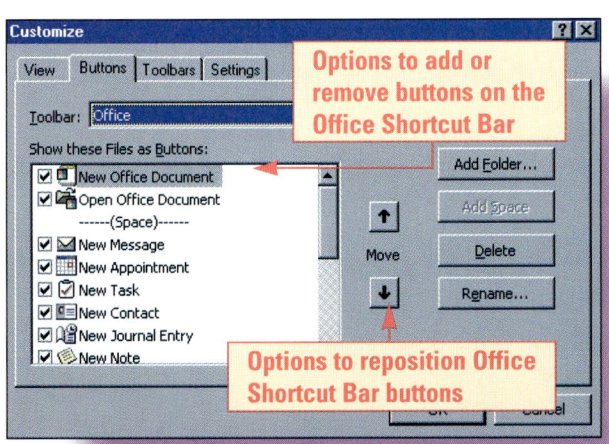

FIGURE 2-10
Office Shortcut Bar

QUICK TIP

The AutoHide command hides the Office Shortcut Bar and displays only a thin border where the Office Shortcut Bar resides. When you position the mouse pointer on the thin border, the Office Shortcut Bar appears. When you move the mouse pointer away from the border, the Office Shortcut Bar hides again.

FIGURE 2-11
Buttons Tab in the Customize Dialog Box

chapter
two

The shortcut button for a particular application or file is visible on the Office Shortcut Bar if a check mark appears in the check box to the left of the application icon in the Show these Files as Buttons: list. To add a shortcut button that opens the Word application:

Step 1	*Scroll*	the Show these Files as Buttons: list to view the check boxes for the Office applications
Step 2	*Click*	the Microsoft Word check box to insert a check mark
Step 3	*Observe*	that a button for the Word application immediately appears on the Office Shortcut Bar

You can easily reposition a button on the Office Shortcut Bar by moving the item into the Show these Files as Buttons: list. To reposition the Word button to the right of the Open Office Document button:

Step 1	*Click*	the Microsoft Word application name to select it in the list
Step 2	*Click*	the Move up arrow until the Microsoft Word application and check box appear immediately below the Open Office Document icon and check box
Step 3	*Observe*	that the Word button on the Office Shortcut Bar is repositioned

You can also delete an application button from the Office Shortcut Bar. To remove the Word application button:

Step 1	*Click*	the Microsoft Word check box to remove the check mark
Step 2	*Move*	the Microsoft Word check box back to its original position above the Excel check box by selecting it and clicking the Move down arrow
Step 3	*Click*	OK

The Office Shortcut Bar may be in the upper-right corner of your screen and sized to fit within an application title bar. This means that Office Shortcut Bar always shows on top of the active application's title bar with small buttons. You can enlarge the buttons and place the Shortcut Bar in its own window so you can move it elsewhere on the screen. You can also hide and redisplay the Shortcut Bar as needed. To close the Office Shortcut Bar:

Step 1	*Right-click*	the Office Shortcut Bar Control-menu icon
Step 2	*Click*	Exit

Summary

▶ When you first start Word, Excel, or PowerPoint, you see personalized menus containing basic commands. As you use different commands, they are automatically added to the personalized menu. Commands that are not used for some time are removed from the personalized menus.

▶ When you first start Word, Excel, or PowerPoint, the Standard and Formatting toolbars share one row below the menu bar. You can reposition the Formatting toolbar to view more or fewer toolbar buttons. The remaining default toolbar buttons that are not visible on the toolbars can be added from the More Buttons list.

▶ FrontPage and Access also provide the personalized menus and toolbars options.

▶ You can turn off or reset the personalized menus and toolbars in the Options tab of the Customize dialog box.

▶ You can hide or view toolbars as you need them by using a shortcut menu.

▶ Toolbars can be docked at the top, bottom, or side of the screen or they can remain floating on the screen in their own window.

▶ You can customize toolbars by adding or deleting buttons and commands, displaying larger-sized buttons, and turning on or off the display of ScreenTips, or adding keyboard shortcut keys to ScreenTips.

▶ The menu bar is a special toolbar that can be customized just like other toolbars.

▶ The Office Shortcut Bar is a customizable toolbar you can position on the desktop and contains shortcuts for opening Office documents and applications.

chapter two

Commands Review

Action	Menu Bar	Shortcut Menu	Toolbar	Keyboard
To display or hide toolbars	<u>V</u>iew, <u>T</u>oolbars	Right-click a toolbar, click the desired toolbar to add or remove the check mark	☒	ALT + V, T
To customize a toolbar	<u>V</u>iew, <u>T</u>oolbars, <u>C</u>ustomize	Right-click a toolbar, click <u>C</u>ustomize		ALT + V, T, C

Concepts Review

Circle the correct answer.

1. A menu is:
- **[a]** a set of icons.
- **[b]** a list of commands.
- **[c]** impossible to customize.
- **[d]** never personalized.

2. The Options tab in the PowerPoint Customize dialog box does not include an option for:
- **[a]** turning on or off ScreenTips for toolbar buttons.
- **[b]** turning on or off Large icons for toolbar buttons.
- **[c]** adding animation to menus.
- **[d]** docking all toolbars.

3. A toolbar is:
- **[a]** a list of commands.
- **[b]** always floating on your screen.
- **[c]** a set of icons.
- **[d]** never docked on your screen.

4. When you right-click an item on your screen, you see:
- **[a]** the Right Click toolbar.
- **[b]** animated menus.
- **[c]** expanded menus.
- **[d]** a shortcut menu.

Circle **T** if the statement is true or **F** if the statement is false.

T F 1. The Standard and Formatting toolbars must remain on the same row.

T F 2. When updating docked personalized toolbars, some buttons may be automatically removed from view to make room for the new buttons.

T F 3. Resetting your usage data affects your toolbars regardless of their size or position.

T F 4. You cannot add animation to menus.

Skills Review

Exercise 1

1. Open the Word application.

2. Open the <u>O</u>ptions tab in the Customize dialog box and reset the usage data, have the Standard and Formatting toolbars share one row, and the menus show recently used commands first.

3. Add the Show/Hide button to the personalized Standard toolbar using the More Buttons list.

4. Add the Font color button to the personalized Formatting toolbar using the More Buttons list.

5. Open the Customize dialog box and reset your usage data in the <u>O</u>ptions tab.

6. Close the Word application.

Exercise 2

1. Open the Excel application.

2. Open the <u>O</u>ptions tab in the Customize dialog box and reset the usage data, have the Standard and Formatting toolbars share one row, and the menus show recently used commands first.

3. View the personalized <u>T</u>ools menu.

4. Add the <u>A</u>utoCorrect command to the personalized <u>T</u>ools menu.

5. Reset your usage data.

6. Close the Excel application.

Exercise 3

1. Open the Office Shortcut Bar. (Do not set it to automatically open when you start your computer.)

2. Customize the Office Shortcut Bar to add the Word, Excel, and PowerPoint shortcut buttons or remove them if they already appear.

3. Customize the Office Shortcut Bar to have large buttons and position it in its own window vertically at the right side of the desktop.

4. AutoFit the Office Shortcut Bar to the title bar with small buttons.

5. Remove the Word, Excel, and PowerPoint application shortcut buttons or add them back, if necessary.

6. Close the Office Shortcut Bar.

Exercise 4

1. Open the Word application.

2. Add the Clear command icon from the Edit category to the menu bar.

3. Reset the menu bar back to its default from the <u>T</u>oolbars tab in the Customize dialog box.

4. Close the Word application.

Exercise 5

1. Open the Excel application.

2. View the Drawing, Picture, and WordArt toolbars using a shortcut menu.

3. Dock the Picture toolbar below the Standard and Formatting toolbars.

4. Dock the WordArt toolbar at the left boundary of the screen.

5. Close the Excel application from the taskbar.

6. Open the Excel with the New Office Document on the Start menu. (*Hint:* Use the Blank Workbook icon.)

7. Float the WordArt toolbar.

8. Float the Picture toolbar.

chapter two

9. Hide the WordArt, Picture, and Drawing toolbars using a shortcut menu.

10. Close the Excel application.

Case Projects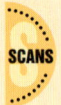

Project 1

As secretary to the placement director for the XYZ Employment Agency, you have been using Word 97. After you install Office 2000, you decide you want the menus and toolbars to behave just like they did in Word 97. Use the Office Assistant to search for help on "personalized menus" and select the appropriate topic from the Office Assistant list. (*Hint:* You may need to view all the topics presented in the Office Assistant balloon.) Review the Help topic you select and write down the steps to make the personalized menus and toolbars behave like Word 97 menus and toolbars.

Project 2

You are the administrative assistant to the controller of the Plush Pets, Inc., a stuffed toy manufacturing company. The controller recently installed Excel 2000. She prefers to view the entire list of menu commands rather than the personalized menus and asks for your help. Use the Office assistant to search for help on "full menus" and select the appropriate topic in the Office Assistant balloon. Review the topic and write down the instructions for switching between personalized menus and full menus.

Project 3

As administrative assistant to the art director of MediaWiz Advertising, Inc. you just installed PowerPoint 2000. Now you decide you would rather view the complete Standard and Formatting toolbars rather than the personalized toolbars and want to learn a quick way to do this. Use the Office Assistant to search for help on "show all buttons" and select the appropriate topic from the Office Assistant balloon. Review the topic and write down the instructions for showing all buttons using the mouse pointer. Open an Office application and use the mouse method to show the complete Standard and Formatting toolbars. Turn the personalized toolbars back on in the Customize dialog box.

Project 4

You are the training coordinator for the information technology (IT) department at a large international health care organization, World Health International. The information technology department is planning to install Office 2000 on computers throughout the organization within the next two weeks. Your supervisor, the IT manager, asks you to prepare a short introduction to the Office 2000 personalized menus and toolbars to be presented at next Monday's staff meeting. He wants you to emphasize the advantages and disadvantages of using the personalized menus and toolbars. Write down in at least two paragraphs the advantages and disadvantages of using the personalized menus and toolbars.

Working With Others Using Online Collaboration Tools

Chapter Overview

I n today's workplace many tasks are completed by several co-workers working together as part of a team called a workgroup. Office applications provide tools to assist workgroups in sharing information. In this chapter you learn about scheduling and participating in online meetings and conducting Web discussions with others in your workgroup.

LEARNING OBJECTIVES

► Schedule an online meeting
► Participate in Web discussions

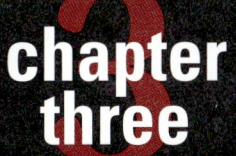

chapter
three

CAUTION TIP

The activities in this chapter assume you have access to directory servers and Web servers with Office Server Extensions installed, Microsoft NetMeeting, and Outlook with Exchange Server service installed. If you do not have access to the appropriate servers and software, you will be able to read but not do the hands-on activities. Your instructor will provide additional server, e-mail address, NetMeeting, and Outlook instructions as needed to complete the hands-on activities.

3.a Scheduling an Online Meeting

Many organizations assign tasks or projects to several workers who collaborate as members of a **workgroup**. Often these workgroup members do not work in the same office or some members travel frequently, making it difficult for the group to meet at one physical location. Office applications, together with Microsoft NetMeeting conferencing software, provide a way for workgroup members to participate in online real-time meetings from different physical locations—just as though everyone were in the same meeting room. In an online meeting, participants can share programs and documents, send text messages, transfer files, and illustrate ideas.

You can schedule an online meeting in advance using Outlook or you can invite others to participate in an online meeting right now by opening NetMeeting directly from Word, Excel, PowerPoint, and Access and calling others in your workgroup. To participate in an online meeting, invitees must have NetMeeting running on their computers.

Calling Others from Office Applications Using NetMeeting

Suppose you are working on an Excel workbook and want to discuss the workbook with another person in your workgroup. You know that they are running NetMeeting on their computer. You can call them while working in the workbook. To open NetMeeting and place a call from within Excel:

Step 1	*Click*	the Start button ![Start] on the taskbar
Step 2	*Click*	the Open Office Document command on the Start menu
Step 3	*Double-click*	the *International Food Distributors* workbook located on the Data Disk
Step 4	*Click*	Tools
Step 5	*Point to*	Online Collaboration
Step 6	*Click*	Meet Now to open NetMeeting and the Place A Call dialog box

The directory server and list of names and calling addresses in the Place A Call dialog box on your screen will be different, but the dialog box should look similar to Figure 3-1.

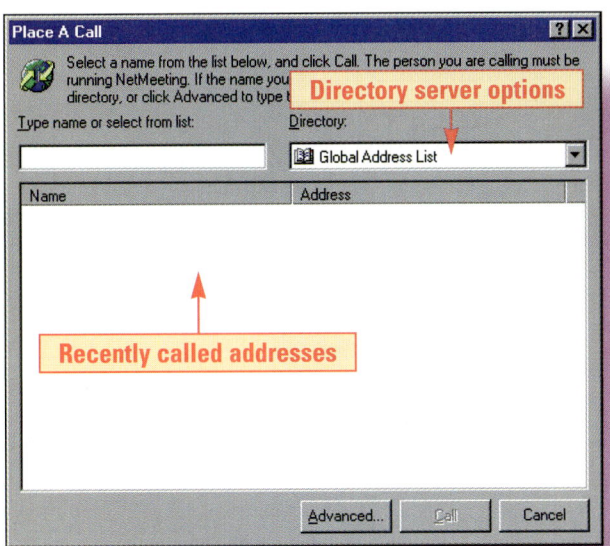

FIGURE 3-1
Place A Call Dialog Box

The person who initiates the meeting call is called the **host**. The person or persons receiving the call are called **participants**. Because you are initiating a call about the open Excel workbook, you are the host for this meeting. You can select a specific directory server and then select the participant to call from a list of persons logged onto the server or select someone from the list of frequently called NetMeeting participants. The *host* now calls a participant in the list:

Step 1	***Right-click*** the name of the person in the list specified by your instructor and click Call

NetMeeting dials the participant. Depending on the participant's NetMeeting configuration, he or she can automatically accept the call or manually accept or ignore the call. If the NetMeeting configuration is set up to manually answer calls, an announcement appears on the participant's screen, allowing him or her to click a button to accept or decline the call.

For the activities in this chapter, the participant's NetMeeting software is configured to automatically accept incoming calls. When the call is accepted, the *International Food Distributors* workbook and the Online Meeting toolbar automatically display on the participant's screen, even if the participant does not have Excel installed. Only the host needs to have the application installed and the file available. Both the *host's* and the *participant's* screens should look similar to Figure 3-2.

The host has **control** of the *International Foods Distributors* workbook when the meeting starts, which means the host can turn on or off collaboration at any time, controlling who can edit the document. When collaboration is turned on, any one participant can control the workbook for editing. When collaboration is turned off,

chapter
three

FIGURE 3-2
Host's and Participant's
Screens

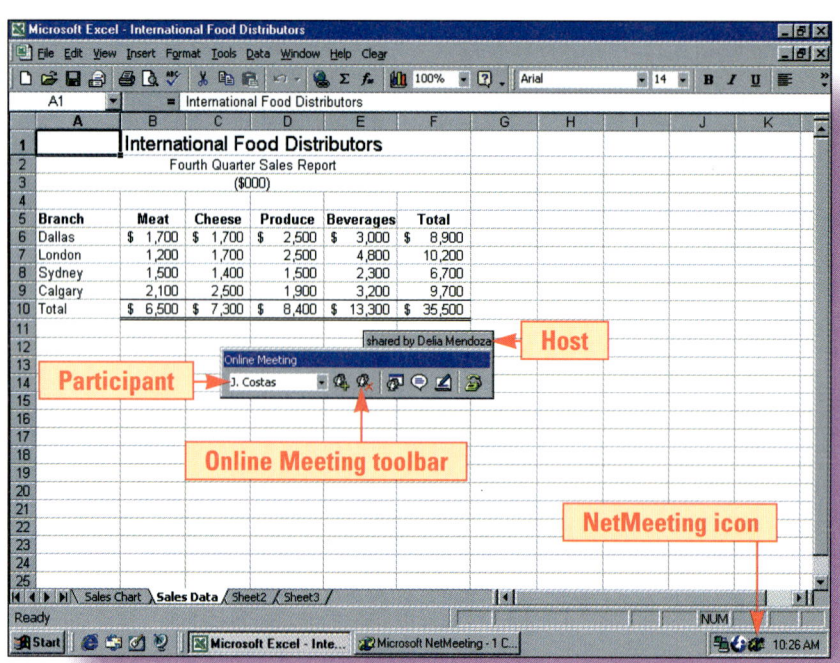

only the host can edit the workbook but all participants can see it. The *host* now turns on collaboration:

Step 1	*Click*	the Allow others to edit button ▣ on the Online Meeting toolbar

The first time a participant wants to take control of the workbook, they double-click it. The host can regain control of the workbook at any time simply by clicking it. To regain control of the workbook after the first time they control it, a participant also clicks it. The initials of the person who currently controls the workbook appear beside the mouse pointer. The *participant* takes control of the workbook for the first time to edit it:

Step 1	*Double-click*	the workbook to take control and place your user initials beside the mouse pointer
Step 2	*Click*	Tools
Step 3	*Click*	Options
Step 4	*Click*	the View tab
Step 5	*Click*	the Gridlines check box to remove the check mark
Step 6	*Click*	OK to turn off the gridlines in the workbook

The *host* regains control of the workbook:

| Step 1 | *Click* | the workbook to regain control and place your initials beside the mouse pointer |
| Step 2 | *Turn on* | the gridlines on the View tab in the Options dialog box |

The **Whiteboard** is a tool that participants can use to illustrate their thoughts and ideas. Only the host can display the Whiteboard during an online meeting that originates from within an Office application. All participants can draw on the Whiteboard at the same time only when the host turns off collaboration. The *host* turns off collaboration:

Step 1	*Click*	the workbook to regain control, if necessary
Step 2	*Click*	the Allow others to edit button [icon] to turn off collaboration
Step 3	*Click*	the Display Whiteboard button [icon] on the Online Meeting toolbar

Your screen should look similar to Figure 3-3.

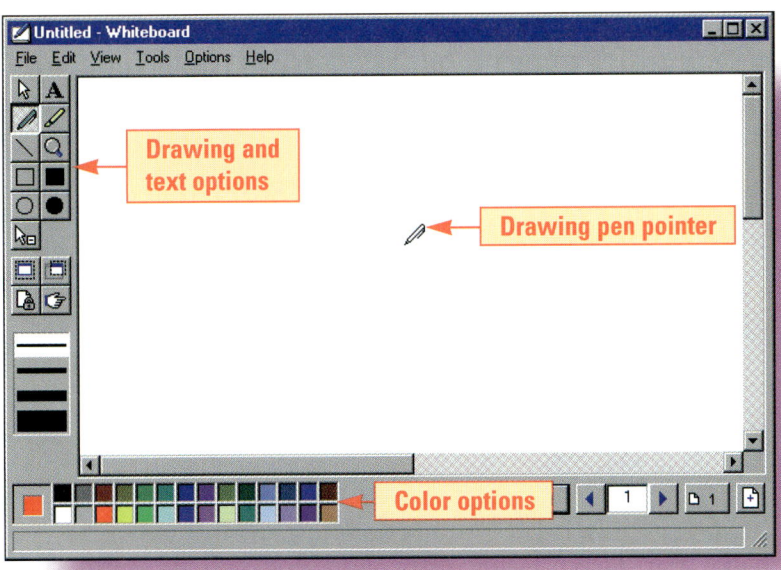

FIGURE 3-3
Whiteboard Window

All participants, including the host, add text, draw shapes, add color, and insert additional pages in the Whiteboard window. The host can save and print Whiteboard pages. The host and participant explore using the drawing, text, and color options for the Whiteboard. First, the *host* selects a color and draws a shape:

chapter
three

MENU TIP

The host can send a copy of the active document to all participants by clicking the File menu, pointing to Send To, and clicking the Online Meeting Recipient command. All participants then receive the file as an e-mail attachment. The host can send the document to one participant by clicking the E-mail button on the Standard toolbar and attaching the document file to an e-mail message.

Step 1	*Click*	Red in the color options
Step 2	*Draw*	a shape by dragging the drawing pen pointer in the Whiteboard drawing area

The *participant* now takes control of the drawing pen, selects a color, and draws a shape:

Step 1	*Click*	the Whiteboard to take control of the drawing pen
Step 2	*Click*	Blue in the color options and draw a shape

The *host* and the *participant*:

Step 1	*Continue*	to share the Whiteboard and explore the different Whiteboard options
Step 2	*Click*	the Close button [X] on the Whiteboard window title bar to close the Whiteboard

CAUTION TIP

Only the host can save and print the document during an online meeting. If a participant in control attempts to print or save the workbook, it is printed at the host's printer and saved to the host's hard disk or originating server.

Each participant can disconnect from the meeting at any time by clicking the End Meeting button on the Online Meeting toolbar. The host can also disconnect any participant by first selecting the participant from the Participants List button and then clicking the Remove Participants button on the Online Meeting toolbar. The host can also end the meeting, which disconnects all the participants. The *host* ends the meeting:

Step 1	*Click*	the End Meeting button [icon] on the Online Meeting toolbar
Step 2	*Close*	the Excel application and workbook from the taskbar without saving changes

Scheduling Online Meetings in Advance Using Outlook

As a host, you can schedule online meetings in advance using Outlook directly or from inside other Office applications. Suppose you are putting the finishing touches on a PowerPoint presentation and want to schedule an online meeting in advance with other workgroup members. You can do this from inside the PowerPoint application. To open a PowerPoint presentation and invite others to an online meeting:

Step 1	*Open*	the PowerPoint application and the *International Food Distributors* presentation located on the Data Disk using the Open Office Document command on the Start menu
Step 2	*Click*	Tools
Step 3	*Point to*	Online Collaboration
Step 4	*Click*	Schedule Meeting

The Outlook Meeting window opens, similar to Figure 3-4.

This window provides all the options for setting up the meeting. You address the message to one or more e-mail addresses, key the subject of the meeting, and select the directory server where the meeting will be held. You also select the date and time of the meeting. The current document is selected as the Office document to be reviewed and a meeting reminder is set to be delivered to the host and attendees 15 minutes prior to the scheduled meeting.

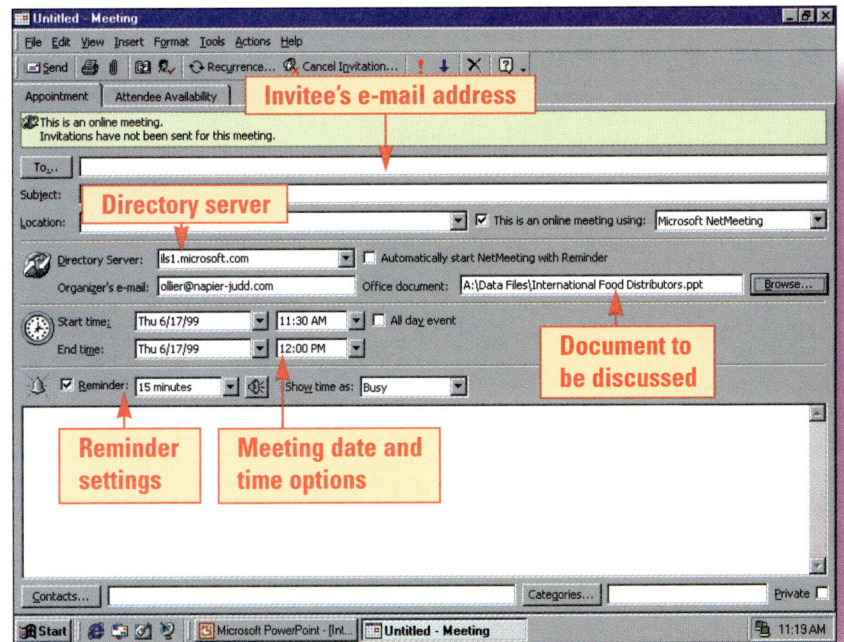

FIGURE 3-4
Outlook Meeting Window

As long as all invitees are using Outlook for their scheduling, you can determine the best time to schedule the meeting by clicking the Attendee Availability tab and inviting others from the Outlook global address book. To review the Attendee Availability tab:

| Step 1 | *Click* | the Attendee Availability tab |

chapter
three

| Step 2 | *Observe* | the meeting scheduling options you can use to compare each invitee's free and busy times from their Outlook calendars and select the best meeting time |
| Step 3 | *Click* | the Appointment tab |

You send the completed meeting invitation by clicking the Send button on the Standard toolbar. Each invitee receives an e-mail message with the meeting information. They can choose to accept, decline, or tentatively accept the invitation by clicking a button inside the message window. If they accept, an Outlook appointment item is added to their calendar. Because you are the host, an appointment item is automatically added to your Outlook calendar. If invitees accept, decline, or accept tentatively, you receive an e-mail notification of their attendance choice and your meeting appointment item is updated to show who is attending and who declined.

Fifteen minutes prior to the scheduled online meeting (if Outlook is running on your computer) a meeting reminder message opens on your screen. If you are the meeting's host, you click the Start this NetMeeting button in the reminder window to begin the meeting. If you are an invited participant, you click the Join the Meeting button in the reminder window to join the meeting or you click the Dismiss this reminder to ignore the meeting invitation.

To close the message window without sending a message:

Step 1	*Click*	the Close button ☒ on the message window title bar
Step 2	*Click*	No
Step 3	*Close*	the PowerPoint application and presentation

Q U I C K   T I P

For more information on scheduling meetings using Outlook, see Outlook online Help.

C A U T I O N   T I P

Special software called Office Server Extensions must be installed on a Web server before discussion items can be created and stored there. For more information on Office Server Extensions software, see the documentation that accompanies Office or online Help.

3.b Participating in Web Discussions

Web discussions provide a way for workgroup members to review and provide input to the same document by associating messages, called **discussion items**, with the document. Discussion items are saved in a database separate from the associated document. This enables the group to consider multiple discussion items related to the same document; it also allows the document to be edited without affecting any discussion items. Discussion items are **threaded**, which means that replies to an item appear directly under the original item. Discussion items are saved as they are entered and are available immediately when the associated document is opened.

Suppose you are working on a Word document and want to solicit input from others in your workgroup. Instead of sending a copy to everyone in the workgroup or routing a single copy to everyone, you decide to use the Web discussion feature. To start a Web discussion:

Step 1	*Open*	the Word application and the *Dallas Warehouse Audit* document located on the Data Disk using the Open Office Document command on the Start menu
Step 2	*Click*	<u>T</u>ools
Step 3	*Point to*	<u>O</u>nline Collaboration
Step 4	*Click*	<u>W</u>eb Discussions

After you connect to your discussion server, the Web Discussions toolbar opens docked above the status bar. See Figure 3-5.

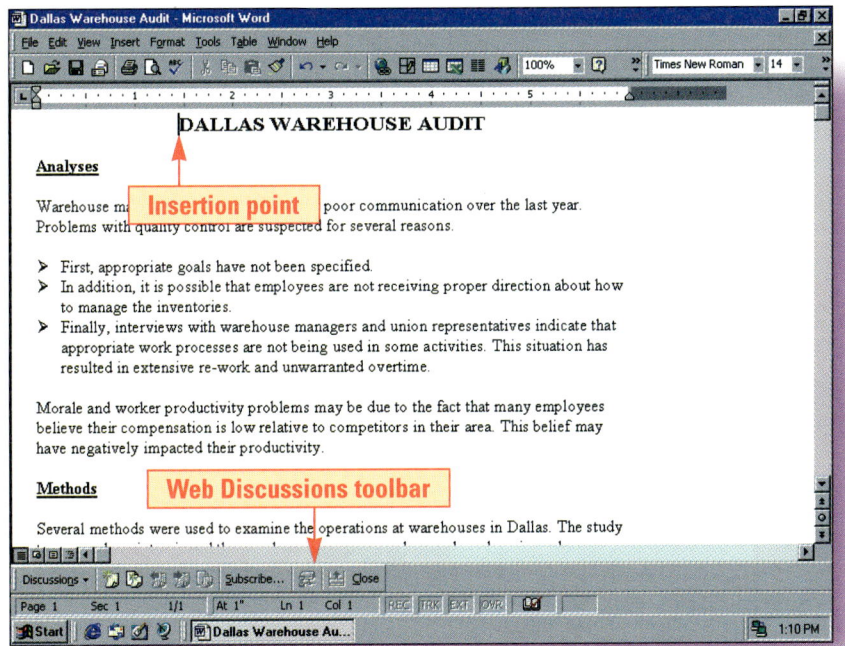

FIGURE 3-5
Document with Web Discussions Toolbar

QUICK TIP

There are two types of discussion items: an **inline discussion item** relates to a specific paragraph, picture, or table, and a **general discussion item** relates to the entire document. Word supports both inline and general discussion items. Excel and PowerPoint support only general discussion items.

First, you add a general discussion item identifying the issues to be discussed in the document. To add a general discussion item:

| Step 1 | *Press* | the CTRL + HOME keys to move the keying position (called the insertion point) to the top of the document |
| Step 2 | *Click* | the Insert Discussion about the Document button  on the Web Discussions toolbar |

The dialog box that opens should look similar to Figure 3-6.

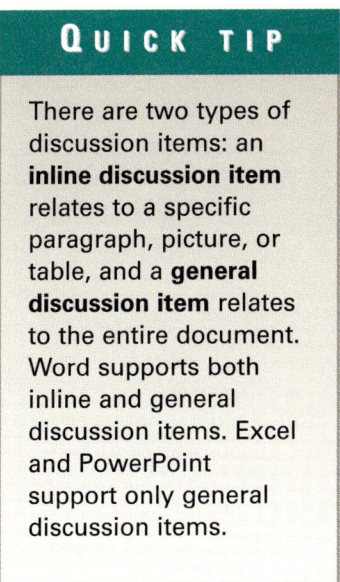

chapter
three

FIGURE 3-6
Enter Discussion Text
Dialog Box

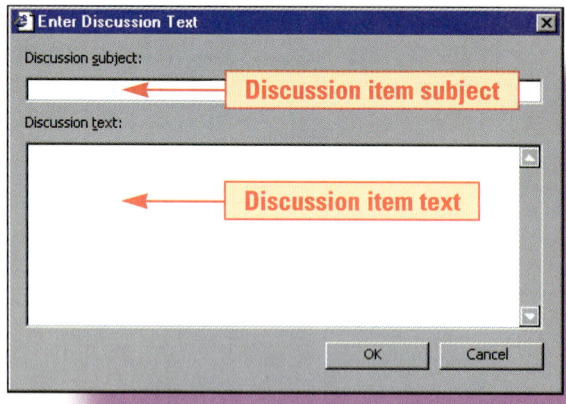

Step 3	*Key*	Problems in Dallas in the Discussion subject: text box
Step 4	*Press*	the TAB key to move the insertion point (the keying position) to the Discussion text: text box
Step 5	*Key*	We have only three weeks to resolve the problems in Dallas.
Step 6	*Click*	OK

The Discussion pane opens and contains information about the active document, the text of the discussion item, and an Action button. You use the Action button to reply to, edit, or delete a discussion item. Your screen should look similar to Figure 3-7.

FIGURE 3-7
Document with
Discussion Pane

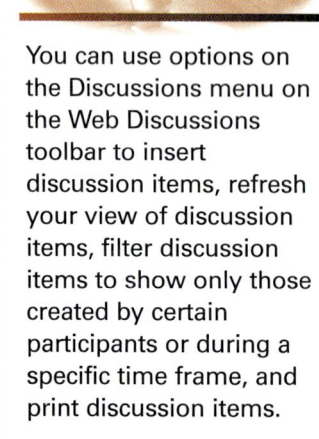

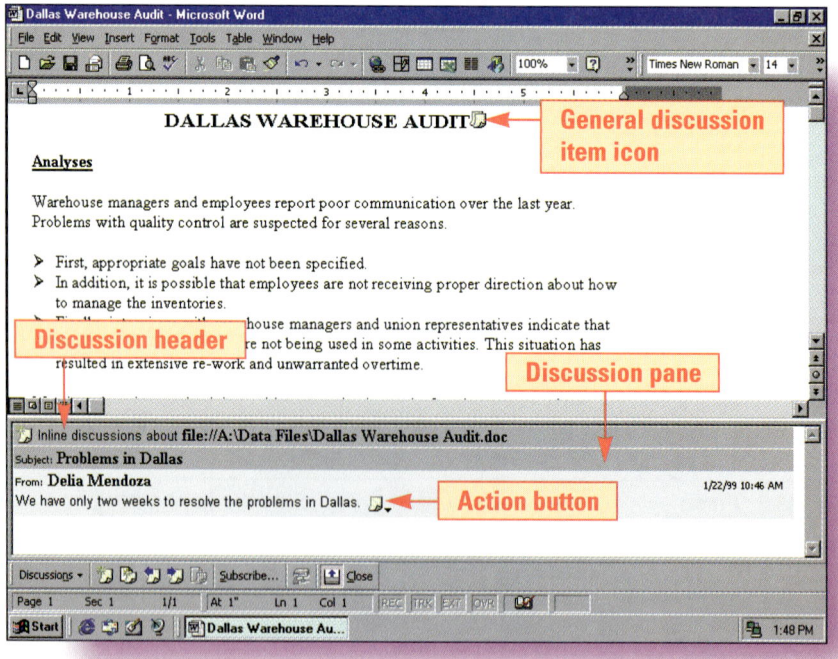

Next you add an inline discussion item to a specific paragraph. To close the Discussion pane and add an inline discussion item:

Step 1	*Click*	the Show/Hide Discussion Pane button on the Web Discussions toolbar
Step 2	*Click*	at the end of the first bulleted item ending in "specified." to reposition the insertion point
Step 3	*Click*	the Insert Discussion in the Document button on the Web Discussions toolbar
Step 4	*Key*	Goals in the Discussion subject: text box
Step 5	*Key*	Doesn't Yong's group have responsibility for setting warehouse goals? in the Discussion text: text box
Step 6	*Click*	OK

The inline discussion item icon appears at the end of the bulleted text and the Discussion pane opens. Your screen should look similar to Figure 3-8.

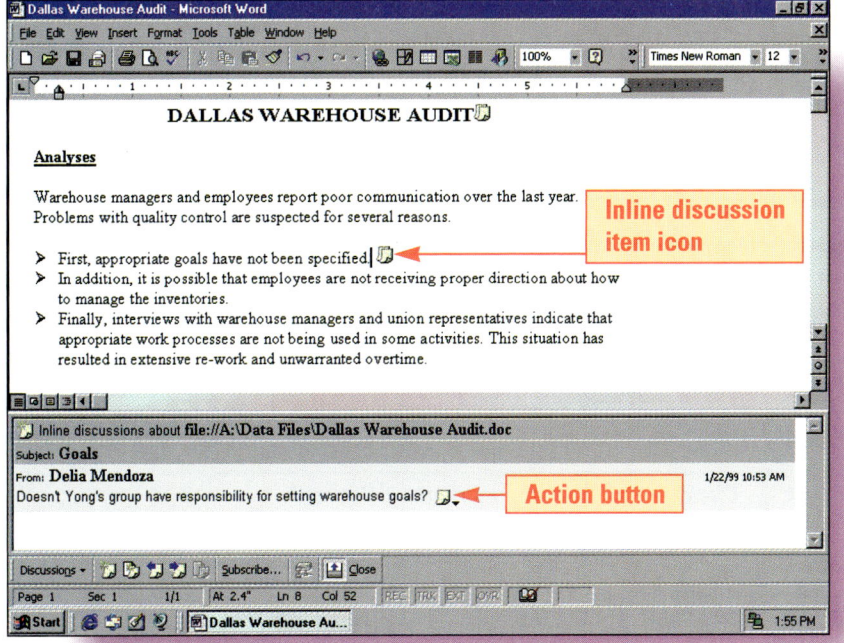

CAUTION TIP

You can modify a document that contains threaded discussions. If you make changes in an area that is not associated with a discussion item, the inline and general discussions are not affected. If you change or delete part of the document associated with a discussion item, any inline discussions are deleted but general discussions are not affected. If you move, rename, or delete a document, all inline and general discussions are lost.

FIGURE 3-8
Inline Discussion Item

| Step 7 | *Click* | the Show/Hide Discussion Pane button on the Web Discussions toolbar to close the Discussion pane |

chapter
three

Others in the workgroup can now open the *Dallas Warehouse Audit* document, log on to the discussion server, and review the inline and general discussion items. They can reply to existing items and create new items. They can edit or delete any discussion items they create. Now assume you are a different member of the workgroup and you just opened the *Dallas Warehouse Audit* document, logged on to the discussion server, and want to participate in the discussion. To thread a reply to the inline discussion item at the end of the bulleted list:

Step 1	*Press*	the CTRL + HOME keys to move the insertion point to the top of the document
Step 2	*Click*	the Next button twice on the Web Discussions toolbar to select the second discussion item and open the Discussion pane
Step 3	*Click*	the Action button in the Discussion pane
Step 4	*Click*	Reply
Step 5	*Key*	Yong's group is currently understaffed and behind schedule. in the Discussion text: text box
Step 6	*Click*	OK to thread your reply immediately below the original discussion item
Step 7	*Close*	the Discussion pane

When discussion items are no longer useful, you can delete them. To open the Discussion pane and delete the discussion items:

Step 1	*Click*	the Show General Discussions button on the Web Discussions toolbar to open the Discussion Pane
Step 2	*Click*	the Action button
Step 3	*Click*	Delete
Step 4	*Click*	Yes to confirm the deletion
Step 5	*Click*	the Next button on the Web Discussions toolbar
Step 6	*Delete*	the first inline discussion item
Step 7	*Delete*	the second inline action item
Step 8	*Click*	Close on the Web Discussions toolbar to close the discussions session
Step 9	*Close*	the Word application and the document without saving any changes

Summary

► You can work with others to complete tasks using Office applications' online collaboration tools: NetMeeting and Web Discussions.

► You can use the NetMeeting conferencing software directly from inside Office applications to host or participate in an online meeting.

► During an online meeting using NetMeeting, participants can take turns editing the current document when the meeting's host turns on collaboration.

► When collaboration is turned off, participants in a NetMeeting online meeting can use the Whiteboard.

► You can chat in real-time during an online meeting and, with a sound card and camera, both see and hear other attendees.

► You can schedule a meeting in advance, either using Outlook or from inside Office applications.

► Another way to work with others on a document is to participate in a Web discussion by associating text comments, called discussion items, with a specific document.

► Inline discussion items relate to specific paragraphs, pictures, or tables in a document. General discussion items relate to the entire document. Only the Word application supports inline discussion items.

Commands Review

Action	Menu Bar	Shortcut Menu	Toolbar	Keyboard
Schedule a meeting using NetMeeting inside Office applications	Tools, Online Collaboration, Meet Now			ALT + T, N, M
Schedule a meeting in advance using Outlook inside Office applications	Tools, Online Collaboration, Schedule Meeting			ALT + T, N, S
Participate in Web Discussions from inside Office applications	Tools, Online Collaboration, Web Discussions			ALT + T, N, W

chapter three

Concepts Review

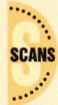

Circle the correct answer.

1. Workgroup members:
- [a] always work in the same physical location.
- [b] never travel on business.
- [c] always work independently of each other.
- [d] often work in different physical locations or travel frequently.

2. A participant in an online meeting:
- [a] can turn collaboration on and off.
- [b] controls access to the Whiteboard.
- [c] can save and print to their own hard drive or printer.
- [d] is the person receiving the call.

3. The first time a participant takes control of a document during an online meeting, the participant must:
- [a] open the Chat window.
- [b] click the document.
- [c] double-click the document.
- [d] press the CTRL + HOME keys.

4. NetMeeting participants use the Whiteboard to:
- [a] key real-time text messages.
- [b] share and edit documents.
- [c] add inline discussion items.
- [d] illustrate their ideas and thoughts.

Circle **T** if the statement is true or **F** if the statement is false.

T T   1. To participate in an online meeting, invitees must be running NetMeeting on their computer.

T F   2. When collaboration is turned on, the host of an online meeting always maintains control of the active document.

T F   3. To gain control of a document during collaboration, participants must double-click it.

T F   4. The active document can be printed and saved to any participant's printer, hard disk, or server during an online meeting.

notes You must be connected to the appropriate directory and discussion servers and have NetMeeting and Outlook running with Exchange server to complete these exercises. Your instructor will provide the server and e-mail address information and any NetMeeting and Outlook instructions needed to complete these exercises.

Skills Review

Exercise 1

1. Open the Word application and the *Dallas Warehouse Audit* document located on the Data Disk.

2. Invite three other people to an online meeting now.

3. Take turns making changes to the document.

4. End the meeting. Close the Word application and document without saving any changes.

Exercise 2

1. Open the Excel application and the *International Food Distributors* workbook located on the Data Disk.

2. Invite four other people to an online meeting next Thursday at 2:00 PM.

3. Open Outlook and read their automatic meeting reply messages.

4. Open the Outlook appointment item created for the message and view the updated attendee information.

5. Delete the appointment item and send a message to all attendees canceling the meeting.

6. Close Outlook. Close the Excel application and workbook without saving any changes.

Exercise 3

1. Open the PowerPoint application and the *International Food Distributors* presentation located on the Data Disk.

2. Create a general Web discussion item using the text "This is an important presentation."

3. Close the Web discussion and the PowerPoint application and presentation without saving any changes.

Exercise 4

1. Open the PowerPoint application and the *International Food Distributors* presentation located on the Data Disk.

2. Reply to the general discussion item using the text "What is the project due date?"

3. Print the discussion items using a command on the Discussions menu.

4. Delete the general discussion items created for the *International Food Distributors* presentation.

5. Close the Web discussion and the PowerPoint application and presentation without saving any changes.

Case Projects

Project 1

As assistant to the accounting manager at Wilson Art Supply, you are asked to find out how to select a discussion server. Open the Word application and use the Office Assistant to search for discussion server topics using the keywords "Web discussions" and select the appropriate topic from the Office Assistant balloon. Review the topic and write down the instructions for selecting a discussion server.

Project 2

You work in the marketing department at International Hair Concepts, a company that imports professional hairdresser supplies. Your department is going to start scheduling online meetings to collaborate on Word documents and you want to be prepared for potential problems. Open the Word application and use the Office Assistant to find the "troubleshoot online meetings" topic. Write down a list of potential problems and their possible solutions.

Project 3

A co-worker at Merton Partners, a public relations firm, mentions that you can subscribe to documents and folders stored on a Web server and then be notified when changes are made to them. Using Word online Help to search for Web discussion topics; review the topic, "About subscribing to a document or folder on a Web server." Write a paragraph about how subscribing to documents and folders could help you in your work.

Project 4

The Women's Professional Softball Teams annual tournament is in two months and 30 teams from around the world will participate. The director wants to review the schedule (created in Word) at one time with the team representatives in the United States, England, France, Holland, Germany, China, Argentina, Mexico, and Australia. Write at least two paragraphs recommending an online collaboration tool and explaining why this is the best choice.

chapter three

Introduction to the Internet and the World Wide Web

Chapter Overview

- ▶ Describe the Internet and discuss its history
- ▶ Connect to the Internet
- ▶ Recognize the challenges to using the Internet
- ▶ Use Internet Explorer
- ▶ Use directories and search engines

M illions of people use the Internet to shop for goods and services, listen to music, view artwork, conduct research, get stock quotes, keep up-to-date with current events, and send e-mail. More and more people are using the Internet at work and at home to view and download multimedia computer files containing graphics, sound, video, and text. In this chapter you learn about the origins of the Internet, how to connect to the Internet, how to use the Internet Explorer Web browser, and how to access pages on the World Wide Web.

chapter
four

4.a What Is the Internet?

To understand the Internet, you must understand networks. A **network** is simply a group of two or more computers linked by cable or telephone lines. The linked computers also include a special computer called a **network server** that is used to store files and programs that everyone on the network can access. In addition to the shared files and programs, networks enable users to share equipment, such as a common network printer. See Figure 4-1.

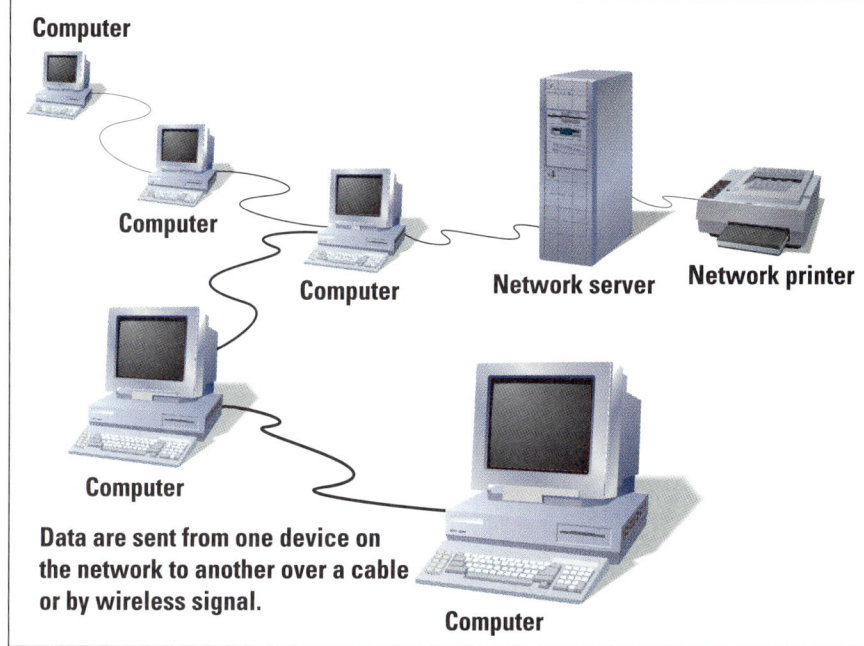

Computer

Computer

Computer

Computer

Network server   Network printer

Computer

Data are sent from one device on the network to another over a cable or by wireless signal.

Computer

FIGURE 4-1
Computer Network

The **Internet** is a worldwide collection of computer networks that enables users to view and transfer information between computers. For example, an Internet user in California can retrieve (or **download**) files from a computer in Canada quickly and easily. In the same way, an Internet user in Australia can send (or **upload**) files to another Internet user in England. See Figure 4-2.

The Internet is not a single organization, but rather a cooperative effort by multiple organizations managing a variety of computers.

A Brief History of the Internet

The Internet originated in the late 1960s, when the United States Department of Defense developed a network of military computers called the **ARPAnet**. Quickly realizing the usefulness of such a network,

chapter
four

FIGURE 4-2
The Internet

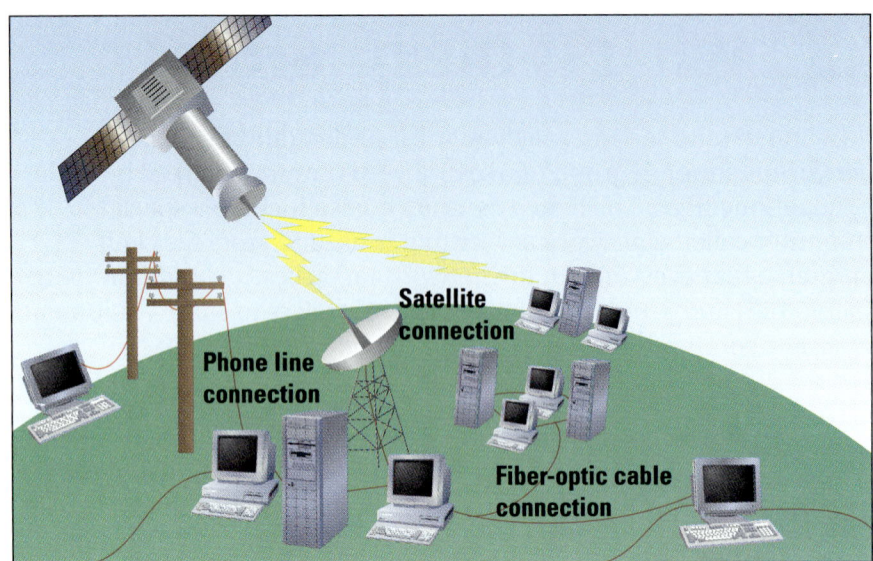

researchers at colleges and universities soon began using it to share data. In the 1980s the military portion of the early Internet became a separate network called the **MILNET**. Meanwhile the National Science Foundation began overseeing the remaining non-military portions, which it called the **NSFnet**. Thousands of other government, academic, and business computer networks began connecting to the NSFnet. By the late 1980s, the term Internet became widely used to describe this huge worldwide "network of networks."

Services Available on the Internet

You find a wide variety of services on the Internet. Table 4-1 explains just some of the options. In this chapter, you learn about using a Web browser and accessing pages on the World Wide Web. Your instructor may provide additional information on other Internet services in the list.

CAUTION TIP

During peak day and evening hours, millions of people are connecting to the Internet. During these hours, you may have difficulty connecting to your host computer or to other sites on the Internet.

4.b Connecting to the Internet

To connect to the Internet you need some physical communication medium connected to your computer, such as network cable or a modem. You also need a special communication program that allows your computer to communicate with computers on the Internet and a Web browser program, such as Microsoft Internet Explorer 5, that allows you to move among all the Internet resources. See Figure 4-3.

Category	Name	Description
Communication	E-mail	Electronic messages sent or received from one computer to another
	Newsgroups	Electronic "bulletin boards" or discussion groups where people with common interests (such as hobbyists or members of professional associations) post messages (called **articles**) that participants around the world can read and respond to
	Mailing Lists	Similar to Newsgroups, except that participants exchange information via e-mail
	Chat	Online conversations in which participants key messages and receive responses on their screen within a few seconds
File Access	FTP	Sending (uploading) or receiving (downloading) computer files via the File Transfer Protocol (FTP) communication rules
Searching Tools	Directories	Tools that help you search for Web sites by category
	Search Engines	Tools to help you find individual files on the Internet by searching for specific words or phrases
World Wide Web (Web)	Web Site	A subset of the Internet that stores files with Web pages containing text, graphics, video, audio, and links to other pages

TABLE 4-1
Internet Services

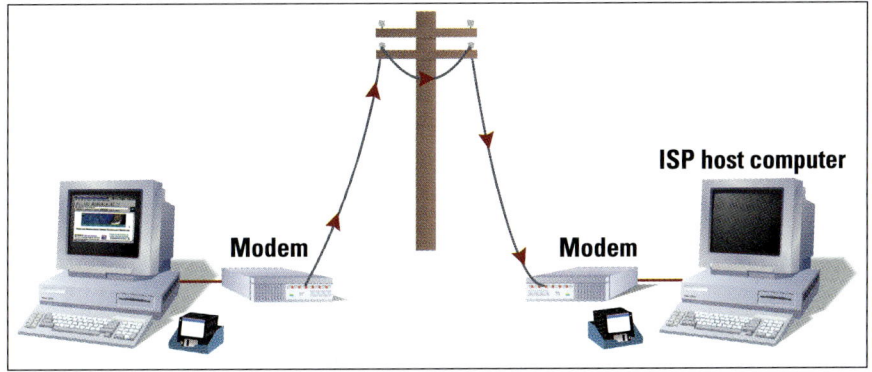

FIGURE 4-3
Internet Connection

chapter
four

Internet Service Providers

After setting up your computer hardware (the network cable or modem) and installing the Internet Explorer Web browser, you must make arrangements to connect to a computer on the Internet. The computer you connect to is called a **host**. Usually, you connect to a host computer via a commercial Internet Service Provider, such as America Online or another company who sells access to the Internet. An **Internet Service Provider (ISP)** maintains the host computer, provides a gateway or entrance to the Internet, and provides an electronic "mail box" with facilities for sending and receiving e-mail. See Figure 4-4.

FIGURE 4-4
Internet Service Providers

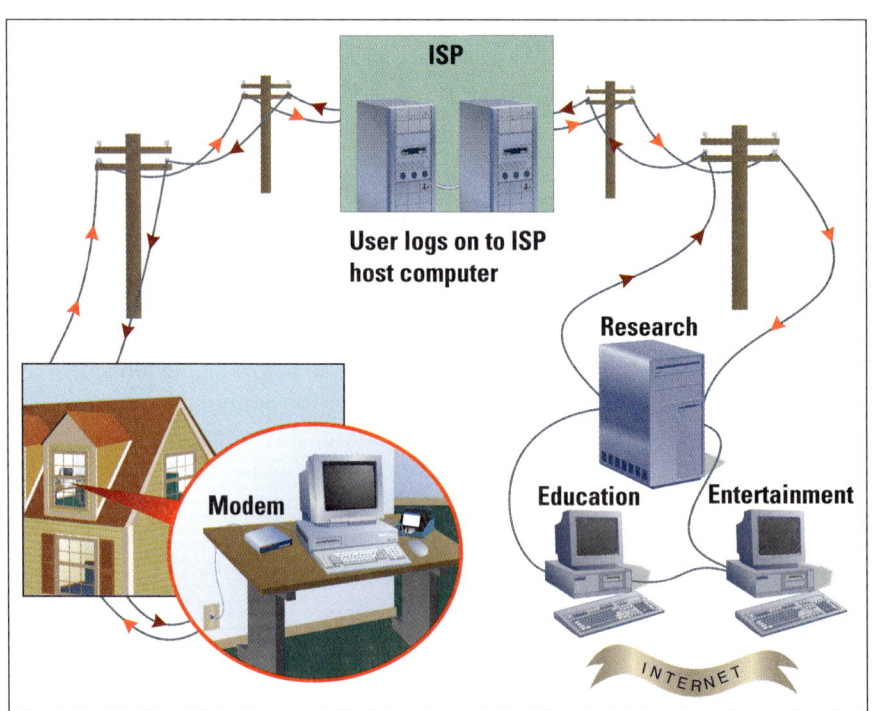

Commercial ISPs usually charge a flat monthly fee for unlimited access to the Internet and e-mail services. Many commercial ISPs generally supply the communication program and browser program you need to access the Internet.

Internet Addresses

A unique Internet address or IP address that consists of a series of numbers identifies each host computer on the Internet. Computers on the Internet use these IP address numbers to communicate with each other, but you will probably need to use one only when you install dial-up networking instructions on your computer. The more important address is the host computer's descriptive address. This address specifies the individual computer within a level of organization, or **domain**, on the Internet. For example, a host computer in the math department at a university might be identified as: *raven.math.uidaho.edu* where "raven" identifies the specific computer, "math" identifies the department, "uidaho" identifies the university, and the suffix "edu" identifies that the address is for an educational institution. You'll find that the descriptive host name is much easier to use and remember than the IP address. Table 4-2 identifies the top-level domain (or highest organizational unit on the Internet) names you see as you work with Internet resources. Other top-level domain names are under consideration but not yet in use.

Top-Level Domain	Organization
.com	Commercial enterprise
.gov	Government institution
.edu	Educational institution
.mil	Military institution
.net	Computer network
.org	Other organizations

TABLE 4-2
Top-Level Domains

User Names

When you make arrangements to access the Internet via an ISP, you also set up a user name that identifies your account with the ISP. Your user name consists of a name you select and the host's descriptive name. User names can be full names, first initial and last names, nicknames, or a group of letters and numbers. For example, the user name for Beth Jackson who accesses the Internet via a commercial ISP named Decon Data Systems might be: *Beth_Jackson@decon.net* where "Beth_Jackson" is the user's name, and "decon.net" is the descriptive name for the ISP's host computer.

4.c Challenges to Using the Internet

Using the Internet to send e-mail, read and post articles to newsgroups, chat online, send and receive files, and search for information is fun and exciting. However, because people use the Internet all over the world, there is a seemingly endless source of data and information available. The sheer size of the Internet can sometimes be intimidating.

Another potential difficulty is the time it takes for messages and files to travel between computers on the Internet. Communication speeds

> ### QUICK TIP
>
> There are several commercial networks that are separate from the Internet. These commercial networks provide users with features such as online newspapers and magazines, chat groups, access to investment activities, computer games, and special-interest bulletin boards as well as Internet access. Popular commercial networks include America Online and the Microsoft Network.

chapter
four

can be improved by using high-speed modems and special telephone lines. Faster Internet communication via cable is also becoming more widely available.

You should also be aware that the Internet is a cooperative effort, with few widely accepted presentation standards. As a result, the presentation of information on the Internet is varied and inconsistent. Some Web sites are well-designed and easy to use, while some are not. The Internet is a dynamic environment that changes daily with new host computers and Web sites being added and existing ones being removed. This means new or different information is available constantly. Also, old or outdated information may still be available on Web sites that are not properly maintained.

Also, there may be questions about the accuracy of information you find on the Internet. Remember that the Internet is a largely unregulated environment with few, if any, controls over what information is published on the Web or contained in files at FTP sites. It is a good idea to get supporting information from another source before using any information you find on the Internet to make critical business decisions.

Another challenge to using the Internet is the lack of privacy and security for your e-mail and file transmissions. Information sent from one computer to another can travel through many computer systems and networks, where it could be intercepted, copied, or altered. When you access a page on the World Wide Web, it is possible that information such as your e-mail address, which Web pages you view, the type of computer, operating system, and browser you are using, and how you linked to that page can be captured without your knowledge. If you are concerned, you can take advantage of security software that prevents this type of information from being captured.

Certain browser and server programs on Internet computers can encrypt (or scramble) information during transmission and then decrypt (or unscramble) it at its destination. Commercial activities, such as buying an item via credit card or transferring money between bank accounts, can occur in this type of secure environment. However, be advised that much Internet activity takes place in an insecure environment. Government regulations, as well as technological methods to assure privacy and security on the Internet, continue to be developed.

4.d Using Internet Explorer

A **Web browser** is a software application that helps you access Internet resources, including Web pages stored on computers called Web servers. A **Web page** is a document that contains hyperlinks (often called links) to other pages; it can also contain audio and video clips. A **hyperlink** is text or a picture that is associated with the location (path and filename) of another page. To open the Internet Explorer Web browser:

QUICK TIP

Many college and university libraries have Web sites with excellent tips on how to use and evaluate information on the Internet.

INTERNET TIP

To change the start page for the Internet Explorer Web browser, click the Internet Options command on the View menu and then click the General tab. Define the start page by keying the URL in the Address: text box or clicking the Use Current, Use Default, or Use Blank buttons. For more information on designating a start page, see Internet Explorer online Help.

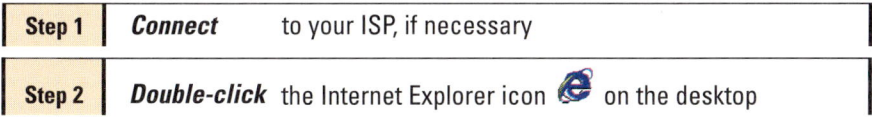

| Step 1 | **_Connect_** | to your ISP, if necessary |
| Step 2 | **_Double-click_** | the Internet Explorer icon 🅔 on the desktop |

When the Web browser opens, a Web page, called the **start page**, loads automatically. The start page used by the Internet Explorer Web browser can be the Microsoft default start page, a blank page, or any designated Web page. Figure 4-5 shows the home page for the publisher of this book as the start page.

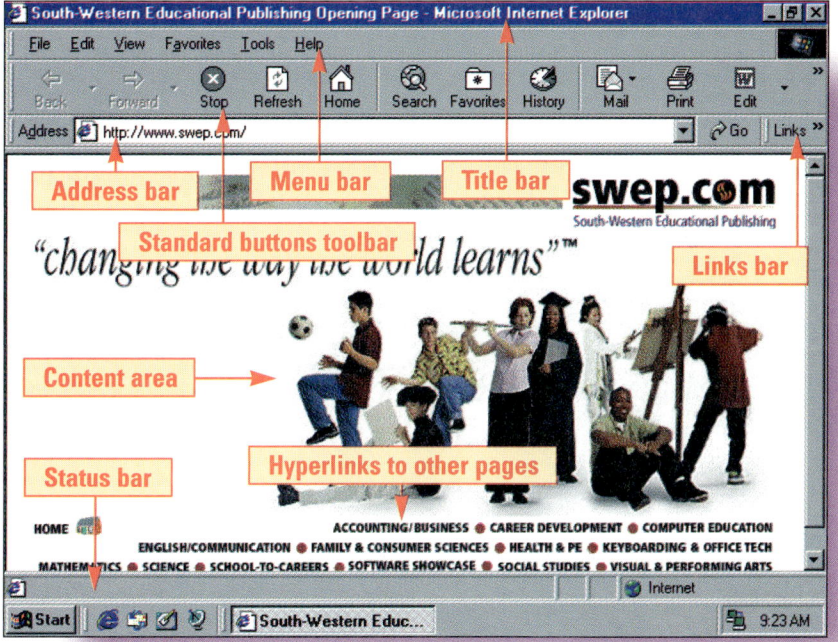

FIGURE 4-5
Internet Explorer
Web Browser

Loading a Web Page

Loading a Web page means that the Web browser sends a message to the computer (called a Web server) where the Web page is stored, requesting a copy of the Web page. The Web server responds by sending a copy of the Web page to your computer. In order to load a Web page, you must either know or find the page's **URL** (Uniform Resource Locator)—the path and filename of the page that is the Web page's address. One way to find the URL for a Web page is to use a search engine or directory or you might find a particular company's URL in one of the company's advertisements or on their letterheads and business cards. Examples of URLs based on an organization's name are:

South-Western Educational Publishing   *www.swep.com*
National Public Radio   *www.npr.org*
The White House   *www.whitehouse.gov*

chapter
four

QUICK TIP

When you start keying the URL of a Web page you have previously loaded, the AutoComplete feature automatically adds a suggested URL to the Address bar. You can continue by keying over the suggested URL or you can accept the suggested URL by pressing the ENTER key.

You can try to "guess" the URL based on the organization's name and top-level domain. For example, a good guess for the U.S. House of Representatives Web page is *www.house.gov.*

You can key a URL directly in the Address bar by first selecting all or part of the current URL and replacing it with the new URL. Internet Explorer adds the "http://" portion of the URL for you. To select the contents of the Address bar and key the URL for the U.S. House of Representatives:

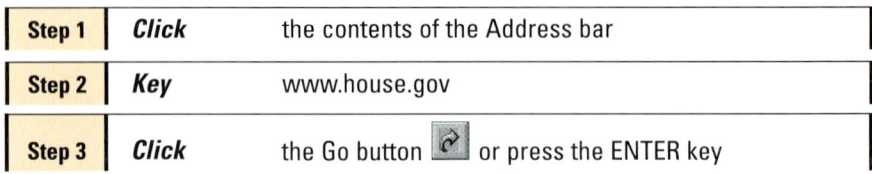

Step 1	*Click*	the contents of the Address bar
Step 2	*Key*	www.house.gov
Step 3	*Click*	the Go button or press the ENTER key

In a few seconds, the U.S. House of Representatives page loads. Your screen should look similar to Figure 4-6.

FIGURE 4-6
U.S. House of Representatives Web Page

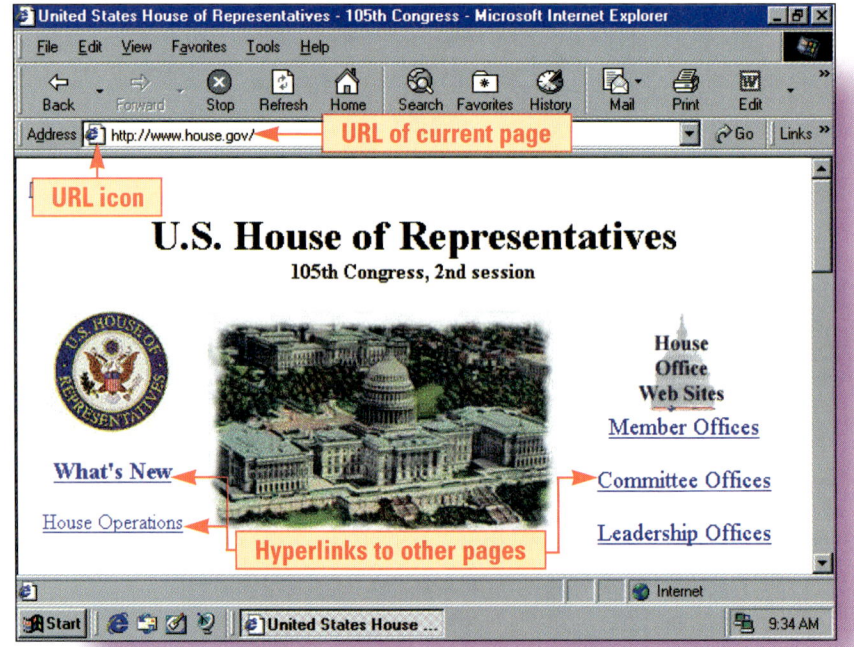

MENU TIP

You can key a URL in the Open dialog box by first clicking the Open command on the File menu.

You can create a favorite by clicking the Favorites command on the menu bar and then clicking Add to Favorites, by right-clicking the background (not a link) on the current Web page and clicking Add to Favorites, or by right-clicking a link on the current Web page and clicking Add to Favorites.

Creating Favorites

Web pages are constantly being updated with new information. If you like a certain Web page or find a Web page contains useful information and plan to revisit it, you may want to save its URL as a **favorite**. Suppose you want to load the U.S. House of Representatives home page frequently. You can create a favorite that saves the URL in a file on your hard disk. Then at any time, you can quickly load this Web page by clicking it in a list of favorites maintained on the Favorites menu.

The URLs you choose to save as favorites are stored in the Favorites folder on your hard disk. You can specify a new or different folder and you can change the name of the Web page as it appears in your list of favorites in this dialog box. To add the U.S. House of Representatives Web page as a favorite:

Step 1	*Click*	Favorites
Step 2	*Click*	Add to Favorites
Step 3	*Click*	OK
Step 4	*Click*	the Home button 🏠 to return to the default start page

One way to load a Web page from a favorite is to click the name of the favorite in the list of favorites on the Favorites menu. To load the U.S. House of Representatives home page from the Favorites menu:

Step 1	*Click*	Favorites
Step 2	*Click*	the U.S. House of Representatives favorite to load the page
Step 3	*Click*	the Home button 🏠 to return to the default start page

The Back and Forward buttons allow you to review recently loaded Web pages without keying the URL or using the Favorites list. To reload the U.S. House of Representatives Home page from the Back button list:

Step 1	*Click*	the Back button list arrow ⬅️▾ on the toolbar
Step 2	*Click*	United States House of Representatives

4.e Using Directories and Search Engines

Because the Web is so large, you often need to take advantage of special search tools, called search engines and directories, to find the information you need. To use some of the Web's numerous search engines and directories, you can click the Search button on the

QUICK TIP

Another way to load a favorite is to use the Favorites button to open the Favorites list in the **Explorer bar**, a pane that opens at the left side of your screen.

CAUTION TIP

Any Web page you load is stored in the Temporary Internet Files folder on your hard disk. Whenever you reload the Web page, Internet Explorer compares the stored page to the current Web page either each time you start the browser or each time you load the page. If the Web page on the server has been changed, a fresh Web page is downloaded. If not, the Web page is retrieved from the Temporary Internet File folder rather than downloaded. To view and change the Temporary Internet File folder options (and other Internet Explorer options), click the Internet Options command on the Tools menu.

chapter
four

QUICK TIP

You can also reload pages from the History folder, which stores the Web pages you load for a specific period of time. You set the number of days to store pages on the General tab in the Options dialog box. Click the History button on the toolbar to open the History list in the Explorer bar.

MOUSE TIP

The Links bar provides shortcuts to various Web pages at the Microsoft Web site. You can also add shortcuts to your favorite Web pages by dragging the URL icon from the Address bar to the Links bar. You can reposition the toolbar, the Address bar, and the Links bar by dragging each one to a new location below the title bar.

You can print the currently loaded Web page by clicking the Print button on the Standard toolbar or the Print command on the File menu.

Standard toolbar to open the Search list in the Explorer bar. To view the Search list:

Step 1	*Click*	the Search button 🔍 on the toolbar
Step 2	*Observe*	the search list options

Search engines maintain an index of keywords used in Web pages that you can search. Search engine indexes are updated automatically by software called **spiders** (or **robots**). Spiders follow links between pages throughout the entire Web, adding any new Web pages to the search engine's index. You should use a search engine when you want to find specific Web pages. Some of the most popular search engines include AltaVista, HotBot, and Northern Light.

Directories use a subject-type format similar to a library card catalog. A directory provides a list of links to broad general categories of Web sites such as "Entertainment" or "Business." When you click these links, a subcategory list of links appears. For example, if you click the "Entertainment" link you might then see "Movies," "Television," and "Video Games" links. To find links to Web sites containing information about movies, you would click the "Movies" link. Unlike search engines, whose indexes are updated automatically, directories add new Web sites only when an individual or a company asks that a particular Web site be included. Some directories also provide review comments and ratings for the Web sites in their index. Most directories also provide an internal search engine that can only be used to search the directory's index, not the entire Web. You use a directory when you are looking for information on broad general topics. Popular directories include Yahoo and Magellan Internet Guide.

To search for Web pages containing "movie guides:"

Step 1	*Key*	movie guides in the search list text box
Step 2	*Click*	the Search button or press the ENTER key
Step 3	*Observe*	the search results (a list of Web pages in the search list)

The search results list consists of Web page titles as hyperlinks. To load a page from the list, simply click the hyperlink. To close the Explorer bar and search list:

Step 1	*Click*	the Search button 🔍 on the toolbar

Guidelines for Searching the Web

Before you begin looking for information on the Web, it is a good idea to think about what you want to accomplish, establish a time frame in which to find the information, and then develop a search strategy. As you search, keep in mind the following guidelines:

1. To find broad, general information, start with a Web directory such as Galaxy or Yahoo.
2. To find a specific Web page, start with a search engine such as Alta Vista or HotBot.
3. Become familiar with a variety of search engines and their features. Review each search engine's online Help when you use it for the first time. Many search engine features are revised frequently so remember to review them regularly.
4. Search engines use spider programs to index all the pages on the Web. However, these programs work independently of each other, so not all search engines have the same index at any point in time. Use multiple search engines for each search.
5. **Boolean operators** allow you to combine or exclude keywords when using a search engine. **Proximal operators** allow you specify that search keywords be close together in a Web page. Boolean and proximal operators are words that allow you to specify relationships among search keywords or phrases using (brackets), OR, NOT, AND, NEAR, and FOLLOWED BY. Not all search engines support Boolean and proximal operators, but use them to reduce the scope of your search when they are available. For example, if you are looking for gold or silver and don't want Web pages devoted to music, try searching by the keywords *metals* not *heavy*. To make sure the keywords are in close proximity use the NEAR or FOLLOWED BY proximal operators.
6. Use very specific keywords. The more specific the phrase, the more efficient your search is. For example, use the phrase "online classes" plus the word genealogy (*"online classes"* + *genealogy*) rather than simply *genealogy* to find Web pages with information about classes in how to trace your family tree.
7. Watch your spelling. Be aware how the search engine you use handles capitalization. In one search engine "pear" may match "Pear", "pEaR", or "PEAR." In another search engine, "Pear" may match only "Pear."
8. Think of related words that might return the information you need. For example, if you search for information about oil, you might also use "petroleum" and "petrochemicals."
9. Search for common variations of word usage or spelling. For example, the keywords deep sea drilling, deepsea drilling, and deep-sea drilling may all provide useful information.
10. The search returns (or **hits**) are usually listed in order of relevance. You may find that only the first 10 or 12 hits are useful. To find more relevant Web pages, try searching with different keywords.

C A U T I O N   T I P

You get varying results when using several search engines or directories to search for information on the same topic. Also, search tools operate according to varying rules. For example, some search engines allow only a simple search on one keyword. Others allow you to refine your search by finding words within quotation marks together, by indicating proper names, or by using special operators such as "and," "or," and "not" to include or exclude search words. To save time, always begin by reviewing the search tool's online Help directions, then proceed with your search.

After you find the desired information, "let the user beware!" Because the Web is largely unregulated, anyone can put anything on a Web page. Evaluate carefully the credibility of all the information you find. Try to find out something about the author and his or her credentials, or the about validity of the origin of the information.

chapter four

Summary

▶ A network is a group of two or more computers linked by cable or telephone lines and the Internet is a worldwide "network of networks."

▶ The Internet began in the late 1960s as the military Internet ARPAnet. By the 1980s the National Science Foundation assumed responsibility for the non-military portions and the term Internet became widely used.

▶ The World Wide Web is a subset of the Internet that uses computers called Web servers to store documents called Web pages.

▶ To access the Internet, your computer must have some physical communication medium, such as a cable or dial-up modem and a special communication program.

▶ An Internet Service Provider (or ISP) maintains a host computer on the Internet. In order to connect to the Internet, you need to connect to the host computer.

▶ Each host computer has an Internet address or IP address consisting of a series of numbers and a descriptive name based on the computer name and domain of the host. In addition to the host computer IP address and descriptive name, each user has a name that identifies their account at the Internet Service Provider.

▶ Large commercial enterprises, colleges, and universities may have a computer network on the Internet and can provide Internet access to their employees or students.

▶ There are many challenges to using the Internet—including the amount of available information, communication speed, the dynamic environment, lack of presentation standards, and privacy/security issues.

▶ You should carefully evaluate the source and author of information you get from the Internet and confirm any business-critical information from another source.

▶ Other external networks related to the Internet are large commercial networks, such as America Online, the Microsoft Network, and USENET.

▶ You use Web browsers, such as Internet Explorer, to load Web pages.

▶ Web pages are connected by hyperlinks, which are text or pictures associated with the path to another page.

▶ Directories and search engines are tools to help you find files and Web sites on the Internet.

Commands Review

Action	Menu Bar	Shortcut Menu	Toolbar	Keyboard
Load a Web page	File, Open			ALT + F, O Key URL in the Address bar and press the ENTER key
Save a favorite	Favorites, Add to Favorites	Right-click hyperlink, click Add to Favorites	Drag URL icon to Links bar or Favorites command	ALT + A, A CTRL + D
Manage the Standard toolbar, Address bar, and Links bar	View, Toolbars	Right-click the Standard toolbar, click desired command	Drag the Standard toolbar, Address bar, or Links bar to the new location	ALT + V, T
Load the search, history, or favorites list in the Explorer bar	View, Explorer Bar			ALT + V, E

Concepts Review

Circle the correct answer.

1. To post messages of common interest to electronic bulletin boards, use:

[a] search tools.

[b] e-mail.

[c] file access.

[d] newsgroups.

2. A network is:

[a] the Internet.

[b] a group of two or more computers linked by cable or telephone wire.

[c] a group of two or more computer networks linked by cable or telephone lines.

[d] a computer that stores Web pages.

3. The Internet began as the:

[a] MILNET.

[b] NSFnet.

[c] SLIPnet.

[d] ARPAnet.

4. Which of the following is not a challenge to using the Internet?

[a] chat groups.

[b] dynamic environment and heavy usage.

[c] volume of information.

[d] security and privacy.

Circle **T** if the statement is true or **F** if the statement is false.

T   F   1. An IP address is a unique identifying number for each host computer on the Internet.

T   F   2. A host computer's descriptive name identifies it by name and organizational level on the Internet.

T   F   3. Commercial networks that provide specially formatted features are the same as the Internet.

T   F   4. USENET is the name of the military Internet.

Skills Review

Exercise 1

1. Open the Internet Explorer Web browser.

2. Open the Internet Options dialog box by clicking the Internet Options command on the View menu.

3. Review the options on the General tab in the dialog box.

4. Write down the steps to change the default start page to a blank page.

5. Close the dialog box and close the Web browser.

chapter four

Exercise 2

1. Connect to your ISP and open the Internet Explorer Web browser.

2. Open the search list in the Explorer bar. Search for Web pages about "dog shows."

3. Load one of the Web pages in the search results list. Close the Explorer bar.

4. Print the Web page by clicking the Print command on the File menu and close the Web browser.

Exercise 3

1. Connect to your ISP and open the Internet Explorer Web browser.

2. Load the National Public radio Web page by keying the URL, *www.npr.org*, in the Address bar.

3. Print the Web page by clicking the Print command on the File menu and close the Web browser.

Exercise 4

1. Connect to your ISP and open the Internet Explorer Web browser.

2. Load the AltaVista search engine by keying the URL, *www.altavista.digital.com*, in the Address bar.

3. Save the Web page as a favorite. Search for Web pages about your city.

4. Print at least two Web pages by clicking the Print command on the File menu and close your Web browser.

Case Projects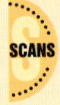

Project 1

Your supervisor asks you to prepare a fifteen-minute presentation describing the Internet Explorer toolbar buttons. Review the toolbar buttons and practice using them. Write an outline for your presentation that lists each button and describes how it is used.

Project 2

Your manager is concerned about Internet security and wants to know more about Internet Explorer security features. Click the Contents and Index command on the Internet Explorer Help menu to locate and review the topics about security. Write a note to your manager discussing two security topics.

Project 3

You are working for a book publisher who is creating a series of books about popular movie actors and actresses from the 1920s to the 1950s, including Humphrey Bogart and Lionel Barrymore. The research director asks you to locate a list of movies on the Web that the actors starred in. Use the Explorer bar search list and the Yahoo directory search tool to find links to "Entertainment." Close the Explorer bar and then, working from the Yahoo Web page, click "Movies" within the Entertainment category, scroll down and click the Actors and Actresses link. Search for Humphrey Bogart in the Actors and Actresses portion of the database. Link to the Web page that shows the filmography for Humphrey Bogart. Print the Web page that shows all the movies he acted in. Use the History list to return to the Actors and Actresses search page. Search for Lionel Barrymore, link to and print the filmography for him. Close the Internet Explorer Web browser.

Project 4

You are the new secretary for the Business Women's Forum. The association's president asked you to compile a list of Internet resources. Connect to your ISP, open Internet Explorer, and search for pages containing the keywords "women in business" (including the quotation marks). From the search results, click the Web page title link of your choice. Review the new Web page and its links. Create a favorite for that page. Use the Back button list to reload the search results and click a different Web page title from the list. Review the Web page and its links. Create a favorite for the Web page. Load and review at least five pages. Return to the default home page. Use the Go menu and the History bar to reload at least three of the pages. Print two of the pages. Delete the favorites you added, and then close Internet Explorer.

Using Outlook 2000

Chapter Overview

I t's a busy world. Every day, the Internet transfers millions of pieces of information. E-mail has replaced U.S. postal mail (snail mail) and, to some extent, the telephone, as *the* standard form of communications in nearly all businesses. In addition to e-mail communication, you need to keep track of all sorts of information about your busy workday. Contact information, including phone numbers, addresses, e-mail and Web site addresses, is just the beginning.

LEARNING OBJECTIVES

- ▶ Identify the components of the Outlook window
- ▶ Customize Outlook
- ▶ Use Outlook as an e-mail client
- ▶ Use the Outlook Calendar
- ▶ Use the Outlook Contact Manager
- ▶ Use the Outlook Task Manager
- ▶ Use the Outlook Journal
- ▶ Use the Outlook Notes Manager
- ▶ Use Advanced Outlook features

Case profile

Walters, Robertson & Associates is a large architectural firm with clients and projects around the world. The firm's principals are constantly on the road, meeting with clients, giving presentations, designing buildings, and visiting job sites. You have been assigned as the project manager to a new multimillion dollar skyscraper project called Nakamichi Plaza. It is your job to coordinate communications between the design team, the project engineers, the contractor, your boss, and the owner of the project.

outlook

notes This text assumes that you have little or no knowledge of the Outlook application. However, it is assumed that you have read Office Chapters 1-4 of this book and that you are familiar with Windows 95 or Windows 98 concepts and common elements of Office 2000 applications.

1.a Identifying the Components of the Outlook Window

Outlook is a personal information manager, or PIM. A **PIM** helps you stay organized, reminds you when it's time for a meeting, keeps track of when you last spoke to an important client, allows you to send e-mail, and keeps track of names and addresses.

Outlook is organized into several folders. Each folder is used to store different items. For example, the Calendar folder is where you schedule meetings, the Tasks folder is where you record tasks you need to get done, and the Inbox folder is where your e-mail is placed when you receive it.

To start Outlook:

Step 1	*Click*	the Start button ![Start] on the taskbar
Step 2	*Point to*	<u>P</u>rograms
Step 3	*Click*	Microsoft Outlook
Step 4	*Click*	the Outlook Today shortcut ![icon] on the left

The Outlook window opens. Your screen should look similar to Figure 1-1. Table 1-1 identifies the important elements of Outlook.

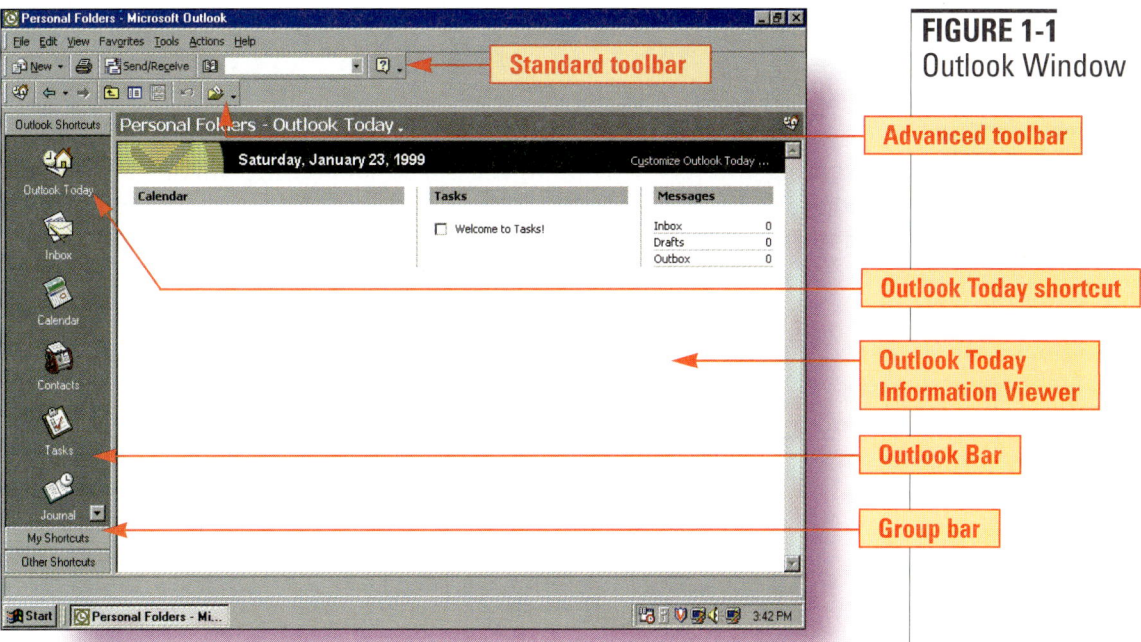

FIGURE 1-1
Outlook Window

Component	Function
Outlook Today	**Outlook Today** provides a quick overview of all the important events happening today. Items listed in Today are hyperlinks, such as those found on a Web page, enabling you to jump quickly to the appropriate folder or item.
Outlook Bar	The **Outlook Bar** is where you access groups and folder shortcuts. When you create a message, an appointment, a note, or other Outlook document, these items are stored in Outlook folders.
Group bar	**Groups** store shortcuts to Outlook folders. Click a group bar to open or close the group.
Folders	**Folders** store items of information, such as appointments, tasks, or e-mail messages.
Shortcuts	**Shortcuts** provide quick access to different features within Outlook, such as the Journal or the Task Manager. You can also use shortcuts to jump to your favorite Web site or to manage important folders on your hard drive without ever leaving Outlook.
Standard Toolbar	The **Standard toolbar** is made up of buttons that start commonly used commands, such as printing or starting a new item. Additional buttons appear on this toolbar when you switch to different Outlook folders. For example, the Standard toolbar in the Inbox folder (one of the Mail folders) contains buttons to reply to or forward a message.
Advanced Toolbar	The **Advanced toolbar** contains buttons to start advanced commands, such as Undo or moving between folders. Additional buttons appear on this toolbar depending on which folder of Outlook you are in. For example, when you are in the Calendar folder, the Advanced toolbar has a button for planning a meeting.

TABLE 1-1
Outlook Components

outlook

1.b Customizing Outlook

As you begin working on the Nakamichi Plaza project, you will begin sending and receiving many messages concerning the project. You can add folders to Outlook for each project you work on. This helps you stay organized.

notes The Office Assistant, which you can use to search for online Help topics, appears automatically when you launch Outlook unless you hide it or turn it off. The default Office Assistant animated graphic is "Clippit." In this book, the Office Assistant is hidden unless you need it for a specific activity. To hide the Office Assistant, right-click it, then click Hide on the shortcut menu.

Creating Groups, Folders and Shortcuts

The Outlook Bar, located to the left of the Outlook window, helps you organize all the items you create, send, and receive while you are using Outlook. Use the Outlook Bar to create groups, folders and shortcuts. The Outlook Bar contains three groups: the Outlook Shortcuts group, the My Shortcuts group, and the Other Shortcuts group. Within each group, shortcuts provide quick access to one of several folders. To change groups:

Step 1	*Click*	the My Shortcuts group bar

The My Shortcuts group contains shortcuts to additional mail folders which you learn about later in the chapter. You want to create a new folder for your project and add a shortcut to this folder in the My Shortcuts group. To create a new folder:

Step 1	*Click*	File
Step 2	*Point to*	New
Step 3	*Click*	Folder to open the Create New Folder dialog box
Step 4	*Key*	Nakamichi Mail in the Name: box
Step 5	*Verify*	that the Folder contains: box contains Mail Items
Step 6	*Click*	the + sign next to Personal Folders, if necessary to display the list of folders
Step 7	*Click*	Inbox as the location of your new folder

Selecting Inbox as the location places your new folder, Nakamichi Mail, as a subfolder in the Inbox. The dialog box on your screen should look similar to Figure 1-2.

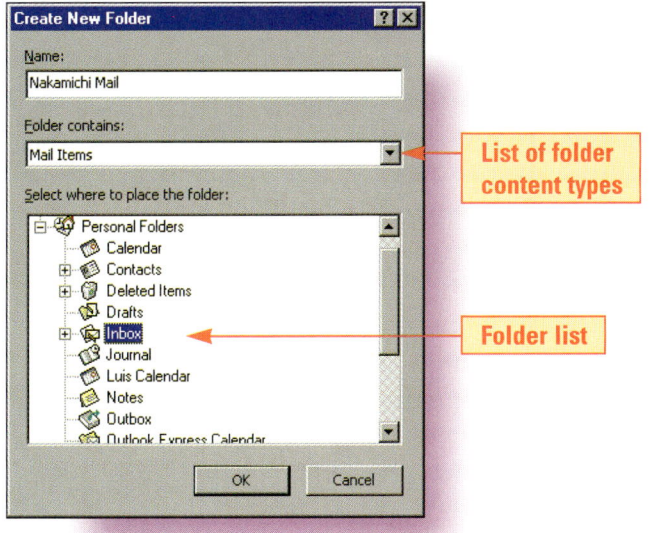

List of folder content types

Folder list

FIGURE 1-2
Create New Folder
Dialog Box

Step 8	*Click*	OK

MOUSE TIP

To add a new group, right-click anywhere in the Outlook Bar, then click Add New Group. To remove a group, right-click the group title bar that you want to remove, then click Remove Group. To rename a group, right-click the group bar you want to rename, then click Rename Group.

Outlook prompts you to add a shortcut for your new folder to the Outlook Bar.

Step 9	*Click*	Yes

Outlook creates a new folder called Nakamichi Mail, and places a shortcut to this folder in the My Shortcuts group.

Changing Information Views

Every folder in Outlook can be viewed several different ways by changing the Current View setting on the Advanced toolbar. When you first start Outlook the Advanced toolbar may not be displayed. To display the Advanced toolbar:

Step 1	*Right-click*	the toolbar area at the top of the Outlook window
Step 2	*Click*	Advanced

QUICK TIP

You can add shortcuts to any group. Right-click inside the shortcut area of the group to which you want to add a shortcut and click Outlook Bar Shortcut. Select the folder name in the Folder name list, or by double-clicking the folder from the tree view below the Folder name list.

outlook

CAUTION TIP

If Advanced already has a check mark next to it on the Toolbars list, do not click it because the toolbar is already displayed.

The Advanced toolbar appears below the Standard toolbar. Today has only one view, so the Current View button does not appear. To switch to another folder and change the current view:

Step 1	*Click*	the Outlook Shortcuts group bar
Step 2	*Click*	the Calendar shortcut 📅 in the Outlook Bar
Step 3	*Click*	the Current View list arrow on the Advanced toolbar
Step 4	*Click*	Active Appointments

The current view list displays different options depending on which folder you are currently viewing. The Calendar folder switches from a calendar planner type view to a list view of any appointments, including holidays, currently on your schedule. Although the views are different for each Outlook folder, you can easily change the view to display data the way you want to see it.

1.c Using Outlook as an E-mail Client

One of Outlook's most important tasks is to help you send, receive, and organize your e-mail. Outlook's default folders are a good start to organizing the many e-mail messages you receive and send. **Inbox** is the default destination for incoming messages. **Drafts** stores messages you have started and saved but aren't ready to send yet. **Outbox** holds messages that will be sent the next time you connect to your ISP or mail server. **Sent Items** keeps copies of messages you have already sent. To open the Inbox folder:

CAUTION TIP

If you don't see the Inbox shortcut in the Outlook Shortcuts group, click the My Shortcuts group bar.

Step 1	*Click*	the Inbox shortcut 📧 in the Outlook Bar

Inbox is the default location for incoming messages. Figure 1-3 shows the Inbox folder. You should see a message with the subject "Welcome to Microsoft Outlook 2000!" in your Inbox. This message is in HTML format, allowing pictures and font formatting to be inserted in the message body.

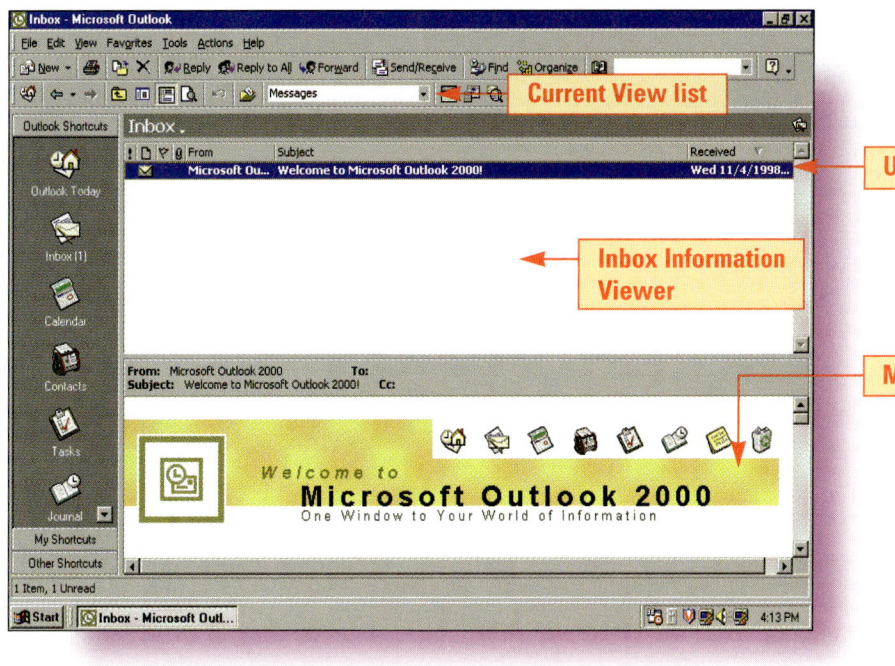

FIGURE 1-3
Inbox Folder

Current View list

Unread message

Inbox Information Viewer

Message Preview window

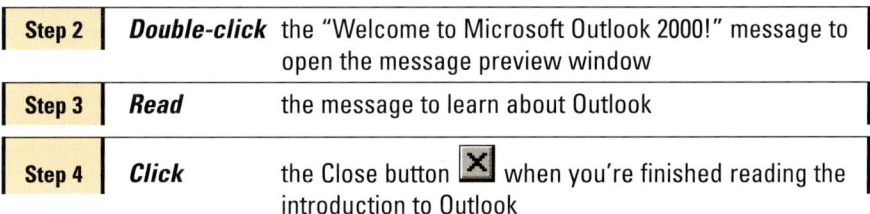

Step 2	**Double-click**	the "Welcome to Microsoft Outlook 2000!" message to open the message preview window
Step 3	**Read**	the message to learn about Outlook
Step 4	**Click**	the Close button when you're finished reading the introduction to Outlook

MENU TIP

Outlook gives you the option of using Word as your e-mail editor. To set Word as your default e-mail editor, click Options on the Tools menu. On the Mail Format tab, click the box next to Use Microsoft Word to edit e-mail messages, then click OK.

Creating and Sending an E-mail Message

You need to send a message to the engineer who will be working on the Nakamichi Plaza project. For these activities, you can send the messages to yourself. If you have a classmate who can exchange messages with you, you can use his or her e-mail address instead of your own. Be sure to have your classmate send you the message as well. To create a message:

Step 1	**Click**	the New Mail Message button [New ▾] on the Standard Toolbar

The e-mail editor opens. See Figure 1-4 for an overview of the e-mail form.

outlook

FIGURE 1-4
E-mail Form

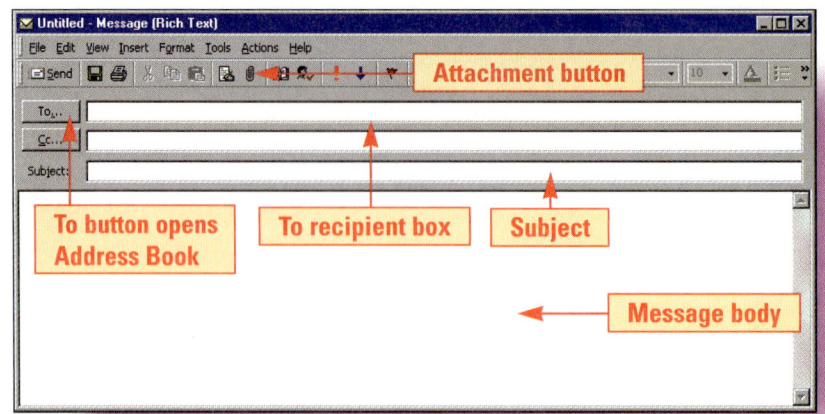

You fill in the e-mail address(es) of the recipient(s) in the **To:** and **Cc:** boxes located at the top of the message form. Some people send **C**ourtesy **c**opies of messages to recipients, even if a reply is not expected. You can send a message to several people at once by keying in as many addresses as you like, separated by a semicolon.

The **Subject:** box summarizes the content or topic of your message. People often scan the subject lines of incoming messages to determine their importance. Be concise and to the point when wording your subject line.

The **message body**, like the body of a letter, contains the content of your message. Although e-mail is easy to use, be concise in your writing. The longer your message is, the longer it takes to send, download, and read. Busy people expect messages to get to the point.

Step 2	*Key*	your e-mail address in the To: box
Step 3	*Press*	the TAB key twice to move to the Subject: box
Step 4	*Key*	ENGINEER: Oval Design for Nakamichi Plaza
Step 5	*Press*	the TAB key to move to the message box
Step 6	*Key*	The design team has proposed using an oval footprint for the Nakamichi Plaza building. Do you see any problems in constructing this shape building?

Your screen should look similar to Figure 1-5.

Step 7	*Click*	the <u>S</u>end button  on the Standard toolbar

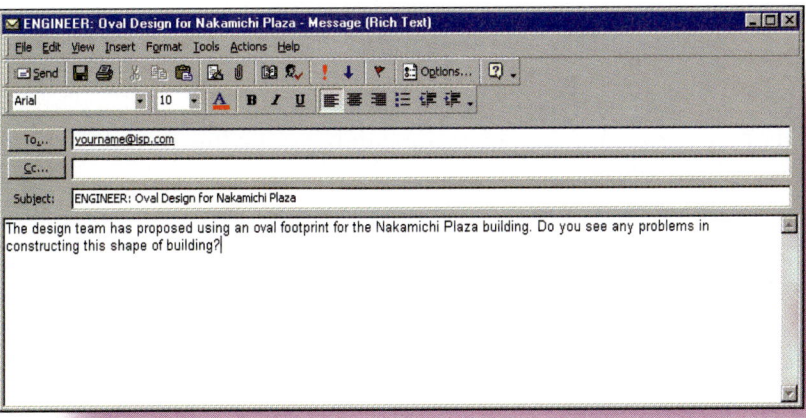

FIGURE 1-5
Completed Message

M O U S E   T I P

You can send any file, like a Word document or Excel workbook, as an attachment to an e-mail message. To do this, start a new message. Click the Insert File button 📎. Use the Insert File dialog box (similar to the Open dialog box) to locate the file you wish to attach, then click Insert.

When you click the Send button, your message is placed in the Outbox folder, where it stays until you click the Send/Receive button. If you are on a network or connected to your ISP, the message may be sent automatically.

| Step 8 | *Click* | the My Shortcuts group bar |
| Step 9 | *Click* | the Outbox shortcut 📬 |

If you see the message in the Outbox, you need to click the Send/Receive button to connect to your ISP or mail server.

| Step 10 | *Click* | the Send/Receive button on the Standard toolbar |

The message is sent to yourself or a classmate. After Outlook sends messages in the Outbox, it retrieves any incoming messages. Outlook notifies you with a tone and displays a dialog box alerting you that you have new messages when you receive new mail.

Replying to and Forwarding Messages

Replying to a message sends the original message along with your response back to the sender. **Forwarding** sends a copy of a message you've received to a different address. You should have received the message you sent to yourself, or sent to you by a classmate. This message is in your Inbox. To open the message:

| Step 1 | *Click* | the Outlook Shortcuts group bar |

Q U I C K   T I P

Outlook allows you to use **name aliases** in the recipient boxes. A name alias is a shortened version of a person's name, like a nickname, that you can key in place of the full e-mail address. Once you enter a contact's information in Contact Manager or the Address Book, use the name alias in one of the addressing boxes.

MOUSE TIP

If you don't see the Inbox shortcut in the Outlook Shortcuts group, click the My Shortcuts group bar.

Step 2	*Click*	the Inbox shortcut

If you don't see your message immediately, wait a few minutes, then click the Send/Receive button again.

Step 3	*Double-click*	the ENGINEER message

The message opens in a new window, as shown in Figure 1-6. Using the toolbar buttons in the message window, you can reply to or forward the message, print it, flag it for importance, move it to another folder, or delete it.

FIGURE 1-6
Message Dialog Box

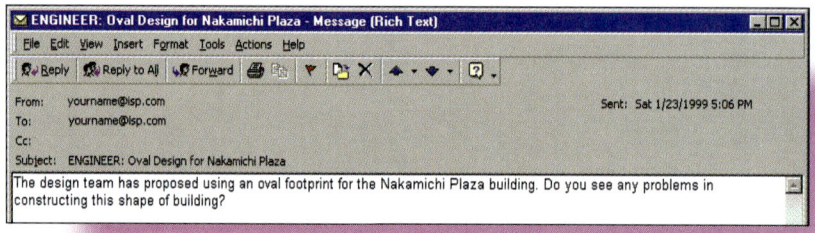

CAUTION TIP

Use caution when replying to (or forwarding) a lengthy message. Cut all but the most essential lines of the original message by selecting the unwanted text and pressing the DELETE key.

Replying to a message by clicking the Reply button creates a copy of the original message, and automatically addresses the new message back to the sender. Also, RE: is added to the subject, indicating that the new message is a reply to the first message. All you need to do is enter your response in the message box. To send a reply to an e-mail message:

Step 1	*Click*	the Reply button [Reply] on the Standard toolbar in the message window
Step 2	*Key*	Structurally, there's no reason why this shape of building can't be built. However, curved glass will be quite expensive. We'll need to discuss the placement and spacing of structural columns as the design progresses.
Step 3	*Click*	the Send button [Send] on the Standard toolbar to deliver the message to your Outbox folder

QUICK TIP

Delete a message from any mail folder by clicking the message to select it, then pressing the DELETE key. You can also click the Delete button X on the Standard toolbar.

Similar to replying to a message, forwarding a message creates a copy of the original message, and adds FW: in front of the subject line to indicate the message has been forwarded. However, when you forward a message, it is sent to another contact. In this case, you have to fill in the recipient's address, in addition to anything you might want to add in the message box. You want to forward a copy of the

ENGINEER message to the builder. If you have the e-mail address of another classmate, you can forward the message to that classmate instead of yourself. To forward the ENGINEER message:

Step 1	*Click*	the For**w**ard button [Forward] on the Message Standard toolbar
Step 2	*Key*	your e-mail address in the To: box
Step 3	*Press*	the TAB key three times to move to the message box
Step 4	*Key*	The design department is considering an oval shape for the Nakamichi Plaza building. Thought you might want to add your comments.
Step 5	*Click*	the **S**end button [Send] on the Standard toolbar
Step 6	*Close*	the ENGINEER message by clicking the Close button [X]
Step 7	*Click*	the Send/Re**c**eive button [Send/Receive] on the Standard toolbar

The messages in the Outbox are sent. You have several meetings to plan for next week. In the next section, you learn to schedule meetings using the Calendar folder.

1.d Using the Outlook Calendar

Next week is going to be a busy week. You have a staff meeting on Monday, a visit to a job site on Tuesday, and you want to review progress on the Nakamichi Plaza plans on Wednesday. Calendar helps you get your schedule under control. You can schedule appointments, meetings, and events. To change the Calendar view:

Step 1	*Click*	the Calendar shortcut [icon]
Step 2	*Click*	the Current View list arrow on the Advanced toolbar
Step 3	*Click*	Day/Week/Month
Step 4	*Click*	the Da**y** button [Day] on the Standard Toolbar

You can change between day, work week, week, or month views by clicking the appropriate button on the Standard toolbar. Figure 1-7

outlook

shows important elements of the Calendar Information Viewer and a sample appointment. Your screen will differ slightly as the date will be different and you should not have any items on your calendar.

FIGURE 1-7
Calendar View

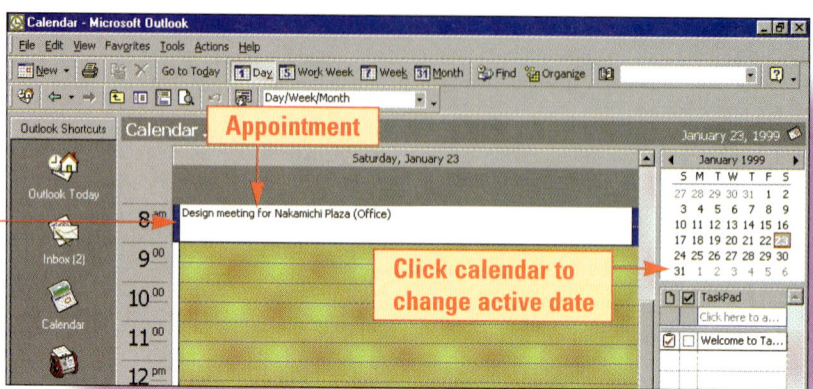

Scheduling Appointments

Monday you will be in your office preparing for your trip. When you schedule an **appointment**, it usually does not involve other people in your office. To create a new appointment:

Step 1	*Click*	the <u>N</u>ew Appointment button [New ▾] on the Standard toolbar

The Appointment dialog box appears, as shown in Figure 1-8.

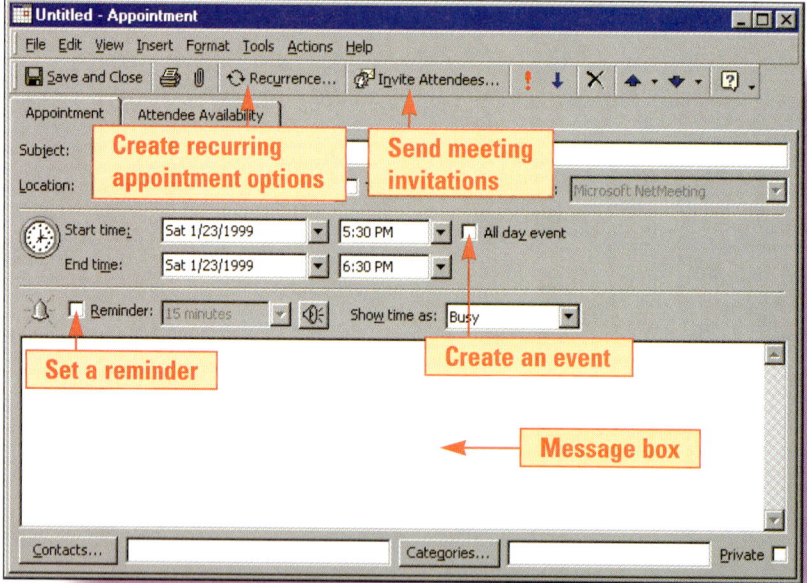

FIGURE 1-8
Appointment Dialog Box

QUICK TIP

When you work in an office, Outlook can help you plan meetings with others. **Meetings** are similar to appointments, but usually involve other people in your office. By sharing your calendar with others, they can view your availability and automatically plan and schedule meetings. To find out more about how to share folders and schedule meetings, use Outlook Help.

| Step 2 | *Enter* | the information provided in Table 1-2 in the corresponding fields of the New Appointment dialog box |

Press the TAB key to move between fields. In the Start time: box where you select the date, key the value shown.

Field	Key/Select
Subject:	In Office
Location:	Office
Start time: (date)	Next Monday
Start time: (time)	10:30 AM
End Time: (time)	5:00 PM
Show time as:	Free

TABLE 1-2
Information for New
Appointment Dialog Box

Step 3	*Verify*	that the Reminder: check box is not selected
Step 4	*Click*	the Save and Close button 🖫 Save and Close on the Standard toolbar in the Appointment window
Step 5	*Click*	the Month button 31 Month on the Standard toolbar

Your appointment is added to the calendar. Next, you schedule an all-day event.

Scheduling Events

Events in Outlook are activities that last at least one full day. Holidays, vacations, and business trips are some examples. You set up an event the same way you do an appointment, but you specify that the appointment is an all day event. The event is displayed differently than an appointment in your calendar. Events display a banner at the top of the calendar day(s). Next Tuesday, you are scheduled to visit one of the firm's job sites out of town. To schedule this event in your calendar:

| Step 1 | *Click* | the New Appointment button ▦ New ▾ on the Standard toolbar |
| Step 2 | *Enter* | the information provided in Table 1-3 in the corresponding fields of the New Appointment dialog box |

QUICK TIP

C Use **natural language dates** in Outlook. Any time you need to enter a date in a date field, try keying a phrase, such as "tomorrow," "ten days from Thursday," or "two weeks ago." Outlook automatically determines the date from your phrase.

MOUSE TIP

Move your pointer over any appointment and "hover" for about a second. A yellow ScreenTip displays the full contents of the appointment's subject line.

outlook

TABLE 1-3
Event Information

Field	Key/Select
Subject:	Nakamichi Plaza Site Visit
Location:	New York City
Start time: (date)	Next Tuesday

Step 3	*Click*	the check box next to All day event

You want to set a reminder to yourself. To set a reminder:

Step 1	*Click*	the check box next to Reminder
Step 2	*Select*	1 day from the Reminder list

Outlook will display a Reminder dialog box one day prior to this event. Now finish entering the information for the reminder.

Step 3	*Click*	in the message box
Step 4	*Key*	Meet at site with owner and civil engineer to discuss site grading
Step 5	*Click*	the Save and Close button 💾 Save and Close on the Standard toolbar in the Appointment window
Step 6	*Click*	the Work Week button 5 Work Week on the Advanced toolbar
Step 7	*Click*	next week in the calendar located in the upper-right corner of the Information Viewer

You have created an event for next Tuesday.

Scheduling a Multi-Day Event

In reviewing your trip itinerary for next week, you realize you won't be able to get everything done in one day. To change your all-day event into a multi-day event:

Step 1	*Move*	the mouse pointer to the right edge of the Nakamichi Plaza site visit banner in your calendar
Step 2	*Click & Drag*	the edge of the appointment to Wednesday
Step 3	*Press*	the ENTER key

The event is now scheduled for two days. See Figure 1-9.

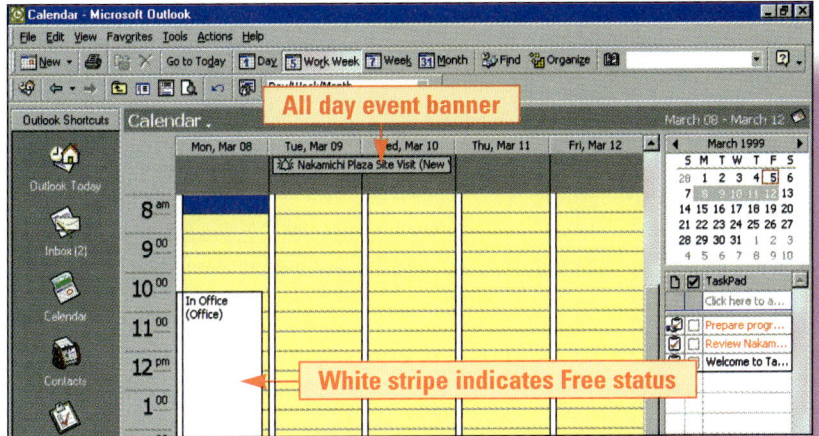

FIGURE 1-9
Sample Schedule

Planning a Recurring Meeting

You try and arrange your schedule so you can be in the office every Monday. It is easy to change any appointment or meeting a recurring one. To set a recurring appointment:

Step 1	***Double-click*** the In Office appointment you set up earlier

Step 2	***Click***	the Recurrence button on the Standard toolbar in the Appointment window

The Appointment Recurrence dialog box opens, as shown in Figure 1-10. You can set up recurring appointments in just about any configuration you like: several times a week, every third month, and so on. You can also set an end date for the recurring appointments.

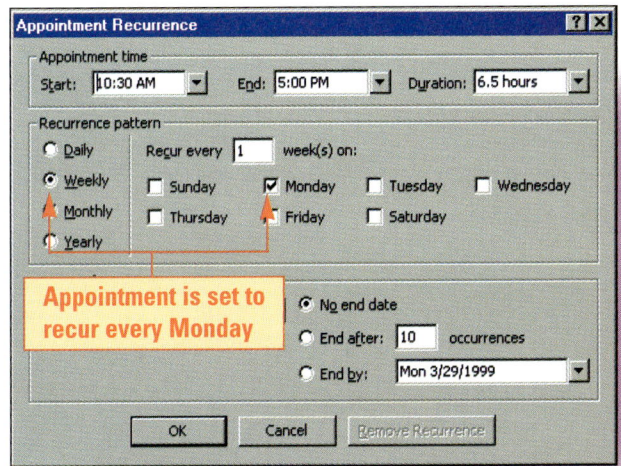

FIGURE 1-10
Appointment Recurrence Dialog Box

outlook

Outlook automatically assumes you want the appointment to occur weekly on Mondays (the same day of the original appointment), with N<u>o</u> end date. If you wanted to change the day, recurrence pattern or range of recurrence, you could set those options here. These options are fine for now.

| Step 3 | *Click* | OK |
| Step 4 | *Click* | the <u>S</u>ave and Close button [💾 Save and Close] on the Standard toolbar in the Appointment window |

Two circular arrows are added next to the appointment, indicating that it is a recurring appointment. In the next section, you use Contact Manager to keep track of contact information.

1.e Using the Outlook Contact Manager

Contact Manager is where you store information about your contacts. Contact Manager gives you easy access to information about all of your contacts. To access the Contact Manager:

| Step 1 | *Click* | the Contacts shortcut [🖼] in the Outlook Shortcuts group in the Outlook Bar |
| Step 2 | *Select* | Address Cards from the Current View list on the Advanced toolbar |

Contacts displays a list view of your contacts in Address Card format, similar to Figure 1-11.

FIGURE 1-11
Contacts Folder

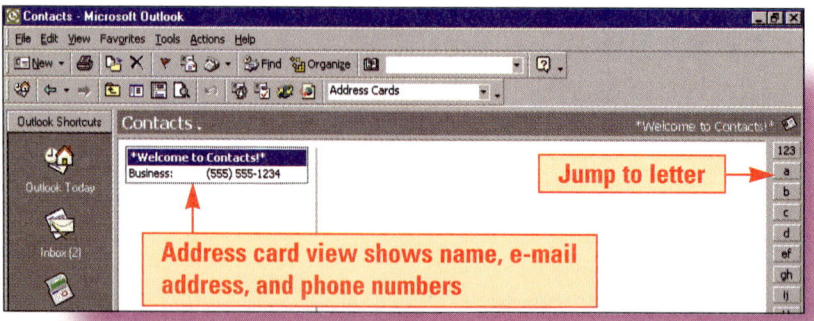

Adding a Contact

Your contact list is a powerful way to organize all your contact information in a central location. To add a contact to the list:

| Step 1 | *Click* | the New Contact button  on the Standard toolbar |

The Contact dialog box appears, as shown in Figure 1-12.

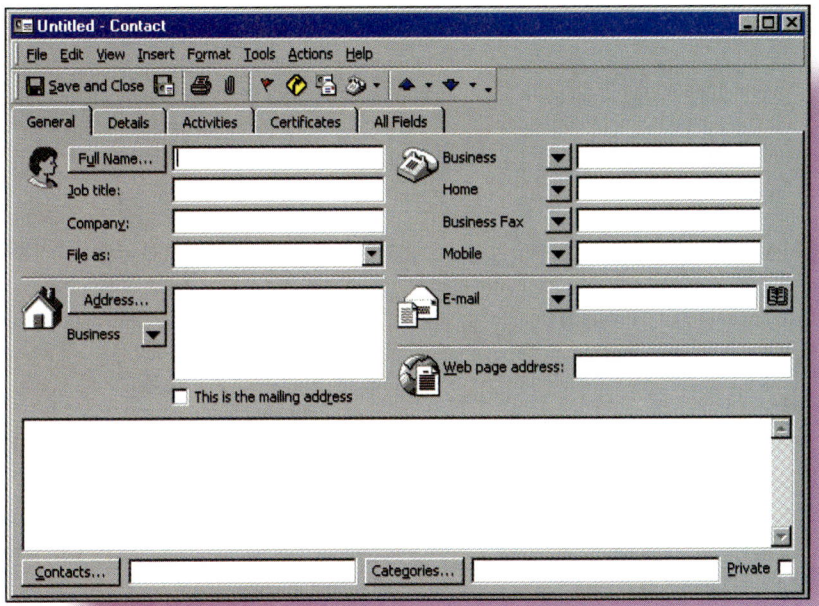

FIGURE 1-12
Contact Dialog Box

QUICK TIP

 You may need to add several contacts who work at the same company. Create the first contact and fill in as much of the company information as you have available. From the Actions menu, click New Contact from Same Company. A new contact is started with the company information automatically entered.

| Step 2 | *Enter* | the information provided in Table 1-4 in the corresponding fields of the Contact dialog box |

TABLE 1-4
Contact Information

Field	Key/Select
F**u**ll Name	Osuro Nakamichi
Job title:	CEO
Compan**y**:	Nakamichi Development
Business phone number	(555) 555-1234
E-mail	Osuro@nakamichidevelopment.com
We**b** page address:	www.nakamichidevelopment.com

outlook

Step 3	*Click*	the Details tab
Step 4	*Key*	February 12 in the <u>B</u>irthday field
Step 5	*Click*	the <u>S</u>ave and Close button ![Save and Close] on the Advanced toolbar

A new address card appears in your contact list. Using Contact Manager, you can store up to 19 phone numbers, three e-mail addresses, a Web site address, a nickname, and the birthdays of both your contact and his or her spouse!

1.f Using the Outlook Task Manager

Many people use a "to-do" list to keep track of important things they need to get done. Outlook uses the **Task Manager** to keep track of these important items. You have several tasks you need to accomplish. To open the Task Manager folder:

Step 1	*Click*	the Task shortcut ![icon] in the Outlook Shortcuts group in the Outlook Bar
Step 2	*Select*	Detailed List from the Current View list on the Advanced toolbar

Figure 1-13 shows the Task Information Viewer in a detailed Task List view.

FIGURE 1-13
Detailed Task List View

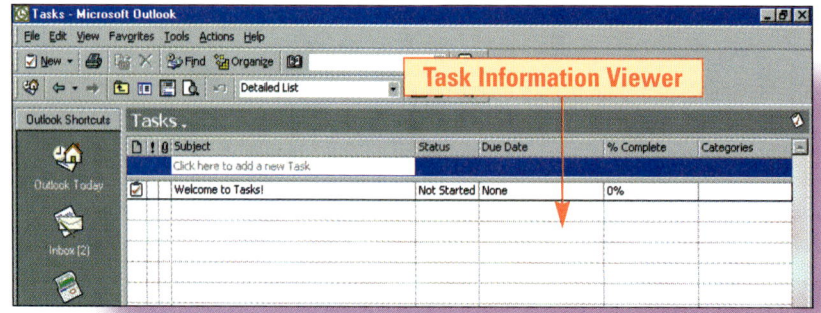

Creating a Task

One of the things you need to accomplish today is to review the schematic drawings for the Nakamichi Plaza project. To create a new task:

| Step 1 | *Click* | the New Task button 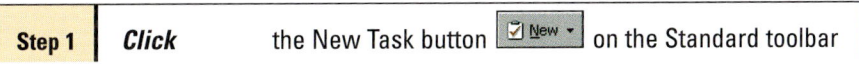 on the Standard toolbar |

The Task dialog box opens, as shown in Figure 1-14.

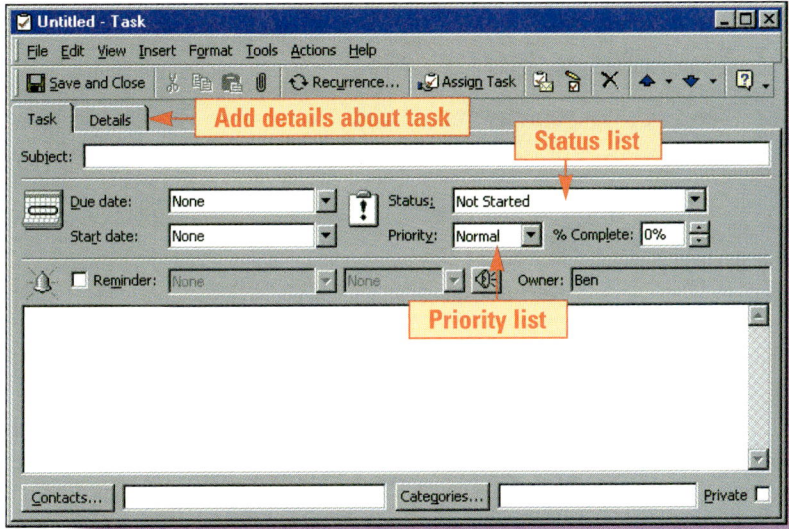

FIGURE 1-14
Task Dialog Box

Step 2	*Key*	Review Nakamichi Plaza schematics in the Subject field
Step 3	*Press*	the TAB key to move to the Due Date field
Step 4	*Key*	Today
Step 5	*Press*	the ENTER key
Step 6	*Click*	the Save and Close button  on the Standard toolbar in the Task dialog box

When you set up this task, you entered a small amount of information about the task. Using the task list, you can add additional detail about the task. To modify your task:

| Step 1 | *Click* | the Status: field of the Review Nakamichi Plaza Schematics task |

Step 2	*Select*	Waiting on someone else
Step 3	*Click*	the % Complete: field of your task
Step 4	*Delete*	the existing percentage
Step 5	*Key*	25 (Outlook fills in the percent sign for you)
Step 6	*Press*	the ENTER key

Many of your tasks are recurring tasks. For example, each week, you need to print a progress report before the weekly coordination meeting. You learn how to create a recurring task in the next activity.

Create a Recurring Task

Tasks, like meetings, can be recurring. You need to remember to print out a progress report before the weekly coordination meeting. To schedule a recurring task:

Step 1	*Start*	a New Task
Step 2	*Enter*	the information provided in Table 1-5 in the corresponding fields of the Task dialog box

TABLE 1-5
Information for
Friday's Task

Field	Key/Select
Subject:	Prepare progress report for coordination meeting
Due date:	Friday
Start date:	Today

Step 3	*Click*	the Recurrence button [↻ Recurrence...] on the Standard toolbar in the Task dialog box

The Task Recurrence dialog box is essentially the same as the Appointment Recurrence dialog box.

Step 4	*Verify*	that the task is set to recur every 1 week
Step 5	*Click*	OK
Step 6	*Click*	the Save and Close button [🖫 Save and Close] on the Standard toolbar in the Task dialog box

Delegate and Track a Task

Working with others is an important skill. As the project manager in charge of a large project, you definitely need to delegate tasks to others. Effective managers also keep track of tasks they've handed off to their co-workers. Once you've created a task, you can assign it to someone on your contact list. You can then track the task to ensure progress is being made. For this activity, you need to add a classmate to your Contacts list (be sure to include his or her e-mail address). To assign and prioritize a task:

Step 1	*Right-click*	the "Prepare progress report…" task
Step 2	*Click*	Assign Task
Step 3	*Click*	To
Step 4	*Double-click*	the classmate from the list of names in the Address Book
Step 5	*Click*	OK
Step 6	*Click*	the Priority list arrow
Step 7	*Click*	High
Step 8	*Click*	Send

Outlook alerts you that you will no longer be reminded about this task.

Step 9	*Click*	OK
Step 10	*Click*	the Inbox shortcut 📩
Step 11	*Click*	the Send/Receive button 📧 Send/Receive on the Standard toolbar
Step 12	*Click*	the Tasks shortcut 📋 to return to the Tasks folder

Once you assign a task to a classmate, he or she can send you updates on the status of the task. Your task list automatically reflects those changes as they are sent to you.

To complete this activity, you should have received a "Prepare Progress report…" task from a classmate. To send a status report:

Step 1	*Change*	the % Complete: field of the "Prepare Progress…" task you received to 50%
Step 2	*Double-click*	the task

Step 3	*Click*	Action
Step 4	*Click*	S̲end status report
Step 5	*Enter*	the e-mail address of the person who assigned the task to you, if necessary
Step 6	*Click*	Send
Step 7	*Close*	the Task dialog box

The task updates automatically to reflect the new status sent by the person assigned to the task. Outlook can help you remember what you did during the day by tracking activities in the Journal folder.

1.g Using the Outlook Journal

The Outlook Journal is a good place to record events that take place during your workday. In addition to items you enter manually, Outlook automatically tracks files you work on in any Microsoft Office 2000 application. It can also record meeting requests, task assignments, and e-mail messages.

Change Journal Settings

You want to view Journal entries and change automatic entry options. To use the Outlook Journal:

Step 1	*Click*	the Journal shortcut 📓 in the Outlook Shortcuts group in the Outlook Bar
Step 2	*Click*	Y̲es, if necessary, to start Journal
Step 3	*Click*	the Current View list arrow Entry List ▾ on the Advanced Toolbar
Step 4	*Select*	Entry List

A list view of your journal entries is shown, showing entry type, file or contact name, start time, and activity duration. See Figure 1-15. Your screen will show no entries or different entries from those in the figure.

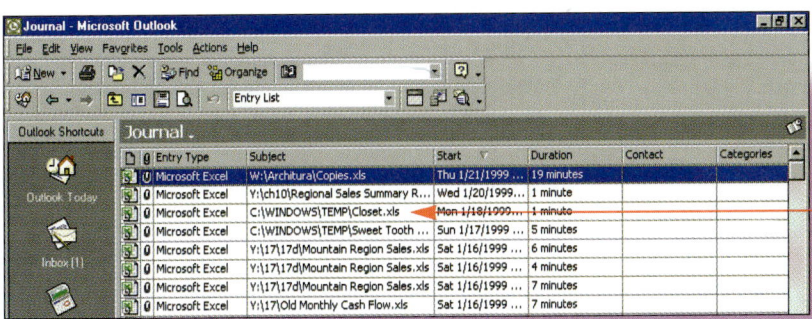

FIGURE 1-15
Journal Entries

Your list will be different

You can change the automatic record options for Journal, using the Options dialog box. To change Journal settings:

Step 1	*Click*	<u>T</u>ools
Step 2	*Click*	<u>O</u>ptions
Step 3	*Click*	the <u>J</u>ournal Options button on the Preferences tab
Step 4	*Click*	the check box next to E-mail Message
Step 5	*Click*	the check box next to Osuro Nakamichi
Step 6	*Click*	OK to close the Journal Options dialog box
Step 7	*Click*	OK to close the Options dialog box

When you receive or send a message to Mr. Nakamichi, a journal entry is recorded automatically. Certain activities cannot be entered automatically. For example, you had an important phone conversation with Mr. Nakamichi this morning. This activity cannot be recorded automatically, but you should create a journal entry to record the decisions you made with Mr. Nakamichi.

Manually Journal an Item

Many businesses depend on accurate, detailed records of conversations, decisions, and meetings. You have just spoken with the owner of the Nakamichi Plaza project. He has approved the preliminary oval design of the building and has authorized your firm to move ahead with the design. Because this is an important decision, record a Journal entry. To manually journal an activity:

Step 1	*Click*	the New Journal entry button [New] on the Standard toolbar
Step 2	*Enter*	the information provided in Table 1-6 in the corresponding fields of the Journal dialog box

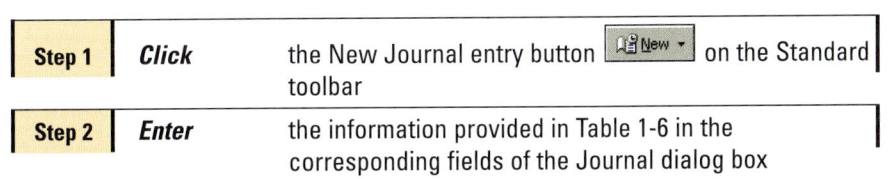

QUICK TIP

One nice Journal feature is the ability to open documents by double-clicking the Journal item. In the Options dialog box, you can enable this feature by clicking the <u>O</u>pens the item referred to by the journal entry option button in the Double-clicking a journal entry group.

outlook

TABLE 1-6
Journal Entry Information

Field	Key/Select
Subject:	Nakamichi Plaza Oval Design Approved by Owner
Entry type:	Phone call
Duration:	10 minutes

TABLE 1-6
Journal Entry Information

Step 3	*Press*	the TAB key twice to move to the memo box
Step 4	*Key*	Owner approved preliminary oval design. We are to proceed with schematic layouts of floors 1-20 and work out elevator/stair/restroom core.

Your screen should look similar to Figure 1-16.

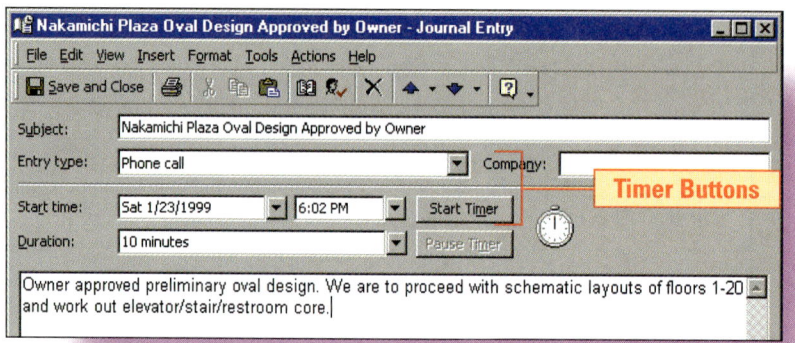

FIGURE 1-16
Journal Entry

Step 5	*Click*	the Save and Close button [Save and Close] on the Standard toolbar in the Journal Entry dialog box

Notes are useful when you want to quickly jot a reminder to yourself. In the next section, you create a note to record an idea you had today about the Nakamichi Plaza project.

1.h Using the Outlook Notes Manager

In 1980, a funny little piece of paper with a non-permanent adhesive started appearing in businesses around the world. Today, it's hard to imagine life without Post-It™ Notes. Notes Manager is like an electronic version of paper adhesive notes. The good news is, you can sort these notes, write as much as you want without running out of space, and they won't get lost. During the day, you have had several ideas about the Nakamichi Plaza project. You want to record these ideas before you forget them. To access the Notes folder:

Step 1	*Click*	the Notes shortcut in the Outlook Shortcuts group
Step 2	*Click*	the Current View list arrow on the Advanced toolbar
Step 3	*Select*	Notes List

The Notes are displayed in list view, which displays the creation date and several lines of each note's content. Your screen should look similar to Figure 1-17.

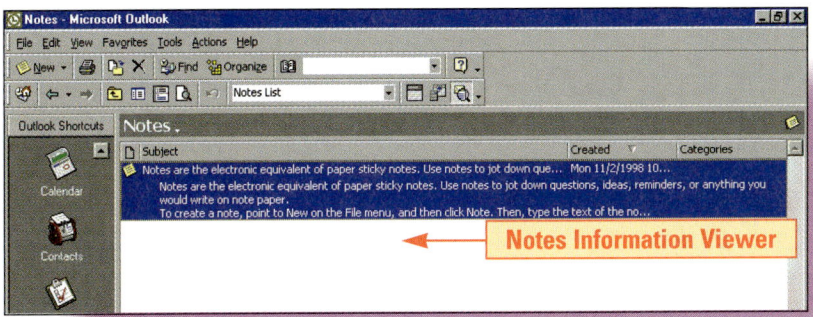

Create a Note

As useful as paper adhesive notes are, you can only stick so many of them on your monitor. Notes Manager keeps track of those important (and even not-so-important) notes in your computer. To create a Note:

| Step 1 | *Click* | the New Note button 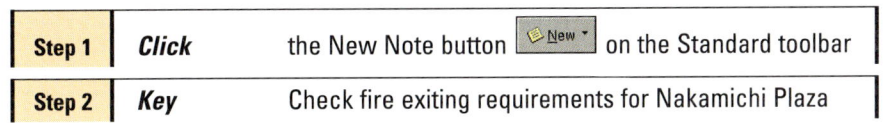 on the Standard toolbar |
| Step 2 | *Key* | Check fire exiting requirements for Nakamichi Plaza |

Figure 1-18 displays the finished Note.

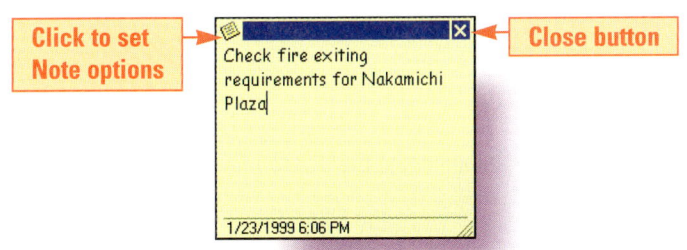

| Step 3 | *Click* | the Close button on the Note |

FIGURE 1-17
Notes Information Viewer

FIGURE 1-18
Finished Note

outlook

1.i Using Advanced Outlook Features

Outlook features many ways to organize information you've created. You can assign items to categories, change the view, and move items to different folders. Another way to find information is by applying filters.

Applying Filters to a View

Filters help sort through the items in your folders. You can filter for keywords, dates, sender or recipient address, categories, message size, or even define your own filter criteria. You want to filter your view to see only notes related to Nakamichi Plaza. To apply a filter:

Step 1	*Click*	View
Step 2	*Point to*	Current View
Step 3	*Click*	Customize current view
Step 4	*Click*	Filter

The Filter dialog box opens, as shown in Figure 1-19.

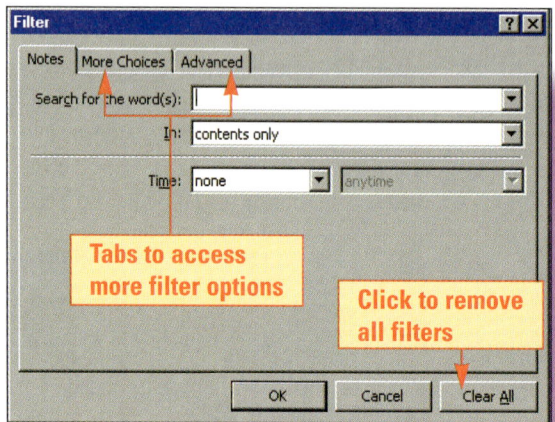

FIGURE 1-19
Filter Dialog Box

Step 5	*Key*	Nakamichi in the Search for the word(s): box
Step 6	*Click*	OK to close the Filter dialog box
Step 7	*Click*	OK to close the View Summary dialog box

The Notes view is filtered to display only messages containing the word "Nakamichi." To the right of the Inbox Information Viewer, a message informs you that a filter has been applied to the current folder. To remove the filter:

Step 1	*Open*	the Filter dialog box
Step 2	*Click*	Clear <u>A</u>ll
Step 3	*Click*	OK
Step 4	*Click*	OK

Printing all Components

You can print any type of item you create in Outlook, including mail messages, calendars, and notes. Depending on which type of item you are printing, you may have different options for printing. For example, Journal items can be printed in a list or memo style. Contacts can be printed in card style, booklet style, or phone directory style. The steps to print each type of item are largely the same. To print a contact list:

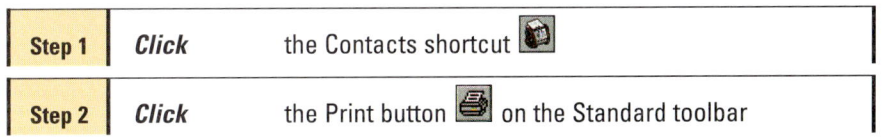

| Step 1 | *Click* | the Contacts shortcut 📇 |
| Step 2 | *Click* | the Print button 🖨 on the Standard toolbar |

The Print dialog box opens, as shown in Figure 1-20.

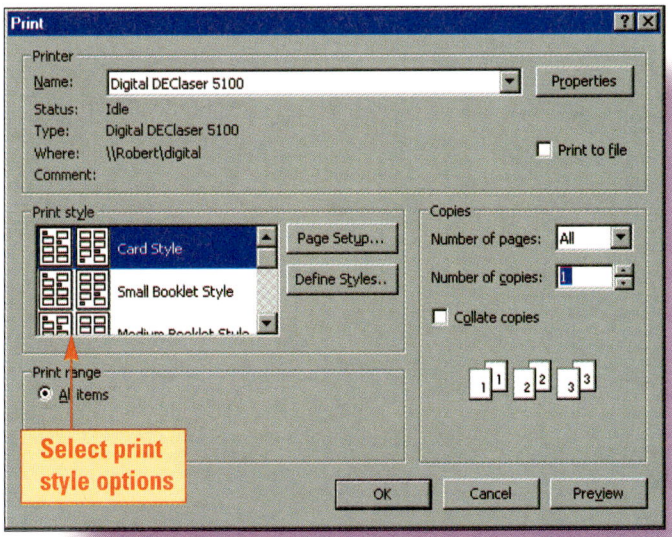

FIGURE 1-20
Print Dialog Box

outlook

Step 3	*Select*	Phone Directory Style in the Print style: list
Step 4	*Click*	Preview
Step 5	*Click*	the Print button on the Print Preview toolbar
Step 6	*Click*	OK

Next you need to remove the Nakamichi Mail folder and shortcut. To remove the Nakamichi Mail folder:

Step 1	*Click*	the Nakamichi Mail shortcut in the My Shortcuts group to open it
Step 2	*Click*	File
Step 3	*Point to*	Folder
Step 4	*Click*	Delete "Nakamichi Mail"

Outlook deletes the folder and moves its contents to the Deleted Items folder. To remove the shortcut:

| Step 1 | *Right-click* | the shortcut icon in the My Shortcuts group |
| Step 2 | *Click* | Remove from Outlook Bar |

Outlook contains many other powerful features to help you get organized and stay in contact with important people. Be sure to use Outlook Help to find out more about Outlook.

Summary

▶ Outlook organizes information in groups and folders. You can access information stored in folders by adding shortcuts to the Outlook Bar.

▶ Change the way items are displayed in any Outlook folder using the Current View button on the Advanced toolbar.

▶ E-mail messages are an essential part of communication in the business world. Subject lines must be concise and catch the reader's attention. Message bodies should also be to the point.

▶ Replying to messages automatically addresses them. Replying to and forwarding messages automatically provides a reference copy of the original.

▶ Appointments are activities that do not involve other people or resources.

▶ Events are activities that last for a day or more.

▶ Contact Manager helps manage contact data. You can send messages to contacts, dial phone numbers, and send contact activities to the Journal.

▶ Tasks are jobs that can be assigned to others and tracked through e-mail.

▶ Journal entries record important activities, such as phone calls to contacts or meeting summaries. Journal can automatically track Office document activity and e-mail communications for selected contacts.

▶ Notes provide an easy way to quickly jot down ideas.

▶ Filters screen information to meet specific criteria.

▶ All Outlook items can be printed in a variety of styles, including table and memo styles.

outlook

Commands Review

Action	Menu Bar	Shortcut Menu	Toolbar	Keyboard
Create a new group		Right-click Outlook Bar, select Add New Group		
Create a new folder	File, New, Folder		New ▾	CTRL + SHIFT + E ALT + F, W, E
Add a shortcut to Outlook Bar	File, New, Outlook Bar Shortcut	Right-click Outlook Bar, select Outlook Bar Shortcut		ALT + F, W, B
Create a new message	File, New, Mail Message	Right-click empty Inbox space, select New Mail Message	New ▾	CTRL + SHIFT + M ALT + F, W, M
Reply to a message		Reply	Reply	
Forward a message		Forward	Reply to All	
Create a new appointment	File, New, Appointment	Right-click Calendar, select New Appointment	New ▾	CTRL + SHIFT + A ALT + F, W, A
Create a new contact	File, New, Contact	Right-click empty Contact space, select New Contact	New ▾	CTRL + SHIFT + C ALT + F, W, C
Create a new task	File, New, Task	Right-click empty Task space, select New Task	New ▾	CTRL + SHIFT + K ALT + F, W, T
Create a new journal	File, New, Journal Entry	Right-click empty Journal space, select New Journal Entry	New ▾	CTRL + SHIFT + J ALT + F, W, J
Create a new note	File, New, Note	Right-click empty Note space, select New Note	📝	CTRL + SHIFT + N ALT + F, W, N
Save any item	File, Save			CTRL + S ALT + F, S
Start Address Book	Tools, Address Book		📖	CTRL + SHIFT + B ALT + T, B
Edit an item	Select item, then File, Open, Selected Items	Right-click item, select Open		CTRL + O ALT + F, O, S
Print an item	File, Print	Right-click item, select Print	🖨	CTRL + P ALT + F, P
Close Outlook	File, Exit	Right-click the application icon, click Close		ALT + F4 ALT + F, X
Undo the previous action	Edit, Undo		↩	CTRL + Z ALT + E, U
Redo an undo action	Edit, Redo		↩	CTRL + Y ALT + E, R

Concepts Review

SCANS

Circle the correct answer.

1. Removing a group deletes:
- [a] shortcuts to folders.
- [b] folders, including any items in those folders.
- [c] items in folders.
- [d] valuable information from your hard drive.

2. Where would you look to find mail messages you have started and saved, but have not yet sent?
- [a] Inbox
- [b] Drafts
- [c] Outbox
- [d] Sent Items

3. **Appointments are calendar items usually involving:**
   [a] you and others for more than one day.
   [b] only you for more than one day.
   [c] only you.
   [d] you and others in your office.

4. **When replying to or forwarding a message, you should:**
   [a] make sure the entire original message stays intact.
   [b] delete the entire original message.
   [c] send only the header information that identifies when the original message was sent and by whom.
   [d] send only portions of the original message to which you are responding.

5. **Events last at least:**
   [a] 24 hours.
   [b] 12 hours.
   [c] 6 hours.
   [d] 1 hour.

6. **Outlook considers an activity a meeting when:**
   [a] you are the only one involved.
   [b] others people or resources are required.
   [c] you don't want to go.
   [d] it lasts more than a day.

Circle **T** if the statement is true or **F** if the statement is false.

T   F   1. When you click the <u>S</u>end button in the message form window, the message is automatically sent directly to the recipient(s).

T   F   2. Journal automatically records everything you do in Outlook.

T   F   3. You can modify the time of a calendar appointment by dragging the edges of an appointment.

T   F   4. Natural language dates let you type in phrases, like "ten days ago" and "in two days," instead of dates.

T   F   5. Recurring and regenerating tasks are the same thing.

T   F   6. Once you assign someone to a task, you have no way of finding out the status of the task.

Skills Review

Exercise 1

1. From your classmates, select at least five people to add to your Contacts list.

2. Include the full name, birthday, e-mail address, a nickname, and a note describing something unique about each person.

3. Create a message addressed to these classmates thanking them for their time.

4. Save the message by clicking the <u>S</u>ave button (this places the message in your Drafts folder).

5. Open the Drafts folder in the My Shortcuts group.

6. Drag the message to the Outbox shortcut.

7. Send the message by clicking on the Send/Re<u>c</u>eive button.

8. Print a copy of the message you sent.

Exercise 2

1. Use Calendar to plan a one-hour appointment tomorrow.

2. Right-click the appointment and click Forward.

3. Click the To: button and select two people from your contact list to send this message to.

4. Add a message in the message box inviting your contacts to come to the meeting.

5. Send the message to your contacts.

6. Print a copy of your calendar for the next week.

Exercise 3

1. Display the Web toolbar by right-clicking any toolbar and selecting Web.

2. Use the Web toolbar to launch your browser by keying in the URL of any search engine.

3. Find the e-mail address of one of the U.S. senators who represents your state.

4. Send the senator a message describing an issue you feel is an important concern for people your age.

5. Print a copy of the message you sent.

Exercise 4

1. Print a phone directory style list of all contacts on your list.

2. Preview your list before you print.

Case Projects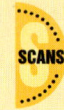

Project 1

You are the office manager of a small business. Create a message reminding everyone about the company's efforts to recycle used ink cartridges. Instead of sending the message, save a copy of it as a text file by clicking Save As on the File menu, then changing the Save as Type to Text Only (*.txt).

Project 2

Time to get your Inbox under control! Create new mail folders for the following items: personal, business, and other messages. Use the Rules Wizard, located on the Tools menu, to create new rules to automatically sort your messages. You will need to create one rule for each of the folders you create. Use the "Move new messages from someone" type for each rule. Follow the directions in the Rule description box, using people you've added to your contact list. Set up the rules so that messages from one contact go to the Personal folder, messages from another contact go to the Business folder, and messages from a third contact go to the Other Messages folder. Have each of those contacts send you a message. The incoming messages should be placed in the appropriate folders automatically. Print a Table style list of your messages in each folder.

Project 3

As the project manager on the Nakamichi Plaza project, you send frequent messages to many people. You want to include contact information about yourself with every message you send out. You need to create an electronic signature. Open the Options dialog box from the Tools menu and click the Mail Format tab, then click the Signature Picker button. Click New to create a new signature, then enter a title, such as "Project Manager." Click Next> then enter the signature text to include with outgoing messages. Include your name, title, the company you work for (Walters, Robertson & Associates), and your business phone number (make one up). When you are finished, click Finish, then OK. Verify that your new signature appears in the Use this signature by default box, then click OK. Create a new message and click the Save button on the Standard toolbar in the Message window to save it in your Drafts folder (your signature should appear automatically).

Project 4

One way to identify important messages is by adding a flag. You want to mark all Nakamichi Plaza messages with a flag to remind yourself to follow up. Open the Inbox folder and use Find to locate all messages with Nakamichi in the message. Right-click each message and click Flag for Follow Up. Assign a different follow-up flag to each message, then print each of the messages.

Microsoft
Word 2000

Quick Start for Word

T**Chapter** **Overview**

This chapter gives you a quick overview of creating, editing, printing, saving, and closing a document. To learn these skills, you create a new document, save and close it, then you open an existing document, revise the text, and save the document with both the same and a different name. This chapter also shows you how to view formatting marks, zoom the document window, and move the insertion point. In addition, you learn to identify the components of the Word window and create a folder on your hard drive to store your documents. You use these basic skills every time you create or edit a document in Word.

LEARNING OBJECTIVES

- ▶ Identify the components of the Word window
- ▶ Compose a simple document
- ▶ Edit a document
- ▶ Save a document
- ▶ Preview and print a document
- ▶ Close a document
- ▶ Locate and open an existing document
- ▶ Create a new document
- ▶ Close Word
- ▶ Send a Word document via e-mail

Case profile

Today is your first day as a new employee at Worldwide Exotic Foods, Inc., one of the world's fastest growing distributors of specialty food items. The company's mission is to provide customers with an unusual selection of meats, cheeses, pastries, fruits, and vegetables from around the world. You report to Chris Lofton, the word processing department manager, to complete an introduction to the Word 2000 word processing application.

chapter one

1

notes This text assumes that you have little or no knowledge of the Word application. It also assumes that you have read Office Chapters 1–4 of this book and that you are familiar with Windows 95 or Windows 98 concepts.

1.a Identifying the Components of the Word Window

Before you can begin to work with Word, you need to open the application. When you open the application, a new, blank document opens as well. To open the Word application and a new, blank document:

Step 1	*Click*	the Start button 🏁Start on the taskbar
Step 2	*Point*	to Programs
Step 3	*Click*	Microsoft Word

When the Word application opens, it contains a blank document with the temporary name *Document1*. Your screen should look similar to Figure 1-1, which identifies the specific components of the Word application window.

notes For the activities in this text, you view your documents in Normal view unless otherwise instructed.

Word has many different ways to view a document. Figure 1-1 shows a new, blank document in Normal view. Changing document views is discussed in more detail in Chapter 2. However, for now, if you need to change the view to Normal view:

| Step 1 | *Click* | View |
| Step 2 | *Click* | Normal |

chapter
one

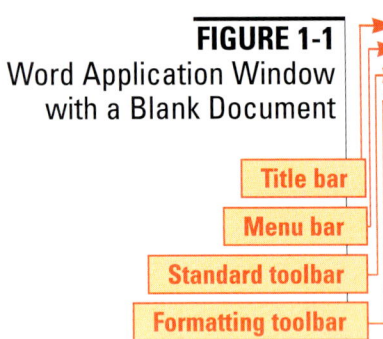

FIGURE 1-1
Word Application Window
with a Blank Document

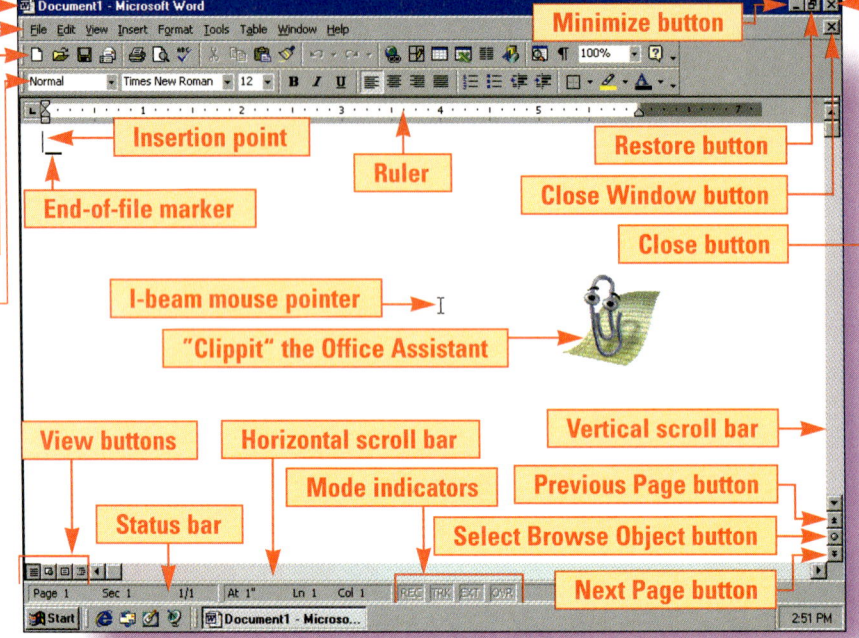

Menu Bar

The **menu bar**, located below the title bar, contains nine drop-down menu commands that contain groups of additional, related commands. For example, the File menu contains commands for opening, closing, previewing, and printing files. You can use the mouse or the keyboard to select a command from the menu bar. The activities in this book instruct you to select menu bar commands with the mouse. The Commands Review section at the end of each chapter provides a summary of both mouse and keyboard techniques to select a menu command.

Standard Toolbar

The **Standard toolbar** is located under the menu bar and is made up of buttons that represent commonly used commands. For example, the Standard toolbar contains buttons for opening, saving, previewing, and printing a file. The Standard toolbar allows you to perform commands quickly by clicking the button that represents that command. You can customize the Standard toolbar (or any other toolbar) by adding or deleting buttons.

Formatting Toolbar

The **Formatting toolbar** is located under the Standard toolbar in Figure 1-1 and is made up of buttons that represent commonly used formats. For example, the Formatting toolbar contains buttons for changing text appearance, such as the font or text alignment.

Ruler

The horizontal **ruler,** located under the Formatting toolbar, provides features you can use to change the tab settings, margins, and indentations in your document.

Insertion Point

The blinking vertical bar in the upper-left corner below the horizontal ruler is the insertion point. The **insertion point** marks the location where text is entered in a document.

End-of-file Marker

The short horizontal line below the insertion point is the **end-of-file marker** that marks the point below which you cannot enter text. This marker moves down as you insert additional lines of text into the document. The end-of-file marker is visible only in Normal view.

Select Browse Object Button

You can use the **Select Browse Object button,** located below the vertical scroll bar, to choose the specific item—such as text, graphics, and tables—you want to use to move or browse through a document.

Previous Page and Next Page Buttons

You use the **Previous Page button** and **Next Page button,** also located below the vertical scroll bar, to move the insertion point to the top of the previous or next page in a multi-page document. When you specify a different browse object, the button name changes to include that object, such as Previous Comment or Next Comment. Clicking the buttons moves you to the previous or next browse object you specified.

View Buttons

Word has several editing views or ways to look at a document as you edit it. The Normal View, Web Layout View, Print Layout View, and Outline View buttons, located to the left of the horizontal scroll bar, can be used to view and work with your document in a different way. Normal view is the best view for most word-processing tasks, such as keying, editing, and basic formatting. Web Layout view shows how your document will look if displayed in a Web browser. Print Layout view shows how your document will look when printed on paper. Outline view displays your document in outline format so you can work on its structure and organization.

QUICK TIP

The Standard and Formatting toolbars appear on the same row when you first install Office 2000. In this position, only the most commonly used buttons of each toolbar are visible. All the other default buttons appear on the More Buttons drop-down lists. As you use buttons from the More Buttons drop-down list, they move to the visible buttons on the toolbar, while the buttons you don't use move into the More Buttons drop-down list. If you arrange the Formatting toolbar below the Standard toolbar, all buttons are visible. Unless otherwise noted, the illustrations in this book show the full menus and the Formatting toolbar below the Standard toolbar.

chapter
one

Status Bar

The **status bar** appears at the bottom of the screen above the taskbar and provides information about your document and a task in progress. It indicates the current page number (Page 1), the current section of the document (Sec 1), and the current page followed by the number of pages in the document (1/1). In the center of the status bar you see indicators for the current vertical position of the insertion point measured in inches (At 1"), the current line number of the insertion point on that page (Ln 1), and the horizontal position of the insertion point (Col 1).

There are five mode indicators at the right of the status bar. These indicators provide mouse shortcuts to: record a macro (REC), track changes (TRK), extend a text selection (EXT), key over existing text (OVR), and check the spelling and grammar in the document (Spelling and Grammar Status). (Note that the Spelling and Grammar Status mode indicator is blank unless the document contains text).

Office Assistant

The **Office Assistant**, which you can use to search for online Help topics, may appear automatically when you work in Word unless you hide it or turn it off. In the illustrations in this book, the Office Assistant is hidden. To hide the Office Assistant, if necessary:

Step 1	*Right-click*	the Office Assistant
Step 2	*Click*	Hide

After you hide the Office Assistant multiple times, you may get a dialog box that asks if you want to turn the Office Assistant off completely. If you turn the Office Assistant off completely, you can then turn it back on by clicking the Show the Office Assistant command on the Help menu.

With the blank document open, you are ready to work. Chris asks you to key in a short company profile that Worldwide Exotic Foods can use in a press release.

1.b Composing a Simple Document

Chris gives you a short paragraph to key. As you key the text, it is visible on the screen and resides in your computer's memory. Word uses a feature called **word wrap** to automatically move words that do not fit on the current line to the next line. As a result, you can key the text without worrying about how much text fits on a line. You do not press the ENTER key at the end of each line. You press the ENTER key only to create a blank line or to end a paragraph.

The paragraph in Step 1 below contains two intentional errors. Key the text exactly as it appears. If you make additional errors, just continue keying the text. You learn two methods of correcting keying errors in the next section. Remember, do not press the ENTER key at the end of each line. To key the text:

| Step 1 | *Key* | Worldwide Exotic Foods, Inc. is one of the fastest-growing distributors of specialty food items. Worldwide Exotic Foods branch offices in Chicago, Illinois, Melbourne, Australia, Vancouver, Canada, and London, England, and specializes in supplying high-quality and unusual food products too customers around the world. |

Next, you correct any keying errors in the paragraph.

1.c Editing a Document

One of the important benefits of using Word is the ability to easily modify a document by inserting, removing, or editing text without having to key the document again. When you position the mouse pointer in a text area, it changes shape to look like a large "I" and is called the **I-beam**. You use the I-beam to position the insertion point in the text area where you want to correct keying errors or add new text. Recall that the insertion point is the blinking vertical bar on your screen that indicates where the next keyed character will appear. The text you just entered contains at least two errors. The first error you need to correct is a missing word in the second sentence. To insert the word "has:"

| Step 1 | *Move* | the I-beam before the "b" in the word "branch" in the second sentence |
| Step 2 | *Click* | the mouse button to position the insertion point |

Your screen should look similar to Figure 1-2.

chapter
one

FIGURE 1-2
Repositioned
Insertion Point

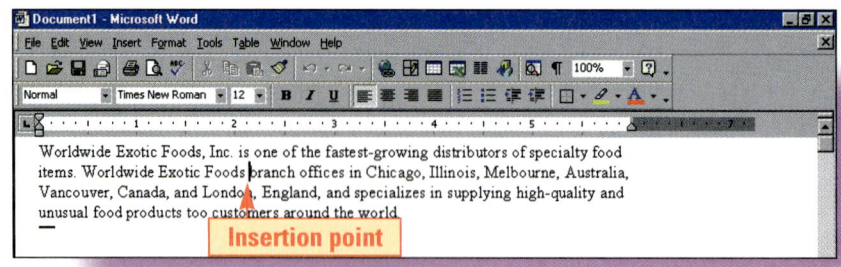

Step 3	*Key*	has
Step 4	*Press*	the SPACEBAR

The second error is an extra letter "o" in the word "too" in the last sentence, which you need to delete. To delete the letter "o":

Step 1	*Move*	the I-beam before the second "o" in the word "too" in the last sentence
Step 2	*Click*	the mouse button to position the insertion point
Step 3	*Press*	the DELETE key
Step 4	*Correct*	any additional errors, if necessary, by repositioning the insertion point and inserting or deleting text

While you are creating or editing a document, every change you make is stored temporarily in your computer's memory. If the power to your computer fails or you turn off the computer, your work will be lost. You can prevent such a loss by frequently saving the document to a disk.

1.d Saving a Document

Word enables you to save files to a floppy disk, an internal hard disk, or a network server. When you save a file for the first time, it does not matter whether you choose the Save command or the Save As command on the File menu or you click the Save button on the Standard toolbar. Regardless of which method you use, the Save As dialog box opens—providing a way for you to give your document a new name and specify the disk drive and folder location where you want to save the document.

After you have specified the location for saving your document, you key the name of the document in the File name: text box. A filename can have up to 255 characters—including the disk drive reference and path—and can contain letters, numbers, spaces, and some special characters in any combination. Filenames cannot include the following special characters: the forward slash (/), the backward slash (\), the colon (:), the semicolon (;), the pipe symbol (|), the question mark (?), the less than symbol (<), the greater than symbol (>), the asterisk (*), and the quotation mark (").

Using longer descriptive filenames helps you locate specific documents when you need to open and print or edit them. For example, the filename *Letter* won't mean much if you have written many letters, but the file-name *Mendez Hire Letter* has meaning even months later.

notes Be sure to check with your instructor if you do not know the disk drive and folder in which to save your documents.

To save your document:

Step 1	**Click**	the Save button  on the Standard toolbar

The Save As dialog box on your screen should look similar to Figure 1-3.

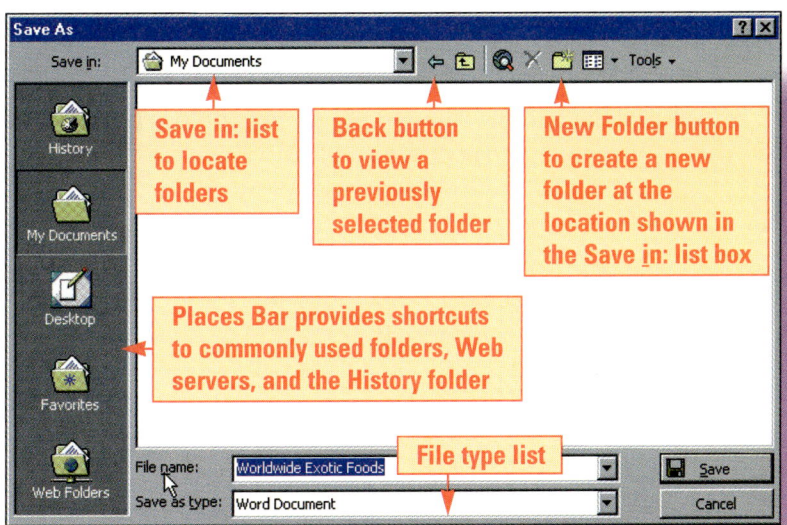

You can quickly locate a folder with the Save in: list, move to the previously viewed folder contents with the Back button, move up one level in the Save in: list, launch the Internet Explorer Web browser and search the Web, delete selected folders, add a new folder to the current location, change the viewing options for the folder icons, and change

FIGURE 1-3
Save As Dialog Box

chapter
one

MENU TIP

To view different save options, click the Options command on the Tools menu, and then click the Save tab in the Options dialog box. Other important Options tabs you should review are User Information, Compatibility, and File Locations.

the file type with options in this dialog box. For easier access to commonly used folders, the Save As dialog box also contains a **Places Bar**, which provides shortcuts for opening the My Documents and Favorites folders. You can view the My Computer, My Documents, and Online Services desktop icons with the Desktop shortcut in the Places Bar. The Web Folders shortcut in the Places Bar allows you to save Web pages you create in Word directly to a Web server.

Step 2	*Click*	the Save in: list arrow
Step 3	*Switch*	to the appropriate disk drive and folder, as designated by your instructor
Step 4	*Key*	*Company Profile* in the File name: text box
Step 5	*Click*	Save

After the document is saved, the document name *Company Profile* appears in place of *Document1* on the title bar.

1.e Previewing and Printing a Document

MENU TIP

You can preview a document with the Print Preview command on the File menu. You can print a document with the Print command on the File menu.

To select print options, you must use the Print command. The Print button prints the document based on the options previously selected in the Print dialog box.

After you create a document, you usually print it. Before printing a document, you can preview it to see what it will look like when printed. You do not have to preview the document before printing it. However, you can save paper by previewing your document and making any necessary changes before you print it.

To preview the *Company Profile* document and then print it:

| Step 1 | *Click* | the Print Preview button 🔲 on the Standard toolbar |

The Print Preview window opens. Your screen should look similar to Figure 1-4.

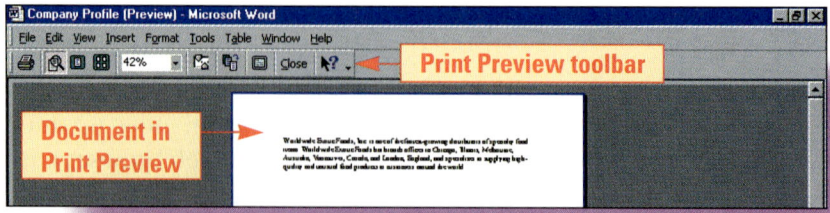

FIGURE 1-4
Print Preview Window

When you preview a document, you are verifying that the document text is attractively and appropriately positioned on the page. If necessary, you can change the document layout on the page, key additional text, and change the appearance of the text as you preview it. For now, you should close Print Preview and return to the original view of the document.

| Step 2 | *Click* | the Close button Close on the Print Preview toolbar |
| Step 3 | *Click* | the Print button 🖨 on the Standard toolbar |

You are finished with the *Company Profile* for now, so you can close the document.

1.f Closing a Document

When you use the Word application, you can have as many documents open in the memory of your computer as your computer resources will allow. However, after you finish a document you should close it or remove it from the computer's memory to conserve those resources. To close the *Company Profile* document:

| Step 1 | *Click* | the Close Window button ☒ in the upper-right corner of the menu bar |

When documents are closed from the File menu or the Close Window button on the menu bar, the Word application window remains open. This window is sometimes called the **null screen**. To continue working in Word from the null screen, you open an existing document or create a new, blank document.

1.g Locating and Opening an Existing Document

When you want to edit an existing document, you need to open a copy of it from the disk where it is stored. From inside the Word application, you can open a document in two ways: (1) with the Open command on the File menu, or (2) with the Open button on the Standard toolbar. Either method opens the Open dialog box. In this dialog box you first select the disk drive and folder where the document is located. Then you can select the specific document you

CAUTION TIP

If you edit a document and then try to close it without saving, Word opens a message window prompting you to save your changes.

chapter
one

want from a list of documents available at that location. Each document you open in Word has its own taskbar button.

Chris asks you to open an existing document that contains several paragraphs so that you can see how to scroll and move the insertion point in a larger document. To open an existing document:

Step 1	*Click*	the Open button on the Standard toolbar
Step 2	*Click*	the Look in: list arrow
Step 3	*Switch*	to the disk drive and folder where the Data Files are stored
Step 4	*Double-click*	New Expense Guidelines

The document contains characters you can see as well as characters you cannot see.

Viewing Formatting Marks

When you create a document Word automatically inserts some characters that you do not see called **formatting marks**. For example, each time you press the ENTER key to create a new line, a paragraph mark character (¶) is inserted in the document. Other formatting marks include tab characters (→) and spaces (·) between words. Sometimes these formatting marks are called **nonprinting characters** because they do not print, but they can be viewed on the screen. You may want to view the formatting marks to help you edit a document. The Show/Hide button on the Standard toolbar turns on or off the view of formatting marks. To show the formatting marks:

| Step 1 | *Click* | the Show/Hide button on the Standard toolbar |

Your screen should look similar to Figure 1-5.

FIGURE 1-5
Formatting Marks

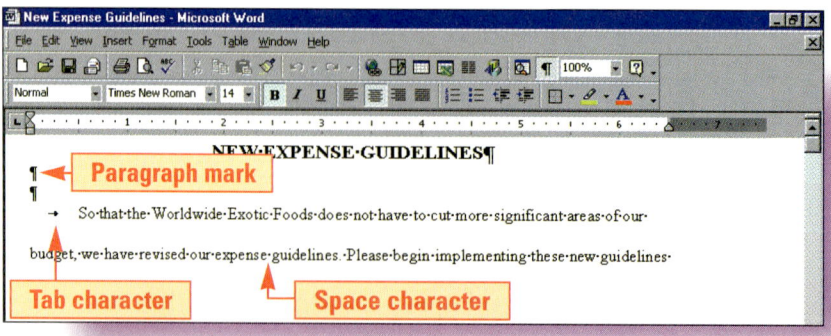

Notice the paragraph marks at the end of each paragraph, the tab character at the beginning of each paragraph, and the space indicators between each word. You won't be formatting this document now, so you can turn off the view of formatting marks. To turn off the view of formatting marks:

Step 1	*Click*	the Show/Hide button ¶ on the Standard toolbar

Whether the formatting marks are visible or not, you can take a closer look at your document.

Zooming the Document Window

When creating a document, you may want to view your document more closely or look at a miniature view of an entire page to see how the text is arranged on the page. This is called **zooming** the document.

You can zoom a document from 10% to 500% of the actual size. You can also resize the view to show the document's entire width by using the Page Width option. To make the text appear larger on the screen, increase the zoom percentage. To make the text appear smaller on the screen, decrease the zoom percentage. Zooming your document changes only the view on the screen; it does not change the size of characters on the printed document. To zoom the *New Expense Guidelines* document:

Step 1	*Click*	the Zoom button list arrow  on the Standard toolbar
Step 2	*Click*	200%

Notice that the Zoom text box indicates 200% and the text is very large.

Step 3	*Click*	the Zoom button list arrow 100% on the Standard toolbar
Step 4	*Click*	Page Width to view the entire width of the document

Being able to change the document view is helpful when you are formatting a document. However, with large zoom percentages or large documents you might need to scroll to view other parts of your document.

chapter
one

Using the Scroll Bars

When you want to view different parts of a document without moving the insertion point, use the vertical and horizontal scroll bars. Scrolling changes only that part of the document you see in the document window; it does not change your keying position in the document. The scroll bars appear on the right side and bottom of the window above the status bar. The **vertical scroll bar** enables you to scroll up and down in your document. The **horizontal scroll bar** allows you to scroll left and right in your document. A scroll bar has two scroll arrows. A gray shaded area containing a scroll box separates these scroll arrows. The **scroll box** represents your viewing position in the document. For example, if the vertical scroll box appears in the middle of the vertical scroll bar, you are viewing the middle of your document. (Figure 1-1 identifies the parts of the vertical and horizontal scroll bars.) Table 1-1 summarizes how to view a document using the scroll bars.

TABLE 1-1
Navigating a Document
with the Scroll Bars

To Scroll	Do This
Down one line	Click the down scroll arrow
Up one line	Click the up scroll arrow
Down one screen	Click the gray shaded area below the vertical scroll box
Up one screen	Click the gray shaded area above the vertical scroll box
Up or down one page	Click and hold the scroll box on the vertical scroll bar to see the current page number. Drag the scroll box to a new page and the new page number will show in a ScreenTip.
End of a document	Drag the vertical scroll box to the bottom of the vertical scroll bar
Beginning of a document	Drag the vertical scroll box to the top of the vertical scroll bar
Right side of document	Click the right scroll arrow
Left side of document	Click the left scroll arrow
Far right side of document	Click the gray shaded area right of the horizontal scroll box
Far left side of document	Click the gray shaded area left of the horizontal scroll box
Beyond the left margin (in Normal view)	SHIFT + Click the left scroll arrow on the horizontal scroll bar
Beyond the right margin (in Normal view)	SHIFT + Click the right scroll arrow on the horizontal scroll bar
To hide the area beyond the left margin (in Normal view)	Click the horizontal scroll box

QUICK TIP

If you are using the IntelliMouse pointing device, you can use the scrolling wheel to scroll a document. For more information on using the IntelliMouse pointing device, see online Help.

In addition to scrolling, you can move the insertion point within a document.

Moving the Insertion Point

You have already learned how to move the insertion point using the I-beam. You can also use the Next Page, Previous Page, and Select Browse Object buttons to move the insertion point, as explained in Table 1-2. (Note that you must be working in a multi-page document to move the insertion point to another page.)

To Move the Insertion Point To	Do This
A new page	Click the Select Browse Object button below the vertical scroll bar and then click the Browse by Page button
The top of the next page	Click the Next Page button below the vertical scroll bar
The top of the previous page	Click the Previous Page button below the vertical scroll bar

TABLE 1-2
Moving the Insertion Point

You can also use the keyboard to move the insertion point in your document. Table 1-3 summarizes the ways you can do this.

To Move	Press	To Move	Press
Right one character	RIGHT ARROW	To the top of the next page	CTRL + PAGEDOWN
Left one character	LEFT ARROW	To the top of the previous page	CTRL + PAGEUP
Right one word	CTRL + RIGHT ARROW	Up one line	UP ARROW
Left one word	CTRL + LEFT ARROW	Down one line	DOWN ARROW
Down one paragraph	CTRL + DOWN ARROW	Up one screen	PAGEUP
Up one paragraph	CTRL + UP ARROW	Down one screen	PAGEDOWN
Beginning of the line	HOME	To the beginning of a document	CTRL + HOME
End of the line	END	To the end of a document	CTRL + END
Back to the previous position of the insertion point or to a previous revision	SHIFT + F5	To go to a specific line or page or section or table or graphic	F5
To the top of the window	ALT + CTRL + PAGEUP	To the bottom of the window	ALT + CTRL + PAGEDOWN

TABLE 1-3
Moving the Insertion Point with the Keyboard

chapter
one

When instructed to scroll to change the view or move the insertion point to a different location, use one of the methods described in Tables 1-1, 1-2, and 1-3. To move the insertion point:

| Step 1 | *Practice* | using the mouse and keyboard to move the insertion point in the *New Expense Guidelines* document |
| Step 2 | *Close* | the *New Expense Guidelines* document without saving any changes |

Chris asks you to add some text to the *Company Profile* document.

Using the Save Command

You can open a copy of an existing document, edit it, and then save it with the same name to update the document on the disk. You want to edit the *Company Profile* document you created earlier. To open the *Company Profile* document:

Step 1	*Click*	the Open button [icon] on the Standard toolbar
Step 2	*Switch*	to the appropriate disk drive and folder
Step 3	*Double-click*	*Company Profile*

The file you selected opens in the document window. You edit the document by inserting text. To add an additional paragraph:

Step 1	*Move*	the insertion point to the end of the last sentence
Step 2	*Press*	the ENTER key twice
Step 3	*Key*	Contact us 24 hours a day, seven days a week at our Web site, www.exoticfoods.com.
Step 4	*Press*	the SPACEBAR

Notice that when you press the SPACEBAR after keying the Web site address and period, Word underlines the Web site address *www.exoticfoods.com* and changes the color to blue. This indicates the text is a hyperlink. A **hyperlink** is text or a picture that is associated with the path to another page. For now, you don't want the Web site address text in your document blue and underlined, so you remove the hyperlink formatting by clicking the Undo button on the Standard toolbar or pressing the CTRL + Z shortcut key combination. Then you save the document to update the copy on the disk.

| Step 5 | *Click* | the Undo button on the Standard toolbar |
| Step 6 | *Click* | the Save button 💾 on the Standard toolbar |

The copy of the document on disk is updated to include the additional paragraph.

Creating a Folder and Using the Save As Command

Sometimes you may want to keep both the original document and the edited document in different files on the disk. This allows you to keep a backup copy of the original document for later use or reference. To do this, you can save the edited document with a different name. If you want to create a new folder in which to store the modified document, you can create it from Windows Explorer or from inside the Word Save As dialog box.

 **notes** Check with your instructor, if necessary, for additional instructions on where to create your new folder.

You need to make an additional edit to *Company Profile* by adding the telephone number. This time, after you edit the document you save it to a new location and with a new name so that the document is available both with and without the phone number. To edit the document, create a new folder, and save the document with a new name:

Step 1	*Key*	You may also contact us at (312) 555-1234.
Step 2	*Click*	File
Step 3	*Click*	Save As
Step 4	*Click*	the Create New Folder button 📁 on the dialog box toolbar
Step 5	*Key*	Completed Files Folder in the Name: text box
Step 6	*Click*	OK to create and open the new folder
Step 7	*Key*	*Company Profile Revised* in the File name: text box
Step 8	*Click*	Save

chapter one

You leave this new copy of the document open while you create a new, blank document.

1.h Creating a New Document

From inside the Word application, you can create a new, blank document in two ways: (1) click the New command on the File menu or (2) click the New Blank Document button on the Standard toolbar. Each document you create in Word is based on a model document called a **template**. When you create a new document using the New Blank Document button on the Standard toolbar, the document is based on the **Normal template**, which is the basic, default Word document model. When you create a document with the New command on the File menu, Word provides a selection of templates for special documents such as letters, memos, and reports. To create a new, blank document:

Step 1	*Click*	the New Blank Document button 🗋 on the Standard toolbar

You should have two documents open, *Company Profile Revised* and a blank document. You can switch easily between open Word documents with the Window command on the menu bar or from the taskbar. To switch to the *Company Profile Revised* document:

Step 1	*Click*	the *Company Profile Revised* taskbar button

You are now viewing the *Company Profile Revised* document. You could work in this document, or return to the new, blank document and work in that document. For now, however, you are finished. When you finish using Word, you should exit or close the application and any open documents.

1.i Closing Word

You can close the Word application without first closing the open documents. If you modify open documents and then attempt to close the Word application without first saving the modified documents, a dialog box prompts you to save the changes you have made.

To close the application:

Step 1	*Click*	<u>F</u>ile
Step 2	*Click*	E<u>x</u>it

The Word application and both open documents close. Because you did not use the blank document, Word did not prompt you to save changes. Also, because you saved the *Company Profile Revised* document after you last modified it, Word closed the document without prompting you to save.

1.j Sending a Word Document via E-mail

If you have Outlook 2000 or Outlook Express 5.0 designated as your e-mail client, you can send e-mail messages directly from Word by clicking the E-mail button on the Standard toolbar. This displays an e-mail message header in which you key the recipient's e-mail address. The open Word document appears in the message content area. To send a Word document as an attachment when working in Word, click the <u>N</u>ew command on the <u>F</u>ile menu, and click the General tab in the New dialog box. Then double-click the E-mail icon to open the message header. Use the Attach File button in the message header to attach the file.

QUICK TIP

For more information on sending e-mail messages from Word, see the Word Integration chapter or online Help.

chapter
one

Summary

- ▶ The components of the Word window in Normal view include the title bar, the Standard and Formatting toolbars, the horizontal ruler, the insertion point, the end-of-file marker, the Previous Page and Next Page buttons, the Select Object Browser button, the View buttons, the vertical and horizontal scroll bars, and the status bar.

- ▶ Pressing the ENTER key creates a blank line or a new paragraph.

- ▶ You can remove text from your document with the DELETE or BACKSPACE keys.

- ▶ When you create or edit text, Word temporarily stores changes in your computer's memory.

- ▶ Word wrap is a word processing feature that automatically moves words that do not fit on the current line to the next line.

- ▶ To preserve changes to your document, you should save the document frequently.

- ▶ To save documents, you must use unique filenames that can be up to 255 characters long, including the disk drive reference and path.

- ▶ When you save a document for the first time, you must specify the disk drive and folder where the document will be stored.

- ▶ Before printing a document, it is a good practice to preview it to see what it will look like when it is printed.

- ▶ You can have as many documents open as your computer's resources will allow; however, it is a good practice to close a document when you finish working with it to conserve those resources.

- ▶ You can move the insertion point with both the mouse and the keyboard.

- ▶ You can view the special formatting marks inserted by Word with the Show/Hide button.

- ▶ Zooming the document window allows you to increase or decrease the viewing size of the text.

- ▶ The vertical and horizontal scroll bars enable you to view different parts of a document without moving the insertion point.

- ▶ When all documents are closed, the Word application remains open and you see the null screen.

- ▶ To edit an existing document, you open a copy of the document stored on a disk.

▶ After opening and editing an existing document, you usually save it again with the same name and in the same location; however, you can save it with a new name or new location.

▶ You can easily create a new folder for storing documents from the Save As dialog box.

▶ When you finish using Word, you should close the application.

Commands Review

Action	Menu Bar	Shortcut Menu	Toolbar	Keyboard
Create a new line or end a paragraph				ENTER
Remove a character to the left of the insertion point				BACKSPACE
Remove a character to the right of the insertion point				DELETE
Save a document for the first time or save a document with a new name or to a new location	File, Save As			ALT + F, A F12
Save a document for the first time or save a previously named and saved document	File, Save		🖫	ALT + F, S CTRL + S SHIFT + F12 ALT + SHIFT + F2
Preview a document	File, Print Preview		🔍	ALT + F, V CTRL + F2
Print a document	File, Print		🖨	ALT + F, P CTRL + P CTRL + SHIFT + F12
Close a document	File, Close	Right-click the document taskbar button, click Close	Close button ☒ on the title bar Close Window button ☒ on the menu bar	ALT + F, C CTRL + W CTRL + F4
Open an existing document	File, Open		📂	ALT + F, O CTRL + O CTRL + F12 ALT + CTRL + F2
Create a new, blank document	File, New		🗋	ALT + F, N CTRL + N
Zoom a document	View, Zoom		100% ▾	ALT + V, Z
Show formatting marks	Tools, Options, View tab, All		¶	ALT + T, O, A
Close the Word application	File, Exit		Application Close button ☒	ALT + F, X ALT + F4
Send e-mail	File, New		📧	ALT + F, N

chapter one

Concepts Review

Circle the correct answer.

1. **The Standard toolbar appears in the Word application window below the:**
   [a] menu bar.
   [b] status bar.
   [c] Formatting toolbar.
   [d] scroll bar.

2. **When you are completely finished working with a document you should:**
   [a] edit it.
   [b] hide formatting marks.
   [c] key it.
   [d] save it.

3. **Zooming the document window:**
   [a] shows the formatting marks.
   [b] allows you to delete text.
   [c] moves text to the bottom of the document.
   [d] increases or decreases the viewing size of text.

4. **The insertion point:**
   [a] is located under the Standard toolbar and contains shortcut buttons.
   [b] indicates the location where text is keyed in a document.
   [c] provides features for changing margins, tabs, and indentations.
   [d] always appears at the bottom of the screen above the taskbar.

5. **To preserve any changes to the document currently visible on your screen, it is a good idea to:**
   [a] save the document frequently.
   [b] preview the document.
   [c] move the document to the null screen.
   [d] scroll the document.

6. **The Select Object Browse button is located:**
   [a] below the Formatting toolbar.
   [b] on the menu bar.
   [c] in the lower-left corner of the Word screen.
   [d] below the vertical scroll bar.

7. **To save a document for the first time, you can click the:**
   [a] Select Browse Object button.
   [b] New Blank Document button.
   [c] Print button.
   [d] Save button.

8. **When you key a document that contains errors, you should:**
   [a] close the document.
   [b] preview and print the document.
   [c] save the document.
   [d] edit the document.

9. **Which of the following characters can be used in a filename?**
   [a] period (.)
   [b] asterisk (*)
   [c] pipe symbol (|)
   [d] question mark (?)

10. **If you edit a document and then try to close the Word application, Word:**
    [a] automatically saves the changes without a message prompt.
    [b] closes without saving any changes to the document.
    [c] opens a message prompt dialog box asking you to save changes.
    [d] requires you to save the changes to the document.

Circle **T** if the statement is true or **F** if the statement is false.

T   F   1. If you are creating or editing a document, any changes you make are stored temporarily in your computer's memory.

T   F   2. When using Word, you need to press the ENTER key at the end of each line of text to move the insertion point back to the left margin.

T   F   3. When you have finished working on a document, Word automatically saves the document to disk.

T   F   4. The Formatting toolbar is located below the ruler and consists of buttons that represent commonly used commands.

T   F   5. The Save As command is used to save a document for the first time.

T   F   6. You cannot use the keyboard to select commands from the menu bar.

T   F   7. When you finish using Word, you should close the application.

T   F   8. You can use letters, numbers, and some special characters in a filename.

T   F   9. When all documents are closed, the null screen appears.

T   F   10. You can move the insertion point to the top of individual pages of a multiple page document with the scroll arrows.

 **notes** The Skills Review exercises sometimes instruct you to create a document. The text you key is shown in italics. Do not format the text with italics unless specified to do so. Your text may word wrap differently from the text shown. Do not press the ENTER key at the end of a line of text to force it to wrap the same way.

Skills Review

Exercise 1

1. Create a new, blank document and key the following text exactly as shown, including the intentional errors. You correct the text in Exercise 2.
   Spreadsheet software is a commmon type of computer application software. Other types of applications include word processing, database management, presentation, communication, and Internet browser.

2. Save the document as *Application Software*.

3. Preview, print, and close the document.

Exercise 2

1. Open the *Application Software* document you created in Exercise 1.

2. Delete the extra "m" in the word "common" in the first sentence and delete the word "applications" and replace it with the word "software" in the second sentence.

chapter one

3. Delete the word "Internet" and replace it with the word "Web" in the second sentence.

4. Save the document as *Application Software Revised.*

5. Preview, print, and close the document.

Exercise 3

1. Create a new, blank document and key the following text exactly as shown, including the intentional errors. You correct the text in Exercise 4.
Word processing provides an individual with an effective and efficient means of preparing documents. You can create documents and quickly make needed changes prior to printing the document. The software allows your to save the document in a file for later use.

2. Save the document as *Word Processing.*

3. Preview, print, and close the document.

Exercise 4

1. Open the *Word Processing* document you created in Exercise 3.

2. Delete the words "and efficient" in the first sentence.

3. Delete the words "the document" and replace them with the word "them" in the second sentence.

4. Delete the character "r" in the word "your" in the last sentence.

5. Save the document as *Word Processing Revised.*

6. Preview, print, and close the document.

Exercise 5

1. Create a new, blank document and key the following text exactly as shown, including the intentional errors. You correct the text in Exercise 6.
The purchasing department will be ordering employee handboooks for the new employees hired during the month of May. Please determine how many handbooks you need and contact Kelly Armstead at ext. 154 by Monday.

2. Save the document as *Employee Handbooks.*

3. Preview, print, and close the document.

Exercise 6

1. Open the *Employee Handbooks* document you created in Exercise 5.

2. Delete the extra "o" in "handboooks" in the first sentence.

3. Insert the word "next" before the word "Monday" in the last sentence.

4. Save the document as *Employee Handbooks Revised.*

5. Preview, print, and close the document.

Exercise 7

1. Create the following document making the noted changes.

> You ⌐monthly sales projection∧is due on ~~Wednesday~~. Please note that the minimum number of units sold per month must be 1,000. Contact Betty McManners or Jim Davidson if you have any questions about preparing your report.
>
> *report* *Thursday*

2. Save the document as *Sales Report*.

3. Preview, print, and close the document.

Exercise 8

1. Open the *New Expense Guidelines* document located on the Data Disk.

2. Practice using the following keyboard movement techniques to move the insertion point in the document:

a. Move the insertion point to the end of the document using the CTRL + END keys.

b. Move the insertion point to the beginning of the document using the CTRL + HOME keys.

c. Move the insertion point to the word "Foods" in the first line of the first paragraph using the CTRL + RIGHT ARROW keys.

d. Move the insertion point to the end of the first line of the first paragraph using the END key.

e. Move the insertion point to the beginning of the first line of the first paragraph using the HOME key.

f. Move the insertion point to the second paragraph (down one paragraph) using the CTRL + DOWN ARROW keys.

g. Move the insertion point to the first paragraph (up one paragraph) using the CTRL + UP ARROW keys.

h. Move the insertion point to the top of the next page using the CTRL + PAGEDOWN keys.

3. Close the document without saving any changes.

Exercise 9

1. Create a new, blank document.

2. Key a paragraph of text describing your favorite hobby.

3. Save the document as *My Favorite Hobby*.

4. Preview, print, and close the document.

chapter one

5. Open *My Favorite Hobby* document you saved in Step 3.

6. Add a second paragraph further describing why you enjoy the hobby.

7. Open the Save As dialog box.

8. Create a new folder named Hobby (check with your instructor, if necessary, to select the appropriate location for the new folder).

9. Save the document in the new Hobby folder with the new name *Why I Enjoy My Hobby*.

10. Preview, print, and close the document.

Case Projects

Project 1

Chris Lofton, the word processing manager at Worldwide Exotic Foods, has asked you to create a new document containing a short paragraph describing two methods of correcting keying errors to include in the Word Processing Training Handbook for new employees. Create, save, preview, and print the document.

Project 2

Create a new document for the Word Processing Training Handbook that contains a short paragraph describing the two methods of opening an existing document from inside the Word application. Save, preview, and print the document.

Project 3

You are working with another new employee at Worldwide Exotic Foods (choose a classmate) to learn how to customize the Office Assistant. Together, review the Office Assistant dialog box options and online Help. Then you and your co-worker each create a document and write at least three paragraphs that describe ways to customize the Office Assistant. Save, preview, and print your documents.

Project 4

Chris asks you to review online Help for several of the buttons on the Standard toolbar and suggests you use the What's This? command on the Help menu to do it. Use the What's This? command on the Help menu to get online Help for three buttons on the Standard toolbar. Create a new document and for each button write one paragraph that describes what the button does and how to use it. Save, preview, and print the document.

Project 5

If you have not yet done so, read Chapter 4 in the Office Unit in this book to learn about the Internet and the World Wide Web (the Web). Many of your assignments at Worldwide Exotic Foods require using the Web to locate information. Chris asks you to learn how to locate information on the Web by using different search engines and directories. Connect to your ISP and use your Web browser's search feature to load the home page for several search engines. Review each search engine's home page and online Help. Print at least three search engine Help Web pages. Close the browser and disconnect from your ISP. Key a brief description of the World Wide Web into a new document. Save, preview, and print the document.

Project 6

Chris asks you to show several new employees how to print multiple documents at one time from the Open dialog box. Using the various tools available on the <u>H</u>elp menu, research how to do this. Create a new document with a short paragraph describing how to print multiple documents from the Open dialog box. Save, preview, and print the document. Using your document as a guide, demonstrate to several co-workers how to print multiple documents at one time from the Open dialog box.

Project 7

Because many of your work assignments at Worldwide Exotic Foods require you to use the Web and your Web browser, Chris wants you to become more familiar with your Web browser's features. Connect to your ISP and load the default home page for your Web browser. Review your Web browser's options to learn how to change the default start page to a page of your choice. With your instructor's permission, change the default start page and close the browser. Open the browser and load the new start page. Reset the option to load the original default start page. Close the browser and disconnect from your ISP. Create a new document and key the steps for changing the default start page in your browser. Save, preview, and print the document.

Project 8

Connect to your ISP and load the home page for a search engine. Use what you learned in Case Project 5 to search for companies on the Web who are similar to Worldwide Exotic Foods. Print at least three Web pages for similar companies. Close the browser and disconnect from your ISP. Create a new document and key the names and URLs of the Web pages you found. Save, preview, and print the document.

chapter one

Creating and Editing a Word Document

Chapter Overview

The basic foundation for every document is creating and editing. This chapter discusses these skills in more detail. You learn to insert dates and text and to select, cut, copy, and delete text. In addition, you learn to use the Overtype mode, the Undo and Repeat commands, and different editing views. With these skills, you can produce finished letters and other documents with minimal rekeying and maximum accuracy.

Case profile

B. D. Vickers, the Administrative Vice President of Worldwide Exotic Foods, requests an assistant in the purchasing department and you get the assignment. You work with Kelly Armstead, Vickers' executive assistant, in preparing correspondence for the department. The first letter is a reply to someone inquiring about distribution possibilities for the company.

chapter two

notes You should review Appendix C, Formatting Tips for Business Documents, before beginning this chapter.

2.a Creating a Letter

Most organizations follow specific formatting for their letters. A common letter format widely used for both business and personal correspondence is the **block format**. When you create a letter in block format, all the text aligns against the left side of the page. This includes the date, the letter address, the salutation, the body, the complimentary closing, the writer's name, reference initials, and any special letter parts such as an enclosure or subject line. The body of the letter is single spaced with a blank line between paragraphs.

Three blank lines separate the date from the letter address information, one blank line separates the letter address information and the salutation, one blank line separates the salutation from the body of the letter, and one blank line separates the body of the letter from the complimentary closing. There are three blank lines between the complimentary closing and the writer's name line. If reference initials appear below the writer's name, a blank line separates them. If an enclosure or attachment is noted, the word "Enclosure" or "Attachment" appears below the initials with two blank lines separating them. Finally, when keying the letter address information, one space separates the state and the postal code (ZIP+4).

Most companies use special paper for their business correspondence called **letterhead** paper because the organization's name and address are preprinted at the top of each sheet. When you create a business letter, you determine the initial keying position based on the depth of the letterhead information on the paper (most letterheads are between one inch and two inches deep) and the amount of the letter text. Figure 2-1 illustrates the parts of a block format business letter.

Kelly asks you to create a new letter in the block format. Before you begin keying the text in your letter, you set the appropriate margins for the document.

Setting Margins

Margins are the distance from the top, bottom, left, and right edges of the page to the text. All text in a document appears within the margins you specify. When printing on letterhead paper, you must consider the depth of the preprinted letterhead when setting top margins and the amount of letter text when setting left and right margins.

chapter two

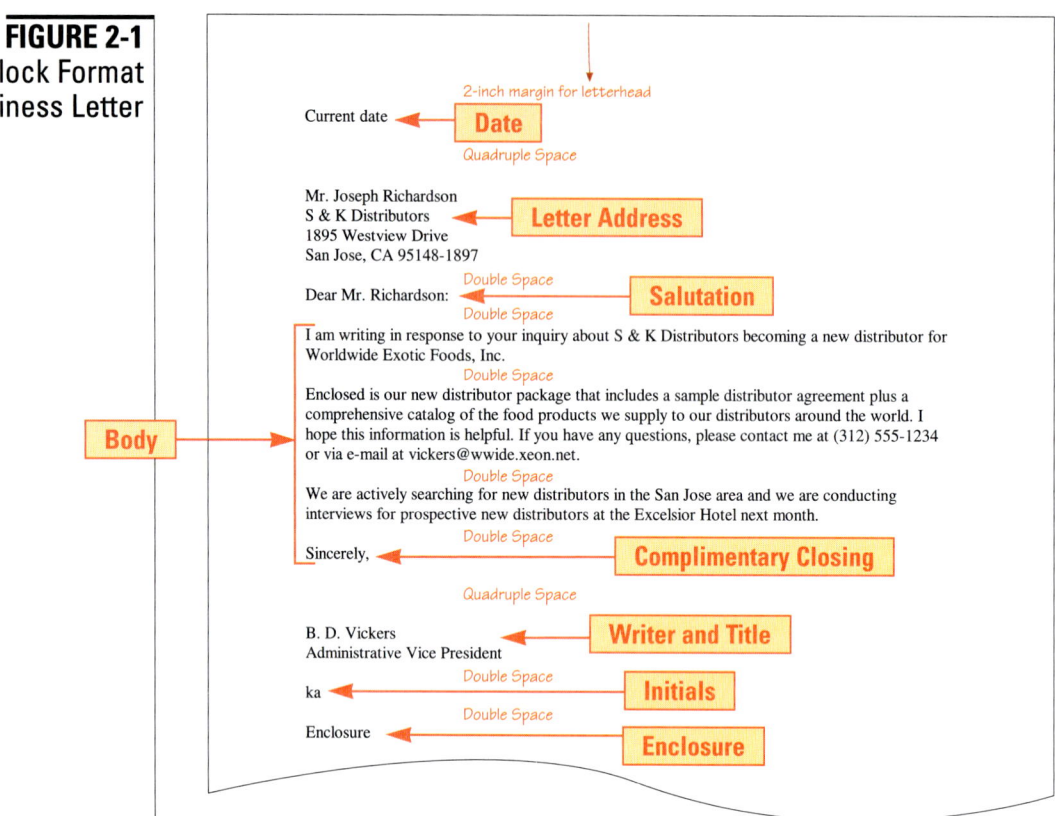

FIGURE 2-1
Block Format
Business Letter

You can change the document margins by clicking the Page Setup command on the File menu to open the Page Setup dialog box. Each margin, Top, Bottom, Left, and Right has a text box indicating the current margin setting. You can key a new margin size number in the text box. You can also click the up and down arrow buttons at the right side of each text box to increase or decrease the margin setting. The new margins you set affect the entire document by default. However, you can change the document margins from the position of the insertion point or for a section of a document.

First, you create the letter shown in Figure 2-1 by creating a new, blank document and then setting the appropriate margins. Then you key the letter text. Worldwide Exotic Foods uses letterhead paper that requires a 2-inch top margin. To create a new, blank document and set the margins:

Step 1	*Click*	the New Blank Document button on the Standard toolbar, if necessary
Step 2	*Click*	File
Step 3	*Click*	Page Setup

Step 4	*Click*	the <u>M</u>argins tab, if necessary

The dialog box on your screen should look similar to Figure 2-2.

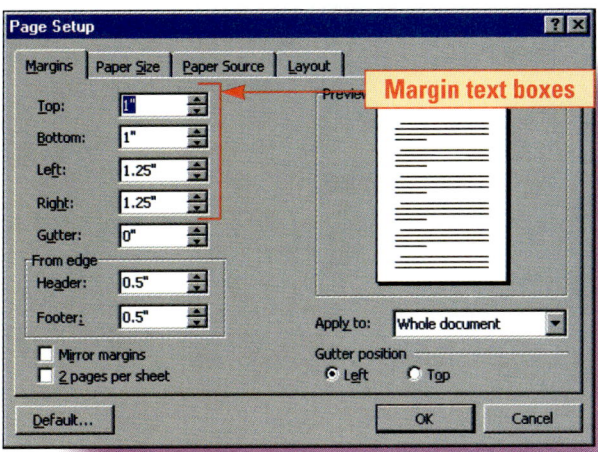

FIGURE 2-2
Margins Tab in the Page
Setup Dialog Box

You can use the dialog box Help button to review the options on the <u>M</u>argins and other tabs in this dialog box. Notice that the blank document is created with preset 1-inch top and bottom margins, and 1.25-inch left and right margins. These **default** margins are preset in the Normal template. You can change the margins as necessary by keying the correct margin in each text box. For this letter, you need to change the top margin to two inches, and the left and right margins to one inch. You can use the TAB key to quickly select the next option in a dialog box.

Step 5	*Key*	2 in the <u>T</u>op: text box
Step 6	*Press*	the TAB key twice
Step 7	*Key*	1 in the <u>L</u>eft: text box
Step 8	*Press*	the TAB key
Step 9	*Key*	1 in the <u>R</u>ight: text box
Step 10	*Verify*	the Appl<u>y</u> to: list box displays Whole document
Step 11	*Click*	OK

After setting the appropriate margins, you begin the letter by inserting the current date.

Inserting the Date and Time

Word provides a variety of special options that allow you to insert a date or date and time without keying it. You can insert the date or date and time as text or as a field of information that is automatically updated with the system date. Instead of keying the date manually in the letter, you can have Word insert the date for you.

Step 1	*Click*	Insert
Step 2	*Click*	Date and Time

The Date and Time dialog box opens. Except for the dates, the dialog box you see on your screen should look similar to Figure 2-3.

FIGURE 2-3
Date and Time Dialog Box

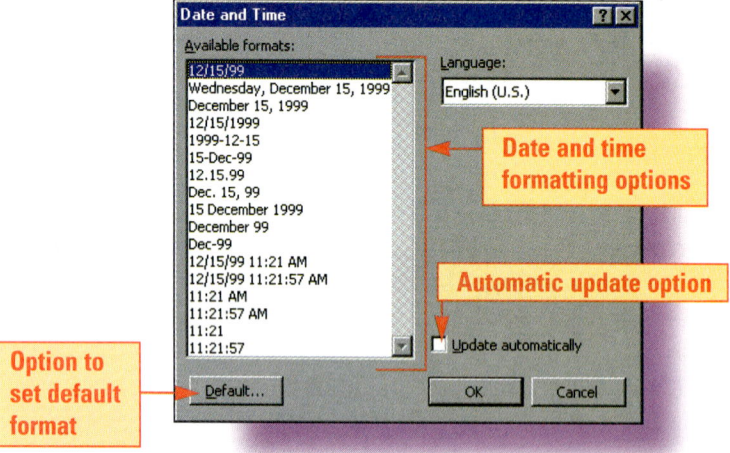

You can change the format of the date by selecting a format option in the Date and Time dialog box. The Update automatically check box provides an option to insert the date as text or as a date field, which automatically updates with the current system date whenever the document is printed. The Default button allows you to set a selected date/time format as the default format for all your Word documents. You use the third date/time format option.

Step 3	*Verify*	the Update automatically check box is blank
Step 4	*Double-click*	the third date format

When the current date is inserted, you are ready to complete the letter by keying the letter text. By default, Word is in **Insert mode**. This means that when you insert text the characters are entered at the position of the insertion point. When you insert text within an existing line of text, the text to the right of the insertion point shifts to make room for the new text. You continue with the letter by inserting the letter address, salutation, body, complimentary closing, initials, and enclosure notation you see in Figure 2-1.

notes

By default, Word capitalizes the first character in the first word of a sentence. When you key your initials, Word automatically capitalizes the first initial. You can manually correct it to lowercase by pressing the SPACEBAR and pressing the CTRL + Z keys after you key your initials.

Also by default, Word changes the color and underlines the path to a Web page or an e-mail address. This allows someone reading the document online to click the e-mail address to open his or her e-mail program. When you press the ENTER key or SPACEBAR after keying an e-mail address, Word changes the e-mail address to a hyperlink. You can remove the hyperlink formatting by clicking the Undo button on the Standard toolbar or pressing the CTRL + Z keys.

To complete and save the letter:

Step 1	*Press*	the ENTER key four times
Step 2	*Key*	the remaining letter text, as shown in Figure 2-1
Step 3	*Save*	the document as *Richardson Letter*

When you create a Word document, it is possible to make changes to characters, complete words, or groups of words at the same time by first selecting the text.

2.b Selecting Text

Selecting text is one of the most important word processing techniques. **Selecting** means to highlight one or more characters of text so that you can edit, format, or delete them. Once a character, word, or group of words is selected, Word recognizes the selected text as one unit that you can modify using Word editing features. For example, if you wanted to underline a group of words for emphasis, you would first select the words and then apply an underline format. You can select text with both the mouse and the keyboard.

chapter
two

Selecting Text with the Mouse

One way to select text with the mouse is to drag the I-beam across the text. To select text by dragging, click at the beginning of the text, hold down the left mouse button, and move the mouse on the mouse pad in the direction you want to highlight. When the desired text is highlighted, release the mouse button.

The **selection bar** is the vertical area to the far left of the document between the horizontal ruler and the View buttons. When the mouse pointer is in the selection bar, it appears as a right-pointing arrow and you can use it to select text. Figure 2-4 identifies the selection bar and the shape of the mouse pointer when it is in the selection bar.

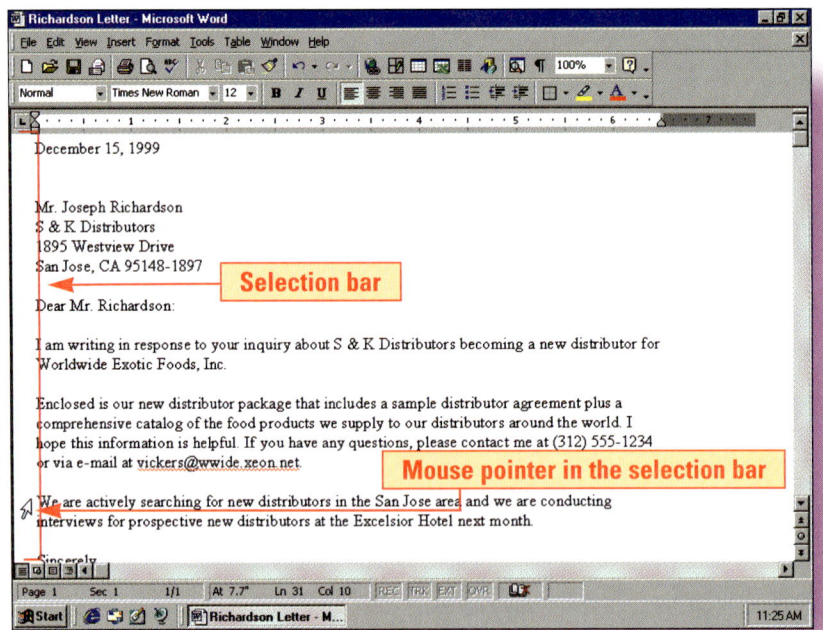

FIGURE 2-4
Selection Bar

Word includes many mouse and keyboard shortcuts for selecting text. Table 2-1 lists some of these frequently used shortcuts.

Deselecting text means to remove the highlighting. You can deselect text by clicking anywhere in the document area outside the selection, by selecting new text, or by pressing a **pointer-movement key** (UP ARROW, DOWN ARROW, LEFT ARROW, RIGHT ARROW) on the keyboard.

 **notes** Chapter 1 and the previous sections of this chapter provided step-by-step instructions for repositioning the insertion point. From this point forward, you are instructed to move the I-beam or insertion point to the appropriate position. Review Chapter 1 to see the step-by-step process for repositioning the insertion point, if necessary.

TABLE 2-1
Keyboard and Mouse
Shortcuts for Selecting Text

To Select	Do This
A word and the trailing space	Double-click a word
A sentence and the trailing space	Hold down the CTRL key and click inside the sentence
A line of text	Move the mouse pointer into the selection bar next to the line and click
Multiple lines of text	Drag in the selection bar next to the lines
A paragraph	Move the mouse pointer into the selection bar next to the line and double-click, or triple-click the paragraph
Multiple paragraphs	Drag in the selection bar
The document	Hold down the CTRL key and click in the selection bar, or triple-click in the selection bar
A vertical selection of text	Hold down the ALT key and drag the mouse down and left or right
A variable amount of text	Place the insertion point at the beginning of the text to be selected then move the I-beam to the end of the text to be selected and hold down the SHIFT key and click the mouse button
The text from the insertion point to the end of the document	Press the CTRL + SHIFT + END keys
The text from the insertion point to the beginning of the document	Press the CTRL + SHIFT + HOME keys

Q U I C K   T I P

You can find comprehensive lists of keyboard shortcuts in online Help by using the Office Assistant to search using the keyword phrase "keyboard shortcuts."

To select a paragraph of your document by dragging:

Step 1	*Move*	the I-beam before the "E" in "Enclosed" in the second body paragraph
Step 2	*Drag*	down until you have highlighted the entire paragraph and the following blank line
Step 3	*Press*	the RIGHT ARROW key to deselect the text

Compare the dragging selection technique to using the selection bar. To select the second body paragraph using the selection bar:

Step 1	*Move*	the mouse pointer into the selection bar before the "E" in "Enclosed" until the mouse pointer becomes a right-pointing arrow
Step 2	*Double-click*	the selection bar
Step 3	*Click*	outside the selected text to deselect it

chapter
two

Selecting Text with the Keyboard

You can select text using the keyboard by pressing F8 (EXT mode) and then pressing a pointer-movement key, or by holding down the SHIFT key and pressing a pointer-movement key. Either method turns on the **Extend mode** at the location of the insertion point. For example, move the insertion point to the beginning of a word, press the F8 key to turn on the Extend mode, then press the CTRL + RIGHT ARROW key to highlight the word. To remove a selection you highlighted with the F8 key, press the ESC key and then press a pointer-movement key.

After text is selected, you can perform other tasks such as deleting it, formatting it, replacing it by keying new text, and copying or moving it to another location.

2.c Cutting, Copying, Inserting, Moving, and Pasting Text

You can move, or **cut and paste,** text from one location to another in a Word document. You can duplicate, or **copy and paste,** text from one location to another in a Word document. You can also cut and paste or copy and paste text into a different Word document or into another Office application document.

Using Collect and Paste

You use the Cut command to remove text, the Copy command to duplicate text, and the Paste command to insert the cut or copied text. The Cut and Copy commands collect selected text from your Word document and insert it in the Office Clipboard. The **Office Clipboard** is a reserved place in the memory of your computer that can be used to store text temporarily. The Office Clipboard can hold up to twelve cut or copy actions.

To cut or copy text, you first select the desired text and then click Cut or Copy on the Edit menu or shortcut menu, or click the Cut or Copy button on the Standard toolbar. To insert the cut or copied text at a new location in your document, first move the insertion point to the location. Then click the Paste command on the Edit menu or shortcut menu, or click the Paste button on the Standard toolbar. You can also use the Clipboard toolbar to paste. The Clipboard toolbar usually appears automatically after you cut or copy a second selection without pasting the first selection you cut or copied.

Kelly reviewed the *Richardson Letter* document and wants you want to move the third body paragraph to the second body paragraph position. To move text with the shortcut menu:

Step 1	*Select*	the third paragraph beginning with "We are" and the following blank line
Step 2	*Move*	the mouse pointer to the selected text
Step 3	*Right-click*	the selected text

A shortcut menu for the selected text appears. Your screen should look similar to Figure 2-5.

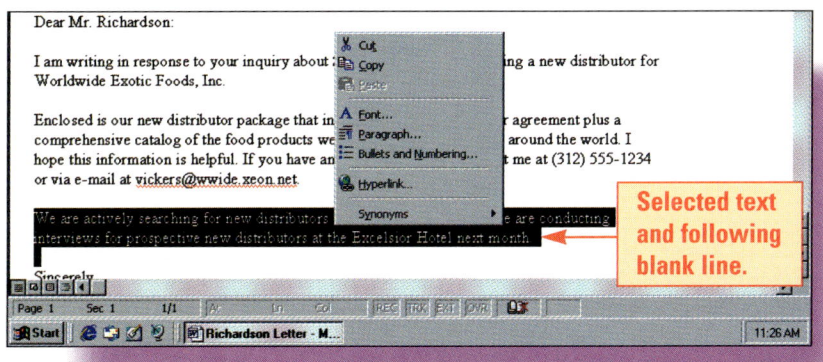

FIGURE 2-5
Text Shortcut Menu

Step 4	*Click*	Cut
Step 5	*Observe*	that the third body paragraph no longer appears in the document because it is temporarily stored on the Office Clipboard
Step 6	*Move*	the I-beam before the "E" in "Enclosed" in the second body paragraph
Step 7	*Right-click*	at the I-beam position to view the shortcut menu
Step 8	*Click*	Paste

The paragraph is inserted in the new location. Kelly also wants you to copy two of the letter address lines to the end of the document. You can copy and paste both lines at one time or you can copy and paste each line separately using the Clipboard toolbar. Before you begin the copy process, you add some additional blank lines at the end of the document. To insert additional blank lines at the bottom of the letter:

| Step 1 | *Move* | the insertion point to the end of the document |

QUICK TIP

When you want to embed or link data copied from another Office application, you use the Paste Special command on the Edit menu. For more information on embedding and linking, see the Word Integration chapter or online Help.

chapter
two

Step 2	*Press*	the ENTER key three times

The **Collect and Paste** feature is a simple way to copy individual lines of the letter address and then paste them all at once. To collect and paste text:

Step 1	*Scroll*	to view the letter address
Step 2	*Select*	the first line of the letter address using the selection bar; include the paragraph mark at the end of the line (turn on the formatting marks, if desired)
Step 3	*Click*	the Copy button 📋 on the Standard toolbar
Step 4	*Select*	the last line of the letter address using the selection bar; include the paragraph mark at the end of the line
Step 5	*Click*	the Copy button 📋 on the Standard toolbar

The Clipboard toolbar appears. The Clipboard toolbar you see on your screen should look similar to Figure 2-6.

FIGURE 2-6
Clipboard Toolbar

Items copied to the Office Clipboard

With the two selections of text copied, you can paste one or both in a new location. To paste text:

Step 1	*Move*	the insertion point to the end of the document
Step 2	*Move*	the mouse pointer to the copied item icons on the Clipboard toolbar and observe the ScreenTip for each item
Step 3	*Click*	the Clipboard toolbar icon for the first line of the letter address (Mr. Joseph Richardson)
Step 4	*Observe*	that the text is pasted into the document and the insertion point moves to the next line
Step 5	*Click*	the Clipboard toolbar icon for the last line of the letter address (San Jose, CA 95148-1897)
Step 6	*Observe*	that the text is pasted into the document and the insertion point moves to the next line

CAUTION TIP

If the Clipboard toolbar was previously turned off, it might not appear automatically. You can right-click the Standard or Formatting toolbar and click Clipboard to show it, if necessary.

You can clear the Clipboard after you no longer need to paste the items stored there. To clear the Clipboard:

Step 1	*Click*	the Clear Clipboard button ▣ on the Clipboard toolbar
Step 2	*Click*	the Close button ☒ on the Clipboard toolbar
Step 3	*Save*	the document as *Revised Richardson Letter* and close it

After reviewing the *Revised Richardson Letter* Kelly wants to make some additional changes. She asks you to work from the original *Richardson Letter*.

Moving and Copying Text with the Mouse

A shortcut for moving and copying text is called the **drag-and-drop** method. This method uses the mouse and does not store the any items on the Office Clipboard. To move text using drag-and-drop, first select the text and then drag the selection to its new location. To copy text using drag-and-drop, select the text, hold down the CTRL key, and then drag the text to its new location, releasing the mouse button before you release the CTRL key.

When you are using the drag-and-drop method, the insertion point changes to a small, dashed, gray vertical line. A small box with a dashed, gray border appears at the base of the mouse pointer. If you are copying text, a small plus sign (+) appears below of the mouse pointer.

You open the *Richardson Letter* from the File menu and move the third body paragraph to the second body paragraph position using the mouse pointer. You can quickly open a recently closed document by clicking the document name on the File menu list of recently closed documents. To use the drag-and-drop method to move text:

Step 1	*Click*	File
Step 2	*Click*	the *Richardson Letter* at the bottom of the File menu
Step 3	*Select*	the paragraph beginning with "We are" and the following blank line
Step 4	*Move*	the mouse pointer to the selected text (the pointer is a left-pointing arrow)
Step 5	*Click*	and hold the mouse button
Step 6	*Observe*	the dashed-line insertion point at the tip of the mouse pointer

MOUSE TIP

You can **right-drag** selected text to move or copy it. Select the text you want to move or copy, and then hold down the right mouse button instead of the left mouse button as you drag the text. Move the dashed-line insertion point to the position where you want to insert it. When you release the mouse button, a shortcut menu containing the Move Here and Copy Here commands appears. Then click the appropriate command to paste the selection.

CAUTION TIP

When copying text with drag-and-drop, do not release the CTRL key until you have first released the mouse button. Releasing the CTRL key first causes Word to move the text instead of copying it.

chapter
two

QUICK TIP

You can use the CTRL + BACKSPACE keys to remove the word before the insertion point and the CTRL + DELETE keys to remove the word after the insertion point.

Step 7	*Drag*	up until the dashed-line insertion point is positioned before the "E" in "Enclosed" in the second body paragraph
Step 8	*Release*	the mouse button
Step 9	*Deselect*	the text

As you edit documents, you often need to delete text previously keyed in a document.

2.d Deleting Text

There are several ways to delete text from a document. The BACKSPACE and DELETE keys delete individual text characters in your document to the left and right of the insertion point, respectively. You can also use the BACKSPACE or DELETE keys to delete selected text. To delete the word "new" in the first body paragraph in the *Richardson Letter* document:

Step 1	*Double-click*	the word "new" in the first body paragraph
Step 2	*Press*	the DELETE key

The text is deleted. You can use this method to delete both small and large selections of text. If you delete a large selection inadvertently, you won't need to re-key the selection. Fortunately, it is possible to reverse your last action.

2.e Using the Undo, Redo, and Repeat Commands

The Undo and Repeat commands come in handy as you edit documents. The **Undo** command enables you to reverse a previous action. The **Repeat** command enables you to duplicate your last action.

You think the word "new" should stay in the letter. Because you just deleted the text, you can use the <u>U</u>ndo command on the <u>E</u>dit menu or Undo button on the Standard toolbar to reverse the action. To restore the word "new" to the letter:

QUICK TIP

Use the CTRL + Y shortcut key combination to quickly repeat your last action.

Step 1	*Click*	the Undo button 🔙▾ on the Standard toolbar

The word reappears in the letter in the original location. You can undo multiple actions sequentially beginning with the last action you performed; just click the Undo button for each command you want to reverse. Similarly, you can also repeat actions and redo actions that were previously undone. Click the <u>R</u>epeat command on the <u>E</u>dit menu to repeat your last action. Click the **Redo** button on the Standard toolbar to redo an action previously undone. After rereading the letter, you decide the word "new" doesn't need to be in the letter. To redo your last undo action:

| Step 1 | *Click* | the Redo button  on the Standard toolbar |

The word "new" is again deleted from the letter. Another way to replace text is to use the Overtype mode and key new text over old text.

2.f Using the Overtype Mode

Word has an **Overtype mode** that allows you to key new text over existing text. When you are in Overtype mode, any character you key replaces the character to the right of the insertion point. The OVR mode indicator on the status bar allows you to turn on or off Overtype mode. To turn on Overtype mode, double-click the OVR mode indicator on the status bar. The OVR mode indicator appears boldfaced to indicate Overtype mode is turned on. When you want to return to Insert mode, double-click the OVR mode indicator to turn off Overtype mode.

You look at Mr. Richardson's original letter and discover his street address is 1895 Westview Place. To edit the street address line using Overtype mode:

Step 1	*Move*	the insertion point before the "D" in "Drive" in the street address line
Step 2	*Double-click*	the OVR mode indicator on the status bar to turn on Overtype mode
Step 3	*Observe*	that the OVR mode indicator is bold, indicating the feature is turned on
Step 4	*Key*	Place

chapter
two

The characters in the word "Place" replace the characters in the word "Drive." Because you are replacing existing characters with new characters, it is important that you turn off Overtype mode and return to Insert mode as soon as you are finished with your changes. This way you won't replace text unintentionally.

Step 5	*Double-click*	the OVR mode indicator on the status bar to turn off Overtype mode
Step 6	*Save*	the document as *Final Richardson Revision* and close it

Word has many ways to view a document for editing. The appropriate editing view depends on the kind of editing you are doing.

2.g Switching Between Different Editing Views

You can view documents in several ways for editing: Normal view, Web Layout view, Print Layout view, Full Screen view, Outline view, and Print Preview. The two most commonly used views for entering and editing text are Normal view and Print Layout view.

Normal View

Normal view is commonly used for keying, editing, and formatting text. It does not display margins, headers and footers, drawing objects, graphics, and text in column format.

Print Layout View

In **Print Layout view**, your document looks more like it looks on the printed page, including headers and footers, columns, graphics, drawing objects, and margins. You also see a vertical ruler in Print Layout view. To view a document in Print Layout view:

Step 1	*Open*	the *Vancouver Warehouse Report* located on the Data Disk
Step 2	*Click*	the Print Layout View button ▣ to the left of the horizontal scroll bar
Step 3	*Zoom*	the document to Whole Page

MENU TIP

You can switch between Normal, Web Layout, Print Layout, Outline, and Full Screen view by clicking the appropriate command on the View menu.

MOUSE TIP

You can switch between Normal, Web Layout, Print Layout, and Outline views using the view buttons to the left of the horizontal scroll bar.

Your screen should look similar to Figure 2-7.

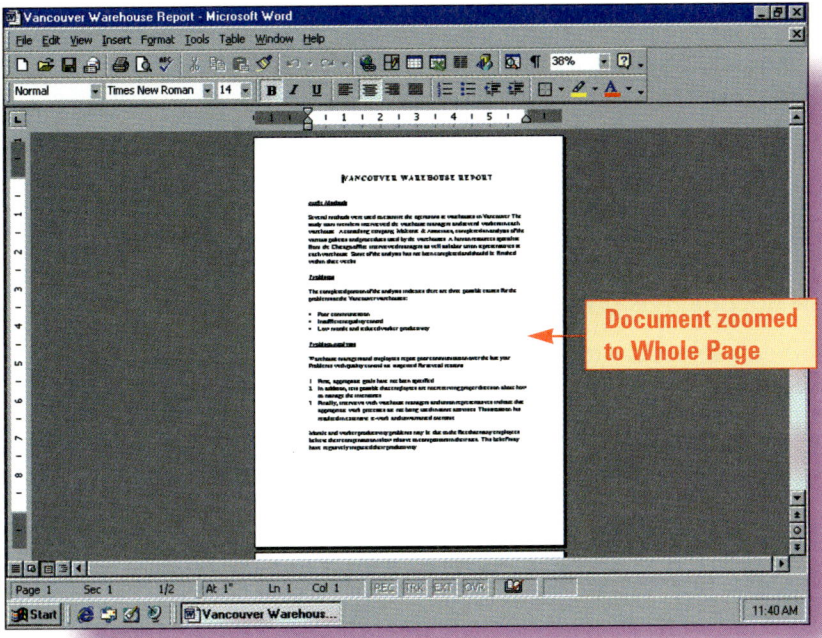
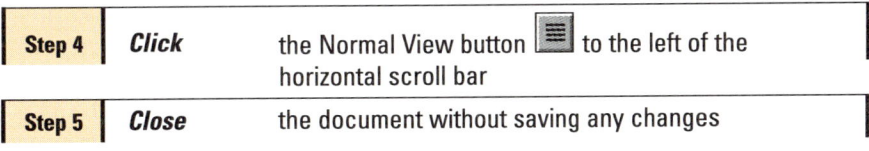

FIGURE 2-7
Print Layout View

CAUTION TIP

You may notice that the I-beam sometimes appears with a text alignment indicator in Print Layout view. This is the Click and Type feature. You use the **Click and Type** feature to double-click anywhere in your document in Print Layout view and key your text.

Step 4	*Click*	the Normal View button ▤ to the left of the horizontal scroll bar
Step 5	*Close*	the document without saving any changes

Full Screen View

When you need to maximize the number of text lines you see on your screen use **Full Screen view**, which hides the title bar, menu bar, toolbars, scroll bars, status bar, and taskbar. You can view a document in Full Screen view by clicking the F<u>u</u>ll Screen command on the <u>V</u>iew menu.

QUICK TIP

For more information on changing Word options click the <u>O</u>ptions command on the <u>T</u>ools menu, then click the General and View tabs. You can use the dialog box Help button to view a description of each option on each tab.

chapter
two

Summary

▶ The block format is a commonly used format for business correspondence.

▶ Word has preset top, bottom, left, and right margins that you can change in the Page Setup dialog box.

▶ The date and time can be inserted in a document as text or as a field that automatically updates to the current system date when the document is printed.

▶ You can select characters, words, or groups of words with the mouse or keyboard.

▶ Selected text can be cut, copied, pasted (inserted), and deleted.

▶ You can collect several cut or copied selections and then paste them individually or all at one time using the Office Clipboard.

▶ You can repeat or undo your last action.

▶ Word has several ways you can view your document, including: Normal view, Web Layout view, Print Layout view, Print Preview, Outline view, and Full Screen view. Use Normal view to key, edit, and format text. Use Print Layout to view and work with margins, headers and footers, columns, graphics, and drawing objects. Use Web Layout view to see how a Web page looks in a Web browser.

Commands Review

Action	Menu Bar	Shortcut Menu	Toolbar	Keyboard
Set margins	File, Page Setup			ALT + F, U
Insert date	Insert, Date and Time			ALT + I, T ALT + SHIFT + D
Update a selected date field		Right-click, then click Update Field		F9
Cut, Copy, Paste	Edit, Cut or Copy or Paste	Right-click then click Cut or Copy or Paste		ALT + E, T or C or P CTRL + C (copy) CTRL + X (cut) CTRL + V (paste)
Turn on or off Overtype			Double-click the OVR mode indicator	INSERT
Undo or Redo actions	Edit, Undo			ALT + E, U CTRL + Z
Repeat actions	Edit, Repeat			ALT + E, R CTRL + Y
Cancel an action				ESC
Change editing views	View, Normal or Web Layout or Print Layout or Outline or Full Screen			ALT + V, N or W or P or U, or O ALT + CTRL + P ALT + CTRL + O ALT + CTRL + N

Concepts Review

Circle the correct answer.

1. You can remove text by selecting the text and pressing the:
[a] EXT key.
[b] ALT + PAGEUP keys.
[c] CTRL key.
[d] DELETE key.

2. You cannot add a date to a document by:
[a] keying the date manually.
[b] inserting a date field that updates automatically.
[c] inserting the date as text.
[d] pressing the Insert key.

3. The selection bar is:
[a] located below the status bar.
[b] used to open other Office applications.
[c] used to select text in different ways.
[d] used to set left and right margins.

4. When you use the block format for a business letter, the:
[a] date and complimentary closing are centered on their respective lines.
[b] letter address is positioned below the salutation.
[c] letter components all begin at the left margin.
[d] letter components all begin at the right margin.

5. Margins refer to the:
[a] distance from the center of the page to the edge of the page.
[b] distance from the top, bottom, left, and right edges of the page to the text.
[c] number of lines you can have on a page.
[d] size of the text on a page.

6. By default, Word is in the:
[a] Overtype mode.
[b] Edit mode.
[c] Online Review mode.
[d] Insert mode.

7. Which of the following is not a selection technique in Word?
[a] Pressing the CTRL + SHIFT + END keys to select from the insertion point to the end of the document.
[b] Double-clicking the selection bar opposite the paragraph you wish to select.
[c] Double-clicking a word.
[d] Pressing the ALT key and clicking a word.

8. Using the mouse to move or copy text is called:
[a] cut-and-drag.
[b] select-and-cut.
[c] copy-and-cut.
[d] drag-and-drop.

9. Overtype mode allows you to:
[a] select text.
[b] key over existing text.
[c] move text.
[d] copy text.

10. Which of the following is not an editing view?
[a] Full Page view
[b] Web Layout view
[c] Print Layout view
[d] Normal view

Circle **T** if the statement is true or **F** if the statement is false.

T F 1. When you are in the Overtype mode and enter new text, any character you key replaces the character to the right of the insertion point.

T F 2. Word automatically defaults to the Edit mode.

T F 3. Word can undo multiple actions.

chapter two

T   F   4. The mouse and the keyboard can both be used to select text in a document.
T   F   5. The EXT mode indicator appears boldfaced when you are using the Extend mode feature.
T   F   6. You can restore text that has been deleted.
T   F   7. You can maximize the number of lines of text displayed on the screen by switching to Full Screen view.
T   F   8. Normal view displays your document closely to the way it looks when printed.
T   F   9. You can insert the date and the time together in a Word document.
T   F   10. The Office Clipboard is a reserved place in the memory of your computer you can use to temporarily store up to 12 items you have cut or copied.

Skills Review

Exercise 1

1. Create the following document. Use the block format with 2-inch top margin and 1-inch left and right margins. Insert the current date in the format of your choice at the top of the document. As you key the text, use the movement techniques and insert/delete actions you learned in this chapter to correct any errors.

Current date

Ms. Gail Jackson
Corporate Travel Manager
International Travel Services
1590 W. Convention Street
Chicago, IL 60605-1590

Dear Ms. Jackson:

Thank you for helping plan business trip to London this winter. I am really looking forward to seeing the sites, as well as taking care of some business. This is my first trip to London, and you were quite courteous in answering my questions.

Yours truly,

Kelly Armstead
Executive Assistant to B. D. Vickers

ka

2. Save the document as *Travel Letter*.

3. Preview, print, and close the document.

Exercise 2

1. Open the *Travel Letter* document created in Exercise 1 in this chapter.

2. At the end of the street address line, add ", Suite 16A"; in the first sentence, add the word "me" after the word "helping"; in the first sentence, add the word "my" after the word "plan" and delete the word "business"; in the first sentence, delete the word "winter" and replace it with the word "summer."

3. Save the document as *Travel Letter Revised*.

4. Preview, print, and close the document.

Exercise 3

1. Create the following document. Use the block format with 2-inch top margin and 1-inch left and right margins. Insert the date as a field at the top of the document. As you key the letter, use the movement techniques and insert/delete actions to correct any errors.

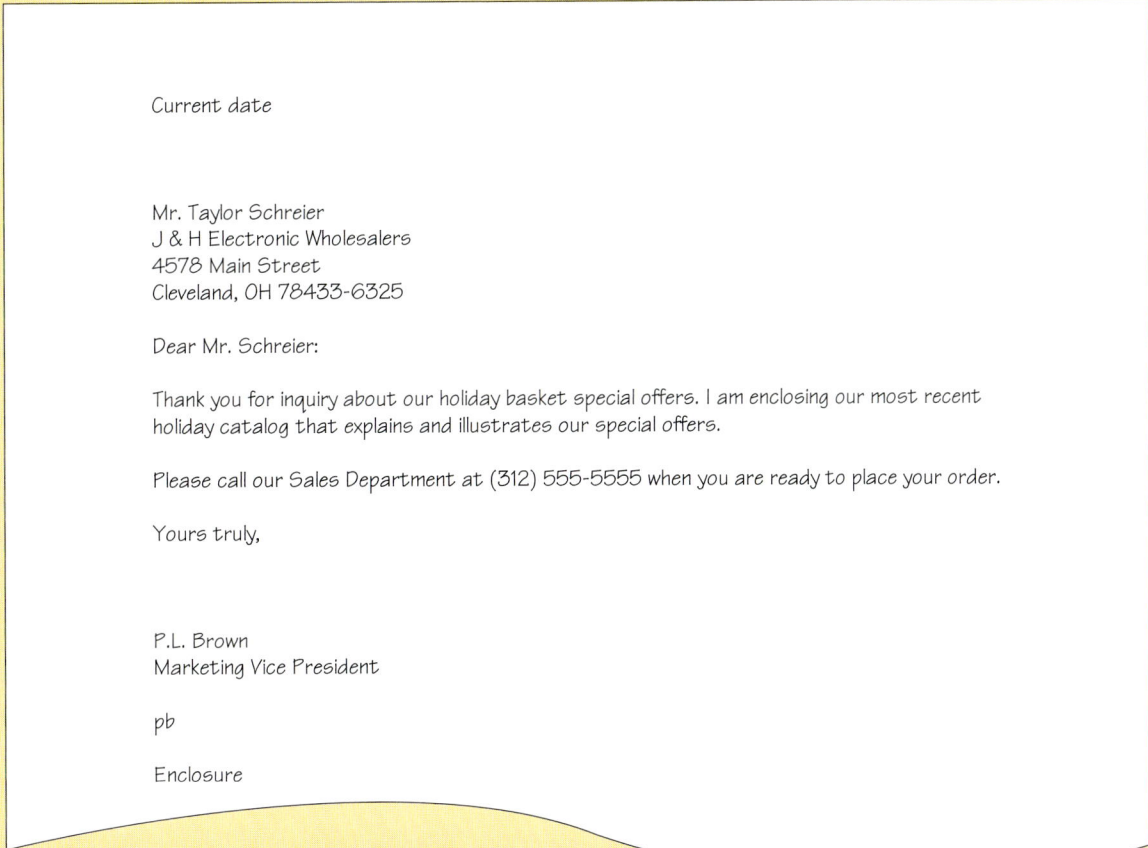

Current date

Mr. Taylor Schreier
J & H Electronic Wholesalers
4578 Main Street
Cleveland, OH 78433-6325

Dear Mr. Schreier:

Thank you for inquiry about our holiday basket special offers. I am enclosing our most recent holiday catalog that explains and illustrates our special offers.

Please call our Sales Department at (312) 555-5555 when you are ready to place your order.

Yours truly,

P.L. Brown
Marketing Vice President

pb

Enclosure

2. Save the document as *Schreier Letter*.

3. Preview, print, and close the document.

chapter two

Exercise 4

1. Open the *Schreier Letter* document created in Exercise 3 in this chapter.

2. In the first sentence, add the word "your" after the word "for" and delete the word "about" and replace it with the word "regarding."

3. Using Overtype mode, replace the text "Yours truly," with the text "Sincerely," in the complimentary close. Delete any extra characters and then turn off Overtype mode.

4. Save the document as *Schreier Letter Revised*.

5. Preview, print, and close the document.

Exercise 5

1. Open the *Employment Application Letter* document located on the Data Disk.

2. Move the second body paragraph to the first body paragraph position using a shortcut menu.

3. Undo the move action.

4. Move the second body paragraph to the first body paragraph position using drag-and-drop.

5. Combine the third body paragraph with the second body paragraph by viewing the formatting marks and deleting the paragraph marks at the end of the second body paragraph and the blank line between the second body paragraph and the third body paragraph. Don't forget to add a space between the two sentences of the revised second body paragraph.

6. Replace the words "Current date" with the current date in the 12 November 1999 format.

7. Save the document as *Employment Application Letter Revised*.

8. Preview, print, and close the document.

Exercise 6

1. Open the *Business Solicitation Letter* located on the Data Disk.

2. Change the margins to a 2-inch top margin and 1-inch left and right margins.

3. Delete the word "own" in the first sentence of the first body paragraph. Use the <u>R</u>epeat command on the <u>E</u>dit menu to delete the text "explaining and" in the first sentence of the second body paragraph.

4. Replace the words "Current date" with the current date in the format of your choice.

5. Save the document as *Business Solicitation Letter Revised*.

6. Preview, print, and close the document.

Exercise 7

1. Create the following document. Use the block format with 1½-inch top margin and 1¼-inch left and right margins. Insert the current date in the format of your choice at the top of the document. As you key the letter, use the movement techniques and insert/delete actions to correct any errors.

Current date

BCH Software Company
4000 Skywalk Way
Ventura, CA 91015-4657

Dear Sir:

Please send by return mail all of products brochures, technical specifications, and price
list for your software related to word processing for IBM PS2/ and IBM-compatible
personal computers.

Additionally, please add your mailing list to update us on any future changes in your
product line.

Sincerely,

B. D. Vickers
Administrative Vice President

ka

2. Save the document as *BCH Software Letter*.

3. Preview, print, and close the document.

Exercise 8

1. Open the *BCH Software Letter* document created in Exercise 7 in this chapter.

2. Edit the document following the proofing notations.

3. Save the document as *BCH Software Letter Revised*.

4. Preview, print, and close the document.

chapter two

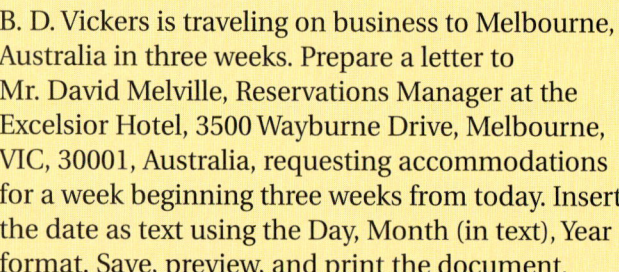

Current date

Mr. James Wilson
BCH Software Company
4000 Skywalk Way
Ventura, CA 91015-4657

Dear ~~Sir:~~ *Mr. Wilson*

Please send by return mail all of *us* products brochures, technical specifications, and price list*s* for ~~your~~ *your* software related to ~~word processing~~ *accounting* for IBM PS2/ and IBM-compatible personal computers.

Additionally, please add *us to* your mailing list ~~to~~ *for* update us on any ~~future~~ changes *to* ~~in~~ your product line.

Sincerely,

B. D. Vickers
Administrative Vice President

ka

Case Projects

Project 1

B. D. Vickers is traveling on business to Melbourne, Australia in three weeks. Prepare a letter to Mr. David Melville, Reservations Manager at the Excelsior Hotel, 3500 Wayburne Drive, Melbourne, VIC, 30001, Australia, requesting accommodations for a week beginning three weeks from today. Insert the date as text using the Day, Month (in text), Year format. Save, preview, and print the document.

Project 2

Kelly Armstead asks you to find out how to use the Paste Special command on the Edit menu. Use the Office Assistant to research embedding and linking data from other Office applications. Open the *Vancouver Branch Sales* workbook (located on the Data Disk) in Excel, copy the data to the Office Clipboard, switch to a blank document, and embed the data using the Paste Special command. Save, preview, and print the document.

Project 3

Kelly Armstead has asked you to find a list of keyboard shortcuts you both can use to prepare correspondence. Using the Office Assistant, search Word online Help for a list of keyboard shortcut keys for moving the insertion point in a document and selecting text in a document. Print the lists. Use the lists to demonstrate the keyboard shortcuts to a classmate.

Project 4

B. D. Vickers is considering ordering several IntelliMouse pointing devices for the Purchasing Department and has asked you to find out how the devices are used to increase productivity in the department. Using the Help menu resources, including Web resources, search for information on the IntelliMouse pointing device. Create a new document containing at least three paragraphs describing how the Purchasing Department employees can improve their productivity by using the IntelliMouse pointing device. Insert the current date as text using the mm/dd/yy format. Save, preview, and print the document.

Project 5

There have been several power failures because of storms in the area and Kelly is concerned that she may lose documents she is working on if the power fails. She has asked you to find out what options Word has to automatically back up documents as she is working and to automatically recover documents lost during a power failure. Using the Help menu, research what backup and document recovery features Word provides. Create a new document, containing at least four paragraphs, that describes how to set backup procedures and recover lost or damaged documents. Insert the date as a field using the format of your choice. Save, preview, and print the document.

Project 6

B. D. Vickers has extended the business trip discussed in Project 1 and now plans to spend two days in Hong Kong and three days in London before returning. Kelly needs a list of possible accommodations in Hong Kong and London and has asked you to search the Web for information on hotels in these cities. She also needs you to review flight schedules and suggest flights from Melbourne to Hong Kong, from Hong Kong to London, and from London to Chicago. Connect to your ISP and search the Web for the information you need. Save at least two URLs as "favorites." Print at least five Web pages. Disconnect from your ISP and close your browser. Create a new, blank document and key the title and URL of the pages you printed. Insert the date as text in the format of your choice. Save, preview, and print the document.

Project 7

Open the document of your choice. Practice using various selection techniques to select text. Delete and restore text using the Delete key and the Undo, Redo, and Repeat commands. Close the document without saving any changes.

Project 8

Worldwide Exotic Foods, Inc. participates in a summer internship program for graduating seniors and has a new group of interns starting the program next week. Margie Montez, the program director, has asked you to make a ten-minute presentation on creating business letters using Word 2000. The presentation is scheduled for next Thursday, at 3:00 PM. Create a new document listing the topics you plan to discuss and the order in which you plan to discuss them. Insert the date and time using the format of your choice. Save, preview, and print the document. Ask a classmate to review the document and provide comments and suggestions on the topics to be covered and the organization of the presentation. With your instructor's approval, schedule a time to give your presentation to your class.

Project 9

Kelly has subscribed to an e-mail mailing list and gets Word 2000 user tips every day via e-mail. You would like to also subscribe to this kind of mailing list and want to know more about how to do this. Connect to your ISP and search the Web for information on locating and subscribing to mailing lists. Create a new, blank document that lists titles and URLs for pages that provide mailing list information. Insert the date using the Day (in text), Month (in text) and Date, Year format. Save, preview, and print the document.

chapter two

Using the Proofing Tools

Chapter Overview

Documents with misspellings and grammar errors indicate sloppiness and inattention to detail—two traits no company wants to convey. Proofing a document before you print it helps ensure it is error-free, allowing readers to focus on its content. Word has several tools to help you proof your documents. In this chapter you learn to use the Spelling and Grammar, Thesaurus, and AutoCorrect proofing tools. You also learn to insert dates automatically with AutoComplete and create, insert, edit, print, and delete AutoText entries.

LEARNING OBJECTIVES

► **Use the Spelling and Grammar**
► **Use the Thesaurus**
► **Use AutoCorrect**
► **Use AutoText**
► **Insert dates with AutoComplete**

Case profile

Worldwide Exotic Foods requires that all correspondence and documents sent out from the company have accurate spelling and grammar. Kelly Armstead asks you to correct any errors in a letter she keyed quickly before it is printed and mailed.

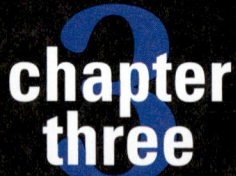

chapter three

3.a Using the Spelling and Grammar Features

Kelly tells you that it is company policy to check the spelling and grammar of any document before you print it. You can check the spelling and grammar in a document with a menu command, a toolbar button, a status bar mode indicator, or a shortcut menu. By default, Word checks the spelling and grammar in your document as you key the text. Using this automatic spelling and grammar feature saves time in editing your document. When you misspell a word or key text that may be grammatically incorrect and then press the SPACEBAR, a wavy red or green line appears below the text. The red line indicates a spelling error and the green line indicates a possible grammar error.

Kelly's letter contains several keying errors. You open the letter and then use the Spelling and Grammar command to correct those errors. To open the letter containing errors:

| Step 1 | *Open* | the *IAEA Letter* document located on the Data Disk |

Notice the wavy red and green lines below text that may be misspelled or grammatically incorrect. In this letter the proper names are correct; therefore, you can ignore the wavy red or green lines underneath them if they appear. When necessary, you can add words like proper names to a custom dictionary. *For the activities in this chapter, do not add any words to a custom dictionary.*

There is one grammar error in the letter, indicated by a wavy green line. To correct the grammar error "an" in the second body paragraph:

| Step 1 | *Right-click* | the word "an" |

The Grammar shortcut menu that appears on your screen should look similar to Figure 3-1.

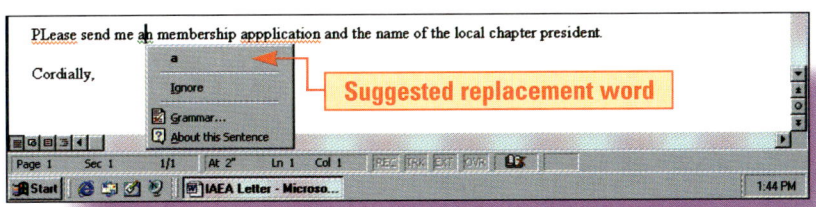

FIGURE 3-1
Grammar Shortcut Menu

chapter
three

MENU TIP

You can right-click a misspelled word or grammar error to correct it. You can also click the Spelling and Grammar command on the Tools menu to correct spelling or grammar errors.

Notice the shortcut menu suggestion to replace the word "an" with "a." You can quickly replace a word by clicking the suggested word in the shortcut menu, or you can display the Grammar dialog box to get more information about the error message. Because this is an obvious error, you can quickly correct it by replacing "an" with "a."

Step 2	*Click*	a on the shortcut menu

Next, you correct the misspellings in the letter. To correct the spelling of the word "intereting" in the first body paragraph:

Step 1	*Right-click*	the word "intereting"

The Spelling shortcut menu that appears on your screen should look similar to Figure 3-2.

FIGURE 3-2
Spelling Shortcut Menu

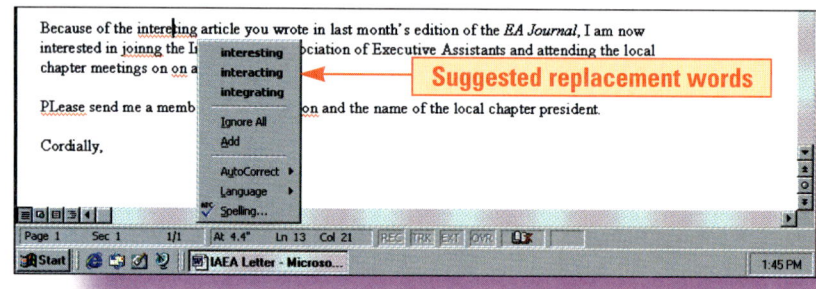

You can click a suggested spelling, ignore the spelling, add the word to a custom dictionary, add the error and suggested replacement word to the AutoCorrect tool, or open the Spelling dialog box. Because the correct spelling is on the shortcut menu, you click it to fix the error.

MOUSE TIP

You can click the Spelling and Grammar button on the Standard toolbar or the Spelling and Grammar Status mode indicator on the status bar to correct spelling or grammar errors.

Step 2	*Click*	interesting on the shortcut menu

You can display the spelling or grammar shortcut menu with the Spelling and Grammar Status mode indicator on the status bar.

To correct the next error, the word "joinng," using the Spelling and Grammar Status mode indicator:

Step 1	*Click*	the word "joinng" to position the insertion point in the word

Step 2	*Double-click*	the Spelling and Grammar Status mode indicator 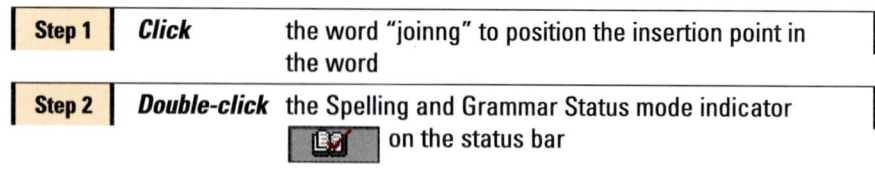 on the status bar

| Step 3 | *Click* | joining on the shortcut menu |

Another way to correct spelling and grammar is to use the Spelling and Grammar dialog box, which shows each error and provides options for you to correct it. To correct the remaining errors using the Spelling and Grammar dialog box:

| Step 1 | *Click* | the Spelling and Grammar button [icon] on the Standard toolbar |

The dialog box on your screen should look similar to Figure 3-3.

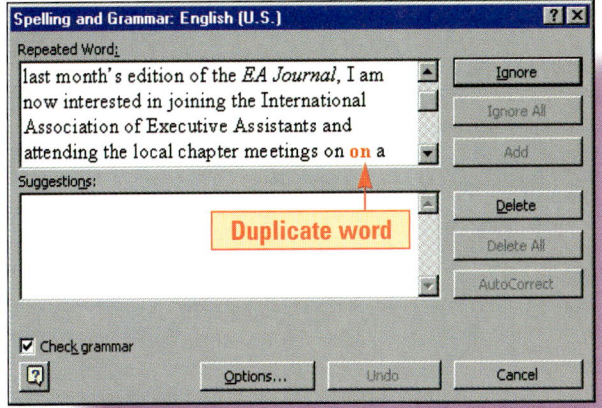

FIGURE 3-3
Spelling and Grammar Dialog Box

The Spelling and Grammar tool detected the duplicate word "on" in the first body paragraph. You want to delete the duplicate word.

| Step 2 | *Click* | Delete |

Word deletes the extra word and moves to the next spelling error. The word "PLease" appears in the dialog box and Word provides a list of possible corrections in the Suggestions: list. Word highlights the most likely suggested correction "Please" for the irregular capitalization.

| Step 3 | *Click* | Change |

The next misspelled word "appplication" appears in the dialog box and Word suggests the correct spelling "application."

| Step 4 | *Click* | Change |

chapter
three

Word highlights the proper name "Armstead." Because this spelling is correct, you can ignore it and proceed to the next error. You can choose to ignore words that are correct but do not appear in the dictionaries. To ignore the remaining possible errors:

Step 5	Click	Ignore until the spelling and grammar checking is complete and a dialog box opens indicating the process is complete
Step 6	Click	OK
Step 7	Save	the document as *IAEA Letter Revised*

In addition to checking the spelling and grammar, you read Kelly's letter and want to find new words to replace certain words in the letter.

3.b Using the Thesaurus

The **Thesaurus** enables you to replace a selected word with another word that has the same or a very similar meaning. Kelly suggests that you substitute a different word for the word "article" in first body paragraph of her letter. To find a synonym:

| Step 1 | Right-click | the word "article" in the first body paragraph |
| Step 2 | Point | to Synonyms |

A shortcut menu of replacement words appears along with the Thesaurus command. You can select a replacement word from the shortcut menu or open the Thesaurus dialog box for additional replacement options. You decide to replace "article" with "commentary."

Step 3	Click	commentary on the shortcut menu
Step 4	Observe	that the word "commentary" replaces the word "article"
Step 5	Save	the document

Another Word proofing tool, AutoCorrect, can automatically correct your keying errors.

3.c Using AutoCorrect

The **AutoCorrect** tool fixes common errors as you key in the text. For example, if you commonly key "adn" for "and," AutoCorrect corrects the error as soon as you press the SPACEBAR. AutoCorrect also corrects two initial capitalized letters (DEar), capitalizes the first letter of a sentence, capitalizes the names of days, and corrects errors caused by forgetting to turn off the CAPS LOCK key (aRTICLE). The AutoCorrect tool contains an extensive list of symbols and words that are inserted whenever you type an abbreviation for the symbol or word and then press the SPACEBAR. You can specify certain words as exceptions to this automatic correction. To verify AutoCorrect is turned on:

Step 1	*Click*	Tools
Step 2	*Click*	AutoCorrect
Step 3	*Click*	the AutoCorrect tab, if necessary

The AutoCorrect dialog box on your screen should look similar to Figure 3-4.

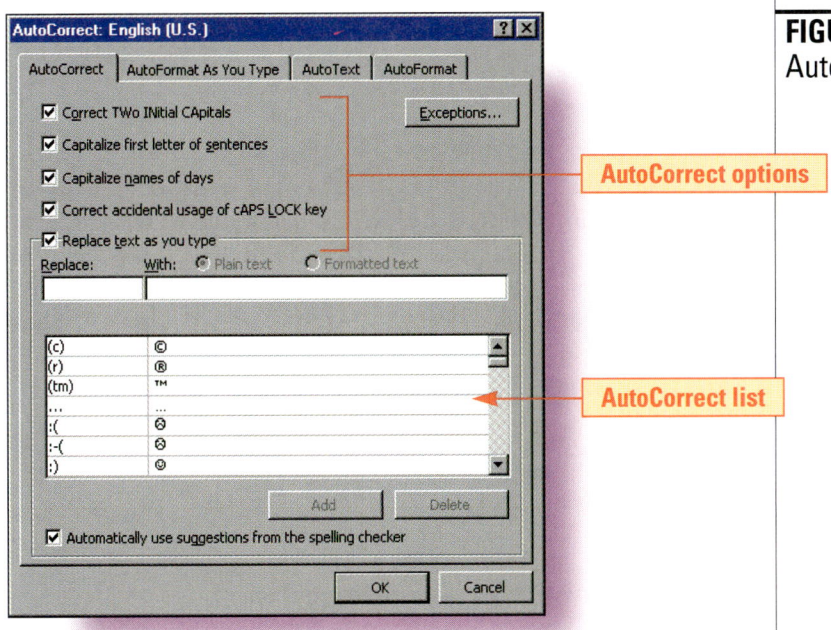

FIGURE 3-4
AutoCorrect Dialog Box

Remember that you can use the dialog box Help button to review the all the options on the AutoCorrect tab.

chapter
three

Step 4	*Verify*	a check mark appears in the Replace text as you type check box
Step 5	*Click*	OK

To test AutoCorrect, you first delete the word "the" before the word "International" in the first body paragraph and then deliberately key the word "teh:"

Step 1	*Delete*	the word "the" before the word "International" in the first body paragraph
Step 2	*Key*	teh
Step 3	*Verify*	that the word is misspelled
Step 4	*Press*	the SPACEBAR
Step 5	*Observe*	the word "teh" is automatically corrected to "the" when you press the SPACEBAR
Step 6	*Save*	the *IAEA Letter Revised* document and close it

Sometimes it is necessary to alter the AutoCorrect tool by adding or removing AutoCorrect items or by setting AutoCorrect exceptions.

Creating and Applying Frequently Used Text With AutoCorrect

You can add and delete items in the AutoCorrect list. You can add not only your own common keying errors or misspelled words, but also words and phrases that you would like to insert whenever you key a certain letter combination and press the SPACEBAR. For example, suppose you want to quickly insert the name of your company into a document by keying an abbreviation and then pressing the SPACEBAR. You can add the name of your company and an abbreviation to the AutoCorrect list. Then, when you key the abbreviation and press the SPACEBAR, your company name is inserted into your document. To add the Worldwide Exotic Foods company name and abbreviation to the AutoCorrect list:

Step 1	*Create*	a new, blank document
Step 2	*Key*	Worldwide Exotic Foods, Inc.
Step 3	*Select*	the text (do not include the paragraph mark at the end of the text)
Step 4	*Click*	Tools

Step 5	*Click*	AutoCorrect
Step 6	*Click*	the AutoCorrect tab, if necessary
Step 7	*Observe*	that the company name is already entered in the With: text box
Step 8	*Key*	wef in the Replace: text box
Step 9	*Click*	Add
Step 10	*Observe*	that the company name and abbreviation are added to the AutoCorrect list
Step 11	*Click*	OK
Step 12	*Delete*	the selected company name text

You decide to test the abbreviation you added to the AutoCorrect list. To insert the company name using AutoCorrect:

Step 1	*Key*	wef
Step 2	*Press*	the SPACEBAR
Step 3	*Observe*	the company name is automatically inserted

Adding words you key frequently to the AutoCorrect list is a great timesaver. When you no longer need an AutoCorrect entry, you should delete it. To delete the company name from the AutoCorrect list:

Step 1	*Click*	Tools
Step 2	*Click*	AutoCorrect
Step 3	*Click*	the AutoCorrect tab, if necessary
Step 4	*Key*	wef in the Replace: text box to scroll the AutoCorrect list
Step 5	*Click*	Worldwide Exotic Foods, Inc. in the AutoCorrect list
Step 6	*Click*	Delete
Step 7	*Click*	OK

You can also create a list of words or exceptions that AutoCorrect leaves untouched.

chapter
three

Setting AutoCorrect Exceptions

AutoCorrect comes with a list of **exceptions**, words or abbreviations that AutoCorrect does not correct automatically. Whenever you key a period (.) in a commonly used abbreviation, AutoCorrect may interpret the period as the end of a sentence and then capitalize the following word. To avoid this, you can set an AutoCorrect exception to ignore capitalization following the period (.) in a specific abbreviation. Worldwide Exotic Foods frequently uses the abbreviation "Qtr." for "quarter" in its documents. You can set an exception for this abbreviation so that the AutoCorrect feature does not automatically capitalize next word. To use AutoCorrect before setting an exception:

Step 1	*Press*	the ENTER key to move the insertion point to the next line
Step 2	*Verify*	the Capitalize the first letter of sentences option is turned on in the AutoCorrect tab of the AutoCorrect dialog box
Step 3	*Key*	Qtr.
Step 4	*Press*	the SPACEBAR
Step 5	*Key*	is
Step 6	*Press*	the SPACEBAR
Step 7	*Observe*	the letter "I" in the word "Is" is capitalized
Step 8	*Delete*	the Qtr. Is text

Many Worldwide Exotic Foods documents use the Qtr. abbreviation for quarters, such as the financial reports. To create an exception for the abbreviation "Qtr.":

Step 1	*Click*	Tools
Step 2	*Click*	AutoCorrect
Step 3	*Click*	the AutoCorrect tab, if necessary
Step 4	*Click*	Exceptions
Step 5	*Click*	the First Letter tab, if necessary

The AutoCorrect Exceptions dialog box on your screen should look similar to Figure 3-5.

QUICK TIP

If the Automatically add words to list option is turned on in the AutoCorrect Exceptions dialog box, you can backspace over the incorrectly capitalized word and key it again. Word then adds the exception to the list. To keep the AutoCorrect feature from automatically correcting text with mixed upper and lowercase letters, you can click the INitial CAps tab in the AutoCorrect Exceptions dialog box and add your exception to the list.

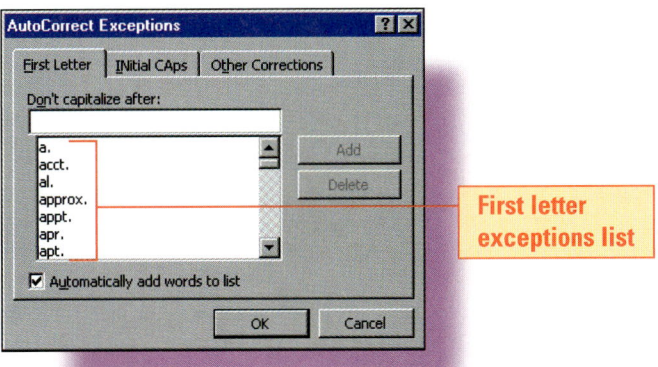

FIGURE 3-5
First Letter Tab in the AutoCorrect Exceptions Dialog Box

First letter exceptions list

QUICK TIP

You can also add formatted text and graphics to an AutoCorrect entry.

You add the words AutoCorrect cannot automatically correct in this dialog box. AutoCorrect exceptions are not case sensitive, so you can enter the text in lowercase letters, uppercase letters, or a combination.

Step 6	*Key*	qtr. in the D<u>o</u>n't capitalize after: text box
Step 7	*Click*	<u>A</u>dd
Step 8	*Click*	OK twice to close the dialog boxes

With the AutoCorrect exception added to the list, you decide to try it out. To test the exception:

Step 1	*Key*	Qtr.
Step 2	*Press*	the SPACEBAR
Step 3	*Key*	is
Step 4	*Press*	the SPACEBAR
Step 5	*Observe*	the word "is" is not capitalized

You can delete exceptions when you no longer need them. To delete the Qtr. exception:

Step 1	*Open*	the AutoCorrect dialog box and view the AutoCorrect tab
Step 2	*Click*	<u>E</u>xceptions
Step 3	*Click*	the <u>F</u>irst Letter tab, if necessary
Step 4	*Key*	qtr. in the D<u>o</u>n't capitalize after: text box to scroll the AutoCorrect list

chapter
three

Step 5	*Observe*	that qtr. is selected in the list
Step 6	*Click*	<u>D</u>elete
Step 7	*Click*	OK twice to close the dialog boxes
Step 8	*Press*	the ENTER key twice to move the insertion point in the document

If you frequently key larger amounts of text, AutoText is a better option than AutoCorrect for inserting text that has already been keyed.

3.d Using AutoText

An **AutoText** entry is a segment of stored text that you can insert into your documents. In this way, it is similar to AutoCorrect; however, AutoText is often used for large amounts of preformatted standard text. Word provides standard AutoText entries or you can create custom AutoText entries.

Inserting Standard AutoText

Word provides standard AutoText entries, such as complimentary closings or mailing instructions for letters. To view the standard AutoText options:

Step 1	*Click*	<u>I</u>nsert
Step 2	*Point to*	<u>A</u>utoText

Your screen should look similar to Figure 3-6.

FIGURE 3-6
Standard AutoText Menu

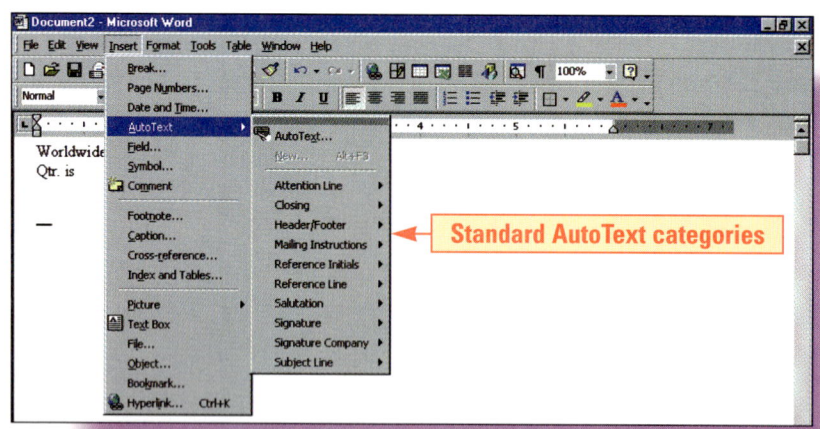

Step 3	*Point to*	Mailing Instructions
Step 4	*Click*	CERTIFIED MAIL
Step 5	*Observe*	the text CERTIFIED MAIL is inserted into the document
Step 6	*Continue*	to explore the standard AutoText entries by viewing the AutoText categories and inserting an AutoText entry into the current document
Step 7	*Press*	the ENTER key twice to move the insertion point

You can create your own custom AutoText entries such as the closing for a letter or standard paragraph text for letters and contracts.

Inserting Custom AutoText

Because you use the same letter closing text for all B. D. Vickers' letters, Kelly suggests you create a custom AutoText closing for the letters instead of keying the closing at the end of each letter. To create a custom AutoText entry, first you create and select the text that you want to insert in documents. If you want the text to have a certain format, you must format the text before you select it.

Each custom AutoText entry must have a unique name that can contain spaces. AutoText names are not case sensitive. If you name an AutoText entry with uppercase letters, you can insert the entry into the document using lowercase letters.

You create a custom AutoText complimentary closing for B. D. Vickers. To key the text for a custom AutoText entry:

> **CAUTION TIP**
>
> Unless you specify another template, an AutoText entry is saved with the Normal template and is available for all documents created with the Normal template.

Step 1	*Key*	Sincerely,
Step 2	*Press*	the ENTER key four times
Step 3	*Key*	B. D. Vickers
Step 4	*Press*	the ENTER key twice
Step 5	*Key*	your initials and press the SPACEBAR
Step 6	*Press*	the CTRL + Z keys to undo the AutoCorrect capitalization
Step 7	*Press*	the ENTER key twice
Step 8	*Key*	Enclosure

chapter
three

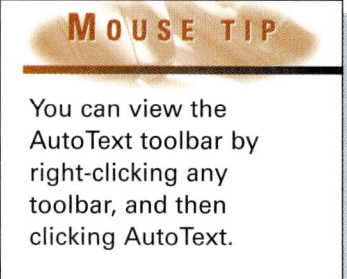

MOUSE TIP

You can view the AutoText toolbar by right-clicking any toolbar, and then clicking AutoText.

After you key the text, and format it if necessary, you can turn it into an AutoText entry. To create the AutoText entry:

Step 1	*Select*	all the lines of text (do not select the paragraph mark at the end of Enclosure)
Step 2	*Click*	Insert
Step 3	*Point to*	AutoText
Step 4	*Click*	AutoText

The dialog box on your screen should look similar to Figure 3-7.

FIGURE 3-7
AutoText Tab in the AutoCorrect Dialog Box

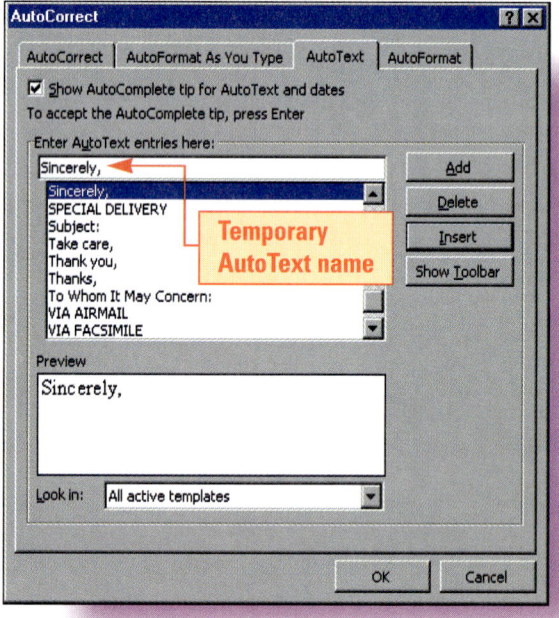

By default, Word inserts text from the first line of the selection as the AutoText name. You can change this to a more descriptive, but brief and unique name that will remind you of its contents.

Step 5	*Key*	closing in the Enter AutoText entries here: text box
Step 6	*Click*	Add
Step 7	*Delete*	the selected text

Now you can insert the closing AutoText entry into your document. You can insert a custom AutoText entry by displaying the AutoText dialog box or by keying the name of the entry and pressing the F3 key. You can also key just enough characters for AutoComplete to identify an AutoText entry's unique name and display an AutoComplete tip, then press the F3 key or the ENTER key. To insert AutoText using the keyboard:

Step 1	*Key*	clos (for closing)
Step 2	*Observe*	the AutoComplete tip that appears above the text with two lines of the AutoText entry
Step 3	*Press*	the F3 key
Step 4	*Observe*	that the AutoText closing entry is inserted into the document

AutoText can be modified to add text or formatting.

Editing AutoText Entries

You can easily edit AutoText entries. You need to include B. D. Vickers' job title in the closing AutoText entry. You can edit an AutoText entry by first changing the text, then selecting the changed text, and adding new AutoText with the same name. To edit the closing AutoText entry:

Step 1	*Move*	the insertion point after the text "B. D. Vickers" in the closing text
Step 2	*Press*	the ENTER key
Step 3	*Key*	Administrative Vice President
Step 4	*Select*	all the lines of the closing, beginning with Sincerely and ending with Enclosure (do not select the paragraph mark following Enclosure)
Step 5	*Click*	Insert
Step 6	*Point to*	AutoText
Step 7	*Click*	AutoText
Step 8	*Click*	closing in the list
Step 9	*Click*	Add
Step 10	*Click*	Yes to redefine the entry with Vickers' title

chapter
three

MENU TIP

You can print AutoText entries by clicking the Print command on the File menu and selecting AutoText entries from the Print what: list box in the Print dialog box.

QUICK TIP

With a special Word AutoText entry, named the **Spike**, you can cut text from several places in one document or from multiple documents and then insert all the text as one entry into a document. For more information on using the Spike, see online Help.

To test the closing entry AutoText:

Step 1	*Delete*	the closing text you just inserted into the document
Step 2	*Key*	Clos
Step 3	*Press*	the F3 key or the ENTER key

The redefined AutoText closing entry is inserted into the document.

Deleting AutoText Entries

When you no longer need an AutoText entry, you should delete it. To delete an AutoText entry, open the AutoText dialog box. Then click the AutoText name in the AutoText list box and click the Delete button. To delete the "closing" AutoText entry:

Step 1	*Click*	Insert
Step 2	*Point to*	AutoText
Step 3	*Click*	AutoText
Step 4	*Click*	closing in the AutoText list
Step 5	*Click*	Delete
Step 6	*Click*	OK

Word has another feature, called AutoComplete, you can use to automatically insert dates and standard AutoText.

3.e Inserting Dates with AutoComplete

The **AutoComplete** feature automatically completes the text of the current date, a day of the week, a month, as well as AutoText entries. As you start to key a date, weekday, month name, or AutoText entry, an AutoComplete tip appears above the insertion point. You press the F3 key or the ENTER key to enter the text or continue keying the text to ignore the AutoComplete suggestion.

To enter the current date using AutoComplete:

Step 1	*Press*	the ENTER key twice to move the insertion point down two lines
Step 2	*Key*	the name of the current month and press the ENTER key when the AutoComplete tip appears
Step 3	*Press*	the SPACEBAR
Step 4	*Observe*	that the AutoComplete tip suggests the current date in the month/day/year format
Step 5	*Press*	the ENTER key to insert the current date as text and then press the ENTER key to move the insertion point to the next line

You can continue keying text as if you had keyed the date yourself. To insert the day of the week using AutoComplete:

Step 1	*Key*	the first four characters of a day of the week
Step 2	*Observe*	the AutoComplete tip suggests the complete name of the day of the week
Step 3	*Press*	the ENTER key to accept the complete name of day of the week
Step 4	*Close*	the document without saving changes

AutoComplete, along with all the proofing tools, will help you ensure all your documents are free from errors.

QUICK TIP

You can turn on or off the display of AutoComplete tips for AutoText and dates in the AutoText tab of the AutoCorrect dialog box.

chapter
three

Summary

► By default, Word automatically checks the spelling and grammar in your document as you type.

► When you display the Spelling and Grammar dialog box, you can choose to ignore the selected word, change it to another word, add the word to a custom dictionary, delete the word from the document, or add the word and its correction to the AutoCorrect list.

► The Thesaurus tool allows you to substitute a word having the same or similar meaning in place of the word that contains the insertion point.

► The AutoCorrect tool allows you to automatically correct commonly misspelled or mistyped words as you type, or to insert text by keying an abbreviation for the text and then pressing the SPACEBAR.

► The AutoCorrect tool is turned on by default.

► You can add items to the AutoCorrect list and create exceptions to the AutoCorrect list.

► The AutoText features allow you to insert standard text—such as mailing instructions—or to create and save custom text, then insert it as needed.

► The Spike is a special AutoText feature that allows you to cut text selections from different documents and insert them at one time.

► The AutoComplete feature allows you to automatically insert the current month, day of the week, and date by pressing the F3 or ENTER key.

Commands Review

Action	Menu Bar	Shortcut Menu	Toolbar	Keyboard
Turn on or off the AutoCorrect tool	Tools, AutoCorrect			ALT + T, A
Check spelling and grammar	Tools, Spelling and Grammar	Right-click a word with a wavy red or green line underneath		ALT + T, S F7 ALT + F7
Substitute words with same or similar meaning	Tools, Language, Thesaurus	Right-click a word, point to Synonyms		ALT + T, L, T SHIFT + F7
Create, edit, insert, delete custom AutoText entry	Insert, AutoText, AutoText			ALT + I, A, X ALT + F3
Insert standard AutoText	Insert, AutoText			ALT + I, A
Print AutoText entries	File, Print			ALT + F, P

Concepts Review

Circle the correct answer.

1. The AutoCorrect tool:
[a] provides statistics about your document.
[b] checks for misspelled words as you key and underlines them with a wavy red line.
[c] checks the grammar in the document.
[d] corrects Caps Lock errors when you press the SPACEBAR.

2. The Thesaurus tool:
[a] adds new words to the custom dictionary.
[b] corrects two initial capitalization.
[c] checks for misspelled words as you type.
[d] allows you to substitute words.

3. The Spelling and Grammar tool does not:
[a] indicate grammatical errors.
[b] identify words with capitalization problems.
[c] show you spelling and grammar errors as you type.
[d] automatically complete dates.

4. The AutoComplete feature:
[a] presents a tip with contents you can insert by pressing the ENTER key.
[b] checks the readability of the document.

[c] checks the spelling in the document.
[d] checks the grammar in the document.

5. An AutoText entry:
[a] must have a unique name.
[b] cannot be saved for future use.
[c] cannot be changed once it is created.
[d] replaces text as soon as you press the SPACEBAR.

6. You can create a new AutoText entry with the:
[a] F3 key.
[b] AutoText subcommand on the Insert menu.
[c] AutoComplete tool and the ENTER key.
[d] INSERT key.

7. The Spike:
[a] allows you to edit text.
[b] allows you to format text.
[c] allows you to cut text from several documents and then insert all the text at one time.
[d] is an AutoComplete feature.

chapter three

8. **You can check the grammar in your document with the:**
   [a] AutoComplete command.
   [b] Thesaurus command.
   [c] Synonyms command.
   [d] Spelling and Grammar Status mode indicator.

9. **You can turn on or off the automatic checking of spelling and grammar in the:**
   [a] AutoCorrect dialog box.
   [b] Options dialog box.

[c] Format dialog box.
[d] AutoText dialog box.

10. **Which of the following options are not available in the Spelling and Grammar dialog box:**
    [a] selecting suggested spellings for a word from a list.
    [b] ignoring the selected word.
    [c] adding the word to the AutoCorrect list.
    [d] adding the word to the AutoText list.

Circle **T** if the statement is true or **F** if the statement is false.

T F   1. You can use the Spelling and Grammar tool to find synonyms for selected words in your document.

T F   2. The AutoText feature allows Word to check for spelling errors as you type.

T F   3. The Synonyms command displays words with the same or similar meaning as that of a selected word.

T F   4. You can check the spelling and grammar of your document only with a toolbar button.

T F   5. The Spelling and Grammar tool presents a ScreenTip containing the complete text of the word you are keying.

T F   6. When the Spelling and Grammar tool does not find a word in the dictionaries, a wavy green line appears underneath the word.

T F   7. AutoText names are case sensitive.

T F   8. The AutoComplete tool finds spelling errors.

T F   9. The AutoCorrect tool automatically corrects commonly misspelled words as you key them.

T F   10. It is not possible to add words to the AutoCorrect list.

Skills Review

Exercise 1

1. Open the *Vancouver Report With Errors* document located on the Data Disk.

2. Correct the spelling errors using the <u>S</u>pelling and Grammar command on the <u>T</u>ools menu.

3. Save the document as *Vancouver Report Revised*.

4. Preview, print, and close the document.

Exercise 2

1. Open the *Solicitation Letter With Errors* document located on the Data Disk.

2. Select the text "Current date" and use AutoComplete to replace it with the actual date.

3. Correct the spelling and grammar errors using the Spelling and Grammar Status mode indicator.

4. Use the Synonyms command to choose another word for "growth" in the first body paragraph.

5. Save the document as *Solicitation Letter Revised*.

6. Preview, print, and close the document.

Exercise 3

1. Open the *Personal Letter With Errors* document located on the Data Disk.

2. Select the text Current date and use AutoComplete to replace it with the actual date.

3. Correct the spelling and grammar errors using the shortcut menus.

4. Use the Thesaurus tool to select another word for "arrangements" in the last paragraph (*Hint*: Right-click the word, point to Synonyms, and then click <u>T</u>hesaurus).

5. Save the document as *Personal Letter Revised*.

6. Preview, print, and close the document.

Exercise 4

1. Create a new, blank document.

2. Create an AutoText entry to insert a standard complimentary closing for the letters signed by R. F. Williams. Use the "Sincerely yours" closing text. Add an Attachment line and your initials. Name the AutoText entry "Williams Closing."

3. Insert the "Williams Closing" AutoText entry into a new, blank document using the F3 key or the ENTER key.

4. Save the document as *Williams Closing*.

5. Preview and print the document.

6. Edit the "Williams Closing" AutoText entry to include the job title "Vice President Marketing."

7. Save the document as *Williams Closing Revised*.

8. Preview, print, and close the document.

Exercise 5

1. Open the *Client Letter* document located on the Data Disk.

2. Select the text "Current date" and use AutoComplete to replace it with the current date.

3. Insert the "Williams Closing" AutoText entry created in Exercise 4 at the bottom of the document. Add any additional blank lines as necessary.

4. Save the document as *Williams Letter*.

5. Preview, print, and close the document.

Exercise 6

1. Print all the current AutoText entries.

2. Delete the "Williams Closing" AutoText entry you created in Exercise 4 in this chapter.

3. Close the Word application to update the Normal template.

Exercise 7

1. Open the *Application Letter With Errors* document located on the Data Disk.

2. Select the text "Current date" and use AutoComplete to replace it with the actual date.

chapter three

3. Move the second body paragraph beginning "Per our conversation" to the first body paragraph position.

4. Move the last body paragraph beginning "If you have" and make it the second sentence of the second body paragraph. Delete any extra blank lines, if necessary.

5. Correct the spelling and grammar using the Spelling and Grammar button on the Standard toolbar.

6. Use the Synonyms command to select another word for "department" in the first paragraph.

7. Save the document as *Application Letter Revised.*

8. Preview, print, and close the document.

Exercise 8

1. Create the following document. Use appropriate margins for a letter to be printed on 2-inch letterhead paper. Correct any spelling or grammar errors as you key the text using the Spelling and Grammar shortcut menus. Use the AutoComplete and standard AutoText features where appropriate to complete the letter—for example, to enter the current date.

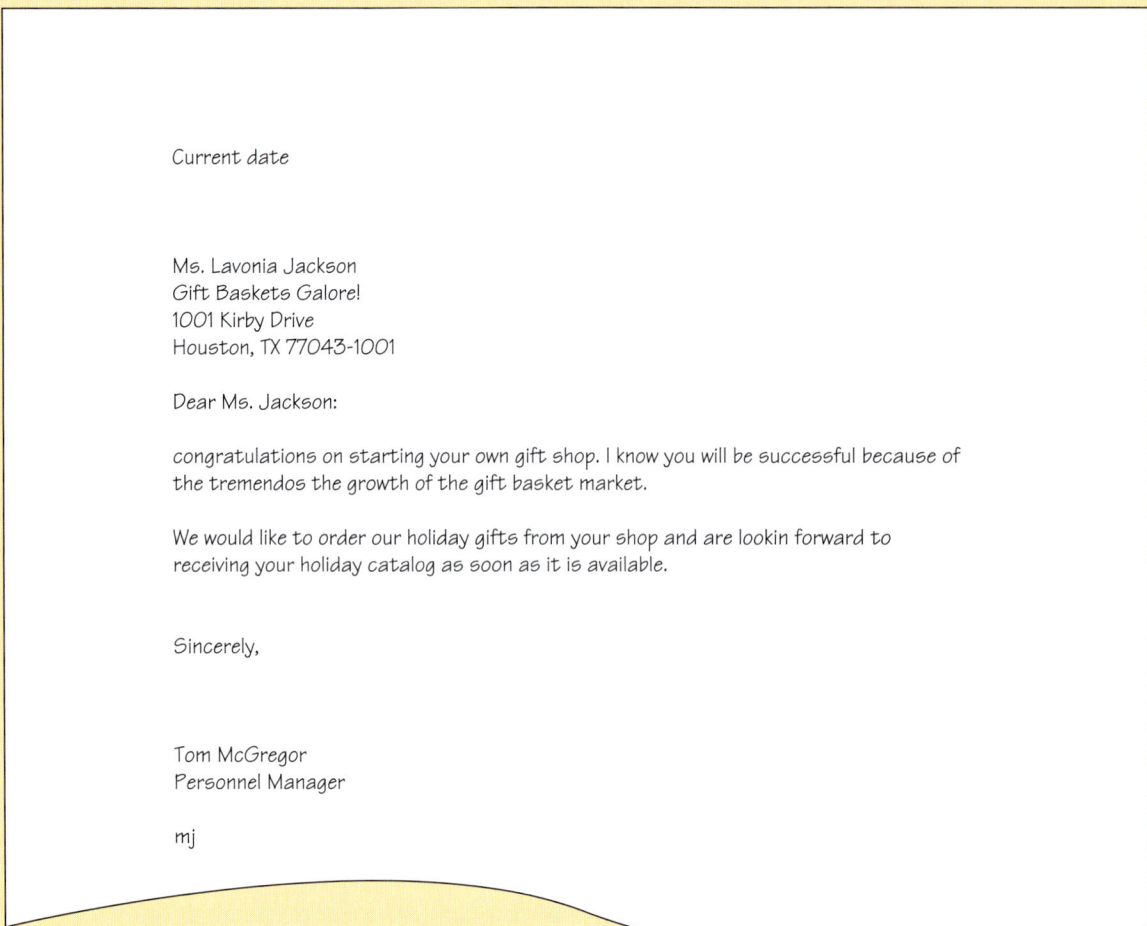

Current date

Ms. Lavonia Jackson
Gift Baskets Galore!
1001 Kirby Drive
Houston, TX 77043-1001

Dear Ms. Jackson:

congratulations on starting your own gift shop. I know you will be successful because of the tremendos the growth of the gift basket market.

We would like to order our holiday gifts from your shop and are lookin forward to receiving your holiday catalog as soon as it is available.

Sincerely,

Tom McGregor
Personnel Manager

mj

2. Save the document as *McGregor Letter.*

3. Preview, print, and close the document.

Case Projects

Project 1

You have been assigned to work in the legal department at Worldwide Foods for two weeks. The department manager has asked you to find some way for the three secretaries in the department to save time using Word to create and proof their documents. Prepare a document describing how the secretaries can use the AutoComplete, AutoText, and AutoCorrect tools to save time. Include spelling and grammar shortcuts. Use the Spelling and Grammar tool to correct any spelling and grammar errors in your document. Use the AutoCorrect tool to quickly enter symbols and text. Use the Thesaurus tool to replace words with more appropriate or descriptive ones. Use the AutoComplete tool to enter the current date. Save and print the document.

Project 2

As Kelly's assistant, you are often called on to solve user problems with the Word application. You received the following list of problems from the secretaries in the Tax Department about the AutoText and AutoCorrect features:

1. How can I store an AutoCorrect entry without its original formatting?

2. My AutoComplete tips are not displaying when I insert AutoText.

3. How can I share AutoText entries with other secretaries in my department?

Using the Office Assistant, research the answers to these questions. Use the keywords "AutoComplete," "AutoText," and "templates" for your search. Create, save, and print a document that describes how to solve these problems. Use the Spelling and Grammar tool to correct any spelling and grammar errors in your document. Use the AutoCorrect tool to quickly enter symbols and text. Use the Thesaurus tool to replace words with more appropriate or descriptive ones. Use the AutoComplete tool to enter the current date. Discuss your proposed solutions with a classmate.

Project 3

One of the legal secretaries asks for your help creating AutoCorrect exceptions. Using the Office Assistant, research the AutoCorrect exceptions list feature. Create a new document containing a short paragraph describing how to use this feature. Use the Spelling and Grammar tool to correct any spelling and grammar errors in your document. Use the AutoCorrect tool to quickly enter symbols and text. Use the Thesaurus tool to replace words with more appropriate or descriptive ones. Use the AutoComplete tool to enter the current date. Save and print the document. Open the AutoCorrect dialog box and add two items of your choice to the AutoCorrect Exceptions list.

Project 4

Mark Lee, a human resources consultant, is giving a 30-minute presentation on creating professional resumes at the next meeting of the International Association of Executive Assistants. He asks you to help prepare a list of topics by looking for Web pages that discuss how to create a resume. Connect to your ISP and open your Web browser. Search the WWW for information about writing a resume. Save at least two URLs as "favorites." Print at least two Web pages. Disconnect your ISP connection and close your Web browser.

Project 5

Using the research on creating resumes you prepared in Project 4, create, print, and save a document Mark can use to prepare his presentation. Use the Spelling and Grammar tool to correct any spelling and grammar errors in your document. Use the AutoCorrect tool to quickly enter symbols and text. Use the Thesaurus tool to replace words with more appropriate or descriptive ones. Use the AutoComplete tool to enter the current date.

chapter three

Project 6

B. D. Vickers has noticed that some letters and reports that contain spelling and grammatical errors are being mailed to clients. He asks you to prepare instructions on using the Spelling and Grammar tool, which he will give to all administrative assistants and secretaries during a special luncheon next week. Create a new document that contains at least four paragraphs outlining how to use the Spelling and Grammar tool *including* custom/special dictionaries, how to add a word to the AutoCorrect list during the spell-checking process, and how to use the various options in the Spelling and Grammar dialog box. Use the Spelling and Grammar tool to correct any spelling and grammar errors in your document. Use the AutoCorrect tool to quickly enter symbols and text. Use the Thesaurus tool to replace words with more appropriate or descriptive ones. Use the AutoComplete tool to enter the current date. Save, preview, and print the document.

Project 7

Kelly wants to purchase several reference books for the company library on how to use Microsoft Word. She doesn't have time to check out the local bookstores so she has asked you to look for the books at several online bookstores. Connect to your ISP and load your Web browser. Search for online bookstores. Load several online bookstore Web pages and search each Web site for books on how to use Microsoft Word. Use the information you gather from the bookstores to prepare a document containing a list of books by title. Include the author's name, the price of the book, and the proposed shipping time. Use the Spelling and Grammar tool to correct any spelling and grammar errors in your document. Use the AutoCorrect tool to quickly enter symbols and text. Use the Thesaurus tool to replace words with more appropriate or descriptive ones. Use the AutoComplete tool to enter the current date. Save and print the document.

Project 8

B. D. Vickers wants to know something about the readability of the documents the administrative staff is preparing and has asked you to find out what feature in Word can provide that information. Using the Office Assistant, research the readability statistics displayed by the Spelling and Grammar tool. Create a new document containing at least three paragraphs describing the readability statistics and formulas. Use the Spelling and Grammar tool to correct any spelling and grammar errors in your document. Use the AutoCorrect tool to quickly enter symbols and text. Use the Thesaurus tool to replace words with more appropriate or descriptive ones. Use the AutoComplete tool to enter the current date. Save, preview, and print the document.

Formatting Text

Chapter Overview

T he ability to format text provides a word processing program much of its power. Word's formatting features give you the ability to create professional-, unique-looking documents. In this chapter you learn how to change the appearance of text using AutoFormat and the character formatting features: fonts, font size, bold, underline, italic, text effects, and text animation. You also learn to repeat and copy character formats and change the case of text. Finally, you learn to add bullets and numbering to text.

LEARNING OBJECTIVES

▶ Format characters as you type
▶ Select and change fonts and font sizes
▶ Apply font formats
▶ Apply character effects
▶ Apply character spacing and animation effects
▶ Duplicate character formats
▶ Change the case of text
▶ Add bullets and numbering
▶ Highlight text in a document
▶ Insert Symbols and special characters

Case profile

Because of your successful performance in the purchasing department, the marketing department has requested you to fill in for Elizabeth Chang, the assistant secretary, who is going on a short holiday. Before she left, Elizabeth left several documents for you to format.

chapter four 4

4.a Formatting Characters as You Type

Word has an **AutoFormat As You Type** feature (in addition to the symbol characters in the AutoCorrect list) that automatically formats certain characters as you type such as replacing ordinals (1st) with superscript (1st), fractions (1/2) with fraction characters (½), and "straight quotes" with "curly quotes." The automatic formatting is applied when you press the SPACEBAR and is turned on by default. You can turn off the automatic formatting of characters on the AutoFormat As You Type tab in the AutoCorrect dialog box.

Before you start formatting the *Library Bulletin* document for Elizabeth, you review the AutoFormat As You Type options. To review the AutoFormat As You Type options:

Step 1	*Open*	the *Library Bulletin* document located on the Data Disk
Step 2	*Click*	Tools
Step 3	*Click*	AutoCorrect
Step 4	*Click*	the AutoFormat As You Type tab

The dialog box you see on your screen should look similar to Figure 4-1.

FIGURE 4-1
AutoFormat As You Type
Tab in the AutoCorrect
Dialog Box

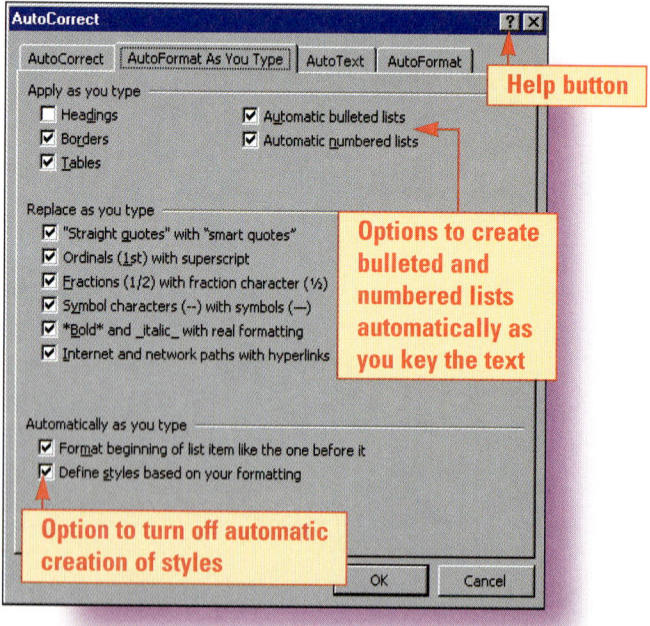

| Step 5 | *Click* | the dialog box Help button to review the options on the AutoFormat As You Type tab |

A **style** is a group of formats you apply to selected text. For now, you turn off the option that automatically creates styles as you format text.

| Step 6 | *Click* | the Define styles based on your formatting check box to remove the check mark |
| Step 7 | *Click* | OK |

Elizabeth wants you to add "on the 1st day of the month" to the document. As you enter the text with an ordinal number, Word automatically formats the number. To add an ordinal number:

| Step 1 | *Select* | the text "on a monthly basis" at the end of the *Library Bulletin* document |
| Step 2 | *Key* | on the 1st day of the month |

The ordinal number "1st" was replaced with "1st." The text on your screen should look similar to Figure 4-2.

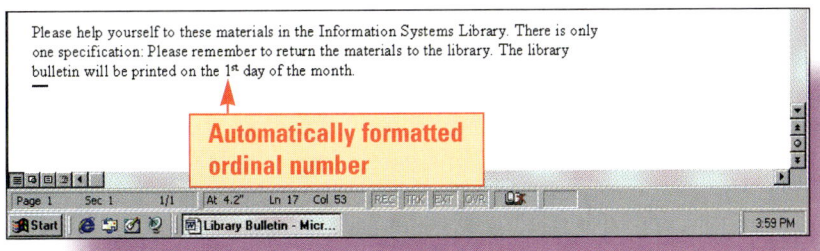

| Step 3 | *Save* | the document as *Library Bulletin Revised* |

You can determine the type of font and the font size you want to use in your documents.

FIGURE 4-2
Automatic Number Formatting

chapter
four

4.b Selecting and Changing Fonts and Font Sizes

A **font** is a set of printed characters with the same size and appearance. A font has three characteristics: typeface, style, and point (font) size.

1. **Typeface** refers to the design and appearance of printed characters. Some typefaces include:

   Times New Roman   Courier New
   Arial   *Brush Script MT*

2. **Style** refers to bold or italic print. *Italic print is slanted to the right* and **bold print is darker**.

3. **Point (font) size** refers to the height of the printed characters. There are 72 points to an inch and the larger the point size, the larger the characters. Some common point sizes include:

   8 point   10 point   12 point

A font may be **monospaced** with the same amount of space between characters or **proportional** with a varying amount of space between characters. Courier is an example of a monospaced font and Times New Roman is an example of a proportional font. Most people who use a word processing application to create text documents use proportional fonts.

There are two main categories of proportional fonts: serif and sans serif. A **serif** is a small line extension at the beginning and end of a character to help the reader's eye move across the text. Serif fonts are often used in documents with a large amount of text. A **sans serif** font is one that does not have the small line extension (*sans* is the French word for without). Sans serif fonts are often used for paragraph headings and document titles. The Times New Roman font is an example of a serif font and the Arial font is an example of a sans serif font.

The default font and font size in Word are the Times New Roman font and 12-point font size. The *Library Bulletin Revised* document, according to Elizabeth's notes, should be in 10-point font size, with the title in Arial font.

notes This book assumes that your computer is connected to a Hewlett-Packard LaserJet printer and you use TrueType fonts. If you have a different printer, make the appropriate selections for your printer.

Changing Fonts

To change the font, first select the text to be changed. For example, if you want to change the font for the entire document, select the entire document. Then select the font you want to use. If the document has not been keyed yet, you can select the font before you key the text. That font selection is then used throughout the document.

Currently, the entire *Library Bulletin Revised* document is formatted with the Times New Roman, 12-point font. To change the font of the title text, "INFORMATION SYSTEMS LIBRARY BULLETIN," to the Arial TrueType font:

Step 1	*Select*	the title "INFORMATION SYSTEMS LIBRARY BULLETIN"
Step 2	*Click*	the Font button list arrow `Times New Roman ▼` on the Formatting toolbar

The font list on your screen should look similar to Figure 4-3.

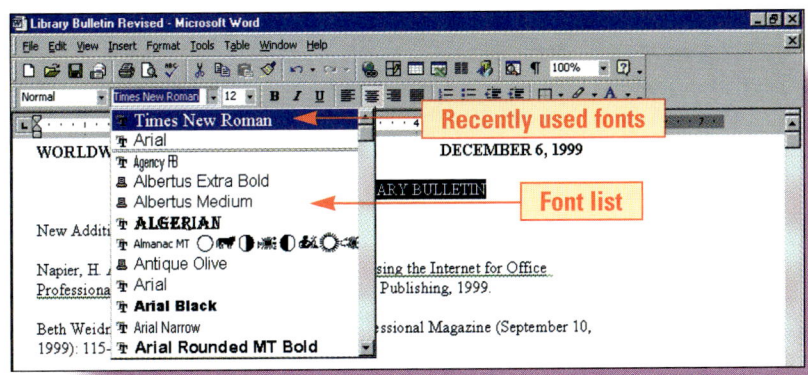

FIGURE 4-3
Font List

Notice that some fonts on the Font drop-down list have a symbol to the left of the font name. A "TT" symbol indicates that the font is a **TrueType font** that prints text exactly the way it is displayed on your screen. A printer symbol next to a font indicates that the assigned printer supports the font. A list of the most recently used fonts may appear at the top of the font list followed by a narrow double line.

Step 3	*Click*	Arial (scroll to view this option, if necessary)
Step 4	*Deselect*	the text

The document title font is different from the text font, making it distinct. You can also change the font size for your documents.

Changing Font Sizes

The point (font) size for the text of the entire document is currently 12 point. The *Library Bulletin Revised* document should be in 10 point. To change the point size for the entire document to 10 point:

Step 1	*Select*	the entire document

Step 2	*Click*	the Font Size button list arrow 12 ▼ on the Formatting toolbar

The Font Size drop-down list that appears on your screen should look similar to Figure 4-4.

FIGURE 4-4
Font Size List

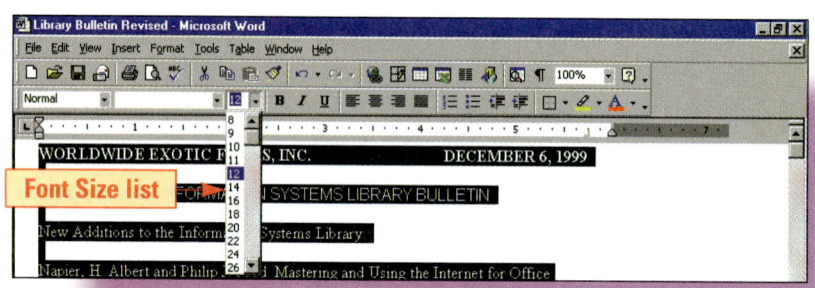

Step 3	*Click*	10

Step 4	*Deselect*	the text

The entire document changes to 10 point. Next you need to add emphasis to certain text by applying font styles, such as bold and italic.

4.c Applying Font Formats

Elizabeth wants certain words emphasized in *Library Bulletin Revised* document. You can do this by applying the bold or italic font formats, or styles, to the text. Font styles are part of **character formatting**, which means only the selected character or characters are affected when you apply the font style.

Applying Bold

The **bold** style makes the selected text darker than other text to attract a reader's attention. When you apply bold style, Word makes the text appear darker on the screen as well as on the printed page.

QUICK TIP

You can use keyboard shortcuts to apply font styles. For example, press the CTRL + B keys to apply the bold style to selected text. Use the Office Assistant to view and print a complete list of keyboard shortcuts.

To apply bold style to the text "New Additions to the Information Systems Library:"

Step 1	*Select*	New Additions to the Information Systems Library (do not select the colon)
Step 2	*Click*	the Bold button **B** on the Formatting toolbar
Step 3	*Deselect*	the text leaving the insertion point in the paragraph

The text appears darker. Notice that the Bold button on the Formatting toolbar appears pressed, indicating the bold style is applied. You remove the bold format the same way you applied it. The first line of the document contains the company name and date formatted with the bold style. Elizabeth's notes tell you to remove the bold. To remove the bold style:

Step 1	*Select*	the first line of the document using the selection bar
Step 2	*Click*	the Bold button **B** on the Formatting toolbar
Step 3	*Deselect*	the text leaving the insertion point in the in the first line

The text is no longer bold and the Bold button on the Formatting toolbar is no longer pressed.

Applying Italic

Italicizing text allows you to emphasize text by slanting the text to the right. You apply and remove italic formatting the same way you do bold formatting: by selecting the text and applying the italic style.

Elizabeth's notes indicate the magazine title in which Beth Weidman's article appears should be italicized. To italicize the magazine title:

Step 1	*Select*	the magazine title "Web Site Professional Magazine" in the second item in the list
Step 2	*Click*	the Italic button *I* on the Formatting toolbar
Step 3	*Deselect*	the text leaving the insertion point in the title

The magazine title is italicized. Notice the Italic button on the Formatting toolbar is pressed, indicating that the italic style is applied to the text. You can remove the italic style the same way you applied it.

MENU TIP

You can apply the bold style to text by clicking the Font command on the Format menu or shortcut menu.

MOUSE TIP

You can apply character formatting to a single, complete word by clicking the word to place the insertion point in it, and then applying the format.

QUICK TIP

You can apply or remove italic formatting from selected text in the Font tab in the Font dialog box.

chapter
four

M ENU TIP

You can underline selected text by clicking the Font command on the Format menu to open the Font dialog box, clicking the Font tab, clicking the Underline Style list arrow, and then clicking the underline style of your choice.

Applying Underlines

Emphasizing text by placing a line underneath the text is called **underlining**. You can choose to underline selected letters, selected words, or selected words and the spaces between them. Word also provides a variety of underlines you can use to enhance text.

You want to add a thick single line below the title "New Additions to the Information Systems Library." The Underline button on the Formatting toolbar formats text and spaces between the text with a thin single line. Instead, you must open the Font dialog box to see a complete list of underline styles.

To apply a thick single underline to text:

Step 1	*Select*	New Additions to the Information Systems Library (do not select the colon)
Step 2	*Right-click*	the selected text
Step 3	*Click*	Font
Step 4	*Click*	the Font tab, if necessary

The Font tab in the Font dialog box that opens on your screen should look similar to Figure 4-5.

FIGURE 4-5
Font Tab in the Font
Dialog Box

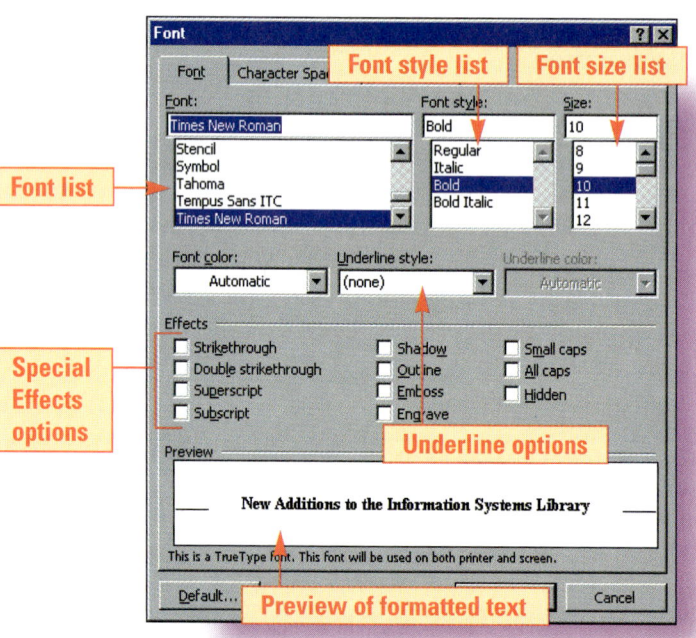

M OUSE TIP

You can underline selected words and spaces with a single underline by clicking the Underline button on the Formatting toolbar.

You can change fonts, font style, font size, underlining, underline color, and color of selected text in the Fo<u>n</u>t tab. The Effects group provides options for applying special effects to selected text. The Preview area provides a sample of the formatting options before they are applied to the selected text.

Step 5	*Click*	the <u>U</u>nderline style: list arrow
Step 6	*Click*	the thick single line option (the fifth option in the list)
Step 7	*Preview*	the underline formatting in the dialog box
Step 8	*Click*	OK
Step 9	*Deselect*	the text

The text is underlined with a thick single line. The book title in the first item in the list should be italicized instead of underlined. You can add or remove a thin single underline to words and spaces with the Underline button on the Formatting toolbar. To remove the underline from the book title and italicize it:

Step 1	*Select*	the book title "Mastering and Using the Internet for Office Professionals"
Step 2	*Click*	the Underline button U on the Formatting toolbar
Step 3	*Click*	the Italic button *I* on the Formatting toolbar
Step 4	*Deselect*	the text leaving the insertion point in the text
Step 5	*Save*	the document

In addition to using bold, italic, and underline to emphasis text, you can use other special text effects such as Superscript, Subscript, Outline, and Small Caps.

4.d Applying Character Effects

Another way to emphasize text is to add special text effects like superscript, subscript, small caps, outline, and strikethrough effects. Elizabeth asks you to add these formats to specified text in the *Library Bulletin Revised* document.

chapter
four

Applying Superscript and Subscript

The **Superscript** format places text slightly above a line of normal printed text. The **Subscript** format places text slightly below a line of normal printed text. This is ^{superscript}, and this is $_{subscript}$. You can apply Superscript or Subscript formats to selected text in the Font tab in the Font dialog box. To experiment with the Superscript and Subscript formats:

Step 1	*Move*	the insertion point to the left margin before the "B" in "Beth"
Step 2	*Key*	1
Step 3	*Select*	the number 1
Step 4	*Click*	Format
Step 5	*Click*	Font
Step 6	*Click*	the Font tab, if necessary
Step 7	*Click*	the Superscript check box to insert a check mark
Step 8	*Click*	OK
Step 9	*Deselect*	the text

The number 1 appears in Superscript format and the text on your screen should look similar to Figure 4-6.

FIGURE 4-6
Superscript Format

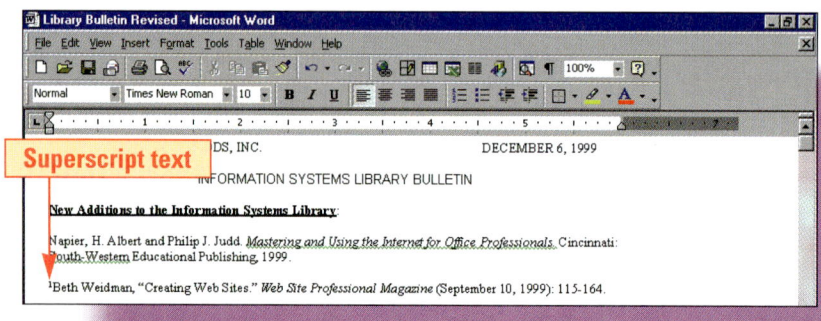

You apply the Subscript format the same way. To apply the Subscript format:

Step 1	*Move*	the insertion point to the left margin before the "R" in "Robert"
Step 2	*Key*	2

Step 3	*Select*	the number 2
Step 4	*Open*	the Font tab in the Font dialog box
Step 5	*Click*	the Subscript check box to insert a check mark
Step 6	*Click*	OK
Step 7	*Deselect*	the text
Step 8	*Observe*	the placement of the superscript and subscript text in relation to the text
Step 9	*Delete*	the superscript and subscript text
Step 10	*Save*	the document

QUICK TIP

You can remove Superscript and Subscript formatting from selected text by removing the check mark from the appropriate check box on the Font tab in the Font dialog box.

Applying Strikethrough

When you edit a document online, you might want to indicate text that should be deleted. One way to do this is to format the text with the **Strikethrough** effect, which draws a line through selected text. To add the Strikethrough effect to the first sentence of the last paragraph:

Step 1	*Select*	in the Information Systems Library
Step 2	*Open*	the Font tab in the Font dialog box
Step 3	*Click*	the Strikethrough check box to insert a check mark
Step 4	*Click*	OK

The selected text now has a line through it, indicating it could be deleted from the document. Because you don't want to delete the text, you remove the Strikethrough.

| Step 5 | *Click* | the Undo button ⟲▾ on the Standard toolbar |
| Step 6 | *Deselect* | the text |

Elizabeth indicated that the library name needs to be distinguished from the rest of the text. You decide to apply the Small Caps effect.

Applying Small Caps

The **Small Caps** effect is a special text effect that displays selected text in uppercase characters and any characters keyed with the SHIFT key pressed are slightly taller than the remaining characters. The

chapter
four

Small Caps format is appropriate for headings and titles, such as Information Systems Library. To apply the Small Caps effect:

Step 1	*Select*	the text "Information Systems Library" in the first sentence of the last paragraph
Step 2	*Open*	the Font tab in the Font dialog box
Step 3	*Click*	the Small Caps check box to insert a check mark
Step 4	*Click*	OK

The text is in uppercase characters, with the first character of each word slightly taller than the remaining characters in the word.

| Step 5 | *Continue* | by applying the Small Caps effect to each instance of "Information Systems Library" |

Another special text effect you can use to emphasize text is the Outline effect.

Applying Outline

The **Outline** effect shows both the inner and the outer border of each character and leaves the interior white. The effect is good for large fonts usually used in titles. To change the font size of the first line and apply the Outline effect:

Step 1	*Select*	the first line beginning "Worldwide" at the top of the document
Step 2	*Open*	the Font tab in the Font dialog box
Step 3	*Change*	the font size to 14 point
Step 4	*Click*	the Outline check box to insert a check mark
Step 5	*Click*	OK
Step 6	*Observe*	the new formatting
Step 7	*Deselect*	the text
Step 8	*Save*	the document

Adding extra spacing between text characters in titles adds variety and interest to a document. Special animation effects are a great way to draw attention to documents that will be read online, such as the *Library Bulletin Revised* document.

4.e Applying Character Spacing and Animation Effects

Character spacing is the amount of white space that appears between characters. You can change the character spacing by scaling the characters to a specific percentage, expanding or condensing the characters a specific number of points, or by kerning. **Kerning** adjusts the space between particular pairs of characters depending on the font.

You want the title of the *Library Bulletin Revised* document to stand out more, so you scale the text. To scale the title text so that it is stretched horizontally to be 120% of its original width:

Step 1	*Select*	the title "INFORMATION SYSTEMS LIBRARY BULLETIN"
Step 2	*Open*	the Font dialog box
Step 3	*Click*	the Character Spacing tab
Step 4	*Key*	120 in the Scale: text box
Step 5	*Press*	the ENTER key

The text is "stretched" horizontally to 120% of its original width. Upon her return, Elizabeth is going to attach the *Library Bulletin Revised* document to e-mail messages so the recipients can read the document online. She wants you to add animation effects to the *Library Bulletin Revised* document that draw attention to the document's title. To add animation effects:

Step 1	*Verify*	the title text is still selected
Step 2	*Open*	the Font dialog box
Step 3	*Click*	the Text Effects tab
Step 4	*Click*	Marching Red Ants in the Animations: list box
Step 5	*Click*	OK
Step 6	*Observe*	that a red dashed moving box now appears around the title
Step 7	*Deselect*	the text
Step 8	*Save*	the document

chapter four

The red marching ants will attract immediate attention to the document. Once you have applied character formatting to text it's often easier to duplicate that formatting to other text rather than reapplying it each time.

4.f   Duplicating Character Formats

Word can duplicate character formats by repeating or copying the formats. If you have already formatted text with a certain character formats (such as font styles) and want to immediately format additional text the same way, you can repeat the character formats with the Repeat command on the Edit menu. If you want to duplicate formats, but you have performed several commands since the formatting command, you can use the Format Painter button on the Standard toolbar to *copy* the formats from one text and paste it to other text.

Repeating Character Formats

You can repeat multiple character formats that have been applied to selected text with the options on the Font tab in the Font dialog box. For example, if you apply the Small Caps and underlining formats with the Font dialog box options, you can then apply both formats to new text at the same time simply by clicking the Repeat command on the Edit menu.

You apply the bold, single underline, and font size formats to selected text and then immediately repeat that formatting to unformatted text. To apply and repeat multiple character formats:

Step 1	*Select*	the phrase "There is only one specification" in the last paragraph (do not select the colon)
Step 2	*Open*	the Font tab in the Font dialog box
Step 3	*Click*	Bold in the Font style: list box
Step 4	*Click*	14 in the Size: list box (scroll to view this option)
Step 5	*Click*	the Underline style: list arrow
Step 6	*Click*	Words only
Step 7	*Click*	OK
Step 8	*Deselect*	the text

The text is formatted with multiple formats. Now you repeat the formats on the next phrase in the document.

Step 9	*Select*	the phrase "Please remember to return the materials to the library" in the last paragraph (do not select the period)
Step 10	*Click*	Edit
Step 11	*Click*	Repeat Font Formatting
Step 12	*Deselect*	the text

The bold, underline, and font size formatting are applied to the selected phrase. You can also apply multiple formats from the Formatting toolbar; just remember that, when you do this, *only the last format applied is repeated.* To apply bold and underline formatting to the last sentence using the Formatting toolbar and then repeat the formatting in the title:

Step 1	*Select*	the last sentence in the document (do not select the period)
Step 2	*Click*	the Bold button **B** on the Formatting toolbar
Step 3	*Click*	the Underline button **U** on the Formatting toolbar
Step 4	*Select*	the title "INFORMATION SYSTEMS LIBRARY BULLETIN"
Step 5	*Click*	Edit
Step 6	*Observe*	that the Repeat command says "Repeat Underline" although you applied both bold and underline formats to the original text

Because you applied multiple formats with the Formatting toolbar buttons, the Repeat Font Formatting command on the Edit menu becomes the Repeat Underline command. Only the last format applied, the underline format, can be repeated. You close the menu and undo the formatting.

| Step 7 | *Press* | the ESC key to close the menu |
| Step 8 | *Click* | the Undo button  on the Standard toolbar twice to undo the bold and underline formats |

When you want to apply the multiple character formatting to different text long after you originally applied the formatting, you can save time by copying the formatting from one text selection to another.

chapter
four

Copying Formats using the Format Painter

Copying formats, rather than recreating them, ensures consistency and saves time. You can copy and paste character formats quickly with the Format Painter button on the Standard toolbar. To use the Format Painter to copy formats, first place the insertion point in the text that contains the formats to be copied. Then click the Format Painter button. When you move the mouse pointer into the keying area, the mouse pointer changes to an I-beam with a paintbrush icon. To paste the formats, drag the Format Painter I-beam across the text to be formatted. The Format Painter pastes *all* the formats from the original text, including *all* formats applied with the Formatting toolbar. You want to copy the formats from "There is only one specification" to different text. To copy formats using the Format Painter:

Step 1	*Move*	the insertion point to the text "There is only one specification"
Step 2	*Click*	the Format Painter button 🖌 on the Standard toolbar
Step 3	*Select*	New Additions to the Information Systems Library (do not select the colon)
Step 4	*Observe*	the copied formats
Step 5	*Deselect*	the text
Step 6	*Save*	the document

4.g Changing the Case of Text

Elizabeth wants you to change the case of the title in the *Library Bulletin Revised* document. You can change the case of text by first selecting the text you want to change, and then clicking the Change Case command on the Format menu. To change the case of the title text:

Step 1	*Select*	the title "INFORMATION SYSTEMS LIBRARY BULLETIN"
Step 2	*Click*	Format
Step 3	*Click*	Change Case

The dialog box on your screen should look similar to Figure 4-7.

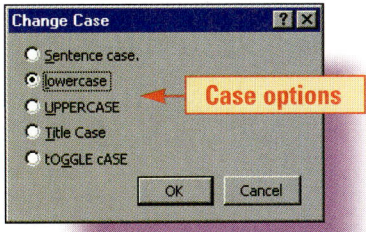

Case options

FIGURE 4-7
Change Case Dialog Box

Step 4	*Click*	the Title Case option button
Step 5	*Click*	OK
Step 6	*Deselect*	the text

Notice that you can now see the small cap formatting you applied earlier to the title.

| Step 7 | *Save* | the document and close it |

Sometimes you need to organize text in a list and add symbols or numbers to each paragraph.

4.h Adding Bullets and Numbering

Special symbols called **bullets** or numbers can precede lists of text, to make the lists more attractive and easier to read. The second document Elizabeth left for you to format is named *Enhanced Text*. Your instructions are to create bulleted and numbered lists from certain paragraphs.

Creating Bulleted Lists

The *Enhanced Text* document contains several short paragraphs to which you must add bullets. The bullets help indicate that the paragraphs are related items. To create a bulleted list:

| Step 1 | *Open* | the *Enhanced Text* document located on the Data Disk |
| Step 2 | *Select* | the text beginning with "Apply" and ending with "listed items." (do not select the title text) |

> **QUICK TIP**
>
> You can remove character formatting from selected text by pressing the CTRL + SHIFT + Z keys.

> **MENU TIP**
>
> You can add numbers or bullets to selected text with options in the Bullets and Numbering dialog box, which you open by clicking the Bullets and Numbering command on the Format menu or a shortcut menu.

chapter
four

| Step 3 | *Click* | the Bullets button ⊞ on the Formatting toolbar |
| Step 4 | *Deselect* | the text |

A bullet symbol is automatically inserted to the left of the paragraphs, which are indented ½ inch. The text you see on your screen should look similar to Figure 4-8.

FIGURE 4-8
Bulleted List

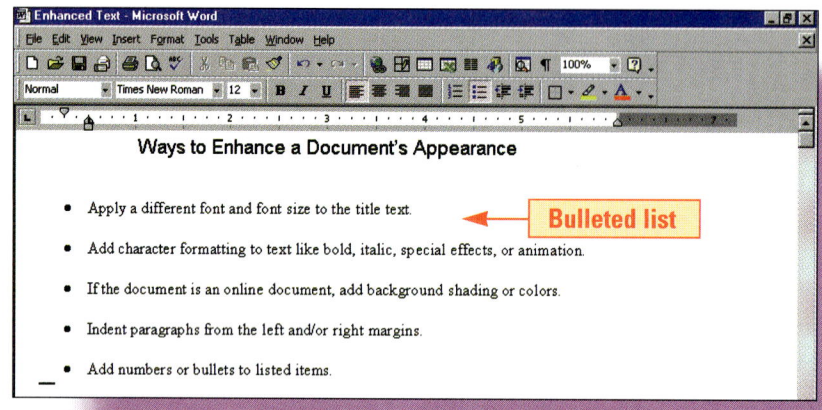

Creating Numbered Lists

Numbered lists are used to organize items sequentially. It is very easy to replace a bulleted list with a numbered list. Simply select the bulleted list paragraphs and then click the Numbering button on the Formatting toolbar. To replace the bullets with numbers:

| Step 1 | *Select* | the bulleted paragraphs beginning with "Apply" and ending with "listed items." |
| Step 2 | *Click* | the Numbering button ⊞ on the on the Formatting toolbar |

Numbers now precede the paragraphs instead of bullets. To change the bullet or numbering style, you can click the Bullets and Numbering command on the Format menu, click the appropriate tab, and select a different bullet or numbering style. You can remove the bullets or numbers from a list by selecting the list and clicking the Bullets or Numbering button on the Formatting toolbar to turn off the formatting.

| Step 3 | *Select* | the numbered paragraphs beginning with "Apply" and ending with "listed items.", if necessary |
| Step 4 | *Click* | the Numbering button ⊞ on the Formatting toolbar |

Step 5	*Reapply*	the Bullets formatting
Step 6	*Deselect*	the text
Step 7	*Save*	the document as *Enhanced Text Revised* and close it

Another way to draw a reviewer's attention to important text in a document being read on a computer screen is to highlight the text.

4.i Highlighting Text in a Document

Elizabeth wants to draw attention to the text "Warning! Warning! Warning!" in the *Policy #152* document. To do this, she asks you to highlight the text in color. To highlight the text:

Step 1	*Open*	the *Policy #152* document located on the Data Disk
Step 2	*Select*	the text Warning! Warning! Warning!
Step 3	*Click*	the Highlight button list arrow ▨▾ on the Formatting toolbar
Step 4	*Click*	Bright Green
Step 5	*Observe*	that the text is highlighted in color

You can also select a highlighter color and then drag the mouse pointer over text to apply the color highlighting. To change the highlighted text color to yellow:

Step 1	*Click*	the Highlight button list arrow ▨▾ on the Formatting toolbar
Step 2	*Click*	Yellow
Step 3	*Position*	the mouse pointer over text and observe that it is now a color pen pointer
Step 4	*Drag*	the color pen pointer over the bright green highlighted text to change the color to yellow
Step 5	*Click*	the Highlight button ▨▾ to turn off the color pen pointer
Step 6	*Save*	the document as *Policy #152 With Highlighted Text* and close it

QUICK TIP

You can turn on or off viewing and printing highlight colors in the View tab of the Options dialog box. Using color to highlight text works best when a document is read on a computer screen. If you print a document with highlighted text, use a light color.

Another way to enhance text appearance is to insert symbols and special characters into your document.

4.j Inserting Symbols and Special Characters

Symbols and special characters can be inserted into a document using the AutoCorrect feature or the Symbol command on the Insert menu. Elizabeth left instructions for you to complete a new marketing department training class announcement by inserting the appropriate symbols and special characters.

Inserting Symbols

First, you need to insert the copyright symbol in the document. To insert the copyright symbol using the AutoCorrect feature:

Step 1	**Open**	the *Quality 2000 Training* document located on the Data Disk
Step 2	**Move**	the insertion point to the end of the "Quality 2000" text in the third title line
Step 3	**Key**	(c) to insert the copyright symbol using AutoCorrect

You can also insert the copyright symbol from a dialog box. To insert the copyright symbol using the Symbol dialog box:

Step 1	**Move**	the insertion point to the end of the "Quality 2000" text in the second body paragraph
Step 2	**Click**	Insert
Step 3	**Click**	Symbol
Step 4	**Click**	the Symbols tab, if necessary
Step 5	**Select**	Symbol from the Font: list, if necessary
Step 6	**Double-click**	the © symbol (12th symbol in the 7th row)
Step 7	**Close**	the dialog box

Now you need to insert a special character.

Inserting Special Characters

Other special characters like the en dash (used in dates), the nonbreaking space, and the em dash (used to insert a break in thought) as well as the copyright symbol can also be inserted from the Special Characters tab in the Symbol dialog box. You want to replace the hyphen in the first paragraph with an em dash character. To select the hyphen and open the dialog box:

Step 1	*Select*	the hyphen following the word "now" in the last sentence of the first body paragraph
Step 2	*Open*	the Symbol dialog box
Step 3	*Click*	the Special Characters tab
Step 4	*Double-click*	the Em Dash option in the list
Step 5	*Close*	the dialog box
Step 6	*Observe*	that the em dash replaces the hyphen in the document
Step 7	*Save*	the document as *Quality 2000 With Symbols* and close it

With Word's formatting features you can make any document look professionally formatted.

chapter
four

Summary

► The AutoFormat As You Type feature automatically formats certain characters you key—such as quote marks, fractions, and ordinals—when you press the SPACEBAR.

► Fonts are sets of printed characters that have the same size and appearance.

► A font has three aspects: typeface, style, and point (font) size.

► The default font in Word is Times New Roman, 12-point font.

► You can apply bold, italic, and underline character formats to selected text for emphasis.

► Superscript or subscript character formats can be applied to selected characters to position the characters slightly above or below the line of normal text.

► You can add animation effects, such as red marching ants, to documents to emphasize text when the document is displayed online.

► Character formats can be duplicated to new text using the Repeat command on the Edit menu or the Format Painter button on the Standard toolbar.

► The case of text characters can be changed to Sentence case, lowercase, UPPERCASE, Title Case, or tOGGLE cASE.

► You can add bullets to group a list of items or add numbers to organize a list of items.

► You can draw attention to text in a document being read on a computer screen by highlighting it in color.

► Symbols and special characters, such as © or ® or em dash, can be inserted into your document.

Commands Review

Action	Menu Bar	Shortcut Menu	Toolbar	Keyboard
Change font	F<u>o</u>rmat, <u>F</u>ont	Right-click the selected text, click <u>F</u>ont	Times New Roman	ALT + O, F CTRL + D CTRL + SHIFT + F, then DOWN ARROW to select the font
Change font size	F<u>o</u>rmat, <u>F</u>ont	Right-click the selected text, click <u>F</u>ont	12	ALT + O, F CTRL + SHIFT + P, then DOWN ARROW to select the font size
Apply or remove bold formatting	F<u>o</u>rmat, <u>F</u>ont	Right-click the selected text, click <u>F</u>ont	**B**	ALT + O, F CTRL + B
Apply or remove italic formatting	F<u>o</u>rmat, <u>F</u>ont	Right-click the selected text, click <u>F</u>ont	*I*	ALT + O, F CTRL + I
Apply or remove underline formatting	F<u>o</u>rmat, <u>F</u>ont	Right-click the selected text, click <u>F</u>ont	<u>U</u>	ALT + O, F CTRL + U
Apply or remove superscript or subscript formatting	F<u>o</u>rmat, <u>F</u>ont	Right-click the selected text, click <u>F</u>ont		ALT + O, F CTRL + = (sub.) CTRL + SHIFT + + (sup.)
Repeat formats	<u>E</u>dit, <u>R</u>epeat			ALT + E, R CTRL + Y
Copy formats				CTRL + SHIFT + C, then CTRL + SHIFT + V
Change case	F<u>o</u>rmat, Change Ca<u>s</u>e			ALT + O, E SHIFT + F3
Remove character formatting				CTRL + SHIFT + Z CTRL + SPACEBAR
Apply or remove bullets and numbering to lists	F<u>o</u>rmat, Bullets and <u>N</u>umbering	Right-click the selected text or at the insertion point and click Bullets and <u>N</u>umbering		Key a number followed by a space or tab character and the text Key an asterisk followed by a space or tab character and the text
Highlight text				
Insert symbols and special characters	<u>I</u>nsert, <u>S</u>ymbol			ALT + I, S Press the appropriate shortcut keys

Concepts Review

Circle the correct answer.

1. You can apply a double underline to text with the:

[a] Underline style: list box in the Font dialog box.

[b] Su<u>p</u>erscript option in the Font dialog box.

[c] Su<u>b</u>script option in the Font dialog box.

[d] Underline button on the Formatting toolbar.

2. Typeface refers to the:

[a] amount of space between the characters.

[b] height of the characters.

[c] design and appearance of the characters.

[d] slant of the characters.

chapter four

3. **You can copy character formats by:**
   [a] clicking the Bullets button.
   [b] using the Format Painter feature.
   [c] clicking the Numbering button.
   [d] pressing the DELETE key.

4. **The Bold, Underline, and Italic buttons on the Formatting toolbar cannot be used to:**
   [a] apply formats.
   [b] remove formats.
   [c] emphasize text.
   [d] repeat multiple formats.

5. **When you use the Repeat command on the Edit menu to repeat formats applied from the Font dialog box:**
   [a] all the formats are repeated.
   [b] none of the formats are repeated.
   [c] the text is changed to uppercase.
   [d] only the last format is repeated.

6. **Which of the following is not a special font effect?**
   [a] Emboss
   [b] Engrave
   [c] Hidden
   [d] Bold

7. **Character spacing options are found in the:**
   [a] Font dialog box.
   [b] AutoCorrect dialog box.
   [c] Formatting dialog box.
   [d] AutoText dialog box.

8. **The Underline button on the Formatting toolbar applies the following underline style:**
   [a] Dotted.
   [b] Single, words only.
   [c] Single, words and spaces.
   [d] Double wavy.

9. **Italics emphasizes text by:**
   [a] making the text darker.
   [b] slanting the text to the right.
   [c] placing the text above the baseline.
   [d] slanting the text to the left.

10. **Which of the following is not an option for changing the case of text?**
   [a] Uppercase
   [b] Lowercase
   [c] Triple case
   [d] Sentence case

Circle **T** if the statement is true or **F** is the statement is false.

T F 1. The Italic button on the Formatting toolbar allows you to create text that looks and prints darker than the rest of the text.

T F 2. You must underline both words and the spaces between them when you apply underlining.

T F 3. Subscript formatting places text slightly below a line of normal printed text.

T F 4. Superscript formatting places text slightly above a line of normal printed text.

T F 5. The Format Painter button on the Standard toolbar allows you to copy only one format at a time.

T F 6. The three characteristics of fonts are: typeface, weight, and point (font) size.

T F 7. You can add Superscript and Subscript buttons to the Formatting toolbar.

T F 8. You can add numbers but not bullet symbols to lists.

T F 9. You cannot turn off the automatic formatting of characters.

T F 10. Typeface refers to the design and appearance of printed characters.

Skills Review

Exercise 1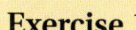

1. Open the *Interoffice Meeting Memo* document located on the Data Disk.

2. Replace the text Current date with the actual date.

3. Apply bold style to the text TO, FROM, DATE, and SUBJECT in the memo form headings. (Do not apply bold to the colons.)

4. Apply bold to the day and time for the meeting in the first paragraph.

5. Single underline the number 20 in the third paragraph.

6. Italicize the topic assignments. (Select only the topic assignments.)

7. Save the document as *Interoffice Meeting Memo Revised*.

8. Preview, print, and close the document.

Exercise 2

1. Open the *Marketing Department Memo* document located on the Data Disk.

2. Replace the text Current date with the actual date.

3. Remove the bold format from the memo form headings. (Do not select the colon.)

4. Remove the italic format from the topic assignments. (Select only the topic assignments.)

5. Select the entire document and change the font to Arial 12 point.

6. Save the document as *Marketing Department Memo Revised*.

7. Preview, print, and close the document.

Exercise 3

1. Open the *Vancouver Sales Report* document located on the Data Disk.

2. Format the title "VANCOUVER BRANCH OFFICE" with the Outline effect.

3. Bold and underline the column titles.

4. Select the entire document and change the font to Arial 12 point.

5. Save the document as *Vancouver Sales Report Revised*.

6. Preview, print, and close the document.

Exercise 4

1. Open the *Commonly Misused Words* document located on the Data Disk.

2. Apply bold style to the commonly misused words. (Do not include the example and definition.)

3. Remove the italic format from the definitions.

4. Highlight in yellow the text "commonly misused words" in the second sentence.

5. Save the document as *Commonly Misused Words Revised*.

6. Preview, print, and close the document.

Exercise 5

1. Open the *Company Correspondence Memo* document located on the Data Disk.

2. Replace the text Current date with the actual date.

3. Change the case of "Memorandum" to all uppercase.

4. Change the character spacing scale of "MEMORANDUM" to 200%.

5. Apply bold style to the text MEMORANDUM, TO, FROM, DATE, and SUBJECT. (Do not apply bold to the colons.)

6. Select the text MEMORANDUM and change the font to Arial 14 point.

7. Select the memo form headings and change the font to Times New Roman 12 point.

8. Save the document as *Company Correspondence Memo Revised*.

9. Preview, print, and close the document.

Exercise 6

1. Open the *Market Research* document located on the Data Disk.

2. Check the spelling and grammar and make the appropriate changes.

3. Insert a superscript number 1 after the word Davidson in the first paragraph.

4. Insert two lines at the end of the document and key the following text (including the superscript; do not apply the italic style to the text):
   [1] One of the leading market research firms in the country.

5. Create a new paragraph beginning with the text "Telephone support" in the last paragraph.

6. Add bullets to the paragraphs beginning "Surveys" and "Telephone support."

7. Change the case of Vancouver branch in the first paragraph to all uppercase.

8. Save the document as *Market Research Revised*.

9. Preview, print, and close the document.

Exercise 7

1. Open the *Policy #152* document located on the Data Disk.

2. Select the text Warning! Warning! Warning! and change the case to uppercase.

3. Apply bold style to the text WARNING! WARNING! WARNING!

4. Select the text WARNING! WARNING! WARNING! and change the font to Arial 24 point.

5. Add animation effects of your choice to the text WARNING! WARNING! WARNING!

6. Change the case of "Only Authorized Personnel" and "May Proceed Beyond This Point" to all uppercase.

7. Select the text "Only Authorized Personnel" and "May Proceed Beyond This Point" and change the font to Arial 14 point bold.

8. Select the remainder of the text and change the font to Arial 12 point.

9. Single underline only the words in the third sentence beginning "Surveillance."

10. Save the document as *Policy #152 Revised*.

11. Preview, print, and close the document.

Exercise 8

1. Open the *Business Information Management* document located on the Data Disk.

2. Select the entire document and change the font to Arial 12 point.

3. Apply bold style to the text BUSINESS INFORMATION MANAGEMENT.

4. Select the text BUSINESS INFORMATION MANAGEMENT and change the font to Arial 18 point.

5. Apply bold style and underline the course number and title for BIM 160.

6. Use the Format Painter feature to copy the formatting to the remaining course numbers and titles.

7. Underline the last two lines in the document.

8. Save the document as *Business Information Management Revised*.

9. Preview, print, and close the document.

Exercise 9

1. Create the following document.

Introduction

Types of Stores
The Mall
The Strip Center
The Boutique
The Gourmet Store

Shopper Personalities
The Sales Hunter
The Gourmet
The Browser
The Catalog Shopper

Conclusion

2. Using the Font dialog box, change the text Introduction, Types of Stores, Shopper Personalities, and Conclusion to all caps, bold, and Arial 14 point. (*Hint:* Use the copy or repeat formatting methods to save time.)

3. Select the text beginning with "The Mall" and ending with "The Gourmet Store" and add bullets.

4. Select the text beginning with "The Sale Hunter" and ending with "The Catalog Shopper" and add bullets.

5. Save the documents as *Stores Outline*.

6. Preview and print the document.

7. Replace the bullets with numbers.

8. Change the text "INTRODUCTION" to "SHOPPING SUMMARY."

9. Save the document as *Shopping Summary*.

10. Preview, print, and close the document.

Exercise 10

1. Open the *Symbols And Special Characters* document located on the Data Disk.

2. Insert the appropriate symbol or special characters as indicated in the text using the Symbol dialog box.

3. Save the document as *Symbols And Special Characters Revised*.

4. Preview, print, and close the document.

5. Open the *Chicago Warehouses Audit* document located on the Data Disk.

6. Highlight the first bulleted list in bright green.

7. Highlight the second bulleted list in pink.

8. Save the document as *Important Chicago Information*.

9. Preview, print, and close the document.

Case Projects

Project 1

Kelly Armstead asks you to show her the different font effect options available in Word. Open an existing document of your choice. Experiment with the special font effects options in the Font dialog box by selecting text and applying special effects formats and animation effects. Create a new Word document listing, describing, and showing the different effects. Use bulleted and numbered lists and character formats as appropriate. Save, preview, and print the document. With your instructor's permission, give a printed copy of the document to a classmate and, using the document as your guide, show your classmate how to use the different fonts and animation options.

Project 2

Marcy Wainwright, who works in the purchasing department, suggests you could save time in applying character formatting to text by using keyboard shortcuts. You decide to research which keyboard shortcuts to use to apply character formatting. Using the Office Assistant, locate, review, and print a list of keyboard shortcut keys used to apply character formatting. Open the document of your choice and apply different character formatting using keyboard shortcuts. Use bulleted and numbered lists and character formats in the document as appropriate. Save, preview, and print the document.

Project 3

You have been assigned to key the text of a new client proposal. Because of the proposal format, you want to use special character spacing for some of the proposal titles but aren't certain what character spacing options are available. Using the Office Assistant and other Word Help features, research how to use the character spacing options. Create a new document, containing at least two paragraphs, to describe how you can use these character spacing options in the client proposal. Include some sample titles with special character spacing. Use bulleted and numbered lists and character formats in the document as appropriate. Save, preview, and print the document.

Project 4

Albert Navarro, in Human Resources, wants to have a "brown bag" lunch for his staff that includes a short presentation on troubleshooting character formatting and using bullets and numbering in documents. He asked Kelly for help and she assigned the presentation to you. Using the Office Assistant, search online Help for tips on how to troubleshoot problems with these topics. Create a new document containing at least three paragraphs that describe possible problems and solutions associated with character formatting or bullets and numbering. Use bulleted and numbered lists and character formats in the document as appropriate. Save, preview, and print the document. With your instructor's permission, present your troubleshooting tips to several classmates.

Project 5

The administrative offices are moving to a new floor in the same building and B. D. Vickers asks you to create a letter announcing the move. The letter should contain the department's new address, phone number, fax number, and e-mail address. Create the letter for B. D. Vickers' signature. Set the appropriate margins, use fictitious data, and apply appropriate character formatting features discussed in this chapter to make the text attractive and easy to read. Use different text effects from the Font dialog box. Use bulleted and numbered lists and character formats in the document as appropriate. Save, preview, and print the letter.

Project 6

Elizabeth left you instructions to create a list of Web sites that are marketing and selling their products on the Web. Connect to your ISP and open your Web browser. Search the Web for pages that contain information on Web-based marketing and direct sales. Print at least three Web pages. Create a new, blank document and list the title of the Web pages and their URLs. Use bulleted and numbered lists and character formats in the document as appropriate. Save, preview, and print the document.

Project 7

Kelly Armstead needs the mailing addresses or e-mail addresses of the senators and congressmen from Illinois. You know that this information is available on the Web. Connect to your ISP and load your Web browser. Locate the home page for the U. S. Senate and U. S. House of Representatives. Follow the links to the names and addresses of the senators and congressmen. Print the appropriate pages. Create a new, blank document and key the information you found. Use bulleted and numbered lists and character formats in the document as appropriate. Save, preview, and print the document.

Project 8

You want to know more about how to use the keyboard to create bulleted and numbered lists automatically. Using the Office Assistant and other Word Help features, research how to create bulleted and numbered lists automatically. Create a new document and practice creating bulleted and numbered lists automatically with the fictitious data of your choice. Save, preview, and print the document.

chapter four

Using the Tabs Command

Chapter Overview

S ome information is more clearly presented in columns and rows than in paragraph text. For example, it's easier to compare monthly expenses when the figures are arranged in columns by month and in rows by item. In this chapter you learn to organize information attractively on the page in rows and columns using tab stops and tab formatting marks.

LEARNING OBJECTIVES

- ▶ Understand tabs
- ▶ Set left tabs
- ▶ Set center tabs
- ▶ Set decimal tabs
- ▶ Set right tabs
- ▶ Set tabs with leaders

Case profile

The accounting department is overwhelmed with special projects and deadlines. Elizabeth Chang was so pleased with your work in the marketing department that she recommended you to Bill Wilson, the accounting manager. Bill wants you to create a summary memo to include with the quarterly sales report.

chapter five

notes

Before beginning the activities in this chapter you should review Appendix C, Formatting Tips for Business Documents, if you have not already done so.

5.a Understanding Tabs

When you need to prepare written communication to someone inside your organization, you can create an interoffice memorandum (or memo) instead of a letter document. Interoffice memorandums generally follow the standard format shown in Figure 5-1. The memorandum should have a 2-inch top margin, 1-inch left and right margins, and the double-spaced heading text TO:, FROM:, DATE:, and SUBJECT: at the beginning of the memorandum followed by paragraphs separated by a blank line. The variable TO:, FROM:, DATE:, and SUBJECT: text that follow each heading should be aligned. You do this with tabs.

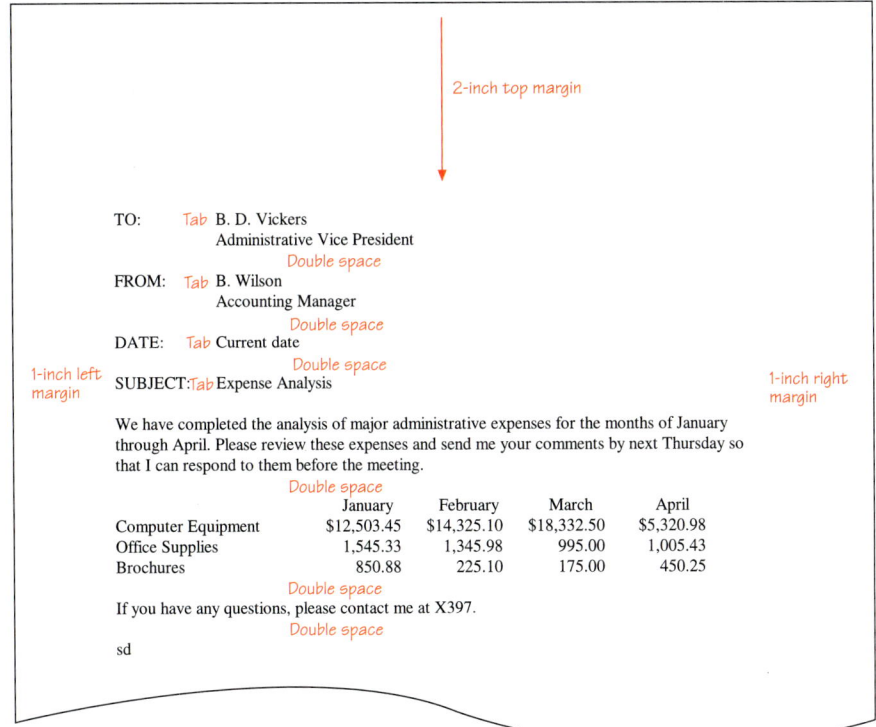

FIGURE 5-1
Standard Interoffice Memorandum

After each heading, you insert a **tab formatting mark,** a nonprinting character you key in your document by pressing the TAB key. Each tab

chapter
five

QUICK TIP

To set custom tab stops that affect all the paragraphs in a new document, set the tab stops before you begin keying the first paragraph. When you press the ENTER key to begin a new paragraph, the tab settings are added to the new paragraph.

formatting mark you insert moves the text to the right of the tab formatting mark to the next tab stop. **Tab stops** are text-alignment icons positioned on the horizontal ruler that indicate where text should align. By default, Word documents have tab stops set at every ½ inch. You can also set custom tab stops at any position between the left and right margins for one or more selected paragraphs or the entire document.

Tab stops are part of **paragraph formatting**. This means that only the selected paragraph or paragraphs are affected when you set or modify tabs stops. To set custom tab stops for individual paragraphs, you must first select the paragraphs. To select a single paragraph, simply move the insertion point into the paragraph. To select multiple paragraphs, use the selection techniques you learned in Chapter 2.

Word has five types of tab alignments: Left, Center, Right, Decimal, and Bar. Text is left-aligned at default tab stops and can be left-, center-, right-, or decimal-aligned at custom tab stops. Table 5-1 describes the five tab text alignments. For more information on Bar alignment, see online Help.

TABLE 5-1
Tab Alignment Options

Tab	Alignment	Icon
Left	Text is left-aligned at the tab	
Center	Text is centered over the tab	
Right	Text is right-aligned at the tab	
Decimal	Text is aligned at the decimal character	
Bar	Inserts a vertical line at the tab stop and aligns text to the right of the line	

MOUSE TIP

You can set the left, center, right, decimal, and bar tab stops by selecting the appropriate tab alignment icon on the Tab Alignment button located to the left of the horizontal ruler, and then clicking at the appropriate position on the horizontal ruler.

Bill Wilson asks you create the interoffice memo to B. D. Vickers shown in Figure 5-1. After you create the memo headings, you insert both the tab stops and the tab formatting marks necessary to align the variable heading text. To create the memo:

Step 1	*Create*	a new, blank document
Step 2	*Set*	a 2-inch top, and 1-inch left and right margins
Step 3	*Click*	the Show/Hide button ¶ on the Standard toolbar

Your screen should look similar to Figure 5-2.

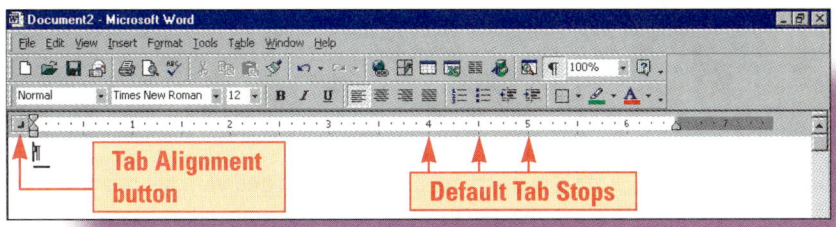

FIGURE 5-2
Formatting Marks, Default
Tab Stops, Tab Alignment
Button

> **MENU TIP**
>
> You can set custom tab stops with the <u>T</u>abs command on the F<u>o</u>rmat menu by specifying where each tab formatting mark is inserted on the page, where each the tab alignment icon is inserted on the horizontal ruler, and the addition of leader characters.

By default, Word sets tab stops every ½ inch on the horizontal ruler. As you key the heading text, you press the TAB key to insert a tab formatting mark, which moves the insertion point to the next default tab stop on the horizontal ruler. Because you displayed the non-printing characters, you'll be able to see the tab formatting marks when you key them. To view the tab formatting marks and create the memo headings:

Step 1	*Observe*	the paragraph formatting mark at the first line
Step 2	*Observe*	the default tab stops set at every ½ inch on the horizontal ruler
Step 3	*Observe*	the Tab Alignment button ▣ to the left of the horizontal ruler
Step 4	*Key*	TO:
Step 5	*Press*	the TAB key
Step 6	*Observe*	the tab formatting mark
Step 7	*Observe*	that the insertion point moves to the next default tab stop at the ½-inch position on the horizontal ruler

Your screen should look similar to Figure 5-3.

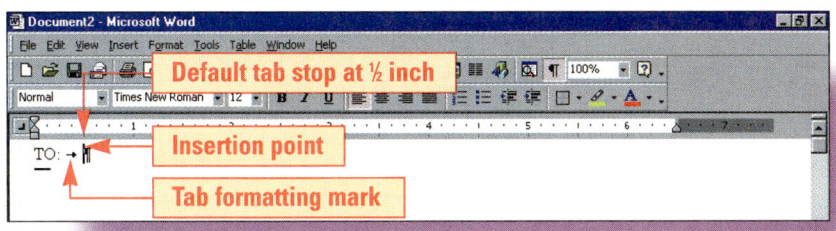

FIGURE 5-3
Insertion Point, Tab
Formatting Mark, and
Default Tab Stop

| Step 8 | *Key* | B. D. Vickers |
| Step 9 | *Press* | the ENTER key |

chapter
five

Step 10	*Press*	the TAB key
Step 11	*Key*	Administrative Vice President
Step 12	*Press*	the ENTER key twice
Step 13	*Continue*	to key the remaining headings and variable heading text you see in Figure 5-1, inserting one tab formatting mark between each heading and the variable text for that heading
Step 14	*Press*	the ENTER key twice following the SUBJECT: heading and variable text
Step 15	*Save*	the document as *Expense Memorandum*

5.b Setting Left Tabs

Notice that the variable heading text is not properly aligned because each line aligned at the first available default tab setting. To properly align the heading text, you need to add a custom left tab stop to the horizontal ruler for all the heading lines. A **left-aligned tab** aligns text along the left at the tab stop position. The quickest way to set custom tab stops is to use the mouse, the Tab Alignment button, and the horizontal ruler. Before you set custom tab stops, you must select the appropriate paragraph or paragraphs, then select the appropriate tab alignment icon with the Tab Alignment button, and finally, click the horizontal ruler to insert the tab stop at the appropriate position. When you click the ruler, the tab alignment icon you select from the Tab Alignment button appears on the ruler. To set a custom left tab for all the heading lines at one time:

Step 1	*Select*	the text beginning with the "TO:" paragraph and ending with the "SUBJECT:" paragraph
Step 2	*Click*	the Tab Alignment button until the left-aligned tab icon appears, if necessary
Step 3	*Move*	the mouse pointer to the 1-inch position on the horizontal ruler
Step 4	*Click*	the horizontal ruler at the 1-inch position
Step 5	*Deselect*	the text

A left-align tab icon appears on the horizontal ruler and the variable text in the heading lines aligns at the 1-inch position. Your screen should look similar to Figure 5-4.

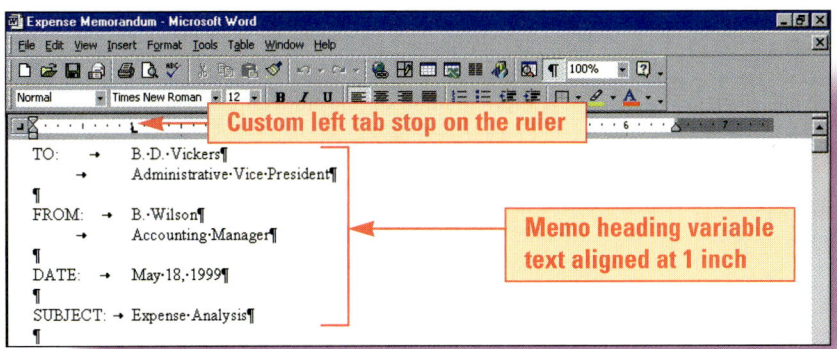

FIGURE 5-4
Custom Left Tab at 1 Inch

You remove tab stops or change the location of tab stops on the horizontal ruler by selecting the appropriate paragraphs and then dragging the tab stops with the mouse pointer. To move the custom left tab to 1½-inch for all the heading paragraphs:

Step 1	*Select*	the heading paragraphs
Step 2	*Position*	the mouse pointer on the left-align tab icon at the 1-inch position on the horizontal ruler (the ScreenTip "Left Tab" appears)
Step 3	*Drag*	the left-align tab icon to the 1½-inch position on the horizontal ruler

The variable text in each heading paragraph shifts to the 1½-inch position. You remove a tab stop by dragging it completely off the ruler. To remove the custom tab at 1½-inch position:

Step 1	*Verify*	the heading paragraphs are still selected
Step 2	*Drag*	the tab icon at the 1½-inch position down off the horizontal ruler

When you remove custom tab stops, the tab settings return to the default settings.

Step 3	*Observe*	that the tab stops on the horizontal ruler indicate the ½ inch default settings and the variable heading text is no longer properly aligned

You set custom tab stops for individual paragraphs just as you do multiple paragraphs. To set a left tab for the first heading paragraph only:

Step 1	*Click*	in the heading paragraph beginning "TO:" to position the insertion point (this selects the paragraph)

Step 2	*Verify*	the Tab Alignment button ⬜ is set for a left tab
Step 3	*Click*	the 1-inch position on the horizontal ruler
Step 4	*Observe*	that the first line of the first paragraph *only* moves right and aligns at the new custom tab stop position
Step 5	*Set*	a 1-inch left-aligned custom tab for the remaining heading paragraphs
Step 6	*Deselect*	the text
Step 7	*Save*	the document

You now key the paragraph text in the body of the memo and then organize the expense analysis data in columns using tab formatting characters and tab stops on the horizontal ruler.

5.c Setting Center Tabs

Center-aligned tabs center text over the tab stop, which is appropriate for creating column headings. Figure 5-1 includes text in columns separated by tab formatting marks. The text is arranged in five columns and includes column headers for the last four columns. You key the first body paragraph and the column headings: To key the first body paragraph:

| Step 1 | *Key* | the first body paragraph from Figure 5-1 on the second line following the SUBJECT: heading line |
| Step 2 | *Press* | the ENTER key twice |

Next you set custom center-aligned tab stops for the expense analysis column headings and key the headings.

Step 3	*Click*	the Tab Alignment button until the center-aligned tab icon ⬜ appears
Step 4	*Click*	the 2.5-, 3.5-, 4.5-, and 5.5-positions on the horizontal ruler to insert the center-aligned tab icons
Step 5	*Press*	the TAB key
Step 6	*Key*	January
Step 7	*Press*	the TAB key

Step 8	*Key*	February
Step 9	*Press*	the TAB key
Step 10	*Key*	March
Step 11	*Press*	the TAB key
Step 12	*Key*	April
Step 13	*Press*	the ENTER key

When you press the ENTER key to create a new paragraph, Word remembers the previous paragraph tab settings. Because you use different tab setting for the text you key in the columns, you should remove the center-aligned tab icons from the ruler for this paragraph. To remove the center-aligned tab icons:

Step 1	*Drag*	each tab stop for the current paragraph off the ruler
Step 2	*Save*	the document

Now you are ready to set tab stops to align the expense analysis data.

5.d Setting Decimal Tabs

You want the expense data to align attractively on the decimal point in each column when you key the data in the columns. This makes reading columns of numbers much easier. A **decimal tab** aligns numbers at the decimal point.

To set decimal tab stops and enter the expense data text in the columns:

Step 1	*Click*	the Tab Alignment button until the decimal-aligned tab icon appears
Step 2	*Click*	the horizontal ruler at approximately the 2.6-, 3.6-, 4.6-, and 5.6-inch positions to insert the decimal-aligned tab stops using the ALT key to view the numbers on the horizontal ruler
Step 3	*Key*	Computer Equipment
Step 4	*Press*	the TAB key
Step 5	*Key*	$12,503.45

chapter
five

Step 6	*Press*	the TAB key
Step 7	*Key*	$14,325.10
Step 8	*Press*	the TAB key
Step 9	*Key*	$18,332.50
Step 10	*Press*	the TAB key
Step 11	*Key*	$5,320.98
Step 12	*Press*	the ENTER key

When you press the ENTER key, the next paragraph retains the tab stop settings from the previous paragraph. These tabs are appropriate for the remaining rows of data. To create the remaining lines:

Step 1	*Key*	Office Supplies
Step 2	*Press*	the TAB key
Step 3	*Observe*	the insertion point moves to the tab and aligns on the decimal point of the number above it
Step 4	*Continue*	to add the remaining two lines of tabbed text and the rest of the memo, as shown in Figure 5-1
Step 5	*Save*	the document and close it

Bill asks you to update the accounting department telephone extension list and add the revision date at the right margin below the phone numbers. You can use a right-aligned tab stop to add the revision date.

5.e Setting Right Tabs

A **right-aligned tab** is appropriate for text that should be aligned at the right of the tab, such as a date at the right margin of a document. To position the date at the right margin, set a right-aligned tab, press the TAB key, and then key or insert the date. To set a right tab and right-align the date at the right margin of the first line:

Step 1	*Open*	the *Telephone List* document located on the Data Disk
Step 2	*Move*	the insertion point to the bottom of the document and add two new blank lines

Step 3	*Click*	the Tab Alignment button to the left of the horizontal ruler until the right-aligned tab icon ◢ appears
Step 4	*Click*	the 5½-inch position on the horizontal ruler to insert the right-aligned tab icon
Step 5	*Drag*	the right-aligned tab icon to the 6-inch position (the right margin)

Your screen should look similar to Figure 5-5.

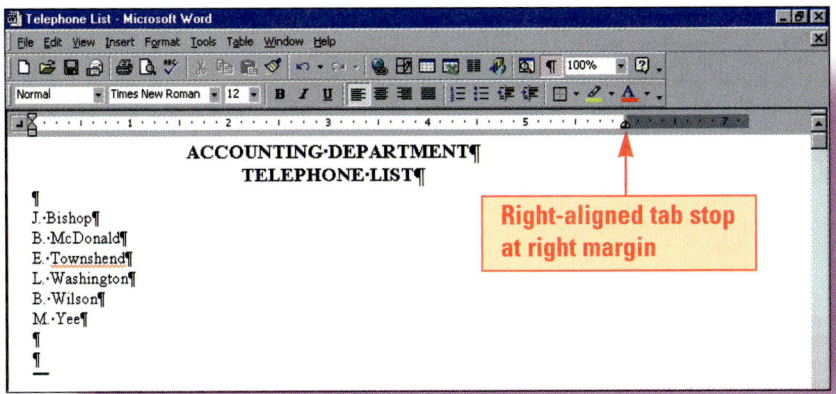

Right-aligned tab stop at right margin

FIGURE 5-5
Right-Aligned Tab

Step 6	*Press*	the TAB key
Step 7	*Key*	today's date using AutoComplete
Step 8	*Observe*	that as you key the date the text flows left from the tab position
Step 9	*Save*	the document as *Telephone List Revised*

Bill asks you to continue the telephone extension list revision by positioning each employee's name at the left margin and their telephone number at the right margin in the telephone list document. He also wants you to insert a dotted or dashed line between the employee's name at the left margin and their extension at the right margin to help guide the reader's eye across the page. You can use right-aligned tab stops with tab leaders to do this.

chapter
five

5.f Setting Tabs with Leaders

Documents that have a large amount of white space between columns of text, such as a table of contents or a phone list, can be difficult for a reader's eye to follow across the page from column to column. **Tab leaders** are dashed or dotted lines you can add to a tab to provide a visual guide for the reader as they read the text from column to column. You add a leader character to a tab in the Tabs dialog box. Before you open the Tabs dialog box to set tab stops and add leaders, you must remember to select the appropriate paragraphs to be formatted. To set a right-aligned tab at the 6-inch position and add the second leader style:

Step 1	*Select*	the lines of text beginning with "J. Bishop" and ending with "M. Yee"
Step 2	*Click*	Format
Step 3	*Click*	Tabs

The Tabs dialog box that opens on your screen should look similar to Figure 5-6.

FIGURE 5-6
Tabs Dialog Box

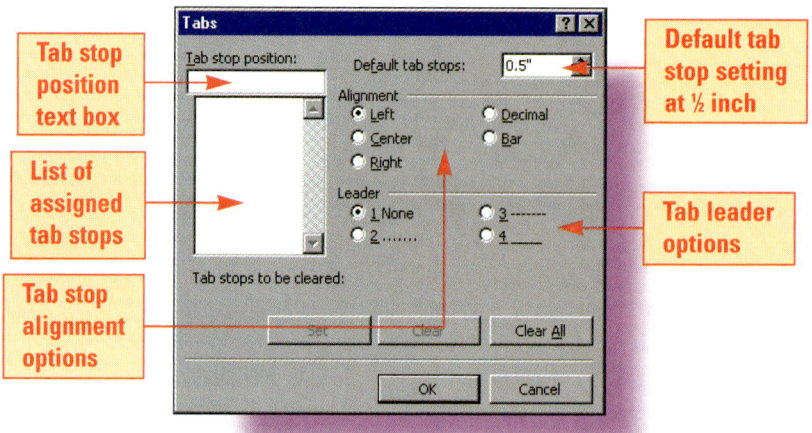

You can use the dialog box Help button to review the options in the dialog box. You set tab stops in the dialog box by keying the tab position and selecting an alignment option. Then you can select a leader style.

| Step 4 | *Key* | 6 in the Tab stop position: text box |
| Step 5 | *Click* | the Right option button |

| Step 6 | *Click* | the 2 .... leader option button |
| Step 7 | *Click* | OK |

With the tab stops and leader set, you can enter the tab formatting marks and telephone extensions for each item. To key the telephone extensions list:

Step 1	*Move*	the insertion point to the end of the J. Bishop text
Step 2	*Press*	the TAB key
Step 3	*Observe*	the leader characters that appear from the J. Bishop text to the tab
Step 4	*Key*	X388
Step 5	*Press*	the DOWN ARROW key to move the insertion point to the end of the B. McDonald text
Step 6	*Continue*	to key the telephone extensions to the document, pressing the TAB key between the name and extension B. McDonald, X391 E. Townshend, X402 L. Washington, X455 B. Wilson, X397 M. Yee, X405
Step 7	*Save*	the document and close it

No matter what type of document you create, you can use tabs to precisely align text in columns.

QUICK TIP

You can use the Click and Type feature to set a left tab stop anywhere in the document when working in Print Layout view or in Web Layout view. Move the I-beam to the desired location. When you see the left-alignment icon next to the I-beam you can double-click the document to insert a left tab stop at that position.

chapter
five

Summary

▶ You can reposition and organize text in columns by setting tab stops on the horizontal ruler and inserting tab formatting marks in the text.

▶ Tab stops are text-alignment icons positioned on the horizontal ruler that indicate where text should align.

▶ Tab formatting marks are nonprinting characters you key in your document by pressing the TAB key.

▶ Left-aligned tab stops position text at the tab and then flow the text to the right.

▶ Right-aligned tab stops position text at the tab and then flow the text to the left.

▶ Center-aligned tab stops are appropriate for column headings and position text at the tab and then flow the text left and right as necessary to center at the tab.

▶ Decimal-aligned tab stops are appropriate for columns of numbers containing decimal points and align the numbers on their decimal points.

▶ To assist the reader's eye in following text from column to column, you can add leader characters to a tab.

Commands Review

Action	Menu Bar	Shortcut Menu	Toolbar	Keyboard
Set custom tab stops	F<u>o</u>rmat, <u>T</u>abs		Click the Tab Alignment button to select an alignment icon, then click the horizontal ruler at the appropriate position ⌞ Left ⌟ Right ⊥ Center ⊥ Decimal	ALT + O, T

Concepts Review

Circle the correct answer.

1. Which of the following is not a tab alignment?
[a] Left
[b] Right
[c] Justify
[d] Decimal

2. To align text at the right of a tab using the Tab Alignment button and the horizontal ruler, select the:
[a] Left alignment icon.
[b] Justify alignment icon.
[c] Right alignment icon.
[d] Center alignment icon.

3. You can insert a tab formatting mark by pressing the:
[a] ENTER key.
[b] TAB key.
[c] HOME key.
[d] END key.

4. To quickly set custom tab stops that affect one paragraph, first:
[a] select the entire document.
[b] select multiple paragraphs.
[c] move the insertion point to the paragraph.
[d] click the horizontal ruler then select the paragraph.

5. The default tab stops are positioned every:
[a] ½ inch.
[b] 1 inch.
[c] ¾ inch.
[d] ¼ inch.

6. To assist the reader's eye in following text from column to column, you can add:
[a] length to the line.
[b] less space between the characters.
[c] leader characters.
[d] lending characters.

7. To view the tab formatting marks in a document, click the:
[a] Show Tabs button.
[b] Show/Hide button.
[c] Format Marks button.
[d] Tab Alignment button.

8. You can manually enter the tab position, change the default tab settings, and add leaders to tab stops with the:
[a] Format, Paragraph commands.
[b] Insert, Tabs commands.
[c] Tools, Options commands.
[d] Format, Tabs commands.

Circle **T** if the statement is true or **F** is the statement is false.

T   F   1. The default setting for tab stops is every ⅛ inch.

T   F   2. You can set tab stops with the mouse and the horizontal ruler.

T   F   3. The Tab Alignment button has four alignment settings.

T   F   4. Use a center-aligned tab to position the date at the right margin.

T   F   5. Use a left-aligned tab to start a new paragraph.

T   F   6. When you create text column headings, you can use the decimal-aligned tab to center the headings over the column.

T   F   7. You cannot remove tab stops with the mouse pointer.

T   F   8. Tab leader characters can be added by clicking the Tab Alignment button.

Skills Review

Exercise 1

1. Create a new, blank document and key the text in columns below:

	1998	1999	2000
Division 1	$200,000	$90,000	$180,000
Division 2	212,000	205,000	79,000
Division 3	140,000	400,000	120,000
Division 4	304,000	107,000	105,000
Division 5	201,000	148,000	195,000

2. Use right-aligned tab stops to align the numbers.

3. Use center-aligned tab stops to align the column headings.

4. Save the document as *Division Data*.

5. Preview, print, and close the document.

Exercise 2

1. Open the *Media Memo* document located on the Data Disk.

2. Replace the text Current date with the actual date.

3. Set the appropriate margins for an interoffice memorandum.

4. Insert tab formatting marks in the heading paragraphs so you can align the variable heading text.

5. Set a left-aligned tab at 1 inch on the horizontal ruler for all the heading paragraphs to align the variable heading text.

6. Insert a new line below R. F. Jones and then insert a tab formatting mark and key the title "Media Buyer."

7. Insert a new line below B. Wilson and then insert a tab formatting mark and key the title "Accounting Manager."

8. Spell check the document.

9. Save the document as *Media Memo Revised*.

10. Preview, print, and close the document.

Exercise 3

1. Create a new, blank document and key the text in columns below:

Branch	Meat	Cheese	Produce
Chicago	$55,900	$125,000	$77,000
Vancouver	33,000	7,890	15,000
London	22,500	12,500	18,000
Melbourne	34,333	40,100	48,550

2. Use right-aligned tab stops to align the numbers.

3. Use center-aligned tab stops to align the column headings.

4. Save the document as *Branch Sales*.

5. Preview, print, and close the document.

Exercise 4

1. Open the *Vendor Phone List* document located on the Data Disk.

2. Select the four lines of text and set a right-aligned tab with the leader of your choice at the 6-inch position on the horizontal ruler.

3. Insert a new line at the top of the document and remove the right-aligned tab from the horizontal ruler.

4. Insert a tab formatting mark, key the column title "<u>Vendor</u>" with the underline, insert a tab formatting mark, and key the column title "<u>Phone List</u>" with the underline.

5. Set two center-aligned tab stops on the horizontal ruler to center the column titles attractively over their respective columns.

6. Save the document as *Vendor Phone List Revised*.

7. Preview, print, and close the document.

Exercise 5

1. Create a new, blank document and key the text in columns below:

Sales District	Telephone	Supplies	Misc.
1	$1,450.25	$744.33	$225.45
2	1,645.33	525.88	214.55
3	985.22	275.90	243.89
4	1,112.98	210.66	423.67
5	1,967.34	678.23	313.56

2. Use decimal-aligned tab stops to align the telephone, supplies, and miscellaneous expense numbers.

3. Use center-aligned tab stops to align the column headings and the sales district numbers.

4. Save the document as *Sales District Expenses*.

5. Preview, print, and close the document.

Exercise 6

1. Create a new, blank document and key the following text in columns.

Item	Budgeted	Actual	Difference
Executive Secretaries	$1,234,000	$1,145,000	$(89,000)
Administrative Assistants	289,500	364,800	75,300
Equipment	850,000	730,000	(120,000)
Telecommunications	365,000	340,500	(24,500)
Miscellaneous	65,000	50,000	(15,000)

2. Use the appropriate tab stops to center the column headings and align the budgeted, actual, and difference numbers.

3. Save the document as *Budget Variance*.

4. Preview, print, and close the document.

Exercise 7

1. Open the *Regional Expenses Memo* document located on the Data Disk.

2. Replace the text Current date with the actual date.

chapter five

3. Select the heading paragraphs and then set a left-aligned tab at 1½ inches on the horizontal ruler.

4. Move the left-aligned tab to 1 inch.

5. Insert the following columnar text separated by tab stops below the first body paragraph of the memo. Use center-aligned tab stops for the column titles. Use decimal-aligned tab stops for the selling, employee, and overhead numbers. Remember to add a single blank line before and after the columnar text.

Region	Selling	Employee	Overhead
Central	$42,000.50	$2,210.00	$12,825.98
Eastern	32,545.78	3,412.44	7,890.66
Midwest	53,897.75	3,508.34	8,454.88
Mountain	49,154.33	6,974.76	5,221.44
Southern	34,675.21	11,242.88	15,111.75
Western	40,876.21	8,417.77	10,445.29

6. Save the document as *Regional Expenses Memo Revised*.

7. Preview, print, and close the document.

Exercise 8

1. Create the following interoffice memorandum.

TO: D. Ingram
             Sales Director

FROM: B. Wilson
             Accounting Manager

DATE: Current date

SUBJECT: Sales Summary   *Analysis*

I have completed the sales analysis you requested and the data appear below.

Name	January	February	March
Davis, Stephen	$65,000	$45,000	$78,000
McCarthy, Rachel	45,000	58,000	76,000
Mills, Cheryl	95,000	99,000	92,000

Please contact me at X397 if you have any questions.

sd

2. Key the current date in the memorandum using AutoComplete.

3. Set appropriate margins for an interoffice memorandum.

4. Set the appropriate tab stops for the text in columns.

5. Apply bold style to the TO:, FROM:, DATE:, and SUBJECT: headings.

6. Save the document as *Ingram Memo*.

7. Preview, print, and close the document.

Case Projects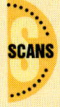

Project 1

Bill Wilson asks you to prepare an interoffice memorandum from him to all regional sales managers advising them of the semi-annual sales meeting to be held in two weeks in the main conference room at corporate headquarters in Chicago. Additionally, everyone attending the meeting must contact you to arrange hotel accommodations, rental cars, and airline tickets. Use character and tab formatting features to make the memo interesting to read and professional in appearance. Save, preview, and print the document.

Project 2

You are preparing a sales analysis for Bill Wilson to take to the semi-annual sales conference and you would like to change the default tab position from every ½ inch to every ¼ inch. Using the Office Assistant and the keyword "tabs" search for help topics on changing the default tab position in a document. Create an interoffice memorandum to Bill Wilson from yourself with the subject line "Default Tabs." Add at least two body paragraphs describing how to change the default tab settings. Save, preview, and print the document.

Project 3

Benji Hori, one of the accounting assistants, asks you if there is a way to vary the alignment of text in a single line. He needs to create a document with the document title, date, and page number all on the same line. He wants the document title left-aligned, the date center-aligned, and the page number right-aligned. If necessary, look up the "Troubleshoot paragraph formatting" topic in online Help using the Office Assistant and review how to align text differently on the same line. Create a sample document with the title "Quarterly Sales Report" left-aligned, the current date center-aligned, and the text "Page Number" right-aligned. Save, preview, and print the document. With your instructor's permission, show a classmate how to align text differently on the same line.

Project 4

Before you begin keying a new accounting report for Bill Wilson, you want to practice setting and removing tab stops in a document. Open an existing document that contains tab stops and tab formatting marks. Remove all the tab stops for the entire document at one time. Explore using left, center, right, and decimal tabs to make the document easier to read. Save the document with a new name, then preview and print it.

Project 5

Bill Wilson is planning an auto trip to Houston, Texas, and he asks you to use the Web to look up the mileage and print driving instructions and a city-to-city trip map from Chicago to Houston. Connect to your ISP, load your Web browser and, using a directory or search engine, locate Web pages that help you plan auto trips by calculating the mileage and creating driving instructions and maps from city to city. Save and print the driving instructions and trip map. Create an interoffice memorandum to Bill outlining the mileage and driving instructions. Save, preview, and print the memorandum.

chapter five

Project 6

Katrina Levy, one of the accounting assistants, asks you for help. She has an old document with tab stops set differently for each of the paragraphs. She wants to remove all the tab stops for the entire document at one time but isn't certain how to do this. Open the Tabs dialog box and use the dialog box Help button to get more information about the Clear and Clear All buttons. Using the Office Assistant and the keywords "clear tabs" search online Help for information on clearing all the tab stops in a document. Create an interoffice memorandum to Katrina describing how to clear all the tabs in document at one time. Save, preview, and print the memo.

Project 7

Kelly Armstead called to ask you how to find someone's e-mail address using the Web. Connect to your ISP, load your Web browser and—using several directories and search engines—locate Web pages that include a feature that allows you to search for e-mail addresses. Print at least three pages. Create an interoffice memorandum to Kelly listing the Web pages and describing how to use them to search for e-mail addresses. Save, preview, and print the memo.

Project 8

Bill Wilson is attending a meeting with the branch vice presidents to discuss the quarterly sales figures. He wants you to create a document he can hand out at the meeting. Using fictitious data for the Chicago, London, Melbourne, and Vancouver branches, create a document with two columns for branch names and total sales data for each branch. Use tab stops with leaders to organize the data attractively on the page. Save, preview, and print the document.

Setting Spacing, Aligning Text, and Using Indentation Options

Chapter Overview

P oorly arranged text can distract readers from the information in a document. When text is attractively spaced and positioned on the page, readers can concentrate on the document content. You can use line spacing, text alignment, and indentation options to position text in your documents. In this chapter you learn different ways to change the line spacing and text alignment, and different ways to indent paragraph text.

Case profile

After completing your assignment in the accounting department, you are asked to return to the purchasing department to help Kelly Armstead create and format the department's correspondence and reports. You begin by keying and formatting the new audit report from the Melbourne branch office.

chapter
six

notes   For this chapter, the automatic creation of styles based on formatting is turned off in the AutoFormat As You Type tab in the AutoCorrect dialog box.

Before beginning the activities in this chapter you should review Appendix C, Formatting Tips for Business Documents, if you have not already done so.

6.a Setting Character, Line, and Paragraph Spacing

Line spacing indicates the vertical space between lines of text. The default setting for line spacing in Word is single spacing. Table 6-1 describes single spacing as well as the other line-spacing options available in Word. The paragraph text in letters and memorandums is usually single spaced. Double spacing is most often used for long reports so that they are easier to read. Also, documents in progress are often double spaced so reviewers can use the extra white space to write their comments and proofing notations.

TABLE 6-1
Line-spacing Options

Option	Description
Single	Accommodates the largest font size in the line plus a little extra space, depending on the font.
1.5 Lines	Sets the line spacing to 1.5 times the single-line spacing.
Double	Sets the line spacing to twice the single-line spacing.
At Least	Sets a minimum line spacing that will adjust to accommodate larger font sizes or graphics.
Exactly	Sets a fixed line spacing that will not adjust for larger font sizes or graphics.
Multiple	Sets the line spacing by a percentage of the single-line spacing. A multiple of 1.3 increases the single-line spacing by 30%. A multiple of 0.7 decreases the single line spacing by 30%.

Figure 6-1 illustrates a report document in the unbound report format with a 2-inch top margin and 1-inch left and right margins. Kelly wants you to key the Melbourne audit report document in Figure 6-1 and then format the text using line spacing and vertical text alignment options to make the text more attractive and easier to read.

FIGURE 6-1
Unbound Report

2-inch top margin

Several methods were used to examine the operations at warehouses in Melbourne. The study team members interviewed the warehouse managers and several workers in each warehouse. A consulting company, Wadell & Associates, completed an analysis of the various policies and procedures used by the warehouses. A human resources specialist from the Chicago office interviewed managers as well as labor union representatives at each warehouse. Some of the analysis has not been completed and should be finished within three weeks.

The completed portion of the analysis indicates there are three possible causes for the problems at the Melbourne warehouses:

1-inch left margin

- Insufficient quality control
- Low morale and reduced worker productivity
- Poor communication

1-inch right margin

Warehouse managers and employees report poor communication over the last year. Problems with quality control are suspected for several reasons.

1. Appropriate goals have not been specified.
2. Appropriate work processes are not being used in some activities.
3. Employees are not receiving proper direction about how to manage the inventories.

Morale and worker productivity problems may be due to the fact that many employees believe their compensation is low relative to competitors in their area. This belief may have negatively impacted their productivity.

In contrast, interviews in Vancouver, Chicago, and London indicate that warehouses in these areas do not seem to have the problems found in Melbourne. Managers and union representatives at these locations stated that all personnel work together in a cooperative manner.

Communications between all warehouse personnel regarding goals, policies, and procedures are effective and employees believe they are fairly compensated.

QUICK TIP

Line spacing is included in paragraph formatting. Whenever you change the line spacing, the new line spacing affects only the selected paragraphs. To change the spacing for a single paragraph, simply move the insertion point to that paragraph. To change the spacing for several paragraphs, you must first select the paragraphs. To set line spacing that affects all the paragraphs in a new document, set the line spacing before you begin typing the first paragraph.

To create the document:

Step 1	*Create*	a new, blank document, if necessary
Step 2	*Set*	2-inch top and 1-inch left and right margins
Step 3	*Key*	the text in Figure 6-1 (do not add any blank lines between the paragraphs)
Step 4	*Create*	the bulleted and numbered lists in the document, as shown in Figure 6-1
Step 5	*Save*	the document as *Melbourne Audit Report*

notes If you are using a 14-inch monitor with 640x480 resolution, you can zoom documents with 1-inch left and right margins to Page Width. This allows you to see all the text at the right margin. For the remainder of this book it is assumed you have zoomed the document to Page Width, if necessary.

chapter
six

To set the line spacing in your document, first select the entire document or the paragraphs you wish to change. Then change the line spacing in the Paragraph dialog box. Kelly wants the entire report double-spaced. To change the line spacing of the entire document to double:

Step 1	*Select*	the entire document
Step 2	*Right-click*	the selected text
Step 3	*Click*	<u>P</u>aragraph
Step 4	*Click*	the <u>I</u>ndents and Spacing tab, if necessary

The dialog box on your screen should look similar to Figure 6-2.

FIGURE 6-2
Paragraph Dialog Box

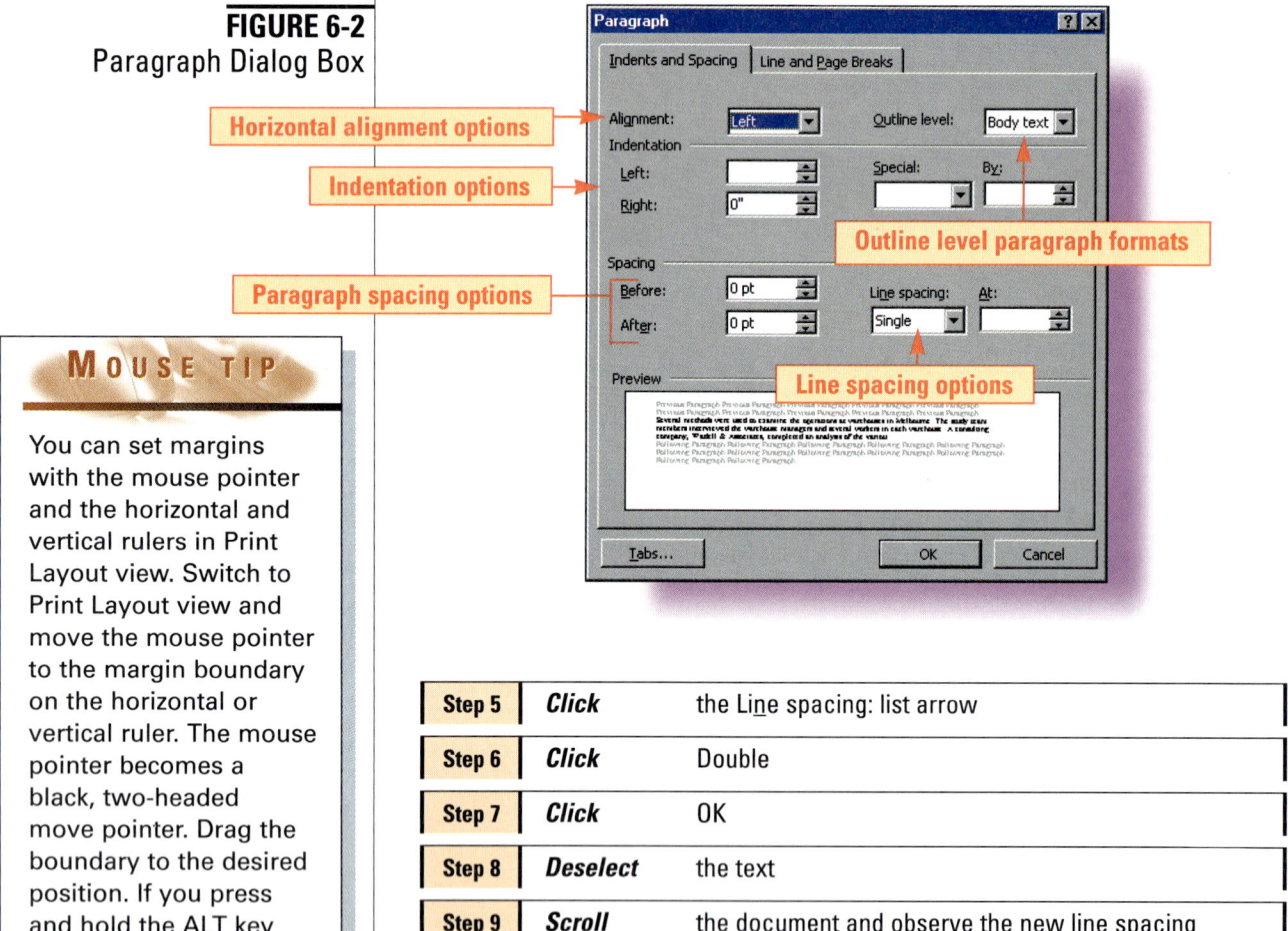

Step 5	*Click*	the Li<u>n</u>e spacing: list arrow
Step 6	*Click*	Double
Step 7	*Click*	OK
Step 8	*Deselect*	the text
Step 9	*Scroll*	the document and observe the new line spacing

Notice that the spacing between each line of text is now two lines, causing the document to extend into a second page. Word inserts a dotted line indicating a page break, which marks the end of page one and the start of page two.

The bulleted and numbered paragraphs in the *Melbourne Audit Report* would look better if they were spaced 1.5 times the single-line spacing. You change only the first two paragraphs in each list because Word inserts the additional space below the line. You want to leave the third paragraph with double spacing so the lists are separated equally from paragraphs above and below them. To change the line spacing for the bulleted and numbered lists:

Step 1	*Select*	the first two bulleted list paragraphs (scroll to view these paragraphs, if necessary)
Step 2	*Right-click*	the selected text
Step 3	*Click*	Paragraph
Step 4	*Click*	the Indents and Spacing tab, if necessary
Step 5	*Click*	the Line spacing: list arrow
Step 6	*Click*	1.5
Step 7	*Click*	OK
Step 8	*Select*	the first two numbered paragraphs (scroll to view the paragraphs, if necessary)
Step 9	*Open*	the Paragraph dialog box
Step 10	*Change*	the line spacing to 1.5
Step 11	*Scroll*	the document and observe the line spacing
Step 12	*Save*	the document

The new line spacing is making the report much easier to read. Kelly wants the *Melbourne Audit Report* to be attractively spaced on one page instead of two pages. She suggests you change the line spacing and use vertical alignment to do this.

6.b Aligning Text Vertically

Vertical alignment affects how the text is placed on the page in relation to the top and bottom margins. Kelly wants the *Melbourne Audit Report* to be attractively spaced on one page. Because the double-spaced report falls onto two pages, you need to change the line spacing to reduce the amount of space between the lines. Once the report is on one page, you can align the text vertically between the

top and bottom margins. To view the document in Print Layout view and change the line spacing:

Step 1	*Switch*	to Print Layout view
Step 2	*Zoom*	the document to Two Pages and observe the two-page layout
Step 3	*Set*	the line spacing for the entire document to 1.5 lines
Step 4	*Observe*	the document is now on one page, but the text is not yet distributed evenly between the top and bottom margins
Step 5	*Zoom*	the document to Whole Page
Step 6	*Click*	File
Step 7	*Click*	Page Setup
Step 8	*Click*	the Layout tab
Step 9	*Click*	the Vertical alignment: list arrow

The dialog box on your screen should look similar to Figure 6-3.

FIGURE 6-3
Layout Tab in the Page Setup Dialog Box

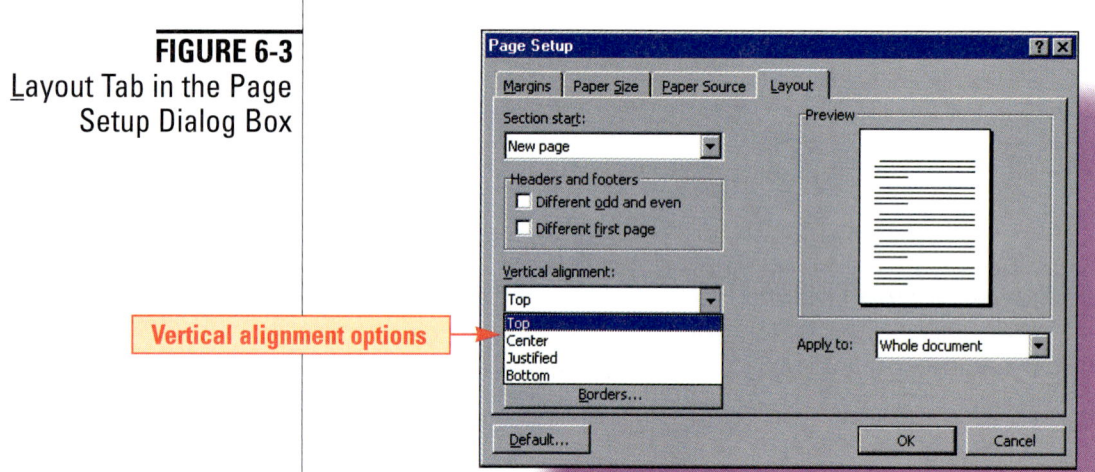

Vertical alignment options

The **Top** vertical alignment option aligns text with the top margin. The **Center** vertical alignment option allows you to center the text between the margins. This option is good for creating report title pages or signs. The **Bottom** vertical alignment option aligns the text at the bottom margin, leaving the extra white space at the top of the page. The **Justified** vertical alignment option distributes full-page text evenly between the top and bottom margins by adding additional line spacing. This option will give the report the look that Kelly wants.

Step 10	*Click*	Justified
Step 11	*Click*	OK
Step 12	*Observe*	the text is distributed evenly between the 2-inch top and 1-inch bottom margins
Step 13	*Switch*	to Normal view and deselect the text
Step 14	*Save*	the document

With the new vertical alignment, the *Melbourne Audit Report* fits nicely on the page. Next Kelly wants the body paragraph text to have evenly aligned left and right margins, the bulleted paragraphs to be centered between the left and right margins, and the numbered paragraphs to be positioned attractively on the page. To create these effects, you must align the text horizontally.

6.c Aligning Text in Paragraphs

Horizontal text alignment affects how the text is placed on the page in relation to the left and right margins. Like line spacing and vertical alignment, horizontal alignment is included in paragraph formatting, which means any horizontal alignment changes affect only selected paragraphs.

The four horizontal text alignment options are left, center, right, and justify. The default horizontal text alignment is left. **Left alignment** lines up text along the left margin and leaves the right margin "ragged," or uneven. **Right alignment** lines up the text along the right margin and leaves the left margin ragged. **Center alignment** centers the text between the left and right margins and leaves both margins ragged. **Justified alignment** aligns the text along both the left and right margins; Word adjusts the spaces between words so that the each line is even at both margins. The quickest way to change the alignment of selected paragraphs is to use the alignment buttons on the Formatting toolbar.

You use each of these alignments in the *Melbourne Audit Report*.

Setting Justified Alignment

Kelly asks you to justify the body text of the report. This way the *Melbourne Audit Report* document will have perfectly even left and right margins for each full line. Justification affects only full lines of text; partial lines are even along the left margin and ragged along the right. To justify all the paragraphs in the document:

Step 1	*Select*	the entire document
Step 2	*Click*	the Justify button ▤ on the Formatting toolbar
Step 3	*Deselect*	the text and scroll the document to verify that all the paragraphs are justified

Although the entire report is justified, notice that the partial lines at the end of each paragraph and the short bulleted and numbered list paragraphs are ragged along the right margin.

Setting Center Alignment

Paragraphs that are center-aligned have each line centered between the left and right margins. Center alignment is appropriate for single-line paragraphs, such as titles, paragraph headings, or bullets. You want to center the bullet paragraphs. To do this:

| Step 1 | *Select* | the bulleted paragraphs (scroll to view, if necessary) |
| Step 2 | *Click* | the Center button ▤ on the Formatting toolbar and deselect the text |

Each bulleted paragraph is centered between the left and right margins. Next you format the numbered list.

Setting Right Alignment

When paragraphs are right-aligned, each line of the paragraph is aligned at the right margin. Right alignment is appropriate for dates, page numbers, or to add a special effect to short one-line paragraphs. You decide to try right alignment for the numbered list. To right-align the numbered paragraphs:

| Step 1 | *Select* | the numbered paragraphs (scroll to view, if necessary) |
| Step 2 | *Click* | the Align Right button ▤ on the Formatting toolbar and deselect the text |

Each numbered paragraph is aligned along the right margin. Kelly comments that right alignment is not the most attractive position for the numbered paragraphs and suggests you realign them to their original position.

Setting Left Alignment

You can remove the horizontal alignment formatting or apply a different horizontal alignment to paragraphs by selecting the paragraphs you want to realign and then clicking the appropriate alignment button. To left-align the numbered paragraphs:

Step 1	*Select*	the numbered paragraphs
Step 2	*Click*	the Align Left button on the Formatting toolbar and deselect the text
Step 3	*Save*	the document

The numbered list looks better left-aligned, but you want to shift the paragraphs right so they stand out more.

6.d Using Indentation Options

Indenting, or moving text away from the margin, helps draw attention to that text. The Word indentation options position some or all lines of a paragraph to the right of the left margin (or to the left of the right margin). Indenting is part of paragraph formatting, which means only selected paragraphs are indented. The other paragraphs in the document remain unchanged.

There are four types of indents: left, right, first line, and hanging. A **Left Indent** moves all the lines of a paragraph to the right away from the left margin. A **Right Indent** moves all lines of a paragraph to the left away from the right margin. A **First Line Indent** moves the first line of a paragraph to the right or the left. A **Hanging Indent** leaves the first line of the paragraph at the left margin and moves the remaining lines to the right away from the left margin.

A tab stop and an indent are very different formatting features. Recall that when you press the TAB key, Word inserts a nonprinting tab formatting mark and moves only that line to the next tab stop on the horizontal ruler. When you apply an indent option, you can specify which lines to move and how many spaces to move them.

Setting a Left Indent

You can use left indents to draw attention to an entire paragraph or to set off quoted material. You indent paragraphs from the left margin by clicking the Increase Indent button on the Formatting toolbar. You

CAUTION TIP

It's easy to accidentally drag the First Line, Hanging, or Left Indent markers on the ruler beyond the document's left margin. In Normal view, if you can still see the indent marker, drag it back to the appropriate position. Then click the scroll box on the horizontal scroll bar to reposition the screen. If you can no longer see the indent markers, switch to Print Layout view, drag the indent markers to the right, and then return to Normal view.

The first paragraph is now indented ¾ inch from both the left and right margins. You can remove the indents by selecting the paragraph and dragging the indent markers back to the left or right margin. To remove the left and right indents from the first paragraph:

Step 1	*Click*	in the first paragraph to select it, if necessary
Step 2	*Drag*	the Right Indent marker back to the right margin
Step 3	*Drag*	the Left Indent marker back to the left margin

The first line of any paragraph can be repositioned to the left or right of the other lines by using the First Line Indent option.

Setting a First Line Indent

You can use the First Line Indent marker on the horizontal ruler to indent just the first line of a paragraph leaving the remaining lines in their original position. You often see first-line indents in long text documents, such as books and reports. You decide to indent the first line of each paragraph in the report. To indent the first line of each text paragraph with the First Line Indent marker:

Step 1	*Verify*	that the insertion point is in the first text paragraph
Step 2	*Move*	the mouse pointer to the First Line Indent marker ▼ on the horizontal ruler (see Figure 6-7)

FIGURE 6-7
First Line Indent Marker

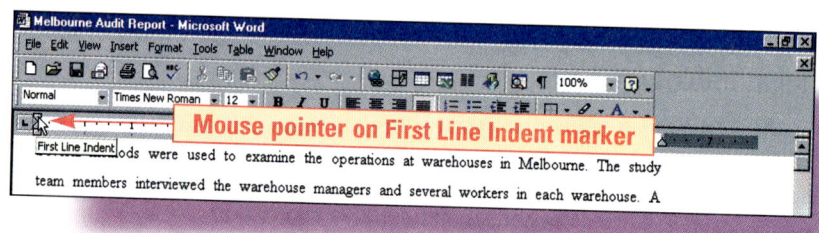

QUICK TIP

By default Word uses a First Line Indent when you press the TAB key for a line of text that is already keyed in the document. You can turn this feature on or off in the Edit tab of the Options dialog box.

Step 3	*Drag*	the First Line Indent marker to the ½-inch position on the horizontal ruler
Step 4	*Observe*	that the first line of the paragraph is indented to the ½-inch position
Step 5	*Continue*	to indent the first line of each of the other five text paragraphs (turn on the formatting marks, if necessary, to see each paragraph mark)

It's easier to find the beginning of each paragraph with the first line indented.

Setting a Hanging Indent

Certain paragraphs need a special kind of indent—a hanging indent, which leaves the first line at its original position and moves all the remaining lines to the right. Hanging indents are often used to create bulleted lists, numbered lists, and bibliographies. You can create a hanging indent with the Hanging Indent marker on the horizontal ruler. To create a hanging indent for the first paragraph:

Step 1	*Move*	the insertion point to the first paragraph
Step 2	*Move*	the mouse pointer to the Hanging Indent marker ⌂ on the horizontal ruler (see Figure 6-8)

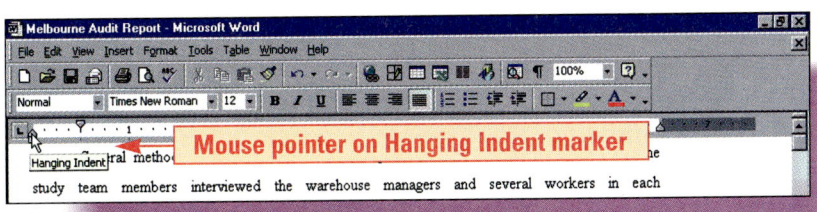

FIGURE 6-8
Hanging Indent Marker

Step 3	*Drag*	the Hanging Indent marker to the 1-inch position
Step 4	*Observe*	that the first line remains at the ¾-inch position and the remaining lines of the paragraph move to the 1-inch position on the horizontal ruler

To undo the hanging indent:

Step 1	*Press*	the CTRL + Z keys to undo the hanging indent
Step 2	*Save*	the document and close it

Indents enable you to position text on the page exactly where you want it.

chapter
six

Summary

▶ Paragraph formatting includes line spacing, vertical and horizontal text alignment, and indents.

▶ When applying paragraph formatting, you must select the paragraph or paragraphs to be formatted before you select the formatting option.

▶ You can select different line-spacing options such as Single, Double, and 1.5 from the Line spacing: list in the Paragraph dialog box.

▶ Text can be aligned vertically from the top margin, centered between the top and bottom margins, and justified between the top and bottom margins.

▶ Horizontal alignment is positioning text between the left and right margins. There are four horizontal alignment options: left, center, right, and justified.

▶ You can indent paragraphs from the left margin, the right margin, or both margins.

▶ Paragraphs can be indented with options in the Paragraph dialog box, buttons on the Formatting toolbar, and by dragging the indent markers on the horizontal ruler. Indentation options include First Line, Hanging, Left, and Right Indents.

Commands Review

Action	Menu Bar	Shortcut Menu	Toolbar	Keyboard
Change line spacing	Format, Paragraph	Right-click selected paragraph(s), click Paragraph		ALT + O, P CTRL + 1 (single) CTRL + 2 (double) CTRL + 5 (1.5)
Change alignment	Format, Paragraph	Right-click selected paragraph(s), click Paragraph	Align Left Center Align Right Justify	ALT + O, P CTRL + L (Left) CTRL + E (Center) CTRL + R (Right) CTRL + J (Justify)
Indent paragraphs	Format, Paragraph	Right-click selected paragraph(s), click Paragraph	Drag the indent marker on the horizontal ruler	ALT + O, P CTRL + M (from Left) CTRL + T (Hanging)
Remove paragraph formatting				CTRL + Q
Review text formatting				SHIFT + F1

Concepts Review

Circle the correct answer.

1. The default line spacing is:
- [a] Justified.
- [b] Single.
- [c] Double.
- [d] Center.

2. To change the line spacing for multiple paragraphs, you must first:
- [a] center the paragraphs.
- [b] justify the paragraphs.
- [c] select the paragraphs.
- [d] apply bold formatting to the paragraphs.

3. The Justified vertical alignment option:
- [a] aligns text with the top margin.
- [b] centers text between the left and right margins.
- [c] distributes text evenly between the top and bottom margins.
- [d] centers text evenly between the top and bottom margins.

4. To format a document with even left and right margins, you should apply the:
- [a] Center vertical alignment.
- [b] Center horizontal alignment.
- [c] Justify horizontal alignment.
- [d] Justified vertical alignment.

5. You cannot indent selected paragraphs by:
- [a] dragging an indent marker on the horizontal ruler.
- [b] clicking the Increase Indent button.
- [c] keying the indent position in the Paragraph dialog box.
- [d] keying the indent position in the Font dialog box.

6. A hanging indent moves:
- [a] all the lines of a paragraph to the right.
- [b] all the lines of a paragraph to the left.
- [c] only the top line.
- [d] all lines except the top line.

7. Which of the following is not part of paragraph formatting?
- [a] underlining
- [b] indenting
- [c] line spacing
- [d] horizontal alignment

8. The Multiple line-spacing option sets the line spacing to:
- [a] twice the single line spacing.
- [b] double the single line spacing.
- [c] 1.5 times the single line spacing.
- [d] a percentage of the single line spacing.

9. Ragged margins are:
- [a] even.
- [b] centered.
- [c] justified.
- [d] uneven.

10. When document text aligns at the left margin and has a ragged right margin, the text is:
- [a] center-aligned.
- [b] left-aligned.
- [c] right-aligned.
- [d] justified.

chapter six

Circle **T** if the statement is true or **F** is the statement is false.

T   F   1. The default horizontal alignment is left alignment.

T   F   2. You can set line spacing with the mouse and the horizontal and vertical ruler.

T   F   3. Word double-spaces your document unless you change the line spacing.

T   F   4. Justified alignment means that text is aligned only along the left margin.

T   F   5. You must press the TAB key to indent a paragraph.

T   F   6. A paragraph can be indented from the right margin.

T   F   7. You can add line-spacing buttons to the Formatting toolbar.

T   F   8. Line spacing means to specify the horizontal space between characters.

T   F   9. Vertical text alignment specifies where the text appears in relation to the top and bottom margins.

T   F   10. When applying paragraph formatting to an entire document, only the first paragraph must be selected.

 **notes**   For the remainder of this text, when you open a letter or memo document from the Data Disk or key a new document from a figure, replace the text "Current date" with the actual date using the AutoComplete feature or the Date and Time command on the Insert menu.

Skills Review

Exercise 1

1. Open the *Expense Guidelines* document located on the Data Disk.

2. Set the appropriate margins for an unbound report.

3. Format the Expense Guidelines title to change the case to uppercase and apply bold, 14 point, centered alignment formats.

4. Justify the body paragraphs between the left and right margins.

5. Double-space the body paragraphs.

6. Save the document as *Expense Guidelines Revised*.

7. Preview, print, and close the document.

Exercise 2

1. Open the *Interoffice Training Memo* located on the Data Disk.

2. Change the margins to the appropriate margins for an interoffice memorandum.

3. Set a tab stop to line up the heading paragraphs.

4. Change the case of the To, From, Date, and Subject headings to uppercase.

5. Indent the two paragraphs beginning "Samantha" and "Steve" ½ inch from both the left and the right margins.

6. Save the document as *Interoffice Training Memo Revised*.

7. Preview, print, and close the document.

Exercise 3

1. Open the *District C Sales Decline* document located on the Data Disk.

2. Set a 2-inch top margin and 1.5-inch left and right margins.

3. Double-space and justify the entire document.

4. Single-space and center the stores paragraphs.

5. Save the document as *District C Sales Decline Revised*.

6. Preview, print, and close the document.

Exercise 4

1. Create the following document.

2. Use the default margins.

3. Right align the current date on the first line.

4. Center align the title four lines below the date and format it with bold, 14-point font.

5. Apply bold formatting to the NAME, ADDRESS, TELEPHONE NUMBER, AGE, and GENDER text.

6. Set left tab stops to position the AGE and GENDER text attractively.

7. Set center tab stops for the column titles to center them over the column text.

8. Set left tab stops for the column text to align the text evenly in columns.

9. Triple-space all the text except the text in columns using the Multiple line-spacing option.

10. Use the 1.5 line-spacing option for the columnar text.

11. Center the text vertically between the top and bottom margins.

12. Save the document as *Order Form*.

13. Preview, print, and close the document.

chapter six

Current date

ORDER FORM

Please fill out the information below using a ballpoint pen. Please print legibly.

NAME:

ADDRESS:

TELEPHONE NUMBER: **AGE:**   **GENDER:**

Please circle the items you wish to order:

Item	Size	Box	Color
12D345	3 pound	round	red
89C367	4 pound	square	green
44F890	6 pound	triangle	black
78B779	2 pound	circle	yellow

Exercise 5

1. Open the *Vancouver Draft* document located on the Data Disk.
2. Set margins for an unbound report.
3. Change the font for the entire document to Times New Roman, 12 point.
4. Center-align, bold, and format with Times New Roman 14-point font the title "Vancouver Warehouse Report."
5. Double-space the entire document.
6. Justify the body paragraphs between the left and right margins.
7. Apply the Small Caps effect and bold formatting to the paragraph heading "Audit Methods."
8. Copy the Small Caps effect and bold formatting to the "Problems," "Problem Analyses," and "Summation" paragraph headings.
9. Create a center-aligned bulleted list with the three paragraphs beginning "Poor Communication."
10. Single-space the bulleted list.
11. Right-align the current date on the second line below the body paragraphs.
12. Save the document as *Vancouver Draft Revised*.
13. Preview, print, and close the document.

Exercise 6

1. Open the *Vancouver Draft Revised* document you created in Exercise 5.

2. Select the entire document.

3. Press the CTRL + Q keys to remove the paragraph formatting.

4. Press the CTRL + SPACEBAR keys to remove the character formatting.

5. Save the document as *Vancouver Draft Without Formatting*.

6. Preview, print, and close the document.

Exercise 7

1. Open the *Policy #113* document located on the Data Disk.

2. Use the default margins.

3. Set the line spacing for the entire document to 4 times the single line spacing.

4. Center-align, apply 14-point Times New Roman font, and apply bold formatting to the text "DANGER! DANGER! DANGER!"

5. Center-align the "Authorized Personnel Only" paragraph.

6. Center-align and apply the All Caps and italic effect to the last line of text.

7. Vertically center the text on the page.

8. Save the document as *Policy #113 Revised*.

9. Preview, print, and close the document.

Exercise 8

1. Open the *Word Division* document located on the Data Disk.

2. Set margins for an unbound report.

3. Set the line spacing for the entire document to 1.5 lines.

4. Format the title "Word Division" with bold, 14-point font, and center align it.

5. Justify the body paragraphs horizontally.

6. Indent the first line of the body paragraphs ½ inch from the left margin using the First Line Indent marker on the horizontal ruler.

7. Create a numbered list with the three paragraphs beginning "A one-letter syllable" and ending with "the contraction doesn't." Right indent the numbered list paragraphs to the 5½-inch position on the horizontal ruler.

8. Save the document as *Word Division Revised*.

9. Preview, print, and close the document.

Exercise 9

1. Create the following document.

2. Set the appropriate margins.

3. Set the appropriate line spacing.

chapter six

4. Use the appropriate horizontal and vertical alignment.

5. Indent the body paragraphs.

6. Format the title.

7. Save the document as *Investment Analysis*.

8. Preview, print, and close the document.

INVESTMENT ANALYSIS

This is an excellent time for you to take a close look at the income you are receiving from the tax-exempt bonds in your portfolio. When you bought the bonds, did you buy fixed income or lifetime maturation?

Essentially any person can earn funds today, but only an informed person will know how to correctly invest their extra money to gain utmost safety of principal and gain the greatest growth in investment appreciation.

To many investors, earnings are the most important part of their investment program. It is their maintenance income, their retirement plan, their self-insurance for children and grandchildren, as well as their trust for charities.

Current date

Case Projects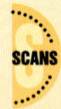

Project 1

Kelly Armstead asks you how to use different paragraph spacing options in the Paragraph dialog box and character spacing options in the Font dialog box. Using Word help features, review information on character and paragraph spacing. Create a new interoffice memorandum to Kelly, containing at least four paragraphs, that describes how to use the character and paragraph spacing options. Open an existing document and change the character and paragraph spacing. Save the document with a new name, and then preview and print it.

Project 2

B. D. Vickers believes you can purchase and print postage over the Internet. Connect to your ISP, launch your Web browser, and search the Web for pages containing information about purchasing and printing postage on the Web. Create a favorite or bookmark for the home page at each site you visit. Create an interoffice memorandum to B. D. Vickers describing how to purchase and print postage from pages on the Web. Save, preview, and print the document.

Project 3

One of the new employees in the purchasing department is having a problem creating evenly spaced lines in a document that contains large text characters on various lines. Using the Office Assistant, search for help topics on setting line spacing for this type of document. Create a new unbound report document containing a title and a numbered list of instructions on changing the line spacing to create evenly spaced lines with mixed-size characters. Save, preview, and print the document. With your instructor's permission, demonstrate these instructions to a classmate.

Project 4

Kelly asks you to prepare an interoffice memorandum to all purchasing department employees reminding them of the annual purchasing conference to be held in three weeks in Vancouver. Anyone who plans to attend the conference must contact her no later than next Thursday to arrange for someone to handle their responsibilities while they are at the conference. Use character, paragraph, and document formatting features to make the memo interesting to read and professional in appearance. Save, preview, and print the document.

Project 5

Kelly tells you that Word provides a special toolbar you can use to open your Web browser and load Web pages from inside Word. Connect to your ISP

and view the Web toolbar using the toolbar shortcut menu. Use the Favorites button to display a Web page with information about purchasing and printing postage on the Web. Create an interoffice memorandum to Kelly describing how to view and use the Web toolbar. Save, preview, and print the document.

Project 6

Kelly wants you to create a one-page cover sheet for an audit report on the Melbourne branch that she is completing. She wants the title of the report to contain B. D. Vickers name and title and the current date triple spaced, in a 14-point font, and centered vertically and horizontally on the page. Create, save, preview, and print the cover sheet.

Project 7

Kelly asks you to present some troubleshooting tips on indenting text at the next meeting of the International Association of Executive Assistants. Using Word help features, review how to indent text. Create a new document containing a list of at least five indenting troubleshooting tips. Save, preview, and print the document. With your instructor's approval demonstrate these troubleshooting tips to several classmates.

Project 8

Rick Johns, a new employee in the purchasing department, asks for your help in setting line-spacing options in a document. Using Word help features, research how to set all the different line-spacing options. Create an interoffice memorandum to Rick containing a description of each of the line-spacing options and how to use them in a document. Include examples of each option in your document. Save, preview, and print the document.

chapter six

Previewing and Printing a Document

Chapter Overview

Previewing documents before printing them enables you to find errors you might otherwise not notice until you print. You can fix any problems you find right in Print Preview, whether they are text edits or formatting changes. In this chapter you learn how to edit a document in Print Preview and set print options.

Case profile

Worldwide Exotic Foods requires all employees to preview their documents and make necessary changes before printing to prevent reprinting and keep costs down. Kelly Armstead needs your help in previewing, editing, and printing several documents previously created.

chapter
seven

7.a Using Print Preview

Print Preview displays your document onscreen exactly as it will print on paper. When viewing a document in Print Preview, you can see one or more pages of your document. Headers, footers, margins, page numbers, text, and graphics can also be seen in Print Preview.

The first document Kelly asks you to finalize and print is an *Analysis Report*. To open and preview a document:

Step 1	*Open*	the *Analysis Report* document located on the Data Disk
Step 2	*Verify*	the insertion point is at the top of the document
Step 3	*Click*	the Print Preview button 🔍 on the Standard toolbar
Step 4	*Click*	the One Page button 🔲 on the Print Preview toolbar to view only the first page of the document, if necessary

The first page of the *Analysis Report* document appears in Print Preview. Your screen should look similar to Figure 7-1.

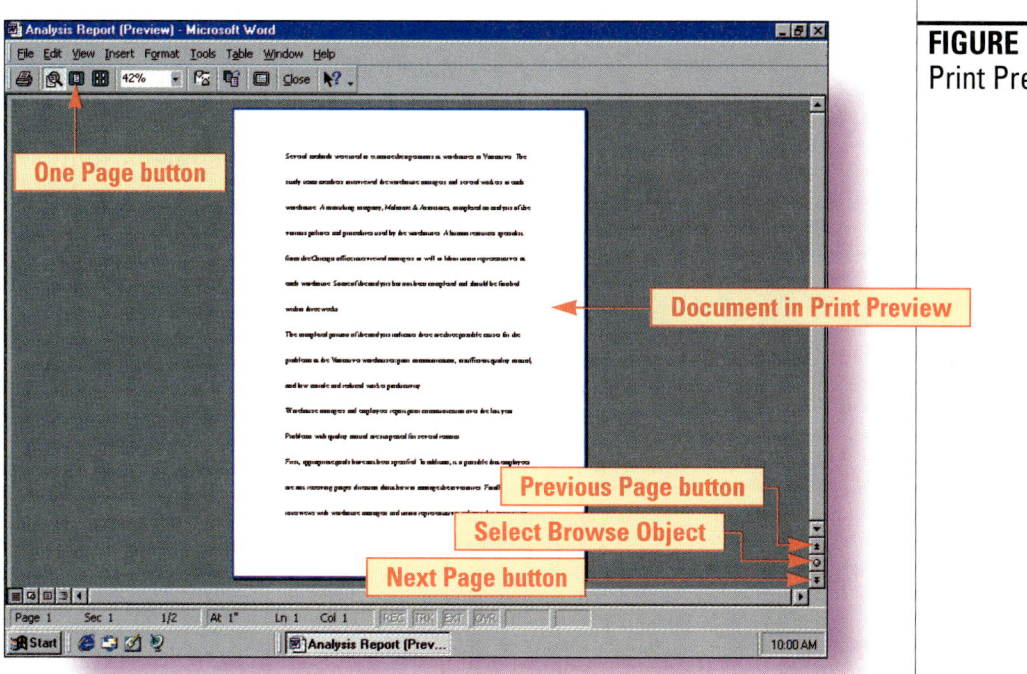

FIGURE 7-1
Print Preview

> **MENU TIP**
>
> You can click the Print Preview command on the File menu to see how your document looks before it is printed.

When viewing only one page of a multiple-page document, you can use the vertical scroll bar or the Previous Page or Next Page buttons located below the vertical scroll bar to scroll among the pages.

You view the second page of the *Analysis Report* document.

chapter
seven

| Step 5 | *Click* | the Next Page button ⬇ below the vertical scroll bar to view page two |
| Step 6 | *Click* | the Previous Page button ⬆ below the vertical scroll bar to view the first page again |

QUICK TIP

The Next and Previous buttons are controlled by the options in the Select Browse Object button. The default option is Page. When the Page option is selected in the Select Browse Object grid, the Next and Previous buttons have black arrows and are used to browse by page in all editing views including Print Preview. When a different option is selected in the Select Browse Object grid, the Next and Previous buttons have blue arrows and become the Next and Previous browse buttons for the option selected in the Select Browse Object grid. To reset the buttons to Next and Previous Page, click the Select Browse Object button and then click Page on the grid.

The One Page button on the Print Preview toolbar displays a single page at a time. You can use the Multiple Pages button on the Print Preview toolbar to view two or more small, thumbnail-sized pages at one time. When you view several thumbnail-sized pages at one time you can compare how the text appears on subsequent pages and where the page breaks occur. To view both pages of the *Analysis Report* document side by side:

Step 1	*Click*	the Multiple Pages button ⊞ on the Print Preview toolbar to view the Multiple Pages grid
Step 2	*Point to*	the second square in the top row of the grid
Step 3	*Observe*	the 1×2 Pages notation at the bottom of the grid
Step 4	*Click*	the second square in the top row
Step 5	*Observe*	both pages of the document display side by side
Step 6	*Observe*	the dark blue border around the first page

The dark border indicates the active page of the document. Your screen should look similar to Figure 7-2.

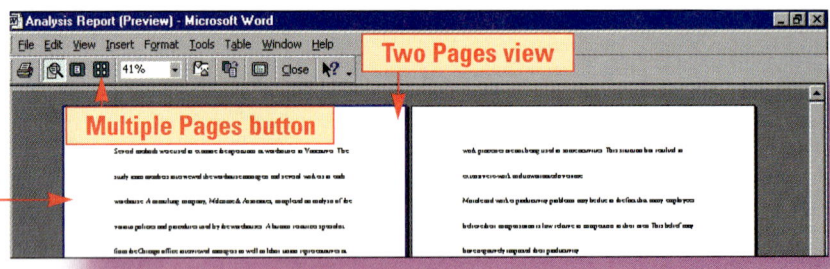

Active Page   **Multiple Pages button**   **Two Pages view**

FIGURE 7-2
Two Pages View

You can zoom or edit individual pages when viewing more than one page by first making a page the active page. To activate a page, simply click it with the mouse pointer.

| Step 7 | *Click* | page two |
| Step 8 | *Click* | page one |

Not only can you see how your document looks before you print it, you can also edit your document in Print Preview. You can key text, apply formatting, set tab stops and paragraph indents, and change margins in Print Preview. For easier viewing, you can magnify, or zoom, a portion of the document with the magnifying pointer or the Zoom button on the Print Preview toolbar.

The **Magnifier** button on the Print Preview toolbar is a toggle switch that turns on or off the zoom pointer. By default, the Magnifier button and the zoom pointer are turned on when you Print Preview a document. When the Magnifier button is turned on and the mouse pointer is positioned on a selected page, it changes into the zoom pointer. If multiple pages are displayed, you should first select a page by clicking it and then position the mouse pointer on it.

To view just single pages and zoom the first page:

Step 1	*Click*	the One Page button 🔲 on the Print Preview toolbar
Step 2	*Move*	the mouse pointer to the beginning of the first paragraph on the page
Step 3	*Observe*	that the mouse pointer changes into a zoom pointer (a magnifying glass with a plus sign in the middle)

Your screen should look similar to Figure 7-3.

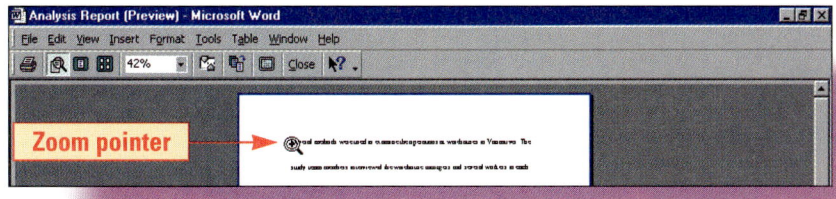

FIGURE 7-3
Zoom Pointer

Step 4	*Click*	the paragraph with the zoom pointer
Step 5	*Observe*	that the document is zoomed to 100% and you are viewing the portion of the first paragraph you clicked
Step 6	*Observe*	that the mouse pointer is still the zoom pointer (a magnifying glass with a minus sign in the middle)
Step 7	*Click*	the document with the zoom pointer

The document is zoomed to one page. You need to change the margins for the *Analysis Report* document. Because you are already viewing the document in Print Preview, you decide to do make the change here. The same formatting features that are available in Normal or Print Layout view are available in Print Preview. For example, you can open the Page

QUICK TIP

You can select and view individual pages of a multiple-page document by pressing the PAGE UP or PAGE DOWN keys. You can show additional toolbars in Print Preview with the toolbar shortcut menu or you can customize the Print Preview toolbar by clicking the More Buttons list arrow and then pointing to Add or Remove Buttons.

You can close the Print Preview of the current document with the taskbar shortcut menu. This does not close the document. It returns you to previous Normal or Print Layout view.

chapter
seven

Setup dialog box from the <u>F</u>ile menu in Print Preview just as you can in Normal or Print Layout view. To set the margins for an unbound report:

Step 1	*Open*	the Page Setup dialog box and click the <u>M</u>argins tab, if necessary
Step 2	*Set*	the appropriate margins for an unbound report
Step 3	*Observe*	the new margins

To key or format selected text in Print Preview, you must first have an insertion point and an I-beam. When you turn off the Magnifier button, the insertion point appears and the mouse pointer becomes an I-beam when you position it over the document. To see the insertion point and the I-beam:

Step 1	*Click*	the Magnifier button on the Print Preview toolbar to turn off the zoom pointer
Step 2	*Move*	the mouse pointer to the top of the page
Step 3	*Observe*	the mouse pointer is now an I-beam and you can see the small, flashing insertion point at the top of the document
Step 4	*Click*	the Zoom button list arrow on the Print Preview toolbar
Step 5	*Click*	75% so you can see the text well enough to edit it

Your screen should look similar to Figure 7-4.

FIGURE 7-4
Document Zoomed to 75%

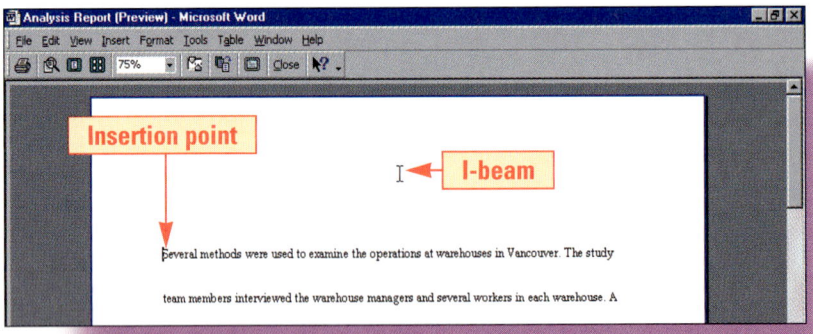

Now you can see the text and the insertion point more easily. You want to indent the first line of all the paragraphs. You can show the horizontal and vertical rulers in Print Preview and then indent individual paragraphs or you can select the entire document, open the Paragraph dialog box, and indent all the paragraphs at the same time.

To indent the first line of each paragraph ½ inch from the left margin:

Step 1	*Select*	the entire document
Step 2	*Open*	the Indents and Spacing tab in the Paragraph dialog box
Step 3	*Click*	the Special: list arrow
Step 4	*Click*	First line
Step 5	*Key*	.5 in the By: text box, if necessary
Step 6	*Click*	OK
Step 7	*Deselect*	the text
Step 8	*Click*	the Zoom button list arrow on the Print Preview toolbar
Step 9	*Click*	Two Pages
Step 10	*Observe*	the indented paragraphs
Step 11	*Zoom*	the first page to 75%

You believe the *Analysis Report* document should have a title. You can key and format that title when the Magnifier button is turned off and you see the insertion point and the I-beam. To key and format a title:

Step 1	*Insert*	a blank line at the top of the first page
Step 2	*Move*	the insertion point to the new blank line
Step 3	*Key*	the title Analysis Report
Step 4	*Select*	the title text using the I-beam
Step 5	*Format*	the title text with Bold using a shortcut menu and the Font dialog box
Step 6	*Center*	the title text using a shortcut menu and the Paragraph dialog box
Step 7	*Zoom*	the first page to One Page (See Figure 7-5)

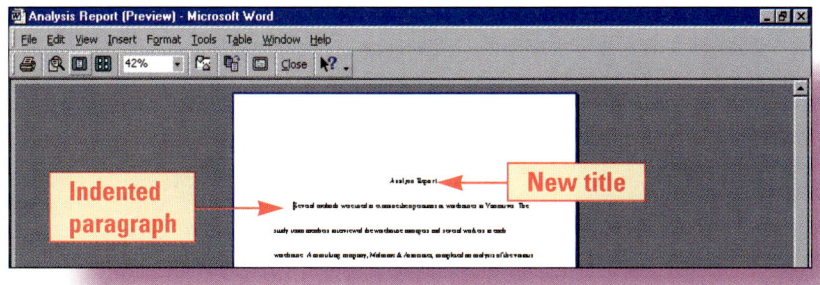

FIGURE 7-5
New Title and
Indented Paragraphs

| Step 8 | *Click* | the <u>C</u>lose button Close on the Print Preview toolbar |
| Step 9 | *Save* | the document as *Revised Analysis Report* |

The document looks good with the correct margins, paragraph indentation, and title. Now you're ready to print it.

 # 7.b Printing A Document

After you correct the margins and paragraph indentations, you are ready to print the document. However, before you print it, you might need to change the paper size, paper orientation, or paper source. The Page Setup dialog box provides options for you to change the paper size, paper orientation, and the paper source before you print a document. Word provides a list of common paper sizes from which to choose, including Letter 8½ × 11 in; Legal 8½ × 14 in, and Envelope #10 4⅛ × 9½ in. You can also choose a paper **orientation** (the direction text is printed on the paper): Portrait or Landscape. **Portrait orientation** means that the short edge of the paper is the top of the page. **Landscape orientation** means that the long edge of the paper is the top of the page. To review the current settings in the Page Setup dialog box:

| Step 1 | *Open* | the Page Setup dialog box |
| Step 2 | *Click* | the Paper <u>S</u>ize tab |

The dialog box on your screen should look similar to Figure 7-6.

FIGURE 7-6
Paper <u>S</u>ize Tab in the Page
Setup Dialog Box

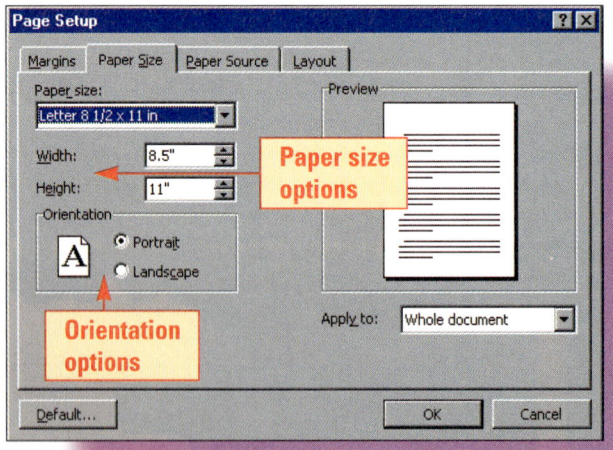

The Paper size: list box provides a list of pre-set paper sizes. You can also select a Custom size from the list and then specify the paper dimensions in the Width: and Height: text boxes. By default, the paper size is Letter (8½ × 11 in) and the orientation is Portrait. You can change the orientation by clicking the appropriate option button. By default, the paper size and orientation settings apply to the whole document. You can change this option with the Apply to: list. As you change the options, the Preview area shows a sample of the document. After you review the options, you can close the dialog box without making changes.

| Step 3 | *Click* | Cancel |

Printing is usually your final activity in document creation. You can print a document by clicking the Print button on the Print Preview toolbar or the Standard toolbar. However, when you click the Print button, you do not get an opportunity to change the print options in the Print dialog box.

The Print command on the File menu opens the Print dialog box, which contains options and print settings you can modify before printing a document. To set the print options for the *Revised Analysis Report*:

| Step 1 | *Click* | File |
| Step 2 | *Click* | Print |

The dialog box on your screen should look similar to Figure 7-7.

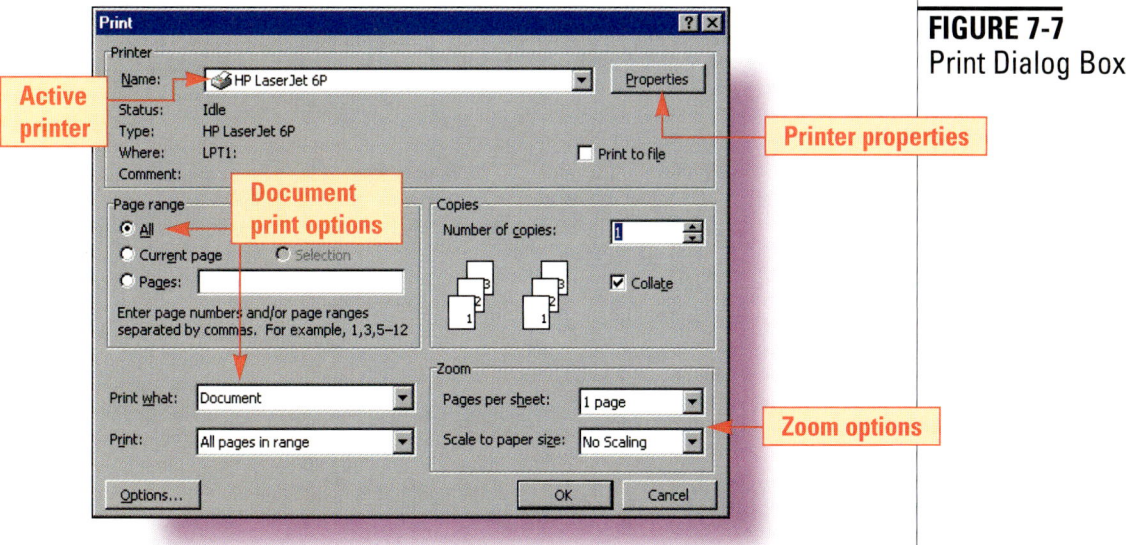

FIGURE 7-7
Print Dialog Box

chapter
seven

QUICK TIP

You can view the properties such as default paper size, default page orientation, graphics resolution for the selected printer with the Properties button in the Print dialog box.

You can specify a number of different print options by clicking the Options button in the Print dialog box or by clicking the Print tab in the Options dialog box.

The active printer is identified in the Name: list box. You can select from a list of available printers by clicking the list arrow and clicking the printer you want to use.

By default, Word prints one copy of your entire document. The Print what: list box provides a list of items you can print other than your document. For example, to print a list of AutoText entries stored in the Normal template, select AutoText entries from this list.

You can specify the number of copies to print in the Number of copies: text box. The Page range group contains options for printing All pages, the Current page that contains the insertion point, the Selection of highlighted text, or the Pages you specify by page number. The Print: list box allows you to print only odd or even pages in a selected page range. By default, Word **collates** or orders copies of a multiple-page document in binding order as it prints. You can turn off the collating option by removing the check mark from the Collate check box.

Printing your document to a file is helpful if you want to print on a higher-quality printer at a different location or on a computer that does not have the Word program. You can print your document to a file on a disk, rather than send it to a printer, by inserting a check mark in the Print to file check box.

Text can be scaled to fit multiple pages on one sheet of paper or scaled to fit to various paper sizes in the Zoom group. Use this feature to scale larger documents to fit smaller paper or print several miniature document pages on one sheet of paper.

| Step 3 | *Click* | Print to print the document |
| Step 4 | *Save* | the document and close it |

The printed *Revised Analysis Report* is ready to be duplicated and distributed to the Worldwide Exotic Foods branch managers.

Summary

- ▶ In order to avoid printing a document that contains errors—which can waste time and money—it is a good practice to preview your document before you print it.

- ▶ You can view one page or multiple pages of your document in Print Preview.

- ▶ Print Preview enables you to view headers, footers, margins, page numbers, text, and graphics.

- ▶ You can edit a document by keying text, applying formatting, setting tab stops, indenting paragraphs, and changing margins in Print Preview.

- ▶ You can turn off the Magnifier button in Print Preview and then key and edit text in the document.

- ▶ In Print Preview, you can zoom in for a closer view of a document either by turning on the Magnifier button and clicking the document with the mouse pointer or by using the Zoom button on the Print Preview toolbar.

- ▶ Before you print your document, you can set print and page setup options in the Print and Page Setup dialog boxes.

- ▶ The Print button on the Print Preview or Standard toolbars prints the document without allowing you to review the settings in the Print dialog box. The Print command on the File menu allows you to open the Print dialog box and confirm or change print options before you print a document.

Commands Review

Action	Menu Bar	Shortcut Menu	Toolbar	Keyboard
Preview a document	File, Print Preview		🔍	ALT + F, V CTRL + F2
View multiple pages in Print Preview			▦	
View one page in Print Preview			▣	
Magnify a document in Print Preview			🔍	
Print a document	File, Print		🖨	ALT + F, P CTRL + SHIFT + F12 CTRL + P

chapter seven

Concepts Review

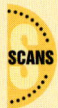

Circle the correct answer.

1. **By default, Print Preview displays your document:**
   [a] in two pages.
   [b] in multiple pages.
   [c] exactly as it will print on paper.
   [d] in Landscape orientation.

2. **The Magnifier button:**
   [a] scrolls to a new page.
   [b] shows the horizontal and vertical rulers.
   [c] shows two pages side by side.
   [d] allows you to zoom your document with the mouse pointer.

3. **You set the default print orientation in the:**
   [a] printer Properties dialog box.
   [b] Page Setup dialog box.
   [c] Page Layout dialog box.
   [d] Options dialog box.

4. **The default paper size and orientation is:**
   [a] 11 × 18 inch, Portrait.
   [b] 8½ × 12 inch, Landscape.
   [c] 8½ × 11 inch, Portrait.
   [d] A4, Portrait.

5. **To key or format selected text in Print Preview, you must use the:**
   [a] zoom pointer.
   [b] horizontal ruler.
   [c] I-beam.
   [d] Magnifier button.

6. **When Word automatically collates a printed document it:**
   [a] saves the document to a file.
   [b] prints AutoText entries.
   [c] prints copies of multiple-page documents in binding order.
   [d] scales larger documents to fit on smaller paper.

7. **The actions of the Next and Previous buttons in Print Preview are controlled by the:**
   [a] vertical scroll bar.
   [b] Magnifier button.
   [c] Zoom button.
   [d] Select Browse Object button.

8. **You can key text in your document in Print Preview by first:**
   [a] minimizing the window.
   [b] viewing multiple pages.
   [c] zooming the document.
   [d] turning off the Magnifier button.

9. **You can view and change print options by clicking the:**
   [a] Printer command on the File menu.
   [b] Options command on the Tools menu.
   [c] Print Options command on the Print Preview menu.
   [d] Set Print Options button in the Print dialog box.

10. **Which of the following options is not available in the Print dialog box?**
   [a] Print to file
   [b] Collate copies
   [c] Set the paper orientation
   [d] Print selected text

Circle **T** if the statement is true or **F** if the statement is false.

T   F   1. To print only the page containing the insertion point, you should select the <u>A</u>ll option in the Print dialog box.

T   F   2. To print the entire document that you are currently editing, you should select the Curr<u>e</u>nt Page option in the Print dialog box.

T   F   3. If you key 1-4 in the Pages text box in the Print dialog box, Word prints only pages 1 and 4 of the document.

T   F   4. The Letter (8½ × 11 in) paper size is the default paper size.

T   F   5. It is not possible to print only odd or even pages.

T   F   6. You can change margins, tab stops, or paragraph indents in Print Preview.

T   F   7. The Print button on the Print Preview toolbar opens the Print dialog box.

T   F   8. You can scale text to fit multiple pages on one sheet of paper.

T   F   9. You can view additional toolbars in Print Preview.

T   F   10. It is possible to print a document in reverse page number order.

Skills Review

Exercise 1

1. Open the *Vancouver Warehouse Report* document located on the Data Disk.

2. Print Preview the document.

3. Print only page 2 and close the document.

Exercise 2

1. Open the *Analysis Report* document located on the Data Disk.

2. Print the entire document using the Print button on the Standard toolbar in Normal view and close the document.

Exercise 3

1. Open the *Interoffice Meeting Memo* document located on the Data Disk.

2. Print Preview the document.

3. Apply bold formatting to the meeting day and time in the first paragraph in Print Preview.

4. Save the document as *Interoffice Meeting Memo Edited*.

5. Print the document from Print Preview and close the document.

Exercise 4

1. Open the *New Expense Guidelines* document located on the Data Disk.

2. Print Preview the document.

chapter seven

3. Format the title with the Arial, 16-point font in Print Preview and leave the insertion point in the title paragraph.

4. Save the document as *New Expense Guidelines Revised*.

5. Print only the current page from Print Preview and close the document.

Exercise 5

1. Open the *Research Results* document located on the Data Disk.

2. Print Preview the document.

3. Change the top margin to 2 inches and the left and right margins to 1 inch in Print Preview.

4. Create numbered paragraphs with the last two single spaced paragraphs in Print Preview.

5. Indent the numbered paragraphs ½ inch from the right margin in Print Preview.

6. Horizontally justify all the paragraphs in the document.

7. Save the document as *Research Results Revised*.

8. Print the document from Print Preview and close the document.

Exercise 6

1. Open the *Understanding The Internet* document located on the Data Disk.

2. Print pages 1 and 3 in Normal view and close the document.

Exercise 7

1. Open the *Understanding The Internet* document located on the Data Disk.

2. Print Preview the document.

3. View the document in multiple pages with 4 pages on 2 rows.

4. Remove the bold, italic formatting and apply bold, Small Caps effect to the side (paragraph) headings in Print Preview. (*Hint:* After selecting and formatting the first bold, italic paragraph heading, use the CTRL + Y shortcut keys to copy the formatting to the other bold, italic paragraph headings.)

5. Save the document as *The Internet And The Web*.

6. Print pages 2, 4, and 6 in Normal view.

7. Use the Zoom options in the Print dialog box to print the entire document two pages per sheet of paper and close the document.

Exercise 8

1. Create the following document.

2. Use the default margins and set the appropriate tab stops for the memo headings.

3. Print Preview the document.

4. Change the margins to the appropriate margins for an interoffice memorandum in Print Preview.

5. Change the font for the entire document to Arial, 12 point in Print Preview.

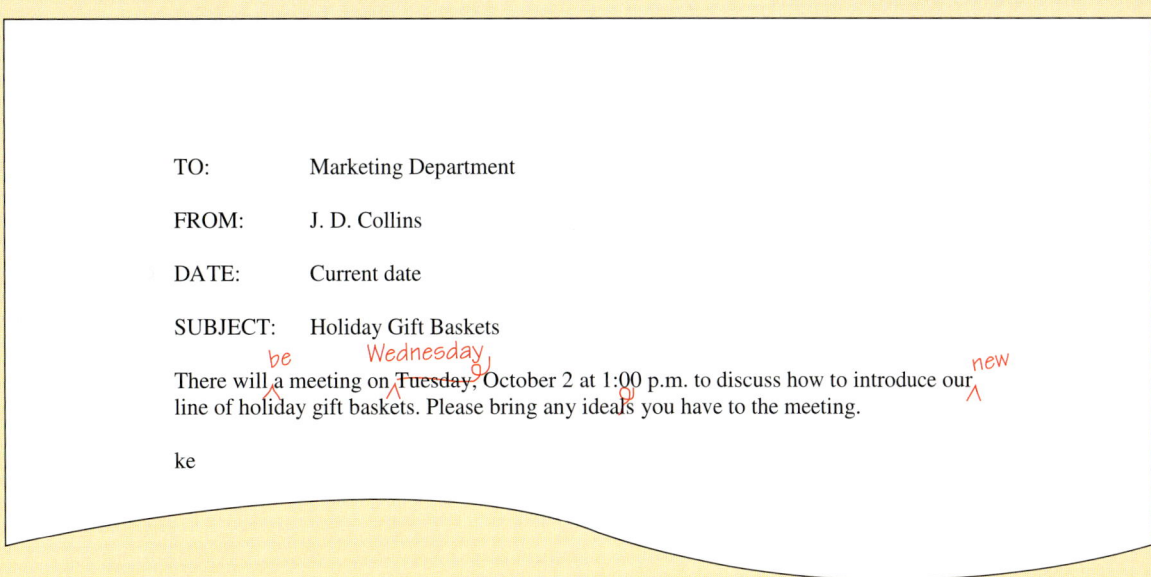

TO: Marketing Department

FROM: J. D. Collins

DATE: Current date

SUBJECT: Holiday Gift Baskets

There will a meeting on Tuesday, October 2 at 1:00 p.m. to discuss how to introduce our line of holiday gift baskets. Please bring any ideals you have to the meeting.

ke

6. bold formatting to the memo heading text TO, FROM, DATE, and SUBJECT (do not include the colon) in Print Preview.

7. Save the document as *Holiday Gift Baskets.*

8. Print the document from Print Preview and close the document.

Case Projects

Project 1

Kelly wants you to review setting different print options and then create a memo to all summer interns describing the print options and how to set them. Using the Word Help tools, review setting print options. Create a new interoffice memorandum to all summer interns, containing at least three paragraphs, that describes how to use at least three print options. Save, preview, and print the document.

Project 2

Dale Metcalf, a purchasing agent, asks you how to view and change the properties for his printer, which is the same model as your printer. Open the Print dialog box and review the Properties for your printer. Create an unbound report document containing at least four paragraphs describing the properties that are set for your printer. Save, preview, and print the document. With your instructor's permission, use the unbound report document as a guide to demonstrate viewing and changing printer properties to one of your classmates.

chapter seven

Project 3

You recently read an article in the company newsletter describing Internet newsgroups (online discussion groups) and would like to know more about how to participate in them. Connect to your ISP, launch your Web browser, and search for Web pages containing information on newsgroups. Save at least two Web pages as favorites or bookmarks. Print at least two Web pages. Create an unbound report, containing at least five paragraphs, that describes newsgroups and how to subscribe to them. Use vertical and horizontal alignment, line spacing, and indentation options to give the report a professional appearance. Save, preview, and print the report.

Project 4

B. D. Vickers needs to purchase several new laser printers for Worldwide Exotic Foods and wants to review which models are currently available. He asks you to use the Web to prepare a list of printers, their features, and cost. Connect to your ISP, launch your Web browser, and search for Web pages for vendors who sell laser printers. Gather printer information on at least three different vendors. Create an interoffice memorandum to B. D. Vickers discussing the results of your research. Save, preview, and print the memo.

Project 5

You are having lunch with Bob Garcia, the new administrative assistant, and he describes several problems he has when printing documents. He frequently gets a blank page at the end of his documents, sometimes the text runs off the edge of the page, he gets a "too many fonts" error when he prints a document, and occasionally the printed text he prints looks different from the text on the screen. You offer to look into the problems and get back to him. Using the Office Assistant, search for troubleshooting tips for printing documents and find suggested solutions to Bob's problems. Write Bob a memo describing each problem and suggesting a solution to the problem. Save, preview, and print the memo.

Project 6

Kelly wants a document she can use to train new employees how to set print options. She also wants to train the new employees to use the Zoom options in the Print dialog box. Open the Options dialog box and click the Print tab. Using the dialog box Help button, review each of the print options. Open the Print dialog box and review the Zoom options. Create an unbound report document titled "Print Options" and describe each of the options on the Print tab and the Print Zoom feature. Save, preview, and print the document. Attach a sample of a two-page document printed on one sheet of paper using the Zoom options.

Project 7

You just purchased a new printer, but do not know how to set up it up and define it as your default printer. Using online Help , research how to set up a new printer and define it as the default printer. Write Kelly Armstead a memo discussing the process. Save, preview, and print the memo.

Project 8

The Melbourne branch office manager is ill and B. D. Vickers wants to send flowers using a shop that accepts orders on the Web but isn't certain how to do this. Connect to your ISP, launch your Web browser, and search for Web pages with information about ordering and paying for flowers for international delivery to Melbourne, Australia. Print at least three Web pages. Create a memo to B. D. Vickers describing how to order and pay for flowers on the Web. Save, preview, and print the memo. Attach the Web pages you print to the memo.

Preparing and Printing Envelopes and Labels

Chapter Overview

Every business depends on its correspondence. Letters and packages need to be sent daily. Each needs an envelope or mailing label before it can be mailed. In this chapter you create, format, and print envelopes and labels.

Case profile

Kelly Armstead asks you to print envelopes and mailing labels. Worldwide Exotic Foods uses the U. S. Postal Service (USPS) guidelines for envelopes and mailing labels that do not have a corresponding letter. Envelopes and labels that do have a corresponding letter follow the punctuation and case of the letter address. You create an envelope that does not have a corresponding letter, an envelope for an existing letter, an envelope and label from a list of addresses, and a sheet of return address labels for B. D. Vickers.

chapter
eight

Before you begin the activities in this chapter, you should review Appendix C, Formatting Tips for Business Documents, if you have not already done so.

8.a Preparing and Printing Envelopes

Printing addresses on envelopes is a word processing task that almost everyone must perform at one time or another. Envelopes do not use the standard 8½ × 11 inch paper on which you normally print letters and reports. A standard Size 10 business envelope is 4⅛ × 9½ inches, and a standard short Size 6¾ envelope is 3⅝ × 6½ inches. You can create envelopes by opening an existing letter and letting Word identify the letter address as the envelope delivery address, or you can key the envelope delivery address in a blank document.

Because different printers have varying setup requirements for envelopes and labels, your instructor may provide additional printing instructions for the activities in this chapter.

Kelly needs an envelope for which there is no corresponding letter. She gives you a copy of the U. S. Postal Service (USPS) guidelines for envelopes and mailing labels to review before you begin (see Appendix C). The USPS delivery address guidelines require a sans serif font, uppercase characters, and no punctuation except for the hyphen in the ZIP + 4 code. Worldwide Exotic Foods uses the USPS guidelines for envelopes and labels that do not have a corresponding letter.

You can create an individual envelope by first creating a blank document. To create an envelope from a blank document:

Step 1	*Create*	a new, blank document, if necessary
Step 2	*Click*	Tools
Step 3	*Click*	Envelopes and Labels
Step 4	*Click*	the Envelopes tab, if necessary

The dialog box you see on your screen should look similar to Figure 8-1.

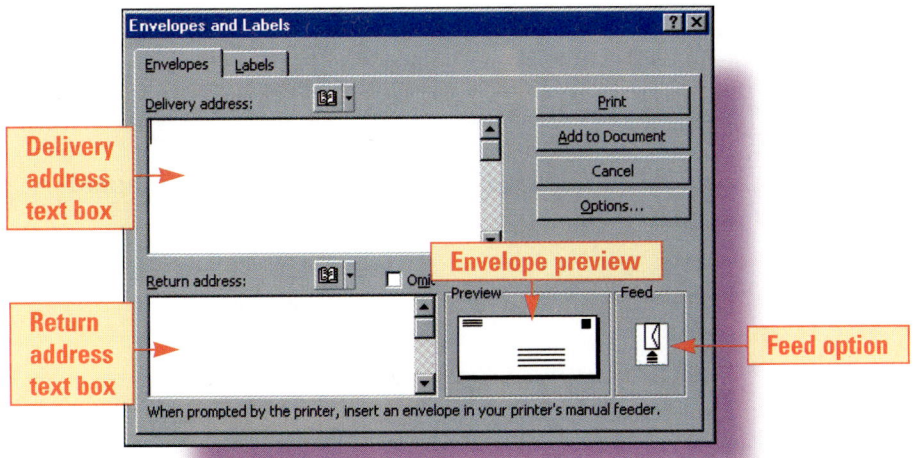

FIGURE 8-1
Envelopes and Labels
Dialog Box

You key the delivery address in the Delivery address: text box. You can edit or key the return address in the Return address: text box, which contains information from the User Information tab in the Options dialog box. If you are using envelopes with a preprinted return address, you can omit printing the return address by inserting a check mark in the Omit check box. The Feed image illustrates how to insert envelopes in the current printer. You click the Options button to change envelope size, select manual or tray feed for blank envelopes, change the feed position, print the Delivery point barcode, or add character formatting to the address text. You send the envelope directly to the printer with the Print button. The Add to Document button attaches the envelope to the current document for saving and printing with the document.

A **style** is a group of formatting attributes saved with a unique name. Word automatically formats the text you key in the Delivery address: text box with the Envelope Address style and the return address with the Envelope Return style. The Envelope Address style contains the sans serif Arial font with a 12-point font size. Next, you key the delivery address using the USPS guidelines. To key the envelope text:

Step 1	*Verify*	the insertion point is in the Delivery address: text box

Step 2	*Key*	MS ELAINE CHANG 719 EAST 35TH STREET ST PAUL MN 55117-1179

Because Worldwide Exotic Foods uses preprinted envelopes for all correspondence, you omit the return address. Then you select the envelope size.

Step 3	*Click*	the Omit check box to insert a check mark, if necessary

> ### QUICK TIP
>
> You can change the font of the delivery or return address in the Envelopes and Labels dialog box by selecting the text and then opening the Font dialog box with a shortcut menu.

chapter
eight

Step 4	*Click*	O̲ptions
Step 5	*Click*	the E̲nvelope Options tab, if necessary

The Envelope Options dialog box you see on your screen should look similar to Figure 8-2.

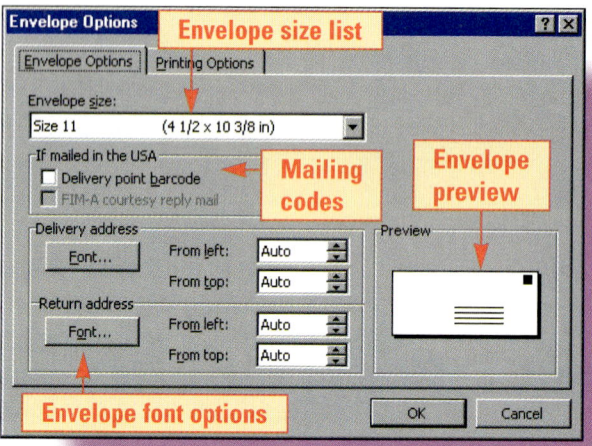

You can select the envelope size in the Envelope s̲ize: list box. Options for using the Facing Identification Mark (FIM-A) and Delivery point b̲arcode to speed mail delivery are in the If mailed in the USA group. For a more detailed explanation of these two codes, see online Help. You can also change the font and position of the envelope addresses. To change the envelope size:

Step 6	*Click*	the Envelope s̲ize: list arrow
Step 7	*Click*	Size 6¾ (3⅝ × 6½ in), if necessary
Step 8	*Observe*	that the sample envelope now displays the 6¾ size

You also set printing options in this dialog box. The current options are set for your printer. However, if necessary, you can specify envelope rotation, face up or down, and manual or tray feed in this tab. You accept the current printing options and envelope size. To review print options:

Step 1	*Click*	the P̲rinting Options tab
Step 2	*Observe*	the different Feed method options
Step 3	*Click*	OK

In order to print the envelope, you may have to manually feed a blank envelope or blank sheet of paper in your printer. If your instructor tells you to print the envelope, follow your printer's envelope setup instructions and print the envelope by clicking the Print button in the Envelopes and Labels dialog box. Otherwise you cancel the Chang envelope by closing the Envelopes and Labels dialog box. To close the dialog box:

| Step 1 | *Click* | Close |

Another way to create an envelope is to open a document that contains a list of frequently used delivery addresses, move the insertion point to one of the addresses, and open the Envelopes and Labels dialog box. Word enters the delivery address for you. Kelly maintains a list of delivery addresses for members of the International Association of Executive Assistants and asks you to create an envelope from this list. To open the address list document and create an envelope:

Step 1	*Open*	the *Envelope And Label List* document located on the Data Disk
Step 2	*Move*	the insertion point to the address for Elaine Fitzsimmons (scroll to view this address)
Step 3	*Click*	Tools
Step 4	*Click*	Envelopes and Labels
Step 5	*Click*	the Envelopes tab, if necessary

The Envelopes tab in the Envelopes and Labels dialog box opens with Elaine Fitzsimmons address in the Delivery address: list box. Unless instructed to print the Fitzsimmons envelope by your instructor, you cancel it by canceling the dialog box.

| Step 6 | *Click* | Cancel |
| Step 7 | *Close* | the document without saving any changes |

When you open an existing letter and then open the Envelopes and Labels dialog box, Word automatically selects the letter address exactly as it appears in the document and places it in the Delivery address: text box. When creating an envelope for an existing letter, Worldwide Exotic Foods uses the letter address punctuation and case in the envelope delivery address. B. D. Vickers' letter to Ms. Neva Johnson needs an envelope.

chapter
eight

To create and format an envelope for an existing letter:

Step 1	*Open*	the *Johnson Letter* located on the Data Disk
Step 2	*Open*	the Envelopes tab in the Envelopes and Labels dialog box
Step 3	*Observe*	the letter address is automatically placed in the Delivery address: text box

You modify the return address text for B. D. Vickers, and select the envelope size and options.

Step 4	*Click*	the Omit check box to remove the check mark, if necessary
Step 5	*Select*	the all text in the Return address: text box or move the insertion point to the text box if it is blank
Step 6	*Key*	B. D. Vickers Administrative Vice President Worldwide Exotic Foods, Inc. Gage Building, Suite 2100 Riverside Plaza Chicago, IL 60606-2000
Step 7	*Click*	Options and click the Envelope Options tab, if necessary
Step 8	*Click*	the Envelope size: list arrow
Step 9	*Click*	Size 6¾ (3⅝ × 6½ in), if necessary
Step 10	*Observe*	the envelope preview
Step 11	*Click*	OK

Often you want to add an envelope to the letter document so that you edit or print both the letter and the envelope at the same time. To add the envelope to the letter:

Step 1	*Click*	Add to Document

A confirmation dialog box opens asking if you want to save the new return address as the default return address for all future envelopes. If you click the Yes button, Word adds the return address information to the User Information tab in the Tools, Options dialog box. You do *not* want to change the default return address.

Step 2	*Click*	No

The envelope is added as Page 0 at the top of the document with a section break separating the envelope from the document. **Section breaks** divide your document into differently formatted parts. You can view and edit both the envelope and the letter in Print Layout view. To view the envelope in Print Layout view:

| Step 1 | *Verify* | the insertion point is in the envelope text |
| Step 2 | *Switch* | to Print Layout view |

Your screen should look similar to Figure 8-3.

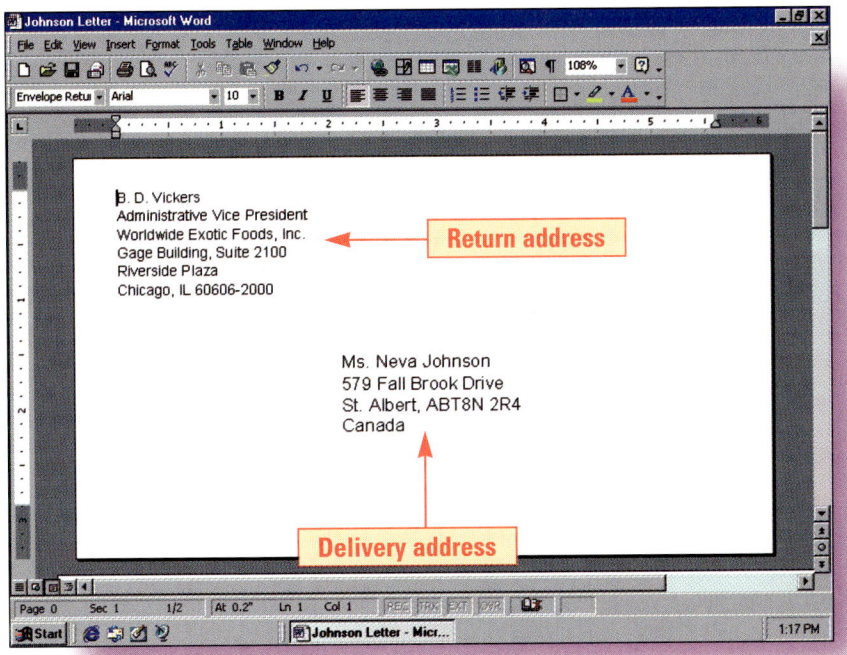

FIGURE 8-3
Envelope in Print Layout View

| Step 3 | *Scroll* | to view both the envelope and the letter and then scroll to view just the envelope |
| Step 4 | *Save* | the document as *Johnson Letter With Envelope* and close it |

Kelly also wants you to create a mailing label for an oversized envelope and a sheet of return address labels for B. D. Vickers.

QUICK TIP

If necessary, you can reposition the delivery address from Print Layout view by moving the frame that Word inserts around the address. A **frame** is a box added to text, graphics, or charts that you drag to reposition these items on a page. To view the frame, move the insertion point into the delivery address. You reposition the delivery address on the envelope by dragging and then deselecting the frame.

chapter
eight

8.b Preparing and Printing Labels

You can create many different types of labels in many different sizes, such as mailing labels, name tags, file folder labels, and computer diskette labels, with the Envelopes and Labels command on the Tools menu. There are labels for dot matrix printers and laser printers. Dot matrix printers use labels that pass through the printer by tractor feed. Laser and ink jet printers use labels on sheets that enter the printer through the sheet feeder. If you are using a laser printer, be sure to buy labels designed specifically for laser printers. Using labels made for a copier in a laser printer may damage your printer. Word has built-in label formats for most types of Avery labels. If you are not using Avery labels, you can specify a similar Avery label format, or you can create a custom label format.

Printing Individual Labels

When you need just one label, you create it and then specify exactly which label on a sheet of labels to use by setting options in the Labels tab of the Envelopes and Labels dialog box. Kelly is sending a large, oversized envelope to one of the contacts on the *Envelope and Label List* document. She asks you to create an individual label for the envelope. The label you use is in the first row and first column on a sheet of Avery 5160-Address labels. To create an individual label:

Step 1	*Open*	the *Envelope And Label List* document located on the Data Disk
Step 2	*Move*	the insertion point to the address for Debbie Gonzales
Step 3	*Open*	the Envelopes and Labels dialog box
Step 4	*Click*	the Labels tab
Step 5	*Observe*	the address is inserted in the Address: text box

The default option is to print a full page of the same label. If you want to print a single label from a sheet of labels, you must specify the exact row and column position of the label. You can print a label that includes the return address in the User Information tab of the Options dialog box by inserting a check mark in the Use return address check box. As with envelopes, clicking the Options button enables you to select a label format or printer. Now you specify the label size and position.

Step 6	*Click*	the Single label option button
Step 7	*Verify*	the Row: and Column: text boxes contain 1 to specify the label prints in the first row and first column of the label sheet
Step 8	*Click*	Options

The Label Options dialog box on your screen should look similar to Figure 8-4.

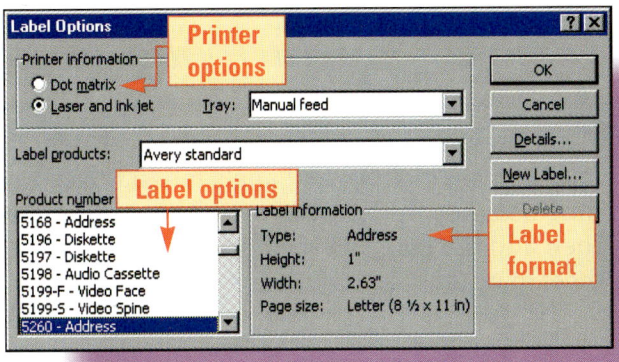

FIGURE 8-4
Label Options Dialog Box

The Printer information group contains options for selecting a Dot matrix or Laser and ink jet printer as well as Tray options. You use the Label products: list box to select an Avery or other label product list. The Product number: list box contains the list of label products by product number. The Label information group contains a description of the label format for the label selected in the Product number: list box. Use the Details button to display margins, height, and width for the selected label. You can also change the **pitch** (space between the labels) and the number of labels in each row or column with the Details button. Use the New Label button to create and save custom labels. When you save a new custom label, it is added to the Product number: list.

Step 9	*Click*	5160 – Address in the Product number: list box (scroll to view this option)

Step 10	*Observe*	that the label type, height, and width appear in the Label information group
Step 11	*Click*	OK

You are ready to print the label, if instructed to do so. Otherwise, cancel the Gonzales label by canceling the dialog box.

Step 12	*Click*	Cancel
Step 13	*Close*	the document without saving any changes

Now you create a sheet of return address labels for B. D. Vickers that Kelly requested.

Printing a Sheet of Return Address Labels

The label product you use for B. D. Vickers return address labels is the Avery 5260-Address label. To create the labels you first create a new, blank document, then open the Labels tab in the Envelopes and Labels dialog box. Key the address, select the appropriate label options, and then add the labels to the document.

To create a sheet of return address labels for B. D. Vickers:

Step 1	*Create*	a new, blank document, if necessary
Step 2	*Open*	the Labels tab in the Envelopes and Labels dialog box
Step 3	*Verify*	the insertion point is in the Address: text box
Step 4	*Key*	B. D. Vickers Administrative Vice President Worldwide Exotic Foods, Inc. Gage Building, Suite 2100 Chicago, IL 60606-2000
Step 5	*Verify*	the Full page of the same label option is selected
Step 6	*Click*	Options
Step 7	*Click*	5260 - Address in the Product number: list box (scroll to view this option)
Step 8	*Click*	OK
Step 9	*Click*	New Document to create a document with labels

CAUTION TIP

Because the Word spelling checker does not work in the Envelopes and Labels dialog box, you should proof the address information you key very carefully.

QUICK TIP

You can use the AutoText feature to quickly insert an address in the Envelopes and Labels dialog box. Simply create the address and store it as AutoText. Then open the Envelopes and Labels dialog box, key the AutoText name, and press the F3 key.

The new document containing a sheet of return address labels appears. Your screen should look similar to Figure 8-5.

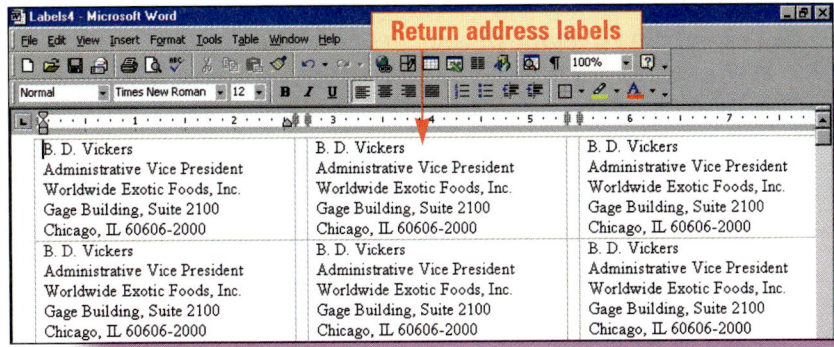

Word organizes label text in a series of columns and rows called a **table**. Each intersection of a column and row is called a **cell**. Each cell of the table represents a label that contains B. D. Vickers return address.

| Step 10 | *Save* | the document as *Return Address Labels* and close it |

Because you saved the new label document you can use it later to create more labels, whenever Kelly needs more return address labels for B. D. Vickers.

chapter
eight

Summary

▶ You can send an envelope or a sheet of labels directly to a printer or you can add them to the current document. An individual label must be sent directly to the printer.

▶ You can create an envelope or label by keying the delivery address in the Envelopes or Labels dialog box or by selecting the delivery address in a document.

▶ When you create an individual envelope for an open letter, Word automatically creates the delivery address from the letter's address.

▶ Word automatically inserts a frame or box around the delivery address on an envelope document that enables you to reposition the delivery address.

▶ Word automatically adds the default return address from data found in the User Information tab of the Options dialog box, which you can change or omit.

▶ You can create an entire sheet of the same label or a sheet with individual labels at a specified position.

▶ You can select from a list of commonly used Avery labels or you can create your own custom label size.

Commands Review

Action	Menu Bar	Shortcut Menu	Toolbar	Keyboard
Create an individual envelope, label, or sheet of the same label	Tools, Envelopes and Labels			ALT + T, E

Concepts Review

Circle the correct answer.

1. To print a single label you must:
[a] open a document that contains the label address.
[b] specify the column and row on the label sheet.
[c] change the return address in the User Information dialog box.
[d] use a name tag label format.

2. A Size 10 business envelope is:
[a] 3⅝ × 6½ inches.
[b] 4⅛ × 9½ inches.
[c] 3⅝ × 9½ inches.
[d] 4⅛ × 6½ inches.

3. Labels are created and displayed in:
[a] table format.
[b] column format.
[c] Landscape orientation.
[d] only Print Preview.

4. You can modify the font, style, and size of addresses in the Envelopes and Labels dialog box with:
[a] the Font command on the menu bar.
[b] the CTRL + Z keys.
[c] the Font command on the shortcut menu.
[d] the Change Formatting button in the Envelopes and Labels dialog box.

5. To reposition the delivery address for an envelope:
[a] view the envelope in Print Preview.
[b] drag the default frame to a new location.
[c] delete the return address.
[d] change the return address in the User Information tab of the Tools, Options dialog box.

6. Which of the following is the default formatting style that Word uses when you key the envelope delivery address?
[a] Normal
[b] Envelope Address
[c] Heading 1
[d] Envelope Return

7. When you create a custom label, it is added to the:
[a] Label products list.
[b] Product number list.
[c] Label options list.
[d] Tray list.

chapter eight

Circle **T** if the statement is true or **F** is the statement is false.

T F   1. You can create file labels in the Envelopes and Labels dialog box.

T F   2. The return address can be omitted when creating envelopes.

T F   3. You can send an envelope directly to a printer or save it with the letter for printing later.

T F   4. If you save an envelope with the letter, Word places the envelope at the bottom of the letter.

T F   5. The USPS approved envelope format is mixed case with punctuation.

T F   6. You cannot create custom labels.

T F   7. Envelopes and labels must be printed on a laser printer.

T F   8. The Details button on the Labels tab allows you to change the margins, pitch, and number of labels on a sheet.

T F   9. The default envelope font is Times New Roman 10 point.

T F   10. You can specify envelope rotation, face up or face down, and manual or tray feed in the Labels Options dialog box.

Skills Review

Exercise 1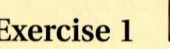

1. Create envelopes for each of the addresses below. Use the Times New Roman 12-point font and the open punctuation, uppercase delivery address format. Create each envelope as a separate document.

   Mr. Thomas Williams   *Ms. Barbara Robins*
   Williams Products Company   *Sunrise Orange Growers*
   293 East Road   *698 Orange Grove Drive*
   Houston, TX 77024-2087   *Miami, FL 33153-7634*

2. the Size 10 (4⅛ × 9½ in) envelope size.

3. Omit the return address.

4. Save the Williams envelope as *Williams Envelope*. Save the Robins envelope as *Robins Envelope*.

5. Preview and print the envelopes and close the documents.

Exercise 2

1. Create envelopes for each of the addresses below. Use the Arial 12-point font and the open punctuation, uppercase delivery address format. Create each envelope as a separate document.

   Mr. Alex Pyle   *Ms. Alice Yee*
   Office Supplies, Inc.   *Raceway Park*
   20343 Blue Sage Drive   *632 Raceway Drive*
   Shreveport, LA 71119-3412   *Sebring, FL 33870-2156*

2. Use the Size 6¾ (3⅝ × 6½ in) envelope size.

3. Omit the return address.

4. Save the Pyle envelope as *Pyle Envelope*. Save the Yee envelope as *Yee Envelope*.

5. Preview and print the envelopes and close the documents.

Exercise 3

1. Create a sheet of labels for the following address. Use the Avery 5160 label product for laser printers.

2. Format the address in the USPS style.
Ms. Ramona Mendez
Southwest Services, Inc
3426 Main Street
Dallas, TX 72345-1235

3. Add the labels to a new document.

4. Save the document as *Mendez Labels*.

5. Preview, print, and close the document.

Exercise 4

1. Open the *Envelope And Label List* document located on the Data Disk.

2. Create a sheet of Avery 5260 product laser labels for John Delany as a new document.

3. Save the document as *Delany Labels*.

4. Preview, print, and close the document.

Exercise 5

1. Open the *Wilson Advertising Letter* located on the Data Disk.

2. Create a Size 10 envelope.

3. Key your name and address as the return address.

4. Add the envelope to the document.

5. Do not save the new return address as the default return address.

6. Reposition the delivery address ½ inch to the right.

7. Save the document as *Wilson Advertising Letter With Envelope*.

8. Preview, print, and close the document.

Exercise 6

1. Open the *Wilson Advertising Letter* document located on the Data Disk.

2. Create a sheet of return labels using the Avery 5160 product for laser printers.

3. Format the labels with Times New Roman 10-point font and the uppercase and open punctuation style. (*Hint:* Remove the punctuation, select the address, right-click the address, and click Font.)

4. Add the labels to a new document.

5. Save the label document as *Wilson Labels*.

6. Preview and print the label document and close both documents.

chapter eight

Exercise 7

1. Create a sheet of name tag labels using the Avery 5362 product for laser printers. Add the labels to a new document.

2. Key the following names into the labels (*Hint:* Press the TAB key to move to the next label):
Janice Greene
Frances Carmichael
Carlos Armondo
Sarah Winters
Felix Martinez

3. Select the entire document and change the font to Arial 20 point.

4. Apply the bold and center align formats.

5. Save the document as *Name Tags*.

6. Preview, print, and close the document.

Exercise 8

1. Create the following letter. Set the appropriate margins for a block format letter.

Current date

Mr. Raul Rodriguez
Rodriguez Food Suppliers
355 Allen Drive
Houston, TX 77042-3354

Dear Mr. Rodriguez:

Congratulations on starting your own business. Given the growth of the specialty food industry, I
know you will be successful.

Please send me a catalog explaining and illustrating your product lines. I hope we can do
business together.

Yours truly,

Davita Washington
Purchasing Agent

ka

2. Create a 6¾ (3⅝ × 6½ in) size envelope and format the delivery address in the approved USPS format.

3. Omit the return address.

4. Add the envelope to the document.

5. Save the document as *Solicitation Letter With Envelope.*

6. Create a sheet of return address labels using the Avery 2160 product for laser printers.

7. Add the labels to a new document.

8. Save the document as *Rodriguez Labels.*

9. Preview and print the sheet of labels and close the documents.

Case Projects

Project 1

One of the purchasing department employees frequently creates return address labels and wants to be able to do this more quickly. You suggest using the AutoText feature. Create an AutoText entry for B. D. Vickers' return address. Using this AutoText entry, create a sheet of return address labels. Save, preview, and print the labels.

Project 2

You have been asked to add the POSTNET code and FIM-A code to an envelope but are not sure what these are. Using the Office Assistant, search online Help for information about these two codes. Create an unbound report document describing these two codes and explaining how to insert them on an envelope. Save, preview, and print the document. Attach a sample envelope with the codes inserted.

Project 3

Kelly Armstead has asked you how to print just the envelope attached to a document. Using the Office Assistant, research how to print only the envelope when it is attached to a document. Create an interoffice memorandum to Kelly explaining how

to do this. Save, preview, and print the memorandum. Then open an existing document with an attached envelope and print only the envelope following the instructions in your memo to Kelly.

Project 4

At next week's "brown bag" lunch and training session for the purchasing department clerical staff, the discussion topic is "Printing Envelopes and Labels." You are presenting information on inserting an address from an electronic address book. Use the Office Assistant to locate information on your topic. Create an unbound report document describing techniques for doing this. With your instructor's permission, describe the process to a group of classmates.

Project 5

The purchasing department is having an "open house" holiday celebration and B. D. Vickers asks you to create a letter inviting three top Chicago-area distributors. Using fictitious data, create three letters in the block format with appropriate margins inviting each distributor. Attach an envelope in the approved USPS format to each letter. Save, preview, and print each document.

chapter eight

Project 6

Several important clients and their families are visiting the Chicago office next week and you have been asked to prepare a list of Chicago-area sites and facilities the families can enjoy during their visit. Connect to your ISP, launch your Web browser, and search for Chicago-area sites of interest to visitors. Print at least five Web pages. Create an interoffice memorandum to B. D. Vickers describing the sites of interest. Save, preview, and print the memorandum.

Project 7

You have been asked to find out how to automatically add the company graphic logo to the return address each time you create an envelope. Using the Office Assistant, research how to do this. Create an interoffice memorandum to Kelly Armstead describing how to add a graphic logo to the return address automatically. Save, preview, and print the memorandum.

Project 8

Worldwide Exotic Foods is going to sponsor an evening at a sports event for Chicago-area youth groups and you need to prepare a list of possible events. Connect to your ISP, launch your Web browser, and search for sports events in the Chicago area. Print at least three Web pages. Create an interoffice memorandum to Kelly Armstead describing the sports events. Save, preview, and print the memorandum.

Working with Documents

Chapter Overview

When you edit existing documents, it is sometimes necessary to quickly locate and replace certain text or formatting with different text or formatting. Also, large documents often require additional identifying text such as the date or page number added to the top or bottom of each page. In this chapter, you learn how to find and replace text, create page and section breaks, create and edit headers and footers, and use hyphenation.

LEARNING OBJECTIVES

➤ Find and replace text
➤ Insert page breaks
➤ Create sections with different formatting
➤ Create and modify headers and footers
➤ Use hyphenation
➤ Set page orientation

Case profile

The human resources department regularly creates documents that are distributed to all Worldwide Exotic Foods employees. Jody Haversham, administrative assistant to B. J. Chang, the Vice President of Human Resources, has several completed documents, including training materials for an Internet class, that need some final editing and formatting before they can be printed and distributed.

chapter nine

9.a Finding and Replacing Text

As you work on existing documents, you may want to move quickly to a certain statement or to each heading in your document. Word can locate a word, phrase, special character, or format each time it occurs in a document. You can search for upper or lowercase text with or without formatting. You can search for whole words or for characters. For example, Word can find the three characters "our" in words such as "hour" or "your" or can find only the whole word "our." **Wildcards**, special search operators, such as "?" or "*", enable you to search for text patterns. The "?" represents any single character. For example, you can use "r?t" to search for three characters beginning with "r" and ending with "t." The "*" represents any series of characters. To search for words ending in "ed" you can use the search pattern "*ed." You can search for words that sound alike but are spelled differently. You can search for all word forms: noun, verb, adjective, or adverb. After Word finds the characters or words, you can edit them manually or replace them automatically with other text.

Finding Text

Jody asks you to open a document, *Internet Training*, find each instance of the uppercase characters "ISP" as a whole word (so you won't stop at that letter combination in other words), and then apply bold formatting to those characters.

To open the document and the Find and Replace dialog box:

Step 1	*Open*	*Internet Training* document located on the Data Disk
Step 2	*Save*	the document as *Internet Training Revised*
Step 3	*Click*	Edit
Step 4	*Click*	Find
Step 5	*Click*	More, if necessary, to expand the dialog box

The Find and Replace dialog box expands to show the options. The dialog box on your screen should look similar to Figure 9-1.

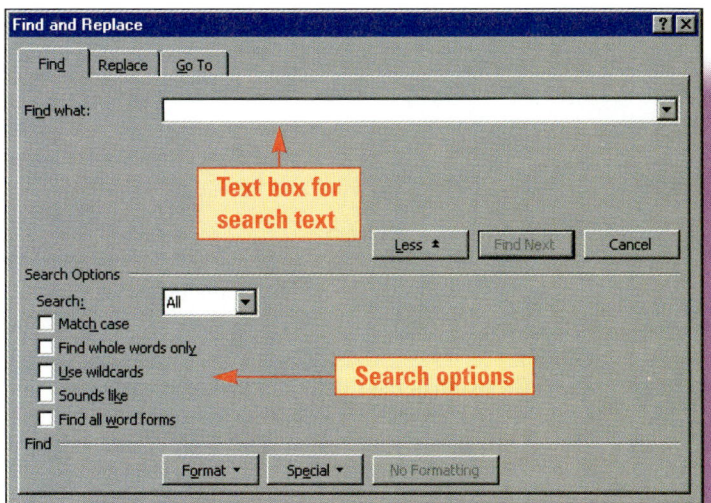

FIGURE 9-1
Find and Replace
Dialog Box

QUICK TIP

C You can find and replace formatting, special characters, and nonprinting elements (such as tab formatting marks) with the Format and Special buttons in the Find and Replace dialog box.

Notice that "All" is the default option selected in the Search Options group. This means that Word will search the entire document, regardless of the position of the insertion point. You can specify that Word find only text with the exact case by turning on the Match case option. To find the uppercase characters "ISP" as a whole word and bold each instance:

Step 1	*Key*	ISP in the Find what: text box
Step 2	*Click*	the Match case check box to insert a check mark, if necessary
Step 3	*Click*	the Find whole words only check box to insert a check mark, if necessary
Step 4	*Remove*	the check marks from the remaining check boxes, if necessary
Step 5	*Click*	Less to collapse the dialog box
Step 6	*Click*	Find Next

The first instance of the text "ISP" is selected. When the Find and Replace dialog box opens it becomes the active window and the Word application window becomes inactive (the title bar is gray). To edit or delete the selected text you must activate the Word document window. If the Find and Replace dialog box hides the selected text or the toolbar buttons, you can drag it out of the way.

Step 7	*Click*	the Word document window to activate the window (the title bar is blue when the window is active)
Step 8	*Click*	the Bold button **B** on the Formatting toolbar

chapter
nine

You continue to find and bold each instance of the text "ISP." When all the instances of the text "ISP" are found, Word opens a Confirmation dialog box telling you the search is finished.

Step 9	*Click*	<u>F</u>ind Next in the Find and Replace dialog box
Step 10	*Click*	the Bold button **B** on the Formatting toolbar to activate the Word window and format the text in one step
Step 11	*Continue*	to find and bold the text "ISP"
Step 12	*Click*	OK to close the Confirmation dialog box when it opens
Step 13	*Click*	Cancel to close the Find and Replace dialog box

Jody instructs you to find each instance of the phrase "electronic mail" in the *Internet Training Revised* document and change it to "e-mail."

Replacing Text

Often you want to search for a word, phrase, special character, or format and replace it with a different word, phrase, special character, or format. You can have Word replace the text or formatting automatically without adding it manually each time. To replace the phrase "electronic mail" with the word "e-mail" in the *Internet Training Revised* document:

Step 1	*Click*	<u>E</u>dit
Step 2	*Click*	R<u>e</u>place
Step 3	*Key*	electronic mail in the Fi<u>n</u>d what: text box
Step 4	*Press*	the TAB key to move the insertion point to the next text box
Step 5	*Key*	e-mail in the Replace wi<u>t</u>h: text box
Step 6	*Verify*	that Options: Match Case appears below the Fi<u>n</u>d what: text box (the Whole words only option automatically turns off when you search for multiple words)
Step 7	*Click*	<u>F</u>ind Next and verify that the phrase "electronic mail" is selected
Step 8	*Click*	<u>R</u>eplace
Step 9	*Drag*	the dialog box out of the way and scroll to view the selected text, if necessary

The first instance of the phrase "electronic mail" is replaced with the word "e-mail" and Word automatically highlights the next occurrence of the phrase. Your screen should look similar to Figure 9-2.

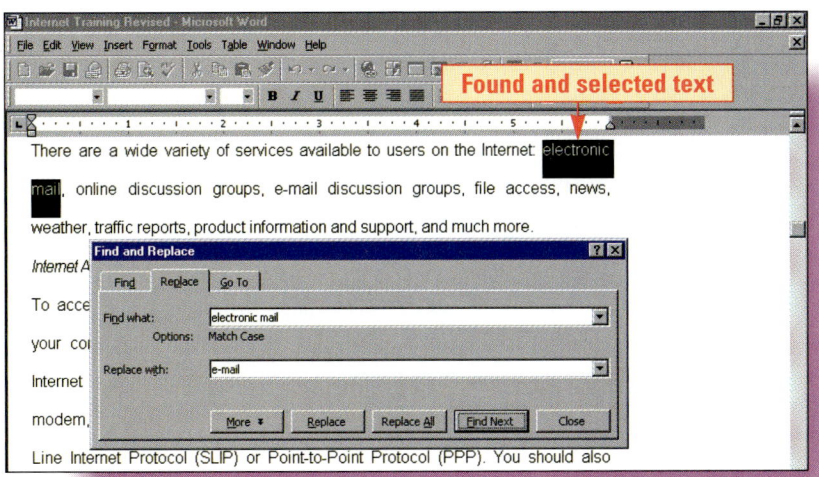

FIGURE 9-2
Replacing Text

> **CAUTION TIP**
>
> Be careful using the Replace All button in the Find and Replace dialog box to replace text in a document with which you are unfamiliar. Replacing all instances of certain characters or words may cause unexpected replacements and create errors in your document.
>
> The Find and Replace dialog box remembers the last search options you set. Always review and turn on or off the search options before each new search. You can also search for and replace formatting as well as text. Always use the No Formatting button to turn off any formatting options set from the previous search before you begin a new search.

When another match is found, you can replace it by clicking the Replace button. If you want to leave the text unchanged, click the Find Next button to skip that occurrence of the text. If you want to replace every occurrence of the text without reviewing each one, click the Replace All button. When no more matches exist, a Confirmation dialog box opens informing you that Word finished searching the document.

Step 10	*Click*	Replace
Step 11	*Click*	OK to close the Confirmation dialog box
Step 12	*Close*	the Find and Replace dialog box
Step 13	*Save*	the document

While reviewing the *Internet Training Revised* document, Jody notices an error on page two and asks you to correct it.

Using Go To to Locate Specific Elements

When you need to edit text on a specific page, you can go to that page quickly. The Go To feature moves a specific item within your document, including a page, section, or line. You can go to that item by clicking the Go To command on the Edit menu to open the Go To tab in the Find and Replace dialog box.

To move the insertion point to the second page and correct the text:

Step 1	*Click*	Edit
Step 2	*Click*	Go To

chapter
nine

The Go To tab in the Find and Replace dialog box opens. The dialog box on your screen should look similar to Figure 9-3.

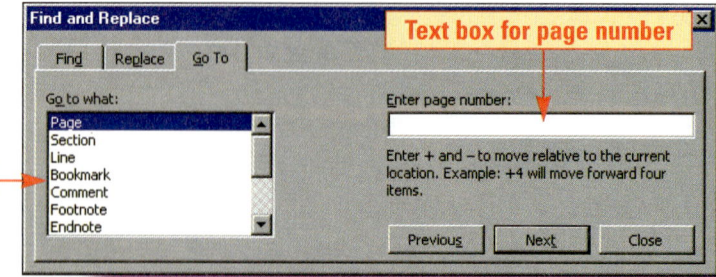

Items to go to

In this tab you select the document item you wish to go to in the Go to what: list. Notice that Page is the default choice. If you want to go to another page, simply enter the page number in the Enter page number: text box and click the Go To button (which appears in place of the Next button when a page number is entered).

Step 3	*Key*	2 in the Enter page number: text box
Step 4	*Click*	Go To

The insertion point moves to the top of page two and the Find and Replace dialog box remains open. The dialog box remains open so you can search through a document and make multiple changes without reopening it. When you are finished, you close the dialog box.

Step 5	*Close*	the dialog box
Step 6	*Move*	the insertion point before the word "computers" in the first line on page two
Step 7	*Key*	of and press the SPACEBAR
Step 8	*Save*	the document

In addition to Go To, Word has other ways to navigate through a document.

Navigating Through a Document

In addition to navigating through a document by using the Go To command, the horizontal and vertical scroll bars, or by moving the insertion point with the mouse and keyboard, you can browse a document by selecting a document item. You use the Select Browse

Object feature to select a field, endnote, footnote, comment, section, heading, picture, or table document item.

You can also open the <u>G</u>o To and Fin<u>d</u> tabs in the Find and Replace dialog box with the Select Browse Object. The default option for the Select Browse Object is to browse by page. To review the Select Browse Object:

| Step 1 | *Click* | the Select Browse Object button 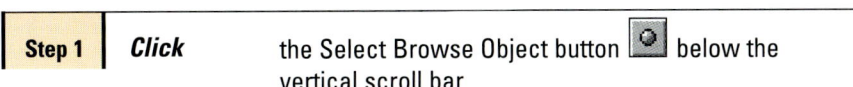 below the vertical scroll bar |

The Select Browse Object grid opens immediately below the Select Browse Object button. The grid on your screen should look like Figure 9-4.

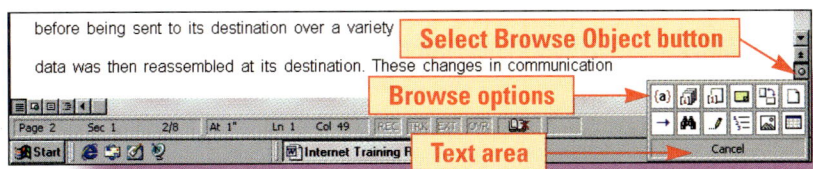

FIGURE 9-4
Select Browse Object Grid

Each icon represents an item by which to browse. You can point to each icon and observe the item name in the text area. When you see the item you want to browse by, click its icon.

Step 2	*Point to*	the first icon on the Select Browse Object grid
Step 3	*Observe*	the text "Browse by Field" in the text area
Step 4	*Continue*	to review each icon on the grid by pointing to it
Step 5	*Point to*	the text area of the grid
Step 6	*Observe*	the text "Cancel"
Step 7	*Click*	Cancel to close the grid without selecting a browse item

The paragraph headings in the *Internet Training Revised* document are italic. Jody asks you to find all the instances of italic formatting and replace it with the Words Only underline style. To use the Select Browse Object to do this:

| Step 1 | *Move* | the insertion point to the top of the document |
| Step 2 | *Click* | the Select Browse Object button 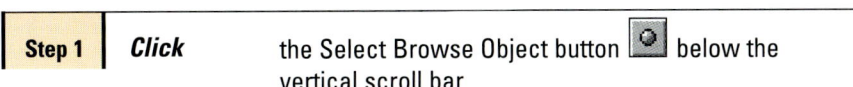 below the vertical scroll bar |

chapter
nine

| Step 3 | *Click* | the Find icon on the Select Browse Object grid |
| Step 4 | *Click* | the Replace tab |

This is the same Find and Replace dialog box you used earlier. First you remove the text you last searched for ("electronic mail"), and then you set the new find options to search for italic formatting.

Step 5	*Delete*	the text in the Find what: text box
Step 6	*Click*	More, if necessary
Step 7	*Click*	Format
Step 8	*Click*	Font to open the Font dialog box
Step 9	*Click*	Italic in the Font style: list in the Font tab
Step 10	*Click*	OK

Next you remove the "e-mail" text from the Replace with: text box and set the underline formatting option. To set the Replace with: formatting:

Step 1	*Press*	the TAB key to select the contents of the next text box
Step 2	*Delete*	the text in the Replace with: text box
Step 3	*Click*	Format
Step 4	*Click*	Font
Step 5	*Click*	Regular in the Font style: list box
Step 6	*Click*	the Underline style: list arrow and click the Words only option
Step 7	*Click*	OK
Step 8	*Click*	the Match case check box to remove the check mark
Step 9	*Click*	the Less button to collapse the dialog box

The dialog box options on your screen should look like Figure 9-5.

QUICK TIP

The Next and Previous buttons below the vertical scroll bar reflect the selected browse object in their ScreenTips. When you click a button, the insertion point moves to the next or previous instance of that object. For example, the Next Page or Previous Page buttons for the default Browse by Page quickly move the insertion point to the top of the next or previous page. When you select an item other than Page, the Next and Previous buttons change color from black (which signifies Page) to blue. To return the Next and Previous buttons to their default page option, click the Page item in the Select Browse Object grid.

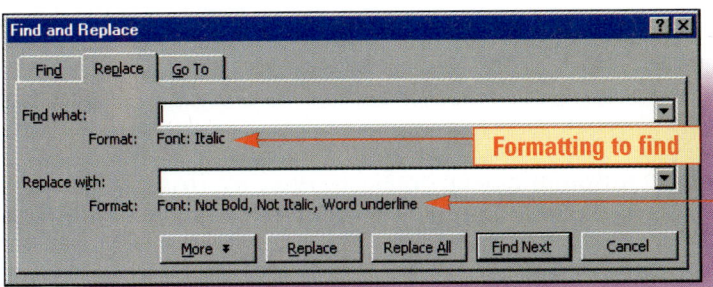

FIGURE 9-5
Find and Replace Options
for Formatting

Step 10	*Click*	Replace All
Step 11	*Click*	OK to confirm Word has replaced all 12 instances of the italic formatting with underlined words
Step 12	*Close*	the dialog box
Step 13	*Scroll*	the document to review the formatting changes to the paragraph headings
Step 14	*Save*	the document

Word inserts an automatic page break when the text you key extends beyond the limits of a single page. Jody reminds you to set the appropriate margins for the unbound report document *Internet Training Revised*, and then review and modify the page breaks.

9.b Inserting Page Breaks

Word automatically determines how much text will fit on a page based on the margins, font, font size, and paper size. A **page break** identifies where one page ends and another begins. There are two types of page breaks: a soft, or automatic, page break and a hard, or manual, page break. Word inserts an **automatic page break** when a page is full of text. In Normal view, an automatic page break appears as a dotted horizontal line from the left to the right margins. You can also create your own **manual page break** at any point on a page; a manual page break appears as a dotted horizontal line from the left to right margins containing the words "Page Break" in the center.

Before you review the pagination of the *Internet Training Revised* document, you need to reset the margins. To set margins for an unbound report:

Step 1	*Set*	2-inch top and 1-inch left and right margins
Step 2	*Zoom*	the document to Page Width, if necessary, to see all the text at the right margin

| Step 3 | *Scroll* | the document to view all the automatic page breaks (the dotted line extending from the left to right margins) then scroll the document to view the first page break |

Some of the automatic page breaks in *Internet Training Revised* occur in awkward places in the document. For example, there is a page break two lines after the paragraph heading "User Names." A better place for that page break to occur is immediately before the paragraph heading so that both the paragraph heading and the following paragraph text are on the same page. Changing the position of the page breaks in a document is called **repagination**. You cannot move or delete an automatic page break. Instead, you must insert a manual page break at some point above the automatic page break. Word then repaginates the entire document from the position of the manual page break.

To insert a manual page break immediately above the paragraph heading "User Names":

Step 1	*Go to*	page 4
Step 2	*Scroll*	to view the User Names paragraph heading at the bottom of the page
Step 3	*Move*	the insertion point to the left margin of the paragraph heading
Step 4	*Click*	Insert
Step 5	*Click*	Break

The Break dialog box that opens on your screen should look similar to Figure 9-6.

FIGURE 9-6
Break Dialog Box

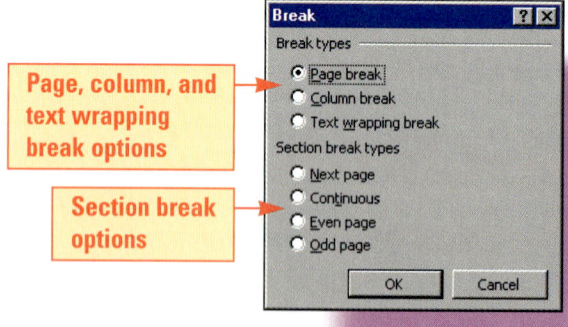

Page, column, and text wrapping break options

Section break options

The default option, <u>P</u>age Break, is already selected.

Step 6	*Click*	OK
Step 7	*Scroll*	the document to see that Word repaginated the document from the new manual page break

As you continue to edit the *Internet Training Revised* document, you can add or remove pages or text or replace the formatting. When you do this, the manual break you just inserted may then be incorrect. If you no longer want a manual page break to occur at a certain position, you can move or delete it.

To delete the manual page break:

Step 1	*Go to*	page 4
Step 2	*Click*	the manual page break dotted line above the paragraph heading "<u>U</u>ser <u>N</u>ames" in the selection bar to select it
Step 3	*Press*	the DELETE key
Step 4	*Observe*	the automatic page break in its original position two lines below the paragraph heading

When you delete the manual page break, Word repaginates the document and inserts automatic page breaks as necessary. Jody wants you to create a title page with 1-inch top and bottom margins using the three lines of text at the top of page one. She wants the text centered vertically and horizontally on the page. Now you create the title page.

9.c Creating Sections with Different Formatting

When you need to format part of a document with different margins, such as a title page, you can insert a section break. A **section break** stores the section formatting such as the margin settings and appears as a double dotted line with the words "Section Break" in the center of the line. Section breaks are inserted automatically when you format a portion of a document with different margins, headers, footers, columns, or page orientation. You also can insert a manual section break and then apply the formatting. To create a new page for title page of the *Internet Training Revised* document:

Step 1	*Move*	the insertion point to the left margin of the first paragraph heading "Introduction To The Internet" on the first page
Step 2	*Open*	the Break dialog box

Table 9-1 describes the four types of section breaks that appear in the Break dialog box.

TABLE 9-1
Types of Section Breaks

Type	Description
<u>N</u>ext Page	creates a page break and begins the new section on the next page
Cont<u>i</u>nuous	begins the new section on the same page
<u>E</u>ven page	begins the new section on the next even-numbered page
<u>O</u>dd page	begins the new section on the next odd-numbered page

Step 3	*Click*	the <u>N</u>ext page option button
Step 4	*Click*	OK
Step 5	*Observe*	the double dotted line with the text "Section Break (Next Page)" above the paragraph heading and the section number, Sec 2, on the status bar
Step 6	*Move*	the insertion point to the top of the document and observe the section number, Sec 1, on the status bar

To change the margins and vertically center the text in Section 1:

Step 1	*Open*	the Page Setup dialog box
Step 2	*Change*	the top margin to 1 inch and verify that the Apply to: list box contains "This section"
Step 3	*Change*	the vertical alignment to Center and verify that that the Apply to: list box contains "This section"
Step 4	*Click*	OK

Now that the appropriate margins are set for each section of the document, you need to verify the remaining page breaks. Whenever a page break occurs one or two lines below a paragraph heading, you insert a manual page break above the paragraph heading to keep the heading and its paragraph together. To review the page breaks:

Step 1	*Scroll*	the document to the next automatic page break at the paragraph heading "How the Internet Began"
Step 2	*Click*	at the left margin of the paragraph heading and insert a manual page break
Step 3	*Continue*	by inserting page breaks at the paragraph headings "Services Available On The Internet" and "Transmission Speeds"
Step 4	*Print Preview* the document in two rows of five pages

Your screen should look similar to Figure 9-7.

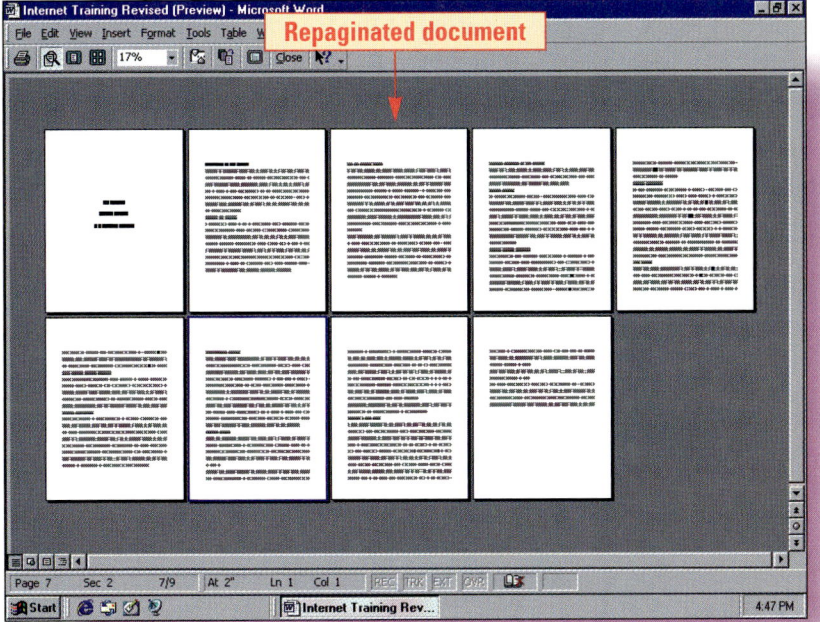

FIGURE 9-7
Document with Section and Page Breaks

| Step 5 | *Close* | Print Preview |
| Step 6 | *Save* | the document |

Because the *Internet Training Revised* document contains many pages, you need to use page numbers. You insert page numbers in the header or footer of a document.

chapter
nine

9.d Creating and Modifying Headers and Footers

Headers and footers allow text to appear on every page of a document above or below the top and bottom margins and body text area. **Header** text appears at the top of each page and **footer** text appears at the bottom of each page. You can specify that headers or footers print on every page or only on certain pages. For example, you can create headers and footers for every page except the first page, or for even- or odd-numbered pages.

Creating, Inserting, and Modifying Page Numbers

Page numbers are always inserted at the top or bottom of a document as a header or footer. One way to insert page numbers is to click the Page Numbers command on the Insert menu, specify either header or footer and the horizontal alignment, indicate whether or not to show the number on the first page, and select a number format.

You won't put a page number on the title page of the *Internet Training Revised* document. To insert page numbers centered in the footer on all pages except the first page:

Step 1	*Move*	the insertion point to the top of the document, if necessary
Step 2	*Click*	Insert
Step 3	*Click*	Page Numbers

The Page Numbers dialog box that opens on your screen should look similar to Figure 9-8.

FIGURE 9-8
Page Numbers Dialog Box

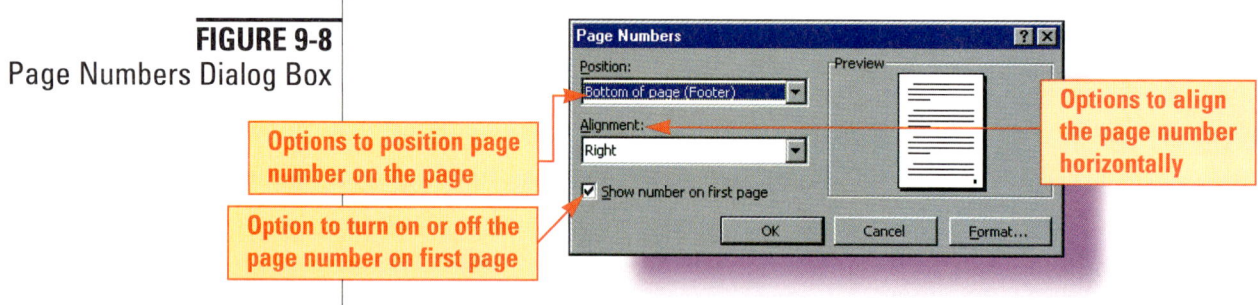

| Step 4 | *Verify* | Bottom of page (Footer) is selected in the Position: list box |

Step 5	*Click*	the Alignment: list arrow
Step 6	*Click*	Center
Step 7	*Click*	the Show number on the first page check box to remove the check mark
Step 8	*Click*	OK

Word switches to Whole Page zoom in Print Layout view.

Step 9	*Scroll*	to view the page number at the bottom of each page except the first page
Step 10	*Zoom*	the document to 100% and scroll to view the bottom of the second page

The page number 2 appears in light gray in the footer area at the bottom of the page. You can change the format of page numbers to be upper and lowercase alphabetic characters or upper and lowercase Roman numerals. To format the page numbers as lowercase Roman numerals:

Step 1	*Open*	the Page Numbers dialog box
Step 2	*Click*	Format

The Page Number Format dialog box that opens on your screen should look similar to Figure 9-9.

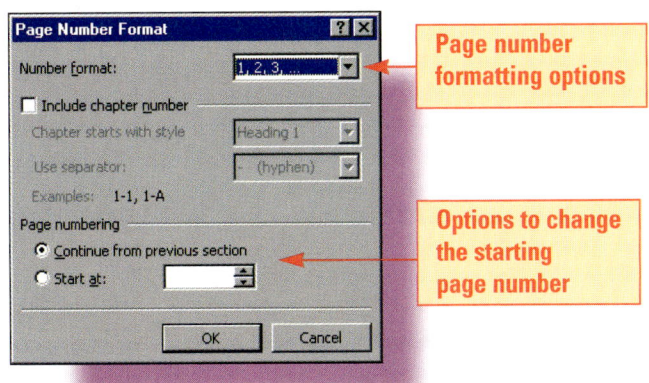

Page number formatting options

Options to change the starting page number

FIGURE 9-9
Page Number Format Dialog Box

You can change the number format by selecting a format from the Number format: list. If you want to change the starting page number, you can click the Start at: option button and then key the new starting page number in the adjacent text box.

Step 3	*Click*	the Number format: list arrow
Step 4	*Click*	the lowercase Roman numeral option (i, ii, iii …)
Step 5	*Click*	OK twice to close both dialog boxes
Step 6	*Scroll*	to view the bottom of page two and observe that the page number is changed from "2" to "ii"
Step 7	*Switch*	to Normal view and move the insertion point to the top of the document
Step 8	*Save*	the document

In addition to the page numbers, the document needs identifying text on each page beginning with page two. Jody wants the company name at the left margin of a header on all even-numbered pages and the text "Internet Training" at the right margin of a header for all odd-numbered pages.

Creating Alternate Headers and Footers

If you want to add more than page numbers to a header or footer, you use the <u>H</u>eader and Footer command on the <u>V</u>iew menu. This command switches to Print Layout view, activates the header or footer pane (in which you can key text and add page numbers or the date), and displays the Header and Footer toolbar. To activate the header and footer panes in the *Internet Training Revised* document:

Step 1	*Click*	<u>V</u>iew
Step 2	*Click*	Header and Footer
Step 3	*Zoom*	the document to Page Width, if necessary, to see the text at the right margin

Your screen should look similar to Figure 9-10.

FIGURE 9-10
Header Pane and Header
and Footer Toolbar

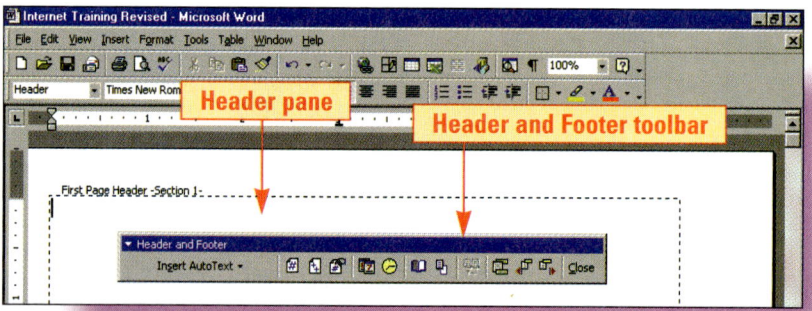

Notice that the First Page Header – Section 1 – pane, enclosed in dashed lines, contains the insertion point. When you removed the page number from the first page, Word created different header and footer panes for the first page and the rest of the text.

Step 4	*Observe*	the First Page Header – Section 1 – pane at the top of the first page
Step 5	*Review*	the Header and Footer toolbar buttons using the ScreenTips feature
Step 6	*Click*	the Show Next button on the Header and Footer toolbar

The Header – Section 2 – pane appears. Any text you key in this pane appears at the top of every page in Section 2 of the *Internet Training Revised* document.

| Step 7 | *Click* | the Switch Between Header and Footer button on the Header and Footer toolbar |

The Footer – Section 2 – pane appears. Any text you key in this pane appears at the bottom of every page in Section 2 of the *Internet Training Revised* document. Notice the footer pane contains the page number you already inserted and modified.

By default the header and footer panes have preset tabs: a Center tab at 3 inches and a Right tab at 6 inches. These tab settings allow you to center and right align text in the pane and are based on the 1¼-inch default left and right margin settings. Because the *Internet Training Revised* document has 1-inch left and right margins, the tab stops in the Footer – Section 2 – pane are not at the correct positions.

| Step 8 | *Remove* | the existing tab stops |
| Step 9 | *Set* | a center-aligned tab stop at the 3¼-inch position and a right-aligned tab stop at the 6½-inch position |

You can create headers and footers for alternate pages, as well as every page. Alternate headers and footers allow flexibility in positioning header and footer text. You want alternate header text on the even-numbered and odd-numbered page. You set the document for

---

QUICK TIP

You key and format text in the header or footer panes just as you do in the body of a document. When the header or footer pane is active, the body text in the document is light gray or "inactive" and cannot be edited.

When you are viewing a header or footer in Print Layout view, you can quickly activate the body text or the header or footer pane by double-clicking whichever is inactive (light gray). Depending on your document's layout, Word creates separate header and footer panes for each section, for the first page of each section, and for odd and even pages in each section.

chapter
nine

alternate header and footer panes in the Layout tab of the Page Setup dialog box.

To create alternate header and footer panes for Section 2:

Step 1	*Click*	the Switch between Header and Footer button 🔲 on the Header and Footer toolbar
Step 2	*Click*	the Page Setup button 📖 on the Header and Footer toolbar to open the Layout tab in the Page Setup dialog box
Step 3	*Click*	the Different odd and even check box to insert a check mark
Step 4	*Click*	OK
Step 5	*Observe*	the Even Page Header – Section 2 – pane

To key the company name at the left margin for each even-numbered page:

Step 1	*Key*	Worldwide Exotic Foods, Inc.
Step 2	*Click*	the Show Next button 🔲 on the Header and Footer toolbar to view the Odd Page Header – Section 2 – pane
Step 3	*Remove*	the existing tab stops
Step 4	*Set*	a 6½-inch right tab stop
Step 5	*Press*	the TAB key
Step 6	*Key*	Internet Training
Step 7	*Print Preview*	the document in two rows of six pages
Step 8	*Observe*	the differently formatted first page in Section 1, page numbers and the odd and even page headers in Section 2 (zoom each page, if necessary, to verify the header and footer)

Your screen should look similar to Figure 9-11.

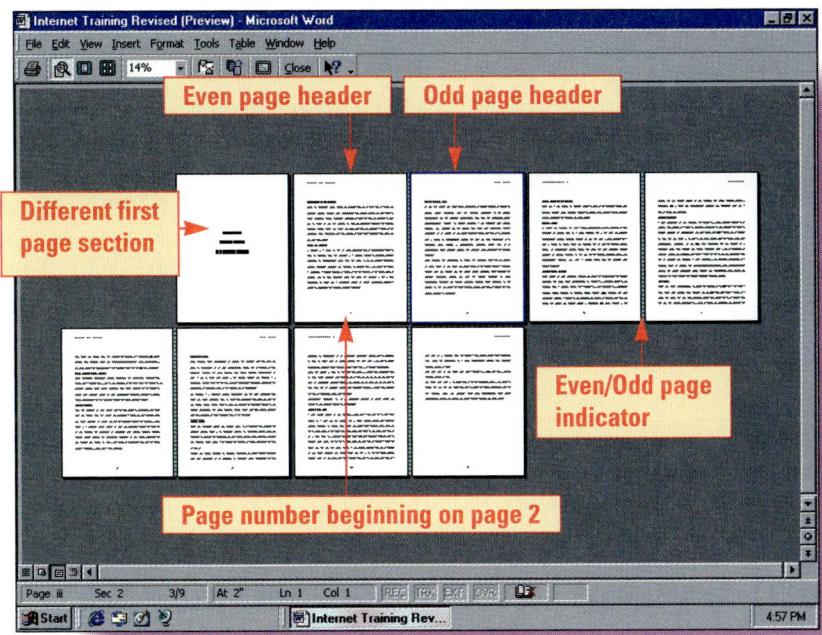

FIGURE 9-11
Different First Page and
Section Formatting

Step 9	*Close*	Print Preview
Step 10	*Save*	the document and close it

The human resources department is beginning computer software training classes next month that are available to all employees. Jody drafted a bulletin to insert in all paycheck envelopes at the next pay period. She is not satisfied with the way the text wraps and asks you hyphenate words in the document.

9.e Using Hyphenation

Hyphens are used to join words, such as "drag-and-drop," and to split long words at the right margin. Because word wrap moves a word to the next line if it is too long to fit within the set right margin, left-aligned text may have a very ragged right margin or justified text may have large spaces between words. The end result is less text on a page. **Hyphenation** splits words at the right margin, creating a smoother right margin or smaller spaces between words and more text on the page. The best time to hyphenate a document is after you have keyed, edited, and formatted the text. The Hyphenation subcommand under the Language command on the Tools menu provides options to hyphenate text automatically or manually.

chapter
nine

You hyphenate the *Training Commitment* document to improve its text wrapping. To open the document and turn on automatic hyphenation:

Step 1	*Open*	the *Training Commitment* document located on the Data Disk
Step 2	*Zoom*	the document to Page Width, if necessary, to view the text at the right margin
Step 3	*Observe*	the ragged right margin
Step 4	*Click*	Tools
Step 5	*Point to*	Language
Step 6	*Click*	Hyphenation

The Hyphenation dialog box that opens on your screen should look similar to Figure 9-12.

FIGURE 9-12
Hyphenation Dialog Box

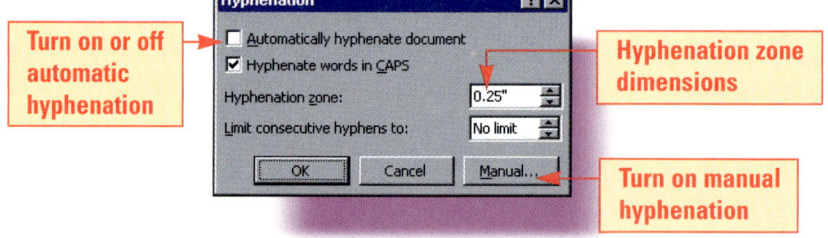

Turn on or off automatic hyphenation

Hyphenation zone dimensions

Turn on manual hyphenation

The **hyphenation zone** defines the distance from the right margin where you want to hyphenate your document. Words that fall into the hyphenation zone are hyphenated. A large zone increases the right margin raggedness because fewer words require hyphens. A small zone reduces the right margin raggedness, because more words require hyphens. Because too many consecutive hyphenated words make a document harder to read, you can limit the number of consecutively hyphenated words.

| Step 7 | *Click* | the Automatically hyphenate document check box to insert a check mark |
| Step 8 | *Click* | OK |

Word automatically hyphenates four words: communication, receive, assigned, and keystrokes. The right margin is less ragged. To control which words are hyphenated, you use manual hyphenation.

QUICK TIP

The en dash, slightly longer than a hyphen, separates words and number ranges such as "5–9." To insert an en dash, press the CTRL + HYPHEN (-) keys on the numeric keypad. An em dash (—) indicates a break in a sentence. To insert an em dash, press the CTRL + ALT + HYPHEN (-) keys on the numeric keypad. You can also insert an en dash or em dash from the Special Characters tab in the Insert, Symbol dialog box.

To undo the automatic hyphenation and manually hyphenate the *Training Commitment* document using a 0.3 inch hyphenation zone:

Step 1	*Click*	the Undo button on the Standard toolbar
Step 2	*Open*	the Hyphenation dialog box
Step 3	*Key*	.3 in the Hyphenation zone: text box
Step 4	*Click*	Manual

The Manual Hyphenation dialog box opens with a suggestion for hyphenating the word "com-mu-ni-ca-tion." The flashing insertion point indicates where the word is hyphenated if you click Yes to accept the suggestion. You can click another hyphenation position to modify the suggestion and then click Yes to accept it. If you don't want to hyphenate that word, click No. To manually hyphenate the document:

Step 1	*Click*	the word at the first (com-) hyphenation position
Step 2	*Click*	Yes
Step 3	*Observe*	the next suggested hyphenation "as-signed"
Step 4	*Click*	No
Step 5	*Accept*	the last suggested hyphenation "key-strokes"
Step 6	*Click*	OK to confirm the hyphenation is complete
Step 7	*Scroll*	the document to review the hyphenation
Step 8	*Save*	the document as *Training Commitment Revised* and close it

Certain hyphenated words (such as e-mail) should not be broken at the right margin.

Nonbreaking Hyphens

The *Fall Schedule* document contains several hyphenated words that you don't want to split between lines. **Nonbreaking hyphens** are used to prevent hyphenated words from breaking at the right margin. To insert nonbreaking hyphens in a document:

Step 1	*Open*	the *Fall Schedule* document located on the Data Disk
Step 2	*Observe*	the hyphenated text "left-aligning" that breaks at the right margin

chapter
nine

QUICK TIP

A nonbreaking space allows words such as 64 MB or B. D. Vickers to stay on the same line if they would ordinarily be placed on two different lines by word wrap. You keep such words together by inserting nonbreaking spaces between the words. To insert a nonbreaking space, press the CTRL + SHIFT + SPACEBAR keys.

Step 3	*Select*	the hyphen following the word "left"
Step 4	*Press*	the CTRL + SHIFT + HYPHEN (-) keys to insert a nonbreaking hyphen
Step 5	*Observe*	the hyphenated text "left-aligned" wrapped to the left margin
Step 6	*Change*	the hyphen in the text "built-in" to a nonbreaking hyphen
Step 7	*Save*	the document as *Fall Schedule Revised*

Sometimes you want to control where a word is hyphenated if it cannot fit at the right margin. You use optional or soft hyphens to do this.

Optional Hyphens

Optional hyphens join words that can be split if they do not fit at the right margin. An optional hyphen breaks a word or phrase only when it does not fit at the right margin. If the word or phrase appears anywhere else in the line, the optional hyphen does not appear in the document. To insert text and an optional hyphen in the *Fall Schedule Revised* document:

Step 1	*Move*	the insertion point after the text "using" and the space at the end of the second line in the large paragraph following the heading "*Intermediate Word Processing*"
Step 2	*Key*	AutoCorrect, using and press the SPACEBAR
Step 3	*Move*	the insertion point between the o and the C in AutoCorrect
Step 4	*Press*	the CTRL + HYPHEN (-) keys to insert an optional hyphen
Step 5	*Observe*	the word AutoCorrect is hyphenated and broken between two lines

To see how the optional hyphen works, you change the margins so that the word "AutoCorrect" does not have to be hyphenated. To view the hyphenated word "AutoCorrect" when it appears at the beginning of the line:

Step 1	*Change*	the right margin to 1½ inch
Step 2	*Observe*	the word "AutoCorrect" at the beginning of the third line of the paragraph and the hyphen disappears
Step 3	*Change*	the right margin to 1¼ inch
Step 4	*Observe*	the word "AutoCorrect" is again hyphenated

| Step 5 | *Save* | the document |

When you need to print a document on paper that is wider than it is tall, you change the page orientation.

9.f Setting Page Orientation

The default page orientation is called **portrait** orientation, which means the paper is taller than it is wide. You can also print documents in **landscape** orientation, which means the paper is wider than it is tall. You want to change the page orientation for the *Fall Schedule Revised* document. To change the orientation:

Step 1	*Open*	the Page Setup dialog box
Step 2	*Click*	the Paper Size tab
Step 3	*Observe*	the default option is Portrait and the document in the preview is taller than it is wide
Step 4	*Click*	the Landscape option button
Step 5	*Observe*	in the preview that the document is now wider than it is tall
Step 6	*Set*	the top margin to 2 inches and the left and right margins to 1.5 inches
Step 7	*Print Preview*	the document to review the new page orientation
Step 8	*Close*	Print Preview
Step 9	*Save*	the document as *Fall Schedule In Landscape Orientation* and close it

Jody will print the training material documents you finished and distribute them at the Internet class.

chapter
nine

Summary

- ▶ Word can locate a character, word, phrase, special character, or format each time it occurs in a document.

- ▶ You can search for characters, words, phrases, special characters, or formats, and replace them with other text or formats individually or all at one time.

- ▶ The Go To command moves the insertion point to a specific item within your document, such as the top of the page.

- ▶ The Select Browse Object button provides options for browsing your document by item, such as pictures, comments, or tables.

- ▶ Word creates an automatic page break when text fills a page whose length is determined by the margins, font, font size, and paper size.

- ▶ You can insert a manual page break to remove an automatic page break.

- ▶ A section break allows you to change the margins and headers or footers for different parts of a document.

- ▶ You can insert page numbers at the top or bottom of every page—or all pages except the first page—and then format the page numbers.

- ▶ Header text appears at the top of the designated pages and footer text appears at the bottom of designated pages.

- ▶ You can use different header or footer text on the first page or on even- or odd-numbered pages.

- ▶ The best time to hyphenate words is after all text is keyed, edited, and formatted.

- ▶ The Hyphenation tool can hyphenate all possible words automatically or can suggest words for you to hyphenate manually.

- ▶ Nonbreaking hyphens are used to prevent hyphenated words from breaking at the right margin.

- ▶ Optional hyphens break a word or phrase only when it does not fit at the right margin.

- ▶ You can print pages in Portrait ($8\frac{1}{2} \times 11$) or Landscape ($11 \times 8\frac{1}{2}$) orientation.

Commands Review

Action	Menu Bar	Shortcut Menu	Toolbar	Keyboard
Search for specific text or item	Edit, Find			ALT + E, F CTRL + F
Search and replace specific text or item	Edit, Replace			ALT + E, E CTRL + H
Go to a specific document element	Edit, Go To		Double-click the status bar (not a mode indicator)	ALT + E, G CTRL + G F5
Navigating through a document by item				
Insert Page or Section Breaks	Insert, Break			ALT + I, B
Creating and modifying Headers and Footers	View, Header and Footer			ALT + V, H
Insert page numbers	Insert, Page Numbers			ALT + I, U
Use Hyphenation tool	Tools, Language, Hyphenation			ALT + T, L, H
Nonbreaking hyphen				CTRL + SHIFT + HYPHEN
Optional hyphen				CTRL + HYPHEN
Nonbreaking space				CTRL + SHIFT + SPACEBAR
Change page orientation	File, Page Setup, Paper Size tab			ALT + F, U, S

Concepts Review

SCANS

Circle the correct answer.

1. Hyphens are used to:
  [a] separate number ranges.
  [b] split long words at the right margin.
  [c] split long words at the left margin.
  [d] add interest to a document.

2. You create alternate header and footer panes in the:
  [a] Margins tab in the Page Setup dialog box.
  [b] Header and Footer tab in the Print Setup dialog box.
  [c] Layout tab in the Print dialog box.
  [d] Layout tab in the Page Setup dialog box.

3. Which Find option allows you to avoid search results that include the individual characters of a word inside other words?
  [a] Match case
  [b] Find whole words only
  [c] Sounds like
  [d] Find all word forms

4. The default option for the Select Browse Object button is to Browse by:
  [a] Picture.
  [b] Comment.
  [c] Find.
  [d] Page.

5. When a page fills with text, Word inserts a(n):
  [a] manual page break.
  [b] temporary page break.
  [c] permanent page break.
  [d] automatic page break.

6. When you want to format part of a document with different margins or page orientation, you insert a:
  [a] manual page break.
  [b] header.
  [c] section break.
  [d] hyphen.

chapter nine

7. Page numbers are always inserted in:
[a] Roman numerals.
[b] a header or footer.
[c] a hyphenated format.
[d] the body text.

8. Repagination means to:
[a] change the line spacing in a document.
[b] format text characters with the Italic format.
[c] insert headers and footers.
[d] change the position of page breaks.

9. The best time to hyphenate text is:
[a] at each page break.
[b] as you key it.
[c] before you format it.
[d] after keying, editing, and formatting it.

10. The actions of the Next and Previous buttons below the vertical scroll bar are controlled by the:
[a] Find and Replace dialog box.
[b] Hyphenation button.
[c] CTRL + SHIFT + HYPHEN (-) keys.
[d] Select Browse Object button.

Circle **T** if the statement is true or **F** if the statement is false.

T   F   1. The <u>F</u>ind command locates a word, phrase, or format in a document and replaces it with a word, phrase, or format.

T   F   2. A page break identifies where one page ends and another begins.

T   F   3. The Select Browse Object button can be used to display only the Find and Replace dialog box.

T   F   4. When you use the <u>R</u>eplace command, you can only replace text from the insertion point forward.

T   F   5. You must be in Print Layout view to see the header and footer panes.

T   F   6. Word automatically changes the position of the center and right tab stops in the header and footer panes when you change a document's margins.

T   F   7. You use Portrait orientation to print on paper that is taller than it is wide.

T   F   8. Word determines how much text fits on a page based on the margins, font, font size, and paper size settings.

T   F   9. An optional hyphen is used to prevent hyphenated words from breaking at the right margin.

T   F   10. You can use special search operators like "?" and "*" to search for text patterns.

Skills Review

Exercise 1

1. Open the *British Columbia Report* document located on the Data Disk.

2. Change the font for the entire document to Arial, 12 point.

3. Change the top margin to 2 inches, the left margin to 1½ inches, and the right margin to 1 inch.

4. Automatically hyphenate the document using the default hyphenation zone.

5. Go to the top of page 2. Change the top margin to 1 inch and apply it from the position of the insertion point forward in the document.

6. Insert a page number at the bottom center of each page.

7. Save the document as *British Columbia Report Revised*.

8. Preview, print, and close the document.

Exercise 2

1. Open the *British Columbia Report* document located on the Data Disk.

2. Find each occurrence of the text "British Columbia" and replace it with "New York." (*Hint:* Remember to clear any formatting that is set in the dialog box.)

3. Change the font for the entire document to Times New Roman 12 point.

4. Change the left margin to 1 inch.

5. Find the text "In contrast" and insert a page break before the paragraph beginning with the text.

6. Create a header with the text "New York Analysis Report" centered, boldfaced, and Times New Roman 12 point. (*Hint:* don't forget to change the center tab stop setting to agree with the left and right margin settings.)

7. Switch to the footer and insert a page number at the bottom center of the page. (*Hint:* Don't forget to change the center tab stop setting to agree with the left and right margin settings.)

8. Omit the header and footer on page 1 by creating blank first page header and footer panes.

9. Save the document as *New York Report*.

10. Preview, print, and close the document.

Exercise 3

1. Open the *Inventory Report* document located on the Data Disk.

2. Find each occurrence of the text "warehouse" and replace it with "plant."

3. Indent the bulleted list ½ inch on the left side.

4. Indent the numbered list ½ inch on the left and right sides.

5. Change the top margin to 2 inches and the left and right margins to 1 inch.

6. Automatically hyphenate the text.

7. Go to the top of page 2. Change the top margin to 1 inch and apply it from the position of the insertion point forward.

8. Create a Section 2 header containing centered and bold text "Inventory Report." (*Hint:* Make sure you turn off the Same as Previous button on the Header and Footer toolbar so the header will not appear in Section 1. Don't forget to adjust the center tab stop.)

9. Switch to the Section 2 footer and insert a page number at the bottom center of the page. (*Hint:* Make sure you turn off the Same as Previous button on the Header and Footer toolbar so the footer will not appear in Section 1. Don't forget to adjust the center tab stop.)

10. Format the page number in the lowercase Roman numeral style.

11. Save the document as *Inventory Report Revised*.

12. Preview, print, and close the document.

Exercise 4

1. Open the *New York Report* document you created in Exercise 2.

2. Zoom the document to Page Width and manually hyphenate it with a 0.4 hyphenation zone.

3. Save the document as *New York Report With Manual Hyphenation*.

4. Preview, print, and close the document.

Exercise 5

1. Create the following document. Use the default font and set the margins for a block format letter.

Current date

Mr. T. J. Olsen
13567 Mason Park Drive
East Melbourne VIC 3002
Australia

Dear Mr. Olsen:

Thank you for your inquiry about teaching positions in our Melbourne office. Our Melbourne office is not currently planning on expanding their training staff. However, we will keep your resume on file for six months and will contact you if there is an opening in the Melbourne office teaching staff.

In the meantime, Mr. Olsen, we are forwarding your resume to the Vancouver branch at your request.

Sincerely,

B. J. Chang
Vice President of Human Resources

jh

2. Find each instance of the name Olsen and replace it with Nance using the Select Browse Object button.

3. Find each instance of the word "Melbourne" and replace it with "Vancouver" except in the letter address.

4. Find each instance of the word "six" without formatting and replace it with the word "*six*" with italic formatting.

5. Create a Size 10 envelope with the Delivery Point barcode and omit the return address.

6. Add the envelope to the document.

7. Save the document as *Nance Letter With Envelope*.

8. Preview, print, and close the envelope and letter.

Exercise 6

1. Open the *Vancouver Warehouse Report* document located on the Data Disk.

2. Create a title page using a Next Page section break immediately before the paragraph heading <u>Audit Methods</u>.

3. Use 1-inch top, bottom, left, and right margins for the title page in Section 1.

4. Center the title text vertically between the left and right margins.

5. Change the Section 2 margins to 2-inch top and 1-inch left and right margins.

6. Move the insertion point to the top of the document and view the Header and Footer toolbar.

7. Using the Header and Footer toolbar buttons create a different first page header and footer pane for Section 1 and leave both the first page header and footer blank.

8. Using the Header and Footer toolbar buttons view the Section 2 header and create a different odd and even header and footer panes for Section 2.

9. Insert a page number at the right margin for the even page header and at the left margin for the odd page header. (*Hint:* Remember to adjust the right-aligned tap stop to the right margin, if necessary.)

10. Save the document as *Vancouver Warehouse Report With Title Page*.

11. Preview, print, and close the document.

Exercise 7

1. Open the *Welcome To The World Wide Web* document located on the Data Disk.

2. Change the margins to the appropriate margins for an unbound report.

3. Using the Replace tab in the Find and Replace dialog box find all instances of the phrase "World Wide Web" and change it to "WWW."

4. Using the Replace tab in the Find and Replace dialog box find all text formatted with the Times New Roman, 14-point font and change it to Times New Roman, 12 point, bold.

5. Horizontally justify the document text below the title.

6. Change the line spacing for the entire document to 1.7.

7. Scroll the document and review the page breaks.

8. Insert a manual page break if an automatic page break occurs 1 to 3 lines below a paragraph heading.

9. Use the Page Numbers command on the Insert menu to insert centered page numbers in footers on all pages. Use the (A, B, C) page number format.

10. Check the spelling and grammar.

11. Save the document as *Welcome To The WWW.*

12. Preview, print, and close the document.

Exercise 8

1. Open the *Welcome To The WWW* document created in Exercise 6.

2. Create a separate title page for the title line.

3. Format the title page with a 1-inch top margin and vertically centered text.

4. Omit the page number on the title page.

chapter nine

5. Change the page number format for Section 2 to uppercase Roman numerals and show the page number on the first page of Section 2.

6. Find the hyphenated text "dial-up and "e-mail" and create nonbreaking hyphens.

7. Save the document at *Welcome To The WWW Revised*.

8. Preview, print, and close the document.

Exercise 9

1. Open the *Legislative Update* document located on the Data Disk.

2. Change the page orientation to landscape.

3. Change the top and bottom margins to .75 inch and the left and right margins to 1 inch.

4. Save the document as *Landscape Legislative Update*.

5. Print and close the document.

Case Projects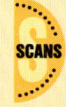

Project 1

Prepare a three-paragraph block format letter for B. J. Chang's signature to Ms. Helen Alexander, 1400 W. Highlands Avenue, Melbourne, VIC, 20006, Australia. Thank Ms. Alexander for her resume and interest in employment as an inventory control specialist with Worldwide Exotic Foods, Inc. Advise Ms. Alexander that there is an opening in the Melbourne warehouse and you are forwarding her resume to the Melbourne warehouse manager who will contact her to set up an appointment for an interview. Save the document but do not close it. Replace each instance of the word "Alexander" with the word "Stackhouse." Replace each instance of the word "Melbourne" in the body of the letter with the word "Sydney." Save the document with a new name. Add an envelope with no return address to each letter, save each letter again, and preview and print both letters and envelopes.

Project 2

Belinda Montez, an assistant secretary in the human resources department, needs help with inserting page breaks and section breaks in her documents. Using the Office Assistant, research troubleshooting page and section breaks. Write

Belinda an interoffice memorandum describing the most common page and section break problems and suggest a solution based on what you learned from your research. Save, preview, and print the document.

Project 3

B. J. Chang asks you to find several Web pages that provide information for human resources professionals, including any online magazines devoted to the human resources field. Connect to your ISP, load your Web browser, and search for Web pages with information for human resources professionals. Print at least four Web pages. Write B. J. Chang an interoffice memorandum describing what you found on the Web. Save, preview, and print the memorandum.

Project 4

You want to practice hyphenating documents automatically and manually. Using the Office Assistant, review how to hyphenate documents—including the use of optional and nonbreaking hyphens. Open three documents of your choice and automatically hyphenate each document. Review each document and create nonbreaking and optional hyphens as necessary. Save each document with a new name and print it. Open two documents of your choice and manually hyphenate the documents. Save the documents with new names and print them. Create a three-page document that includes a title page and two pages of text. The title page should include the title "Using Word Features," your name, and the current date centered vertically and horizontally on the page. The text pages should describe in your own words how to search for and replace text and formatting, how to use the Select Browse Object feature, how to create different types of headers and footers, and how to use different hyphenation options. Create different first page headers and footers and leave them blank. Insert page numbers centered at the bottom of the page on pages two and three beginning with number 2. Insert your name as a header at the left margin of each even-numbered page and your school's name at the right margin of each odd-numbered page (except the first page). Use hyphenation as necessary. Save, preview, and print the document.

Project 5

B. J. Chang wants to post several open positions on the Web and asks you which Web sites to use. Connect to your ISP, load your Web browser, and search for Web sites that allow companies to post job openings. Print at least three pages. Write an interoffice memorandum to B. J. Chang recommending at least two Web sites. Discuss the reasons for your recommendations. Save, preview, and print the memorandum.

Project 6

You are working with Jody and Belinda on the new employee handbook and they have questions about creating the headers and footers for the handbook. Jody asks how to adjust the horizontal and vertical position of headers and footers and Belinda asks how to insert the chapter number and title in footers. Using online Help, look up

answers to these questions. Create an interoffice memorandum to both Jody and Belinda listing their questions and your answers. Save, preview, and print the document. With your instructor's permission, use the memo as a guide to show a classmate how to adjust the horizontal and vertical position of headers and footers and how to insert a chapter number and title in footers.

Project 7

Jody wants to know how to use the Special button in the expanded Find and Replace dialog box. Open a large document of your choice and experiment finding items on the Special button list. Also experiment finding items and replacing them with other items on the Special button list. Write Jody an interoffice memorandum describing how to use the Special button and suggesting how she can use the list to expedite editing her documents.

Project 8

Belinda has a large document and she wants to find every instance of a three-letter word that begins with "s" and ends with "t." It does not matter what the middle character is. She also misspelled the name "Cathy" throughout the document by spelling it "Kathy" and wants to find and correct each instance. Finally, she needs to find all words that begin with "program" such as "programming" and "programmed" and apply bold formatting. Using Word Help features determine the Find and Replace options Belinda can use to accomplish her goals with the large document. Create a two-page, unbound report for Belinda describing in your own words how to use all the options in the Find and Replace dialog box, and giving specific examples of how to use each option. Insert page numbers in the top right corner on both pages in a header using the Roman numeral style. Add your name at the left margin and the current date at the right margin in a footer on both pages. Save, preview, and print the report.

chapter nine

Working with Columns and Drawing Objects

Chapter Overview

Columns are used in many documents—from annual reports to brochures to newsletters. Often lines and shapes are added to documents to make certain text stand out or to create an interesting and attractive format. In this chapter, you learn how to key and edit text in columns and create and modify lines and objects.

LEARNING OBJECTIVES

▶ Creating and using newspaper-style columns
▶ Using the drawing toolbar

Case profile

The human resources department distributes the company newsletter each month. Jody Haversham assigns you the task of creating and formatting the company newsletter for September. The newsletter is one page of text, formatted with a title and two-column body text. As space permits, Jody asks you to insert an AutoShape object to add interest and draw attention to some aspect of the newsletter.

chapter ten

10.a Creating and Using Newspaper-Style Columns

So far, you've worked with documents that have only a single column of text from margin to margin. You can also create multi-column documents, such as advertising brochures or newsletters, using **newspaper-style columns**, which divide a document into two or more vertical columns placed side-by-side on a page. When you format a document with columns, text fills the length of one column before moving to the next column. You can create two, three, four, or more newspaper-style columns of equal or unequal width for an entire document or for selected text in a document.

The Columns button on the Standard toolbar displays a grid from which you specify the number of equally spaced columns you want. By default, the Columns button applies column formatting to the whole document or to the active section. To apply column formatting to a portion of the document, first select the text to be formatted and then select the number of columns from the Columns button grid. Word automatically inserts a continuous section break before and, if necessary, after the selected text in columns.

Jody hands you a hard copy of the September newsletter text, shown in Figure 10-1. After you key and format the text, you change the body text to a two-column format.

To create the September newsletter:

Step 1	*Key*	the document in Figure 10-1
Step 2	*Save*	the document as *September Newsletter*
Step 3	*Zoom*	the document to Page Width, if necessary, to view all the text at the right margin

You create a continuous section break at the first paragraph heading and then apply the column formatting to the body text section.

Step 4	*Move*	the insertion point to the left margin of the first paragraph heading "Annual Conference"
Step 5	*Open*	the Break dialog box
Step 6	*Click*	the Continuous option button
Step 7	*Click*	OK

chapter ten

FIGURE 10-1
September Newsletter
Text

Set 1 inch top, bottom, left, and right margins

WORLDWIDE EXOTIC FOODS, INC.
SEPTEMBER NEWSLETTER

Use 14-point, Bold, Times New Roman font for title text

Annual Conference
Worldwide Exotic Foods, Inc. hosted the annual food distributor conference last month in Vancouver, Canada. Our Chairman, Jason Smythe, presented the keynote address entitled "Challenge 2000" on the final evening of the conference. Also attending the conference were Communications Vice President, Ellen Nguyen, and Marketing Vice President, Robin Conroy.

Use an en dash between the dates

Annual Meeting
The annual stockholders meeting is November 28–December 2 in the ballroom at the Huntington Hotel. There are rooms available if you would like accommodations at the hotel rather than commuting from the office. Stockholders are eligible for a special discount of $75 per night. Please contact Jody Haversham if you would like more information.

New Clients and Distributors
Several major new clients placed orders with Worldwide Exotic Foods, Inc. last quarter, raising our quarterly results to a 5-year high: AMC Company of Vancouver, BC, and Wolson, Inc. of San Francisco, CA, are new distributors for our holiday baskets that become available on October 1.

Use a nonbreaking space between the month and the day

New Employees
Welcome! We have several new employees this month. Please extend a welcome to Julia Brown, finance; Oliver Hunt, human resources; and James Sharp, computer support.

Happy Birthday!
Warm Happy Birthday wishes to all our employees with September birthdays. This month's birthday bunch includes Beverly Denton, Mark Cohn, Ross James, Samantha Washington, and Belinda Huang. The monthly birthday celebration will be held in Conference Room 2 on the 15th.

Issue Awareness Committee
The IAC has distributed packets containing important employee information to each employee. Each packet should contain:

• New insurance forms for medical, life, and disability plans
• Information on the company 401(k) plan
• Stock and money market fund options
• Company-provided day care information
• Carpool matching forms

Use 12-point, Times New Roman font for nontitle text

Brown Bag Workshop
Register soon for a lunchtime workshop on September 12. The topic this month is "Advanced Graphic Features in Word 2000." The workshop begins promptly at 11:45.

The title is in Section 1 of the document and the body text is in Section 2. You create two equally spaced newspaper-style columns in Section 2.

Step 8	*Verify*	the insertion point is in Section 2
Step 9	*Click*	the Columns button ▦ on the Standard toolbar
Step 10	*Move*	the mouse pointer to the second column indicator on the grid
Step 11	*Observe*	the text "2 Columns" at the bottom of the grid

Step 12	*Click*	the second column indicator on the grid

Word creates the newspaper-style columns and automatically switches to Print Layout view. You can view multiple columns in Print Layout view or Print Preview, but not in Normal view. When the text in the first column reaches the bottom of the page, the remaining text shifts automatically to the next column. This can create uneven columns lengths. For example, the second column in the *September Newsletter* document is not as long as the first column. To view the columns:

Step 1	*Zoom*	the document to Whole Page to view the two newspaper-style columns
Step 2	*Zoom*	the document to 75% so you can read the text

To make the newsletter more attractive, you can balance the column length.

Balancing Column Length

To balance column length, you can insert manual column breaks that force text into the next column. Manual column breaks are inserted with an option in the Break dialog box. Manual column breaks can be deleted and recreated, if necessary, as you continue to edit the document. To insert a manual column break in the *September Newsletter* document:

Step 1	*Move*	the insertion point to the left margin of the line beginning with the text "Brown" below the paragraph heading "New Employees" in column one
Step 2	*Open*	the Break dialog box
Step 3	*Click*	the Column Break Option button
Step 4	*Click*	OK
Step 5	*Zoom*	the document to Whole Page and review the more even column lengths
Step 6	*Click*	the Undo button 🔄 on the Standard toolbar to remove the manual column break

Another way to use manual column breaks is to keep related text together in columns. For example, look at the heading and two lines of the following paragraph at the bottom of column one in the *September Newsletter* document. The remaining paragraph text flows to the top of

QUICK TIP

You can have Word balance column length automatically by inserting a continuous section break at the end of the columns you want to balance.

A fast way to insert a column break is with shortcut keys. Move the insertion point to the desired position and press the CTRL + SHIFT + ENTER keys to insert a column break.

chapter
ten

column two. It would be easier to read if both were in the same column. You can keep both the paragraph heading and following paragraph text together by inserting a manual column break. To insert a manual column break at the bottom of column one:

Step 1	*Zoom*	the document to 75% so you can read the text
Step 2	*Move*	the insertion point to the left margin of the last paragraph heading in column one
Step 3	*Insert*	a manual column break

The paragraph heading and two lines move to the top of column two with the remaining paragraph text. However, this column break does not create even column lengths. You decide to see how the document looks with other column formats.

Revising the Column Structure

The Columns dialog box provide a variety of formatting options that save you time creating newspaper-style columns. The five preset newspaper-style column formats are: <u>O</u>ne column, <u>T</u>wo columns, <u>T</u>hree columns, <u>L</u>eft column, and <u>R</u>ight column. The <u>O</u>ne, <u>T</u>wo, and <u>T</u>hree column formats create even column widths. The <u>L</u>eft and <u>R</u>ight column formats create uneven column widths. You can also add a horizontal line as a divider between the columns.

Word cannot remove a manual column break when it applies a different column format to text. So to reformat columns, you should first remove any manual column breaks. You do this moving the insertion point to the right of the column break and pressing the BACKSPACE key. To revise the column structure:

Step 1	*Verify*	the insertion point is at the top of column two
Step 2	*Press*	the BACKSPACE key
Step 3	*Click*	F<u>o</u>rmat
Step 4	*Click*	<u>C</u>olumns

The Columns dialog box that opens on your screen should look similar to Figure 10-2.

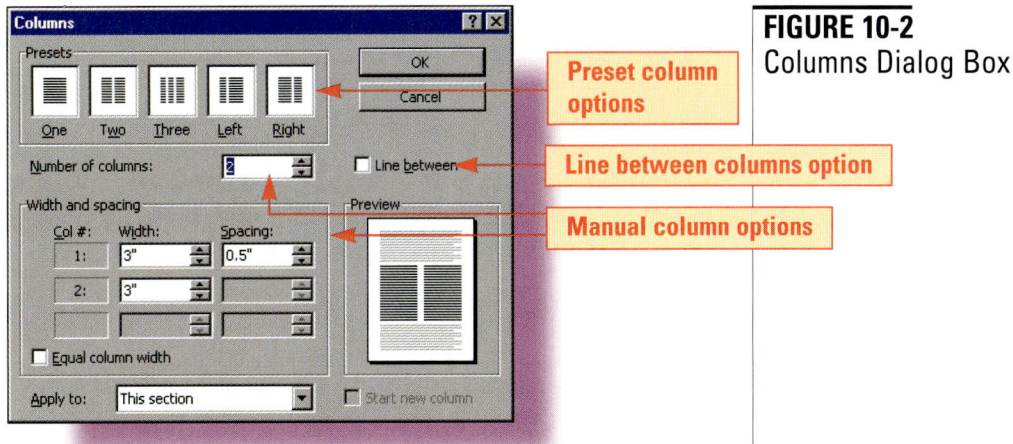

FIGURE 10-2
Columns Dialog Box

First you try two newspaper-style columns with uneven widths.

Step 5	*Click*	Right in the Presets group
Step 6	*Click*	OK
Step 7	*Zoom*	the document to Whole Page and review the columns

The text is in a wide left column and narrow right column. To try three evenly spaced columns with lines between them:

Step 1	*Open*	the Columns dialog box
Step 2	*Click*	Three in the Presets group
Step 3	*Click*	the Line between check box to insert a check mark
Step 4	*Click*	OK

The text now appears in three evenly spaced columns with a vertical line between each column. You decide you liked two evenly spaced columns for the document. To modify the *September Newsletter* document:

Step 1	*Open*	the Columns dialog box
Step 2	*Click*	Two in the Presets group
Step 3	*Click*	the Line between check box to remove the check mark
Step 4	*Click*	OK
Step 5	*Insert*	a manual column break before the last paragraph heading at the bottom of column one

M O U S E   T I P

You can change column widths by dragging the column indicator on the horizontal ruler with the mouse.

chapter
ten

| Step 6 | *Zoom* | the document to 75% so you can read the text |
| Step 7 | *Save* | the document |

To make the *September Newsletter* document more interesting to readers, Jody asks you to create and format an attractive drawing object at the bottom of column two.

10.b Using the Drawing Toolbar

Word provides a special toolbar, called the Drawing toolbar, which provides tools for creating and editing drawing objects in a document. **Drawing objects** are graphic items such as shapes, curves, and lines that can be created and edited with tools on the Drawing toolbar. For example, you can draw lines, arrows, rectangles, squares, ovals, special preset shapes called **AutoShapes**, and three-dimensional shapes by selecting the kind of object you want and then drawing the object with the mouse pointer. You can edit drawing objects to add text and color.

notes It is a good idea to use the ScreenTips feature to review the buttons on each toolbar with which you are unfamiliar. For the remainder of this book it is assumed that each time a new toolbar is introduced you review the toolbar buttons before continuing with the step-by-step activities.

Jody suggests you draw a line below the text in column two and then add a "Congratulations!" banner below the text in column two. To view the Drawing toolbar and draw a line below the text in column two:

Step 1	*Move*	the insertion point to the bottom of column two
Step 2	*Click*	the Drawing button on the Standard toolbar to display the Drawing toolbar
Step 3	*Click*	the Line button on the Drawing toolbar
Step 4	*Move*	the mouse pointer to the left margin of column two approximately ¼ inch below the text (it becomes a drawing crosshair pointer)
Step 5	*Press & Hold*	the left mouse button

Step 6	*Drag*	approximately three inches to the right
Step 7	*Release*	the mouse button to create the line

Notice the small white squares at either end of the line. These are **sizing handles**, which you drag with the mouse pointer to change the size and shape of a drawing object. When you place the mouse pointer on a sizing handle, it becomes a black, two-headed sizing pointer that you use to drag the sizing handle in the desired direction. If you drag a corner sizing handle, the object maintains its vertical and horizontal proportion. The sizing handles also indicate an object is selected. To deselect the line object:

Step 1	*Click*	in the document outside the line object

You use the AutoShapes tool to quickly draw special shapes such as stars and banners.

Using the AutoShapes Tool

The AutoShapes tool has many different preset shapes you can draw with the mouse pointer. To draw an AutoShape, you first select the shape to draw, move the mouse pointer to the appropriate location in the document, press and hold the left mouse button, and then drag downward and to the right to draw the shape. When the AutoShape object is the correct size, you release the mouse button.

To create the banner AutoShape in the newsletter:

Step 1	*Click*	the AutoShapes button `AutoShapes ▾` on the Drawing toolbar
Step 2	*Point to*	Stars and Banners

The AutoShapes menu and Stars and Banners palette you see on your screen should look similar to Figure 10-3.

QUICK TIP

To view a collection of pictures (also called **clips**) drawn with the AutoShapes tool, click the More AutoShapes command on the AutoShapes menu. Scroll to view the individual AutoShapes clips. To insert a clip in your document, right-click the clip and then click Insert.

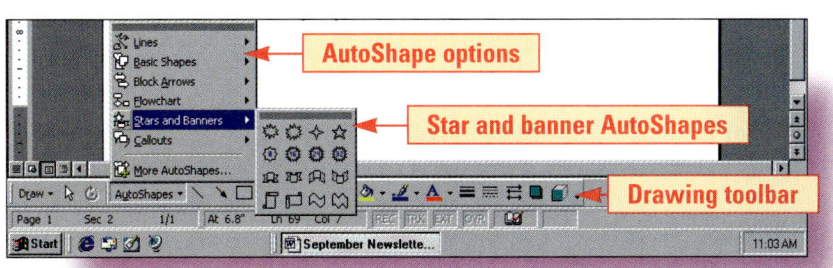

FIGURE 10-3
AutoShapes Stars and Banners Palette

chapter
ten

Step 3	*Click*	the Down Ribbon option on the Stars and Banners grid (second column, the third row)
Step 4	*Move*	the mouse pointer to the left boundary of column two in the white space approximately ¼ inch below the line drawing object
Step 5	*Press & Hold*	the mouse button
Step 6	*Drag*	down approximately two inches and to the right approximately three inches
Step 7	*Release*	the mouse button to create the banner drawing object
Step 8	*Observe*	the sizing handles on the boundary of the banner object, indicating the object is selected
Step 9	*Deselect*	the banner object

The banner object on your screen should look similar to Figure 10-4.

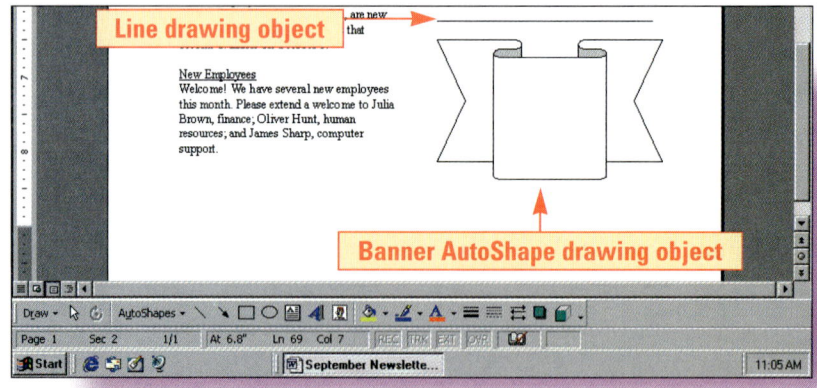

The banner drawing object is no longer selected. You can add text, shadow, and color to a drawing object.

Modifying Drawing Objects

To modify, or edit, a drawing object, you must first select it. Then you can use buttons on the Drawing toolbar to add fill (inside) color, line (border) color, a shadow effect, and even a three-dimensional effect to the object. You can also edit a drawing object with a shortcut menu and dialog box options.

You change the fill and line color, and add a blue shadow effect to the banner object. To modify the banner object:

Step 1	*Right-click*	the banner object

QUICK TIP

You can select AutoShapes, WordArt, drawing objects, and graphic objects, and then drag them to a new position or delete them.
You can also right-click an AutoShape, WordArt, or graphic object and click the Format *object* command to position the object on the page.

FIGURE 10-4
Down Ribbon
Drawing Object

CAUTION TIP

Word provides the Click and Type feature in Print Layout view and Web Layout view. With this feature, you can move the mouse pointer anywhere in the document and double-click to position the insertion point without pressing the ENTER key to add blank lines. The Click and Type I-beam displays a horizontal alignment indictor (left, center, right, and justified).

Step 2	*Click*	Format Aut<u>o</u>Shape

Step 3	*Click*	the Colors and Lines tab, if necessary

The Format AutoShape dialog box that opens on your screen should look similar to Figure 10-5.

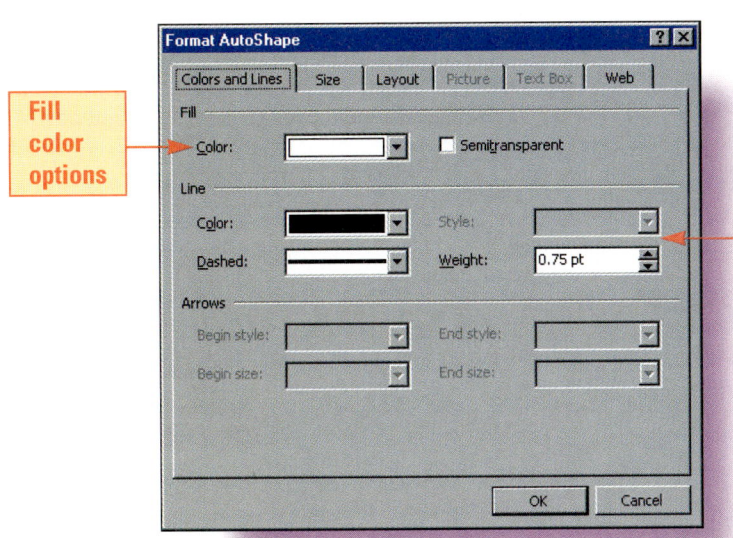

Fill color options

Line size, weight, and color options

FIGURE 10-5
Colors and Lines Tab in the Format AutoShape Dialog Box

Step 4	*Click*	the Fill <u>C</u>olor: list arrow
Step 5	*Click*	Red (first column, third row)
Step 6	*Click*	the Line C<u>o</u>lor: list arrow
Step 7	*Click*	Blue (sixth column, second row)
Step 8	*Click*	OK
Step 9	*Click*	the Shadow button 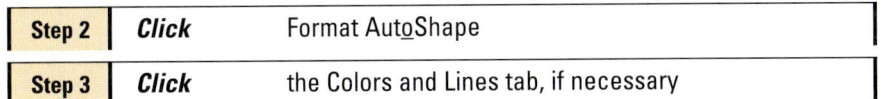 on the Drawing toolbar
Step 10	*Click*	Shadow Style 2 on the Shadow grid (second column, first row)
Step 11	*Click*	the Shadow button on the Drawing toolbar
Step 12	*Click*	<u>S</u>hadow Settings to display the Shadow Settings toolbar
Step 13	*Click*	the Shadow Color button list arrow on the Shadow Settings toolbar
Step 14	*Click*	Blue on the Shadow Color grid (sixth column, second row)
Step 15	*Close*	the Shadow Settings toolbar

M O U S E   T I P

You can insert pictures in your document by clicking the Insert Clip Art button on the Drawing toolbar to open the Clip Gallery. Then select and insert a picture.

You can insert specially formatted text by clicking the Insert WordArt button on the Drawing toolbar.

chapter
ten

QUICK TIP

C Word supports two basic kinds of graphics: drawing objects and pictures. The two kinds of pictures you can insert are **metafiles** (pictures you can ungroup and convert to objects) and **bitmaps** (pictures you cannot ungroup). For more information on inserting and editing graphics see online Help.

Because the banner is meant to draw attention to the New Employees, you add the text "Congratulations!" to the banner. You can add text to a drawing object with a shortcut menu. To add and edit text to the banner object:

Step 1	*Right-click*	the banner object
Step 2	*Click*	Add Te<u>x</u>t
Step 3	*Observe*	the insertion point inside the banner object
Step 4	*Press*	the ENTER key twice to move the insertion point down two lines
Step 5	*Key*	Congratulations!
Step 6	*Select*	the text
Step 7	*Center*	the text
Step 8	*Change*	the font size to 14
Step 9	*Click*	the Font Color button list arrow [A] on the Drawing toolbar
Step 10	*Click*	Blue (sixth column, second row)

If the text area in the banner object is too small to contain the formatted text on one line, the text wraps to the next line. You can increase the size of the object, if necessary, so the text fits on one line. To size the banner object, if necessary:

Step 1	*Move*	the insertion point to the lower-right corner sizing handle (the mouse pointer becomes a black, two-headed sizing pointer)
Step 2	*Drag*	the sizing handle down and right approximately ¼ inch or until the formatted text fits inside the banner object without wrapping to the next line
Step 3	*Deselect*	the banner object
Step 4	*Save*	the document

The banner drawing object on your screen is now red with a blue boundary, blue shadow effect, and blue text. Some drawing objects can have a three-dimensional shape. Instead of the banner object, you decide to use a three-dimensional rectangle object.

Creating and Modifying 3-D Shapes

When you no longer want a drawing object in your document, you can select and delete it. To select an object that contains text, move the mouse pointer to the object's boundary. The mouse pointer then becomes a move or selection pointer. (If you move the pointer to the text area of an object, it becomes an I-beam.) To select and delete the banner object:

Step 1	*Move*	the mouse pointer to the banner object's boundary
Step 2	*Click*	the banner object's boundary with the move or selection pointer to select the object
Step 3	*Press*	the DELETE key

In place of the banner object, you draw a rectangle and then add color, text, and a three-dimensional effect. To create and modify a rectangle drawing object:

Step 1	*Click*	the Rectangle button ▢ on the Drawing toolbar
Step 2	*Move*	the mouse pointer to the left margin of column two in the white space below the line
Step 3	*Drag*	down approximately one inch and to the right approximately three inches to create the rectangle object
Step 4	*Select*	the rectangle drawing object, if necessary
Step 5	*Click*	the Fill Color button list arrow 🎨 on the Drawing toolbar
Step 6	*Click*	Orange on the Fill Color grid (second color, second row)
Step 7	*Click*	the 3-D button 🔲 on the Drawing toolbar
Step 8	*Click*	3-D Style 1 on the grid (first style, first row)
Step 9	*Click*	the 3-D button 🔲 on the Drawing toolbar
Step 10	*Click*	3-D Settings to view the 3-D Settings toolbar

QUICK TIP

C You can add interest to your documents by adding borders and shading to selected paragraphs. Select the paragraph text and then click the Borders and Shading command on the Format menu to view border and shading options.

chapter
ten

You can turn on or off the 3-D effect, tilt the 3-D object, change its shape and direction, change the lighting effect for any side, change the surface composition, and change the color with buttons on this toolbar. You lighten the color on the front surface of the object.

Step 11	Click	the Lighting button on the 3-D Settings toolbar
Step 12	Click	the button in the center of the grid
Step 13	Close	the 3-D Settings toolbar

Next you key text in the rectangle and format it. To add text:

Step 1	Right-click	the 3-D rectangle object
Step 2	Click	Add Text
Step 3	Key	Congratulations! two lines from the top of the object
Step 4	Select	the text
Step 5	Format	the text with 22 point, bold, white color font, and center alignment

Now that the rectangle is complete, you can resize and reposition it. To size and move the rectangle object:

Step 1	Verify	the rectangle object is selected
Step 2	Drag	the lower-right sizing handle down and to the right approximately ¼ inch with the black, double-headed sizing pointer
Step 3	Drag	the rectangle object from the bottom boundary of the object with the selection or move pointer until it is positioned attractively below the line
Step 4	Deselect	the object
Step 5	Click	the Drawing button on the Standard toolbar to close the Drawing toolbar
Step 6	Save	the document and close it

The completed newsletter looks much more attractive and interesting with the added drawing objects.

Summary

- ▶ Newspaper-style columns are appropriate for documents like brochures or newsletters.

- ▶ When you use newspaper-style columns, the text fills the length of one column before moving to the next column.

- ▶ You can create newspaper-style columns for an entire document or for a section of a document.

- ▶ You can select text and create columns from the selected text, or you can insert a section break and then create columns for the text in a specific section.

- ▶ You can view text columns in Print Layout view or Print Preview, but not in Normal view.

- ▶ When you use the Columns button on the Standard toolbar, Word creates columns that are equal in width by default.

- ▶ You can create columns of unequal width by using one of the two preset unequal-width column options or by specifying the exact column width in the Columns dialog box.

- ▶ You can add a vertical divider line between columns.

- ▶ Drawing objects—such as shapes, lines, and curves—are graphic items that you draw and edit with buttons on the Drawing toolbar.

- ▶ AutoShapes are special preset shapes—such as stars, banners, and flowchart symbols—that you draw with the mouse pointer.

- ▶ You can add fill and line color and three-dimensional shapes to drawing objects with buttons on the Drawing toolbar.

chapter ten

Commands Review

Action	Menu Bar	Shortcut Menu	Toolbar	Keyboard
Create columns of text	Format, Columns		(icon)	ALT + O, C
Insert a column break	Insert, Break			ALT + I, B CTRL + SHIFT + ENTER
View the Drawing toolbar	View, Toolbars, Drawing	Right-click any toolbar, click Drawing	(icon)	ALT + V, T, DOWN ARROW, ENTER
Format a drawing object		Right-click the object, click Format (object name)	Various buttons on the Drawing toolbar	

Concepts Review

Circle the correct answer.

1. **Which of the following is not a preset option for creating columns in the Columns dialog box?**
   [a] Right
   [b] Center
   [c] Left
   [d] Two

2. **Which of the following is not an AutoShapes category?**
   [a] Basic Shapes
   [b] Block Arrows
   [c] Hearts and Flowers
   [d] Stars and Banners

3. **When you use the Columns button, columns are automatically created with:**
   [a] unequal column widths.
   [b] equal column widths.
   [c] divider lines.
   [d] justified alignment.

4. **To add a special effect to a drawing object, you can click the:**
   [a] Shadow button on the Drawing toolbar.
   [b] 3-D button on the Standard toolbar.
   [c] Fill Color button on the Formatting toolbar.
   [d] AutoShapes command on the menu bar.

5. **To balance columns of uneven length, you should insert a(n):**
   [a] page break.
   [b] even page section break.
   [c] column break.
   [d] line break.

6. **To prevent a document title from becoming part of a column you can:**
   [a] insert a section break below the title.
   [b] apply a 14-point font to the title.
   [c] center and bold the title.
   [d] indent the title.

7. **When you add text to a drawing object, and move the mouse pointer to the text area, it becomes a(n):**
   [a] move pointer.
   [b] sizing handle.
   [c] sizing pointer.
   [d] I-beam.

8. **Before you apply different column formats, you should remove the manual:**
   [a] page breaks.
   [b] section breaks.
   [c] column breaks.
   [d] line breaks.

9. You can use sizing handles to:
  [a] format drawing objects.
  [b] position text in newspaper-style columns.
  [c] change the size and shape of drawing objects.
  [d] draw preset stars, banners, and other graphic items.

10. To draw a straight line, square, or oval you use a button on the Drawing toolbar and the:
  [a] CTRL key
  [b] ALT key.
  [c] SHIFT key.
  [d] TAB key.

Circle **T** if the statement is true or **F** is the statement is false.

T F 1. With newspaper-style columns, text fills one column before moving to the next column on a page.

T F 2. Columns appear on the screen only in Print Layout view.

T F 3. You can redistribute text in columns by inserting a manual page break.

T F 4. The insertion point must be in the document section formatted in columns to revise the number of columns.

T F 5. You can change column width by dragging the column marker on the horizontal ruler.

T F 6. You can view vertical lines between columns in Normal view.

T F 7. You cannot create a manual column break with shortcut keys.

T F 8. Columns are created in unequal width when you use the Columns button.

T F 9. To draw an AutoShape you first select the shape, press the left mouse button, and drag down and to the right.

T F 10. You create three-dimensional shapes with a button on the Formatting toolbar.

Skills Review

Exercise 1

1. Open the *Legislative Update* document located on the Data Disk.

2. Insert a continuous section break below the second title line "LEGISLATIVE UPDATE."

3. Format the text in Section 2 with two columns of even width.

4. Insert column breaks so that the columns are approximately the same lengths.

5. Add a vertical line between the columns.

6. Switch to Normal view and select the two lines of title text in Section 1.

7. Expand the characters in the title text by 0.5 points. (*Hint:* Use the Character Spacing tab in the Font dialog box.)

8. Save the document as *Legislative Update With Columns*.

9. Preview, print, and close the document.

chapter ten

Exercise 2

1. Create a new, blank document.

2. Display the Drawing toolbar.

3. Draw a rectangle and fill it with blue. Change the line color to yellow. Change the line style to 2¼ point.

4. Draw an arrow to the right of the rectangle and format it with red using the Line Color button. Change the arrowhead style to Arrow Style 7 using the Arrow Style button.

5. Draw an oval below the rectangle and fill it with yellow. Change the line color to red. Change the line style to 6 point (three narrow and one wide line option). Add the text "Oval" in red, 14-point font in the center of the oval.

6. Using the SHIFT key and the Rectangle button, draw a square below the arrow and fill it with orange. Add the 3-D Style 17 to the square. Change the lighting effect to brighten the top of the 3-D object. Change the 3-D color to gold. (*Hint:* Use the 3-D Color button on the 3-D Settings toolbar.)

7. Using the SHIFT key and the Oval button draw a circle below the square and fill it with purple. Change the line color to orange. Add a light orange shadow effect to the circle.

8. Save the document as *Drawing Objects*.

9. Preview, print, and close the document.

Exercise 3

1. Open the *Announcements* document located on the Data Disk.

2. Find all instances of underlined text and replace it with no underline and Small Caps effect.

3. Format the entire document in two columns of uneven width using the <u>R</u>ight preset option.

4. Select the entire document and justify the text.

5. Save the document as *Announcements Revised*.

6. Preview, print, and close the document.

Exercise 4

1. Create a new, blank document.

2. Center the title "AutoShapes" in Arial, 14-point, bold font.

3. Display the Drawing toolbar.

4. Using the AutoShapes tool, draw five AutoShapes of your choice anywhere in the document.

5. Use fill and line color as desired.

6. Add text to two of the AutoShapes.

7. Format the text as desired.

8. Save the document as *AutoShape Examples*.

9. Preview, print, and close the document.

Exercise 5

1. Open the *Chicago Warehouses Audit* report located on the Data Disk.

2. Format the body text (not the title) in two columns of even width.

3. Insert a manual column break at the paragraph beginning "A consulting company...."

4. Save the document as *Chicago Warehouses Audit With Columns*.

5. Preview, print, and close the document.

Exercise 6

1. Create the following document. Use a 2-inch top and 1-inch left and right margins. Use the Times New Roman 10-point font for the body text and 12-point bold font for the title text.

2. Use newspaper-style columns for the body text beginning with "Pink Beach" paragraph heading.

3. Insert a manual column break to more evenly space the columns.

WORLDWIDE EXOTIC FOODS, INC.
TRAVEL SERVICES SPRING RECOMMENDATION
BONAIRE

On this sleepy island only 50 miles off the coast of Venezuela, where pink flamingos outnumber people, scuba diving is the sport of choice among visitors. Bonaire takes an enlightened approach to its marine environment, with the entire perimeter of the island from the high-water mark to 200 feet below deemed a protected park with restricted coral taking and spear fishing. Many attractions are described below.

Pink Beach
The prettiest stretch of sand on the island, Pink Beach lies on the southwestern shore and really does takes on a pinkish hue in the late afternoon sun. The powder-soft sand and bathwater-calm water makes it perfect for swimming, snorkeling, and scuba diving.

Salt Flats and Slave Huts
On the southern end of the island, huge white pyramids of industrial salt—looking like misplaced mounds of snow—are harvested by the Akzo Salt Antilles Company. The salt industry, which began in the early 19th century, formerly employed African slaves, who worked the fields by day, then slept in cramped huts (which can still be seen along the roadside) by night, returning to their homes in Rincon only on weekends.

Kralendijk
The quiet capital city of this serene island has only one main street—J. A. Abraham Boulevard, which turns into Kaya Grandi.

Boca Cai
At the mouth of La Bay on the eastern side of the island, this serene beach boasts mountainous heaps of conch shells, left there by fishermen. On weekends, particularly Sundays, Boca Cai is the place to be as two snack shacks open their doors, a meringue band strikes up the tunes, and locals and in-the-know visitors congregate for food, fun, music, and cold beverages.

---

4. Save the document as *Travel Services Recommendation*.

5. Preview, print, and close the document.

chapter ten

Exercise 7

1. Create the following document. Use a 2-inch top and 1-inch left and right margins. Use the Arial 10-point font for the body text and 12-point bold font for the title text.

2. Use three columns of equal width for the body text and insert the appropriate manual column breaks. Add a vertical line between the columns.

3. Save the document as *Office Technology Society*.

4. Preview, print, and close the document.

OFFICE TECHNOLOGY SOCIETY

OTS PURPOSE
Our primary purpose is to offer a symposium to exchange ideas among business and academic members. This knowledge facilitates research that helps the office workplace.

Secondarily, we advise the public on changes in office information technology in the areas of analysis, design, and administrative decision support.

OTS ACTIVITIES
- **Newsletter** – Published monthly. Update activities, conferences, research projects.

- **Journal** – Contains major excerpts from the research projects taken on by the members.

- **Research Conference** – A two-day annual conference where ideas and trends in office technology are discussed and papers are presented.

OTS MEMBERSHIP
1. Faculty members and students in the office technology field.

2. Administrators in business and government who manage office technology for their organizations.

3. Administrators, research directors, and vendors in the field of office technology.

Exercise 8

1. Open the *Training Commitment* document located on the Data Disk.

2. Create two newspaper-style columns of even width for the entire document.

3. Insert a column break at the "About Our Courses" paragraph.

4. Display the Drawing toolbar.

5. Draw a straight line across the bottom of the columns from the left margin of column one to the right margin of column two.

6. Draw a 24-point star AutoShape approximately two inches tall and two inches wide below the line and fill it with yellow. Change the border around the star to blue. (*Hint:* Use the Line Color button list arrow.)

7. Center the text "Our Training Commitment" on three lines near the center of the object and format the text with 14-point font.

8. Size the star, if necessary, to accommodate the new font size.

9. Zoom the document to Whole Page and reposition the star object close to the center of the page below the line with the mouse pointer then zoom back to 100%.

10. Select the line object and use the Line Style button to format the line with the 2¼ point style. (*Hint:* Click the line to select it.)

11. Save the document as *Training Commitment With Columns*.

12. Preview, print, and close the document.

Case Projects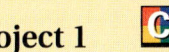

Project 1

You are the secretary for the local chapter of the Office Technology Society and you prepare a quarterly newsletter for all chapter members. Create a newsletter titled "OFFICE TECHNOLOGY BULLETIN" with two newspaper-style columns of body text containing fictitious data for the following paragraph headings:

> Membership Drive
>
> New Members
>
> Annual Conference
>
> User Tips for Word 2000
>
> Hot Internet Sites

Add a line between the columns. Add an appropriate drawing object at the bottom of column two. Using online Help, review the "about graphics" topic, then use the Insert Clip Art and Insert WordArt buttons on the Drawing toolbar to insert metafiles, bitmaps, WordArt and other graphic objects in the newsletter. Insert at least five objects. Reposition two objects. Delete two objects. Use the Borders and Shading dialog box to apply borders and shading to selected paragraphs in the newsletter. Save, preview, and print the document.

Project 2

Jody Haversham is transferred to another department. Bill Martin, the new administrative assistant to B. J. Chang, is having trouble preparing the monthly employee newsletter. He does not know how to change column widths or balance the column text so that the newsletter has an attractive appearance; he asks you for help. Create an interoffice memorandum to Bill describing how to use the Office Assistant to troubleshoot problems with columns. Include two paragraphs explaining how to change column widths and balance column text. Save, preview, and print the memorandum.

chapter ten

Project 3

Your new assignment in the human resources department is to fill in for the corporate librarian while she is at a conference. Joe Beck in the finance department requests a list of investment-oriented online magazines and newsletters. Connect to your ISP, load your Web browser, and search for investment-oriented online newsletters and magazines. Print at least two Web pages. Write an interoffice memo to Joe describing the results of your search. Use two evenly-spaced columns separated by a line for the Web page descriptions. Add an appropriate AutoShape drawing object to the memo. Attach the Web pages you printed.

Project 4

Bill Martin drops by your desk to tell you about the AutoShape pictures he discovered. You want to experiment using these AutoShapes and then tell Kelly Armstead and Jody Haversham about them. Create a new, blank document. Display the Drawing toolbar, click the More AutoShapes command on the AutoShapes menu. Explore the contents of the More AutoShapes dialog box. Explore inserting AutoShape pictures in the blank document. Write an interoffice memorandum to both Kelly and Jody describing the AutoShapes pictures and suggesting ways they can use them in their documents. Save, preview, and print the memo.

Project 5

Chris Lofton, the manager of the word processing department, calls and asks for your help. The word processing department is experiencing delays in getting final documents to the authors. Chris thinks a flowchart illustrating an efficient workflow in the department will help identify any bottlenecks. You agree to help by creating the flowchart. Use the Flowchart and Lines options on the AutoShapes button to create a flowchart of an efficient workflow that includes keying, proofreading, editing, and printing documents. Add text and color to the drawing objects in the flowchart. Save, preview, and print the flowchart.

Project 6

The human resources department is helping a neighborhood civic association to hold its annual fund-raising bake sale by providing clerical support for the association. You are asked to create a flyer announcing the bake sale that can be copied and posted at neighborhood stores. Create an 8½ × 11-inch flyer using fictitious data announcing the bake sale. Include a map showing the major roads and specific intersections and address of the building where the bake sale is to be held. (*Hint:* Use AutoShapes and other drawing objects to create the map.) Include formatting drawing objects to highlight the event. Assume the flyer is to be printed on white paper on a color printer. Use color in the fonts and drawing objects. Save, preview, and print the flyer.

Project 7

Bill Martin calls and asks for help. B. J. Chang wants a list of Web-based training classes covering office technology topics and Bill is not familiar with the WWW. You agree to search for the Web sites and write a memo to Chang. Connect to your ISP, load your Web browser, and search for Web sites providing online classes in office technology topics. Print at least three Web pages. Write an interoffice memorandum to B. J. Chang describing the results of your search. Use columns and drawing objects to make the memo more interesting. Save, preview, and print the memorandum. Attach the Web pages to the memorandum.

Project 8

While working on the September newsletter, you noticed three AutoShape lines with which you are unfamiliar: the Curve, the Freeform, and the Scribble lines. You want to know how to use these line drawing tools. Using the Office Assistant, research how to use these three tools. Create a new, blank document and experiment using each of the tools. Save, preview, and print the document.

Using Tables to Organize Information

Chapter Overview

Certain columnar data included in a document, such as budgets and price lists, needs to be organized in a logical manner so that it is easier to read and understand. You could use tabs to organize this data, but usually it is simpler to place it in a table. In this chapter you learn how to create and edit tables, format them attractively, use formulas to perform calculations, and switch text to tables and back again.

LEARNING OBJECTIVES

- ▶ Create and format tables
- ▶ Revise tables and modify table structure
- ▶ Use special table features
- ▶ Switch between text and tables

Case profile

The marketing and sales departments at Worldwide Exotic Foods, Inc. are getting ready for the busy holiday shopping season and need assistance preparing correspondence and reports. You are assigned to handle the work overflow for both departments. First you create a letter about advertising budgets, then you create a holiday price list cover sheet, and finally you format the latest phone extension list for the company's sales representatives. You use tables in each document.

chapter eleven

11.a Creating and Formatting Tables

R. D. Jacobson, the media director for the marketing department, gives you a page of handwritten notes and asks you to use the notes to create a letter to the advertising agency that develops the media buying plans for Worldwide Exotic Foods. The letter contains the media budget for this year's holiday season. Jacobson's executive assistant, Maria Betancourt, suggests you organize the budget data in a table. You begin by creating a new, blank document and keying part of text. To create the letter:

Step 1	*Create*	a new, blank document
Step 2	*Set*	the appropriate margins for a block format letter
Step 3	*Key*	the current date, letter address, salutation, and first two body paragraphs shown in Figure 11-1
Step 4	*Press*	the ENTER key twice
Step 5	*Zoom*	the document to Page Width, if necessary, to view the text at the right margin

The next part of the letter contains the table of information. A **table** is a grid organized into columns and rows. A **column** is a set of information that runs down the page. A **row** runs across the page. A **cell** occurs at a column and row intersection. First, you create the table grid and key the data in the table cells. You can then add or remove the table border, format the text using the same formatting features you use for the body text, size the table, and position the table on the page.

The Insert Table button on the Standard toolbar displays a grid from which you select the number of rows and columns for the table by dragging the mouse pointer down and across the grid. To create a table with 5 rows and 4 columns:

Step 1	*Click*	the Insert Table button ⊞ on the Standard toolbar
Step 2	*Move*	the mouse pointer to the upper-left cell in the grid
Step 3	*Observe*	the text "1 x 1 Table" at the bottom of the grid, indicating one row and one column are selected
Step 4	*Drag*	the mouse pointer down five rows and across four columns (until you see 5 x 4 Table at the bottom of the grid)

FIGURE 11-1
Completed Dynamic
Advertising Letter

Current date

Ms. Sue Wong
Account Executive
Dynamic Advertising Agency
3268 West International Blvd.
Dallas, TX 75211-1052

Dear Ms. Wong:

Please extend our thanks and congratulations to everyone at the Dynamic Advertising Agency
who works on the Worldwide Exotic Foods, Inc. account. Because of the outstanding media
program developed by your team last year, we experienced outstanding holiday sales.

We anticipate holiday sales for this year to exceed last year. Therefore, we are increasing this
year's media budget by 20%. The budget is detailed below:

	Worldwide Exotic Foods, Inc. Media Budget			
Branch Office	**Holiday Baskets**	**Beverage Baskets**	**Gift Certificates**	**Total**
Chicago	$133,175.45	$55,321.89	$11,500.98	$199,998.32
London	74,768.90	46,987.37	10,589.32	132,345.59
Melbourne	97,509.52	30,890.00	1,561.25	129,960.77
Vancouver	458,321.89	138,079.43	15,345.95	611,747.27
Total	$763,775.76	$271,278.69	$38,997.50	$1,074,051.95

We can discuss these budget figures in detail at our media program meeting next week.

Sincerely,

R. D. Jacobson
Media Director

xx

Step 5	**_Release_**	the mouse button to create the table
Step 6	**_Save_**	the document as _Dynamic Advertising Letter_

The insertion point automatically appears in the first cell of the table. Whenever the insertion point is in the table, column markers also appear on the horizontal ruler. Word inserts table nonprinting formatting marks, called end-of-cell and end-of-row marks, in the table. You use these formatting marks to select cells, rows, and columns.

Step 7	**_Click_**	the Show/Hide button ¶ on the Standard toolbar to view the table formatting marks, if necessary

chapter
eleven

Your screen should look similar to Figure 11-2.

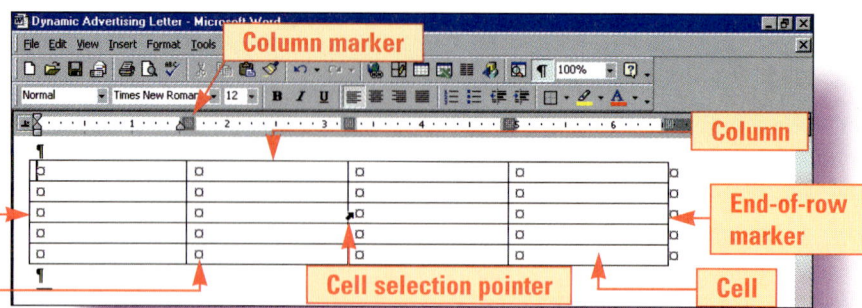

FIGURE 11-2
Table Grid,
Column Markers, and
Formatting Marks

FIGURE 11-2
Table Grid,
Column Markers, and
Formatting Marks

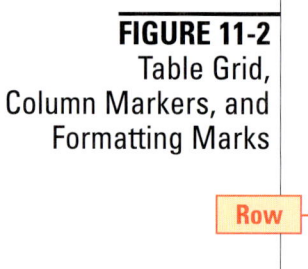

QUICK TIP

Remember that the selection bar runs from the ruler to the View buttons along the document's left margin.

To key text in a table you must move the insertion point from cell to cell.

Moving the Insertion Point in a Table

You can use the I-beam and the keyboard to move the insertion point from cell to cell. You do not press the ENTER key. Pressing the ENTER key creates a new line inside the cell. To move the insertion point with the I-beam, just click in the appropriate cell. To use the keyboard, press the appropriate ARROW key, press the TAB key to move one cell to the right, or press the SHIFT + TAB keys to move one cell to the left. Table 11-1 lists keyboard methods for moving the insertion point in a table.

TABLE 11-1
Table Movement Keys

Location	Keys	Location	Keys
One cell down	DOWN ARROW	First cell in a row	ALT + HOME
One cell right	TAB (RIGHT ARROW, if the cell is empty)	Last cell in a row	ALT + END
One cell left	SHIFT + TAB (LEFT ARROW, if the cell is empty)	First cell in a column	ALT + PAGE UP
One cell up	UP ARROW	Last cell in a column	ALT + PAGE DOWN

CAUTION TIP

By default, the table is created with thin, black borders that print. If you do not want to print a border you can remove it by moving the insertion point inside the table, opening the Borders and Shading dialog box, and clicking the None preset option on the Borders tab.

To move the insertion point in the table:

Step 1	*Click*	the middle of the first cell of the second row
Step 2	*Press*	the UP ARROW key
Step 3	*Continue*	to practice moving the insertion point in the table using Table 11-1 as your guide

Step 4	*Move*	the insertion point to the first cell (upper-left corner) in the table

Now you are ready to key the text in the table.

Keying Text in Tables

You key the column headings in the first row of the table, called the **heading row**, and then key the branch office budget data in the following rows. Do not worry about keying the Totals row or column now; you add these later. As you key the numbers, do not align them in the cells. You align the numbers later. If you accidentally press the ENTER key while keying data in a cell, press the BACKSPACE key to remove the paragraph mark and blank line from the cell. To key the column headings:

Step 1	*Verify*	the insertion point is in the first cell in the first row
Step 2	*Key*	Branch Office and press the TAB key
Step 3	*Key*	Holiday Baskets and press the TAB key
Step 4	*Key*	Beverage Baskets and press the TAB key
Step 5	*Key*	Gift Certificates and press the TAB key

The insertion point moves to the first cell in the second row. Now you can key the rest of the data.

Step 6	*Key*	Chicago and press the TAB key
Step 7	*Continue*	to key the remaining data in the Branch Office, Holiday Baskets, Beverage Baskets, and Gift Certificates columns for the Chicago, London, Melbourne, and Vancouver branches, as shown in Figure 11-1 (*do not key the total text or numbers*)
Step 8	*Save*	the document

In addition to moving the insertion point from cell to cell, you also select cells, rows, and columns to format or delete the contents or to insert or delete the cells, rows, and columns.

Selecting Cells, Rows, and Columns

Before you can format the table contents, you must select the cells that contain the text. If you move the mouse pointer to the lower-left corner of a cell, to the selection bar to the left of a row, or to the top of

chapter
eleven

a column, the mouse pointer becomes a selection pointer. You can also select parts of a table with the keyboard. Table 11-2 lists mouse pointer and keyboard selection techniques.

TABLE 11-2
Table Selection Methods

Selection	Mouse	Keyboard
Cell	Move the mouse pointer inside the left boundary of a cell and click	Move the insertion point to the cell and press the SHIFT + END keys
Several cells	Drag across the cells with the selection pointer or the I-beam	Move the insertion point to the first cell, press and hold the SHIFT key, and then press the UP, DOWN, LEFT, or RIGHT ARROW key
Column	Move the mouse pointer to the top of the column until it becomes a vertical selection pointer then click, or press and hold the ALT key and click a cell in the column with the I-beam pointer	Move the insertion point to the first cell in the column, hold down the SHIFT key, and press the ALT + PAGE DOWN keys
Row	Click the selection bar at the left of the row, or double-click any cell in a row with the selection pointer	Move the insertion point to the first cell in the row, hold down the SHIFT key, and press the ALT + END keys
Table	Drag to select all rows or all columns (including the end-of-row marks) with the selection pointer	Move the insertion point to any cell, press the NUMLOCK key on the numeric keypad to turn off the Number Lock feature, and press the ALT + 5 keys (the 5 key on the numeric keypad).

MENU TIP

You can point to the Select command on the Table menu and then click Table, Column, Row, or Cell to select all or part of the table containing the insertion point.

To select a row, column, and cell in the table:

Step 1	*Move*	the mouse pointer to the left of the first row in the selection bar
Step 2	*Click*	the selection bar
Step 3	*Move*	the mouse pointer to the top of the second column (the mouse pointer becomes a small black selection pointer)
Step 4	*Click*	the column with the selection pointer
Step 5	*Move*	the mouse pointer just inside the left cell boundary in last cell in the last row (the mouse pointer becomes a small black selection pointer)
Step 6	*Click*	the cell with the selection pointer

| Step 7 | *Continue* | to select cells, rows, columns, and the entire table using Table 11-2 as your guide |
| Step 8 | *Move* | the insertion point to the first cell in the first row |

You can delete both the contents of a table and the table grid. To delete the contents of a cell, row, or column, simply select the cell, row, or column and press the DELETE key. To delete the entire table grid or a cell, row, or column, you must use a menu command. First move the insertion point to the table column, row, or cell, point to the Delete command on the Table menu, and click Table, Columns, Rows, or Cells. To delete the first row of the table:

Step 1	*Click*	Table
Step 2	*Point to*	Delete
Step 3	*Click*	Rows

The row is deleted. Because you want to use the entire table in the letter, you restore it.

| Step 4 | *Click* | the Undo button  on the Standard toolbar |

Now you are ready to format the table text.

Changing Cell Formats

To help distinguish the column labels from the rest of the data, you format them. You format text in a table just like you do in the body of a document. To add bold and center the column headings:

Step 1	*Select*	the first row containing the column headings
Step 2	*Click*	the Bold button **B** on the Formatting toolbar
Step 3	*Click*	the Center button on the Formatting toolbar
Step 4	*Click*	any cell to deselect the row
Step 5	*Save*	the document

Later you shade the cells. Now, you add the table heading and the column and row totals.

chapter
eleven

11.b Revising Tables and Modifying Table Structure

Once you create a table, you often need to modify it by inserting rows or columns for additional data, or by deleting unused rows and columns. For the table in the letter, you need to insert a row at the top of the table for the table heading, a row at the bottom of the table for the column totals, and a column at the right of the table for the row totals.

Inserting Rows and Columns

To insert rows or columns, first select the number of rows or columns you want to insert. For example, to insert two rows, select two rows in the table. Then you click the Insert command on the Table menu to insert the rows or columns above or below the selected row and left or right of the selected column. The inserted row retains the formatting from the original row. To add a new row at the top of the table using the Table menu:

Step 1	*Move*	the insertion point to any cell in the first row
Step 2	*Click*	Table
Step 3	*Point to*	Insert
Step 4	*Click*	Rows Above

A new row is inserted at the top of the table. To insert a column at the end of the table, you select the end-of-row marks just like you select a column. To insert a new column at the end of the table:

Step 1	*Select*	the end-of-row marks with the vertical selection pointer
Step 2	*Right-click*	the selection
Step 3	*Click*	Insert Columns
Step 4	*Observe*	the new column inserted to the left of the end-of-cell marks
Step 5	*Click*	the first cell in the new column
Step 6	*Observe*	that the cell is set for bold font and centered alignment, the same as other cells in the row

MOUSE TIP

When you select a table row, the Insert Table button on the Standard toolbar becomes the Insert Rows button. When you select a cell or column, the Insert Table button becomes the Insert Cell or Insert Column button.

The cells in the new column retain the same formatting as other cells in their respective rows. When you add a new column, the overall table size doesn't change but the column widths adjust to accommodate the new column. Notice the column heading "Beverage Baskets" now wraps to two lines and the row height increases to accommodate the new line. The remaining column labels fit on the first text line in each cell. The column labels are more attractive if they are aligned vertically at the bottom of each cell. There are nine cell alignment options, which combine the horizontal options (left, right, and center) with the vertical options (top, bottom, and center). To change the vertical alignment:

Step 1	*Select*	the column labels row
Step 2	*Right-click*	the selected row
Step 3	*Point to*	Cell Alignment
Step 4	*Click*	Align Bottom Center button on the palette
Step 5	*Move*	the insertion point to any cell in the first column

A table heading in the first row helps identify the data in the table. Currently the first row has five cells, one for each column. You only need one cell for a table heading.

Merging Cells

You can combine, or **merge**, cells vertically or horizontally by first selecting the cells to be merged and then clicking the Merge Cells command on the Table menu or a shortcut menu. You can also divide, or **split**, cells vertically or horizontally. Before you key and format the table heading, you must combine or merge the five cells in the first row into one cell. To merge the cells in the first row:

Step 1	*Select*	the first row
Step 2	*Right-click*	the selected row
Step 3	*Click*	Merge Cells

The first row of the table now contains one large cell. To key the two-line table heading:

Step 1	*Key*	Worldwide Exotic Foods, Inc.
Step 2	*Press*	the ENTER key to create a new line in the cell

chapter
eleven

| Step 3 | *Key* | Media Budget |
| Step 4 | *Observe* | that the two-line table heading is centered and bold and the row height increases to accommodate the second line of the heading |

You now need to add a row at the bottom of the table for the category totals. You can do this with the TAB key. To add a row to the bottom of the table:

| Step 1 | *Move* | the insertion point to the last cell in the last row |
| Step 2 | *Press* | the TAB key to add a new row to the bottom of the table |

Your screen should look similar to Figure 11-3 with the insertion point in the first cell of the new row.

FIGURE 11-3
Table with New Row and Column

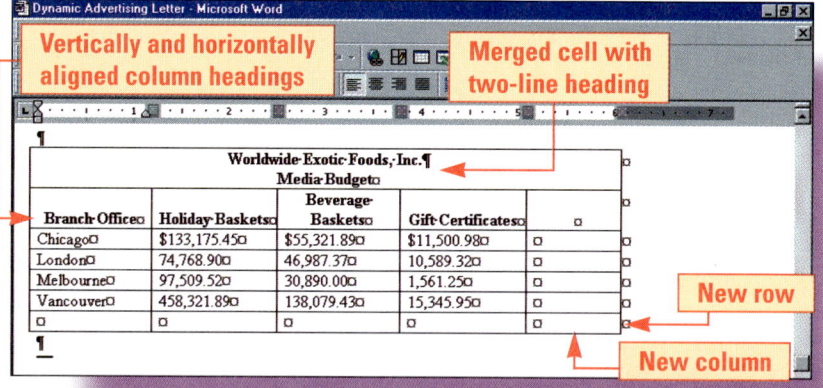

| Step 3 | *Save* | the document |

Now that the total column and row are inserted, you calculate the total for each row and column.

Performing Calculations in a Table

You could manually calculate the total for each column and each row and then key it in the appropriate cell; however, if you later change the numbers or insert additional rows or columns, you must manually recalculate and rekey the totals. Instead, you can insert a formula that adds the contents of all the cells in the column or row. Then if you make any changes, you can update the formula to show the new total. You insert formulas with the Formula command on the

Table menu. You insert the column totals first. To insert the row heading and total formulas in the last row:

Step 1	*Key*	Total in the first cell in the last row
Step 2	*Press*	the TAB key
Step 3	*Click*	Table
Step 4	*Click*	Formula

The Formula dialog box that opens on your screen should look similar to Figure 11-4.

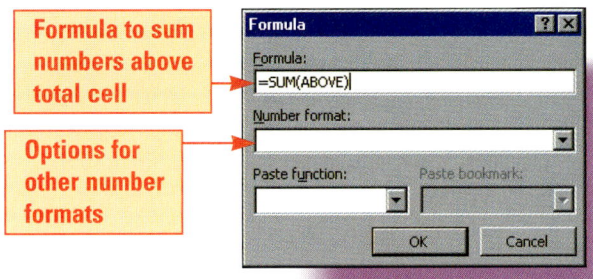

Formula to sum numbers above total cell

Options for other number formats

The most common calculation for a table is addition. You can also subtract, multiply, divide, and calculate averages, percentages, and minimum or maximum values in a table. Unless you indicate otherwise, Word assumes the calculation you want to perform is addition. Based on the position of the insertion point and the cells containing numbers, Word inserts an addition formula in the Formula: text box. For example, if the insertion point is in a column, Word inserts a formula to sum the numbers in the cells *above* the insertion point. If the numbers are in a row, Word inserts a formula in the Formula: text box to sum the numbers in the cells to the *left* or *right* of the insertion point.

Because the insertion point is in the last cell of a column, Word assumes you want to add the numbers in the cells above the insertion point. You accept the =SUM(ABOVE) formula.

| Step 5 | *Click* | OK |

The sum of the numbers in the Holiday Baskets column appears in the cell. Once you create a formula, you can repeat it in other cells by using the Repeat Formula command on the Edit menu or by pressing

chapter
eleven

the CTRL + Y keys. To calculate the totals for the Beverage Baskets and Gift Certificates columns:

Step 1	*Press*	the TAB key to move the insertion point to the Beverage Baskets column
Step 2	*Press*	the CTRL + Y keys
Step 3	*Press*	the TAB key
Step 4	*Press*	the CTRL + Y keys

The totals for the Beverage Baskets and Gift Certificates columns appear in the cells. Now you can create a formula to calculate the total media budget for the Chicago branch office and then repeat that formula for the other branch offices and the grand total. To key the column heading and insert the row totals:

Step 1	*Move*	the insertion point to the last cell in the heading row
Step 2	*Key*	Total
Step 3	*Press*	the DOWN ARROW key
Step 4	*Open*	the Formula dialog box
Step 5	*Verify*	that the formula in the Formula: text box is =SUM(LEFT)
Step 6	*Click*	OK
Step 7	*Repeat*	the formula for the remaining cells in the column
Step 8	*Save*	the document

The table is almost complete; however, you need to align the numbers on the decimal points.

Using Tab Stops in Tables

You can set tab stops for table cells in the same way you set them for body text by selecting the tab alignment and clicking the tab-stop position on the horizontal ruler. You can set tab stops for individual cells or a group of selected cells.

To align all the numbers for each column at one time, you first select all the cells containing numbers. When you select cells containing numbers and then insert a tab stop, Word automatically aligns the numbers without inserting a tab character in the cell. To select the cells and insert a decimal tab stop:

Step 1	*Select*	all the cells containing numbers
Step 2	*Select*	the Decimal Tab alignment button
Step 3	*Move*	the mouse pointer to the 2¼-inch position on the horizontal ruler

Your screen should look similar to Figure 11-5.

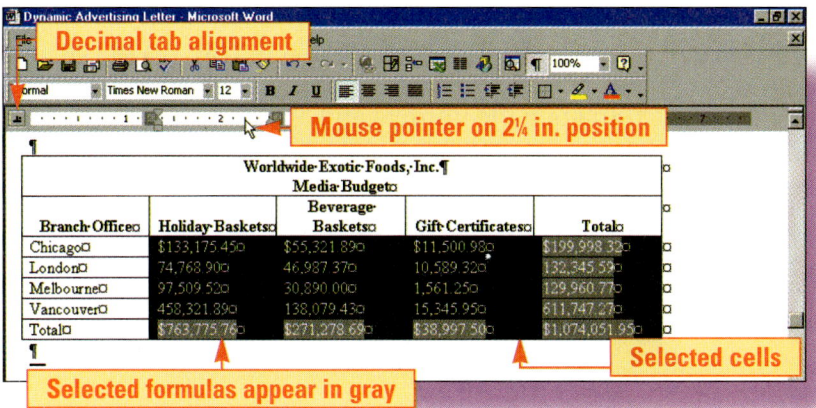

Step 4	*Click*	the horizontal ruler at the 2¼ position
Step 5	*Deselect*	the cells

Now that the numbers are aligned, you can resize the table.

Changing Row Height and Column Width

Now that the table contents are complete, you want to resize the cells' heights and widths to fit the data. A quick way to resize the table is to use the Auto**F**it options on the **Ta**ble menu. You can have Word size or fit each column to match the column's contents. This method creates a column width that accommodates the widest cell contents in that column. Word can also resize the entire table to fit within the document margins or format rows for uniform height and columns for uniform width.

To have Word fit the entire table with evenly distributed columns (columns with the same width):

Step 1	*Verify*	the insertion point is in the table

QUICK TIP

A quick way to align values with the same number of decimal places is to right-align the values in the cells.

To insert a tab formatting mark in a table cell press the CTRL + TAB keys.

FIGURE 11-5
Table with Selected Cells

CAUTION TIP

If you change a number in a cell that is part of a calculation, the formula does not recalculate automatically. To recalculate a formula, select the formula and press the F9 key. If you copy and paste a formula to a new cell, you must update the formula.

chapter
eleven

Step 2	*Click*	T<u>a</u>ble
Step 3	*Point to*	<u>A</u>utoFit
Step 4	*Click*	Distribute Columns Evenl<u>y</u>

You decide to see how the table looks without a border and with shaded column label cells.

Adding Borders and Shading to Tables

Borders and shading can make a table more attractive and easier to read. When you create a table using the Insert Table button on the Standard toolbar or <u>I</u>nsert Table command on the T<u>a</u>ble menu, Word automatically adds a border around each cell in the table. You can modify or remove this border and add shading from the Borders and Shading dialog box. To open the Borders and Shading dialog box:

Step 1	*Right-click*	the table
Step 2	*Click*	<u>B</u>orders and Shading
Step 3	*Click*	the <u>B</u>orders tab, if necessary

The border options for tables appear on the <u>B</u>orders tab. You can select one of the five preset border options or customize the table border. If you remove the table's printing border, the table appears with light gray gridlines. These nonprinting **gridlines** provide a visual guide as you work in a table. The nonprinting gridlines can be turned on or off with the Show <u>G</u>ridlines or Hide <u>G</u>ridlines commands on the T<u>a</u>ble menu. You remove the border and view the nonprinting gridlines.

Step 4	*Click*	the <u>N</u>one border option in the Setting: group
Step 5	*Click*	OK

The light gray nonprinting gridlines should appear. However, if the gridlines were previously turned off they do not appear. To turn on the gridlines, if necessary, and Print Preview the document:

Step 1	*Click*	T<u>a</u>ble
Step 2	*Click*	Show <u>G</u>ridlines, if necessary
Step 3	*Print Preview*	the document to see that the light gray gridlines do not print

| Step 4 | *Close* | Print Preview |

You realize that the information in the table was easier to read with the default border. To reapply the default border and add shading to the column label row:

Step 1	*Open*	the Borders tab in the Borders and Shading dialog box
Step 2	*Click*	the Grid option
Step 3	*Click*	OK
Step 4	*Select*	the second row, which contains the column heading text
Step 5	*Open*	the Shading tab in the Shadings and Borders dialog box
Step 6	*Click*	the Gray-10% color on the color grid (the third color in the first row)
Step 7	*Click*	OK
Step 8	*Deselect*	the row

The table is now complete and you need to finish the letter. To key the remaining body text and closing:

Step 1	*Move*	the insertion point to the blank line below the table
Step 2	*Press*	the ENTER key
Step 3	*Key*	the last body paragraph, closing, and your initials, using Figure 11-1 as your guide
Step 4	*Save*	the document and close it

The finished letter is ready for R. D. Jacobson's signature.

11.c Using Special Table Features

Bill Blake, an account executive in the marketing department, asks you to help create the new holiday sales price list. While he compiles the price list, he wants you to create a cover sheet for the document. You decide to do this by drawing tables in which you key the cover sheet text. Figure 11-6 shows the finished cover sheet.

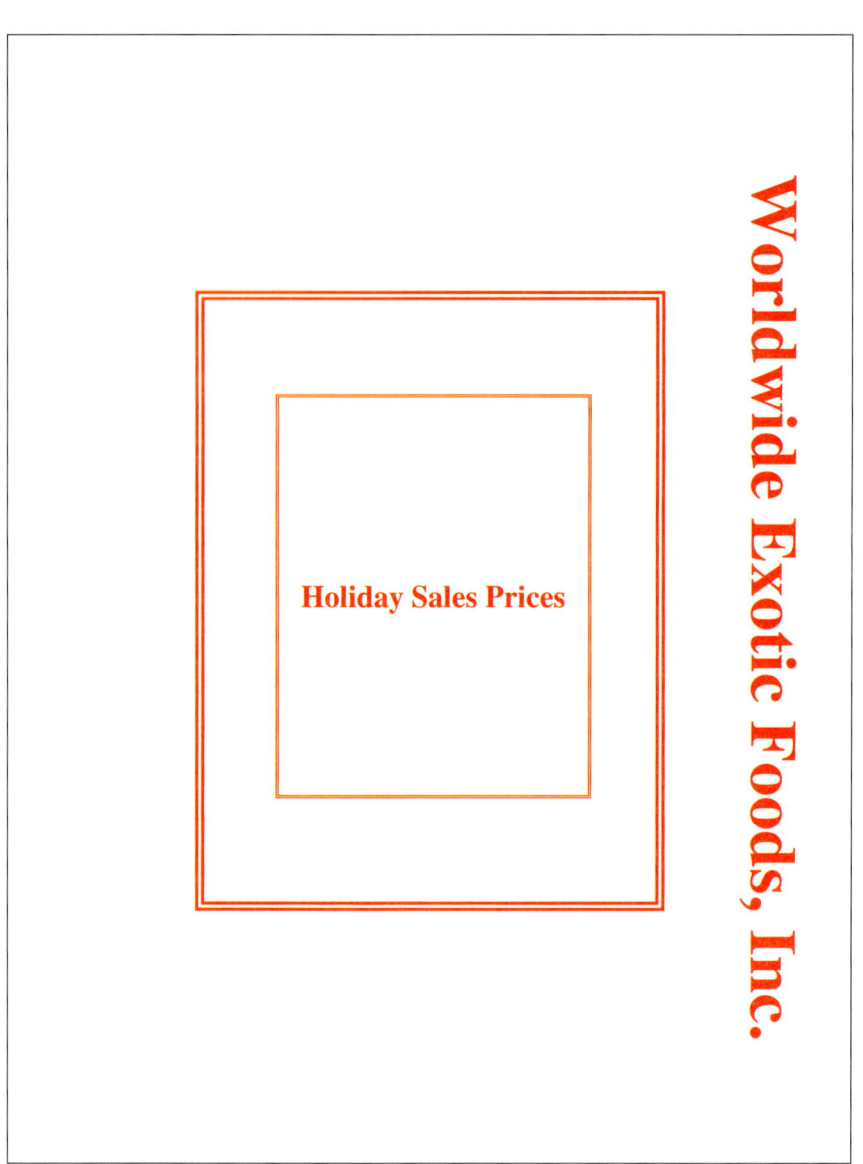

FIGURE 11-6
Completed Holiday
Price List Cover Sheet

Several features enable you to be very creative with tables. You can draw complex tables that have cells of different heights or a different number of columns per row, create side-by-side tables, change text direction inside a table cell, and even create a table inside a table cell. You can also reposition and size a table you draw with the mouse pointer.

Drawing Tables

You can also draw a table with the mouse pointer. When you use the Insert command on the Table menu or the Insert Table button on the Standard toolbar, you create a table grid of uniformly sized and positioned columns and rows. Drawing a table with the mouse pointer gives you the flexibility to determine the size and position of rows and columns. The Tables and Borders toolbar contains tools for drawing, erasing, and formatting a table. To begin the holiday sales price cover sheet, you create a new, blank document, change the margins, and view the Tables and Borders toolbar:

Step 1	*Create*	a new, blank document
Step 2	*Set*	the top, bottom, left, and right margins to ½ inch
Step 3	*Click*	the Tables and Borders button ⊞ on the Standard toolbar

Word switches to Print Layout view, the mouse pointer changes to the pencil pointer when positioned in the document, and the Tables and Borders toolbar opens. Unless it has been previously repositioned, the Tables and Borders toolbar appears in its own window near the top of the document. You reposition the Tables and Borders toolbar below the Formatting toolbar to keep it out of the way.

| Step 4 | *Drag* | the Tables and Borders toolbar by its title bar up until it attaches directly below the Formatting toolbar |
| Step 5 | *Click* | the Draw Table button ✎ on the Tables and Borders toolbar to display the pencil pointer, if necessary |

Before you draw a table, you set the table border style, width, and color, or you can turn off the default border. To select a border style, line width and color:

Step 1	*Click*	the Line Style button list arrow [_____ ▼] on the Tables and Borders toolbar
Step 2	*Click*	the thin double line border option (the eighth option)
Step 3	*Click*	the Line Weight button list arrow [½ ▼] on the Tables and Borders toolbar
Step 4	*Click*	the 2¼ pt option
Step 5	*Click*	the Border Color button ✎ on the Tables and Borders toolbar
Step 6	*Click*	Red (the first color in the third row)

To draw the table, you position the pencil pointer in the document where you want the upper-left corner of the table to begin. Thin

guidelines appear on the horizontal and vertical ruler, indicating the current position of the pencil pointer. You then drag diagonally toward the location of the lower-right corner of the table to create the external table boundaries. You continue to use the pencil pointer to draw the row and column boundaries inside the table. To draw the table:

| Step 1 | *Move* | the pencil pointer 1 inch below the top margin and 1 inch to the right of the left margin |

Your screen should look similar to Figure 11-7.

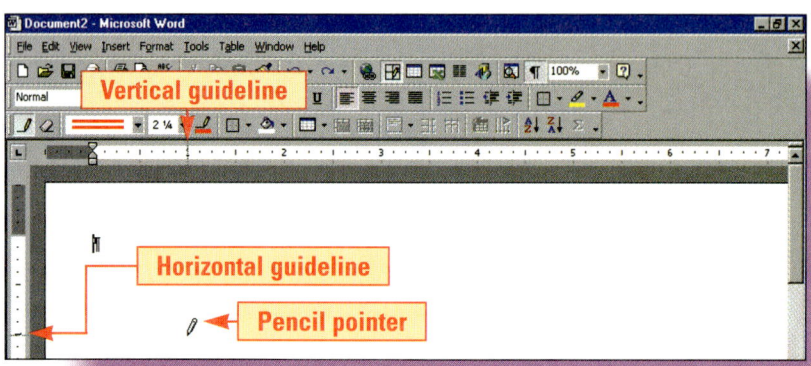

Step 2	*Drag*	diagonally to the right until the guideline on the horizontal ruler is at the 6-inch position and the guideline on the vertical ruler is at the 8½-inch position
Step 3	*Release*	the mouse button to create the external table boundaries
Step 4	*Zoom*	the document to Whole Page, if necessary

You use the pencil pointer to draw row and column boundaries inside the table. To create column and row boundaries with a red, 1-point, single border style:

Step 1	*Click*	the single line option (the second option) in the Line Style button list on the Tables and Borders toolbar
Step 2	*Click*	the 1 pt option in the Line Weight button list on the Tables and Borders toolbar
Step 3	*Click*	Red (the first color in the third row) in the Border Color button on the Tables and Borders toolbar
Step 4	*Move*	the pencil pointer inside the top boundary of the table approximately 1 inch from the left boundary of the table

Step 5	*Drag*	down to the bottom boundary until a dashed line column boundary appears
Step 6	*Release*	the mouse button to create the column boundary
Step 7	*Draw*	a second column boundary at any position inside the table
Step 8	*Draw*	a row boundary approximately 1 inch from the top of the table
Step 9	*Draw*	two additional row boundaries at any position

You now have a 4 × 3 table (four rows and three columns) with unevenly distributed columns and rows. You can turn off the Draw Table feature to switch back to an I-beam.

| Step 10 | *Click* | the Draw Table button to turn off the pencil pointer |

You can move the insertion point; select cells, rows, and columns; size the cells, rows, and columns; and key text in the cells just as you can when you create a table using the toolbar or menu commands. You sized the previous table using AutoFit sizing options; you can also size individual column widths or row heights. A quick way to do this is with the mouse pointer. To widen the first column and row:

Step 1	*Zoom*	the document to 75% so that it is easier to see
Step 2	*Move*	the mouse pointer to the right boundary of the first column (the mouse pointer becomes a sizing pointer)
Step 3	*Drag*	the column boundary to the right approximately ½ inch
Step 4	*Move*	the mouse pointer to the bottom boundary of the first row (the mouse pointer becomes a sizing pointer)
Step 5	*Drag*	the row boundary up approximately ½ inch

Actually, you don't need the table divided into rows and columns for the cover sheet. If you draw a column or row boundary that you don't need, or draw it in the wrong place, it is easy to erase it by turning the pencil pointer into an eraser. To erase the row and column boundaries:

Step 1	*Zoom*	the document to Whole Page
Step 2	*Click*	the Eraser button  on the Tables and Borders toolbar
Step 3	*Drag*	the eraser pointer over a column boundary to erase it

chapter
eleven

Step 4	*Drag*	the eraser pointer over a row boundary to erase it
Step 5	*Erase*	the remaining column and row boundaries leaving only the external table boundaries
Step 6	*Click*	the Eraser button 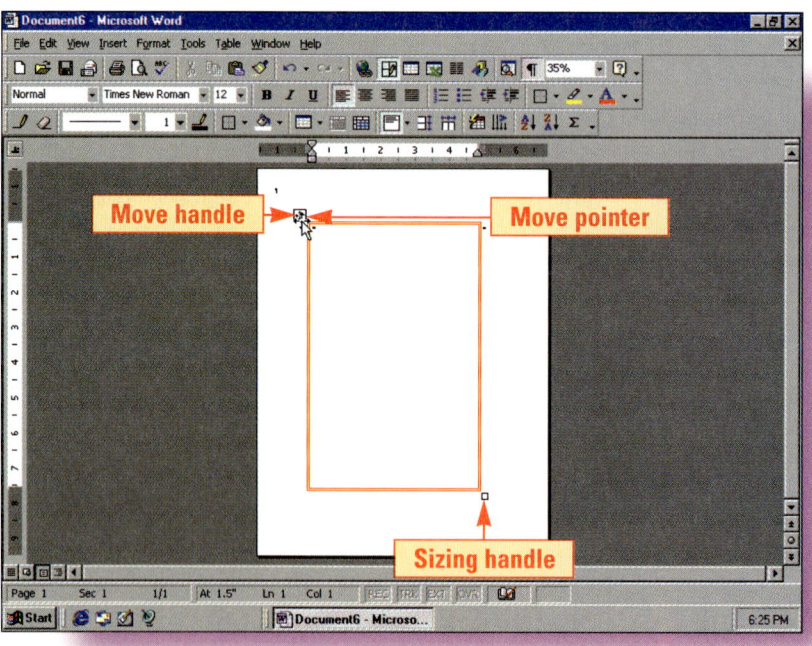 on the Tables and Borders toolbar to turn it off

Q U I C K   T I P

You can press the SHIFT key to turn the pencil pointer into the eraser pointer.

When the pencil and eraser pointers are turned off, the mouse pointer becomes the I-beam when positioned over a table cell. When you place the I-beam in the table, two new objects are added to the table: a move handle that appears above the upper-left corner of the table and a sizing handle that appears below the lower-right corner of the table. You drag the **move handle** to reposition the table and the **sizing handle** to resize the entire table. You decide to move the table up on the page and make it a little smaller. To reposition and resize the table using the move handle and the sizing handle:

| Step 1 | *Move* | the mouse pointer to the move handle above the upper-left corner of the table (the mouse pointer becomes a move pointer with four black arrows) |

Your screen should look similar to Figure 11-8.

FIGURE 11-8
Table Move Handle and Move Pointer

| Step 2 | *Drag* | the move handle up approximately ¼ inch to reposition the table |

| Step 3 | *Move* | the mouse pointer to the sizing handle below the lower-right corner of the table |
| Step 4 | *Drag* | the sizing handle up approximately 1 inch |

To make the cover page more interesting, you key title text in a second table inside the first table.

Nesting Tables

To help organize text on a page, you can create a table inside another table cell. Creating tables inside other tables is called **nesting**. You can nest tables when you need to organize a subset of data inside a larger table or to create a decorative effect. To create a nested table:

QUICK TIP

You can also create nested tables using the Insert Table button or command.

Step 1	*Set*	a thin double line, ¾ point, red boundary using buttons on the Tables and Borders toolbar
Step 2	*Click*	the Draw Table button 🖉 on the Tables and Borders toolbar to turn on the pencil pointer, if necessary
Step 3	*Draw*	a smaller table inside the larger table, approximately 2½ inches wide and 3 inches long and equidistant from the top, bottom, left, and right boundaries of the larger table
Step 4	*Position & Size*	the smaller table attractively near the center of the larger table
Step 5	*Zoom*	the document to 75% and scroll to view the smaller table
Step 6	*Verify*	the insertion point is inside the smaller table
Step 7	*Key*	Holiday Sales Prices
Step 8	*Format*	the text with bold and change the font to a larger point, red font

You decide to try different text alignment options. To change the vertical and horizontal alignment of the text in the nested table:

Step 1	*Verify*	the insertion point is in the smaller table
Step 2	*Click*	the Align button list arrow 🔲▾ on the Tables and Borders toolbar
Step 3	*Click*	the Align Center button 🔲
Step 4	*Deselect*	the text

chapter
eleven

The text is aligned vertically and horizontally between the nested table boundaries.

Creating Side-by-Side Tables

Side-by-side tables provide greater flexibility in organizing information on a page. For example, in a sales brochure you might have lists of products in multiple side-by-side tables. You could also use side-by-side tables without borders to add a special text effect on a page. You do this for the holiday sales prices cover sheet. To create a new table without borders to the right of the nested tables:

Step 1	*Zoom*	the document to Whole Page
Step 2	*Select*	the No Border option from the Line Style list
Step 3	*Draw*	a long narrow table to the right of the nested tables beginning at the top margin and ending at the bottom margin leaving at least ½ inch between the tables

In addition to the horizontal and vertical alignment of text in a table cell, you can also change the text direction. You add the name of the company rotated so that it is read from top to bottom in the table.

Rotating Text in Tables

Changing the direction of text in a table cell allows you to add a special effect to the text. It also works well to rotate long column headings over narrow columns of data. Rotated text retains its horizontal and vertical formatting. You want the company name to appear vertically against the right boundary of the new table. To change the text direction:

Step 1	*Zoom*	the document to 75%
Step 2	*Click*	the Draw Table button on the Tables and Borders toolbar to turn off the pencil pointer, if necessary
Step 3	*Verify*	the insertion point is in the new table
Step 4	*Click*	the Change Text Direction button on the Tables and Borders toolbar until the directional arrows on the button face are pointing up
Step 5	*Change*	the alignment to Align Center Right using the Alignment button on the Tables and Borders toolbar
Step 6	*Key*	Worldwide Exotic Foods, Inc.
Step 7	*Format*	the text with bold, 48 point, red font

| Step 8 | *Zoom* | the document to Whole Page |

Before you complete the cover sheet, you want to center the nested tables vertically and horizontally on the page.

Positioning Tables on the Page

You can horizontally align a table in relation to the edge of the page, the margins, or column boundaries. Tables can also be vertically aligned in relation to the top and bottom of the page, the top and bottom margins, or the top and bottom of a paragraph. The Table tab in the Table Properties dialog box provides options for positioning a table on the page. To position the table:

Step 1	*Right-click*	the large table in the nested tables
Step 2	*Click*	Table Properties
Step 3	*Click*	the Table tab, if necessary

The Table Properties dialog box that opens on your screen should look similar to Figure 11-9.

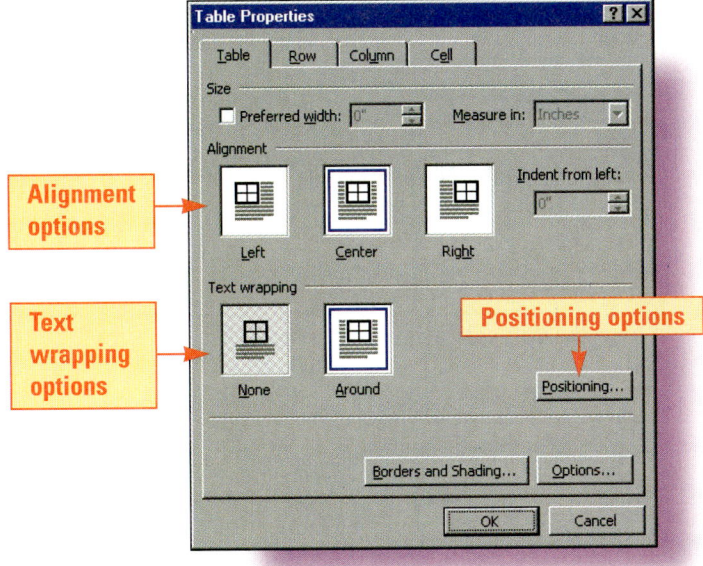

Alignment options

Text wrapping options

Positioning options

FIGURE 11-9
Table Properties
Dialog Box

| Step 4 | *Click* | Positioning |

chapter
eleven

The Table Positioning dialog box that opens on your screen should look similar to Figure 11-10.

FIGURE 11-10
Table Positioning
Dialog Box

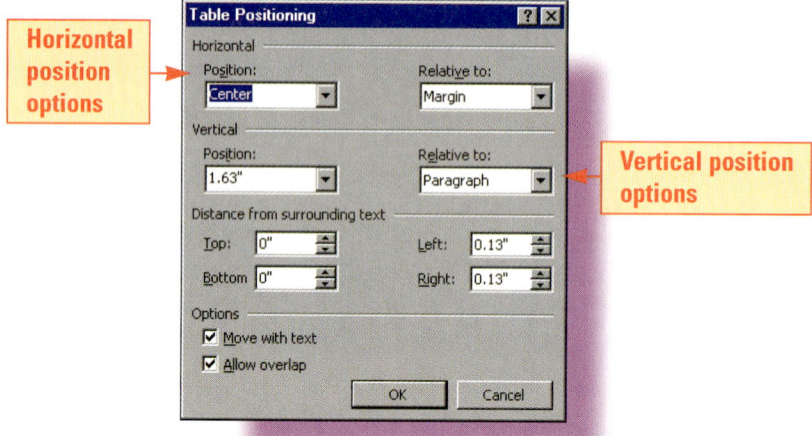

The options in the Horizontal and Vertical groups allow you to specify the position of the table in relation to the edges of the page, the margins, a newspaper-style column, or a text paragraph. You can also specify the distance the table boundaries should be from surrounding text. You center the table between the left and right margins.

Step 5	*Click*	the Horizontal Position: list arrow
Step 6	*Click*	Center, if necessary
Step 7	*Click*	the Horizontal Relative to: list arrow
Step 8	*Click*	Margin, if necessary
Step 9	*Click*	the Vertical Position: list arrow
Step 10	*Click*	Center
Step 11	*Click*	the Vertical Relative to: list arrow
Step 12	*Click*	Margin, if necessary
Step 13	*Click*	OK in each dialog box

The nested tables are centered vertically and horizontally between the margins. To center the long, second table between the top and bottom margins:

| Step 1 | ***Right-click*** | the long, second table |
| Step 2 | *Click* | Table Properties |

Step 3	*Click*	Positioning
Step 4	*Select*	Center from the Vertical Position: list
Step 5	*Select*	Margin, if necessary, from the Vertical Relative to: list
Step 6	*Click*	OK in each dialog box
Step 7	*Save*	the document as *Holiday Sales Prices* and close it
Step 8	*Close*	the Tables and Borders toolbar

Now Bill can add the holiday price list to the cover sheet.

11.d Switching Between Text and Tables

Selena Jackson, a secretary in the sales department, asks you to format a list of sales representatives and their telephone extensions. She already created the list using tab stops and tab characters to separate the information for each sales representative, but she thinks the list is easier to work with in a table. Instead of creating a table and keying the list again, you decide to convert the existing list to a table.

Data in tables is usually easier to manipulate, format, and calculate than the same data in text columns separated by tabs or other characters. You can convert text columns separated by tab characters, commas, or other characters to a table. You can also convert a table of rows and columns into text columns.

Converting Text to a Table

To convert text to a table you first select the text and then point to the Convert command on the Table menu and click the Text to Table command. To open Selena's existing document and select the text to convert to a table:

Step 1	*Open*	the *Sales Representatives* document located on the Data Disk
Step 2	*Select*	the columns of text separated by tab formatting marks, beginning with the Jones row and ending with the Aguilar row
Step 3	*Click*	Table
Step 4	*Point to*	Convert

chapter eleven

Step 5	*Click*	Te<u>x</u>t to Table

The Convert Text to Table dialog box that opens on your screen should look similar to Figure 11-11.

FIGURE 11-11
Convert Text to Table
Dialog Box

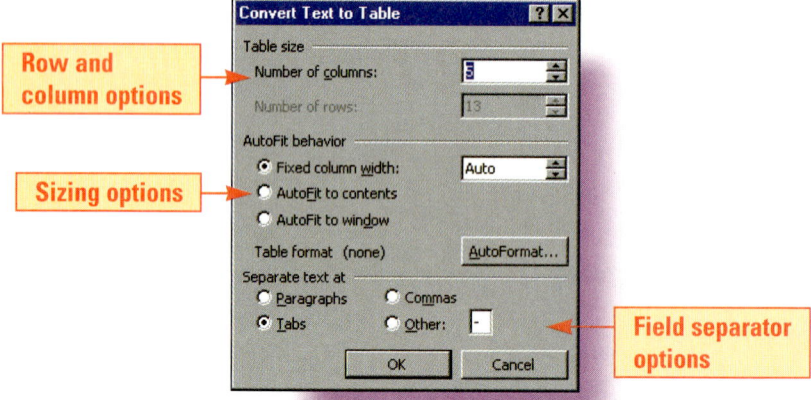

You specify the number of columns and rows as well as the size of the cells using AutoFit options in this dialog box. You also identify the character that separates columns so Word knows when to create a new column in the table. For example, the data in the *Sales Representatives* document is separated by tab formatting marks. Each time Word identifies a tab formatting mark, it places the data to the right of the tab formatting mark in the next column in the table. Word recognizes that the selected text contains five columns of text separated by tab formatting characters and sets those options for you. You can change the AutoFit option to control column width. Word also provides several automatic formats you can apply to a table. These automatic formats contain column width settings, shading, and font formatting.

To create a five-column table formatted with the Colorful 2 AutoFormat:

Step 1	*Verify*	the Number of <u>c</u>olumns: text box contains five and the <u>T</u>abs option button is selected
Step 2	*Click*	<u>A</u>utoFormat

The Table AutoFormat dialog box that opens on your screen should look similar to Figure 11-12.

You can preview how a table looks with each of the AutoFormats in the Forma<u>t</u>s: list in the Preview area of the dialog box. Some AutoFormats can be modified to remove or add borders and shading to specific columns and rows in the table. Because your table does not have a heading row, you select the Colorful 2 AutoFormat and then remove the heading row formatting.

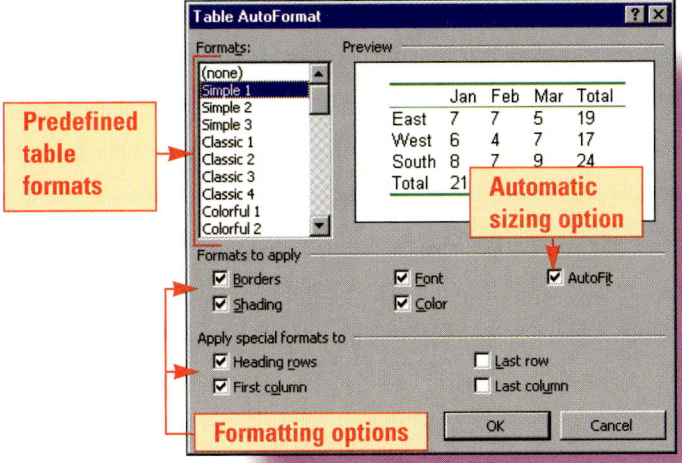

Step 3	*Click*	Colorful 2 in the Formats: list box
Step 4	*Observe*	the table preview and the darkly shaded heading row
Step 5	*Click*	the Heading rows check box to remove the check mark
Step 6	*Observe*	the table preview heading row is formatted like the remaining rows
Step 7	*Observe*	the AutoFit (to contents) check box contains a check mark
Step 8	*Click*	OK in each dialog box

The table is created with the Colorful 2 AutoFormat and the column widths automatically are sized to fit the contents. By default the table is left aligned. You can horizontally align a table by selecting the entire table and clicking a horizontal alignment button on the Formatting toolbar.

To center the table horizontally:

Step 1	*Verify*	the entire table is selected, including the end-of-row marks
Step 2	*Click*	the Center button  on the Formatting toolbar
Step 3	*Deselect*	the table
Step 4	*Save*	the document as *Sales Representatives Revised*

Selena finds the new format much easier to read.

MENU TIP

To save formatting time, you can apply one of the Word automatic table formats to any table by first selecting the table and then clicking the Table AutoFormat command on the Table menu or the Table AutoFormat button on the Tables and Borders toolbar.

CAUTION TIP

If you select the entire table by selecting columns, remember to also select the end-of-row marks.

chapter
eleven

Converting a Table to Text

Sometimes you need to convert data organized in a table to text separated by a tab formatting mark, a paragraph mark, comma, or some other character in order to import the data into another application. Suppose you need to convert the table data in the *Sales Representatives Revised* document to text columns separated by a comma. To begin:

Step 1	*Move*	the insertion point inside the table
Step 2	*Click*	Table
Step 3	*Point to*	Convert
Step 4	*Click*	Table to Text
Step 5	*Click*	the Commas option button to select the column separator character
Step 6	*Click*	OK
Step 7	*Deselect*	the text
Step 8	*Observe*	that the data in each row of text is now separated by commas rather than a table columns
Step 9	*Save*	the document as *Converted Table* and close it

Converting table data to text columns enables you to format the same information in different ways without having to rekey it.

Summary

► You can place data in a table so that it is easier to read and understand.

► A table is a grid organized into rows and columns.

► A column is a set of information that runs down a page, and a row is a set of information that runs across a page.

► A cell is the intersection of a column and a row.

► You can move the insertion point between cells in a table using the mouse or the keyboard.

► Cells, rows, and columns in a table can be selected to insert, delete, or format the cells, rows, or columns.

► You can merge multiple cells vertically and horizontally into one cell.

► You can create formulas in tables to add, subtract, multiply, divide, and calculate averages, percentages, and identify minimum or maximum values in a column or row.

► You can change the column widths for one column in a table or multiple columns, using the mouse or the AutoFit commands on the Table menu.

► You position tables on the page with options in the Table Properties dialog box or with the mouse pointer.

► You can set tab stops for one or more table columns.

► Word provides several preset table formats, called AutoFormats, you can apply to a table.

► You can draw a complex table with the Draw Table feature, and then format the table and its contents with the Tables and Borders toolbar options.

► You can nest tables by drawing a table inside another table cell, and you can place tables side by side.

► Text separated by commas, paragraph marks, or other characters can be converted to a table.

► Tables can be converted to text that is separated by commas, paragraph marks, or other characters.

► You can format text in table cells just as you format paragraph text.

chapter eleven

Commands Review

Action	Menu Bar	Shortcut Menu	Toolbar	Keyboard
Create a table	Table, Insert, Table or Draw Table			ALT + A, I, T or ALT + A, B
Delete a table or table component	Table, Delete, Table, or Columns, or Rows, or Cells	Right-click selected table component, click Delete		ALT + A, D, T or C or R or E
Insert rows, columns, or cells in a table	Table, Insert, Columns to the Left Columns to the Right Rows Above Rows Below Cells	Right-click selected table component, click Insert		ALT + A, I, L or R or A or B or E
Change column width for selected column(s)	Table, Table Properties or AutoFit		Drag the column boundary or the column marker on the horizontal ruler	ALT + A, R or A
To align a table on the page	Table, Table Properties	Right-click table, click Table Properties	Drag move pointer	ALT + A, R
Align text horizontally and vertically		Right-click cell, click Cell Alignment		
Add formula to a table	Table, Formula			ALT + A, O
Repeat formulas	Edit, Repeat Formula			ALT + E, R CTRL + Y F4
Update a selected formula		Right-click a formula field, click Update Field		F9
Merge cells vertically or horizontally	Table, Merge Cells	Right-click selected cells, Merge Cells		ALT + A, M
Insert a tab formatting mark in a cell				CTRL + TAB
Add borders and shading to a table	Format, Borders and Shading	Right-click table, Borders and Shading		ALT + O, B
Change text direction		Right-click cell, click Text Direction		
Draw a table	Table, Draw Table			ALT + A, B
Apply a built-in automatic format	Table, Table AutoFormat			ALT + A, F
Convert text to a table	Table, Convert, Text to Table			ALT + A, V, X
Convert a table to text	Table, Convert, Table to Text			ALT + A, V, B
Split cells vertically or horizontally	Table, Split Cells			ALT + A, P
Split a table	Table, Split Table			ALT + A, T
Distribute rows and columns evenly	Table, Autofit, Distribute Rows Evenly or Distribute Columns Evenly	Right-click selected columns or rows, click Distribute Columns Evenly or Distribute Rows Evenly		ALT + A, N or Y
Repeat a heading row on all pages of the table	Table, Heading Rows Repeat			ALT + A, H
Change pencil pointer to eraser pointer				SHIFT

Concepts Review

Circle the correct answer.

1. A table:
  [a] is a grid organized in columns and rows.
  [b] must be created with a button on the Standard toolbar.
  [c] cannot be formatted with character formats like bold and paragraph formats like borders and shading.
  [d] has columns labeled 1, 2, 3 and rows labeled A, B, C.

2. You can change the width of a column in a table by:
  [a] pressing the TAB key.
  [b] dragging a row boundary between two rows.
  [c] clicking the Column Width command on the Table menu.
  [d] dragging a column boundary on the horizontal ruler.

3. The gray table gridlines:
  [a] automatically appear when you create a table.
  [b] cannot be turned on and off.
  [c] print with the table.
  [d] provide visual help when working in a table without borders.

4. A cell is:
  [a] a set of information that runs down a page.
  [b] a set of information that runs across the page.
  [c] the intersection of a column and row.
  [d] a grid of columns and rows.

5. You cannot move the insertion point in a table with the:
  [a] I-beam.
  [b] TAB key.
  [c] UP ARROW and DOWN ARROW keys.
  [d] SPACEBAR.

6. You can create a table with the:
  [a] Insert, Table commands on the Table menu.
  [b] Draw Table button on the Standard toolbar.
  [c] Table command on the Format menu.
  [d] Insert Table button on the Formatting toolbar.

7. To update a formula in a table, press the:
  [a] F8 key.
  [b] SHIFT + F9 keys.
  [c] ALT + F9 keys.
  [d] F9 key.

8. Nested tables allow you to:
  [a] move a table with the mouse pointer.
  [b] size a table with the mouse pointer.
  [c] place a table inside another table.
  [d] add, subtract, multiply, and divide values.

9. The best way to align the numbers 973.32, 734.871, 34.972 in table columns is to:
  [a] left-align the numbers.
  [b] set a decimal tab stop.
  [c] right-align the numbers.
  [d] center the numbers.

10. Which of the following formatting options is not available on the Tables and Borders toolbar?
  [a] vertical and horizontal text alignment
  [b] text rotation
  [c] line color, style, and width
  [d] bold

chapter eleven

Circle **T** if the statement is true or **F** if the statement is false.

T   F   1. You cannot repeat the heading row when the table flows to a second page.

T   F   2. To delete a table's content and structure, first select the table and then press the DELETE key.

T   F   3. Rows can be inserted above or below the selected rows.

T   F   4. Cells can be merged horizontally but not vertically.

T   F   5. To move the insertion point to the next cell, press the ENTER key.

T   F   6. Tab stops are set for table cells in the same manner as body text.

T   F   7. The default table border cannot be removed or modified.

T   F   8. The pencil pointer is used to draw tables.

T   F   9. Creating tables inside other tables is called stacking.

T   F   10. Once text is converted to text in a table, it cannot be converted back to plain text.

Skills Review

Exercise 1

1. Open the *Annual Sales Data* document located on the Data Disk.

2. Change the top margin to 1½ inches and the left margin and right margins to one inch.

3. Select text separated by tab formatting marks and convert the text to a table using the Classic 2 table AutoFormat. Modify the AutoFormat to remove the borders.

4. Center the table on the page using the Center button on the Formatting toolbar.

5. Right-align the column headings and numbers in their cells.

6. Add a row to the bottom of the table and a column at the end of the table.

7. Key the word "Total" in the first cell of the new row and column.

8. Insert a formula in the last cell of the 1997 column to sum the values.

9. Repeat the formula for the 1998 and 1999 columns.

10. Insert a formula in the last cell of the Chicago row to sum the values.

11. Repeat the formula for the London, Melbourne, and Vancouver branches.

12. Save the document as *Annual Sales Data Revised*.

13. Preview, print, and close the document.

Exercise 2

1. Open the *Regional Deli Sales* document located on the Data Disk.

2. Select the five rows of text and convert the text to a table. (*Hint:* The separator character is a dash.)

3. Insert a row between North and East regions using the Insert Rows button on the Standard toolbar.

4. Key the following text in the row: Central, 28,975.33, 54,333.45, and 78,125.54.

5. Insert a column at the end of the table.

6. Key "Total Sales" in the first cell of the column.

7. Insert a row at the bottom of the table and title it "Total Sales."

8. Calculate the total for each column and row.

9. Right-align the numbers in the cells.

10. Adjust the column widths by dragging the column boundaries with the mouse pointer so that each column is just wide enough for the largest cell contents.

11. Center and bold the heading row.

12. Align the heading row text at the bottom center of each cell.

13. Center the table on the page.

14. Save the document as *Regional Deli Sales Revised*.

15. Preview, print, and close the document.

Exercise 3

1. Open the *Annual Sales Data Revised* document you created in Exercise 1.

2. Remove the automatic formatting. (*Hint:* Click in the table, click the Table AutoFormat command on the Table menu, click the (none) option in the Formats: list.)

3. Display the Tables and Borders toolbar.

4. Use the pencil pointer to draw a double-line, ¾-point, black border around the table.

5. Use the pencil pointer to draw single-line, ¾-point, black border column boundaries.

6. Add Gray-10% shading to the top and bottom row. (*Hint:* Use the Shading Color button on the Tables and Borders toolbar.)

7. AutoFit the table to the window (between the left and right margins).

8. Save the document as *Annual Sales Data With AutoFit*.

9. Preview, print, and close the document.

Exercise 4

1. Create a new, blank document.

2. Create a 7 × 4 table with the Insert Table button on the Standard toolbar

3. Key the data below:

District	Selling Expenses	Employee Expenses	Overhead
Central	$49,100.60	$12,421.00	$13,921.99
Eastern	41,756.72	5,523.42	8,992.33
Midwest	64,871.86	4,819.89	9,655.76
Mountain	59,256.36	7,085.07	6,332.99
Southern	45,817.32	12,253.57	16,322.86
Western	51,857.52	9,528.88	11,661.30

4. Select the first row and add bold formatting to the text.

5. Insert a row at the bottom of the document and a column at the left of the document.

6. Add the text "Total" to the first cell in the new row and column.

7. Display the Tables and Borders toolbar.

chapter eleven

8. Use the AutoSum button on the Tables and Borders toolbar to insert the total for each column. (Do not repeat the first formula.)

9. Use the Formula command on the Table menu to add the Central row. Repeat the formula for the remaining rows.

10. Change the value for Chicago Selling Expenses to $59,100.60. (*Hint:* The Selling Expenses total, Central total, and grand total do not change automatically.)

11. Select the Selling Expenses total cell and press the F9 key to update the formula. Select the Central total cell and press the F9 key to update the Central total. Select the grand total cell and press the F9 key to update the grand total.

12. Set a decimal tab for the cells that contain numbers.

13. AutoFit the table to the contents.

14. Select the first row and align the contents centered at the bottom of the cell using the Alignment button on the Tables and Borders toolbar.

15. Insert a row at the top of the document and merge the cells using buttons on the Tables and Borders toolbar.

16. Key the following title text in the new first row.
Worldwide Exotic Foods, Inc.
District Expense Report
Fourth Quarter

17. Change the font to 14 point.

18. Use the Borders and Shading dialog box to apply a 1½-point grid border to the table.

19. Center the table between the left and right margins.

20. Save the document as *District Expense Report*.

21. Preview, print, and close the document.

Exercise 5

1. Open the *Adjusted Costs Memo* document located on the Data Disk.

2. Display the Tables and Borders toolbar.

3. Draw a 7 × 4 table with no border below the memo body text.

4. Distribute the rows and columns evenly.

5. Merge the cells in the first row.

6. Key the following heading text centered and bolded in two lines in the first row.
EXECUTIVE SUPPORT DIVISION
Adjusted Costs for Second Fiscal Quarter

7. Key the following data in the remaining rows.

Item	Budgeted	Actual	Difference
Executive Secretaries	$2,455,000	$2,256,000	–$199,000
Administrative Assistants	390,600	475,900	85,300
Equipment	960,000	840,000	–120,000
Telecommunications	476,000	450,600	–25,400
Miscellaneous	76,000	60,000	–16,000

8. Align the numbers at the bottom right using the Align button on the Tables and Borders toolbar.

9. Underline and center the column heading text in the second row at the bottom of each cell.

10. Align the "Item" titles at the bottom left of the cell.

11. AutoFit the table to the contents.

12. Center the table between the left and right margins.

13. Save the document as *Adjusted Costs Memo Revised*.

14. Preview, print, and close the document.

Exercise 6

1. Create a new, blank document and insert the text TRIVIA INFORMATION ABOUT SELECTED STATES centered in 14-point font at the top of the document.

2. Display the Tables and Borders toolbar and draw two side-by-side tables beginning at the left margin using the border style of your choice. Make the first table approximately 1½ inches wide and 5 inches long and the second table approximately 4 inches wide and 5 inches long. Leave ½ inch white space between the tables.

3. Draw a narrow column approximately .3 inch at the left side of each table.

4. Format the first cell in each table to rotate the text vertical up (read from bottom to top) and align center left.

5. Key NAME in the first cell in the first table and format the text with the 18-point, bold font.

6. Key NICKNAME in the first cell in the second table and format the text with the 18-point, bold font.

7. Format the second cell in each table to align the text centered vertically and horizontally in the cell.

8. Key the following double-spaced text in the second cell of the first table: *Arkansas, Arizona, Colorado, Connecticut, Nebraska, New Mexico, Texas, Washington*.

9. Key the following double-spaced text in the second cell of the second table: *The Natural State, Grand Canyon State, Centennial State, Constitution State, Cornhusker State, America's Land of Enchantment, The Lone Star State, The Evergreen State*.

10. Center each table vertically between the top and bottom margins.

11. Save the document as *State Trivia*.

12. Preview, print, and close the document.

Exercise 7

1. Create the following document. Set the appropriate margins for a block format letter.

2. The company information and column titles in the table should be centered and boldfaced. Use the default black grid. The expense data should be right aligned. Finally, the Sales District numbers should be centered.

3. Calculate the total for each column.

4. Change the column width of each column as necessary.

5. Center the table horizontally.

6. Save the document as *Burns Letter With Table*.

chapter eleven

Current date

Mr. Daniel Burns
Vice President
Burns Consulting, Inc
250 Main, Suite 1230
Chicago, IL 60615-1203

Dear Daniel:

We finally completed the second quarter expense report for the Vancouver office and look forward to your suggestions on reducing these expenses. See the details below:

VANCOUVER OFFICE EXPENSE REPORT			
Second Quarter			
Sales District	Telephone	Supplies	Misc.
1	$1,400.60	$806.86	$300.60
2	1,660.36	736.96	334.36
3	986.30	85.00	453.56
4	1,246.88	443.77	564.33
5	1,766.99	999.99	434.66
Total	$7,061.13	$3,072.58	$2,087.51

I will be meeting with the managers of each sales district to review these expenses next week. After the reviews, I will e-mail our estimated expenses for the fourth quarter to you.

Sincerely,

Lisa Harrison
Accounting Manager

xx

Exercise 8

1. Create a new, blank document.
2. Use the Draw Table feature to create the following document.
3. Draw the first table beginning at the left margin with a single, 3-point, red border. Make the table approximately 3½ inches wide and 3 inches long. Center the table horizontally.
4. Draw the second table inside the first table with a single 1½-point, red border. Make the second table approximately 2¾ inches wide and 2 inches long. Center the table horizontally.
5. Draw a column boundary (vertical line) down the middle of the second table.
6. Draw five row boundaries (horizontal lines) across the second table.

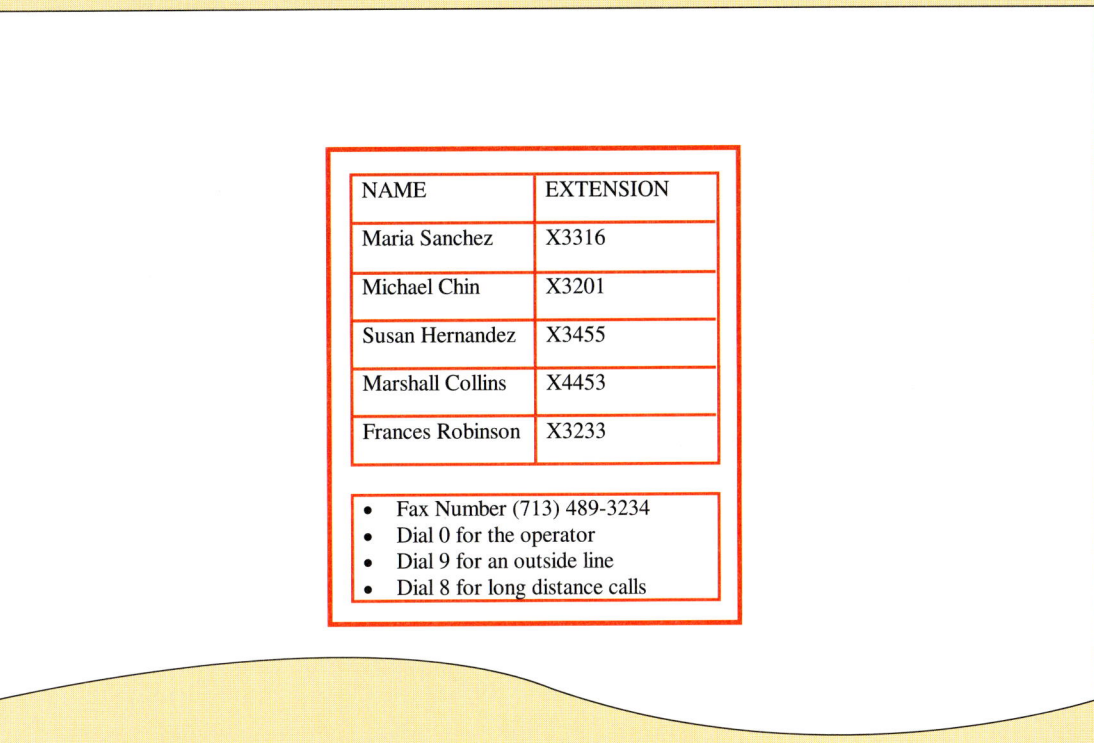

NAME	EXTENSION
Maria Sanchez	X3316
Michael Chin	X3201
Susan Hernandez	X3455
Marshall Collins	X4453
Frances Robinson	X3233

- Fax Number (713) 489-3234
- Dial 0 for the operator
- Dial 9 for an outside line
- Dial 8 for long distance calls

7. Distribute the rows and column evenly.

8. Draw a third table below the second table. Make this table approximately 2¾ inches wide and ½ inch long. Center the third table horizontally.

9. Key the text shown in the table.

10. Save the document as *Extension List*.

11. Preview, print, and close the document.

Case Projects

Project 1

A marketing department coworker, Ella Cohen, wants to know how to insert information from a database or other data source into a Word document as a table. Use online Help to locate the topic "Inserting information from a database into a Word document." Write an interoffice memorandum to Ella describing the process. Save, preview, and print the memo.

Project 2

R. D. Jacobson asks you to create an interoffice memo to five Vancouver sales representatives advising them of the profit (sales minus expenses) for the third quarter on the Extravaganza Basket product. Use a table to present the data for the five sales representatives by listing the sales, expenses, and profit for each. Then calculate the total sales, total expenses, and total profit for the branch. Use fictitious data. Format and position the table attractively on the page. Save, preview, and print the memo.

chapter eleven

Project 3

Maria Betancourt does not understand the concept of Word fields, such as the formula field or date and time field, and asks for your help. Use the Office Assistant to search online Help for information on Word fields. Print and review the information. Open the Options dialog box and use the Help button to review the Field options in the View tab. Create an interoffice memorandum to Maria describing Word fields and how to use the options on the View tab to view the fields. Use a table to organize the information about the View tab options. Save, preview, and print the memo. With your instructor's permission, use the memo as a guide to describe Word fields to a classmate. Then open a document that contains a date and time or formula field and demonstrate how to use the View tab field options.

Project 4

R. D. Jacobson asks you to help locate a list of firms that provide Web-based advertising. Connect to your ISP, load your Web browser, and search for companies who provide advertising services on the Web. Print at least five home pages. Create an interoffice memorandum to R. D. Jacobson listing your Web sources and a brief description of their services. Organize your Web source list in an attractively formatted and positioned table. Save, preview, and print the memo.

Project 5

Create a letter and an accompanying envelope to the president of WholeSale Food Distributors from M. D. Anderson, Sales Director, advising the president of the total sales data for the first quarter for five products. Use an attractively formatted and positioned table to itemize the product sales for January, February, and March. Calculate the total sales by product and month. Use fictitious data. Save, preview, and print the letter.

Project 6

Bill Blake has a big marketing presentation he will be putting together soon. In preparation for helping him, you practice drawing and formatting tables with the Tables and Borders toolbar. Create a new, blank document and display the Tables and Borders toolbar. Explore drawing various tables including nested tables. Use all the buttons on the toolbar, including changing the text orientation inside a cell to format the tables. Save, preview, and print the document.

Project 7

R. D. Jacobson assigns you to write a memorandum to all sales and marketing department employees advising them how to save a Word document to the company FTP site on the Internet. Use the Office Assistant to research how to save a Word document to an FTP site. Use the keywords "saving to FTP," click the Save a Document topic and follow appropriate links. Create a memorandum that describes an FTP site with step-by-step instructions on how to save a document to an FTP site. Use a table to organize the steps. Save, preview, and print the document.

Project 8

During lunch Maria Betancourt tells you that the features on the Tables and Borders toolbar can also be used to create and format borders around text. You want to explore doing this. Open an existing document that contains several text paragraphs. Display the Tables and Borders toolbar and use the toolbar buttons to draw borders around the paragraphs. Select a paragraph and convert it to a table with a border. Modify several borders. Save the document with a new name, preview it, and print it.

Using Styles and Templates

Chapter Overview

Styles and templates help reduce the time you need to format documents you create repeatedly, such as schedules, fax coversheets, or reports. Styles let you try out various looks for your document quickly, or you can create a template containing styles so you focus on the content rather than the formatting of future documents. This chapter shows you how to use built-in styles and templates, as well as how to create and modify custom styles and templates.

LEARNING OBJECTIVES

▶ Create and apply styles
▶ Edit styles
▶ Use templates and wizards to create documents

Case profile

Worldwide Exotic Foods, Inc. human resources department often distributes documents to employees throughout the company. Bill Martin asks you to format the winter training schedule for him. He asks you to use styles so he can add items to the schedule using the same formats. The public affairs officer, Viktor Winkler, handles investor and customer inquiries from around the world. Viktor's assistant is out of the office for two weeks and he asks you to prepare several fax coversheets and a calendar.

chapter twelve

12.a Creating and Applying Styles

Instead of copying formats from one paragraph or character to another, you can create styles. A **style** is a group of formats assigned a unique name. A style allows you to format text easily by applying all the specified formats at one time. You can use multiple styles within the same document. Styles are saved with the current document or a template, such as the Normal template, upon which the document is based. Table 12-1 below lists the two kinds of Word styles.

TABLE 12-1
Types of Word Styles

Style	Description
Paragraph	Determines the appearance of a paragraph, including text alignment, tab stops, indentation, line spacing, page breaks, borders and shading, numbered and bulleted lists, numbered headings, and the paragraph's position in the page layout
Character	Determines the appearance of selected text, including font, size, bold, italic, underline, and effects such as all caps

You can use the styles that come with Word or you can create your own.

Applying Built-in Styles

Word provides more than 90 built-in paragraph and character styles for formatting a document. You can apply the built-in styles to format selected text from the Style Preview list (also called simply the Style list), which you view by clicking the Style button list arrow on the Formatting toolbar. By default, only five built-in styles appear in the Style Preview. You can view the other built-in styles by holding down the SHIFT key as you view the Style Preview. Built-in styles can be used as is or they can be modified for the current document. If no built-in style contains the formats you want, you can create a custom style.

Bill creates a notice of future training schedules to be posted on the employee bulletin boards and asks you to format the document in a way that draws the attention of employees. You use styles to quickly format the document. To view the Style Preview:

| Step 1 | *Open* | the *Winter Schedule* document located on the Data Disk |
| Step 2 | *Click* | the Style button list arrow `Normal ▼` on the Formatting toolbar |

The list of built-in styles that appears on your screen should look similar to Figure 12-1.

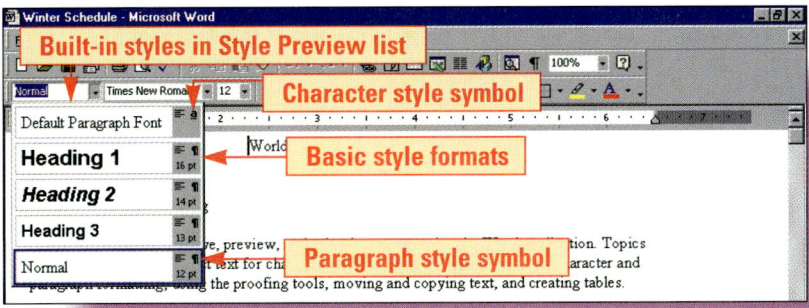

FIGURE 12-1
Style Preview

A bold, underlined letter "**a**" indicates a character style. A paragraph mark (¶) indicates a paragraph style. Notice the alignment and font size indicators. Each style name is displayed with its character formatting, providing an example of the style. The character style Default Paragraph Font formats selected text with the underlying paragraph style font, which is based on the paragraph style Normal. The paragraph style Normal is Times New Roman, 12 point, single-spaced, and left-aligned. By default, the Normal paragraph style is applied to all the text in a document that is based on the Normal template. The paragraph styles Heading 1, 2, and 3 format selected paragraphs to stand out from the Normal text as titles by making the font larger, boldfaced, or italicized—or by changing spacing above and below the paragraph.

Step 3	Press	the ESC key to close the style list

Because a paragraph style affects entire paragraphs, you can position the insertion point anywhere in a paragraph to select the paragraph before you apply a paragraph style. To apply character styles to an entire word, you position the insertion point in the word. If you are formatting a group of characters, you must select all the characters you want to format.

To format the document title, paragraph headings, and date line paragraphs, you decide to use Word built-in styles. To apply the Heading 1 style to the two title lines of the *Winter Schedule* document:

Step 1	Select	the two title lines
Step 2	Click	the Style button list arrow 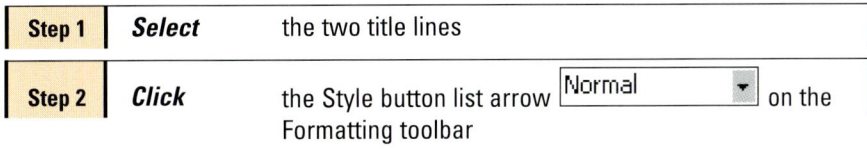 on the Formatting toolbar

CAUTION TIP

When you open a document created with an earlier version of Word, the five basic styles shown in the Style Preview reflect the styles in the original Normal template on which the document is based, not on the Word 2000 Normal template. For example, the default font size for the Normal style is 10 point for documents created in Word 97. If you open a document created in Word 97 the Style Preview shows the Normal style as 10 point.

MENU TIP

You can apply a style to selected characters or paragraphs by clicking the Style command on the Format menu.

chapter
twelve

Step 3	*Observe*	that the Heading 1 style contains bold, left-aligned, 16-point font formatting
Step 4	*Click*	Heading 1 in the Style Preview
Step 5	*Move*	the insertion point to the top of the document

Your screen should look similar to Figure 12-2.

FIGURE 12-2
Heading 1 Style Applied to Title Text

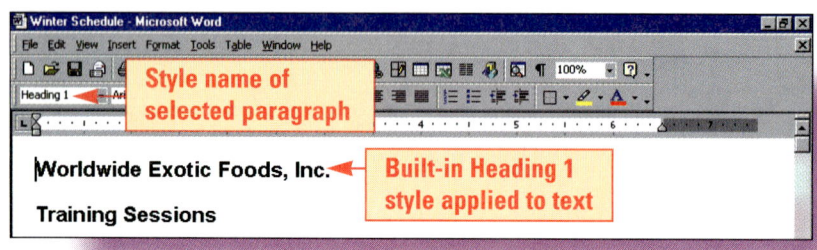

The Heading 1 style is applied to the selected text. Notice that the spacing between the two lines is also altered. In addition to the formatting you observed in the Style Preview, the Heading 1 style adds white space above and below each line. You can view the formatting components of each style from within the document.

Viewing Styles in a Document

When you position the insertion point in a paragraph, the Style button on the Formatting toolbar lists the name of the style used to format the paragraph. Figure 12-2 shows the insertion point in the first paragraph (the first title line) and the Heading 1 style name in the Style button. However, you cannot always tell the exact formatting from the style name or even by looking at the formatted text. If you want to see a list of all the formatting elements contained in the style, you click the paragraph with the What's This? help pointer.

To convert the mouse pointer to the What's This? help pointer and view the Heading 1 style formatting:

| Step 1 | *Press* | the SHIFT + F1 keys |
| Step 2 | *Click* | the first title line |

The Reveal Formats box, itemizing the paragraph and character styles of the Heading 1 style, appears. Your screen should look similar to Figure 12-3.

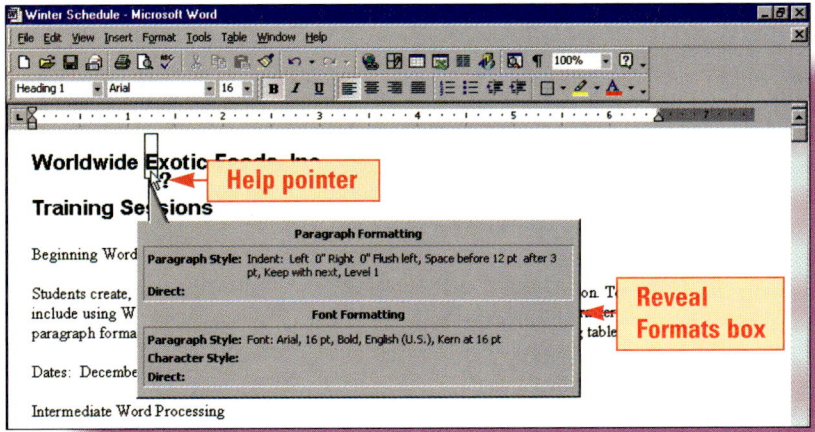

FIGURE 12-3
Heading 1 Style Paragraph
and Font Formatting

Any paragraph or character style applied to the selected text appears in the box. The list also includes any formatting you applied to the text using the Font or Paragraph command on the Format menu or the Formatting toolbar. After reviewing the formats in the Reveal Formats box, you can close it.

Step 3	*Press*	the ESC key

When working in Normal view, you can see the names of all the paragraph styles applied in the document without moving the insertion point from paragraph to paragraph. To do this, you set a space, called the **Style area**, to the left of the left margin and the selection bar on the screen. To create a ¾ inch Style area:

Step 1	*Click*	Tools
Step 2	*Click*	Options
Step 3	*Click*	the View tab, if necessary
Step 4	*Key*	.75 in the Style area width: text box
Step 5	*Click*	OK

The Style area appears at the left of the screen, which should look similar to Figure 12-4.

FIGURE 12-4
Document with Style Area

Style area

You can size the Style area by dragging the boundary left or right with the mouse pointer. You can quickly remove the Style area by dragging the boundary all the way to the left edge of the screen. To remove the Style area:

Step 1	*Move*	the mouse pointer to the Style area boundary line (it becomes a sizing pointer)
Step 2	*Drag*	the Style area boundary line left until it disappears

When there is no built-in style with the formatting combination you want, you can create a custom style.

Creating Custom Styles

Custom styles can be created in the Style dialog box or by example from formatted text. When you create styles in the Style dialog box, you can base the new style on another style or specify the style to be applied to the following paragraph.

To create styles by example, change the formatting of the selected text, click in the text box of the Style button, key a new style name, and press the ENTER key. Word creates the new style. You want to format all the paragraph headings for the *Winter Schedule* with the 12 point, bold, Arial, Small Caps, and a 2¼-inch text shadow border. First you reformat the "Beginning Word Processing" paragraph heading, and then you create a custom style by example based on the reformatted text. To change the font size and font style, and add a special text effect to the "Beginning Word Processing" paragraph heading:

MENU TIP

You can click the Style command on the Format menu to open the Style dialog box and create a custom style.

Step 1	*Select*	the "Beginning Word Processing" paragraph
Step 2	*Open*	the Font tab in the Font dialog box
Step 3	*Select*	the Arial, Bold, 12 point, Small Caps options
Step 4	*Click*	OK

The text shows the new font, font style, font size, and Small Caps effect. To add a 2¼-inch shadow border to the paragraph heading text:

Step 1	*Verify*	the "Beginning Word Processing" paragraph heading is selected
Step 2	*Open*	the Borders tab in the Borders and Shading dialog box
Step 3	*Click*	the Shadow Setting: option
Step 4	*Click*	2¼ pt in the Width: list
Step 5	*Click*	Text in the Apply to: list
Step 6	*Click*	OK
Step 7	*Deselect*	the text and leave the insertion point in the paragraph

A 2¼ pt shadow border is added to the paragraph. Your screen should look similar to Figure 12-5.

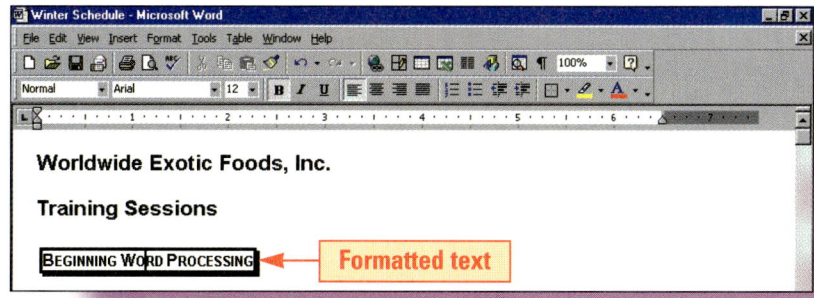

You can create a style based on the formatted text by moving the insertion point to the formatted text and then keying the style name in the Style button text box. By keying custom style names in all uppercase, you can distinguish your custom styles from the built-in styles. To create a custom style:

Step 1	*Verify*	the insertion point is in the "Beginning Word Processing" paragraph heading
Step 2	*Click*	the Style button text box  on the Formatting toolbar
Step 3	*Key*	COURSE LEVEL
Step 4	*Press*	the ENTER key
Step 5	*Observe*	the COURSE LEVEL paragraph style name in the Style button text box

---

FIGURE 12-5
Formatted Heading Text

chapter
twelve

The custom style makes it quick and easy to format other paragraphs the same way. You can apply the COURSE LEVEL style to the remaining paragraph headings by selecting the style from the Style Preview or by repeating the last action. To apply the custom style to the remaining paragraph headings:

Step 1	*Select*	the paragraph heading "Intermediate Word Processing"
Step 2	*Click*	the Style button list arrow [Normal ▼] on the Formatting toolbar
Step 3	*Observe*	that the custom style, COURSE LEVEL, is added to the Style Preview for this document
Step 4	*Click*	COURSE LEVEL
Step 5	*Select*	the paragraph heading "Advanced Word Processing"
Step 6	*Press*	the CTRL + Y keys to repeat the style formatting

The COURSE LEVEL paragraph style is applied to the title paragraphs.

Step 7	*Save*	the document as *Winter Schedule Revised*

notes

Word can also automatically create styles as you key text. For example, when you key and format a document title or paragraph heading, Word interprets your formatting choices as modifications to a heading style. If you want to use the automatic style creation feature you can turn the option on (or off) in the AutoFormat As You Type tab in the AutoCorrect dialog box.

After reviewing the *Winter Schedule Revised* document you decide to change some of the style formatting. You can modify styles by overriding the style formatting with different formatting or by redefining the formatting contained in the style.

12.b Editing Styles

You override formatting applied by style when you select the text and apply different formatting from the Formatting toolbar or a dialog box. When you override style formatting, the new formats apply to only the selected text. The style itself is not affected. The Heading 1 style has left aligned the two title lines. You want to center the lines but retain the rest of the Heading 1 style formatting. To override the Heading 1 style by centering the lines manually:

Step 1	Select	the first title line
Step 2	Click	the Center button ▤ on the Formatting toolbar
Step 3	Observe	that the second title line formatted with the Heading 1 style is not affected
Step 4	Center	the second title line

When you want to edit a style and have the changes automatically applied to all text in the current document formatted with that style, you redefine (or modify) the style itself. To redefine a style by example, you select text formatted with the style, change the formatting, and then rename the style with the same name.

You want to emphasize the date lines by applying a style. To apply the Heading 3 style to the date lines:

Step 1	Select	the first date line
Step 2	Apply	the Heading 3 style from the Style Preview
Step 3	Select	the second date line
Step 4	Press	the CTRL + Y keys

The 13-point font in the Heading 3 style is too large for the date line. Also, Bill inserted tab formatting marks between the dates and there are no custom tab stops set to arrange the dates attractively. You want to edit the Heading 3 style to have a 12-point font and left tab stops set at the 1-inch, 2.5-inch, and 4-inch positions. To reformat the text:

Step 1	Select	the first date line
Step 2	Change	the font size to 12
Step 3	Set	a left-aligned tab at the 1- , 2.5- , and 4-inch positions on the horizontal ruler
Step 4	Click	the Heading 3 style name in the Style button text box to select it
Step 5	Press	the ENTER key to rename the style with the same name

The Modify Style dialog box that opens on your screen should look similar to Figure 12-6.

> **MENU TIP**
>
> You can redefine a style with options in the Style dialog box. Open the Style dialog box by clicking the Style command on the Format menu.

chapter
twelve

FIGURE 12-6
Modify Style Dialog Box

Option to update style with formatting changes

Option to revert to previous style formats

The default option is to redefine, or update, the style based on the changes made to the selected text. The other option is to return the selected text to its original, unmodified style. When you select the default option, all text formatted with the modified style is automatically reformatted.

Step 6	*Click*	OK
Step 7	*Observe*	that the second date line is automatically reformatted with the redefined Heading 3 style
Step 8	*Deselect*	the text
Step 9	*Save*	the document

CAUTION TIP

You can delete custom styles, but you cannot delete built-in styles.

When you no longer need a custom style in a document, you can delete it. This keeps the Style Preview shorter and easier to use. When you delete a custom style, any text in the document formatted with the custom style returns to the Normal style. To delete the COURSE LEVEL style:

Step 1	*Click*	Format
Step 2	*Click*	Style
Step 3	*Click*	COURSE LEVEL in the Styles: list box
Step 4	*Click*	Delete
Step 5	*Click*	Yes in the confirmation dialog box
Step 6	*Close*	the Style dialog box
Step 7	*Observe*	that the Course Level style is deleted and the Normal style is applied to the paragraph headings
Step 8	*Close*	the document without saving any changes

QUICK TIP

The Organizer enables you to copy styles from document to document and from template to template. You open the Organizer dialog box by clicking the Templates and Add-Ins command on the Tools menu and then clicking the Organizer button or by clicking the Organizer button in the Style dialog box.

You can use the Style Gallery button in the Theme dialog box to preview sample documents based on Word templates, the current document with styles from templates, or a list of styles. To open the Theme dialog box, click T̲heme on the F̲ormat menu. When you copy a template in the Style Gallery to your document, styles with the same name override the style formatting currently in the document. Styles with names not in your document are added to the document. Unique styles in your document are not affected.

Viktor Winkler sends many faxes in response to customer and investor inquiries. He asks you to create a fax cover sheet. You can base the new cover sheet document on one of the Word fax templates.

12.c Using Templates and Wizards to Create Documents

Every document you create in Word is based on a template. A **template** is a master document or model that contains any text, formats, styles, macros, and AutoText that you want to include in a particular kind of document. Templates enable you to prepare documents more quickly because they supply many of the settings that you would otherwise need to create—such as margins, tabs, alignment, and formatted non-variable text. Each time you click the New button on the Standard toolbar you create a new document based on the Normal template. Another example is a letter template that contains the margin settings for a block format letter, the date field, and a standard closing including the writer's signature area.

There are two types of templates: global templates and document templates. The Normal template is an example of a **global template**, which means its settings are available for all documents. **Document templates** supply settings that affect only the current document and help you automatically format letters, faxes, memos, reports, manuals, brochures, newsletters, and special documents, such as Web pages. Word provides many built-in document templates and you can easily create your own.

You use a document template to create the cover sheet. To create a fax cover sheet based on a template:

Step 1	*Click*	F̲ile
Step 2	*Click*	N̲ew

QUICK TIP

To use settings from another template you can load it as a global template and attach it to your document. For more information on using and attaching global templates, see online Help.

CAUTION TIP

It is assumed that the Word templates used in the activities and exercises in this chapter are already installed on your computer. See your instructor if the templates are not installed.

chapter twelve

Step 3	*Click*	the Letters & Faxes tab, if necessary
Step 4	*Double-click*	the Contemporary Fax icon
Step 5	*Observe*	that a new document is created based on the Contemporary Fax template and Word switches to Print Layout view
Step 6	*Zoom*	the document to 75%

The document is preformatted with graphics, text boxes, heading text, lines, and placeholders. **Placeholders** are areas in which you key the variable information. Your screen should look similar to Figure 12-7.

FIGURE 12-7
Document Based on the
Contemporary Fax
Template

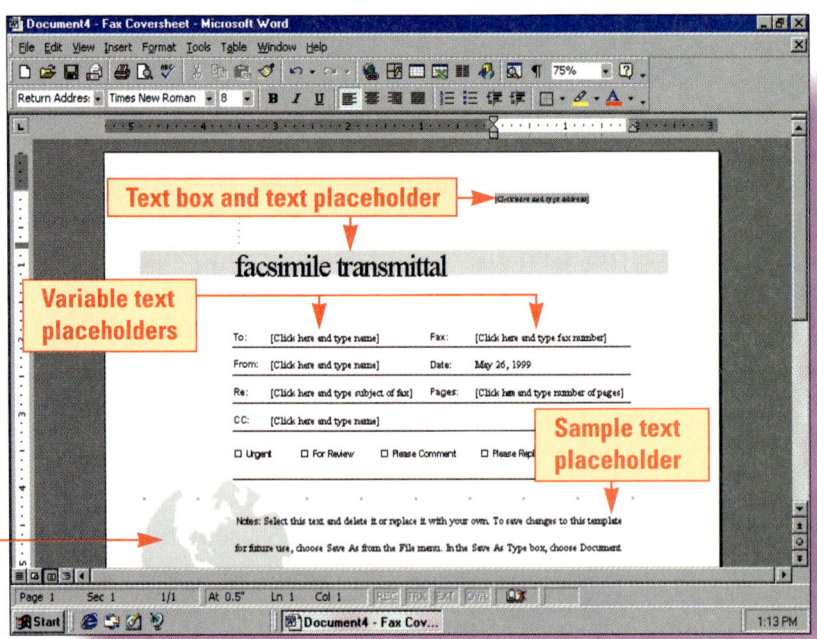

All you need to do to complete the fax is to key the appropriate variable information in the [Click here and type…] placeholders. After you click a variable text placeholder to select it, you key the appropriate text. Then press the F11 key to move to the next placeholder. To key the company name and address:

Step 1	*Zoom*	the document to 100% so you can read the text and placeholders
Step 2	*Observe*	that the current date already appears in the Date: placeholder because the date area contains a date field
Step 3	*Click*	the address placeholder text box in the upper-right corner of the document

Step 4	*Key*	Worldwide Exotic Foods, Inc. Gage Building, Suite 1200 Riverside Plaza Chicago, IL 60606-2000
Step 5	*Press*	the F11 key to select the next placeholder

To key the remaining variable text:

Step 1	*Key*	John Washington, Software Inc.
Step 2	*Press*	the F11 key
Step 3	*Key*	312-555-0098 in the Fax: placeholder
Step 4	*Press*	the F11 key
Step 5	*Key*	Viktor Winkler in the From: placeholder
Step 6	*Press*	the F11 key twice
Step 7	*Key*	Speaking Engagement in the Re: placeholder
Step 8	*Press*	the F11 key
Step 9	*Key*	2 in the Pages: placeholder
Step 10	*Press*	the F11 key
Step 11	*Press*	the Delete key to delete the CC: placeholder
Step 12	*Press*	the F11 key
Step 13	*Key*	X in the Urgent placeholder check box
Step 14	*Select*	the Notes: text below the check box placeholders (do not select the word and colon "Notes:")
Step 15	*Key*	I am happy to accept your invitation to speak at the Software Inc. executive committee luncheon tomorrow. Attached is a draft of my speech.
Step 16	*Save*	the document as *Washington Fax* and close it

During the day, Viktor Winkler asks you to create several fax cover sheets for him. To save time, you decide to create a custom fax cover sheet template that already contains the company name, address, and Viktor Winkler's name.

Creating a Custom Template

You can create your own templates by making changes to the current document and saving it as a template. You can also use one of the Word templates as a basis for your custom template. You use the

QUICK TIP

By default, custom templates are stored in the Templates folder located in the Windows\Application Data\Microsoft location. An icon for each template stored in the Templates folder appears on the General tab in the New dialog box, making it easy to create documents from a custom template. You can create additional tabs in the New dialog box by creating folders inside the Templates folder. Word uses the folder name as the new tab name.

You can change the default location for templates from the Templates folder by changing the User Templates location in the File Locations tab in the Options dialog box. For more information about storing templates, see online Help.

Contemporary Fax template as the basis for the Winkler fax template. To create a custom template:

Step 1	***Open***	the Letters & Faxes tab in the New dialog box
Step 2	***Click***	the Template option button to create a new template based on another template
Step 3	***Double-click***	the Contemporary Fax icon

A template document named Template1 – Fax Coversheet opens. Now you can replace the placeholders with text that never changes. To add text to the template:

Step 1	***Select***	the address placeholder text box in the upper-right corner of the document
Step 2	***Key***	Worldwide Exotic Foods, Inc. Gage Building, Suite 1200 Riverside Plaza Chicago, IL 60606-2000
Step 3	***Press***	the F11 key three times
Step 4	***Key***	Viktor Winkler
Step 5	***Delete***	the Notes: text (do not delete the word and colon "Notes:")

Next you customize the heading text at the top of the document.

Step 6	***Select***	the text "facsimile transmittal" near the top of the document
Step 7	***Key***	Fax Cover Sheet

You need to save the changes you made to the template, just as you do with a document. To save the template:

Step 1	***Open***	the Save As dialog box
Step 2	***Observe***	that Save in location defaults to the Templates folder
Step 3	***Observe***	the file type is Document Template
Step 4	***Save***	the template as *Winkler Coversheet* and close it

The next time Viktor asks for a fax cover sheet, you can create one quickly based on the *Winkler Coversheet* template. To test the custom template:

Step 1	*Open*	the General tab in the New dialog box
Step 2	*Observe*	the new *Winkler Coversheet* template icon
Step 3	*Double-click*	the *Winkler Coversheet* template icon
Step 4	*Create*	a one-page fax to Beryl Davis, 312-555-7890, for review with a note confirming receipt of the new brochure listing government offices in the Chicago area
Step 5	*Save*	the fax as *Davis Fax* and close it

When you no longer use a template, you can delete it by opening the New dialog box, right-clicking the template icon, and clicking <u>D</u>elete. Your fax assignments for Viktor are complete so you want to delete the template. To delete the *Winkler Coversheet* template:

Step 1	*Open*	the General tab in the New dialog box
Step 2	*Right-click*	the *Winkler Coversheet* icon
Step 3	*Click*	<u>D</u>elete
Step 4	*Click*	<u>Y</u>es to confirm the deletion
Step 5	*Cancel*	the New dialog box

You can also modify the Normal template to change the default settings. Common defaults that users change are the font style, font size, and margin settings. Viktor Winkler uses the same margins and fonts for all public affairs correspondence. You can create a custom template for his correspondence or you can modify the margins and font settings in the Normal template so that every document you create contains the preferred margin and font settings.

Creating a New Document with a Wizard

A **wizard** is a series of dialog boxes that asks questions and uses your answers to lay out and format a document. You can use wizards to create legal pleadings, letters, fax cover sheets, envelopes, labels, memos, meeting agenda, calendars, resumes, and Web Pages. The wizard icons are located in the various tabs in the New dialog box along with the template icons. Viktor Winkler asks you to create a calendar he

> **QUICK TIP**
>
> The Normal template contains default formats and settings that are appropriate for most common documents. The most common changes to the Normal template are to the font and font size and margin settings. These changes can be made to the Normal template from the Font and Page Setup dialog boxes

can use to plan his travel schedule for next month. You use the Calendar Wizard to do this quickly. To create a one-month calendar:

Step 1	*Open*	the New dialog box
Step 2	*Click*	the Other Documents tab
Step 3	*Double-click*	the Calendar Wizard icon
Step 4	*Observe*	the Calendar Wizard dialog box options

When you work in a Wizard, you can cancel your actions with the Cancel button, return to the previous step with the <Back button, move to the next step with the Next> button, and complete the document with the Finish button. These buttons appear at the bottom of the dialog box.

Step 5	*Click*	Next> to choose a style for your calendar
Step 6	*Click*	the Boxes and borders option button
Step 7	*Click*	Next> to choose a the paper orientation
Step 8	*Click*	the Landscape option button
Step 9	*Click*	Next> to choose the calendar date
Step 10	*Select*	the next month and current year from the Month and Year list boxes
Step 11	*Click*	Next> to complete your calendar choices
Step 12	*Click*	Finish

The completed calendar document appears on your screen. You can click inside each day block and key text. When you click the calendar you can see the object's boundaries, which you can click to select the content and change its formatting. To review the calendar:

Step 1	*Scroll*	to view the calendar
Step 2	*Click*	the first blank day box at the top of the calendar to view the calendar border
Step 3	*Click*	the calendar object border to select the contents
Step 4	*Change*	the font size to 18 and remove the bold formatting
Step 5	*Save*	the document as *Viktor's Calendar* and close it

Wizards, templates, and styles make it easy to create consistently formatted documents quickly, letting you focus on the content of your documents.

Summary

► A style is a group of formats assigned a unique name.

► Styles help you save time by applying several different formats at once.

► There are two kinds of styles: paragraph styles and character styles.

► Styles are saved with the document and can be added to the template on which the document is based so that the styles are available to all new documents based on that template.

► Word has more than 90 built-in styles; however, only five built-in styles appear in a new document by default. You can choose to display all the built-in styles, if desired.

► Styles can be viewed in a Style area on the screen to the left of the document text.

► You can review the formatting components of a style by changing the mouse pointer to the What's This? help pointer and clicking the formatted text.

► You can create custom styles and can modify built-in styles in the Style dialog box. You can also create styles by example, using the Style button on the Formatting toolbar.

► A template is a model document. The default model is the Normal template.

► You can modify the Normal template by opening it and making changes to it. Also, you can change the font, font size, and margin settings in the Normal template in the Font and Page Setup dialog boxes.

► Word has many letter, fax, Web page, and other templates you can use to create your own documents.

► You can create a custom template by using another Word document as an example and saving it as a template. You can also use a Word template as the basis for the new custom template.

► You can create a variety of documents following a step-by-step process called a wizard.

chapter twelve

Commands Review

Action	Menu Bar	Shortcut Menu	Toolbar	Keyboard
Apply a style to selected text	Format, Style		Normal ▼	ALT + O, S CTRL + SHIFT + S CTRL + SHIFT + N (Normal style) ALT + CTRL + 1 (Heading 1 style) ALT + CTRL + 2 (Heading 2 style) ALT + CTRL + 3 (Heading 3 style) CTRL+ SHIFT + L (List style)
Repeat a style	Edit, Repeat Style			ALT + E, R CTRL + Y F4
Display all built-in styles			Press the SHIFT key and click the Normal ▼ list arrow	
Display the formatting applied to text in a box	Help, What's This?			ALT + H, T SHIFT + F1
Close the box containing formatting information				ESC
Display styles in the Style Area of the document	Tools, Options View tab			ALT + T, O
Create custom styles	Format, Style		Click the text area of Normal ▼ and type style name	ALT + O, S
Modify a style	Format, Style		Click the text area of Normal ▼ and press ENTER	ALT + O, S
View and/or copy styles from Word templates to the current document	Tools, Templates and Add-Ins			ALT + T, I
Base a document on a template or wizard	File, New			ALT + F, N
Go to the next field in a document based on a Word template				F11
Go to the previous field in a document based on a Word template				SHIFT + F11

Concepts Review

Circle the correct answer.

1. A paragraph style does not:
- **[a]** include font, font size, and line spacing.
- **[b]** affect the entire selected paragraph.
- **[c]** determine the overall appearance of a paragraph.
- **[d]** affect only selected text characters.

2. Which of the following is not a basic style in the Style Preview?
- **[a]** Heading 1
- **[b]** Heading 3
- **[c]** Default Character Font
- **[d]** Normal

3. **You cannot see which style is applied to a paragraph by:**
   [a] selecting the paragraph and observing the Style button.
   [b] clicking the Style Gallery command on the Format menu.
   [c] setting a Style area down the left side of the screen.
   [d] moving the insertion point to a paragraph and then opening the Style dialog box.

4. **A template is a:**
   [a] place to store documents.
   [b] tool to apply a combination of formats at one time.
   [c] model document.
   [d] way to view the styles in your document.

5. **To view the entire list of styles in the Style Preview press the:**
   [a] ALT key and click the Style Preview list arrow.
   [b] CTRL key and click the Style Preview list arrow.
   [c] BACKSPACE key and click the Style Preview list arrow.
   [d] SHIFT key and click the Style Preview list arrow.

6. **A character style:**
   [a] determines the overall appearance of a paragraph.
   [b] must be applied to entire words.

   [c] must be created by example.
   [d] determines the appearance of selected text.

7. **The Normal template:**
   [a] must be opened before you can edit it.
   [b] is used to create documents when you click the Open button on the Standard toolbar.
   [c] cannot be edited in the Font and Page Setup dialog boxes.
   [d] contains the default font and margin settings.

8. **Entering a custom style name in uppercase characters:**
   [a] defines the style as a paragraph style.
   [b] makes the name easier to read.
   [c] distinguishes the custom style from a built-in style.
   [d] creates a style by example.

9. **Which template do you use each time you click the New button on the Standard toolbar?**
   [a] Paragraph template
   [b] Normal template
   [c] Font template
   [d] Formatting template

10. **The bold, underlined letter "a" indicates:**
    [a] a paragraph style.
    [b] the Normal template.
    [c] a character style.
    [d] the Style Gallery.

Circle **T** if the statement is true or **F** if the statement is false.

T   F   1. A style allows you to format text easily by applying many different formats at one time.

T   F   2. Word provides exactly 65 built-in styles.

T   F   3. You can create custom styles with the Formatting toolbar or the Style command on the Format menu.

T   F   4. You can delete built-in styles.

T   F   5. You can use the Style Gallery button on the Formatting toolbar to apply, create, or modify styles.

T   F   6. A character style determines the overall appearance of a paragraph.

T   F   7. The Reveal Formats box shows only character styles.

chapter twelve

T F   8. After you edit a style, you must manually reapply the style to the formatted text.

T F   9. Built-in styles cannot be modified.

T F   10. You can use the Style Gallery to preview and copy styles to your document.

Skills Review

Exercise 1

1. Open the *Word Outline* document located on the Data Disk.

2. Apply the built-in Heading 1 style to the title "WORD FOR WINDOWS."

3. Apply the built-in Heading 2 style to the topic headings. (The topic headings are in 12-point font.)

4. Save the document as *Word Outline With Built-in Styles*.

5. Preview, print, and close the document.

Exercise 2

1. Open the *Word Outline* document located on the Data Disk.

2. Create a style by example to center and add bold formatting to the title "WORD FOR WINDOWS." Name the style TITLES.

3. Create a style by example to bold and underline the topic headings. (The topic headings are in 12-point font.) Name the style HEADINGS.

4. Apply the HEADINGS style to the topic headings.

5. Apply the built-in List Bullet 2 style to the subtopics. (The subtopics are in 10-point font.) (*Hint:* Use the SHIFT key to view all the style in the Style Preview.)

6. Save the document as *Word Outline With Custom Styles*.

7. Preview, print, and close the document.

Exercise 3

1. Open the *Word Outline With Custom Styles* document created in Exercise 2.

2. Modify the TITLES style using the Style list box on the Formatting toolbar so that the title is Arial, 16 point, italic, no bold.

3. Modify the HEADINGS style using the Style list box on the Formatting toolbar so that the headings are Arial, 12 point, bold, Small Caps effect, no underline.

4. Save the document as *Word Outline With Custom Styles Revised*.

5. Preview, print, and close the document.

Exercise 4

1. Open the *Preparing For A Speech* document located on the Data Disk.

2. Create a style that indents the body of the document 0.25 inches from the left and right margins, double spaces the body of the document, and uses justified alignment. Name the style LAYOUT.

3. Create a style that makes the document title boldfaced and centered. Name the style TITLES.

4. Create a style to format the paragraph headings with a double underline and 1.5 line spacing. Name the style SIDEHEAD.

5. Apply the styles in the document.

6. Save the document as *Preparing For A Speech With Styles*.

7. Preview, print, and close the document.

Exercise 5

1. Open the *Preparing For A Speech With Styles* document created in Exercise 4.

2. Edit the SIDEHEAD style so that the side headings are bold and italic instead of underlined.

3. Change the LAYOUT style so that the line spacing is 1.5.

4. Save the document as *Preparing For A Speech Revised*.

5. Preview, print, and close the document.

Exercise 6

1. Use the Elegant Memo template to create a memorandum to Viktor Winkler from yourself with a copy to Bill Martin.

2. Describe the new Winkler Coversheet template and how to use it in the body of the memorandum.

3. Save the memorandum as *Winkler Memo*.

4. Preview, print, and close the document.

Exercise 7

1. Create a new custom fax coversheet for Bill Martin, with a copy to B. J. Chang, based on the Professional Fax template. (*Hint:* Enlarge the text box that contains the company name so that the text does not wrap to two lines.)

2. Save the custom template as *Martin Fax*.

3. Preview, print, and close the document.

Exercise 8

1. Create an interoffice memo using the Memo Wizard.

2. Use the Contemporary style, the default title text, and the Date, From, and Subject header lines. Send the memo to Jody Haversham with a copy to Viktor Winkler. Add your initials as the writer's initials. Do not include a header or footer. The subject is "Using Wizards."

3. Key a brief paragraph describing how to create a document using a wizard.

4. Save the document as *Memo Created With A Wizard*.

5. Preview, print, and close the document.

Exercise 9

1. Create the following document using built-in styles.

2. Save the document as *Public Affairs Officer*.

3. Preview, print, and close the document.

chapter twelve

Public Affairs Officer

Viktor Winkler

Investor and Customer Inquiries

Annual Reports

401(k) Reports

Customer Service

Government Liaison

13ᵗʰ District Election Committee

Food Distributors PAC

Registered Lobbyist

Civic and Business Liaison

Heltrep Foundation

Speakers Bureau

Youth First Committee

Mayor's Council

Case Projects

Project 1

Viktor Winkler's assistant, Bob Thackery, returns from vacation and is impressed with the documents you formatted. He wants to know how to apply, create, and modify styles using the Style dialog box and asks you for help. Because you created your custom styles using the Style button, you need to research how to use the Style dialog box. Open the Style dialog box with the Style command on the Format menu. Use the dialog box Help tool to review the options and buttons in the dialog box, and then close it. Use the Office Assistant to research creating and modifying paragraph and character styles using the options in the Style dialog box. Write Bob an interoffice memorandum, based on a memo template, explaining how he can use the Style dialog box to save time formatting documents. Save, preview, and print the memo.

Project 2

The human resource department frequently receives unsolicited resumes from people around the world who want to work for Worldwide Exotic Foods. Company policy is to thank the sender for the resume and advise them that their resume will be kept on file for six months. If a position becomes available, the sender will be contacted to arrange for an interview. To save time in responding to unsolicited resumes, Bill asks you to create a block format custom letter template with B. J. Chang's signature line. The only variable data keyed in documents based on this new custom template is the letter address and the name portion of the salutation. The date, the "Dear" portion of the salutation, the body text, the closing, the signature line, and the typist's initials are fixed text, sometimes called boilerplate text, in the template. Create, save, preview, and print the template. Then create two letters, including attached envelopes, to fictitious persons using the new custom letter template. Save, preview, and print the letters and envelopes.

Project 3

Viktor Winkler needs a list of government Web sites containing information of interest to Worldwide Exotic Foods, Inc. management and employees. He asks you to compile such a list. Connect to your ISP, load your Web browser, and search the Web for government Web pages of interest. Print at least five Web pages. Create a list of the Web sites of interest. Use built-in and custom styles to format the list. Save, preview, and print the list.

Project 4

Lydia Montez, a receptionist in the human resources department, is having trouble using styles. Sometimes her styles change unexpectedly, some paragraphs formatted with the same style look different, and she cannot see all the styles she wants to use in the Style Preview. You agree to research these problems and then tell her how to solve them. Using the Office Assistant, review how to troubleshoot problems you might encounter when using styles. Create a new document, with at least four paragraphs, that describes each of Lydia's style problems and suggests a solution for each one. Use styles to format the document. Save and print the document. With your instructor's approval, use the document as a guide to show a classmate how to solve these and other style problems.

Project 5

Bill Martin wants to preview the styles used in several Word templates and then copy the styles into a new document he is creating. He asks you

how to do this. Using the Office Assistant, research how to view or copy styles from another template into your document using the Style Gallery. Write Bill and interoffice memorandum explaining how to do this. Use styles to format your memorandum. Save, preview, and print the memorandum.

Project 6

Viktor Winkler wants to include current U. S. government international travel warnings in a bulletin he wants faxed to each branch office and posted in the employee lounge area to warn traveling employees. He asks you to locate the government page where international warnings are listed. Print the page. Create a document that lists the travel warnings. Format the document using custom paragraph and character styles. Save, preview, and print the document.

Project 7

Several human resources employees ask you how they can access styles contained in other documents when working in their documents. Using the online Help features, research how to use settings from another document by attaching a different template to a document and by using the Organizer feature. Practice attaching a different template and updating styles and copying styles to a document using the Organizer. Create a document itemizing how to use both techniques to use settings from other documents. Save, preview, and print the document. With your instructor's permission, demonstrate these techniques to several classmates.

Project 8

To save time in creating interoffice memos, Lydia asks you to create a human resources interoffice memorandum template. She wants you to use the Professional Memo template as the basis for the custom template, but she does not want the page number at the bottom of the page. Create the custom memo template—making any other changes you think appropriate to styles, layout, and formatting. Save, preview, and print the document.

chapter twelve

Generating an Outline

Chapter Overview

An outline is a way to structure information logically. You can use an outline to organize ideas and information into topics and subtopics for a large document, such as a report, proposal, or presentation. An outline is also a good way to construct multilevel lists. In this chapter you learn to create and modify outlines.

LEARNING OBJECTIVES

► **Organize a document in Outline view**
► **Modify an outline**
► **Use Outline Numbered formats to create outlines**

Case profile

Worldwide Exotic Foods, Inc. is planning a major presentation for investors, distributors, and other invited guests, during a company-sponsored picnic at the International Food Distributors annual conference in London. The executive assistant, Marisa DaFranco, asks you to help prepare the food list for the caterers and the chairperson's presentation outline.

13
chapter thirteen

13.a   Organizing a Document in Outline View

An **outline** consists of headings and body text organized by level of importance into major headings and subheadings. Body text is paragraph text below an outline heading. Major headings are called level one headings. Each major heading can have subheadings, called level two headings. Each level two heading can have its own subheadings at level three, and so forth.

Marisa is preparing the food list for the company picnic and needs to organize the information for the caterer. She gives you the handwritten document in Figure 13-1 and asks you to create an outline with three heading levels.

QUICK TIP

You can use built-in heading styles or the <u>O</u>utline level: formats from the Paragraph dialog box to indicate an outline level in a document. For example, you can format a major heading with the "Heading 1" style. If you do not want to change its formatting, you use the <u>O</u>utline level: format "Level 1" instead. Either method designates the paragraph heading as a level one heading in an outline.

FIGURE 13-1
Catering List Outline

chapter
thirteen

MENU TIP

You can view a document in Outline view by clicking the Outline command on the View menu.

You begin by keying the text in Figure 13-1 in one single spaced column at the left margin. Do not manually indent any of the text. The text is indented when you create the outline.

To key the menu:

| Step 1 | *Key* | the text in Figure 13-1 in one single spaced column at the left margin |
| Step 2 | *Save* | the document as *Catering Food List* |

Word has two tools you can use to create outlines. You can create an outline in Outline view using heading or level styles and you can create outlines using formats in the Outline Numbered tab in the Bullets and Numbering dialog box.

To create the outline using styles:

| Step 1 | *Click* | the Outline View button  to the left of the horizontal scroll bar |

The *Catering Food List* document appears in Outline view. Your screen should look similar to Figure 13-2.

FIGURE 13-2
Outline View

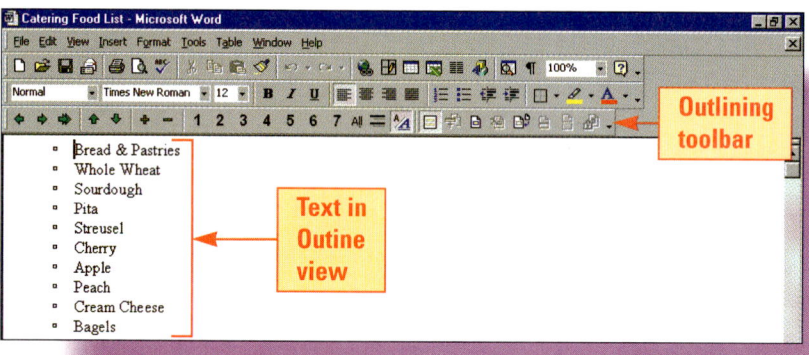

The Outlining toolbar appears below the Formatting toolbar whenever you are in Outline view. To create an outline in Outline view, you "promote" or "demote" headings to different levels of importance in the outline. You can do this as you key text into a blank document, or you can open an existing document, select the heading, and promote or demote it to the appropriate level. You use the Promote and Demote buttons on the Outlining toolbar to apply heading styles that indicate the outline levels.

Figure 13-1 indicates the text "Bread & Pastries," "Meat & Cheese," "Produce," and "Snack Foods" are major headings. To begin the outline by promoting the "Bread & Pastries" major heading to level one:

Step 1	*Verify*	the insertion point is in the first heading "Bread & Pastries"
Step 2	*Click*	the Promote button ◀ on the Outlining toolbar
Step 3	*Observe*	the Bread & Pastries text is formatted with the Heading 1 style, making it a major or level one heading

The text beginning with "Whole Wheat" and ending with "Streusel" are level two subheadings. To demote the next four paragraphs to level two:

Step 1	*Select*	the text beginning with "Whole Wheat" and ending with "Streusel"
Step 2	*Click*	the Demote button ▶ on the Outlining toolbar

Word indents the level two headings and applies the Heading 2 style. The headings beginning with "Cherry" and ending with "Cream Cheese" are level three headings. To demote the next four paragraphs to level three:

Step 1	*Select*	the text beginning with "Cherry" and ending with "Cream Cheese"
Step 2	*Click*	the Demote button ▶ on the Outlining toolbar

The level three headings are indented and formatted with the Heading 3 style. To promote the heading "Bagels" to level two:

Step 1	*Select*	the text Bagels
Step 2	*Click*	the Promote button ◀ on the Outlining toolbar twice

Bagels is promoted to level two. To promote the "Meat & Cheese" text to level one:

Step 1	*Select*	the "Meat & Cheese" text
Step 2	*Click*	the Promote button ◀ on the Outlining toolbar twice

chapter
thirteen

Your screen should look similar to Figure 13-3.

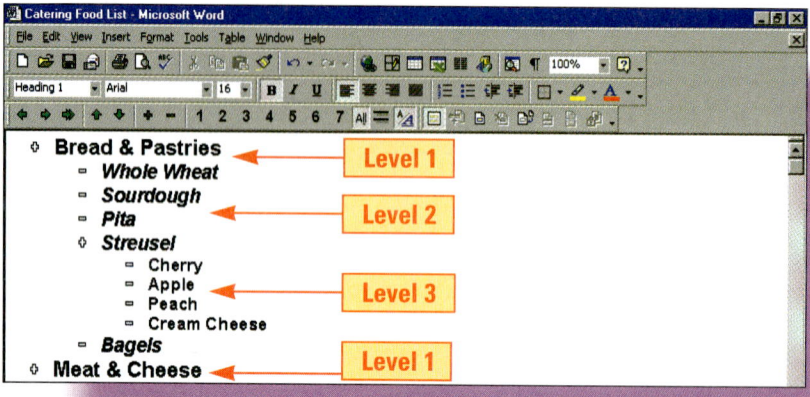

The plus sign (+) next to an outline level indicates that the outline level contains subheadings. The minus sign (–) next to an outline level indicates that the outline level does not contain subheadings. You can use the TAB key to demote text to a lower outline level and the SHIFT + TAB keys to promote text to a higher outline level. To demote the text beginning with "Turkey" and ending with "Beef" to level two:

Step 1	*Select*	the text beginning with "Turkey" and ending with "Beef"
Step 2	*Press*	the TAB key
Step 3	*Select*	the text beginning with "Sliced" and ending with "Chopped"
Step 4	*Press*	the TAB key to demote the selected text to level three

Next you use the SHIFT + TAB to promote text to a higher outline level. To promote "Cheeses" to level two:

Step 1	*Select*	the text "Cheeses"
Step 2	*Press & Hold*	the SHIFT key
Step 3	*Press*	TAB key twice to promote the text to level two
Step 4	*Release*	the SHIFT key
Step 5	*Complete*	the outline using Figure 13-1 as your guide
Step 6	*Save*	the document as *Catering List Outline*

Because you use outlines to organize ideas and information for large documents or presentations, you sometimes want to review outlines by heading level. This allows you to focus on the document structure. You can review an outline by heading level with the Show Heading buttons on the Outlining toolbar. Outline view indicates that a section contains more detail in two ways. The plus sign (+) to the left of a heading indicates it contains subheadings. When you hide the subheadings, a gray line appears below headings that contain additional detail, whether a subheading or body text. To see different level headings:

Step 1	*Click*	the Show Heading 1 button ☐1 on the Outlining toolbar
Step 2	*Observe*	only the level one headings are visible
Step 3	*Observe*	the gray line below the level one headings
Step 4	*Click*	the Show Heading 2 button ☐2 on the Outlining toolbar
Step 5	*Observe*	both the level one and two headings are visible
Step 6	*Click*	the Show All Headings button ☐All on the Outlining toolbar
Step 7	*Observe*	all the headings are visible

Marisa likes the way the outline looks, but asks you to add two new subheadings under "Candy" and add a numbering scheme so that each outline level is numbered differently. She also asks you to move the entire Meat & Cheese group headings to the top of the outline.

13.b Modifying an Outline

After you create an outline, you can change it by adding and moving headings. To add a heading to the outline, move the insertion point to the location where you want the heading to begin, press the ENTER key to create a new line, and key the new heading. You can promote or demote the new headings as needed. To add two new headings:

Step 1	*Move*	the insertion point to the end of the document
Step 2	*Press*	the ENTER key
Step 3	*Click*	the Demote button ➡ on the Outlining toolbar

chapter
thirteen

Step 4	*Key*	Chocolate
Step 5	*Press*	the ENTER key
Step 6	*Key*	All Other

You can move a heading by selecting it and clicking the Move Up or Move Down buttons on the Outlining toolbar. This moves the heading and all its subheadings up or down one position at a time in the outline. To select a heading and all its subheadings, click the plus sign (+) to the left of the heading.

A quick way to move a heading and its subheadings up or down several positions in the outline is to drag the heading's plus sign. As you drag the plus sign a horizontal positioning line appears on the screen indicating where the heading group is placed when you release the mouse pointer.

To select and move the Meat & Cheese major heading and subheadings to the top of the list:

| Step 1 | *Drag* | the plus sign (+) to the left of the Meat & Cheese level one text up until the horizontal line is positioned above the Bread & Pastries heading at the top of the document |

Your screen should look similar to Figure 13-4.

FIGURE 13-4
Repositioning a Major Heading

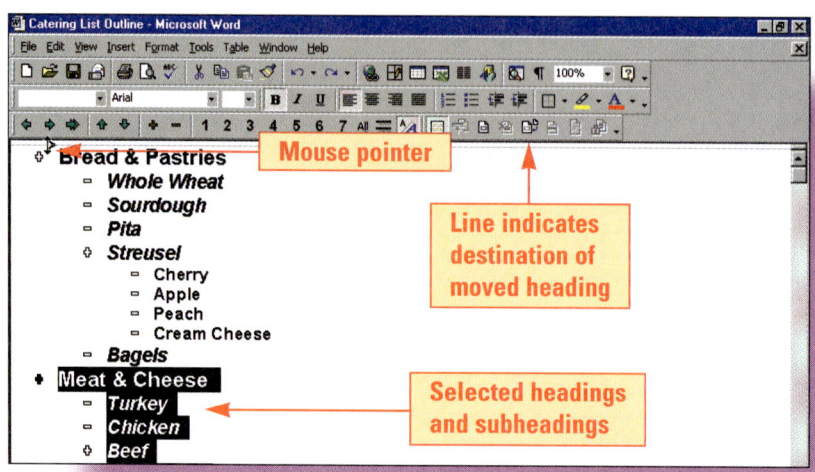

Step 2	*Release*	the mouse button to position the Meat & Cheese heading and subheadings at the top of the document
Step 3	*Deselect*	the text
Step 4	*Save*	the document

Creating an Outline Style Numbered List

Another way to modify an outline is to add numbers to each outline heading. This helps the reader follow the document structure from more important to less important headings. You can add numbers to the outline levels using the O̲utline Numbered tab in the Bullets and Numbering dialog box. This is more effective than numbering the levels manually because if you rearrange the outline order Word updates the numbers automatically. To add numbers to the outline:

Step 1	*Move*	the insertion point to the top of the document, if necessary
Step 2	*Click*	F̲ormat
Step 3	*Click*	Bullets and N̲umbering
Step 4	*Click*	the O̲utline Numbered tab, if necessary

The dialog box you see on your screen should look like Figure 13-5. You select and customize the numbering scheme in this dialog box.

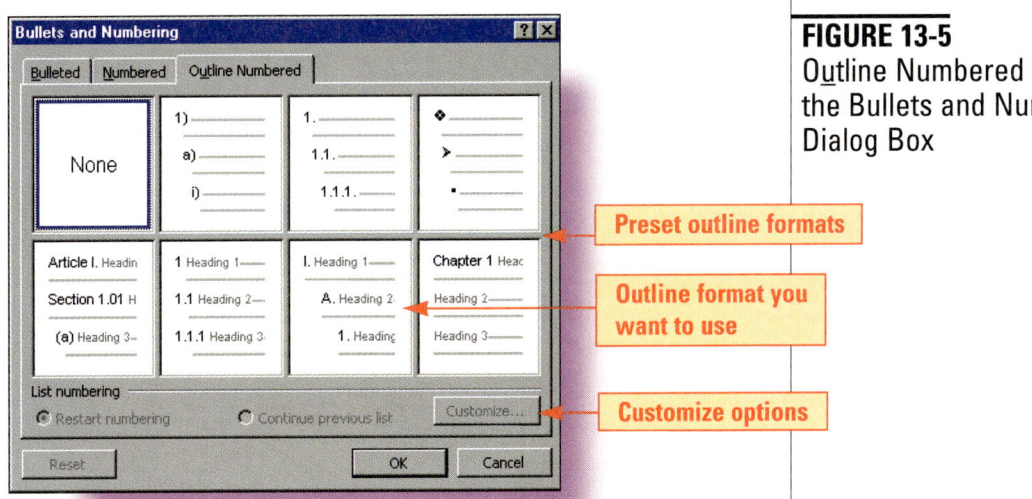

FIGURE 13-5
O̲utline Numbered Tab in the Bullets and Numbering Dialog Box

notes

Unless otherwise noted, the activities in this chapter assume the O̲utline Numbered formats contain their default settings. If the formats are customized, the Reset button is active when the format is selected. Click the Reset button, if it is active, to return the format to its default settings. It is recommended that you return all O̲utline Numbered formats to their default settings before you proceed with the remaining activities in this chapter.

chapter thirteen

To apply the I., A., 1. (Heading 1, 2, 3) format:

| Step 1 | **Double-click** | the third format option in the second row |
| Step 2 | **Observe** | the numbering added to the outline headings and subheadings |

In Outline view you cannot view the horizontal ruler with the indent marker and tab stops settings that control the position of the heading and subheadings in the outline. To view these settings, you must switch to Print Layout or Normal view.

Step 3	**Switch**	to Normal view
Step 4	**Scroll**	to view the entire list
Step 5	**Scroll**	to view the "Produce" and "Snack Foods" major headings on the screen
Step 6	**Observe**	the spacing between the heading number and the heading text for both headings

Your screen should look similar to Figure 13-6.

FIGURE 13-6
Heading Number and Text
Spacing

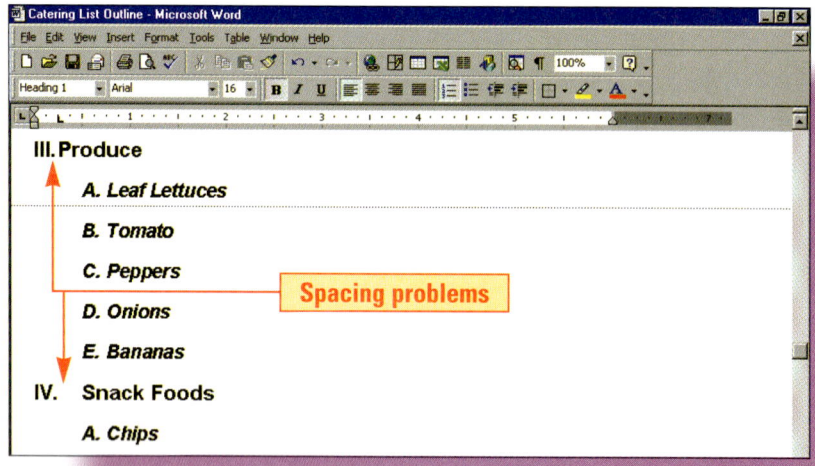

The "Produce" heading aligns immediately to the right of the heading number and the "Snack Foods" heading aligns at the next default tab stop. Word automatically indents each heading level in ½-inch increments beginning with level two. Also, Word inserts a custom left-aligned tab stop ¼ inch to the right of each heading's indent marker. When the heading number increases to three positions, the default ¼-inch tab stop position is not sufficient to properly align the heading text. Also notice that the level three headings appear indented too far to the right. To more attractively align the level one and level three headings, you must customize the outline number format for both levels. To customize the Outline Numbered format:

Step 1	*Open*	the Outline Numbered tab in the Bullets and Numbering dialog box
Step 2	*Verify*	the I., A., 1. (Heading 1, 2, 3) format is selected
Step 3	*Click*	Customize
Step 4	*Click*	the More button to expand the dialog box

The dialog box you see on your screen should look similar to Figure 13-7.

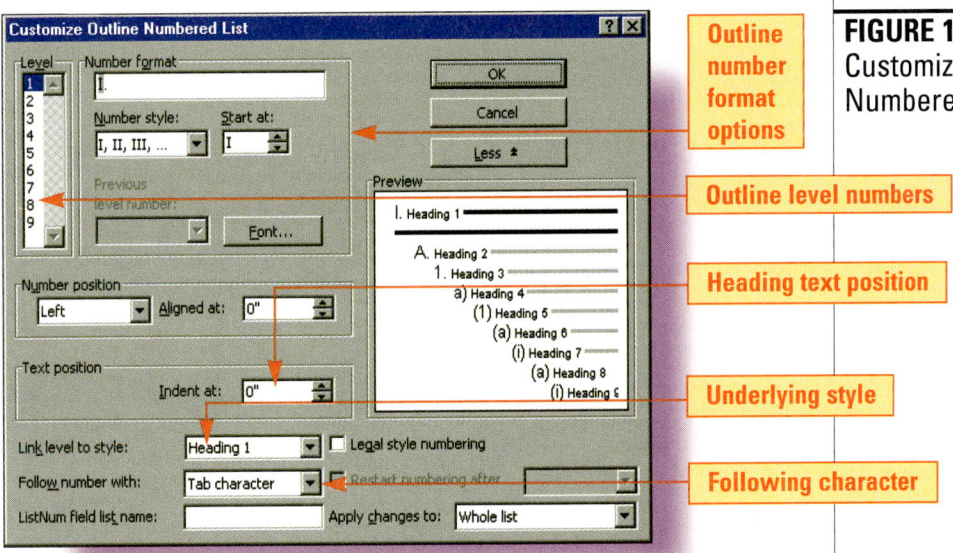

FIGURE 13-7
Customize Outline Numbered List Dialog Box

When you customize the Outline numbered format, you do it one level at a time. First select the heading number you want to modify from the Level list and then change the numbering style, font, beginning number, or indentation positions. You can apply your changes to the whole list or at the position of the insertion point. To change the level one heading indentation so that it's ½ inch to the right of the heading number:

| Step 1 | *Verify* | that 1 is selected in the Level list |
| Step 2 | *Observe* | the position of the Heading 1 text in the Preview |

chapter
thirteen

| Step 3 | *Key* | .5 in the Indent at: text box |
| Step 4 | *Observe* | the new position of the Heading 1 text in the Preview |

Now you change the indentation for the level three number and heading text to ¾ inch.

Step 5	*Click*	3 in the Level list
Step 6	*Key*	.75 in the Aligned at: text box to change the number indentation
Step 7	*Key*	.75 in the Indent at: text box to change the heading text indentation
Step 8	*Click*	OK
Step 9	*Scroll*	to view the new level one and level three heading positions
Step 10	*Save*	the document

Marisa wants you to add a title to the outline. The best way to add a title to an outline created with heading styles in Outline view is to switch to Normal view, create a blank line at the top of the document, and then key and format the text. If you create a title in Outline view, you may not be able to see the title's formatting changes or its positioning.

To key and center the title "Catering Menu:

Step 1	*Verify*	the document is in Normal view
Step 2	*Move*	the insertion point to the top of the document
Step 3	*Press*	the ENTER key
Step 4	*Move*	the insertion point to the top of the document
Step 5	*Press*	the BACKSPACE key to remove the outline number
Step 6	*Key*	and center the title Catering Food List
Step 7	*Save*	the document and close it

Now Marisa wants you to add paragraph numbering to a report and create the chairperson's presentation as a formal topic outline.

MOUSE **TIP**

You also can insert body text below an outline topic while in Outline view. To do this, move the insertion point to the end of the heading under which you plan to add text, press the ENTER key to add a line, and click the Demote to Body Text button on the Outlining toolbar.

13.c Using Outline Numbered Formats to Create Outlines

Using Outline view is one way to create an outline. Another way is to work directly with the Outline Numbered formats in the Bullets and Numbering dialog box in Normal or Print Layout view. You can use the Outline Numbered formats to add numbering to text paragraphs or lists.

Outlining a Document by Assigning Outline Levels to Paragraphs

Numbered text paragraphs are often used in reports and proposals. While in London, the chairperson is also meeting with the London branch manager to discuss a research report on stores in the London branch. Marisa asks you to add paragraph numbering to the research report. To open the document and add paragraph numbering:

Step 1	*Open*	the *London Research* document located on the Data Disk
Step 2	*Select*	the entire document
Step 3	*Open*	the Outline Numbered tab in the Bullets and Numbering dialog box
Step 4	*Double-click*	the third option in the first row (1, 1.1, 1.1.1)
Step 5	*Deselect*	the text and review the new paragraph numbering

Paragraphs 3. and 4. are subparagraphs of paragraph 2 so you need to modify the paragraph numbering by demoting the paragraphs to the next lower level. You can use the TAB and SHIFT + TAB keys to promote and demote numbered paragraphs just like in an outline. To demote paragraphs 3. and 4.:

Step 1	*Select*	paragraphs 3. and 4.
Step 2	*Press*	the TAB key
Step 3	*Deselect*	the paragraphs and observe the new subparagraph numbering (2.1 and 2.2)
Step 4	*Save*	the document as *London Research Revised* and close it

Creating a Formal Topic Outline

When you need to create a formal topic outline, you can use a modified Outline Numbered format. A formal topic outline has a 2-inch top margin with an uppercase, centered title followed by three blank lines. Each major heading is numbered with Roman numerals followed by a period. The numerals are decimal aligned on the periods (for example, the I. and IV. heading numbers are aligned on the period). You double space before and after each major heading. The subheadings are single spaced and the number for each new subheading level (A., 1.) begins immediately below the text of the previous heading.

To create the chairperson's presentation as a formal topic outline, you apply a modified Outline Numbered format and then key the text in the outline. The chairperson will expand the outline later by providing the appropriate body text and formatting. To create the margins and title of a formal outline:

Step 1	*Create*	a new, blank document
Step 2	*Set*	a 2-inch top margin
Step 3	*Center*	the title "PRESENTATION OUTLINE" on the first line
Step 4	*Press*	the ENTER key four times
Step 5	*View*	the formatting marks
Step 6	*Move*	the insertion point to the left margin

Next you select and customize an Outline Numbered format. To create and customize the formal outline:

Step 1	*Open*	the Outline Numbered tab in the Bullets and Numbering dialog box
Step 2	*Click*	the second outline option (1, a, i) in the first row
Step 3	*Click*	Customize

To conform to the formatting standards for a formal topic outline, you must change the number style to Roman numerals for level one, uppercase alphabetic characters for level two, and Arabic numbers for level three. The character following the number must be changed to a period. The level one number alignment must be changed to Right aligned so that the numbers align on the period at the end of each number. The indentation for levels two and three must be modified to align the number with the text above it. You start by modifying the outline format for level one.

Step 4	*Verify*	1 is selected in the Level list
Step 5	*Click*	the Number style: list arrow
Step 6	*Click*	I, II, III
Step 7	*Click*	in the Number format text box
Step 8	*Replace*	the closing parenthesis with a period
Step 9	*Change*	the Number position to Right
Step 10	*Key*	.25 in the Aligned at: text box
Step 11	*Observe*	the changes to the level one heading in the Preview

You repeat the same series of actions for the level two headings. To modify the level two indentations, numbering style and following character:

Step 1	*Click*	2 in the Level list
Step 2	*Change*	the Number style to A, B, C
Step 3	*Replace*	the closing parenthesis with a period
Step 4	*Change*	the Aligned at: text box to .5 inch
Step 5	*Change*	the Indent at: text box to .85 inch

To modify the level three indentations, numbering style, and following character:

Step 1	*Click*	3 in the Level list
Step 2	*Change*	the Number style to 1, 2, 3
Step 3	*Change*	the closing parenthesis to a period
Step 4	*Change*	the Aligned at: text box to .85 inches
Step 5	*Change*	the Indent at: text box to 1.2 inches
Step 6	*Click*	OK

The indented first number automatically appears. You promote or demote headings by clicking the Increase or Decrease Indent buttons on the Formatting toolbar or by pressing the TAB key or the SHIFT + TAB keys before you key the text.

chapter
thirteen

To key the first heading:

Step 1	*Key*	MARKETING FORECAST
Step 2	*Press*	the SHIFT + ENTER keys to insert a New Line formatting mark (small return arrow) at the end of the MARKETING FORECAST heading and move the insertion point to a new line

Your screen should look similar to Figure 13-8.

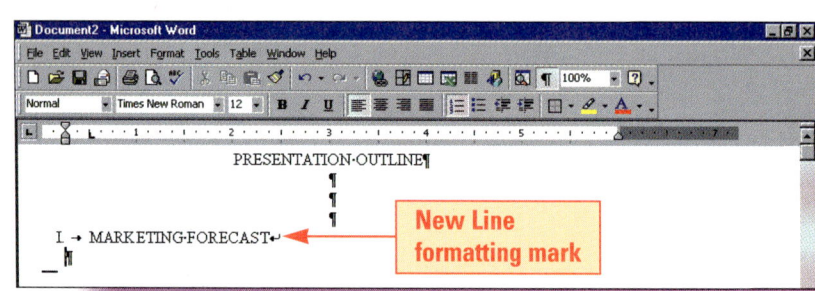

FIGURE 13-8
New Line Formatting Mark

Step 3	*Press*	the ENTER key to move the insertion point to the next line and continue the outline numbers

The next outline heading is automatically numbered at the same level as the previous heading which is level one. However, you now want to key level two headings. You demote the insertion point to the next level.

Step 4	*Click*	the Increase Indent button on the Formatting toolbar to move the insertion point to the next level and insert the A. outline number
Step 5	*Key*	Projected Sales
Step 6	*Press*	the ENTER key
Step 7	*Key*	Sales Stars!
Step 8	*Press*	the ENTER key

Next, key the level three headings below "Sales Stars!"

Step 9	*Press*	the TAB key
Step 10	*Key*	Wilson, Betancourt, and Fontaine, pressing the ENTER key after each heading

Step 11	*Key*	Lu
Step 12	*Press*	the SHIFT + ENTER keys to insert a New Line formatting mark
Step 13	*Press*	the ENTER key

The next heading is level one. To promote the insertion point and key the second level one heading:

Step 1	*Click*	the Decrease Indent button ⊟ twice on the Formatting toolbar
Step 2	*Key*	ADVERTISING CAMPAIGN
Step 3	*Press*	the SHIFT + ENTER keys to insert a New Line formatting mark
Step 4	*Press*	the ENTER key to create the next heading line
Step 5	*Press*	TAB key to demote the insertion point to level two
Step 6	*Key*	Media Budget
Step 7	*Press*	the ENTER key
Step 8	*Press*	the TAB key to demote the insertion point
Step 9	*Key*	TV, Radio, and Web banners, pressing the ENTER key after each heading
Step 10	*Press*	the SHIFT + TAB keys to promote the insertion point
Step 11	*Key*	Print Ads
Step 12	*Press*	the ENTER key
Step 13	*Press*	the TAB key to demote the insertion point
Step 14	*Key*	Newspapers and Magazines pressing the ENTER key after Newspapers
Step 15	*Save*	the document as *Presentation Outline* and close it

The chairperson will base the conference presentation on this outline.

> ### CAUTION TIP
>
> When you customize an Outline Numbered format, it remains customized until you reset the format's options. Unless you want to permanently change the options, you should open the Outline Numbered tab in the Bullets and Numbering dialog box, select the customized format, and reset it when you are finished using the format.

chapter thirteen

Summary

▶ An outline is a way of organizing the ideas and information presented in a long document or presentation.

▶ Outline view automatically creates outlines from text formatted with built-in heading styles or Outline level: formats from the Paragraph dialog box.

▶ You can view different levels of an outline in Outline view.

▶ After you create an outline, you can change it by adding headings at any level or by moving headings to different levels and adding numbering or body text.

▶ You can modify headings by promoting them to a higher level or demoting them to a lower level.

▶ You can apply numbering to outline headings or document paragraphs using the Outline Numbered options in the Bullets and Numbering dialog box.

▶ The New Line formatting mark can be used to create a blank line inside an existing paragraph formatting mark.

Commands Review

Action	Menu Bar	Shortcut Menu	Toolbar	Keyboard
Display your document in Outline view	View, Outline			ALT + V, O ALT + CTRL + O
Display your document in Normal view	View, Normal			ALT + V, N ALT + CTRL + N
Promote a heading		Right-click a heading, click Decrease Indent		ALT + SHIFT + LEFT ARROW TAB
Demote a heading		Right-click a heading, click Increase Indent		ALT + SHIFT + RIGHT ARROW SHIFT + TAB
Expand the view of a heading				ALT + SHIFT + PLUS SIGN
Collapse the view of a heading				ALT + SHIFT + HYPHEN
Move a heading up or down			Drag the selected heading up or down	

Concepts Review

Circle the correct answer.

1. Outlines created in Outline view are not:
[a] a way of viewing a document to organize ideas and information.
[b] a way to arrange text in a document.
[c] easily created using built-in heading styles or Outline level: formats.
[d] automatically numbered.

2. You can add numbers to an outline created with the built-in heading styles by clicking the:
[a] Borders and Shading command on the Insert menu.
[b] Page Numbering command on the Insert menu.
[c] Heading Numbering command on the Format menu.
[d] Bullets and Numbering command on the Format menu.

3. Outline body text is:
[a] text added below an outline heading.
[b] the body of a letter.
[c] a subheading.
[d] an index.

4. Which of the following buttons is not on the Outlining toolbar?
[a] Expand
[b] Collapse
[c] All
[d] Show Level 12

5. The Outline level: formats are located in the:
[a] Font dialog box.
[b] Paragraph dialog box.
[c] Bullets and Numbering dialog box.
[d] Tabs dialog box.

6. To hide the subheadings for a selected major heading, click the:
[a] Expand button.
[b] Demote to Body Text button.
[c] All button.
[d] Show Heading 1 button.

7. You can reposition a major heading and its subheadings at one time by dragging:
[a] the minus sign (–) to the left of the major heading.
[b] the major heading text.
[c] the plus sign (+) to the left of the major heading.
[d] a subheading text.

8. Outlines created in Outline view are composed of:
[a] headings and body text.
[b] paragraph numbers.
[c] body text and numbers.
[d] formatting and fonts.

9. To create a formal topic outline, you can:
[a] modify and apply an Outline Numbered format.
[b] apply the Formal Topic Outline style.
[c] indent each subheading 1 inch.
[d] click the Formal Topic Outline command on the Insert menu.

10. Which numbering scheme is used for numbering paragraphs in reports and proposals?
[a] I, II, III
[b] Heading 1, Heading 2, Heading 3
[c] 1, 1.1, 1.1.1
[d] A, B, C

chapter thirteen

Circle **T** if the statement is true or **F** is the statement is false.

T F 1. An index is a way of organizing the ideas and information that you want to present in a long document or report.

T F 2. Outlines cannot have more than two levels.

T F 3. You use the Promote button to move a major heading and its subheadings to the top of the document.

T F 4. The Demote button moves a heading level to the next lower level.

T F 5. When you press the ENTER key, Word automatically creates a new heading at the same level.

T F 6. You can key an outline using Outline Numbered formats only in Outline view.

T F 7. When you customize an Outline Numbered format, it automatically reverts to its original default settings the next time you open Word.

T F 8. When you key and format an outline document title in Normal view, you can see the formatting and positioning changes you make.

T F 9. You should use the Outline level: formats in the Paragraph dialog box when you do not want to change heading formats.

T F 10. Press the SHIFT + ENTER keys to create a New Line formatting mark.

Skills Review

Exercise 1

1. Open the *Different Documents* document located on the Data Disk.

2. Select the text.

3. Open the Outline Numbered tab in the Bullets and Numbering dialog box and reset any customized formats.

4. Apply the fourth format in the first row to the document.

5. Center the title BUSINESS CORRESPONDENCE two lines above the outline.

6. Save the document as *Different Documents Outline*.

7. Preview, print, and close the document.

Exercise 2

1. Open the *Understanding The Internet* document located on the Data Disk.

2. Insert a centered page number at the bottom of each page including the first page.

3. Select all the text below the document title.

4. Apply paragraph numbering using the 1, 1.1, 1.1.1 Outline Numbered format to the selected paragraphs.

5. Use the TAB key or SHIFT + TAB keys to promote or demote the paragraph headings and following text paragraphs appropriately. The paragraph headings in all uppercase are level one headings; they should be numbered 1, 2, 3, and so forth. The paragraph text following the level one headings should be numbered as level two (1.1, 2.1). The paragraph headings in mixed case bold and Italic are level three headings and should be numbered 1.1.1, 1.1.2 and so forth. The paragraph text following the level three headings is level four (1.1.1.1, 1.1.2.1).

6. Save the document as *Numbered Paragraphs*.

7. Preview, print, and close the document.

Exercise 3

1. Open the *Suppliers And Distributors* document located on the Data Disk.

2. Move the "Suppliers" subheadings so that they appear in alphabetical order.

3. Move the "Distributors" subheadings so that they appear in alphabetical order.

4. Switch to Normal view and add the centered title Suppliers and Distributors at the top of the document.

5. Save the document as *Suppliers And Distributors Revised*.

6. View Level 2 headings in Outline view.

7. Print the document in Outline view showing only level one and two headings.

8. Show all levels of detail.

9. Switch to Normal view.

10. Preview, print, and close the document.

Exercise 4

1. Open the *Top Sales* document located on the Data Disk in Outline view. Promote and demote the headings beginning with UNITED STATES. The headings in all uppercase are level one headings. The bold headings are level two headings. The remaining headings are level three.

2. Apply the 1, 1.1, and 1.1.1 Outline Numbered format.

3. Add the centered title TOP SALES at the top of the document in Normal view.

4. Save the document as *Top Sales Outline*.

5. Preview, print, and close the document.

Exercise 5

1. Open the *Top Sales Outline* document you created in Exercise 4 in Outline view.

2. Move the "AUSTRALIA" major heading and all subheadings above the "UNITED STATES" major heading.

3. Move the "UNITED STATES" major heading and all subheadings below the "GREAT BRITAIN" heading.

4. Save the document as *Top Sales Outline Revised*.

5. Preview, print and close the document.

Exercise 6

1. Use the data in the following document and a modified Outline Numbered format to create a formal topic outline following the rules outlined in this chapter. Title the outline "SALES OPPORTUNITIES."

2. Save the document as *Sales Opportunities*.

3. Preview, print, and close the document.

chapter thirteen

```
        INTRODUCTION
        TYPES OF STORES
                The Mall
                        Suburban

                        Inner city

                The Strip Center
                The Boutique
                        Mom-and-Pop Stores
                        The Eclectic Boutique
                The Gourmet Store
        SHOPPER PERSONALITIES
                The Sale Hunter
                The Gourmet
                The Browser
                The Catalog Shopper
        CONCLUSION
```

Exercise 7

1. Open the *Sales Opportunities* document created in Exercise 6.

2. Move the "SHOPPER PERSONALITIES" major heading and subheadings above the "TYPES OF STORES" heading.

3. Key the following information below the "SHOPPER PERSONALITIES" heading and subheadings. Do not apply the italic formatting:
SHOPPING SEASONS
       Valentine's Day
       Easter
       Mother's Day
       Father's Day
       Fall
       Christmas

4. Save the document as *Sales Opportunities Revised*.

5. Reset the Outline Numbered format you modified back to its defaults.

6. Preview, print, and close the document.

Exercise 8

1. Create a new blank document and key the following text in Outline view. Promote or demote the text to the appropriate heading level as you key it. Do not apply the italic formatting.

Using the Proofing Tools
 Using the Spelling and Grammar Command
 Using the Thesaurus Command
 Using AutoCorrect
  Customizing AutoCorrect
  Setting AutoCorrect Exceptions
 Creating and Applying Frequently Used Text
  Inserting Standard AutoText
  Inserting Custom AutoText
  Editing, Saving, Printing, and Deleting AutoText Entries
 Inserting Dates with AutoComplete

2. Apply the Chapter 1 Heading 1 Outline Numbered format.

3. Save the document as *Proofing Topics*.

4. Preview, print, and close the document.

Case Projects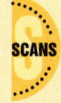

Project 1

Marisa wants to know which keyboard shortcuts she can use to create an outline. Using the online Help tools, identify the keyboard shortcuts used to create an outline in Outline view. Create an Outline Numbered list document itemizing these keyboard shortcut key combinations. Save, preview, and print the document.

Project 2

Because of your experience creating outlines, you are asked to prepare a short presentation to the executive staff of Worldwide Exotic Foods on the differences between creating an outline in Outline view and creating an outline using an Outline Numbered formats. Use the Office Assistant to review the differences between these methods. Create an outline for your presentation using either of the methods. Save, preview, and print the outline. With your instructor's permission, use your outline to discuss and demonstrate the differences between the two methods.

Project 3

Marisa wants you to create an outline from an existing document, but she does not want you to change the formatting. You know you can use the Outline level: formats in the Paragraph dialog box to do this, but you have never used this method. Use the Office Assistant and the dialog box Help tool to review how to use the Outline level: formats. Create an outline using an Outline numbered format itemizing the steps for using the Outline level: formats. Open two documents of your choice and use the Outline level: formats in the Paragraph dialog box to create an outline. Save, preview, and print the document.

Project 4

The chairperson wants to stay at an historic inn and visit several historic sites following the conference in London. Marisa asks you to locate several inns and suggest sites of interest around the London area. Connect to your ISP, load your Web browser, and search the Web for historic inns

chapter thirteen

and sites of interest in the London area. Print at least five Web pages. Create an interoffice memorandum to Marisa that itemizes and describes your research. Use an outline in the memorandum to list the inns and historic sites. Key the outline using an Outline Numbered format. Save, preview, and print the memo.

Project 5

Marisa tells you she would like to be able to see the actual formatting of a document when working in Outline view but finds it time-consuming to switch back and forth between Normal and Outline view as she works. You think she can view a document in both Normal and Outline view at the same time by splitting the screen. Use the Office Assistant to look up how to split the screen into two independent viewing panes. Also look up working in Outline view and viewing document formatting at the same time in Normal or Print Layout view. Create an outline itemizing how to see an outline in Normal or Print Layout view while you create it in Outline view. Save, preview, and print the outline. With your instructor's permission, use your outline as a guide and demonstrate the process to a classmate.

Project 6

The chairperson is extending the trip to London to include side trips to Wales and Scotland. Marisa asks you to find information on accommodations, ground transportation (auto rental, train), and guided tours to Wales and Scotland. Connect to your ISP, load your Web browser, and search for this information on the Web. Print at least five Web pages. Create an outline listing your research results. Save, preview, and print the outline.

Project 7

The current issue of the International Association of Executive Assistants monthly newsletter includes an article on creating outlines in Word. The article mentions using a shortcut menu in the Document Map to expand or collapse level headings in an outline. You want to see how this works and then show Marisa how to use the Document Map with outlines. Use the Office Assistant to review the Document Map feature, if necessary. Open several outlines of your choice and view the Document Map. Use a shortcut menu in the Document Map to show different outline levels and to expand and collapse outline levels. Write an interoffice memorandum to Marisa that includes an outline of the steps needed to view the Document Map and use the shortcut menu to view different levels of detail. Save, preview, and print the memo.

Project 8

The chairperson compliments you on the quality of your work and asks you to create an outline listing each department at Worldwide Exotic Foods, Inc. in which you worked and the Word features you used to create documents for the department. Create a formal topic outline using a modified Outline Numbered format. List each department in which you worked as major headings and the Word features you used to create documents for the department as subheadings. Include at least three levels of detail. Save, preview, and print the outline.

Creating Documents for the Internet or an Intranet

Chapter Overview

Organizations of every kind use Web sites to advertise and sell their products and services to the millions of potential customers who browse the Web each day. In addition, companies have intranets where they post Web pages that only their employees can access. In this chapter, you learn how to save documents as HTML, how to create your own Web pages from a template, and how to test and publish your Web pages to the Internet.

Case profile

The Worldwide Exotic Foods, Inc. Web site development committee wants to create a corporate Web site with a home page and individual branch office pages. You are assigned to assist Nat Wong, the committee chairperson, in creating the Web site using Word 2000. You create a home page for Worldwide Exotic Foods to promote the company's specialty food products and branch offices, and provide support to employees creating individual Web pages.

chapter
14
fourteen

notes The activities in this chapter assume you have read Chapter 4 in the Office unit and are familiar with the Internet and the World Wide Web. It is also assumed that you are using the Internet Explorer 4.0 or later version Web browser.

14.a Saving as a Web Page

CAUTION TIP

When you save a Word document as a Web page, some of the Word formatting may not be visible when you view the Web page in your Web browser. When you reopen the Web page in Word, all the original formatting is available. This is called "roundtrip HTML" or "roundtrip documents." For more information, see online Help.

QUICK TIP

The Web Page Wizard in the Web Pages tab in the New dialog box allows you to create multipage Web sites by entering a title and location, specifying the pages types to include, and applying a design theme.

Many organizations are using the Web to communicate with customers and suppliers. Additionally, many organizations use their internal Web or intranet to communicate with employees by publishing Web pages that contain employee handbooks, policies and procedures, computer help-desk tips, and other useful information. Typically, this kind of information was previously made available to employees in printed form.

You can quickly publish documents to the Web or your company intranet by converting Word documents to Web pages. You do this by saving them as HTML documents. An HTML document is a document formatted as a Web page. All Web pages are based on HyperText Markup Language, or **HTML**, which uses codes, called **tags**, to identify the parts of a Web page—such as the title, headings, body—or graphic images, such as bullets. When a Web browser reads the Web page, it formats the Web page for the screen based on these HTML tags. You can save any existing Word document as an HTML document simply by clicking the Save as Web Page command on the File menu. Word automatically inserts the appropriate HTML tags for you.

Kelly Armstead needs help converting the *Vancouver Warehouse Report* to a Web page. She already created the document in Word, and wants to publish the document to the company intranet. You agree to create the Web page for her. To create a Web page from an existing document:

Step 1	*Open*	the *Vancouver Warehouse Report* document located on the Data Disk
Step 2	*Click*	File
Step 3	*Click*	Save as Web Page

The Save As dialog box that opens on your screen should look similar to Figure 14-1.

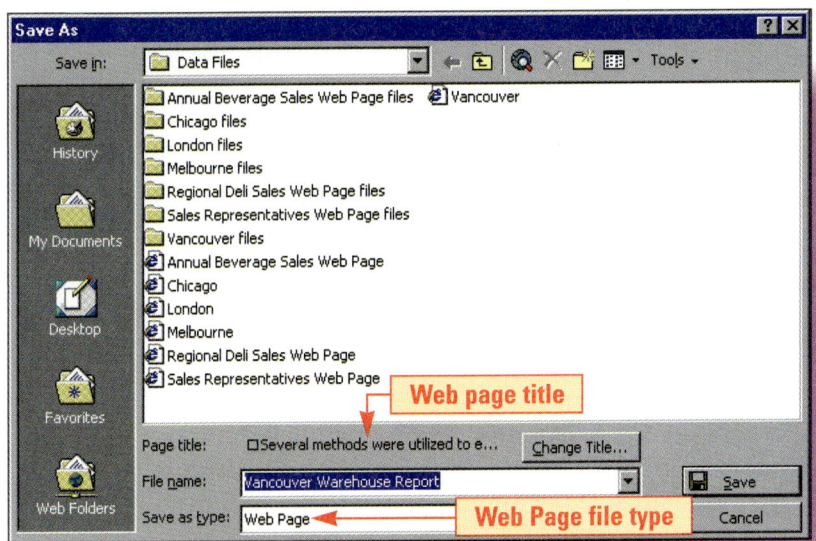

FIGURE 14-1
Save As Dialog Box

CAUTION TIP

As you save an existing Word document as HTML, a warning dialog box opens if the document contains formatting features that are not supported by HTML. You can cancel the save, continue saving the document by accepting any modifications made for the browser, or view online Help.

MOUSE TIP

The HTML format is a Clipboard format so you can drag and drop selected text or graphics from a Web page in a browser to a Word 2000 document.

The Save As dialog box opens with Web Page in the Save as type: text box. In addition to the filename identification, you can create a title for the Web page. The **title** of a Web page is the text that appears in the title bar of a Web browser when the page loads. This information becomes part of the bookmark or URL when you save a bookmark or favorite URL in a Web browser and some search engines use this text as the keywords for indexing a Web page. If you don't supply a document title, Word uses the first few words of unformatted document text as the title. You want the filename to be the title of the document.

Step 4	*Observe*	the Page title: text
Step 5	*Click*	Change Title
Step 6	*Key*	Vancouver Warehouse Report in the Page title: text box
Step 7	*Click*	OK
Step 8	*Observe*	the new Page title: text
Step 9	*Save*	the Web page as *Vancouver Warehouse Report Web Page* in the location specified by your instructor
Step 10	*Click*	Continue to save the document and accept any automatic modifications made for the browser

After the save is complete, Word automatically switches to Web Layout view. You work in Web Layout view when you want to view the background color, text wrapping, or the position of graphics in Web pages or in Word documents that are to be read online. To see how your document looks in a Web browser, click the Web Page Preview command on the File menu. When you preview your document as a Web page,

chapter
fourteen

QUICK TIP

You can save Word documents in HTML format so that anyone with a Web browser can read them. When viewing an HTML document created in Word 2000 in the Internet Explorer browser, you can click the Edit button on the Internet Explorer toolbar to launch Word and edit the document using Word features.

MENU TIP

You can view the HTML tags that structure a Web page in its source file. You open the source by clicking the Source command on the View menu in the Internet Explorer Web browser or a similar command in other browsers. You can also view HTML tags in Web Layout view in Word by clicking the HTML Source command on the View menu.

Word saves a copy of your document as a temporary file and then opens the copy in your default Web browser. To preview the Web page:

Step 1	*Click*	File
Step 2	*Click*	We**b** Page Preview to view the *Vancouver Warehouse Report* Web page in the Web browser
Step 3	*Scroll*	to review the Web page
Step 4	*Close*	the browser and then the document

Kelly can publish the document on the company intranet. Nat Wong has created the branch office Web pages for the Worldwide Exotic Foods Web site and is ready for you to create the home page.

14.b Creating a Web Page

To create a Web page in Word 2000, you can use one of the Web templates on the Web Pages tab in the New dialog box. The templates contain preset formatting and sample text you replace with your own text. You can also create a blank, unformatted Web page with the Web Page icon on the General tab in the New dialog box. Use this icon when you want to create a Web page with your own formatting and text options.

After selecting the appropriate template, you use many familiar word processing tools, such as tables, styles, alignment, and font formatting to help you create attractive and professional-looking Web pages.

The Worldwide Exotic Foods home page contains information about the company's business purpose, and a list of the branch office locations followed by the company's contact information. You begin the home page by creating a new, blank Web page. Then you add a title, apply a design theme, insert text, bullets, and a horizontal divider line. To create a new, blank Web page:

Step 1	*Open*	the General tab in the New dialog box
Step 2	*Double-click*	the Web Page icon

A blank Web page appears in Web Layout view. Nat wants you to use the company name as the title for the home page. You add a Web page title to a blank Web page in the document's properties. To add a title:

Step 1	*Click*	File

Step 2	*Click*	Properties
Step 3	*Click*	the Summary tab, if necessary
Step 4	*Key*	Worldwide Exotic Foods, Inc. in the Title: text box
Step 5	*Click*	OK

The Word title bar shows the blank document temporary name, not the new title. The new title appears in the title bar only when the page is loaded in a Web browser. It is a good idea to preview the Web page in a browser as you create or modify it so you can verify the quality and accuracy of your work before you complete the page. You want to verify that the new title "Worldwide Exotic Foods, Inc." appears in the browser title bar. To preview the Web page:

Step 1	*Click*	File
Step 2	*Click*	Web Page Preview
Step 3	*Observe*	the new title in the title bar of the Web browser
Step 4	*Close*	the Web browser

Now you want to add a design theme to the page. It is faster to apply a design theme to your Web page than to format each element individually. The Theme command on the Format menu allows you to preview and select a Web page **theme** that contains coordinated background, horizontal divider line, bullet, and text colors. You decide to look at the various themes that come with Word. To preview different themes:

Step 1	*Click*	Format
Step 2	*Click*	Theme

The Theme dialog box that opens on your screen should look similar to Figure 14-2.

notes It is assumed that all the themes are installed. See your instructor, if necessary, to install missing themes.

chapter
fourteen

FIGURE 14-2
Theme Dialog Box

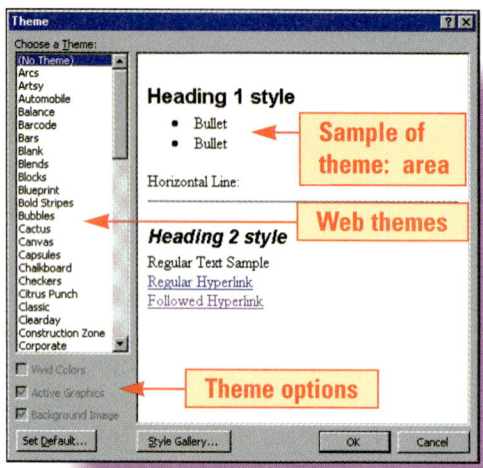

You can select a theme from the Choose a Theme: list box and preview the background, headings, bullet, horizontal divider line, and text formats associated with the theme in the Sample of theme: area. Some of the themes' colors, graphics, and background images can be modified with options in this dialog box. You can set a default theme from the Theme dialog box. When you select a theme, Word sets the Bullets button on the Formatting toolbar with the theme bullet color and style, adds the theme horizontal divider line button to the Borders palette on the Formatting toolbar, and modifies the Normal and heading styles to match the theme.

Step 3	*Click*	Blends in the Choose a Theme: list
Step 4	*Observe*	the sample theme in the Sample of theme Blends: area
Step 5	*Continue*	to review the different themes
Step 6	*Click*	Geared Up Factory in the Choose a Theme: list
Step 7	*Click*	the Vivid Colors, Active Graphics, and Background Image check boxes to insert a check mark, if necessary
Step 8	*Click*	OK

The background image is applied to the page, the Bullets button option is modified, the horizontal divider line style is added to the Borders palette, and the Style Preview contains styles based on the chosen theme. To add the company name as a centered heading at the top of the page:

Step 1	*Click*	the Heading 1 style in the Style Preview
Step 2	*Key*	WORLDWIDE EXOTIC FOODS, INC.

Step 3	*Center*	the text
Step 4	*Press*	the ENTER key

Because tabs and newspaper-style columns are not supported by HTML, tables are used to organize information like the branch office names attractively on Web pages. You key the company's business purpose, called a mission statement, into a 1 × 1 table centered below the heading. Below the mission statement you key the branch office names as a bulleted list inside another 1 × 1 table. To insert the mission statement:

Step 1	*Create*	a 1 × 1 table on the line below the heading
Step 2	*Remove*	the table border
Step 3	*Show*	the gridlines, if necessary
Step 4	*Key*	Worldwide Exotic Foods, Inc. is the world's fastest growing distributor of specialty food items. Our mission is to provide our customers with an extensive and unusual selection of meats, cheeses, pastries, fruits, vegetables, and beverages.
Step 5	*Center*	the table horizontally
Step 6	*Center*	the text inside the table cell
Step 7	*Click*	at the left margin below the table
Step 8	*Click*	File
Step 9	*Click*	Save as Web Page
Step 10	*Save*	the Web page as *Worldwide Home Page* to the location specified by your instructor
Step 11	*Preview*	the Web page to make sure the text looks like what you expected
Step 12	*Close*	the Web browser

Nat wants viewers who load the home page to be able to locate each branch office. You create a bulleted list of the branch office locations below the mission statement. To add a table and the branch office bulleted list:

Step 1	*Press*	the ENTER key to move the insertion point down one line
Step 2	*Create*	a 1 × 1 table and remove the border

chapter
fourteen

Step 3	*Drag*	the right table boundary to the left until the table is approximately two inches wide
Step 4	*Center*	the table horizontally
Step 5	*Move*	the insertion point into the table
Step 6	*Apply*	the Heading 4 style
Step 7	*Key*	Visit Our Branch Offices
Step 8	*Center*	the text in the cell
Step 9	*Press*	the TAB key to create a new row
Step 10	*Apply*	the Normal style

Your screen should look similar to Figure 14-3.

FIGURE 14-3
Tables in a Web Page

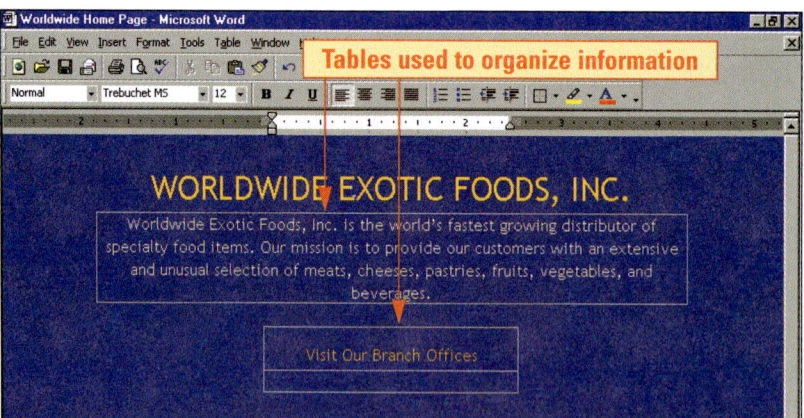

Step 11	*Click*	the Bullets button ▦ on the Formatting toolbar
Step 12	*Key*	Chicago and press the ENTER key
Step 13	*Continue*	by adding London, Melbourne, and Vancouver to the bulleted list
Step 14	*Save*	the Web page
Step 15	*Preview*	the Web page and close the Web browser

Horizontal lines are used frequently in Web pages to break the text into logical segments. You want to insert a horizontal line to separate the branch office names from the end-of-page contact information. In Web Layout view you can use the Click and Type feature to position the insertion point anywhere on the page. To add a centered horizontal divider line below the branch office names:

| Step 1 | *Double-click* | the center position below the bulleted list with the Click and Type pointer shown in Figure 14-4 |

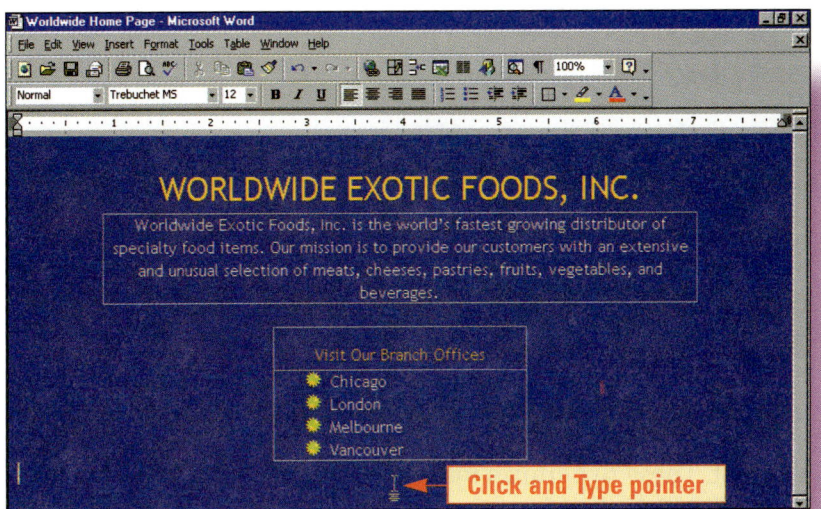

FIGURE 14-4
Click and Type Pointer

Step 2	*Click*	the Borders button list arrow ▣▾ on the Formatting toolbar
Step 3	*Click*	the Horizontal Line button on the Borders palette
Step 4	*Save*	the Web page
Step 5	*Preview*	the Web page and close the Web browser

It is important that viewers of your Web page have a way to contact you about the Web page. Because most viewers are looking for current information, it is also important to include the date the Web page was updated. Finally, to protect the contents of your Web page, you should add a copyright notice. To key the contact, update date, and copyright information below the horizontal divider line:

| Step 1 | *Move* | the insertion point to the left margin below the horizontal divider line |

> **QUICK TIP**
>
> The Click and Type feature is available in Print Layout or Web Layout view. **Click and Type** automatically applies the formatting needed to center, left align, or right align the text when you double-click the center, right side, or left side of a blank page. It also can left indent and apply left or right text wrapping. As you move the Click and Type pointer to a new position, it changes shape to show you which formatting will be applied. For more information on using Click and Type, see online Help.

chapter
fourteen

QUICK TIP

You can insert the © symbol with AutoCorrect by keying (c).

Step 2	*Key*	Worldwide Exotic Foods, Inc. Gage Building, Suite 2100, Riverside Plaza Chicago, IL 60606-2000 Contact us with questions or comments about this Web site. Updated 11/21/99 © 1999, Worldwide Exotic Foods, Inc.
Step 3	*Select*	all the text below the horizontal divider line
Step 4	*Apply*	the Heading 6 style
Step 5	*Center*	the text and then deselect it
Step 6	*Save*	the Web page
Step 7	*Preview*	the Web page and close the Web browser

Because the Web page is longer than one screen, Nat suggests you add a hyperlink at the bottom of the page that viewers can click to move quickly back to the top of the page. Nat asks you to create hyperlinks to each branch office Web page using the branch office bulleted list. These hyperlinks make it convenient for viewers to access each branch office page from the home page.

Creating Hyperlinks

A **hyperlink**, commonly called a **link**, is text or a picture that provides a shortcut to another document or to another location in the same document. When you position the mouse pointer on a hyperlink, it becomes a hand pointer. When you click a hyperlink, the associated document opens.

When viewers browse the Web looking for information, they often decide whether or not to explore a Web site based on the information they can see as a Web page loads. Because of this, you should position all important information and hyperlinks as close to the top of the page as possible. To help viewers navigate easily through a Web site, each page should include **navigational links**, hyperlinks to important areas of the same page and to all other significant pages at the site. A well-designed Web page contains an internal navigational link at the bottom of each page to move viewers quickly back to the top of the page without scrolling. You add an internal navigational link below the contact information at the bottom of the page. Internal links can be made to text formatted with the Word built-in heading styles or to a reference point at the destination position called a **bookmark**. Because the Web page formatting may change later, Nat asks you to use a bookmark. To insert a bookmark at the top of the page:

INTERNET TIP

You can create hyperlinks between two Word documents or between a Word document and a Web page. Additionally, you can create hyperlinks between different Office 2000 applications.

| Step 1 | *Move* | the insertion point to the top of the page |

| Step 2 | *Click* | <u>I</u>nsert |
| Step 3 | *Click* | Boo<u>k</u>mark |

The Bookmark dialog box that opens on your screen should look similar to Figure 14-5.

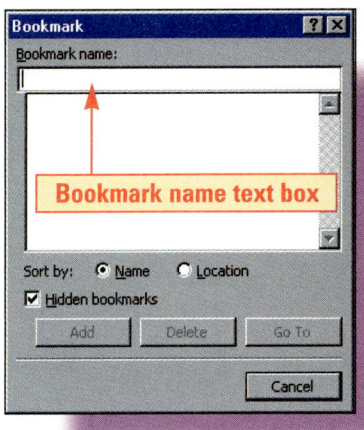

FIGURE 14-5
Bookmark Dialog Box

You create a bookmark by assigning it a name and adding it to a list of available bookmarks. Bookmark names must begin with an alphabetic character. You can use numbers following the first character but you cannot use spaces. Use the underscore to separate words in a bookmark name instead of a space. You should use a descriptive name so that you can easily remember what the bookmark references later.

QUICK TIP

 You can insert graphic objects in a Web page. When you save your document as a Web page, all graphic objects, including pictures, AutoShapes, WordArt, text boxes, and so forth, are saved in GIF, JPEG, or PNG format. For more information on graphic file types for Web pages, see online Help.

| Step 4 | *Key* | Top in the <u>B</u>ookmark name: text box |
| Step 5 | *Click* | <u>A</u>dd |

Next you create a hyperlink between text at the bottom of the page and the bookmark. To insert the hyperlink text:

Step 1	*Move*	the insertion point to the bottom of the document
Step 2	*Press*	the ENTER key
Step 3	*Center*	the insertion point
Step 4	*Key*	Top of Page
Step 5	*Select*	the Top of Page text
Step 6	*Click*	the Insert Hyperlink button [icon] on the Standard toolbar

chapter
fourteen

The Insert Hyperlink dialog box that opens on your screen should look similar to Figure 14-6.

FIGURE 14-6
Insert Hyperlink
Dialog Box

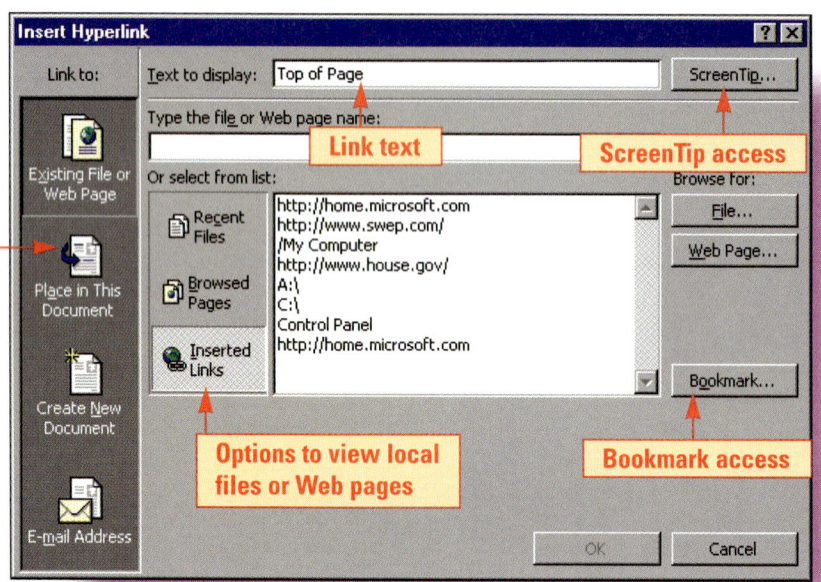

Link to: Places Bar

Hyperlinks can be text, pictures, or drawing objects. You can insert pictures and drawing objects in a Web page with the Picture or Object commands on the Insert menu and you can use the AutoShapes feature to add drawing objects to a Web page.

You can create hyperlinks to existing external files or Web pages, locations in the current document, new external documents, and e-mail addresses in this dialog box. The selected text "Top of Page" appears in the Text to display: text box and appears on the Web page. You can create a custom ScreenTip for the hyperlink that appears whenever a viewer points to a link. You create a hyperlink to the Top bookmark and include a customized hyperlink ScreenTip.

Step 7	*Click*	the Place in This Document icon in the Link to: Places Bar
Step 8	*Observe*	the list of headings and bookmarks
Step 9	*Click*	Top in the Select a place in this document: list box
Step 10	*Click*	ScreenTip to open the Set Hyperlink ScreenTip dialog box
Step 11	*Key*	Return to the Top of the Page in the ScreenTip text: text box
Step 12	*Click*	OK to close the Set Hyperlink ScreenTip dialog box
Step 13	*Click*	OK to close the Insert Hyperlink dialog box

After you create hyperlinks, whether internal or external, you should test them to ensure they work correctly.

To test the Top internal navigational link:

Step 1	*Save*	the Web page
Step 2	*Preview*	the Web page
Step 3	*Position*	the mouse pointer on the Top of Page link at the bottom of the page to see the hand pointer and custom ScreenTip.

Your screen should look similar to Figure 14-7.

FIGURE 14-7
Hand Pointer and Custom ScreenTip

Step 4	*Click*	the Top of Page link
Step 5	*Observe*	that you are viewing the top of the Web page
Step 6	*Close*	the Web browser

Often viewers who visit your Web page will want to contact you. To make it easy for them to provide feedback or request information you can add your e-mail address as a hyperlink on every Web page at your Web site. When clicked, the link opens the viewer's e-mail message composition window and automatically inserts your e-mail address in the To: address line. This type of hyperlink is called a **mailto: link**. To create a mailto: link in the contact information at the bottom of the home page:

Step 1	*Move*	the insertion point immediately before the word "with" in the sentence beginning "Contact us" at the bottom of the Web page
Step 2	*Key*	at staff@wwide.xeon.net
Step 3	*Press*	the SPACEBAR to have Word automatically create the mailto: link
Step 4	*Position*	the mouse pointer on the new link to view the mailto: ScreenTip

chapter
fourteen

Step 5	*Save*	the Web page
Step 6	*Preview*	the Web page and close the Web browser

Now you are ready to create external hyperlinks to the branch office Web pages.

Creating External Hyperlinks

You can create hyperlinks to other pages at your Web site and to pages at other Web sites. As with internal hyperlinks, external hyperlinks can be both pictures and text. You need to create external hyperlinks to each of the branch office pages that Nat created. To create an external hyperlink to the Chicago branch office home page:

Step 1	*Select*	the text Chicago in the bulleted list
Step 2	*Right-click*	the selected text
Step 3	*Click*	Hyperlink to open the Insert Hyperlink dialog box
Step 4	*Click*	the Existing File or Web Page icon in the Link to: Places Bar

You can key the path and filename of the external file to which you are linking, select the path and filename from lists of recently viewed local files or Web pages, or browse through the files stored on a diskette, hard drive, or network server to locate the appropriate file. You locate the Chicago branch office page by browsing.

Step 5	*Click*	File in the Browse for: area to open the Link to File dialog box
Step 6	*Switch*	to the disk drive and folder where the Data Files are stored
Step 7	*Double-click*	*Chicago*
Step 8	*Change*	the hyperlink ScreenTip to Chicago Branch Office
Step 9	*Click*	OK in each dialog box
Step 10	*Continue*	to create external hyperlinks with custom ScreenTips to the London, Melbourne, and Vancouver branch office home pages
Step 11	*Save*	the Web page
Step 12	*Preview*	the Web page and close the Web browser

If you decide you don't want to use a particular theme you can remove it or replace it with another theme. Before you test the links, Nat reviews the Web page and decides that the theme colors are too dark. He suggests you replace it with the theme he used for the branch office pages. To replace the theme:

Step 1	*Open*	the Theme dialog box
Step 2	*Double-click*	Cactus in the Choose a Theme: list box
Step 3	*Observe*	the changes to the background, text, bullets, horizontal line, and hyperlinks
Step 4	*Save*	the Web page
Step 5	*Preview*	the Web page and close the Web browser
Step 6	*Close*	the *Worldwide Home Page* document

After you complete all the Web pages at a Web site, you should review the pages and test all the links.

14.c Testing and Publishing Web Pages

Remember that potential viewers of a Web site can live anywhere in the world. Because of this, it is very important that you test the "look" of your Web pages by previewing them in different browsers, if possible. If you have access to a browser other than the one you already used to preview your pages, you should use it to open the *Worldwide Home Page* and observe any differences between how the page looks in your default browser and the other browser. To open the Web browser and load the *Worldwide Home Page*:

Step 1	*Open*	the Web browser
Step 2	*Click*	File
Step 3	*Click*	Open
Step 4	*Click*	Browse to locate and then open *Worldwide Home Page* Web page
Step 5	*Observe*	how the Web page looks

chapter
fourteen

Before you give the home page file to Nat, you should test all the hyperlinks. This way you can ensure they work and ensure viewers can focus on your message (rather than any problems). To test the hyperlinks and review the Web site:

Step 1	*Click*	the Chicago hyperlink
Step 2	*Test*	all the hyperlinks on the Chicago page and then return to the home page
Step 3	*Continue*	to load and review all the branch office pages from the home page
Step 4	*Close*	the browser when all the pages are reviewed and all the hyperlinks are verified

The final test of your Web pages is to have several people (both inside and outside of your organization) review the pages for their look, clarity, ease of use, interest, and so forth. Weigh their suggestions carefully, and revise your Web pages as necessary. It is a good idea to also carefully proofread the Web page text.

When you are satisfied with the look and content of your Web pages, you can make them available on the Web by publishing them to a Web server. **Publishing** is the process of transferring your Web pages to a Web server. You can save your Web pages directly to a Web server with options in the Save As dialog box or you can publish your Web pages using an FTP (File Transfer Protocol) program to transfer your Web page files over the Internet to a Web server. Once your Web pages are stored on the Web server, other users can access them.

Summary

- ▶ Word 2000 contains HTML editing tools that are shortcuts for entering HTML tags to create a Web page.

- ▶ You can use the Web Page Wizard and Web page templates to create new Web page documents. You can also save an existing Word document as a Web page.

- ▶ You can add a Web page title to the document's properties or in the Save As dialog box.

- ▶ Word provides Web page themes with coordinated background color and graphics, bullets, horizontal lines, and text.

- ▶ A table is an effective way to organize Web page content.

- ▶ Horizontal lines break a Web page into logical segments.

- ▶ You can use bulleted lists to itemize text on a Web page.

- ▶ Text, pictures, and drawing objects can be used to create external hyperlinks to other documents or internal hyperlinks to different locations in the same document.

- ▶ You should include navigational links to the home page, the top of the current page, and all other Web pages to each Web page at your site.

- ▶ You can add a custom ScreenTip to each hyperlink.

- ▶ After you complete all the pages at your Web site you should review them by testing all the links, running the spelling checker and proofreading the contents, and having others review the pages for their look, clarity, and ease of use.

- ▶ When you are satisfied with the look and content of your Web pages, you can make them available on the Web by publishing them to a Web server.

chapter fourteen

Commands Review

Action	Menu Bar	Shortcut Menu	Toolbar	Keyboard
Create a Web page	File, New		⬛ in Web Layout View	ALT + F, N
Switch to Web Layout view	View, Web Layout		⬛	ALT + V, W
Save a Web page	File, Save as Web Page			ALT + F, G
Preview a Web page	File, Web Page Preview			ALT + F, B
Add a title to a Web page	File, Properties			ALT + F, I
Create a bulleted list			⬛	ALT + O, N
Insert a horizontal line			⬛▾	
Apply a design theme	Format, Theme			ALT + O, H
Create a hyperlink	Insert, Hyperlink	Right-click selected link text, click Hyperlink	⬛	ALT + I, I
Create a bookmark	Insert, Bookmark			ALT + I, K

Concepts Review

Circle the correct answer.

1. **To add a title to a Web page, you click the:**
   [a] Options command on the Edit menu.
   [b] Properties command on the Edit menu.
   [c] Internet Options command on the View menu.
   [d] Properties command on the File menu.

2. **To apply a preset design to a Web page click the:**
   [a] Color command on the Format menu.
   [b] Scheme command on the Insert menu.
   [c] Theme command on the Format menu.
   [d] Background command on the View menu.

3. **You organize information on a Web page with:**
   [a] columns.
   [b] bookmarks.
   [c] tables.
   [d] links.

4. **The Web page title appears in the:**
   [a] title bar in Web Layout view.
   [b] Insert Hyperlink dialog box.
   [c] top of a Web page of a Web browser.
   [d] title bar of a Web browser.

5. **When you save a Web page, Word automatically:**
   [a] opens the Insert Hyperlink dialog box.
   [b] creates a subfolder at the same location as the Web page.
   [c] applies a theme.
   [d] browses for files.

6. **Horizontal lines are used in Web pages to:**
   [a] link external pages.
   [b] format text.
   [c] break text into logical segments.
   [d] move quickly to the top of a Web page.

7. **Publishing is the process of:**
   [a] setting a document's properties.
   [b] adding a Web page title.
   [c] creating a bookmark.
   [d] transferring a Web page to a Web server.

8. **In order to encourage viewers to provide feedback on your Web site, you should:**
   [a] have fewer than 10 Web pages.
   [b] link to other Web sites.
   [c] use a consistent color scheme.
   [d] insert a mailto: link on each page at the site.

9. The final test of your Web pages is to:
[a] check the spelling and grammar.
[b] proofread them.
[c] have others review them.
[d] publish them.

10. HTML is an abbreviation for:
[a] Hyperbolic Markup Language.
[b] HyperText Formatting Language.
[c] HyperText Markup Language.
[d] Hypersensitive Formatting Language.

Circle **T** if the statement is true or **F** is the statement is false.

T   F   1. Animated graphics can be viewed only in Web Layout view.

T   F   2. Hyperlinks can be text but not pictures.

T   F   3. Web pages are created with HTML.

T   F   4. You cannot use the Word proofing tools to check the spelling and grammar of your Web pages.

T   F   5. A Web page title is the heading text often centered at the top of the page.

T   F   6. It is not important to preview your Web page in a Web browser as you create it.

T   F   7. After you create and test your Web pages, you can publish them to a Web server so others can access them.

T   F   8. A hyperlink is commonly called a link.

T   F   9. You can view the HTML tags that structure a Web page by viewing the source file.

T   F   10. The Click and Type feature allows you to double-click anywhere on a document in Web Layout or Print Layout view to position the insertion point.

Skills Review

Exercise 1

1. Create a new Web page using the Personal Web Page template.

2. Add your name as the title in the document properties.

3. Replace the main heading sample text with your name in all uppercase characters.

4. Complete the Work Information, Favorite Links, Contact Information, Current Projects, Personal Interests, and Revised Date using your own information.

5. Preview the Web page and make any necessary corrections.

6. Change the theme to a theme of your choice.

7. Save the Web page with your name as the filename.

8. Preview, print, and close the Web page.

chapter fourteen

Exercise 2

1. Create a new Web page using the Frequently Asked Questions template.

2. Complete the Web page by stating and answering the following questions:
How do I create a Web page from a template?
Where can I find the Web page templates?
What is a template?

3. Select and delete the table of contents text and buttons and related text for the questions:
Why doesn't…?
Who is…?
When is…?

4. Insert the current date as the last revised date.

5. Apply the theme of your choice.

6. Save the Web page with the title and filename *Frequently Asked Questions*.

7. Preview, print, and close the Web page.

Exercise 3

1. Open the *Office Information Automation Society* document located on the Data Disk.

2. Apply the Nature theme with vivid colors, animated graphics, and background image.

3. Format the main heading with the Heading 2 style and center it.

4. Add a centered horizontal line below the main heading.

5. Format the paragraph headings with the Heading 3 style.

6. Add bullets to the items below each paragraph heading.

7. Insert a top of page bookmark at the top of the page.

8. Use the AutoShapes feature to draw a blue filled up arrow object centered approximately 1½ lines below the last line of text. Insert a hyperlink from the arrow object to the top of page bookmark. Use the text "Top of the Page" as a customized ScreenTip. (*Hint:* Right-click the selected up arrow drawing object to open the Insert Hyperlink dialog box)

9. Save the Web page as *OIAS Web Page*.

10. Preview, print, and close the Web page.

Exercise 4

1. Open the *Commonly Misused Words* document located on the Data Disk.

2. Apply the Loose Gesture theme with vivid colors, animated graphics, and background image.

3. Center the major heading COMMONLY MISUSED WORDS formatted with the Heading 1 style one line above the first paragraph.

4. Format the first paragraph with the Heading 3 style.

5. Insert a centered horizontal line between the first paragraph and the list of descriptions.

6. Format the list of descriptions with the Heading 4 style.

7. Add bullets to the list of descriptions.

8. Insert a bookmark at the top of the page.

9. Insert a hyperlink to the top of the page bookmark centered below the text.

10. Save the Web page with the title "Commonly Misused Words" and filename *Misused Words Web Page*.

11. Preview, print, and close the Web page.

Exercise 5

1. Create a new Web page with the Web Page icon on the General tab in the New dialog box or the New Web Page button on the Standard toolbar in Web Layout view.

2. Add the title Worldwide Sales Department to the file properties.

3. Apply the Blueprint theme with vivid colors, active graphics, and background image.

4. Center the major heading "SALES INFORMATION" formatted with the Heading 1 style.

5. Insert a centered horizontal line below the major heading.

6. Create a 1 × 1 centered table approximately four inches wide and remove the border.

7. Apply the Heading 2 style.

8. Key and center the text "Sales Report Links" in the table.

9. Create a new row and apply the Heading 4 style.

10. Turn on the Bullets feature and key the following filenames in the second row.
    Sales Representatives Web Page
    Annual Beverage Sales Web Page
    Regional Deli Sales Web Page

11. Browse to create a hyperlink from each bulleted item to the file on the Data Disk. Modify the ScreenTip for each hyperlink to contain the filename.

12. Save the Web page as *Sales Information Web Page*.

13. Print and close the Web page.

14. Open the Web browser, load the *Sales Information Web Page* and test the links.

15. Close the Web browser when finished.

Exercise 6

1. Open the *Winter Schedule* document located on the Data Disk.

2. Select the two date paragraphs and convert the text to a table without a border.

3. Bold the date table contents.

chapter fourteen

4. AutoFit the table to the contents and then center the table horizontally. (*Hint:* Select all the columns and double-click any column boundary.)

5. Apply the Expedition theme with vivid colors and active graphics. Turn off the background image.

6. AutoFit the table to the contents again.

7. Apply the Heading 1 style to the major heading and center it.

8. Apply the Heading 2 style to the "Training Sessions" subheading and center it.

9. Apply the Heading 3 style to each of the paragraph headings.

10. Insert a centered horizontal divider line following the "Training Sessions" subheading, each date table, and the last paragraph on the page.

11. Create a bulleted list from the text following each paragraph heading. (*Hint:* Each sentence in the paragraph should be a new paragraph with a bullet.)

12. Add a top of page bookmark and an AutoShape hyperlink with the modified ScreenTip "Top of Page" below the last horizontal divider line.

13. Save the document as a Web page with the title "Training Schedule" and the filename *Winter Schedule Web Page*.

14. Preview, print, and close the Web page.

Exercise 7

1. Open the *Policy #113* document located on the Data Disk.

2. Apply the theme of your choice and format the document attractively using the theme options.

3. Save the document as a Web page with the title "Policy #113" and filename *Policy #113 Web Page* then preview, print and close it.

4. Open the *Policy #152* document located on the Data Disk.

5. Apply the theme of your choice and format the document attractively using the theme options.

6. Save the document as a Web page with the title "Policy #152" and filename *Policy #152 Web Page* and then preview, print and close it.

7. Create a new, blank Web page and apply the theme of your choice. Use the theme formatting options to format the page as desired.

8. Insert the major heading PERSONNEL POLICIES centered at the top of the page and text hyperlinks to the *Policy #113 Web Page* and *Policy #152 Web Page* files. Modify the ScreenTip for each hyperlink appropriately.

9. Save the new Web page with the title "Personnel Policies" and the filename *Personnel Policies Web Page*.

10. Open the Web browser, load the *Personnel Policies* Web page, and test the links.

11. Close the Web browser when finished.

Exercise 8

1. Open the *Preparing For A Speech* document located on the Data Disk.

2. Save the document as a Web page formatted with a theme of your choice. Use the title "How to Prepare for a Speech" and the filename *Preparing For A Speech Web Page*.

3. Add the appropriate navigational links.

4. Preview, print, and close the Web page.

Case Projects

Project 1

The sales manager, Dick Montez, asks you to create a Web page describing Worldwide Exotic Foods new holiday products. Create a blank Web page and apply the theme of your choice. Use fictitious information about five holiday products for the headings, text, and bulleted lists. Format the page attractively. Save, preview, and print the Web page.

Project 2

Nat Wong thinks it would be helpful for you to learn more about creating a Web page with the HyperText Markup Language (HTML) and suggests you locate online guides for working with HTML. Connect to your ISP, load your Web browser, and search for Web sites that provide information on how to create Web pages using HTML. Print at least four Web pages. Write Nat an interoffice memorandum describing the results of your research. Save, preview, and print the memo.

Project 3

Jody Haversham calls to ask for help formatting and saving an existing document as a Web page. Create an outline detailing the steps Jody should follow to open, apply a theme, format, preview, and save an existing document as a Web page. Save, preview, and print the outline. With your instructor's permission, use the outline to demonstrate the process to a classmate.

Project 4

Mary Boyer, the marketing department representative to the Web site development committee, asks you to research online options for getting the company Web site noticed. Connect to your ISP, load your Web browser, and search for Web sites that provide information on publicizing Web sites. Print at least five Web pages. Write an interoffice memorandum to Mary with a CC: to the Web site development committee describing your research. Include your recommendation on how to use these options to publicize the Worldwide Exotic Foods Web site. Save, preview, and print the memo.

Project 5

Nat wants to know how to use the Web Page Wizard icon in the Web Pages tab of the New dialog box to create multiple Web pages at one time and he asks you review the process. Use the Web Page Wizard icon to launch the wizard. Review each of the wizard steps using the dialog box Help tool. Follow the Wizard instructions to create a sample multiple-page Web site. Write Nat an interoffice memorandum describing how to use the wizard. Save, preview, and print the memo.

chapter fourteen

Project 6

Viktor Winkler, the public affairs officer, wants to add a Web page to the company intranet that provides hyperlinks to important government Web sites. He asks you to create the Web page. Using the template and theme of your choice, create a Web page that contains hyperlinks to ten local, state, and federal Web sites. Save, preview, and print the Web page.

Project 7

The human resources department decides to place the employee newsletter on the company intranet. Jody asks you to create the employee newsletter Web page for December. Use one of the columnar Web page templates and create an employee newsletter Web page using fictitious data. Replace the template theme with a theme of your choice. Using online Help, review the different file formats for graphic objects inserted in a Web page, then insert clip art, WordArt, photographs, and other graphics to enhance the Web page. After saving the Web page, review the associated graphics folder and identify the file type for each graphic—GIF, JPEG, or PNG. Create a document that contains a list of the graphics by file type. Save, preview, and print the Web page and document.

Project 8

Kelly Armstead is having trouble creating Web pages and asks for your help. When she saves existing Word documents as Web pages, some of the formatting is different when she views the Web page in a browser. Use the Office Assistant to search for information on Web pages. Look for an explanation of the formatting differences when Word documents are saved as Web pages and then viewed in the Microsoft Internet Explorer Web browser. Create an outline itemizing the differences. Save, preview, and print the outline.

Microsoft
Excel 2000

Quick Start for Excel

Chapter Overview

In this chapter, you learn about the components of the Excel workbook window. You open an existing workbook, create a new workbook, enter and revise data, and save your work. You also learn about Excel's "workhorses"–formulas and functions.

Case profile

Amy Lee runs a rapidly growing candy business called Sweet Tooth. Today, her confections are sold to retail outlets in many states. Because Sweet Tooth is growing so rapidly, the company has hired you to computerize the company records. In this chapter, you use Excel to track how many items were sold at each location.

LEARNING OBJECTIVES

▶ Explore the Excel components
▶ Locate and open an existing workbook
▶ Navigate a worksheet
▶ Enter text, dates, and numbers
▶ Select cells
▶ Edit cell content
▶ Clear contents and formatting of cells
▶ Use Undo and Redo
▶ Enter formulas and functions
▶ Save workbooks
▶ Close workbooks and exit Excel

chapter one

notes This text assumes that you have little or no knowledge of Excel. It assumes that you have read Office Chapters 1–4 of this book and that you are familiar with Windows 95 or Windows 98 concepts.

1.a Exploring the Excel Components

Spreadsheet applications, such as Excel, help you organize and analyze information, especially information involving numbers. A **spreadsheet** is a computer file specially designed to organize data into cells, which are containers that hold individual pieces of data. Cells are organized into rows and columns to create a **worksheet**. Worksheets, in turn, are collected in a file called a **workbook**.

Before you can begin to work with Excel, you must open the application. When you open the application, a new, blank workbook opens as well. To open Excel and a new, blank workbook:

Step 1	*Click*	the Start button on the taskbar
Step 2	*Point to*	<u>P</u>rograms
Step 3	*Click*	Microsoft Excel

Within a few seconds, Excel starts. Your screen should look similar to Figure 1-1.

Worksheets

Each new workbook contains three worksheets, which are similar to pages in a notebook. You switch between worksheets by clicking the **tabs** near the bottom of the Excel window. Each workbook can hold as many as 255 worksheets, which you can name individually. The default names are Sheet1, Sheet2, and so on. The **current** worksheet is the worksheet that appears to be in front of the other worksheets.

Worksheets are made up of columns and rows. **Columns** run vertically up and down a worksheet. Across the top of each worksheet you see **column headings,** lettered from A to Z, AA to AZ and so on to column IV (256 in total). **Rows** run from left to right across a worksheet. On the left side of each worksheet are **row headings,** numbered from 1 to 65,536 (the maximum number of rows in a worksheet).

chapter
one

FIGURE 1-1
Excel Program Window

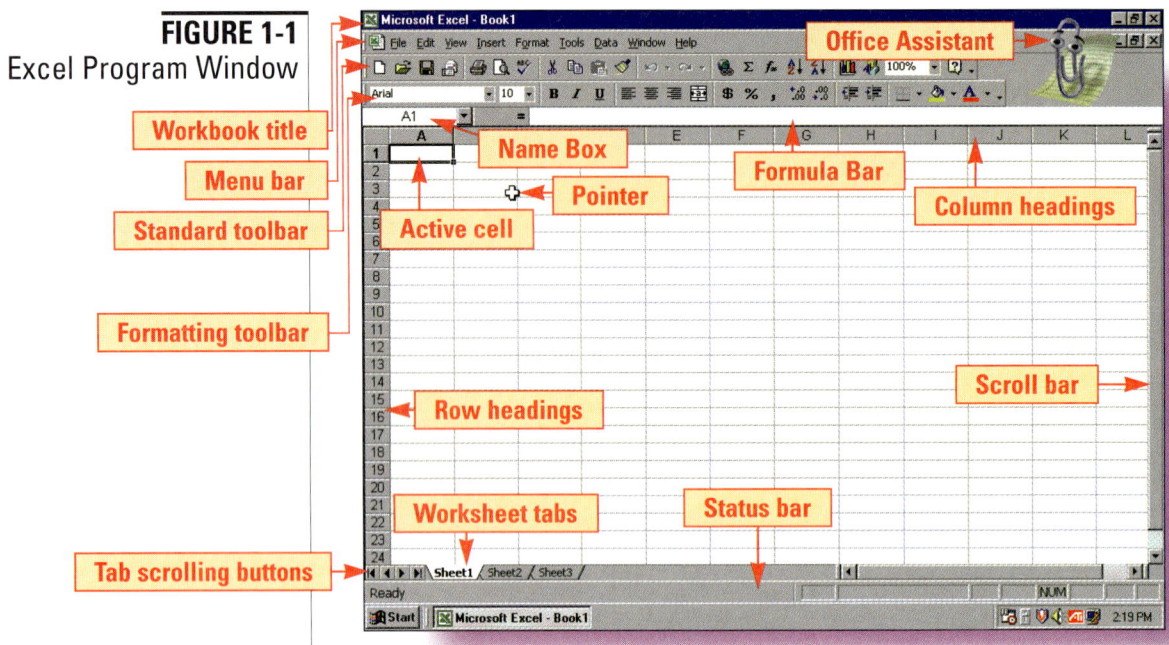

Workbook title
Menu bar
Standard toolbar
Formatting toolbar
Tab scrolling buttons
Name Box
Pointer
Active cell
Row headings
Worksheet tabs
Office Assistant
Formula Bar
Column headings
Scroll bar
Status bar

Cells, the intersection of rows and columns, store values. **Values** are numbers, text, hyperlinks, formulas, and functions. A **cell reference** is the column letter and row number that identifies a cell; for example, cell A1 refers to the cell at the intersection of column A and row 1. Each cell can contain as many as 32,000 characters. When you move your mouse pointer over a worksheet, it changes to a large white cross. This pointer changes shape depending on what you are doing. When you click a cell, it becomes the **active cell**, and a thick border surrounds it. Any values you enter are stored in the active cell.

Top of the Program Window

The **title bar** displays the application name as well as the current document name. The default name for the blank workbook that appears when you start Excel is Book1. On the right side of the title bar are the Minimize, Maximize/Restore, and Close buttons. The **menu bar**, located below the title bar, contains drop-down menu commands that contain groups of additional, related commands. The activities in this book instruct you to select menu bar commands with the mouse; if you prefer, however, you can press the ALT key plus the underlined letter in the menu command to open the menu, then press the underlined letter in the command on the menu. In addition, many menu commands have an associated keyboard shortcut. For example, to open a file, you could click the File menu, then click Open; you could press the ALT + F keys, then press the O key; or you could press the CTRL + O keys. The Commands Review section at the end of each chapter summarizes both the mouse and keyboard techniques to select a menu command.

The **Standard toolbar**, beneath the menu bar, provides easy access to commonly used commands, such as Save, Open, Print, Copy, and Paste, as well as many other useful commands. The **Formatting toolbar**, below the Standard toolbar, provides easy access to commonly used formatting commands, such as Style, Font, Font Size, Alignment, Fill Color, and Font Color. The **Name Box**, below the Formatting toolbar, displays the current cell or cells. Use the **Formula Bar**, to the right of the Name Box, to create and edit values. The Formula Bar becomes active whenever you begin keying data into a cell. When the Formula Bar is active, the Enter, Cancel, and Edit Formula buttons appear.

Bottom of the Program Window

The **tab scrolling buttons** allow you to navigate through the tabs, or worksheets, contained in your workbook. The right- and left-pointing triangles scroll one tab to the right or left, respectively. The right- and left-pointing triangles with the vertical line jump to the first and last tabs in the notebook, respectively. Scrolling the tabs does not change your active worksheet. The **status bar** at the bottom of the Excel window indicates various items of information, such as whether NUM LOCK or CAPS LOCK is active. If you select a range of cells containing numbers, the sum of the selected cells is displayed on the status bar.

Office Assistant

The **Office Assistant**, which you can use to search for online Help topics, appears automatically when you launch Excel unless you hide it or turn it off. In this book, the Office Assistant is hidden unless you need it for a specific activity. To hide the Office Assistant, if necessary:

Step 1	*Right-click*	the Office Assistant
Step 2	*Click*	Hide

Amy, Sweet Tooth's president, would like you to review the workbook she has been using to track candy sales.

1.b Locating and Opening an Existing Workbook

When you want to edit an existing workbook, you must open the workbook from the disk where it is stored. Amy asks you to review the *Sweet Tooth 1998 Sales* workbook she created.

QUICK TIP

Press the CTRL + O keys to display the Open dialog box.

FIGURE 1-2
Open Dialog Box

CAUTION TIP

Your system may be set up to show file extensions, which are three letters at the end of filenames that identify the file type. The Excel file extension is xls. The illustrations in this book do not show file extensions.

MENU TIP

To change the Excel default of creating three worksheets in a new workbook, select Options from the Tools menu. On the General tab, use the spinner control next to Sheets in new workbook to set the number of worksheets.

To open an existing workbook:

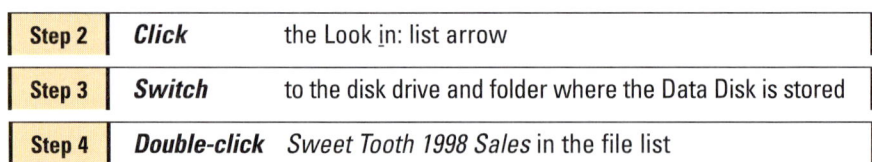

The Open dialog box that appears should look similar to Figure 1-2.

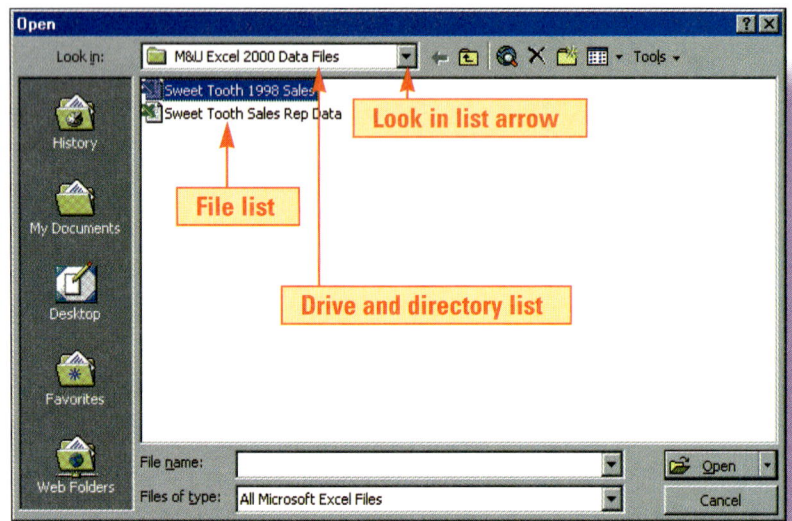

Step 2	*Click*	the Look in: list arrow
Step 3	*Switch*	to the disk drive and folder where the Data Disk is stored
Step 4	*Double-click*	*Sweet Tooth 1998 Sales* in the file list

The *Sweet Tooth 1998 Sales* workbook opens. Amy created this workbook last year to keep track of how many items were sold to each client for the first quarter of 1998.

1.c Navigating a Worksheet

Recall that the active cell is the cell with the thick black border around it. When the pointer is over the cell you want to make active, click the cell. To activate a cell with the mouse:

Step 1	*Point to*	cell B6

Step 2	*Click*	cell B6
Step 3	*Verify*	that cell B6 is active by looking in the Name Box

You can also use the ARROW keys and other keyboard shortcuts to move the active cell. Table 1-1 summarizes some of the keyboard shortcuts for moving around in Excel.

To Move	Press
Up one cell	UP ARROW
Down one cell	DOWN ARROW
Right one cell	TAB or RIGHT ARROW
Left one cell	SHIFT + TAB or LEFT ARROW
To the first active cell of the current row	HOME
To the last active cell of the current row	END and then ENTER
Down one page	PAGE DOWN
Up one page	PAGE UP
To cell A1	CTRL + HOME
To the last cell with data in it in a worksheet	CTRL + END or END and then HOME
To the edge of the last cell containing a value or to the edges of a worksheet	CTRL + ARROW

TABLE 1-1
Using the Keyboard to Navigate a Workbook

MOUSE TIP

You can also scroll through the worksheet by clicking the arrows to scroll one row or column at a time; drag the scroll boxes to scroll several rows or columns.

To navigate a worksheet using the keyboard:

Step 1	*Press*	the CTRL + HOME keys to move to cell A1
Step 2	*Press*	the CTRL + END keys to move to the last cell with data in it in the worksheet
Step 3	*Press*	the HOME key to move to the first cell in the current row
Step 4	*Press*	the CTRL + PAGE DOWN keys to move to Sheet2
Step 5	*Press*	the CTRL + PAGE UP keys to move back to Sheet1

QUICK TIP

With the IntelliMouse pointing device, you can use the scrolling wheel to scroll a worksheet. For more information on using the IntelliMouse pointing device, see online Help.

1.d Entering Text, Dates, and Numbers

You can enter numbers, letters, and symbols into the active cell. When you enter data in a cell, Excel recognizes the type of data you are entering. For example, if you enter your name in a cell, Excel knows that this is a text value and therefore cannot be used in calculations. If

chapter
one

you enter a date in a cell, such as 1/1/99 or January 1, 1999, Excel automatically identifies it as a date value and applies a date number format that closely corresponds to the way you entered the date.

Amy gives you a copy of her records for candy sales in January, February, and March of 1999, as shown in Table 1-2.

TABLE 1-2
Sweet Tooth Sales Data

Location	January	February	March
Widgit, Inc.	45	57	52
Firehouse 451	123	97	101
Clothes Horse	36	23	28

QUICK TIP

You can also start a new workbook by pressing the CTRL + N keys, or by clicking the File menu, and then clicking New.

MENU TIP

You can change the default behavior of the ENTER key by using the Options dialog box. On the Tools menu, click Options. On the Edit tab, locate the Move selection after Enter check box. To turn the behavior off, remove the check mark. To force the active cell in a different direction, select a new direction from the Direction: list box.

You enter this data in the blank worksheet. Before you do this, you need to open a new workbook. To open a new workbook:

Step 1	*Click*	the New button on the Standard toolbar

To enter data in a worksheet:

Step 1	*Verify*	that Sheet1 is the active worksheet
Step 2	*Click*	cell A1, if necessary
Step 3	*Key*	Location

Your screen should look similar to Figure 1-3. As you enter data, the status bar displays the word "Enter." The Formula Bar displays the contents of the active cell, while the cell itself shows the results of any formula entered in the cell. In the case of numbers or text, no calculation takes place, so you see exactly what you enter. Notice that the Cancel and Enter buttons appear next to the Formula Bar. Also note that the mouse pointer changes to an I-beam pointer to indicate that you are entering a value in a cell, and a blinking **insertion point** appears in the cell to indicate where the next character that you key will go.

FIGURE 1-3
Entering Data

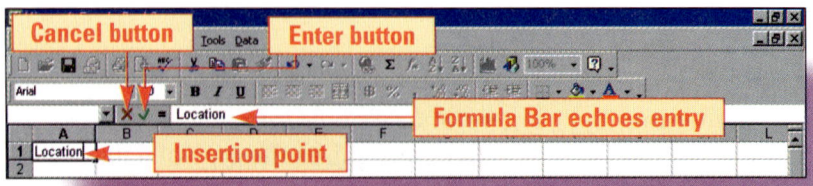

| Step 4 | *Press* | the ENTER key |

When you press the ENTER key, the entry is accepted and the active cell moves down one row by default.

Step 5	*Click*	cell B1 to activate it
Step 6	*Key*	January
Step 7	*Press*	the TAB key
Step 8	*Key*	February
Step 9	*Press*	the TAB key
Step 10	*Continue*	to enter the rest of the data as shown in Table 1-2

When you finish, your worksheet should look similar to Figure 1-4. You cannot see some of the text in column A. You learn how to widen a column in Chapter 2.

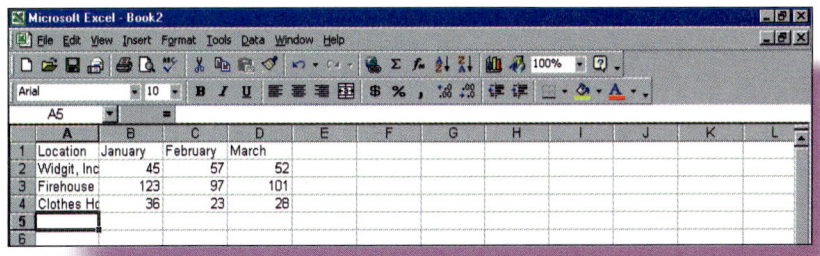

FIGURE 1-4
Sweet Tooth Sales Data

1.e Selecting Cells

Selecting cells is one of the most fundamental skills used when working in Excel. You select cells for editing, moving, copying, and formatting. To select cells using the mouse:

| Step 1 | *Click* | cell A1, *but do not release* the mouse button |
| Step 2 | *Drag* | to cell A4 |

You have selected a range of cells. A **range** is any group of contiguous cells. To refer to a range, you specify the cells in the upper-left and lower-right corners. In this step, you selected the range A1:A4. As you

select the range, the status bar displays the sum of all cells in the selected range containing number values and the Name Box displays a running count of rows and columns in your selected range. In this example, the Name Box shows 4R x 1C, meaning four rows and one column are selected. As soon as you release the mouse button to close your selection, the Name Box displays the group's active cell reference.

| Step 3 | *Release* | the mouse button |

The first selected cell, A1, remains unshaded to indicate that it is the active cell in the group, as shown in Figure 1-5.

Selected range of cells

FIGURE 1-5
Selecting a Range

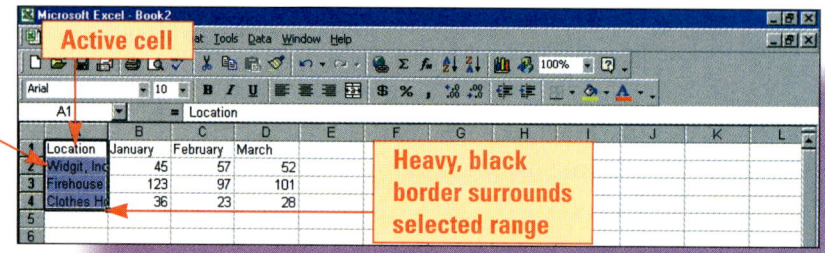

Active cell

Heavy, black border surrounds selected range

You often want to select an entire row or column to apply the same alignment or number format over the entire row or column. To select rows and columns:

| Step 1 | *Click* | the row 3 heading at the left of your worksheet to select row 3 |
| Step 2 | *Click* | the column B heading at the top of your worksheet to select column B |

You can also use keys to select cells. To select cells using keys:

Step 1	*Click*	cell B4 to make it the active cell
Step 2	*Press & Hold*	the SHIFT key
Step 3	*Press*	the RIGHT ARROW key twice to select cells B4 and C4
Step 4	*Press & Hold*	the SHIFT + CTRL keys
Step 5	*Press*	the UP ARROW key

| Step 6 | *Release* | the SHIFT + CTRL keys to select the range B1:C4 |
| Step 7 | *Click* | any cell in the worksheet to deselect the range |

Using the SHIFT key starts a selection that you control using only the ARROW keys. Using the CTRL key in combination with the ARROW keys causes the selection to jump in the direction you specify until it reaches the last cell containing data. If the cells in the direction you specify with an ARROW key are blank, the selection moves to the limits of the worksheet. Now that you can select cells, you're ready to continue modifying your worksheet.

1.f Editing Cell Content

Amy has given you updated data for your spreadsheet. Rather than starting a new workbook, you can edit the data in each cell in your existing workbook. To revise cell B2:

Step 1	*Activate*	cell B2
Step 2	*Key*	47 to replace the previous entry
Step 3	*Press*	the TAB key
Step 4	*Key*	55 in cell C2
Step 5	*Press*	the RIGHT ARROW key
Step 6	*Key*	60 in cell D2
Step 7	*Click*	the Enter button ✔ on the Formula Bar

Editing in the Active Cell

Often, you need to revise only part of an entry. To edit in the active cell:

| Step 1 | *Double-click* | cell B4 to place the blinking insertion point in the cell |
| Step 2 | *Drag* | the I-beam pointer ⌶ over the value in cell B4 to select it |

See Figure 1-6. The value in cell B4 is **selected**, or highlighted. Anything you type will replace the selected text.

chapter
one

FIGURE 1-6
Editing in the Active Cell

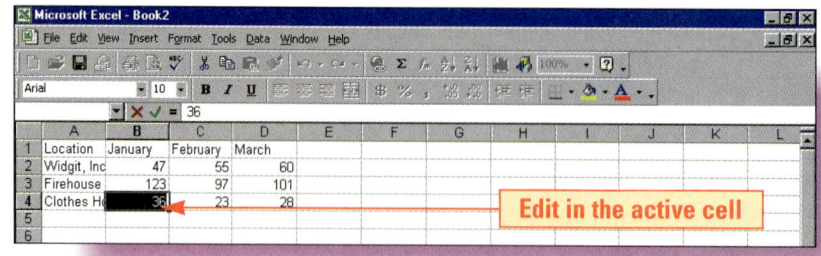

Edit in the active cell

QUICK TIP

Sometimes it's difficult to select text in a cell precisely with the mouse, especially when you're highlighting only a few characters in the middle of a long formula or text entry. The next time that you need to select a few characters, try this: Click to position the insertion point near the start of your selection. Press and hold the SHIFT key while you press the right ARROW key to move across the text. When you've selected the text, release the SHIFT key and continue your editing.

Step 3	*Key*	40
Step 4	*Press*	the ENTER key
Step 5	*Use*	either of the previous methods to change the contents of cell C4 to 37 and the contents of cell D4 to 38

Editing with the Formula Bar

You can edit the contents of the active cell in the Formula Bar by either moving the insertion point where you want to make changes or highlighting the text you want to change and then keying new text. To edit from the Formula Bar:

Step 1	*Activate*	cell B3
Step 2	*Click*	the I-beam pointer to the right of 1 in the Formula Bar to place the insertion point
Step 3	*Press*	the DELETE key to delete one character to the right
Step 4	*Key*	4
Step 5	*Click*	the Enter button ✓ on the Formula Bar
Step 6	*Activate*	cell C3
Step 7	*Click*	to the right of 7 in the Formula Bar
Step 8	*Press*	the BACKSPACE key to delete one character to the left
Step 9	*Key*	5
Step 10	*Press*	the TAB key to move to cell D3
Step 11	*Click*	to the left of the 0 in the Formula Bar
Step 12	*Key*	1
Step 13	*Press*	the DELETE key
Step 14	*Press*	the ENTER key

1.g Clearing Contents and Formatting of Cells

In Excel, you can clear the contents or formatting of a cell, or both, using the Clear Contents, Clear Formats, or Clear All commands available from the Clear command on the Edit menu. The Delete command on the Edit menu deletes a cell's contents and formatting, shifting the surrounding cells to replace the deleted cell. This command is generally used far less often than the Clear Contents command.

To clear values from a cell or cells:

| Step 1 | *Select* | cells A2 through A4 using any of the methods you learned earlier in this chapter |
| Step 2 | *Press* | the DELETE key |

The values contained in cells A2:A4 are deleted. You can also, of course, clear the contents and formatting of only the active cell.

1.h Using Undo and Redo

The **Undo** command reverses your previous action or actions. Although you can undo most commands, such as formatting, moving, or data entry, certain commands, such as printing and file operations, like Save or Save As, cannot be undone. The **Redo** command reinstates the action or actions you previously undid. You can Undo and Redo one action at a time, or you can select a number of actions to Undo and Redo from a list of up to 16 previous actions. To undo the last action, click the Undo button on the Standard toolbar. The Redo button will not be active until you have used Undo. Click the Redo button to undo the last Undo command.

You realize you didn't need to delete the store locations from your worksheet. Rather than rekeying the text, use Undo. To use the Undo and Redo commands:

| Step 1 | *Click* | the Undo button 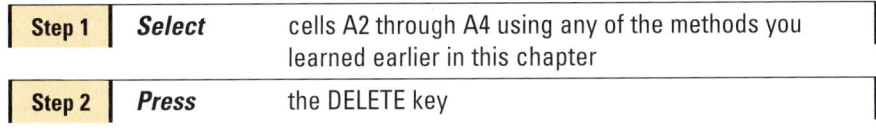 on the Standard toolbar |

The contents of cells A2 through A4 should return to their previous values of Widgit, Inc., Firehouse 451, and Clothes Horse.

chapter one

| Step 2 | *Click* | the Redo button ⟳ on the Standard toolbar to clear the contents of cells A2:A4 again |
| Step 3 | *Click* | the Undo button ↺ on the Standard toolbar again to restore the values to A2:A4 |

Use the Undo list to quickly Undo several commands at once. To use the Undo list:

| Step 1 | *Change* | the value in cell D4 to 50 |
| Step 2 | *Change* | the value in cell C3 to 175 |

You have performed two actions, both data entry. The Undo list allows you to select multiple actions to Undo.

Step 3	*Click*	the Undo button list arrow ↺▾ on the Standard toolbar
Step 4	*Move*	the pointer down the list, highlighting the top two "Typing" actions
Step 5	*Click*	the second "Typing" action

Cell D4 returns to its previous value of 38, and cell C3 returns to its previous value of 95. The Redo list works in the same way.

MENU TIP

Click the Undo command on the Edit menu to reverse your last action. Click the Redo command on the Edit menu to reverse the previous Undo action.

1.i Entering Formulas and Functions

Spreadsheet programs would not be very useful if they didn't work with formulas and functions. A **formula** is like a recipe. When you combine ingredients in a specific way and cook the mixture for the right amount of time, a particular result comes out.

All formulas in Excel begin with the equal sign (=). Some formulas are simple, such as those that add, subtract, multiply, and divide two or more values; for example, =2+2 is a simple formula. Other formulas can be very complex and include a sequence of **functions**, or predefined formulas.

All functions require **operands**, which can be either values or references to cells containing a value, or both. Some functions require **operators** to indicate the type of calculation that will take place. Common mathematical operators include **+** for addition, **–** for subtraction, ***** for multiplication, **/** for division, and **^** for exponentiation.

Following Formula Syntax and Rules of Precedence

Formulas follow a syntax. The **syntax** is the structure, or order, of the elements (operands and operators) in a formula. It signifies that the contents of the cell will evaluate to some result.

Excel evaluates formulas using mathematical rules of precedence to determine what gets calculated first. Excel calculates a formula from left to right, first evaluating any operations between parentheses, then any exponentiation, then multiplication and division, followed by addition and subtraction. Consider the following formulas: =5+2*3 and =(5+2)*3. In the first formula, 2*3 is calculated first and then added to 5, giving a result of 11. In the second example, 5+2 is calculated first and then multiplied by 3, giving a result of 21.

Amy would like to know the total items sold at Widgit, Inc. for the first three months of 1999. To create a formula:

Step 1	*Click*	cell E2
Step 2	*Key*	=47+55+60
Step 3	*Click*	the Enter button ☑ on the Formula Bar

This simple mathematical formula adds 47+55+60, the total sales for Widgit, Inc., resulting in a value of 162, which is displayed in the cell. Notice that the Formula Bar displays the formula, not the calculated result, as shown in Figure 1-7.

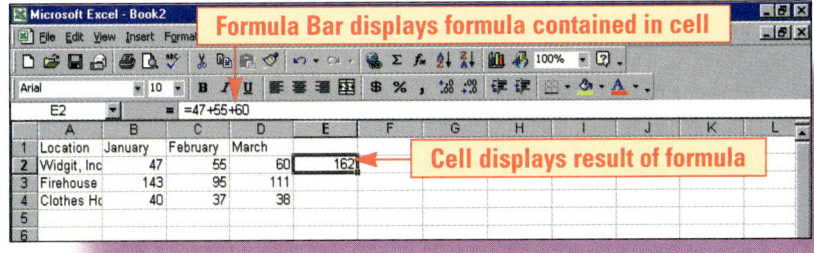

FIGURE 1-7
Formula Displayed in the Formula Bar

Adding Cell References to a Formula

The real power of formulas lies in their ability to use cell references. Using cell references allows you to quickly change values, leaving the formula intact. To replace the numerical values in cell E2 with cell references:

Step 1	*Drag*	to select the entry in the Formula Bar

chapter
one

| Step 2 | *Key* | =b2+c2+d2 in the Formula Bar |
| Step 3 | *Press* | the ENTER key |

The result of adding cells B2, C2, and D2—162—appears in the Formula Bar and in cell E2.

| Step 4 | *Change* | the value in cell B2 to 55 |

When you press the ENTER key, the value in cell E2 automatically recalculates to 170 to reflect the change in the value of B2.

Using the Sum Function and AutoSum

The SUM function is one of the most commonly used functions. It is very useful for adding the values of many cells. The syntax of the SUM function is **SUM(number1**,number2,…). The terms in bold in a function's syntax are required; the terms that are not bold are optional. The terms between the parentheses are the **arguments**, values that must be supplied for the function to perform the calculation correctly. The ellipses (…) indicate you can supply as many optional arguments to the function as you like. Use the SUM function to total the number of pieces of Sweet Tooth's candy that each location sold during January, February, and March. To start keying the SUM function:

| Step 1 | *Activate* | Cell E3 |
| Step 2 | *Key* | =sum(|

Next, you need to select the range of cells to sum. To select a range of cells in a formula:

| Step 1 | *Select* | cells B3:D3 using the mouse |

See Figure 1-8. The range B3:D3 is the number1 argument of the SUM function.

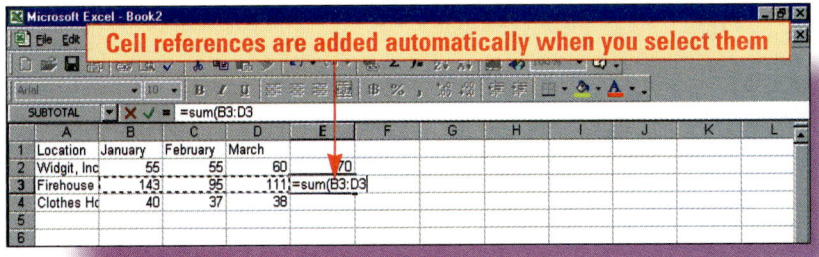

FIGURE 1-8
Using the SUM Function

Now complete the SUM function. To complete the SUM function:

Step 1	*Click*	the Enter button on the Formula Bar

QUICK TIP

Need help in a hurry? Press the F1 key to bring up the Office Assistant.

If you want to sum the values in a second range, separate each argument with a comma. For example, to sum the ranges B3:D3 and B5:D5, the SUM function would be written as =SUM(B3:D3, B5:D5).

When you use the AutoSum button on the Standard toolbar, Excel inserts the SUM function and scans cells above and to the left for values to add together. If it finds any, it adds the reference as an argument. To use the AutoSum button:

Step 1	*Activate*	cell E4

Step 2	*Click*	the AutoSum button  on the Standard toolbar

The formula =SUM(B4:D4) is inserted in cell E4. The range B4:D4 is surrounded by a flashing border.

Step 3	*Press*	the ENTER key

The formula is accepted in cell E4. Next, you use the Min and Max functions to work with your data.

Using the Min and Max Functions

Finding the minimum and maximum values of a set of numbers are commonly performed operations. Excel uses the MIN and MAX functions to calculate these values. One way to analyze Sweet Tooth's sales data is to find these values. To use the MIN and MAX functions:

Step 1	*Key*	MIN in cell A6

chapter
one

Step 2	*Press*	the ENTER key
Step 3	*Key*	MAX in cell A7
Step 4	*Press*	the ENTER key
Step 5	*Activate*	cell B6
Step 6	*Key*	=min(
Step 7	*Select*	cells B2:D4 using the mouse
Step 8	*Press*	the ENTER key

The lowest, or minimum, value in the selected range, 37, appears as the results of the formula in cell B6.

Step 9	*Key*	=max(
Step 10	*Select*	cells B2:D4 using the mouse
Step 11	*Press*	the ENTER key

The highest, or maximum, value in the selected range, 143, appears as the results of the formula in cell B7.

1.j Saving Workbooks

The first rule of computing is: Save Your Work Often! The second rule of computing is: Follow the First Rule of Computing.

There are two distinct saving operations: Save and Save As.

Using the Save As Command

When you use the Save As command, you provide a filename and specify the disk drive and folder location where the workbook should be saved. A filename can have as many as 255 characters, including the disk drive reference and path, and can contain letters, numbers, spaces, and some special characters in any combination. If you use the Save As command on a previously saved workbook, you actually create a new copy of the workbook, and any changes you made appear only in the new copy. To save the current workbook:

| Step 1 | *Click* | File |

Step 2	*Click*	Save As

Because the workbook does not have a filename yet, you can click Save instead of Save As when you save a new workbook the first time.

Step 3	*Click*	the Save in: list arrow
Step 4	*Switch*	to the disk drive and folder where you are storing your Data Files
Step 5	*Drag*	to select the text in the File name: box
Step 6	*Key*	Sweet Tooth 1999 Sales in the File name: text box

Figure 1-9 shows the Save As dialog box.

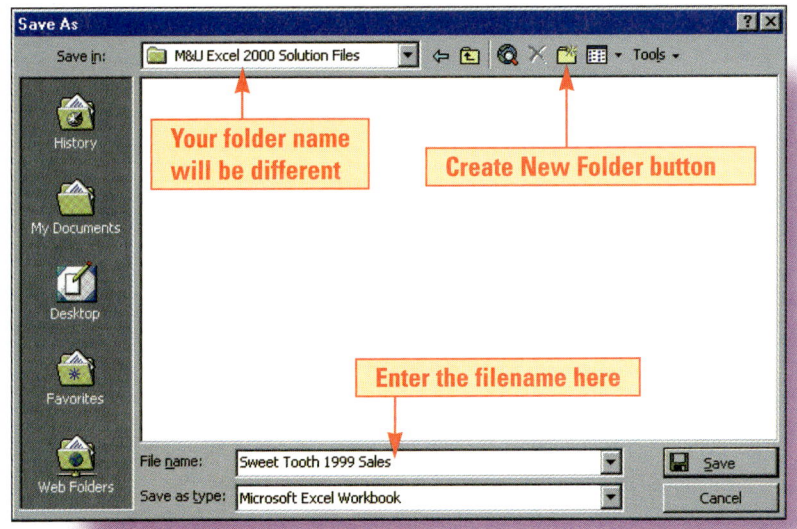

Step 7	*Click*	Save

The workbook is saved to your file folder as *Sweet Tooth 1999 Sales*. Notice that your title bar includes the new filename.

Using the Save Command

When you save a previously saved workbook with the Save command, no dialog box appears. Instead, the changes are saved to

---

CAUTION TIP

Filenames cannot include the following special characters: the forward slash (/), the backward slash (\), the colon (:), the semicolon (;), the pipe symbol (|), the question mark (?), the less than symbol (<), the greater than symbol (>), the asterisk (*), and the quotation mark (").

FIGURE 1-9
Save As Dialog Box

QUICK TIP

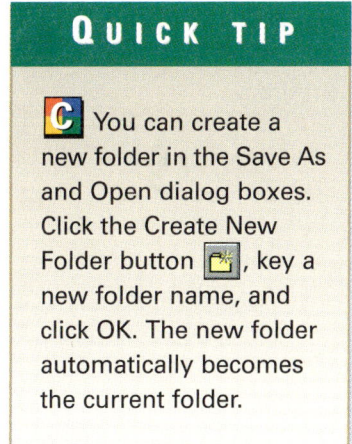 You can create a new folder in the Save As and Open dialog boxes. Click the Create New Folder button , key a new folder name, and click OK. The new folder automatically becomes the current folder.

chapter
one

CAUTION TIP

Computers and computer programs are not perfect. Avoid losing data from computer crashes by saving your work every 10 to 15 minutes.

MOUSE TIP

Click the Close Window button at the top of the worksheet window, just below the Excel title bar, to close the workbook.

Click the Close button on the Excel title bar to quickly exit the Excel program.

QUICK TIP

Press the CTRL + F4 or CTRL + W keys to close a workbook.

Press the ALT + F4 keys to exit the Excel program.

your current workbook and location and you go back to work. To modify your workbook and save the changes:

| Step 1 | *Change* | the value in cell B3 to 98 |
| Step 2 | *Click* | the Save button 💾 on the Standard toolbar |

No dialog box appears because you already named the workbook.

1.k Closing Workbooks and Exiting Excel

You can close individual workbooks without closing the Excel application. If you have modified the workbook you are closing, Excel prompts you to save your work. To close the *Sweet Tooth 1999 Sales* workbook:

| Step 1 | *Click* | File |
| Step 2 | *Click* | Close |

Excel displays the next open workbook, if there is one. If no workbooks are open, you see a blank workspace. The *Sweet Tooth 1998 Sales* workbook that you were using earlier appears.

| Step 3 | *Close* | the *Sweet Tooth 1998 Sales* workbook |
| Step 4 | *Click* | No to reject any changes, if prompted |

When you finish working in Excel, you should exit the program. If any workbooks that you modified remain open, Excel prompts you to save your work before closing the program. If you change your mind about exiting, click Cancel. To exit Excel:

Step 1	*Click*	File
Step 2	*Click*	Exit
Step 3	*Click*	Yes to save any edited workbooks, if necessary

Summary

▶ A worksheet is an electronic spreadsheet. A workbook is a collection of worksheets.

▶ Cells are containers in worksheets for text, numerical values, and formulas that calculate data. Cells are organized into rows and columns. A cell reference identifies a particular cell through a combination of the column letter and the row number.

▶ You can open multiple workbooks in Excel.

▶ Use keyboard shortcuts like HOME, CTRL + HOME, TAB and SHIFT + TAB to navigate around a worksheet. You can also use the mouse to activate a cell or to scroll to other cells.

▶ By default, new workbooks are created with three worksheets.

▶ Enter number and text data by keying the information directly into the cell or in the Formula Bar.

▶ Select cells with the mouse by pressing and holding the left mouse button as you drag across cells. Select cells with the keyboard by pressing and holding the SHIFT key plus the ARROW keys, and other shortcut keys, such as the CTRL, HOME, and END keys.

▶ Modify data by keying data over a cell, double-clicking or pressing the F2 key and then editing directly in the cell, or clicking the cell and then using the Formula Bar to edit cell contents.

▶ Clear cell contents quickly by selecting ranges and pressing the DELETE key. Clear cell formatting by using the Clear command on the Edit menu.

▶ Use the Undo list to quickly undo as many as 16 commands at once, including formatting, data entry, editing, and deletion. The Undo command cannot be used to reverse File and Print operations, such as the Save As command.

▶ Formulas evaluate mathematical operations or predefined functions, returning a new value. Formulas must be preceded by an equal sign (=).

▶ Functions are predefined formulas that perform complex operations. They must receive valid input for all required arguments if they are to perform calculations correctly.

▶ Use the SUM function to sum the values of several cells. Use the AutoSum button to automatically insert the SUM formula.

chapter one

▶ Use the MIN function to find the minimum, or lowest, value in a set of numbers.

▶ Use the MAX function to find the maximum, or highest, value in a set of numbers.

▶ Use the Save command to save a new workbook or to save changes to a previously named workbook.

▶ Use the Save As command when you want to make a copy of an existing workbook.

▶ When you close a new or modified workbook, Excel reminds you to save your work.

▶ When you close the Excel application, Excel reminds you to save any unsaved workbooks.

Commands Review

Action	Menu Bar	Shortcut Menu	Toolbar	Keyboard
Open a workbook	File, Open	Right-click empty Excel workspace, click Open		CTRL + O ALT + F, O
Create a new workbook	File, New	Right-click empty Excel workspace, click New		CTRL + N, ALT + F, N
Save a workbook	File, Save			CTRL + S, ALT + F, S
Save a workbook with a new name, location, or type	File, Save As			ALT + F, A
Edit a cell				F2
Accept a cell entry				ENTER
Cancel a cell entry				ESC
Use AutoSum				ALT + =
Close a workbook	File, Close			CTRL + F4 ALT + F, C CTRL + W
Close multiple workbooks	Press and hold the SHIFT key, then File, Close All			SHIFT + ALT + F, C
Close Excel	File, Exit	Right-click the application icon, click Close		ALT + F4 ALT + 5, X
Undo the previous action	Edit, Undo			CTRL + Z ALT + E, U
Redo an undo action	Edit, Redo			CTRL + Y ALT + E, R

Concepts Review

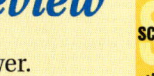

Circle the correct answer.

1. Excel worksheets contain:
[a] 30 rows.
[b] 256 rows.
[c] 20,000 rows.
[d] 65,536 rows.

2. Excel worksheets contain:
[a] 30 columns.
[b] 256 columns.
[c] 20,000 columns.
[d] 65,536 columns.

3. To cancel an entry in a cell that has not yet been accepted, press the:
[a] TAB key.
[b] ENTER key.
[c] ESC key.
[d] DELETE key.

4. The status bar displays:
[a] text and formulas you are entering.
[b] results of the formula you are entering.
[c] important worksheet and system information.
[d] the filename of your workbook.

5. To finish editing a cell:
[a] press the CTRL + ALT + ESC keys.
[b] stop keying and wait for the previous value to return.
[c] press the ENTER key.
[d] press the ESC key.

6. You can Undo or Redo as many as:
[a] 1 operation.
[b] 10 operations.
[c] 16 operations.
[d] unlimited number of operations.

7. All formulas start with:
[a] @.
[b] the keyword "Formula."
[c] =.
[d] $$.

8. To perform calculations correctly, formulas must employ the correct:
[a] functions.
[b] operands.
[c] operators.
[d] syntax.

9. Functions require the use of:
[a] arguments.
[b] documents.
[c] formulas.
[d] values.

10. An operand is:
[a] the same as an operator.
[b] a value or cell reference containing a value.
[c] not required in some formulas.
[d] a calculation performed by Excel.

Circle **T** if the statement is true or **F** if the statement is false.

T   F   1. Excel can open many workbooks at once.

T   F   2. Cells can contain numbers, text, or formulas.

T   F   3. The formula =(5+5)*2 gives the same result as the formula =5+5*2.

T   F   4. The Undo command can undo any type of command in Excel.

T   F   5. Skipping optional arguments in a function is acceptable.

T   F   6. Changing the order of required arguments in a function is acceptable, as long as they are all there.

chapter one

T F 7. Rows run vertically down the worksheet.

T F 8. The key combination of CTRL + HOME closes the Excel application and saves any open workbooks.

T F 9. By default, new workbooks contain five worksheets.

T F 10. Editing cell contents in the Formula Bar works just as well as editing directly in the cell.

Skills Review

Exercise 1

1. Create a new workbook and enter the data below on Sheet1. Enter the label TIME SHEET in cell A1. (*Hint:* Enter the dates with forward slashes and the times with colons. Use 24-hour clock times as shown in the table.)

TIME SHEET		
Date	Start Time	End Time
5/10/99	8:00	17:00
5/11/99	8:05	16:30
5/12/99	8:00	16:55

2. Save the workbook as *Time Sheet* and close it.

Exercise 2

1. Open the *Time Sheet* workbook that you created in Exercise 1.

2. Save the workbook as *Time Sheet Revised.*

3. Change the start time for 5/10/99 to 8:15.

4. Change the end time for 5/12/99 to 17:35.

5. Enter the following values in row 6:

   5/13/99   8:45   17:00

6. Save your changes and close the workbook.

Exercise 3

1. Create a new workbook and enter the data below on Sheet1. Enter the label CHECKBOOK TRANSACTIONS in cell A1.

CHECKBOOK TRANSACTIONS			
Date	Description	Expense	Income
10/12/99	Paycheck		1542.90
10/14/99	Groceries	142.57	
10/20/99	Bonus		300.00
10/21/99	House payment	842.50	

2. Save the workbook as *Checkbook Transactions* and close it.

notes Your worksheet may display several ##### signs, indicating that the value stored in the cell is too wide for proper display. Also, trailing zeros, such as the one in 1,542.**90,** are dropped by default. We discuss how to fix this in the next chapter.

Exercise 4

1. Open the workbook *Checkbook Transactions* that you created in Exercise 3.

2. In cell B7, key Totals.

3. Use AutoSum in cell C7 to add all of the expense items.

4. Use AutoSum in cell D7 to add all of the income items.

5. Enter MAX in cell B9 and MIN in cell B10.

6. Find the maximum and minimum values in columns C and D and place them in cells C9 and C10.

7. Save the modified workbook as *Checkbook Transactions Revised* and close it.

Exercise 5

1. Open the workbook *Checkbook Transactions Revised* that you created in Exercise 4.

2. Change cell A1 to read "Personal Checkbook Transactions."

3. Save the file as *Personal Checkbook Transactions*.

4. Delete the four transactions found in cells A3 through D6.

5. Save and close the workbook.

Exercise 6

1. Open the workbook *Personal Checkbook Transactions* that you created in Exercise 5.

2. Enter two deposits (income) and two expense transactions using fictitious data.

3. Save the workbook as *Personal Checkbook Transactions Revised* and close it.

chapter one

Exercise 7

1. Create a new workbook and enter the data below on Sheet1. Enter the label STATE CAPITALS in cell A1.

STATE CAPITALS	
State	Capital City
Utah	Salt Lake City
Delaware	Dover
California	Sacramento
Arizona	Tempe
New York	Albany
Florida	Tallahassee
Texas	Dallas
Colorado	Denver

2. Save the workbook as *State Capitals* and close it.

Exercise 8

1. Open the *State Capitals* workbook that you created in Exercise 7.

2. Display the Web toolbar, if necessary, by clicking <u>V</u>iew, pointing to <u>T</u>oolbars, then clicking Web.

3. Search the Web for a list of state capitals.

4. Correct any errors you find in the workbook.

5. Save the workbook as *State Capitals Revised*.

6. Close the workbook and exit Excel.

Case Projects

Project 1

You are the office manager of a small business. One of your duties is to keep track of the office supplies inventory. Create a workbook using fictitious data for at least 20 items. Include a column for each of the following: name of item, current amount in stock, and estimated price for each item. Save your workbook as *Office Supplies Inventory*.

Project 2

As the payroll clerk at a college bookstore, you must calculate the hours worked by each student employee during the week. Create a worksheet containing fictitious employee names in column A. In columns B, C, D, E, and F, list the day names Monday through Friday, then list the number of hours that each student works each day. In column G, add up the total hours that each student is available during the week. For each student, the total hours worked should be between 10 and 25 hours per week. Save your workbook as *Employee Work Hours*.

Project 3

You are a teacher who uses Excel to record student scores. Create a workbook containing 15 fictitious student names with five assignment columns and a total column. Record data indicating each student's scores for the five assignments, then use the Total column to show each student's assignment total. Switch to Sheet2 to enter data from another class, and enter 15 more student names, five assignment columns, and a total column. Record new data and add each student's totals as you did before. Save your workbook as *Student Scores*.

Project 4

You are thinking of investing money in the stock market. Use the Internet to find the most current stock price of five companies in which you are interested. Create a new workbook to record the company name, company stock ticker symbol, opening share price, closing share price, and the date. Include a formula to calculate the net loss/gain. Save your workbook as *Stock Prices*.

Project 5

You make purchasing recommendations for computer systems to your boss. Use the Internet to obtain prices for systems offered by at least three different vendors. Create a new workbook to record the vendor name, Web address, system price, processor speed, amount of RAM, hard drive size, and monitor size. When you enter a Web address, Excel automatically formats it with blue text and underline. Save your workbook as *Computer Prices*.

Project 6

You are planning a road trip. Use the Internet to find the driving distance from your city to at least five other cities you would like to visit. (*Hint*: Search for the keywords "driving directions.") Create a new workbook to record the starting city, destination city, and driving distance. Use a formula to calculate the estimated driving time if you travel at 60 miles per hour. Calculate the minimum and maximum estimated driving times. Save your workbook as *Road Trip*.

Project 7

You must teach new employees how to use Excel. Your first lesson will cover how to open workbooks. Using the Office Assistant, find out how to open workbooks on an intranet and the World Wide Web (WWW). Use Word to create a document of at least two paragraphs explaining how to open Excel workbooks on a hard drive or from an intranet or the WWW. Save and print your document as *Open an Excel Workbook*.

Project 8

You are working on a statistics project. Over the next five days, count the number of students attending each of your classes. Create a new workbook. In row 1, enter the dates you used for your survey. In column A, enter the class names. Enter the data you collected each day for each class. Save the workbook as *Attendance Statistics*.

chapter one

Formatting Worksheets

Chapter Overview

In this chapter, you become familiar with Excel's wide selection of formatting tools. Thoughtful application of formatting styles can enhance the appearance of your worksheets not only on-screen, but also in printed documents. In addition, good formatting increases the usefulness of a worksheet. Poorly formatted worksheets may provide correct calculations, but if the results are difficult to find, the worksheet will not live up to its potential. The goal of any well-designed worksheet is to provide information in a clear, easy-to-read fashion.

Learning Objectives

- Merge cells to create a worksheet title
- Work with a series to add labels
- Modify the size of columns and rows
- Change fonts and font styles
- Modify the alignment of cell contents
- Rotate text and change indents
- Apply number formats
- Apply cell borders and shading

Case profile

Sweet Tooth is growing, and Amy Lee has hired several new employees to keep up with the increase in business. You have been given the task of setting up a time sheet workbook. Employees will use the workbook to keep track of how much time they spend servicing each client throughout the month. To make the worksheet easier to use, you add formatting to emphasize important parts of the worksheet.

chapter two

2.a Merging Cells to Create a Worksheet Title

Titles provide a clear indication of what type of information can be found on the worksheet. To start your time sheet workbook:

Step 1	*Start*	Excel
Step 2	*Key*	Sweet Tooth Employee Time Sheet in cell A1
Step 3	*Press*	the ENTER key

Typically, the title should be centered over the area you will use, in this case cells A1:J1. To center the title:

Step 1	*Select*	cells A1:J1
Step 2	*Click*	the Merge and Center button  on the Formatting toolbar to merge cells B1:J1 into cell A1
Step 3	*Save*	your new workbook as *Employee Time Sheet*

Your worksheet should look similar to Figure 2-1.

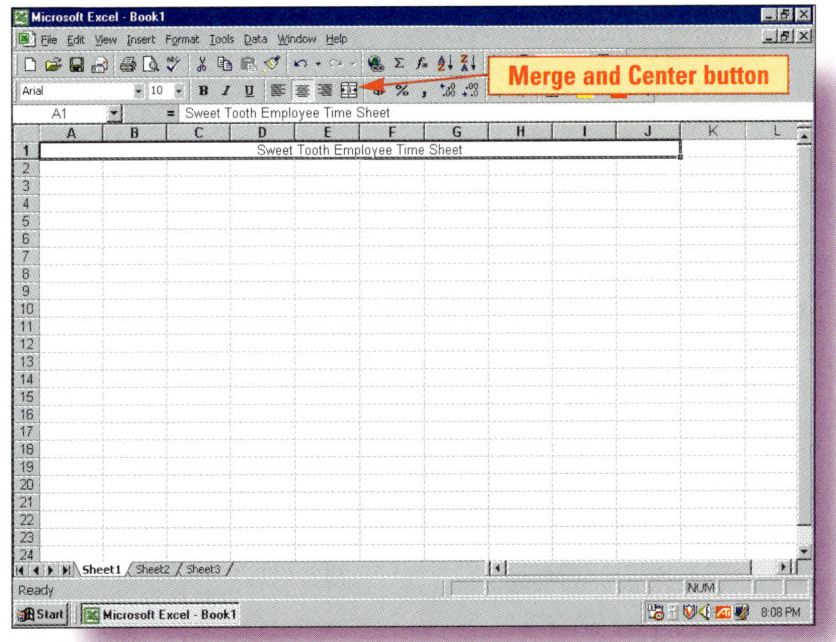

FIGURE 2-1
Using Merge and Center to Create Titles

chapter
two

2.b Working with a Series to Add Labels

Sweet Tooth's employees typically service several companies each day. In the company's time sheet, you need to provide a column for each day of the week. To add a column label:

Step 1	*Activate*	cell B3
Step 2	*Key*	Monday
Step 3	*Click*	the Enter button ✓ on the Formula Bar to keep the active cell in place

Excel uses a feature called **AutoFill** to save time when you must enter a series of data. Numbers, days, months, and other series can be automatically filled in through AutoFill. To fill a series, you drag the fill handle. The **fill handle** is in the lower-right corner of the active cell. To AutoFill the days of the week:

Step 1	*Move*	the pointer over the fill handle, as shown in Figure 2-2, so that it changes to a thin black cross

FIGURE 2-2
Fill Handle and Pointer

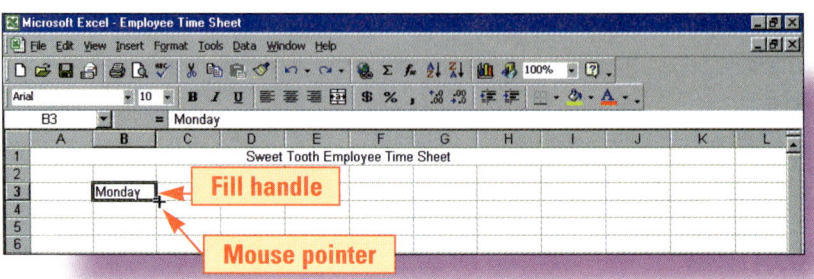

Step 2	*Drag*	the fill handle to cell F3

As you drag the fill handle, a ScreenTip appears, displaying the new values being added to each cell, as shown in Figure 2-3. When you release the mouse button, your new series of days appears in cells B3:F3. You can drag the fill handle down, left, and up as well as to the right.

MENU TIP

Point to Fill on the Edit menu to access the Fill Down, Right, Up, and Left commands.

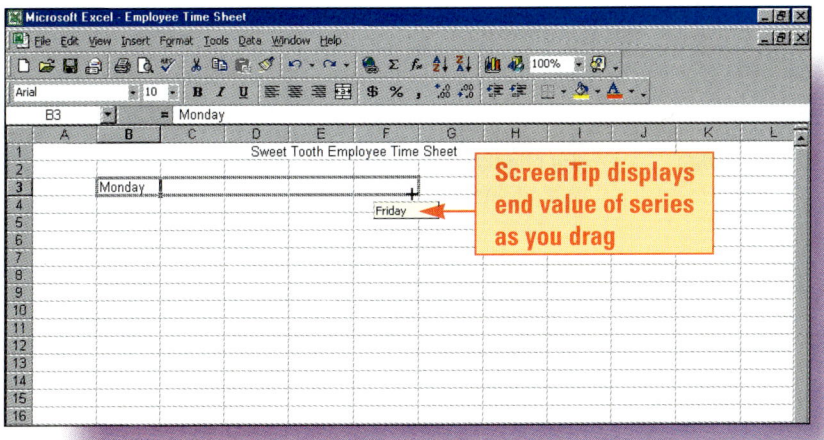

To add the day of the month below the day column heads:

Step 1	*Click*	cell B4
Step 2	*Key*	1
Step 3	*Click*	the Enter button ✅ on the Formula Bar
Step 4	*Right-drag*	the fill handle to cell F4 to open a shortcut menu
Step 5	*Select*	Fill Series from the shortcut menu to fill in the dates from 1 to 5

notes

In this book, the instruction to *enter* a value or formula in a cell means to activate that cell, key the text specified, then accept the entry using the ENTER key, the ARROW keys, the TAB key, or the Enter button on the Formula Bar. Occasionally, you will be instructed to input the data using a specific method. At those times, you will be instructed to key the data, then follow specific instructions to accept the entry.

Step 6	*Enter*	Total in cell G3
Step 7	*Enter*	Client in cell A3

The Total label creates a column in which to sum the time spent servicing each of Sweet Tooth's clients during the week. The Client label creates a column label for the client names you will add. Row

chapter
two

labels identify the contents of information stored in those rows. To add row labels:

Step 1	*Enter*	the clients listed below, beginning in cell A5:
		Widgit, Inc.
		Firehouse 451
		Clothes Horse
		Mendoza Engineering Supply
		ZAZ Printing
		Jungle Planet
		Aquanatics
		Ribbon Steel Co.
Step 2	*Enter*	Total in cell A13
Step 3	*Click*	the Save button on the Standard toolbar

2.c Modifying the Size of Columns and Rows

By default, Excel columns are wide enough to display only eight characters. The number of characters in these cells exceeds this width. Because the cells next to the row labels are blank, Excel allows the full contents to spill over. When a column is too narrow to display the text value contained in a cell, Excel displays as many characters as the column width allows, hiding the rest of the characters. If a column is too narrow to display numerical values, it displays a series of # signs. One way to display the full contents of a cell is to change the column width. If a cell is selected, the **AutoFit** command automatically resizes the entire column to the width of that cell's contents. If a range is selected, AutoFit resizes the column to accommodate the cell with the longest value. To resize a column using AutoFit:

| Step 1 | *Move* | the mouse pointer to the column divider between columns A and B until the pointer changes to the horizontal resize pointer ✛ |
| Step 2 | *Double-click* | the column divider |

The column widens to accommodate the longest entry in the column. See Figure 2-4. The AutoFit command works the same way on rows; double-click the row divider line below the row whose height you want to change.

MENU TIP

You can use AutoFit from the Format menu. Point to Column, then click AutoFit Selection.

MENU TIP

To access the Column Width dialog box, use the Format menu. Point to Column, then click Width. To open the Row Height dialog box, point to Row on the Format menu, then click Height.

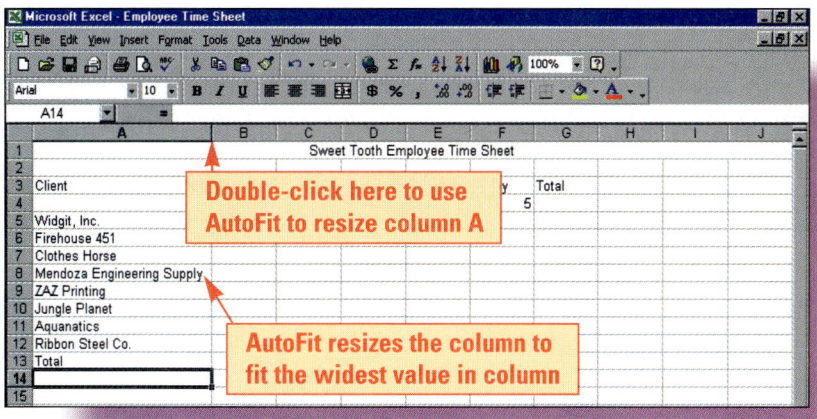

FIGURE 2-4
Using AutoFit to Resize
a Column

QUICK TIP

Right-click a row
heading and select <u>R</u>ow
Height to adjust the row
height precisely with the
Row Height dialog box.

Another way to resize a column is to specify an exact width. Column width is measured in terms of how many characters can appear in the column before they spill into another column. A column 10 units wide, for example, can display 10 characters before spilling over. Excel's default width is 8.43 units. To resize columns and rows:

Step 1	*Drag*	the column headings B:G to select those columns
Step 2	*Right-click*	the selected cells
Step 3	*Click*	<u>C</u>olumn Width
Step 4	*Key*	12
Step 5	*Click*	OK to resize columns B through G
Step 6	*Deselect*	the columns by clicking cell A1
Step 7	*Drag*	the row divider between rows 3 and 4 down until the ScreenTip indicates 24.00

MOUSE TIP

Resize columns by
dragging the divider
line between headings,
and resize rows by
dragging the divider
line between rows.

2.d Changing Fonts and Font Styles

A **font** is a set of printed characters with similar characteristics. Fonts are a combination of three factors: typeface, style, and point size. **Typeface** is the design and appearance of the font in printed form. The **style** refers to whether the font is displayed with *italic,* **bold,** <u>underlined</u>, or normal print. The **point size** refers to the print height. You can also add **effects**, such as strikethrough, superscripts, and subscripts. Some common typefaces include the following:

Arial   Times New Roman

Courier New   Book Antiqua

MENU TIP

On the F<u>o</u>rmat menu,
click C<u>e</u>lls, then click
the Font tab to choose
font settings.

chapter
two

Changing Font and Font Size

To maintain consistency in its documents, Sweet Tooth has selected the Impact font style, set to point size 20, for worksheet titles. To change the font and font size:

Step 1	*Click*	the Font list arrow `Arial ▾` on the Formatting toolbar to display the available fonts
Step 2	*Click*	Impact (or another font if Impact is not available)
Step 3	*Click*	the Font Size list arrow `10 ▾` on the Formatting toolbar
Step 4	*Click*	20
Step 5	*Change*	the font in cells A5:A12 to Garamond 12 point
Step 6	*Click*	cell A8
Step 7	*Press*	the CTRL + 1 keys to open the Format Cells dialog box
Step 8	*Click*	the Alignment tab
Step 9	*Click*	the Shrink to fit check box to select it
Step 10	*Click*	OK

Changing Font Color

Using different font colors can enhance the visual impact of your worksheets. Sweet Tooth uses red text on its corporate logo, in its letterhead, and in worksheet titles. To change the font color:

Step 1	*Click*	cell A1
Step 2	*Click*	the Font Color list arrow `A ▾` on the Formatting toolbar
Step 3	*Move*	the pointer to the Red square (look at the ScreenTip)
Step 4	*Click*	the Red square to change the title color
Step 5	*Select*	cells B3:G3
Step 6	*Select*	the Blue square from the Font Color list
Step 7	*Change*	cells A5:A12 to Dark Red

Changing Font Style

Changing the font style to use bold, italics, or underline is another way to draw attention to or emphasize certain cells. To change the font style:

Step 1	*Select*	cells B4:F4
Step 2	*Click*	the Bold button **B** on the Formatting toolbar
Step 3	*Activate*	cell G3
Step 4	*Press & Hold*	the CTRL key while clicking cell A13
Step 5	*Click*	the Italic button *I* on the Formatting toolbar

QUICK TIP

Press CTRL + B to bold selected cells. Press CTRL + I to italicize selected cells. Press CTRL + U to underline selected cells.

2.e Modifying the Alignment of Cell Contents

Values can be aligned horizontally and vertically within a cell. By default, text values are left-aligned, and numbers, dates, and times are right-aligned. Typically, column labels are centered in the column, while row labels are left-aligned. To change the alignment of cells:

Step 1	*Select*	cells B3:G4
Step 2	*Click*	the Center button ☰ on the Formatting toolbar

QUICK TIP

When you need to make several formatting adjustments, use the Format Cells dialog box instead of the Formatting toolbar.

The day and date labels are centered horizontally in their respective columns. Now center the labels in row 3 vertically. To center the labels vertically:

Step 1	*Select*	cells B3:G3
Step 2	*Press*	the CTRL + 1 keys to open the Format Cells dialog box
Step 3	*Click*	the Alignment tab
Step 4	*Click*	the Vertical: list arrow
Step 5	*Select*	Center
Step 6	*Click*	OK

MENU TIP

Click the Format menu and then click Cells to open the Format Cells dialog box.

chapter
two

The column labels are now centered vertically and horizontally in the cells, as shown in Figure 2-5.

FIGURE 2-5
Aligning Data Vertically
and Horizontally

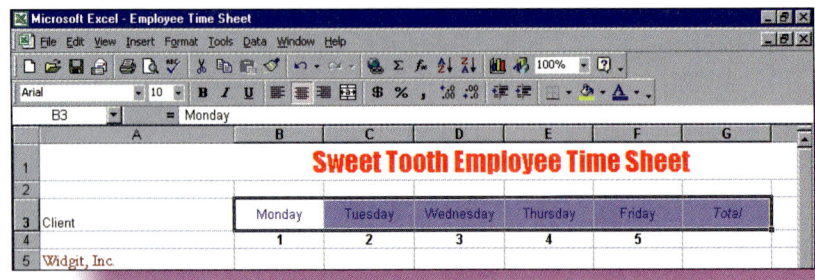

2.f Rotating Text and Changing Indents

In Sweet Tooth's worksheet, the data for cells B5:F12 will be entered in decimal format to denote hours and minutes worked; for example, 4 hours and 15 minutes would be recorded as 4.25 hours. The columns do not need to be 12 characters wide to accommodate this data. Instead, you can decrease the width of those columns by rotating the column labels. To rotate text:

Step 1	*Verify*	that cells B3:G3 are selected
Step 2	*Press*	the CTRL + 1 keys to open the Format Cells dialog box
Step 3	*Double-click*	in the Degrees spinner control box
Step 4	*Key*	60
Step 5	*Click*	OK
Step 6	*Double-click*	the row divider between rows 3 and 4 to AutoFit the row height
Step 7	*Select*	columns B:G
Step 8	*Right-click*	the selected cells
Step 9	*Click*	Column Width
Step 10	*Key*	7
Step 11	*Click*	OK
Step 12	*Activate*	cell A1

Your worksheet should look similar to Figure 2-6.

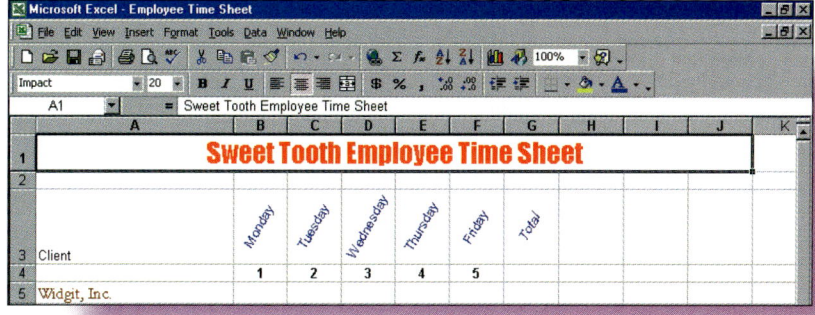

FIGURE 2-6
Rotated Text

> **QUICK TIP**
>
> To increase the Indent more, click the Increase Indent button multiple times. To decrease the Indent, click the Decrease Indent button on the Formatting toolbar.

To emphasize the break between the client names and the Total row heading, you decide to indent the Total heading in row 13. To indent text:

Step 1	*Activate*	cell A13
Step 2	*Click*	the Increase Indent button on the Formatting toolbar

2.g Applying Number Formats

As you enter numeric data, Excel attempts to identify the type of numeric format best suited to the input and automatically applies the appropriate setting. For example, if you enter **1/1/99** in a cell, Excel guesses that you are inputting a date and applies the default date number format to that cell, changing it to 1/1/1999. If you want to display the date as January 1, 1999 you can simply change the format with the Format Cells dialog box, and Excel automatically converts your entry to the desired format.

Sweet Tooth rounds each employee's time worked to the nearest five-minute increment. You need to create a list of decimal equivalencies for five-minute increments. To enter the list of five minute increments:

Step 1	*Key*	Decimal in cell I3
Step 2	*Press*	the TAB key

The text you keyed in cell I3 inherits the same formatting characteristics as the text in the rest of the list, B3:G3. If you had started in cell J3, the Extend List Format command would not have

chapter
two

extended the formatting, because two blank columns (H and I) would have separated your entry from the rest of the list.

MENU TIP

You can turn on or off the Extend List Formats feature. On the Tools menu, select Options. On the Edit tab, select or deselect the check box next to Extend list formats and formulas, according to your preferences.

Step 3	*Enter*	Time (Minutes) in cell J3
Step 4	*Enter*	5 in cell J4
Step 5	*Enter*	10 in cell J5
Step 6	*Enter*	15 in cell J6
Step 7	*Select*	cells J4:J6
Step 8	*Italicize*	the selection
Step 9	*Drag*	the fill handle to cell J14

Now you add a formula in column I to calculate the decimal equivalent. To add the formula:

Step 1	*Activate*	cell I4
Step 2	*Key*	=j4/60 to divide the time in minutes in cell J4 by the total number of minutes in an hour
Step 3	*Click*	the Enter button ✓ on the Formula Bar
Step 4	*Drag*	the fill handle to cell I14

The formula is copied, but the resulting values are a mess. Some cells display only one digit after the decimal; others display as many as six digits. See Figure 2-7. At most, your users will need two significant digits.

FIGURE 2-7
Decimal Equivalent of
Five Minutes

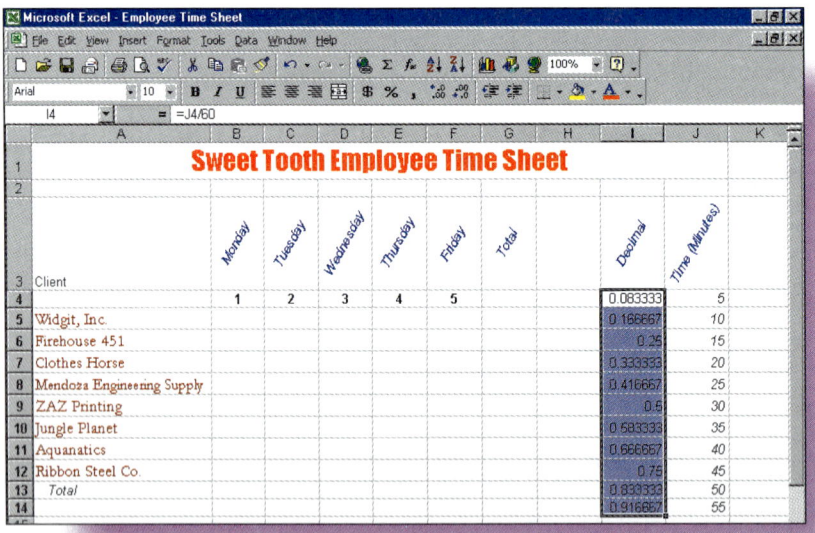

To adjust the decimal place:

Step 1	*Click*	the Decrease Decimal button [.00/.0] on the Formatting toolbar
Step 2	*Continue*	to decrease the decimal until only two digits appear after the decimal

The main data entry area in cells B5:G13 should be formatted this way as well. This time, use the Format Cells dialog box to set the format.

Step 3	*Select*	cells B5:G13
Step 4	*Open*	the Format Cells dialog box
Step 5	*Click*	the Number tab
Step 6	*Click*	Number from the Category: list
Step 7	*Verify*	that Decimal places: is set to 2 (see Figure 2-8)

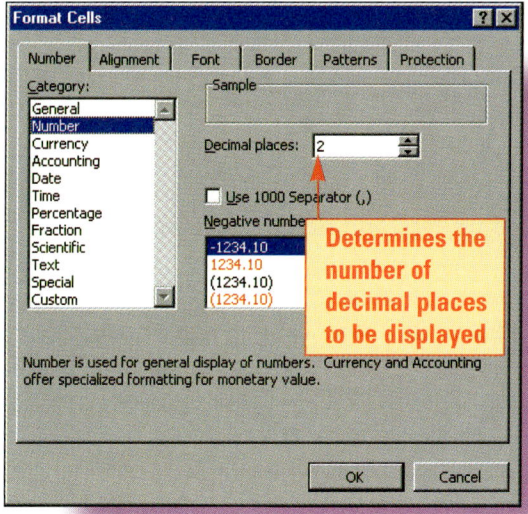

FIGURE 2-8
Number Tab of the Format Cells Dialog Box

Step 8	*Click*	OK

Understanding how and when to apply number formats is very important. Using Excel's extensive set of number formats, you can display numerical values as times, dates, currency, percentages, fractions, and more. When you apply a numerical format to a value,

the manner in which the value is displayed may vary dramatically, but the actual value held in the cell remains the same. Table 2-1 illustrates how a common numerical value of 1054.253 would be displayed with different number formats applied.

TABLE 2-1
Comparing Number
Formats

Category	Description	Default Display (Value = 1054.253)
General	No specific number format	1054.253
Number	Default of two decimal places; can also display commas for thousand separators	1054.25
Currency	Default of two decimal places, comma separators, and $, the U.S. dollar sign	$1,054.25
Accounting	Aligns currency symbol, two decimal places, and comma separators	$ 1,054.25
Date	Displays serial equivalent of date	11/19/1902
Time	Displays serial equivalent of time	11/19/1902 6:00 AM
Percentage	Multiplies value by 100 and displays result with % sign	105425%
Fraction	Displays decimal portion of value as fraction	1054 1/4
Scientific	Displays number in scientific notation	1.05E+03

It is important to understand how Excel deals with time and date values. In Excel, all time and date values are calculated using serial values. **Serial values** are real numbers that are converted to display a date or time. Starting with 1, which Excel displays as January 1, 1900, each day is represented by a whole-number value. Times are calculated as a decimal portion of a day. For example, Excel interprets the value 1.0 as January 1, 1900 12:00 AM. A value of .25 corresponds to 6:00 AM (25% of the day), .5 corresponds to 12:00 PM (50% of the day), and so on.

2.h Applying Cell Borders and Shading

Borders and shading are two of the more dramatic visual effects available to enhance your worksheets. Borders can be used to separate row and column labels from data. Shading can be used to emphasize important cells.

QUICK TIP

When you activate a cell containing a date or time format, the Formula Bar displays the date or time value—not the serial, or number, value. To view the serial value of a date, you must change the cell's format to another number format.

Adding Borders

Although you see gridlines on your screen, the default for printed worksheets is for no gridlines to appear. If you want only some of the gridlines to appear, you can apply a border. When applying borders to cells, Excel treats the entire selection as though it were a single cell. With one cell selected, you can apply borders to all of the cell's edges at once or to a single edge. For example, you can apply a border along the bottom edge of a cell to denote the sum line. When you select a group of cells and apply a border, however, the border is applied to the group as though the entire group was one cell. If you apply a left border to the selection, for example, only the cells on the left edge of the selection receive the border. To add a border:

Step 1	*Select*	cells B5:F12
Step 2	*Click*	the Borders list arrow ▦ on the Formatting toolbar
Step 3	*Click*	the All Borders button ▦ on the Borders drop-down list

The All Borders command applies a border to all edges surrounding and within the selection. See Figure 2-9.

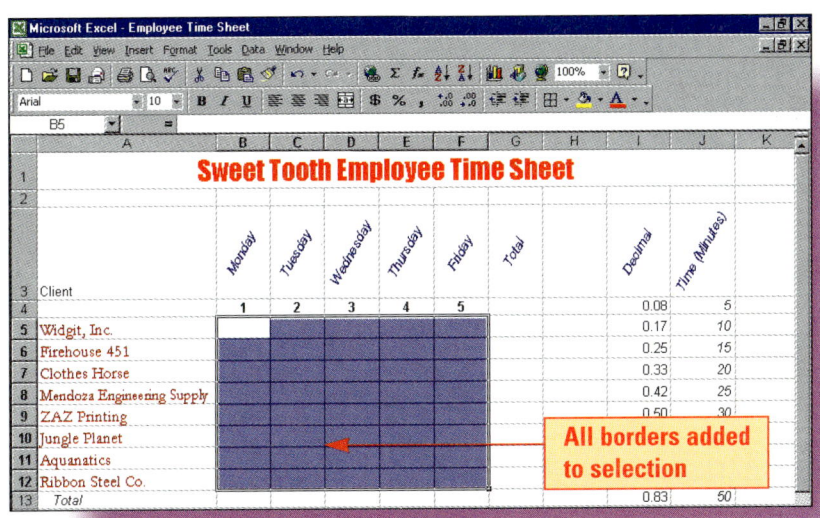

FIGURE 2-9
Adding All Borders to the Worksheet

You are not limited to the 12 choices appearing on the Borders button list. In fact, you can use the Borders tab of the Format Cells dialog box to select different line styles, change line colors, and choose additional

chapter two

border options, such as inserting diagonal lines and applying borders to only the inside of a selection. To create a custom border:

Step 1	*Select*	cells A13:G13
Step 2	*Open*	the Format Cells dialog box
Step 3	*Click*	the Border tab
Step 4	*Select*	the heavy solid line style from the Style: box
Step 5	*Click*	the top edge of the Border preview diagram
Step 6	*Click*	the bottom edge of the Border preview diagram

Your Border tab should look similar to Figure 2-10.

FIGURE 2-10
Creating Custom
Border Settings

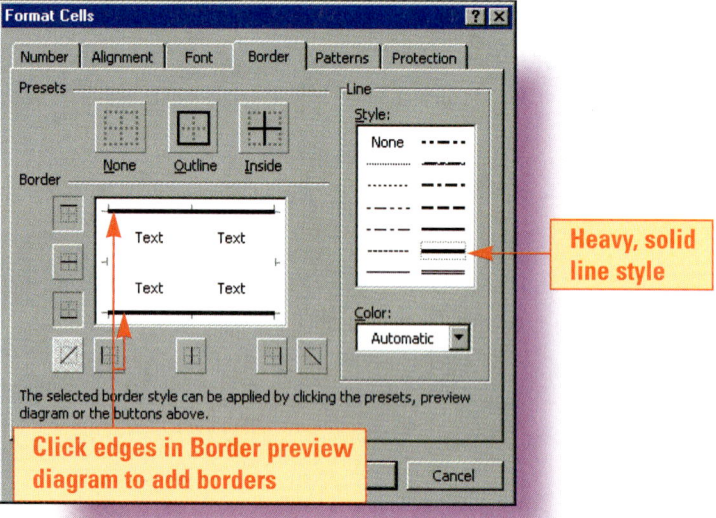

Heavy, solid line style

Click edges in Border preview diagram to add borders

Step 7	*Click*	OK

Your custom border is applied to the selection.

Adding Shading

One way you can make row 4, which contains the date numbers, stand out is to use a "reverse text" effect. To create this effect, you apply a dark fill color to the cells, then change the font color to white. To add shading to a cell:

Step 1	*Select*	cells A4:G4

Step 2	*Click*	the Fill Color list arrow  on the Formatting toolbar
Step 3	*Select*	the Blue square from the Fill Color list
Step 4	*Click*	the Font Color list arrow on the Formatting toolbar
Step 5	*Select*	the White square from the Font Color list
Step 6	*Activate*	cell A1 to deselect the cells
Step 7	*Click*	the Save button on the Standard toolbar to save your workbook

Compare your final worksheet with Figure 2-11.

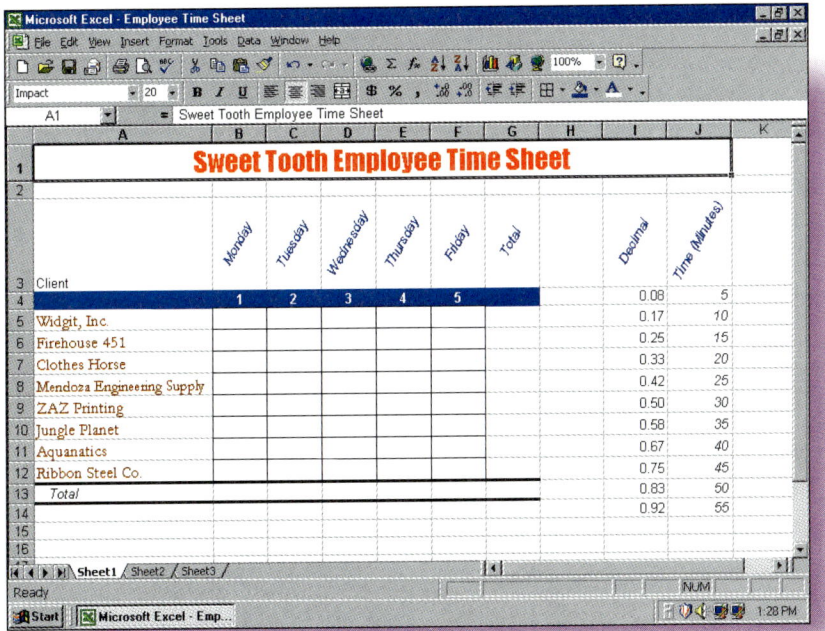

FIGURE 2-11
Finished Time Sheet

You can now distribute the *Employee Time Sheet* workbook to Sweet Tooth's different divisions. Formatting a worksheet doesn't take much time, but it can have a dramatic impact on the worksheet's appearance and legibility.

chapter
two

Summary

▶ Titles add visual impact and provide a guide to the worksheet's contents.

▶ Column and row labels aid in understanding data contained in a worksheet.

▶ Expand the width of a column by using AutoFit, by working with the Column Width dialog box, or by clicking and dragging column heading borders.

▶ Judicious use of font formats can enhance a worksheet's appearance and make it easier to read. Use Format Painter to copy formats to other cells. Use the Font tab of the Format Cells dialog box to apply several settings simultaneously.

▶ Expand the height of a row by using AutoFit, by working with the Row Height dialog box, or by clicking and dragging row heading borders. Row heights expand automatically with font size changes.

▶ Align cell contents to enhance visual clarity. The default for text is left-alignment. For numeric entries, such as currency, dates, and times, the default is right-alignment.

▶ Rotate text to add visual interest or to decrease the width of a column. Indent text to provide visual breaks or to indicate that a list has a certain hierarchical structure. Use the Alignment tab of the Format Cells dialog box to apply these settings.

▶ Use number formats to change how cells' numerical contents are displayed. Excel detects date and time entries and formats the cell accordingly.

▶ Borders and shading can add visual impact to worksheets. Create custom borders using the Borders tab of the Format Cells dialog box.

Commands Review

Action	Menu Bar	Shortcut Menu	Toolbar	Keyboard
Merge and center a cell			⊞	
Fill	Edit, Fill, Series	Right-click and drag fill handle		ALT + E, I, S
Fill Right	Edit, Fill, Right			CTRL + R ALT + E, I, R
Fill Down	Edit, Fill, Down			CTRL + D ALT + E, I, D
AutoFit a column	Format, Column, AutoFit		Double-click column divider	ALT + O, C, A
Change width of a column	Format, Column, Width	Right-click column heading, click Column width	Drag column divider	ALT + O, C, W
AutoFit a row	Format, Row, AutoFit		Double-click row divider	ALT + O, C, A
Change height of a row	Format, Row, Height	Right-click column heading, click Row height	Drag row divider	ALT + O, C, E
Format cells	Format, Cells	Right-click selected range, click Format Cells		CTRL + 1 ALT + O, E
Align cell contents (see Alignment tab of Format Cells dialog box)			▤ ▤ ▤	
Font Color (see Font tab of Format Cells dialog box)			**A** ▾	
Bold (see Font tab of Format Cells dialog box)			**B**	CTRL + B
Italics (see Font tab of Format Cells dialog box)			*I*	CTRL + I
Underline (see Font tab of Format Cells dialog box)			U	CTRL + U
Increase/decrease indent (see Alignment tab of Format Cells dialog box)			▤ ▤	
Apply number formats (see Number tab of Format Cells dialog box)			$ % , ⁺⁰.₀₀ .₀₀⁺⁰	
Add borders (see Borders tab of Format Cells dialog box)			▦ ▾	
Apply outline border				CTRL + SHIFT + &
Remove outline border				CTRL + SHIFT + _
Add shading to cells (see Patterns tab of Format Cells dialog box)			◇ ▾	
Indent text (see Alignment tab of Format Cells dialog box)			▤ ▤	
Use Format Painter			✎	

chapter two

Concepts Review

Circle the correct answer.

1. To select multiple, nonadjacent ranges, press and hold the:
[a] SHIFT key.
[b] END key.
[c] ALT key.
[d] CTRL key.

2. To select a range using the keyboard, press and hold the:
[a] SHIFT key.
[b] END key.
[c] ALT key.
[d] CTRL key.

3. To center a title across multiple cells, use the:
[a] Center button.
[b] Merge button.
[c] Merge and Center button.
[d] Center Alignment button.

4. One reason a cell might display ###### is because:
[a] the text value of the cell exceeds the width of the column.
[b] an incorrect argument has been entered in a function.
[c] the numeric value of the cell exceeds the width of the column.
[d] the number format is not recognized.

5. Typeface refers to:
[a] print density.
[b] upright or italic print.
[c] print height.
[d] design and appearance of a font.

6. Which of these is *not* a valid method of changing the height of a row?
[a] Increase the font size of the contents in the row.
[b] Use Format, Row, Hide.
[c] Use Format, Row, Height.
[d] Drag the border between row labels.

7. Which of the following data types is *not* right-aligned by default?
[a] Dates
[b] Text
[c] Times
[d] Numbers

8. To apply multiple changes to a font, use the _____ tab of the Format Cells dialog box.
[a] Font
[b] Border
[c] Patterns
[d] Number

9. To apply custom border styles, use the _____ tab of the Format Cells dialog box.
[a] Font
[b] Border
[c] Patterns
[d] Number

Circle **T** if the statement is true or **F** if the statement is false.

T F   1. You can access the Format Cells dialog box by pressing the CTRL + 1 keys.

T F   2. You can apply a border diagonally across a cell (or cells).

T F   3. You cannot use too many fonts in a worksheet.

T F   4. Increasing the font size automatically increases the row height.

T F   5. The fill handle is found on the upper-left corner of the selection border.

T   F   6. You can create an AutoFill by using the Fill command on the <u>E</u>dit menu.

T   F   7. AutoFit resizes columns to accommodate the longest entry in the column, regardless of whether the cell is selected.

T   F   8. Rotating text automatically adjusts the row height.

Skills Review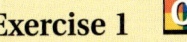

Exercise 1

1. Open the *Project Expense Log* workbook on your Data Disk.

2. Change the numeric format of column A to the MM/DD/YY date format.

3. Expand the width of column B to show the full contents of the longest entry in the column.

4. Change the number format of column C to currency style by clicking the Currency Style button on the Formatting toolbar.

5. Merge and center cell A1 across cells A1:C1.

6. Center the column labels in row 3.

7. Save your changes as *Project Expense Log Revised*.

Exercise 2

1. Open a new, blank workbook.

2. Create a title called "Calendar" at the top of your worksheet. Apply font settings so that the title stands out clearly. Center the title across columns A through G.

3. Using your knowledge of adjusting row heights and column widths, create a one-month calendar grid consisting of six rows and seven columns. Adjust row heights to 60 and column widths to 12 so that each cell is approximately square.

4. Use AutoFill to create the weekday series, starting with Sunday. Center this series vertically and horizontally.

5. Use AutoFill to create the date numbers in each cell as follows:

a.   Starting with the first Sunday as the first day of the month, Fill Series to the right.

b.   Select the first row of dates, and right-click and drag the fill handle to the fourth week of the calendar.

c.   Select S<u>e</u>ries, then enter 7 as the <u>S</u>tep value.

d.   Add the final three dates to your calendar so that Tuesday is the 31st day of the month.

e.   Use the Alignment tab of the Format Cells dialog box to align the date number in the upper-left corner of each cell.

6. Apply shading to days on the calendar that follow the end of the month.

7. Apply shading to the column labels. Apply a border to the calendar.

8. Save your workbook as *Calendar*.

chapter two

Exercise 3

1. Enter the following data in a new workbook. (Enter Employee Name in cell A1.)

Employee Name	Current Wage	Proposed Wage	Increase per Month
Mark Havlaczek	7.50	8	
Roberta Hernandez	8.25	9	
Eric Wimmer	8.25	8.85	
Micah Anderson	7.75	8.5	
Allyson Smith	9.5	10.35	
Total Increase			

2. Increase the column width to show the full contents of each cell.

3. Apply the currency format with two decimal places to cells B2:D7.

4. Create a formula in cell D2 that calculates how much *more* each employee will make per month as a result of the proposed wage increase. Assume that each employee works 168 hours per month. (*Hint:* Subtract the Current Wage from the Proposed Wage, then multiply the result by 168.)

5. Sum the amounts in column D to show the additional cost to the owner as a result of the proposed wage increases.

6. Save your workbook as *Proposed Wage Increase*.

Exercise 4

1. Open the *Proposed Wage Increase* workbook that you created in Exercise 3.

2. Use the Format Cells dialog box to format cell A1 as follows:

   a. Change the font to Times New Roman.

   b. Increase the font size to 12.

   c. Change the font color to Blue.

   d. Change the font style to Bold.

3. With cell A1 still active, click the Format Painter button on the Standard toolbar, then drag to select cells B1:D1.

4. Decrease the column widths of columns A–D to 11.

5. Turn on Wrap Text for cells A1:D1 and center the column labels.

6. Make cells A7:D7 bold and add a Gray-25% shade.

7. Clear the formatting in cells A7:C7 by pointing to Clear on the Edit menu, then clicking Formats.

8. Add a thick bottom border to cells A1:D1.

9. Indent cell A7.

10. Increase the width of column A to display the employee names correctly.

11. Save your workbook as *Proposed Wage Increase Revised*.

Exercise 5

1. Open the *Number Formatting* workbook on the Data Disk.

2. Center the column labels and apply a Light Green shade.

3. Apply the All Borders border to all cells that hold data.

4. Use the number format indicated by each column label to format the columns. Use the default settings unless otherwise directed.

   a. In the Number column, select the Use 1000 Separator (,) check box in the Number format settings.

   b. In the Date column, set the Date type to 3/14/1998. (Notice that Excel converts numbers into dates, starting with 1 equal to 1/1/1900.)

   c. In the Time column, set the Time type to 3/14/1998 1:30 PM. (If you don't have this format, set it as 3/14/98 1:30 PM.)

   d. In the Fraction column, set the Fraction type to Up to two digits (21/25). (Because many of the numbers are whole numbers, no fraction will appear in the worksheet, but the number will move to the left side of the cell to allow proper alignment of fractions when present.)

5. Use AutoFit to increase the column widths so as to fully display the numbers in each cell.

6. Save your workbook as *Number Formatting Revised*.

Exercise 6

1. Create a new workbook.

2. Enter the data as shown in the table below:

Important Dates of World War II	
Date	**Event**
9/1/1939	Germany invades Poland
6/14/40	German troops occupy Paris
7/10/40	Battle of Britain begins
6/22/1941	German troops invade Russia
12/7/1941	Japan attacks U.S. forces at Pearl Harbor, Hawaii
12/8/1941	U.S. declares war on Japan
12/11/1941	U.S. declares war on Germany and Italy
6/4/1942	Battle of Midway starts (turning point of Pacific war)
1/23/1943	Casablanca Conference decides on Cross Channel Invasion of Continental Europe
7/10/43	Allies invade Sicily
6/6/1944	D-Day Allied invasion of Western Europe commences in France
5/7/1945	Germany surrenders to Allies at Reims, France
7/16/1945	U.S. tests 1st atomic bomb in New Mexico
8/6/1945	U.S. drops atomic bomb on Hiroshima, Japan
8/9/1945	U.S. drops atomic bomb on Nagasaki, Japan
8/14/1945	Japan agrees to surrender
9/2/1945	Japan formally surrenders in Tokyo Bay

3. Merge and center the title in row 1.

4. Bold and center the labels in row 2.

5. Change the format of the Date column to the Month DD, YYYY format.

chapter two

6. Format cell A1 with a black fill and white text.

7. Format the text in cell A1 as bold and increase the font size to 16 points.

8. Format row 2 with a dark gray fill and white text.

9. Save the workbook as *WWII*.

Exercise 7

1. Open the *WWII* workbook you created in Exercise 6.

2. Change the width of column B to 45.

3. Turn on wrap text with column B selected.

4. Left align cells A3:A19.

5. Italicize cells A3, A7, A13, A14, and A19.

6. Activate cell A1, then save the workbook as *WWII Revised*.

Exercise 8

1. Open the *New Computer Prices* workbook on the Data Disk.

2. Change the title in row A1 to 16 point, bold text.

3. Merge and center cell A1 across A1:G1.

4. Bold and center the labels in row 3.

5. Resize columns A-G to fit the data.

6. Format column C with Comma format.

7. Change cells E4:F6 to right aligned.

8. Save your workbook as *New Computer Prices Formatted*.

Case Projects

Project 1

You work in a large bank. You are frequently asked about the current exchange rate for U.S. dollars relative to a variety of foreign currencies. Search the Internet for a site that reports currency exchange rates. Create a new workbook to keep track of recent updates. Include the URL of the site(s) you find in your workbook, which will allow you to access these sites easily later. Record the date and currency exchange rate for converting U.S. dollars into the euro currency and the currencies of at least six countries, including those of Japan, Germany, France, and the United Kingdom. Apply currency formats displaying the appropriate currency symbol for each country (if available). Set up your workbook so that you can monitor the changes in exchange rates over time. Center and bold column labels, and italicize row labels. Save your workbook as *Foreign Currency Exchange*.

Project 2

You work for an insurance company processing accident claims. One of your tasks is to determine how many days have elapsed between the date of an accident and the date that a claim was filed. You know that Excel stores dates as numbers, so you must be able to create a formula that calculates this information. Use the Office Assistant to look up more information about how Excel keeps track of dates. Can you figure out the trick? Create a workbook with column labels for Accident Date, Claim Filed Date, and Elapsed Days. Save your workbook as *Claim Lapse Calculator*.

Project 3

You work in a warehouse run by a large furniture retailer. Your company uses a unique numbering system to track inventory in the warehouse. Inventory numbers look similar to the following: 1-234-5678. Unfortunately, it's difficult to remember the pattern of dashes when entering data in the inventory workbook. You've noticed that Excel has a custom number format option in the Format Cells dialog box, and wonder if it might be the answer to your problem. Use the Office Assistant to look up how to create a custom number format. Create a new number format and try using it to enter at least five inventory items. (*Hint:* The format should automatically supply all dashes; you should simply have to type in the numbers.) Bold and center any column headings you use, such as Part Number. Save your workbook as *Warehouse Inventory*.

Project 4

Your mom, a quilter, has come to you with an interesting project. She needs to organize her quilt pattern, but because of the number of pieces, it's very difficult to keep track of everything. You know that Excel can shade cells in different colors. That gives you an idea. Can you use shading and borders to create a fun geometrical pattern? Don't be afraid to modify column widths and row heights to achieve a more artistic pattern. Save your workbook as *Quilt*.

Project 5

You have just started a new business—a bookstore. As a small business owner, you're not sure where to turn for advice—you just know you need some.

Use the Web toolbar in Excel to search the Internet for Small Business Guides. In particular, search for topics dealing with education, training, taxes, and technology. Print the home pages of at least three different sites.

Project 6

You have used the AutoFill command to automatically create series of day names, months, and all sorts of number variations. What else could you do with series fill? What about a list of color names? Use the Office Assistant to help you find out how to create a custom fill series. Create a new series using the following colors: red, orange, yellow, green, blue, and purple. Test your new fill series by entering "red" in cell A1, then AutoFilling the series to the right. Then select the values and AutoFill the series down. Save your workbook as *Color Series*.

Project 7

Use the Internet to locate a timeline showing major events of the 20th century. Create a workbook to record the date and a description of the event. Include at least one event from each decade of the 20th century. Do not include more than three events from any decade. Save your workbook as *20th Century Timeline*.

Project 8

Use the Internet to locate information about current events. Print at least one story of national importance, and one of local importance.

chapter two

Organizing Worksheets Effectively

Chapter Overview

Effective organization of worksheets is essential to providing timely, accurate information. Mastering the use of cell references and naming ranges helps you develop accurate formulas more quickly. You can rearrange information by inserting and deleting columns, rows, and worksheets to provide additional information.

Creating outlines using the Subtotals command offers an easy way to summarize data.

LEARNING OBJECTIVES

▶ Perform single and multi-level sorts
▶ Copy and move data
▶ Rename a worksheet
▶ Insert, move, and delete worksheets
▶ Insert and delete cells, rows, and columns
▶ Use absolute, relative, and mixed references
▶ Create and use named ranges
▶ Freeze and unfreeze rows and columns
▶ Use grouping and outlines
▶ Check spelling in a worksheet

Case profile

For reporting and organizational purposes, Sweet Tooth divides the country into four regions: the East Coast, Mountain, West Coast, and Central. Each region is further classified into North, South, East, and West divisions. Amy Lee, the company president, has asked you to study the financial impact of paying various commission percentages to the company's sales force and to calculate the total sales for each region.

chapter three

3.a Performing Single and Multi-level Sorts

The *Sweet Tooth Sales Rep Data* workbook contains gross sales data for each salesperson employed by Sweet Tooth. You want to work with these data, but—recognizing that a lot of work has gone into creating this information—leave the original data intact. Your first task is to save a new copy of the file, enabling you to manipulate it without worrying about losing the original data. To open a file and save it with a new name:

Step 1	*Open*	the *Sweet Tooth Sales Rep Data* file on your Data Disk
Step 2	*Save*	the file as *Sweet Tooth Sales Rep Data Revised*

When dealing with long lists of data, such as the sales data in your workbook, it can be helpful to sort the information. Column A contains the column label, Region. This column label acts as your sort **criteria**, indicating the type of data you want to sort by. If you place the active cell in this column, Excel knows which column to sort. To sort the sales representative data:

Step 1	*Activate*	cell A4
Step 2	*Click*	the Sort Ascending button on the Standard toolbar

The column is sorted in ascending order (alphabetically) by region. When Excel works with lists, it assumes that the top row of the list contains the column labels and does not sort that row. Using the Sort dialog box, you can sort by as many as three criteria. To sort on multiple columns:

Step 1	*Click*	<u>D</u>ata
Step 2	*Click*	<u>S</u>ort

The Sort dialog box appears, as shown in Figure 3-1. When you open the Sort dialog box, Excel scans for the header row of the active list and adds the column headings to the criteria list boxes. It also assumes that the Sort by criteria is the column containing the active cell.

chapter
three

FIGURE 3-1
Sort Dialog Box

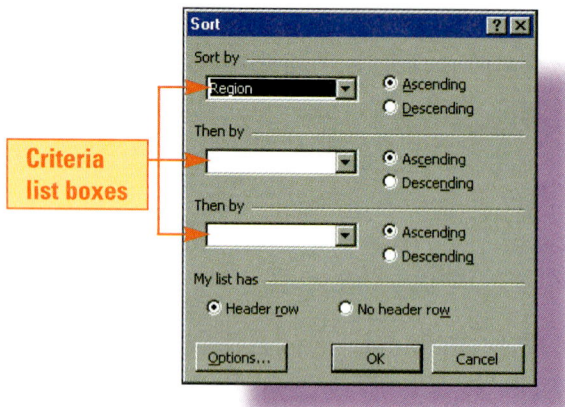

Step 3	*Click*	the upper Then by list arrow
Step 4	*Select*	Division from the list
Step 5	*Click*	the lower Then by list arrow
Step 6	*Select*	Gross Sales from the list
Step 7	*Click*	the Descending option button next to Gross Sales
Step 8	*Click*	OK

Your list is sorted by region, then alphabetically by division, then from highest to lowest by gross sales within each division.

3.b Copying and Moving Data Using Drag and Drop

In Chapter 2, you learned to copy data by using the fill handle. Another way to move and copy data is to use **drag and drop**. To drag selected cells, click the selection border using the left mouse button. Hold the left mouse button down as you *drag* the cells to a new location, then *drop* them by releasing the left mouse button. To move data using drag and drop:

Step 1	*Select*	cells A4:D19
Step 2	*Move*	the pointer over the border of your selection

The cross pointer changes to an arrow pointer ↖. At this point, you can click the border and drag the entire range to a new location.

| Step 3 | *Drag* | the range to cells F4:I19 |

A ScreenTip and a range outline guide you in moving the cells. The data are moved from A4:D19 to F4:I19. See Figure 3-2.

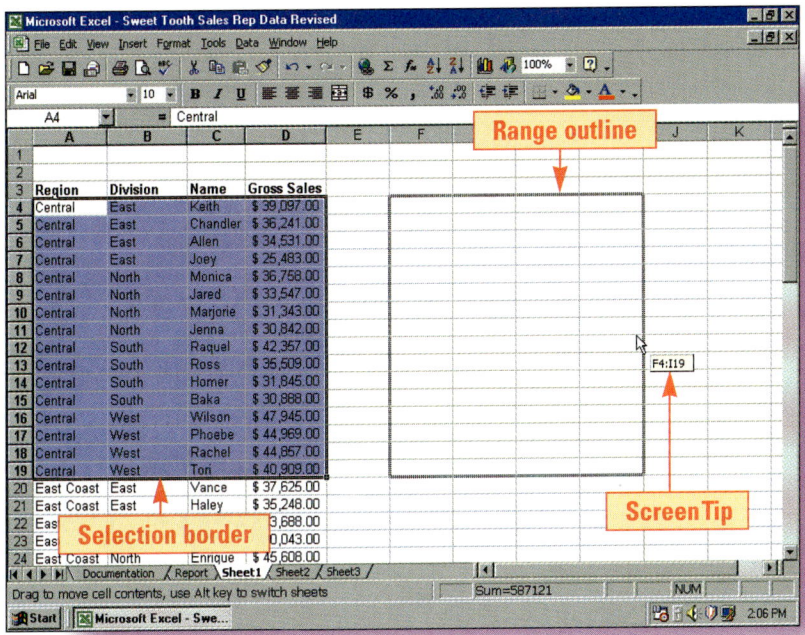

FIGURE 3-2
Dragging and Dropping the Border to Move Cells

To copy data using drag and drop, simply press the CTRL key before you start to drag a range of cells. To copy data using drag and drop:

| Step 1 | *Press & Hold* | the CTRL key |
| Step 2 | *Drag* | the border of the selected range F4:I19 to cells A4:D19 |

As you drag, the pointer changes to ⬚⁺, indicating that you are creating a copy of the selected data. You realize that you copied the data by mistake. To delete the data and save your work.

Step 1	*Select*	cells F4:I19
Step 2	*Press*	the DELETE key
Step 3	*Save*	your workbook

QUICK TIP

To move data from one sheet to another using drag and drop, press and hold the ALT key as you drag the range onto the new worksheet tab. To copy data to another worksheet using drag and drop, press and hold the CTRL + ALT keys as you drag the range onto the new worksheet tab.

chapter
three

3.c Renaming a Worksheet

Naming worksheet tabs simplifies the process of locating information in a workbook. To name a worksheet tab:

Step 1	*Right-click*	the Sheet1 tab
Step 2	*Select*	Rename to highlight the current tab name
Step 3	*Key*	Sales Report Data
Step 4	*Press*	the ENTER key
Step 5	*Repeat*	steps 1–4 to rename Sheet2 as Central Region
Step 6	*Repeat*	steps 1–4 to rename Sheet3 as East Coast Region

3.d Inserting, Moving, Copying, and Deleting Worksheets

By default, Excel creates new workbooks with three worksheets. You can add or delete worksheets from your workbook at any time. Each workbook can hold a maximum of 255 worksheets. You can also change the order of worksheets as you further refine your workbook design.

Inserting a Worksheet

You need to add several new worksheets to Sweet Tooth's workbook. To add a new worksheet to a workbook:

Step 1	*Right-click*	the Sales Report Data worksheet tab
Step 2	*Click*	Insert to open the Insert dialog box
Step 3	*Select*	the Worksheet icon
Step 4	*Click*	OK

A new worksheet is inserted to the left of the selected worksheet.

Step 5	*Repeat*	steps 1–4 to insert another worksheet

Step 6	*Rename*	Sheet1 as Mountain Region

Step 7	*Rename*	Sheet2 as West Coast Region

When you finish, the workbook should include a total of seven worksheets.

Moving and Copying a Worksheet

You can reorganize your worksheets in any order by dragging worksheet tabs to a new location. In your workbook, the Sales Report Data should appear first, followed by each of the Region worksheets in alphabetical order. To move a worksheet:

Step 1	*Point to*	the Mountain Region tab

Step 2	*Press & Hold*	the left mouse button

The pointer changes to to indicate that you are moving a tab, and a small black triangle appears at the left of the tab to indicate the tab's position.

Step 3	*Drag*	the Mountain Region tab to the right of the East Coast Region tab

As you drag, the small black triangle moves with the pointer to indicate the tab's new position, and the tabs scroll left. See Figure 3-3.

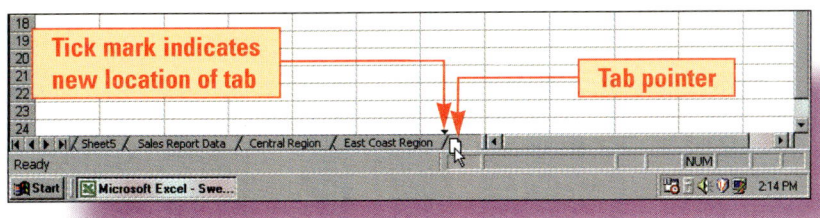

Step 4	*Release*	the mouse button

The tab moves to the new location.

The tab scrolling buttons help you navigate when you can't see all of the tabs. The right tab scrolling button ▶ scrolls one tab to the right. The left tab scrolling button ◀ scrolls one tab to the left. The right end tab scrolling button ▶| scrolls to the tab at the extreme right, and the left end tab scrolling button |◀ scrolls to the tab to the extreme left. To

chapter
three

MOUSE TIP

Drag the horizontal scroll bar resize handle at the left of the horizontal scroll bar to the right to decrease its size and view more worksheet tabs.

scroll past several tabs at once, hold the SHIFT key down when you click the right tab arrow button ▶ or the left tab arrow button ◀. Note that scrolling tabs does not change the active tab.

| Step 5 | *Click* | the left end tab scrolling button ⏮ to scroll to the leftmost tab |
| Step 6 | *Repeat* | steps 1–4 to move the West Coast Region tab to the right of the Mountain Region tab |

3.e Copy and Move Data Using Cut, Copy, and Paste

You can also move and copy data using the Cut, Copy, and Paste commands. You're probably familiar with these commands from other programs, such as Microsoft Word.

Moving Data Using Cut and Paste

The Cut command removes date from the worksheet. To move data:

Step 1	*Scroll*	the Sales Report Data worksheet until you can see rows 52 to 67
Step 2	*Select*	cells A52:D67
Step 3	*Click*	the Cut button ✂ on the Standard toolbar

A moving, dotted border, shown in Figure 3-4, surrounds the selected area. The status bar provides instructions about how to select a destination cell. The destination can be on another worksheet or even another open workbook.

Step 4	*Right-click*	the right tab scrolling button ▶
Step 5	*Click*	West Coast Region
Step 6	*Click*	cell A4
Step 7	*Click*	the Paste button 📋 on the Standard toolbar
Step 8	*Click*	cell A4 to deselect the range

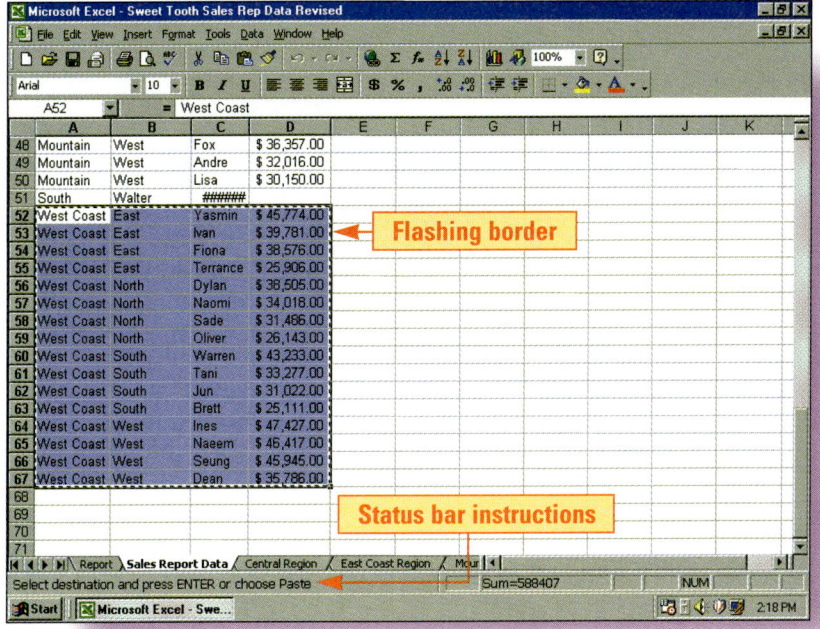

FIGURE 3-4
Dotted Border Indicating
Cut or Copy Operation

> **CAUTION TIP**
>
> Use extreme caution when deleting worksheets. This Excel command cannot be undone. Once you've deleted a worksheet, you cannot get it back.

The Cut command in Excel works slightly differently than in other programs, such as Microsoft Word. Excel does not remove the selected text until you take one of two actions: (1) complete the move by selecting a destination and clicking Paste (or pressing the ENTER key), or (2) press the DELETE key. If you change your mind before pasting or deleting, press the ESC key to cancel the cut operation.

Copying Data Using Copy and Paste

The Copy and Paste commands enable you to create a copy of the data. Rather than using the mouse to select the cell range, you can work with the Name Box to create a selection by entering cell references. To select cells using the Name Box:

> **MENU TIP**
>
> Cut, Copy, and Paste are available on the Edit menu. To cut a selection, click Cut. To copy a selection, click Copy. To paste a selection, click Paste.

Step 1	*Click*	in the Name Box
Step 2	*Key*	a4:d19
Step 3	*Press*	the ENTER key

The desired data range is selected, and you're ready to copy it. To copy data using the Copy and Paste commands:

Step 1	*Click*	the Copy button  on the Standard toolbar

> **QUICK TIP**
>
> The shortcut keys for cut, copy, and paste are: CTRL + X to cut, CTRL + C to copy, and CTRL + V to paste.

chapter
three

CAUTION TIP

If the Clipboard did not appear, click the <u>V</u>iew menu, point to <u>T</u>oolbars, and click Clipboard.

FIGURE 3-5
The Office Clipboard

QUICK TIP

The Office Clipboard stores as many as 12 items from any Office 2000 application, including Word, Access, PowerPoint, and Excel. For example, you can use the Office Clipboard to copy several cells in Excel, copy a picture inserted in a PowerPoint slide, and then paste both items into a Word document. Items are stored in the Office Clipboard as long as any Office 2000 application remains open.

The Office Clipboard toolbar appears, similar to Figure 3-5. As you move the pointer over the clips on the Clipboard, a ScreenTip displays a portion of the contents of the clip.

| Step 2 | *Click* | the left end tab scrolling button |
| Step 3 | *Click* | the Sales Report Data tab |

Cells A52:D67 are still selected.

| Step 4 | *Click* | the clip on the Clipboard toolbar |

The West Coast data are pasted into the Sales Report Data worksheet. Using the Clipboard, you can copy the data by clicking the clip on the Clipboard whenever necessary.

To copy the Mountain region data:

| Step 1 | *Scroll* | the Sales Report Data worksheet to view rows 36 to 51 |
| Step 2 | *Select* | cells A36:D51 |

Notice that a data entry error appears in row 51. You will correct this error in the next section.

Step 3	*Click*	the Copy button on the Standard toolbar to add the clip to the Clipboard
Step 4	*Click*	the Mountain Region tab
Step 5	*Click*	cell A4
Step 6	*Press*	the ENTER key

When you press the ENTER key to paste a selection, it ends the Copy command in Excel. Likewise, activating a cell will stop the Copy command and gray out the Paste button on the Standard toolbar. You may want to close the Clipboard when you have finished pasting data. To close the Clipboard:

| Step 1 | *Click* | the Close button on the Clipboard toolbar |
| Step 2 | *Click* | cell A19 to deselect the range |

3.f Inserting and Deleting Cells, Rows, and Columns

As you organize worksheets, you will find many occasions when you need to insert a few cells into a list—or entire rows or columns—to add new information to a worksheet. You may also need to delete rows or columns.

Inserting and Deleting Cells

In some instances, you may need to insert extra cells without inserting an entire row or column. To insert extra cells:

Step 1	*Right-click*	cell A19
Step 2	*Click*	Insert to open the Insert dialog box
Step 3	*Click*	the Shift cells right option button
Step 4	*Click*	OK to shift all cells to the right of the selected cell to the right
Step 5	*Key*	M

As you began typing "Mountain" in cell A19, Excel automatically filled the rest of the word for you. This feature is called **AutoComplete**. As you enter data in columns or rows, Excel builds a list of unique data entries, which it scans as you type. When it senses that you are duplicating an item on its list, the program fills in the rest of the entry automatically. To accept the AutoComplete entry, press the ENTER key. If you are entering a different item, continue inputting the text or data as usual.

| Step 6 | *Press* | the ENTER key |

Don't forget to fix the Sales Report Data worksheet.

chapter
three

| Step 7 | *Scroll* | left to the Sales Report Data worksheet tab |
| Step 8 | *Repeat* | steps 1–6 on the Sales Report Data worksheet to correct the entry error |

Inserting and Deleting Rows and Columns

You want to insert a new row. To insert a new row:

Step 1	*Click*	the Report tab
Step 2	*Right-click*	the row 9 heading
Step 3	*Select*	Insert to insert a new row and shift row 9 to row 10

To insert columns, you use the same technique:

| Step 1 | *Right-click* | the column A heading |
| Step 2 | *Click* | Insert |

All data in the selected column and in the columns to the right are shifted to the right to make room for the new column.

You realize that you don't need the extra column. To delete columns:

Step 1	*Right-click*	the column A heading
Step 2	*Click*	Delete to delete the column from your worksheet
Step 3	*Click*	cell A1 to deselect the column
Step 4	*Save*	your workbook

3.g Using Absolute, Relative, and Mixed References in Formulas

Using cell references in formulas allows you to quickly update values in referenced cells. All formulas referencing those cells will automatically recalculate their results based on your changes. Excel

---

MOUSE TIP

If you accidentally delete a row or column, click the Undo button to restore it.

MENU TIP

To insert a new row, or column click the Insert menu, then click Rows or Columns.

To delete rows or columns, select the row(s) or column(s), click Delete on the Edit menu.

QUICK TIP

To insert multiple rows, select the number of rows you want to insert, then right-click the row heading and click Insert.

uses three types of references: absolute, relative, and mixed references. Each of these reference types affects how a formula is copied. Amy Lee, the president of Sweet Tooth, wants you to calculate the commission for each of the company's sales people to find the total cost of the 20% sales commission.

Using Relative References in Formulas

When you copy a formula containing a **relative cell reference**, the references change relative to the cell from which the formula is being copied. If cell C1 contains the formula =A1+B1, when this formula is copied to cell D2, it changes to =B2+C2. Cell D2 is one row down and one row over from C1; cells B2 and C2 are correspondingly one row down and one row over from cells A1 and B1. To use relative cell references in a formula:

Step 1	*Activate*	the Central Region tab
Step 2	*Enter*	Planned Commission % in cell A1
Step 3	*Enter*	20% in cell A2
Step 4	*Key*	=D4*A2 in cell E4
Step 5	*Click*	the Enter button ✓ on the Formula Bar
Step 6	*Drag*	the fill handle to cell E6 to copy the formula
Step 7	*Click*	cell E5

The formula in cell E6 is =D5*A3. Because there is no value in cell A3, the result of the formula is 0, which is displayed as a dash in the currency style number format.

Step 8	*Click*	cell E6

The error message #VALUE! appears in cell E6, because the value of cell A3 is not a numerical value. See Figure 3-6.

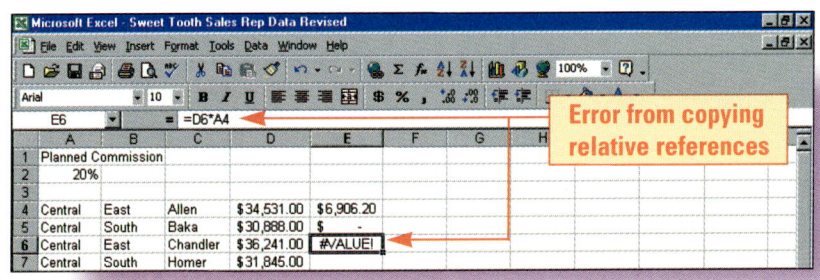

FIGURE 3-6
Errors Due to Copying Formulas with Relative References

chapter
three

You must fix these formulas so that they multiply the value in column D by cell A2, which contains the percentage needed for your formula.

Using Absolute and Mixed References in Formulas

Sometimes you don't want one or more of the cell references in a formula to change, no matter where you copy a formula. For example, in the formula that calculates the commission for Sweet Tooth's sales representatives, the second reference in the formula should always refer to cell A2. In such a case, you would use an **absolute cell reference**, which always refers to a specific cell. In an absolute reference, the dollar sign ($) precedes the column and row designation. In the formula you set up in cell E5, for example, an absolute reference to cell A2 would look like this: =D5***A2**.

To edit the formula and add an absolute reference:

Step 1	*Activate*	cell E4
Step 2	*Click*	in the Formula Bar to the left of A2
Step 3	*Press*	the F4 key to change the reference from A2 to A2
Step 4	*Click*	the Enter button ✔ on the Formula Bar
Step 5	*Copy*	the formula in cell E4 to cells E5:E19
Step 6	*Click*	cell E6

The relative reference in the Formula Bar correctly changes to reference the cell directly to the left, while the absolute reference remains fixed on cell A2.

In addition to absolute and relative references, Excel uses mixed references. A **mixed cell reference** maintains a reference to a specific row or column. For example, suppose you need to copy the formula in cell E5 to cell G5. With a relative reference to cell D5, the formula would change to: =F5*A2. Using a mixed reference, however, you could maintain the reference to column D, but allow the row to change as you copied the formula down column G. A mixed reference would look like this: =$D5*$A$2.

3.h Creating and Using Named Ranges

Giving meaningful names to cells and ranges makes it easier to refer to them.

Add and Delete a Named Range

To continue preparing the report for Amy Lee, you calculate each region's total sales commissions. Using named ranges, you can easily refer to the cells containing those calculations. To name ranges:

Step 1	*Select*	cells E4:E19 on the Central Region sheet
Step 2	*Click*	the Name Box
Step 3	*Key*	Central
Step 4	*Press*	the ENTER key

Once you've named a range, it is added to the list in the Name Box. You can then use this list to select the named range. To select a named range:

Step 1	*Press*	the RIGHT ARROW key to move to cell F4
Step 2	*Click*	the Name Box list arrow
Step 3	*Select*	Central

You use the Define Name dialog box to add, delete and modify your named ranges. To use the Define Name dialog box to name ranges:

Step 1	*Click*	Insert
Step 2	*Point to*	Name
Step 3	*Click*	Define

The Define Name dialog box appears, as shown in Figure 3-7.

The cell reference in the Refers to: text box begins with an equal sign (=), because the reference is essentially a formula that calculates the range name you chose. The sheet name appears next, enclosed between single quotation marks. An exclamation point separates the sheet name from the cell references. Finally, notice that the cell

chapter
three

FIGURE 3-7
Define Names
Dialog Box

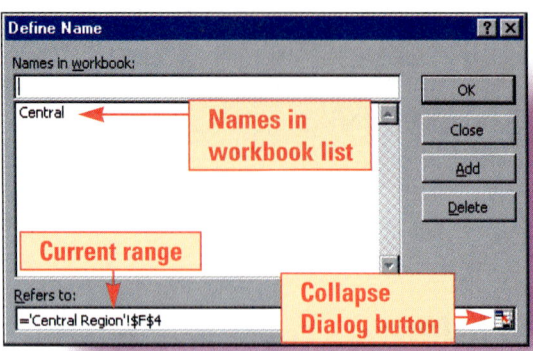

reference is an absolute reference. You can modify the cell references in the text box, select new ones from the worksheet by clicking the Collapse Dialog button, add new named ranges, or delete existing ones. To create a named range using the Define Names dialog box:

| Step 1 | *Key* | Commission in the Names in workbook: text box |
| Step 2 | *Click* | the Collapse Dialog button in the Refers to: text box |

The dialog box collapses to show only the Refers to: box, and the status bar prompts you to point to add cells to your named range.

Step 3	*Select*	cell A2
Step 4	*Click*	the Expand Dialog button in the dialog box
Step 5	*Click*	Add to add the new named range to the Names in workbook list
Step 6	*Click*	OK to close the Define Name dialog box

Using a Named Range in a Formula

You can use range names instead of cell references in formulas. In Sweet Tooth's workbook, the Report worksheet has been started for you. You create a formula using a named range to calculate the Central region's total commissions. To create a formula using a named range:

Step 1	*Click*	the Report tab
Step 2	*Key*	=sum(in cell B5
Step 3	*Click*	Insert

Step 4	*Point to*	Name
Step 5	*Click*	Paste to open the Paste Name dialog box
Step 6	*Click*	Central
Step 7	*Click*	OK
Step 8	*Click*	the Enter button ☑ on the Formula Bar

Excel automatically adds the closing parenthesis for the SUM argument. Your formula should match the one shown in Figure 3-8, with the correct result appearing in cell B5.

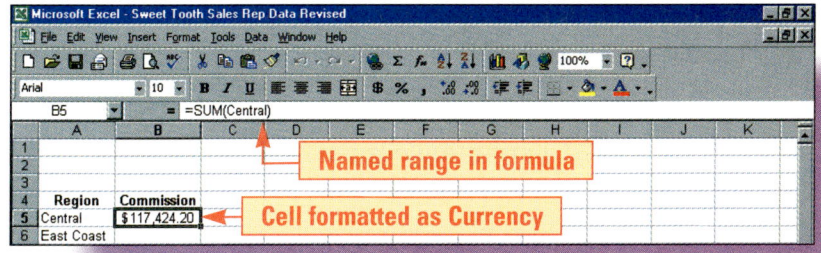

FIGURE 3-8
Using Named Ranges in Formulas

3.i Freezing and Unfreezing Rows and Columns

When working with large worksheets, it can be helpful to retain row and column headings on the screen as you scroll through your worksheet. When you need to view row or column labels while scrolling through a worksheet, use the Freeze Panes command. This command freezes the rows above, and the columns to the left of, the active cell and prevents them from scrolling off the screen. Suppose you want to see the column headings as you scroll the list on the Sales Report Data worksheet. To freeze panes:

Step 1	*Click*	the Sales Report Data tab
Step 2	*Press*	the CTRL + HOME keys to move to cell A1
Step 3	*Activate*	cell A4
Step 4	*Click*	Window
Step 5	*Click*	Freeze Panes

chapter three

A thin, black line appears on your workbook, indicating that rows 1 through 4 are frozen. This black line will not print when you print the worksheet. These frozen rows will not scroll with the rest of your worksheet.

Step 6	*Press & Hold*	the DOWN ARROW key until your worksheet begins scrolling down

The rows of data disappear off the screen under the column labels. When you no longer need the frozen panes, you can unfreeze them. To unfreeze panes:

Step 1	*Click*	Window
Step 2	*Click*	Unfreeze Panes

The panes are removed, permitting normal worksheet scrolling.

3.j Using Grouping and Outlines

Outlines offer a powerful option for viewing data in a worksheet. An **outline** allows you to view data in hierarchies, or levels. An easy way to create outlines is to use the Subtotals command. When you create subtotals, you specify at what points subtotals should be calculated. Excel automatically inserts the SUBTOTAL function at the specified points, then creates a grand total at the end. The information appearing above each subtotal is called **detail data**. Applying the Subtotals command automatically creates an outline, and a set of outline symbols appears on the left of the worksheet, providing the controls to display or hide detail data.

Using the Subtotals command, you can gather the totals requested by Amy Lee. At the same time, you can provide totals by region and for the company as a whole. To create a subtotal outline:

Step 1	*Click*	cell A4

| Step 2 | *Click* | D̲ata |
| Step 3 | *Click* | Su̲btotals |

The Subtotal dialog box appears. When the Subtotal dialog box opens, Region—the first column in the data set—is automatically selected in the A̲t each change in list. The Region column is sorted alphabetically. Whenever a new value appears in the Region column, a subtotal will be calculated. The SUM function is automatically selected in the U̲se function list. In the A̲dd subtotal in list, Gross Sales—the last column in the data set—is selected. See Figure 3-9.

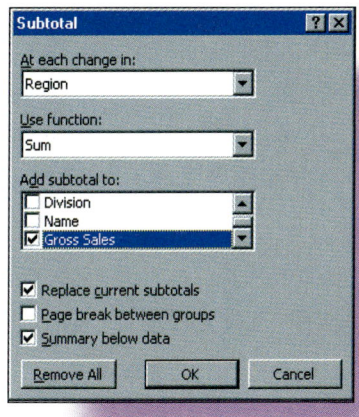

FIGURE 3-9
Subtotal Dialog Box

Step 4	*Click*	OK
Step 5	*Double-click*	the column divider line between columns D and E to widen the column
Step 6	*Scroll*	the worksheet down until you can see row 72

New rows are inserted at each change in the Region column, and Excel calculates a subtotal for each region. Outline symbols showing a two-level outline appear on the left. At the bottom of the list, a grand total is calculated. See Figure 3-10.

M E N U T I P

You can create an outline by clicking the D̲ata menu, pointing to G̲roup and Outline, then clicking A̲uto Outline. Use G̲roup and U̲ngroup to create single levels of data. Note that your worksheet must be set up properly for this function to work. Use the Office Assistant to find out more about creating an outline manually.

chapter
three

FIGURE 3-10
Outline Created Using
the Subtotals Command

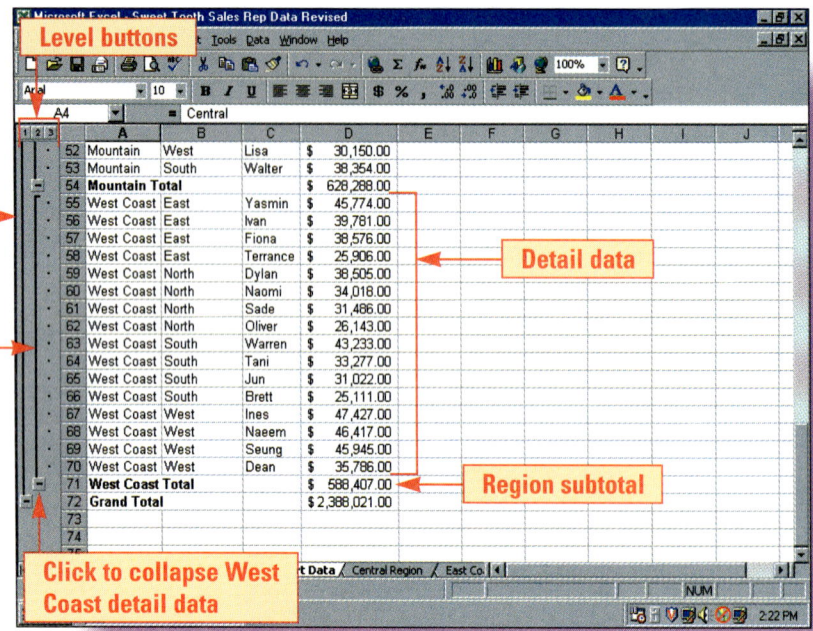

Level buttons

Outline symbols

Identifies rows added to
calculate West Coast subtotal

Detail data

Region subtotal

Click to collapse West
Coast detail data

Amy has requested the totals for each region. You can hide the detail data by collapsing the outline. To collapse outline levels:

Step 1	*Click*	the Collapse Level button ⊟ to the left of row 71 to hide the detail for the West Coast Region
Step 2	*Click*	the 2 Level button ② at the top of the outline to display only subtotals for each region
Step 3	*Scroll*	to the top of the worksheet to view all of the subtotals

Your outline can include up to eight levels. Anticipating that Amy might need to view each division's totals, you decide to add a third level to the outline. To add another level to an outline:

Step 1	*Click*	cell B20
Step 2	*Click*	Data
Step 3	*Click*	Subtotals
Step 4	*Select*	Division from the At each change in list
Step 5	*Click*	the Replace current subtotals check box to deselect it
Step 6	*Click*	OK

Each division now has a subtotal, as shown in Figure 3-11.

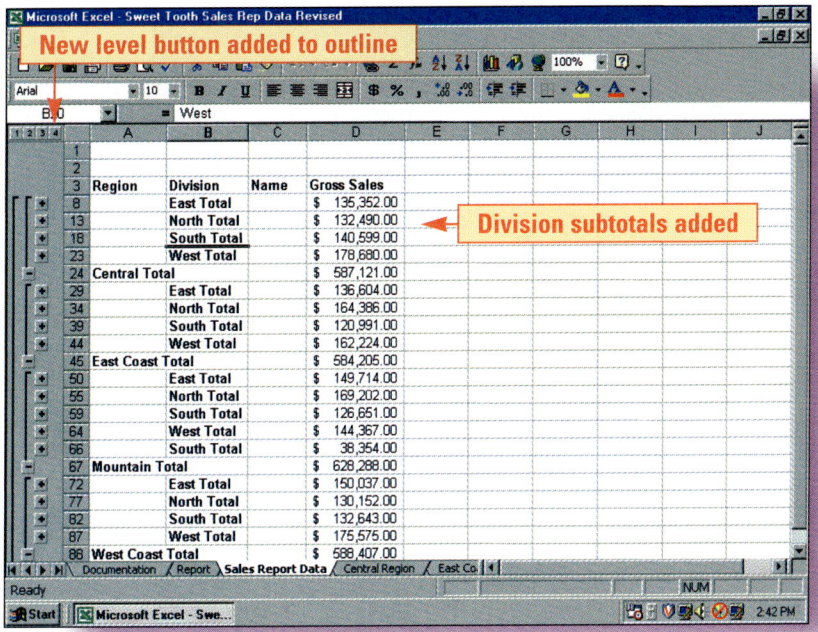

FIGURE 3-11
Adding Additional
Levels to an Outline

MENU TIP

To run spell check from
the menu bar, click
Tools, then click
Spelling.

3.k Checking Spelling in a Worksheet

Excel can check the spelling in your workbook. To spell check a worksheet:

Step 1	*Click*	the Documentation tab
Step 2	*Click*	the Spelling button on the Standard toolbar

The Spelling dialog box opens. Near the top of the dialog box, you will see the first misspelled word found on the worksheet. Suggested corrections appear in the Suggestion list box. See Figure 3-12.

notes

The dictionary that Excel uses to spell check your document does not include many proper names, so your name may be identified as the first misspelled word in this activity. If so, click Ignore to skip your first and last name, then continue the exercise.

The first word that Excel locates is part of the filename, *Revised.xls*. Because it is part of the filename, you can ignore the word by clicking the Ignore button.

QUICK TIP

A documentation worksheet is useful to other users. This page documents the contents of the workbook and provides other useful information, such as the creation date and date the workbook was last modified. Study the Documentation tab to familiarize yourself with the various sections.

chapter
three

FIGURE 3-12
Spelling Dialog Box

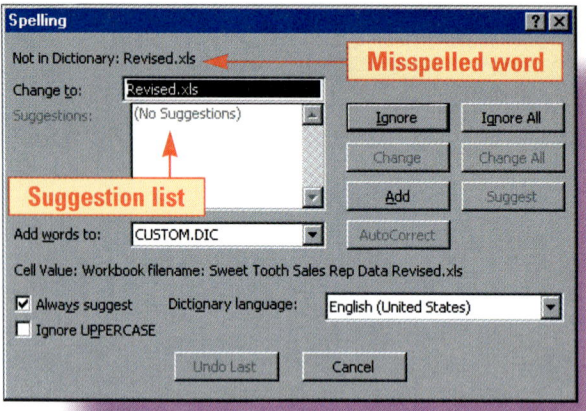

| Step 3 | *Click* | Ignore |

Next, the spell checker finds *Reprot* next. It offers two suggested spellings. The first one is correct and is listed in the Change to: box.

| Step 4 | *Click* | Change |

The next misspelled word Excel locates is *comissions*. The Spelling dialog box offers only one suggested spelling, and it is the correct one.

| Step 5 | *Click* | Change |
| Step 6 | *Click* | Change to accept the suggested correction for *Paramters* |

The next misspelled word, *comission*, has been misspelled several times in the worksheet. You can quickly correct all instances of a misspelling by clicking the Change All button.

| Step 7 | *Click* | Change All |

When you have finished, Excel notifies you that the spelling check of the worksheet is complete.

| Step 8 | *Click* | OK |
| Step 9 | *Save* | your workbook and close it |

You are now ready to present the requested information to Amy Lee, Sweet Tooth's president.

Summary

▶ Sort data using as many as three levels of sort criteria.

▶ Drag selection borders to move data. Press the CTRL key and drag selection borders to copy data. Press the ALT key to move or copy data to another worksheet.

▶ Name worksheet tabs to make information easier to find.

▶ Insert, move, and delete worksheets to organize workbooks.

▶ Use Cut, Copy, and Paste to move or copy information.

▶ Insert and delete rows and columns as needed to organize worksheets. Insert cells by shifting them up or to the right when it is necessary to maintain surrounding information.

▶ Relative cell references change relative to the source cell when copied.

▶ Use absolute cell references to maintain links to a specific cell when copying formulas. Absolute cell references use the dollar sign ($) in front of the column and row identifiers: A1.

▶ Mixed cell references maintain links to a specific row or column when copying formulas. Mixed references use the dollar sign ($) in front of either the row or column identifier: $A1 or A$1.

▶ Create named ranges to quickly select ranges and to use the specified ranges in formulas.

▶ Freeze panes to prevent rows and/or columns from scrolling along with the worksheet.

▶ Use subtotals to create outlines automatically. Add as many as eight levels of subtotals. Use outline symbols to hide or reveal detail.

▶ Use the Spelling command to quickly spell check a worksheet or several worksheets at once.

chapter three

Commands Review

Action	Menu Bar	Shortcut Menu	Toolbar	Keyboard
Sort data	Data, Sort			ALT + D, S
Name a worksheet tab	Format, Sheet, Rename	Rename		ALT + O, H, R
Insert a worksheet	Insert, Worksheet	Insert		ALT + I, W SHIFT + F11 SHIFT + ALT + F1
Move a worksheet	Edit, Move or Copy Sheet	Move or Copy		ALT + E, M
Delete a worksheet	Edit, Delete Sheet	Delete		ALT + E, L
Cut	Edit, Cut	Cut		CTRL + X ALT + E, T
Copy	Edit, Copy	Copy		CTRL + C ALT + E, C
Paste	Edit, Paste	Paste		CTRL + V ALT + E, P
Insert cells	Insert, Cells	Insert		ALT + I, E CTRL + SHIFT + + (plus key)
Insert rows	Insert, Rows	Insert		ALT + I, R
Insert columns	Insert, Columns	Insert		ALT + I, C
Delete rows and columns	Edit, Delete	Delete		ALT + E, D
Cycle reference type between absolute, mixed, and relative				F4
Open Define Name dialog box	Insert, Name, Define			ALT + I, N, D CTRL + F3
Open Paste Name dialog box	Insert, Name, Paste			ALT + I, N, P F3
Freeze/unfreeze pane	Window, Freeze Panes Window, Unfreeze Panes			ALT + W, F
Hide/Unhide rows or columns		Hide Unhide		
Create a named view	View, Custom Views			ALT + V, V
Open Subtotal dialog box	Data, Subtotals			ALT + D, B
Expand an outline level	Data, Group, Show detail			ALT + D, G, S
Collapse an outline level	Data, Group, Hide detail			ALT + D, G, H
Spelling	Tools, Spelling			ALT + T, S F7

Concepts Review

Circle the correct answer.

1. To copy a selection while dragging, press and hold the:
[a] SHIFT key.
[b] END key.
[c] CTRL key.
[d] ALT key.

2. To copy a selection to another worksheet, press and hold the:
[a] SHIFT + CTRL keys.
[b] CTRL + ALT keys.
[c] SHIFT + ALT keys.
[d] CTRL + SPACEBAR keys.

3. Which of the following formulas is an absolute reference?
[a] A1
[b] $A1
[c] A1
[d] A$1

4. Copying the formula =A1+B1 from cell C1 to cell E3 would make what change to the formula?
[a] =A1+B1
[b] =A1+C3
[c] =B3+C1
[d] =C3+D3

5. Copying the formula =$A1+B$2 from cell C1 to cell E3 would make what change to the formula?
[a] =$A3+D$2
[b] =$A1+B$2
[c] =$A2+E$2
[d] =$A3+C$2

6. Cell A1, named AMT, contains a value of $100.00. Cell B1, named TAX, contains a value of 6%. Cell C1 contains the formula =AMT*TAX. What is the result of this formula?
[a] none, you can't use cell names in formulas
[b] $106.00
[c] $6.00
[d] an error

7. Identify the type of reference for the row and column of the following cell reference: X$24.
[a] absolute, absolute
[b] absolute, relative
[c] relative, absolute
[d] relative, relative

8. You can sort data using as many as _____ levels of sort criteria.
[a] one
[b] two
[c] three
[d] four

9. You can create outlines with as many as _____ levels of detail.
[a] five
[b] six
[c] seven
[d] eight

chapter three

Circle **T** if the statement is true or **F** if the statement is false.

T   F   1. You can use the F7 key to open the Paste Name dialog box.

T   F   2. The freezing pane command prevents rows or columns from scrolling with the worksheet.

T   F   3. Formulas containing relative references do not change when copied.

T   F   4. You can use the F4 key to cycle through cell reference options when editing formulas.

T   F   5. You must hold the ALT key down while selecting multiple worksheet tabs for spell checking.

T   F   6. Clicking one of the Sort buttons will sort based on the column of the active cell.

T   F   7. Using the Subtotals command automatically creates an outline.

T   F   8. Spell check catches all spelling errors.

T   F   9. Spell check checks only the current active worksheet unless you select multiple worksheets.

T   F   10. Documenting a workbook is important when other users will use the workbook.

Skills Review

Exercise 1

1. Open the *Employee Time* workbook on your Data Disk.

2. Insert a new worksheet into the workbook.

3. Name the tab Revised Data.

4. Rename the Employee Time tab to Original Data.

5. Copy all of the data to the Revised Data tab (the worksheet includes data in 349 rows).

6. Save the file as *Employee Time 1*.

Exercise 2

1. Open the *Employee Time 1* workbook that you created in Exercise 1.

2. Switch to the Revised Data tab, if necessary.

3. Insert a new column at column A.

4. Move all of the data (including the column heading) under Project to the new column A.

5. Delete the empty column C.

6. Change column C to Number format with two decimal places.

7. Increase the width of column A to show the project names in full.

8. Bold and center the column labels.

9. Move the title in cell B1 to cell A1.

10. Bold the title, then merge and center it across columns A through C.

11. Delete the blank rows 2, 3, and 4 under the worksheet title.

12. Save your work as *Employee Time 2*.

Exercise 3

1. Open the *Employee Time 2* workbook that you created in Exercise 2.

2. Scroll the worksheet until row 3 is the top row you can see.

3. Activate cell A4.

4. Use freeze panes to lock the column labels in place.

5. Scroll to the bottom of the worksheet.

6. Save your work as *Employee Time 3*.

Exercise 4

1. Open the *Employee Time 3* workbook that you created in Exercise 3.

2. Unfreeze the column labels.

3. Delete all blank rows separating data (leave row 2 blank).

4. Sort the data by Project (ascending order), then by Hours (descending order).

5. Create an outline of the data by creating subtotals for each Project.

6. Collapse the outline to level 2.

7. Save your work as *Employee Time 4*.

Exercise 5

1. Open the *Employee Time 4* workbook that you created in Exercise 4.

2. Remove the subtotals from the data by opening the Subtotal dialog box, and then clicking the Remove all button.

3. Select cells C4:C328. Name this range Hours.

4. Save the workbook as *Employee Time 5*.

Exercise 6

1. Open the *Employee Time 5* workbook that you created in Exercise 5.

2. Insert a new worksheet and name it Report.

3. In cell A2, enter the row label "Number of Projects."

4. In cell A3, enter the row label "Average Hours."

5. In cell A4, enter the row label "Total Hours."

6. Widen column A so the text fits.

7. Use the Office Assistant to look up the COUNT function. Insert the COUNT function in cell B2 using the named range Hours.

8. Use the Office Assistant to look up the AVERAGE function. Insert the AVERAGE function in cell B3 to calculate the average hours spent by each employee on each of the company's projects.

9. Enter the SUM function in cell B4 to calculate the total number of hours worked.

chapter three

10. Format column B using the number style with two decimal places.

11. Save the workbook as *Employee Time 6*.

Exercise 7

1. Open the *Employee Time 6* workbook that you created in Exercise 6.

2. Check the spelling on the Report worksheet.

3. Check the spelling on the other two worksheets in the workbook.

4. Add the title Time Sheet Report to cell A1 in the Report worksheet, then merge and center it across columns A and B.

5. Insert two rows below row 1.

6. Format the Report worksheet as you see fit.

7. Save the workbook as *Employee Time 7*.

Exercise 8

1. Open the *Groceries* workbook on your Data Disk.

2. Select rows 3 through 6.

3. Click Data, point to Group and Outline, then click Group.

4. Click Data, point to Group and Outline, then click Hide Detail.

5. Activate any cell in row 9.

6. Click Data, point to Group and Outline, then click Auto Outline. Click OK when prompted to modify the existing outline.

7. Click the level 1 outline button to collapse the outline.

8. Print your worksheet.

9. Save the workbook as *Groceries with Outline*.

Case Projects

Project 1

You are an instructor at a community college who teaches working adults about Excel. Several of your students have asked you for additional resources. Use the Web toolbar to search the Internet for Excel books. Print at least three summary pages showing the title, author name, and ISBN number for each book.

Project 2

You are in charge of the accounting office at a large department store. Recently, several computational errors have occurred in various reports. In reviewing the work of junior staff members, you find that some of them are having problems understanding the difference between absolute and relative cell references. Prepare a workbook with samples of the four types of references. Use this workbook to demonstrate what happens when you move data or copy formulas containing these different types of references. Use the Office Assistant to help you brush up on your knowledge of the topic. Save the workbook as *Cell Reference Training*.

Project 3

You have just been promoted to programming director at the radio station where you work. The station manager wants to completely reorganize the way in which the station keeps track of which songs are played. Prepare a workbook that can sort songs by number of times played in a week, duration, artist, and musical classification. Be sure to format the cells so that they display the correct units. Add the titles of at least 10 songs, and create fictitious data for the number of times played and duration. Save the workbook as *Record Tracker*.

Project 4

You are a serious baseball card collector. Create a worksheet to organize your card collection by player, card manufacturer, or value. Use the Internet to locate Web sites devoted to baseball card collectors. Create a workbook containing the names, card manufacturers, card years, and values for 20 cards. Include at least three different cards for three of the players. Organize the data so that they can be sorted by player name, card manufacturer, year, or value. Save the workbook as *Baseball Card Collection*.

Project 5

You are the manager of a pizzeria. Create a worksheet with fictitious data that shows how many pizzas were sold last month. Calculate the total sales, figuring each pizza sold for $8.00. Show column headings for Overhead, Labor, Ingredients, Advertising and Profit. Calculate the amount spent in each category, figuring 15% for overhead, 30% for labor, 25% for ingredients, 10% for advertising, and the remainder for profit. Save the workbook as *Pizzeria*.

Project 6

You plan on selling your car soon and want to find out how much it is worth. Use the Web toolbar and search the Internet for used car prices. Try finding a listing for your car and two other cars built the same year. (*Hint*: Search for "Blue Book values.") Print Web pages showing the trade-in value of the cars you selected.

Project 7

Using Excel online Help, find out how to outline a list of data manually (rather than using the Subtotals command). Write a ½ page summary of the information you find out. Be sure to describe, in your own words, how to organize data to create an outline. Point out how to troubleshoot outlines that aren't working correctly. Save your work as *Manually Outlining Data.doc*.

Project 8

As an assistant to the accountant for a medium-sized accounting firm, you have been asked to ensure that the company's worksheets use consistent documentation. Create a "template" documentation page that you can copy and paste into each of the company's many Excel files, similar to the documentation sheet in the *Sweet Tooth Sales Rep Data* worksheet you used in this chapter. Be creative in your use of fonts and colors to make the documentation page easy to read and follow, and interesting to look at. Save your workbook as *Documentation Template*.

chapter three

4.a Previewing and Modifying Page Setup Options

Previewing worksheets and setting page setup options are important tasks when it comes to printing worksheets. Because spreadsheets aren't really shaped like pages, and because *each* worksheet can hold as many as 256 columns and 65,536 rows, your poor printer may be working overtime. Before you can print calendars for next week's planning meeting, you need to preview the print job and modify the page setup options.

Setting the Print Area

The *12 Month Calendar* workbook contains a calendar you can print for Sweet Tooth's semi-annual meeting. To open and save the calendar file:

Step 1	*Start*	Excel
Step 2	*Open*	the *12 Month Calendar* workbook from your Data Disk
Step 3	*Save*	the workbook as *12 Month Calendar Revised*

The month titles in this calendar are formatted with the Month-YY date format. By default, Excel prints all data on the current worksheet. If you need to print only a portion of a worksheet, however, you can define a print area using the Set Print Area command. To set the print area:

Step 1	*Select*	cells A1:G18
Step 2	*Click*	File
Step 3	*Point to*	Print Area
Step 4	*Click*	Set Print Area

This action defines a print area covering the months January-99 and February-99.

Using Print Preview

You should always preview your print jobs before sending them to the printer. To preview the print area:

Step 1	*Click*	the Print Preview button  on the Standard toolbar

chapter
four

If your computer is attached to a color printer, your print preview appears in color; otherwise, the print preview is in black and white. See Figure 4-1. The Print Preview toolbar appears at the top of the window. The status bar indicates the number of pages in the print job.

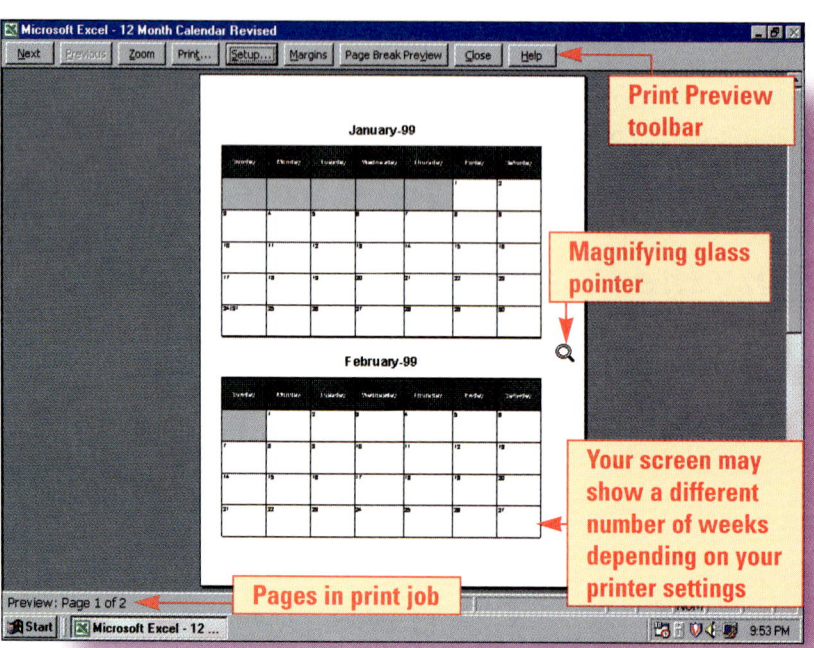

| Step 2 | *Click* | the Next button on the Print Preview toolbar to view the next page in the print job |

As you can see, page 2 of the print job contains one row (or two rows, depending on your printer) of the calendar.

Changing Page Orientation and Scale

The Page Setup dialog box provides many settings through which you can arrange the page, including scaling, orientation, and paper size settings. Scaling a document allows you to fit a report to a certain number of pages. For Sweet Tooth's meeting notes, the January and February calendars should fit on a single page. To scale a print job:

| Step 1 | *Click* | the Setup button on the Print Preview toolbar |
| Step 2 | *Click* | the Page tab, if necessary |

The Page Setup dialog box is shown in Figure 4-2.

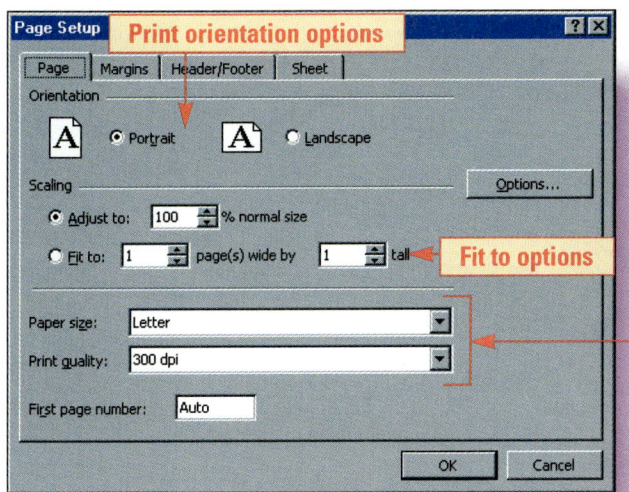

FIGURE 4-2
Page Tab of Page Setup
Dialog Box

Step 3	*Click*	the Fit to: option button
Step 4	*Verify*	that the Fit to: boxes are set to 1
Step 5	*Click*	OK

The print job scales the print area so that it fits on a single page, which you can see by looking at the Print Preview window.

Most business documents, including letters, memos, and financial reports are printed in **portrait orientation**, or across the width of the page. In working with Excel, you may find **landscape orientation** more suitable, because it prints across the length of the page, as if you were holding the paper sideways. To change the orientation:

Step 1	*Click*	the Setup button on the Print Preview toolbar
Step 2	*Click*	the Landscape option button
Step 3	*Click*	OK

The worksheet appears in landscape orientation. You decide this print job will look better in portrait orientation.

Step 4	*Switch*	back to Portrait orientation, as shown in Figure 4-3

MENU TIP

You can access the Page Setup dialog box from the File menu by clicking Page Setup.

chapter
four

FIGURE 4-3
Portrait Orientation

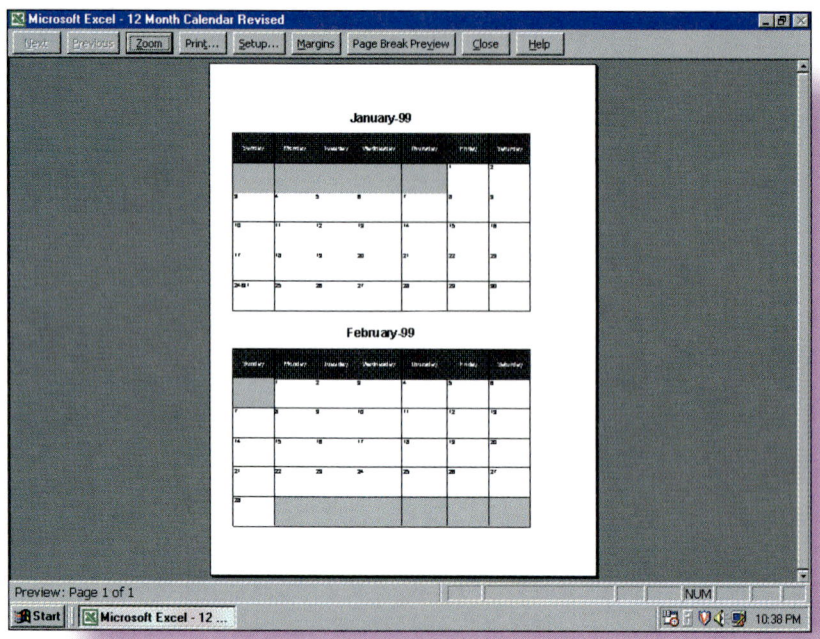

Setting Page Margins and Centering

Sweet Tooth's calendar is not centered on the page, so you want to adjust its margins. To adjust the margins in print preview:

Step 1	*Click*	the <u>M</u>argins button on the Print Preview toolbar

Vertical and horizontal lines appear on your preview page, indicating the left, right, top, and bottom margins, as well as the header and footer margins. Tick marks at the top indicate worksheet column widths. Your screen should look similar to Figure 4-4.

FIGURE 4-4
Adjusting Margins

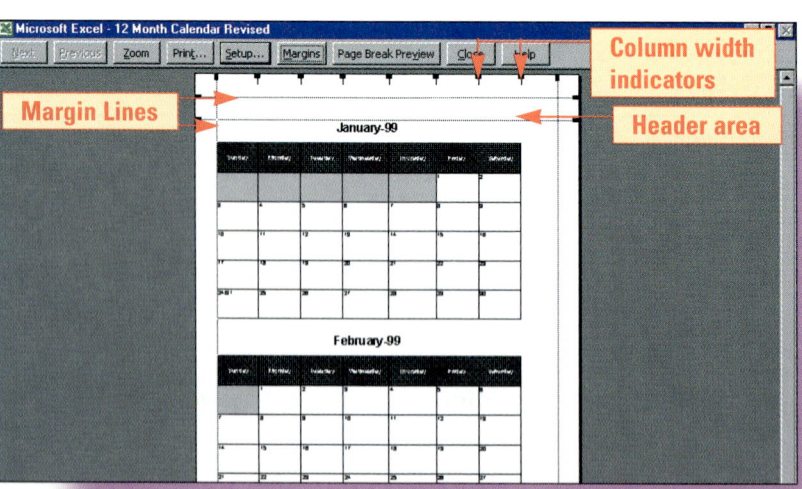

You can change the margins by clicking the line and dragging it to a new location. As you drag the margin, watch the status bar, which indicates the margin setting.

| Step 2 | *Drag* | the right margin line to the left until the status bar reads Right Margin: 1.00 |
| Step 3 | *Click* | the Margins button on the Print Preview toolbar |

The margin lines disappear. You want to center each page of the calendar. To do this, you must use the Margins tab of the Page Setup dialog box. To center a print area on the page:

| Step 1 | *Click* | the Setup button on the Print Preview toolbar |
| Step 2 | *Click* | the Margins tab |

See Figure 4-5. You can use the Margins tab to set margins precisely and to specify centering options.

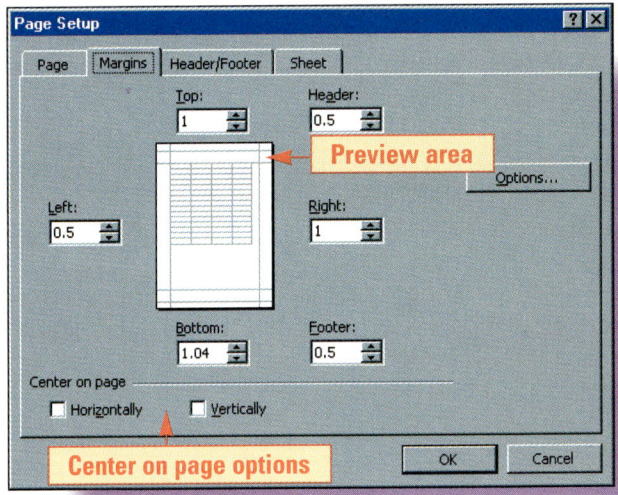

FIGURE 4-5
Margins Tab of Page Setup
Dialog Box

Step 3	*Click*	the Horizontally check box in the Center on page section
Step 4	*Click*	the Vertically check box in the Center on page section
Step 5	*Double-click*	in the Right: margin box
Step 6	*Enter*	0.5
Step 7	*Click*	OK

chapter
four

Excel updates the print preview so that it now displays the months centered on the page. You add a header and footer to your print job.

Setting Up a Header and Footer

Headers and footers appear on every page of your print job. A **header** appears above the top margin of every page you print. A **footer** appears below the bottom margin of every page you print. Excel has several predefined headers and footers, using the most common options. You can also create a custom header and footer. You can specify separate font options for the header and footer. In addition to including any desired text, you can insert special codes that print the date, time, page number, filename, or sheet tab name in either the header or footer. To add a predefined header:

Step 1	*Click*	the Setup button on the Print Preview toolbar
Step 2	*Click*	the Header/Footer tab
Step 3	*Click*	the Header: list arrow

The Header list contains preset headers to print the current page number, filename, user name, company name, current page number, and total number of pages in the print job, as well as several variations and combinations of these elements.

Step 4	*Click*	12 Month Calendar Revised

This choice will print the filename as the header. The mini-preview above the Header list shows what your header will look like. To add a custom footer to your document:

Step 1	*Click*	Custom Footer

The Footer dialog box opens. The Header and Footer dialog boxes, which look identical, contain buttons to insert special print codes. Table 4-1 lists the function of each of these buttons.

Text you enter in the left section will be left-aligned, text in the center box will be center-aligned, and text in the right section will be right-aligned.

Step 2	*Key*	*Your Name* in the Left section: box
Step 3	*Click*	in the Right section: box

To	Use	Code Inserted
Change the text font	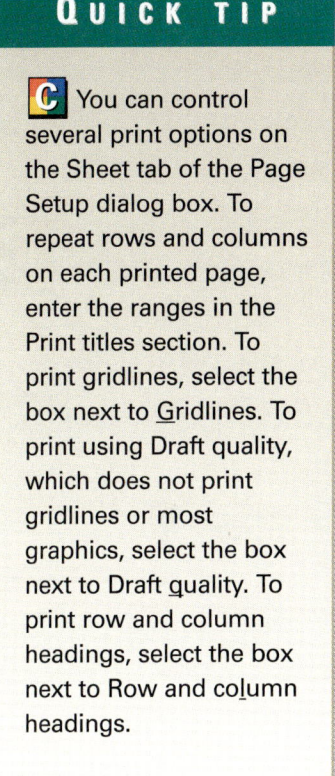	
Insert a page number		&[Page]
Insert the total number of pages		&[Pages]
Insert the current date		&[Date]
Insert the current time		&[Time]
Insert the workbook filename		&[File]
Insert the worksheet tab name		&[Tab]

TABLE 4-1
Button Functions

Step 4	*Click*	the Date button
Step 5	*Click*	in the Center section: box
Step 6	*Click*	the Page Number button
Step 7	*Press*	the SPACEBAR
Step 8	*Key*	of
Step 9	*Press*	the SPACEBAR
Step 10	*Click*	the Total Pages button (see Figure 4-6)

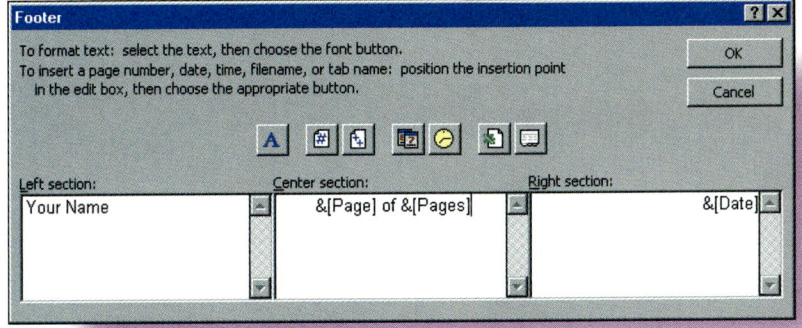

FIGURE 4-6
Header/Footer Dialog Box

| Step 11 | *Click* | OK |

Your footer appears in the Footer list box, and the mini-preview below the Footer list box shows what the footer will look like.

Step 12	*Click*	OK to apply the header and footer

Now print the print area you set earlier. To print a print area:

Step 1	*Click*	the Print button on the Print Preview toolbar
Step 2	*Click*	OK to print the print area and return to Normal view

Clearing a Print Area

The January and February calendars print. When the Print dialog box closes, Print Preview closes as well and you return to the worksheet. You can now clear the print area. To clear the print area and restore the print scale:

Step 1	*Click*	File
Step 2	*Point to*	Print Area
Step 3	*Click*	Clear Print Area
Step 4	*Open*	the Page setup dialog box
Step 5	*Click*	the Page tab
Step 6	*Click*	the Adjust to: option button
Step 7	*Key*	100 in the Adjust to: box
Step 8	*Click*	OK
Step 9	*Press*	the CTRL + HOME keys

4.b Inserting and Removing Page Breaks

When printing multiple page print jobs, you may need to adjust the position of page breaks so that information appears on the correct page. To do this, you use Page Break Preview mode. For Sweet Tooth's meeting, you would like to print all the calendars for 1999 two to a page. To change the worksheet view to Page Break Preview:

Step 1	*Click*	View

Step 2	*Click*	Page Break Preview

The Welcome to Page Break Preview dialog box might appear, containing instructions for adjusting page breaks.

Step 3	*Click*	OK to close the Welcome to Page Break Preview dialog box if it appears on your screen

See Figure 4-7. Dashed blue lines represent Excel's automatic page breaks. A light gray page number indicates the order in which pages will print. You can drag the page break to a new location to change how pages are printed.

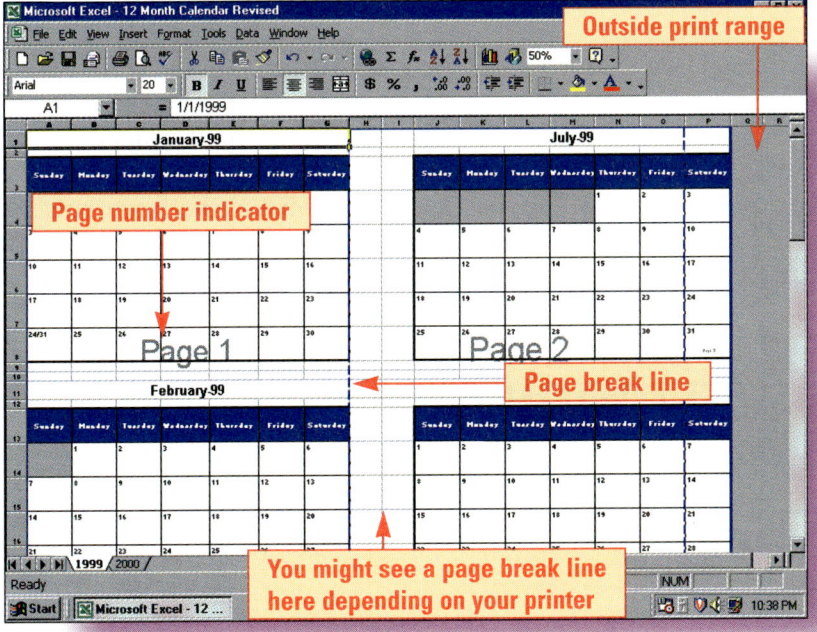

FIGURE 4-7
Page Break Preview Mode

MOUSE TIP

You can insert or remove page breaks by right-clicking in the Page Break Preview window. Select Insert Page Break to insert additional page breaks above and to the left of the active cell. Right-click a cell to the right of a vertical page break or below a horizontal page break and then select Remove Page Break to remove page breaks. You can also select Reset All Page Breaks to return to Excel's default page breaks.

Step 4	*Scroll*	the worksheet to view rows 16–24
Step 5	*Drag*	the first horizontal page break between rows 20 and 21

The dashed blue line changes to a solid blue line, representing a manually adjusted page break. Notice that the page break between columns G and H automatically shifted.

Step 6	*Drag*	the dashed blue page break line between columns I and J to columns H and I

chapter four

| Step 7 | *Scroll* | the worksheet to verify that the other page break appears between rows 40 and 41 |

Your calendar will now print as two months per page.

| Step 8 | *Click* | the Print Preview button [icon] on the Standard toolbar |
| Step 9 | *Click* | the Close button on the Print Preview toolbar |

To return to Normal view:

| Step 1 | *Click* | View |
| Step 2 | *Click* | Normal |

Returning to Normal worksheet view, you see dotted black lines indicating the page break settings. Because Sweet Tooth's meeting will cover long-range planning for two years, you need to print calendars from both tabs of the workbook. Until now, you have been working with areas on only one worksheet. In the next section, you learn how to print multiple worksheets.

4.c Printing an Entire Workbook

As noted earlier, you can print an area of a worksheet, an entire worksheet, or an entire workbook. You have already learned how to print a named range, how to clear the print area, and how to set page breaks for an entire worksheet. You still need to print all the months from both worksheets for the planning meeting, however. Before you can print the year 2000 calendars, you should check the page breaks on that worksheet.

To print the entire workbook:

| Step 1 | *Click* | File |
| Step 2 | *Click* | Print |

The Print dialog box opens, as shown in Figure 4-8.

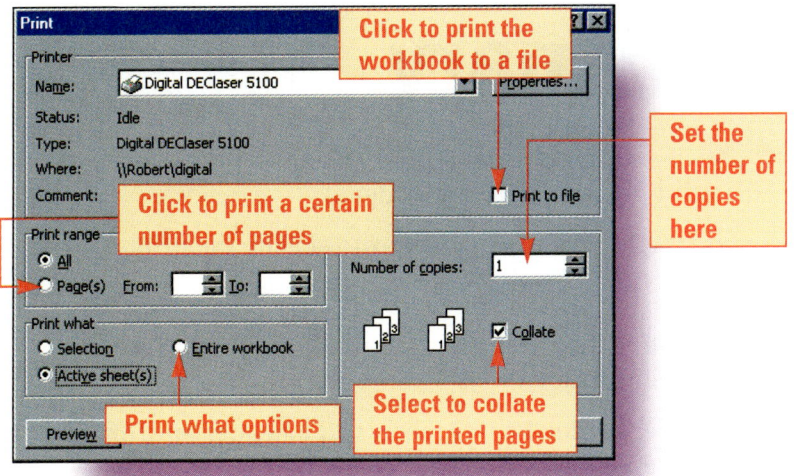

Step 3	*Click*	the Entire workbook option button in the Print what section
Step 4	*Click*	the up spin arrow in the Number of copies: box, to change it to 2
Step 5	*Click*	Preview at the bottom of the dialog box
Step 6	*Verify*	that the pages will print as desired
Step 7	*Verify*	that your instructor wants you to print two copies of all 12 pages

notes

Because you're not really going into a meeting, your instructor probably doesn't want to print two copies of all 12 pages. At this point, you can change the Number of copies back to 1, click the Page(s) option button, key 1 in the From: box, click in the To: box, and key 2. Excel will then print one copy of the first two pages of the workbook. Alternatively, you can click the Print to file check box, then click OK to open the Print To File dialog box. Key a filename in the File name: box, verify the drive and directory location, then click OK. If you print the workbook to a file, skip to step 10.

Step 8	*Click*	the Print button on the Print Preview toolbar
Step 9	*Save*	your workbook
Step 10	*Close*	the *12 Month Calendar Revised* workbook

You're all set for the meeting!

MENU TIP

You can print a selected area or a worksheet without setting the print area. If you want to print a worksheet, click Print on the File menu, then click the Active sheet(s) option button in the Print what group. If you want to print a selection, select the area you want to print, then click Print on the File menu. Click the Selection option button in the Print what group, then click OK.

QUICK TIP

The Collate check box in the Print dialog box organizes the order of your print job. When the Collate option is checked, Excel prints a complete copy of the document before starting the next copy.

**chapter
four**

Summary

▶ Preview worksheets and print options before printing. Zoom in on a print preview to see more detail.

▶ Use the Page Setup dialog box to specify the print options.

▶ Use the Page tab to set the print job's orientation and scaling options.

▶ Use the Margins tab to adjust margin settings and select page centering options.

▶ Use the Header/Footer tab to add a header and/or footer to a print report.

▶ Use the Sheet tab to select print areas, select draft quality, and toggle gridline and row and column heading printing.

▶ Work in Page Break view to manually adjust page breaks.

▶ Print selected areas by selecting File, Print area, then Set Print Area.

▶ Print a workbook by clearing print areas. Select Entire Workbook from the Print dialog box.

Commands Review

Action	Menu Bar	Shortcut Menu	Toolbar	Keyboard
Preview the printed workbook	File, Print Preview			ALT + F, V
Display Page Setup dialog box	File, Page Setup			ALT + F, U
View page breaks	View, Page Break Preview			ALT + V, P
View normal worksheet	View, Normal			ALT + V, N
Print	File, Print			CTRL + P ALT + F, P

Concepts Review

Circle the correct answer.

1. To select multiple ranges for printing, press and hold the _____ key while selecting areas.
[a] SHIFT
[b] END
[c] CTRL
[d] ALT

2. To set centering options for a print report, use the _____ tab of the Page Setup dialog box.
[a] Page
[b] Margins
[c] Header/Footer
[d] Sheet

3. To set a page to print in landscape orientation, use the _____ tab of the Page Setup dialog box.
[a] Page
[b] Margins
[c] Header/Footer
[d] Sheet

4. What does the print formula &[Page] do when you include it in a header or footer?
[a] Prints **&[Page]** on every page.
[b] Prints the total page count on every page.
[c] Prints the current page number on each page.
[d] Prints a box where you can write in the page number by hand.

5. In Normal view, page breaks are indicated by a:
[a] heavy blue line.
[b] heavy black line.
[c] dotted black line.
[d] thin blue line.

6. In Page Break Preview view, default page breaks are indicated by a:
[a] dotted blue line.
[b] heavy black line.

[c] solid blue line.
[d] thin blue line.

7. You just printed a named range, January. Now you need to print the entire worksheet. When you switch to Print Preview, however, all you see is the January range. What should you do?
[a] Close Print Preview, then try opening Print Preview again to see whether the problem goes away.
[b] Click the Print button and hope it prints correctly.
[c] Clear the print area.
[d] Click the Margins button on the Print Preview toolbar and widen the margins.

8. You set up page breaks on Sheet1 of a workbook and select Entire workbook from the Print dialog box. Sheet2 doesn't print correctly. What should you do?
[a] Click the Print button again to see whether the problem goes away.
[b] Check to see whether the printer is working properly.
[c] Clear the print area.
[d] Use Page Break Preview mode to check page breaks for both worksheets.

9. To set collating options for a print job, you use the:
[a] Page Setup dialog box.
[b] Page Break Preview.
[c] Print dialog box.
[d] Options button in the Page Setup dialog box.

10. When you manually adjust page break lines, what is displayed?
[a] dotted blue line
[b] heavy black line
[c] solid blue line
[d] thin blue line

chapter four

Circle **T** if the statement is true or **F** if the statement is false.

T   F   1. You should always preview before you print.

T   F   2. Clicking the Print button on the Standard toolbar displays the Print dialog box.

T   F   3. The dotted black page preview lines cannot be turned off.

T   F   4. To center a print area on a page, you must drag it in the Print Preview window until it looks centered.

T   F   5. Once you change page break locations, you can't undo them.

T   F   6. You can see page breaks only in Page Break Preview mode.

T   F   7. You can scroll in a zoomed Print Preview window using the ARROW keys.

T   F   8. Headers and footers must use the same font.

T   F   9. You can set margins in the Print Preview window or by pressing the Margin tab of the Page Setup dialog box.

T   F   10. You need to set footer options for each page in your printed report.

Skills Review

Exercise 1

1. Open the file *24 Month Calendar* from your Data Disk.

2. Set the view to Page Break preview.

3. Select the January-00, February-00, and March-00 calendars.

4. Set the print area with these ranges selected.

5. Print preview your report.

6. Give this multiple selection the name Qtr1_2000 in the Name Box for printing later.

7. Print the report if instructed to do so.

8. Change the view to Normal view.

9. Activate cell A1.

10. Save the workbook as *24 Month Calendar Revised 1*.

Exercise 2

1. Open the *24 Month Calendar Revised 1* workbook that you created in Exercise 1.

2. Insert the filename as the header.

3. Modify the header by clicking Custom Header; select the text in the center section, then change the text to 16 point, bold.

4. Set the May-99 calendar as the print area using the Name Box to select the range.

5. Center the print area vertically and horizontally.

6. Preview your print job.

7. Print the report if instructed to do so.

8. Save the workbook as *24 Month Calendar Revised 2*.

Exercise 3

1. Open the *24 Month Calendar Revised 2* workbook that you created in Exercise 2.

2. Set up a named range covering all months of 2000. Name this range Year2000.

3. Set this area as the print area.

4. Use the Fit to option to print all of the calendars on one page.

5. Set the print options to center the calendars vertically and horizontally.

6. Print the report if instructed to do so.

7. Save the workbook as *24 Month Calendar Revised 3*.

Exercise 4

1. Open the *24 Month Calendar Revised 3* workbook that you created in Exercise 3.

2. Set July99 as the print area.

3. Set the page orientation to landscape.

4. Scale to 125%.

5. Print the report if instructed to do so.

6. Save the workbook as *24 Month Calendar Revised 4*.

Exercise 5

1. You will be distributing the *24 Month Calendar Revised* to all employees in your company. Write a step-by-step description explaining how to print the January-99 calendar only. Save the document as *Printing a Calendar*. Include the following instructions:

    a. Explain how to add "1999" as the header for the printed report.

    b. Explain how to print the calendar in landscape orientation.

2. Print your document or e-mail it to a classmate. Have your classmate follow your directions *exactly* and print the report. See how well he or she was able to follow your instructions.

3. Save your document as *Printing a Calendar.doc*.

Exercise 6

1. Open the *Sweet Tooth Q2 1998 Sales* workbook on your Data Disk.

2. Set print options to print the worksheet centered horizontally and vertically using Portrait orientation.

3. Print the worksheet.

chapter four

4. Set print options to print the worksheet centered horizontally but not vertically using Landscape orientation.

5. Print the worksheet.

6. Save the workbook as *Sweet Tooth Q2 1998 Sales Revised*.

Exercise 7

1. Open the *Sweet Tooth Q2 1998 Sales Revised* workbook you created in Exercise 6.

2. Change the print options to print gridlines and row and column headings.

3. Create a custom footer displaying the filename on the left, date in the center, and time on the right.

4. Print the worksheet.

5. Save the workbook as *Sweet Tooth Q2 1998 Sales Revised 2*.

Exercise 8

1. Open the *Sweet Tooth Q2 1998 Sales Revised 2* workbook you created in Exercise 7.

2. Set the print scale to 150%.

3. Set the print quality to Draft quality on the Sheet tab.

4. Print the worksheet.

5. Save the workbook as *Sweet Tooth Q2 1998 Sales Revised 3*.

Case Projects

Project 1

Your job is to train employees in the use of Excel. Search the Internet for Excel tips to include in your weekly "Excel Training Letter." Select one tip and create a Word document of at least two paragraphs describing it. Provide the URL of any sites that you used as references for your tip. Save the document as *Excel Training Letter.doc*.

Project 2

As part of your job, you track inventory at a used car dealership. You must record the number of cars sold by type per month. Create a worksheet providing data on at least four different makes of cars. Enter fictitious data for sales of each make of car for a period of four months. Sort the list by make of car, and then print it. Rearrange the data to display the months in order, then print the list again. (*Hint:* Add an index column in front of the month column with the number of each month next to the month name—for example, January=1, February=2, and so on.) Save the workbook as *Car Sales*.

Project 3

You're an office manager for a busy construction company. You have a lot of names, phone numbers, and addresses to manage. Create a worksheet containing the following column headings: Last Name, First Name, Address, City, State, Zip, Phone number. Enter fictitious data for 20 people. Your data should use at least four but not more than six states. Sort the list by state, then move the records for each state to separate worksheets (insert new worksheets as necessary). Be sure to copy the column headings and name tabs. Print the entire workbook. Save the workbook as *Phone List*.

Project 4

You are a travel agent. To stay competitive, you use the Internet to find out about your competitors' offers. Use the Web toolbar to locate at least three Web sites offering five- to seven-night packages to Cancun, Mexico. Print pages showing information about each of these packages.

Project 5

You are interested in increasing your productivity while using Excel. Using Office Assistant, search for the topic "keyboard shortcuts." Print one of the pages containing keyboard shortcuts for any of the shortcut key categories. Instructions for printing are included on each page in the Help file.

Project 6

As manager of a growing software company, you want to begin selling your products over the Internet. Use the Web toolbar to search for information regarding secure transactions over the Internet. (*Hint:* Search for the Secure Sockets Layer [SSL] protocol.) Write a two-paragraph document in Word describing what SSL is and how it works. Save your document as *Secure Transactions.doc*.

Project 7

In order to be better organized, you decide to create a day planner. Create a worksheet that breaks the day into 1-hour segments starting from when you get up in the morning to when you go to bed at night. Fill in the planner with your usual schedule for seven days. Print the worksheet(s). Save the workbook as *Day Planner*.

Project 8

You are the accounts manager of a graphic design company. Create a list of 10 clients who owe your company money. Use fictitious client names and amounts due (between $500 and $2,000). Add a column indicating how many days the account is overdue. Sort the list by the number of days the account is overdue. Print the worksheet. Save the workbook as *Overdue Accounts*.

chapter four

Creating Charts

Chapter Overview

As more information becomes available to us, the skills of analyzing and summarizing information are even more vital today than they were in past years. Charts offer a great way to summarize and present data, providing a colorful, graphic link to numerical data collected in worksheets. Creating such an explicit relationship helps other people analyze trends, spot inconsistencies in business performance, and evaluate market share.

Case profile

Each quarter, Sweet Tooth's regional managers meet with the company president, Amy Lee, to review sales figures and set goals for the next quarter. You have collected data from each of the region offices and are now ready to compile a report for the meeting. You decide to use charts to show the company's final sales figures.

5.a Using Chart Wizard to Create a Chart

A chart provides a graphical interface to numerical data contained in a worksheet. Almost anyone can appreciate and understand the colorful simplicity of a chart. The data found in the *Sweet Tooth Sales Rep Data Q1 1999* workbook represents Sweet Tooth's sales for the first quarter. Your job is to create and format a chart for use in tomorrow's sales meeting. To open the workbook and save it with a new name:

Step 1	*Start*	Excel
Step 2	*Open*	the *Sweet Tooth Sales Rep Data Q1 1999* workbook from your Data Disk
Step 3	*Save*	the workbook as *Sweet Tooth Sales Rep Data Q1 1999 Revised*

Excel's Chart Wizard walks you step-by-step through a series of four dialog box boxes to quickly create a chart. You can create charts as separate workbook sheets called **chart sheets**, or you can place them directly on the worksheet page as **embedded charts**. One type of chart, called a column chart, helps you compare values across categories. To create a chart using the Chart Wizard:

Step 1	*Activate*	cell A5 on the Summary worksheet
Step 2	*Click*	the Chart Wizard button 📊 on the Standard toolbar

See Figure 5-1. In step 1, you select the type of chart you want to create from the list of chart types on the left side of the dialog box. Clicking a chart type on the left displays chart subtypes on the right side of the dialog box. A description of the chart subtype is given beneath the preview window. You decide to create three-dimensional charts, which provide an interesting visual alternative to two-dimensional charts.

Step 3	*Verify*	that Column is selected in the <u>C</u>hart type: list
Step 4	*Click*	the Clustered column with a 3-D visual effect from the Chart sub-<u>t</u>ype: box
Step 5	*Click*	Next >

chapter five

FIGURE 5-1
Step 1 of the Chart Wizard

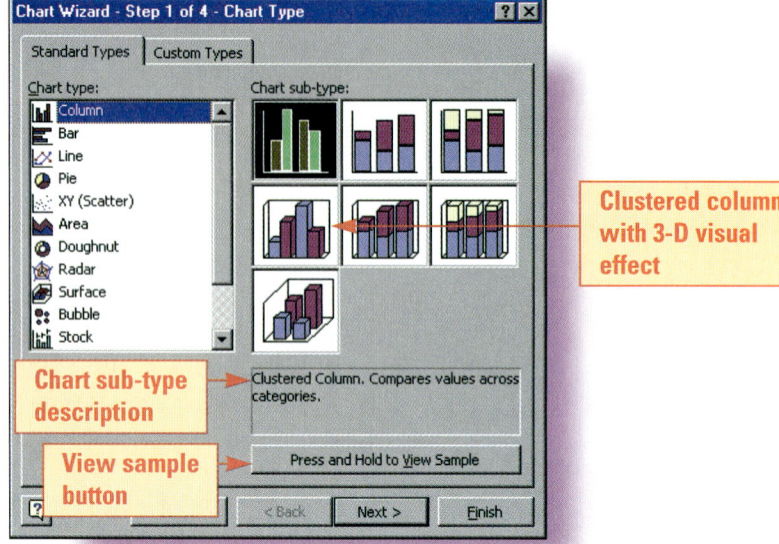

In step 2, you select or modify the chart's source data. A preview of the selected data appears at the top of the Data Range tab. Notice the moving, dotted line border around the range in the worksheet in the background.

| Step 6 | *Click* | Next > |

Step 3 of the Chart Wizard appears with the Titles tab on top. See Figure 5-2. In this step, you enter chart options such as titles, legends, and data labels. Each type of chart produces different tabs here.

FIGURE 5-2
Step 3 of the Chart Wizard

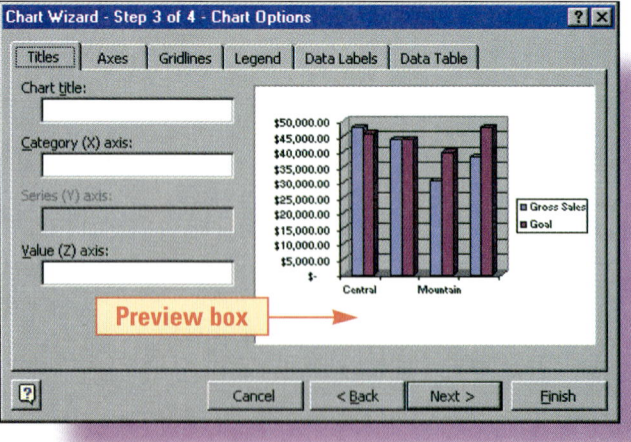

Step 7	*Click*	in the Chart title: box
Step 8	*Key*	Gross Sales by Region
Step 9	*Press*	the TAB key to move to the Category (X) axis: box
Step 10	*Key*	Region Name
Step 11	*Click*	the Legend tab
Step 12	*Click*	the Bottom option button
Step 13	*Click*	Next >

See Figure 5-3. In step 4 of the Chart Wizard, you specify the location of the new chart. You can create the chart as a new sheet or as an object in another worksheet.

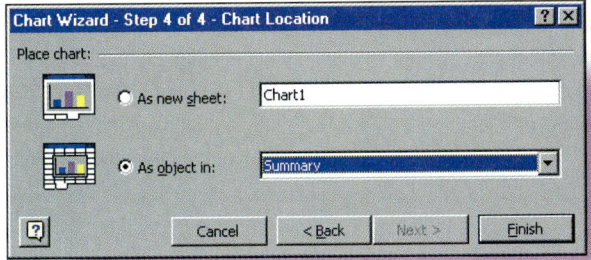

FIGURE 5-3
Step 4 of the Chart Wizard

Step 14	*Click*	the As new sheet: option button
Step 15	*Key*	Gross Sales by Region Chart in the As new sheet: box
Step 16	*Click*	Finish

The chart appears on a new worksheet in your workbook. See Figure 5-4.

When you create a chart, the Chart toolbar appears, and the Chart menu replaces the Data menu in the menu bar. The Chart menu and Chart toolbar contain chart-specific tools to aid in the creation and modification of charts and the elements that make up the chart, called **chart objects**. To enhance the chart even more for Sweet Tooth's meeting, you can modify the formatting of individual chart objects.

MOUSE TIP

You can change the chart to a different type any time. Right-click the chart you want to change, then click Chart Type. Select a new chart type and subtype, then click OK.

chapter
five

FIGURE 5-4
Chart Created with
Chart Wizard

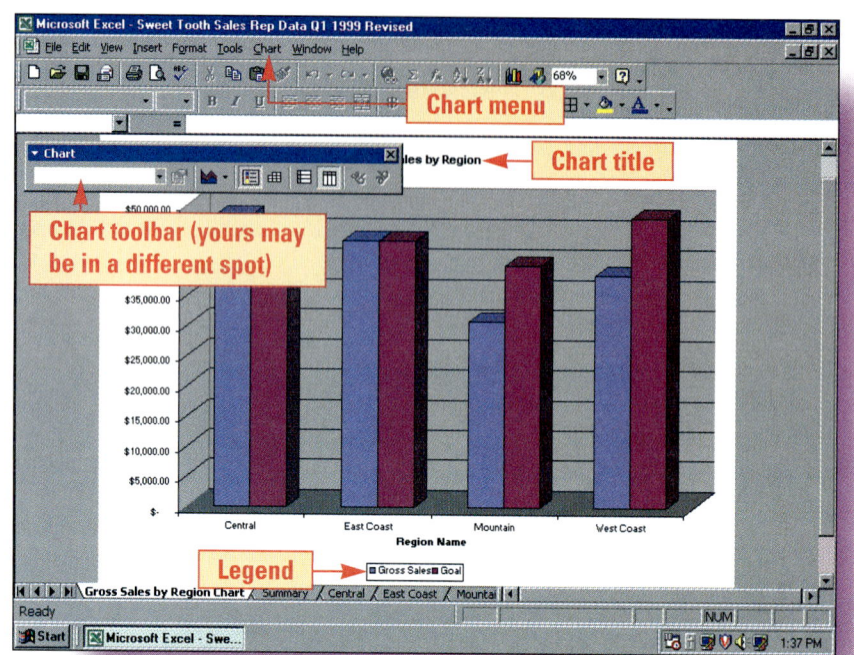

MOUSE TIP

You can change the location of a chart by right-clicking the chart and clicking Location.

MENU TIP

Do you use a certain type of chart most of the time? You can change the default chart type. First, create a chart. From the Chart menu, click Chart Type. Choose the type of chart and the subtype that you use most often, then click Set as default chart at the bottom of the dialog box.

5.b Formatting and Modifying a Chart

Every element of a chart, such as the title, legend, and plot area, is considered an object. An **object** is a graphical element added to a worksheet that you can manipulate, by moving, resizing or reformatting. Some of the more important chart objects are defined here. The **legend** is a key used to identify the colors assigned to categories in a chart. **Tick marks** are small marks on the edges of the chart that delineate the scale or separate the data categories. **Data points** represent the numerical data in your worksheet. In the current chart type, the data points are represented by horizontal bars. Data points, however, can also be represented by bars, columns, pie slices, and a variety of other shapes and marks. A **data series** represents all related data points in a set. On Sweet Tooth's chart, the Gross Sales bars are a data series, as are the Goal bars. The **plot area** of a chart is the area including only the chart itself. **Data labels** identify the data points with the category name, the data values, or the percentages.

Each chart object can be formatted by double-clicking the object, or right-clicking the object, then clicking F_ormat *object* (*object* is the name of the object you selected, such as legend). The Format dialog box displays options unique to each object.

Changing Chart Fonts

You can change font settings for all text on the chart simultaneously, or you can select individual text objects and then customize their font settings. For Sweet Tooth's chart, the title should stand out from the other elements of the chart. To change fonts for individual objects:

| Step 1 | *Move* | the pointer over the Chart Title object at the top of the chart to see the ScreenTip |
| Step 2 | *Double-click* | the Chart Title object |

Double-clicking any chart object opens the Format dialog box for that object.

Step 3	*Click*	the Font tab in the Format Chart Title dialog box
Step 4	*Select*	Impact from the Font: list
Step 5	*Select*	20 from the Size: list
Step 6	*Click*	the Color: list arrow
Step 7	*Click*	Red
Step 8	*Click*	the Patterns tab
Step 9	*Click*	the Automatic option button in the Border group
Step 10	*Click*	OK
Step 11	*Press*	the ESC key to deselect the Chart Title object

The chart title is now formatted with your selections. Next, you learn to format the Legend object.

Formatting the Axes

You can modify both axes of the chart. The **category axis**, sometimes called the *x*-axis, is the axis along which you normally plot categories of data. The **value axis** is the axis along which you plot values associated with various categories of data. The value axis is the *y*-axis in two-dimensional charts, but the *z*-axis in three-dimensional charts. In bar charts in Excel, the category axis serves as the vertical axis and the value axis represents the horizontal axis.

Excel gives you full control over the scale of the axes, the number format, and the appearance of the axis labels. You decide to modify

chapter
five

When a chart object is selected, you can cycle to other chart objects by pressing the ARROW keys. The UP and DOWN ARROW keys cycle through major chart objects such as Chart Title, Data Series, Plot Area, and Chart Area. The LEFT and RIGHT ARROW keys cycle through minor chart objects, such as Legend, Value Axis, and individual data points.

the number format of the value axis by dropping the decimal amount. To modify the value axis scale:

Step 1	**Double-click**	the value axis
Step 2	**Click**	the Number tab in the Format Axis dialog box
Step 3	**Click**	the down spin arrow next to <u>D</u>ecimal places: twice to set it to 0
Step 4	**Click**	OK

Your screen should look similar to Figure 5-5.

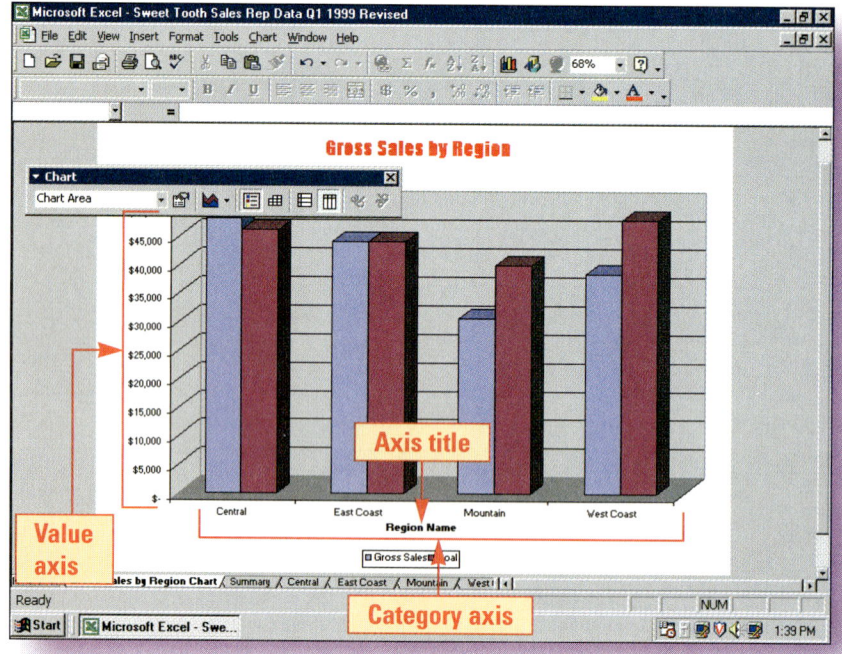

FIGURE 5-5
Changing Value Scale
Options

Data labels show the exact values of data points on a chart. You can add data labels by right-clicking the data series, then clicking the Data Labels tab. Select an option button, then click OK.

Adding a Data Table to a Chart

A **data table** displays the actual data used to create the chart. Sometimes you may find it helpful to show this information on the chart worksheet. To add a data table to the chart:

Step 1	**Click**	the Data Table button ⊞ on the Chart toolbar

The data table is added beneath the value axis, as shown in Figure 5-6.

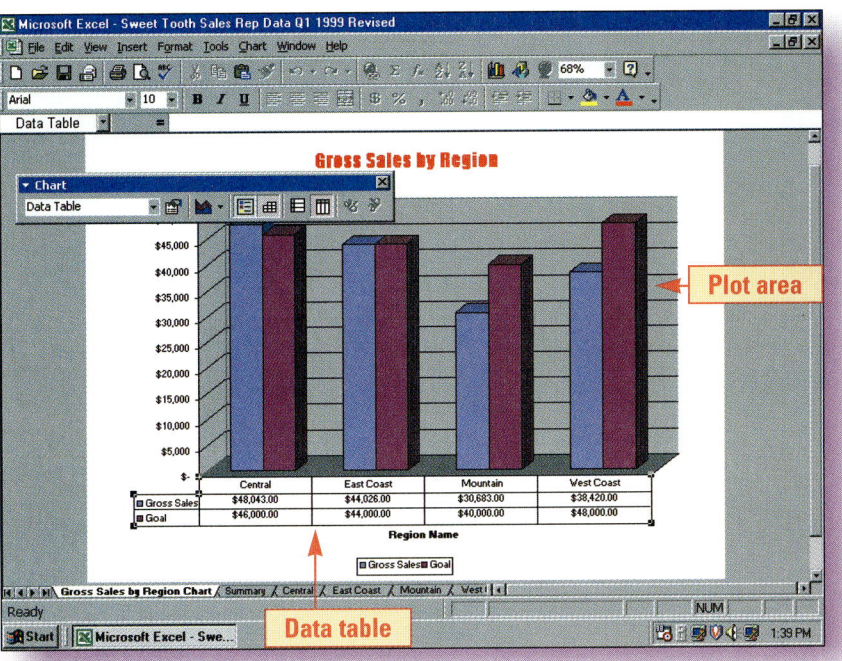

FIGURE 5-6
Adding a Data Table to
a Chart

MOUSE TIP

Some types of charts
allow you to do
interesting things with
the data points. For
example, you can drag
a "slice" of a pie chart
away from the rest of the
"pie" by clicking the slice
once to select the data
series. Click the slice
again to select the
individual point, then
drag the slice to its new
location.

| Step 2 | **Save** | your workbook |

The Gross Sales by Region chart is complete. In the next section, you
print the chart for your upcoming meeting.

5.c Previewing and Printing Charts

Before you print your chart for the meeting, you should preview it in
Print Preview to make sure that everything looks the way you expected.
You can preview a chart, change print setup options, and print the
chart from the Print Preview window. To change chart printing options:

| Step 1 | **Click** | the Print Preview button on the Standard toolbar |

The chart appears in print preview. If your default printer is a color
printer, the preview will show the chart in color; otherwise, you will
see a black-and-white preview of your chart. Your screen should look
similar to Figure 5-7.

chapter
five

FIGURE 5-7
Previewing the Chart

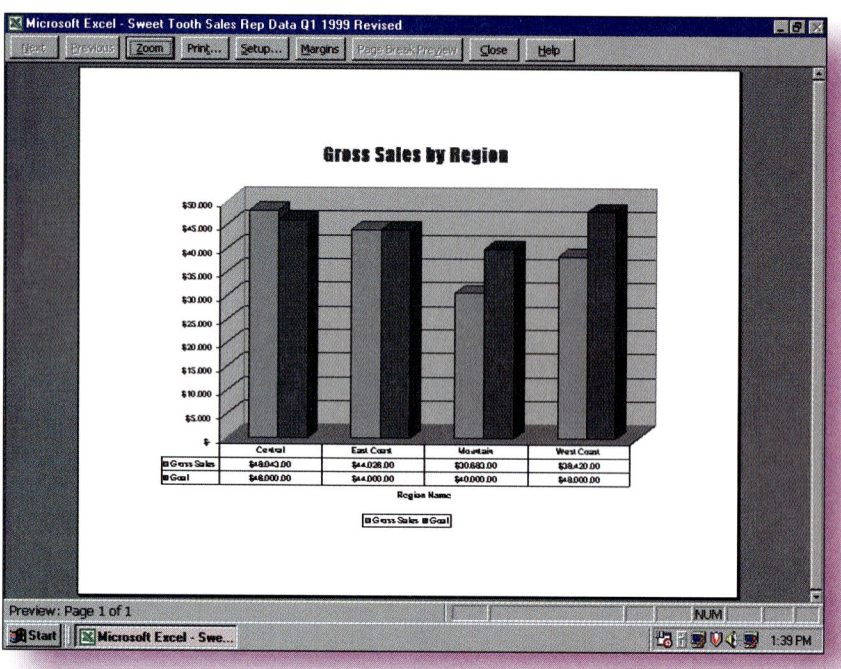

FIGURE 5-7
Previewing the Chart

Step 2	*Click*	the Setup button on the Print Preview toolbar
Step 3	*Click*	the Chart tab
Step 4	*Click*	the Scale to fit page option button

This option scales the chart until either the height or the width of the chart hits a page margin. The Use full page option scales the chart until both the height and the width touch the page margins on all sides.

Step 5	*Click*	OK
Step 6	*Click*	the Print button on the Print Preview toolbar
Step 7	*Click*	OK
Step 8	*Save*	your workbook

5.d Working with Embedded Charts

An embedded chart appears in a worksheet rather than on a chart sheet by itself. Because an embedded chart "floats" over the data on a worksheet, it may cover data that you need to see. You can move an embedded chart by dragging it to a new location. In addition, you can resize the chart by clicking the size control handles and stretching the chart as desired. As with chart sheet charts, you can modify all chart objects.

The embedded chart on the West Coast worksheet has already been created for you. You decide to reposition the chart. To reposition the embedded chart:

Step 1	*Click*	the right end tab scroll button ▶|
Step 2	*Click*	the West Coast worksheet tab
Step 3	*Move*	the pointer over the chart until you see the Chart Area ScreenTip
Step 4	*Drag*	the chart to the right side of the data until it is approximately in the range D2:J19

To resize the embedded chart:

Step 1	*Move*	the pointer over the lower-right resize handle

The pointer changes to a two-headed sizing pointer.

Step 2	*Press & Hold*	the CTRL key
Step 3	*Drag*	the handle to shrink the chart until it approximately fills the range D3:J17

Using the CTRL key resizes the chart uniformly from the center.

Step 4	*Click*	the worksheet outside the chart object to deselect the chart object

The chart is deselected and you can edit the worksheet again.

Step 5	*Save*	your workbook and close it

With your printed chart in hand, you're ready for the sales meeting.

QUICK TIP

You can print an embedded chart by itself or with the data on the worksheet. To print an embedded chart by itself, select the chart by clicking it once, then click the Print Preview button on the Standard toolbar.

MOUSE TIP

To resize the chart proportionally from the edge, press and hold the SHIFT key while dragging a resize handle.

QUICK TIP

To delete an embedded chart, select the chart, then press the DELETE key. To delete a chart sheet, right-click the chart sheet tab, then click Delete.

chapter
five

Summary

▶ Use the Chart Wizard to create a chart. Create a new default chart by pressing the F11 key.

▶ Charts can be placed on a separate chart tab, or they can be embedded on a worksheet. You can move and resize embedded worksheets as you like. Chart locations can be changed at any time.

▶ Charts contain many types of objects, including titles, legends, data tables, and plot areas. Each of these objects can be formatted independently.

▶ Change formatting elements for all chart objects at any time by using the Format dialog box.

▶ Add a data table to a chart to show the actual data used to create the chart.

▶ Preview charts before printing them so you can set print options. Embedded charts can be printed separately or as part of the active worksheet.

Commands Review

Action	Menu Bar	Shortcut Menu	Toolbar	Keyboard
Use the Chart Wizard	Insert, Chart			ALT + I, H
Create a default chart				F11 ALT + F1
Format a selected chart object	Format, Selected (chart object name)	Right-click chart object, click Format (chart object name)		ALT + O, E CTRL + 1
Change chart type	Chart, Chart Type	Chart Type		ALT C + T
Change chart options	Chart, Chart Options	Chart Options		ALT C + O
Show Chart toolbar	View, Toolbars, Chart			ALT + V, T
Add a data table to a chart				

Concepts Review

Circle the correct answer.

1. A data label:
  [a] displays the name of a chart object when the pointer is over that object.
  [b] displays the actual data used to create a chart.
  [c] is a key used to identify patterns, colors, or symbols associated with data points on a chart.
  [d] supplies information about a data point.

2. A legend:
  [a] displays the name of a chart object when the pointer is over that object.
  [b] displays the actual data used to create a chart.
  [c] is a key used to identify patterns, colors, or symbols associated with data points on a chart.
  [d] can show the value of a data point on a chart.

3. To create a default chart, select the data range, then press the:
  [a] CTRL + 1 keys.
  [b] F4 key.
  [c] F11 key.
  [d] CTRL + C keys.

4. A data point:
  [a] represents a series of data.
  [b] represents a single value.
  [c] can be shown as a pie slice, column, bar, or other graphical representation.
  [d] both b and c.

5. Which of the following does *not* bring up the Format (chart object) properties dialog box?
  [a] Double-click (chart object)
  [b] Right-click (chart object), select Format (chart object)

  [c] Select object, click Edit, click Format (chart object)
  [d] Click the Chart Objects list arrow on the Chart toolbar to select the chart object, then click the Format (chart object) button on the Chart toolbar

6. The F11 shortcut key allows you to:
  [a] create an embedded chart.
  [b] choose whether to use the Chart Wizard.
  [c] create only a chart sheet chart.
  [d] create either an embedded chart or a chart sheet chart.

7. The Chart Wizard allows you to:
  [a] create either an embedded chart or a chart sheet chart.
  [b] create only an embedded chart.
  [c] create only a chart sheet chart.
  [d] change the data values used to create the chart.

8. If you change your mind while using the Chart Wizard, click:
  [a] Cancel and start over.
  [b] Finish, delete the chart, and start over.
  [c] Next >.
  [d] < Back.

9. To change the location of a chart, right-click the chart and select:
  [a] Chart Type.
  [b] Source Data.
  [c] Chart Options.
  [d] Location.

chapter five

Circle **T** if the statement is true or **F** if the statement is false.

T F 1. Charts make data easier to understand.

T F 2. Embedded charts cannot be moved on the worksheet.

T F 3. A data point is a graphical means of displaying numerical data.

T F 4. You cannot change the default chart style created when you press the F11 key.

T F 5. The Format (chart object) dialog box is the same no matter which object is selected.

T F 6. Once you create a chart on a chart sheet, you cannot change it into an embedded chart.

T F 7. A data table cannot be displayed on the same worksheet as a chart.

T F 8. Chart objects can be moved and modified.

T F 9. You cannot print an embedded chart by itself.

Skills Review

Exercise 1

1. Open the workbook *Sales Data* on your Data Disk.

2. Using the data on the Summary tab, create a new Clustered Column chart with a three-dimensional effect.

3. Title the chart "Sales by Region."

4. Insert the chart on a new chart sheet called "Sales by Region Chart."

5. Print the Sales by Region Chart.

6. Save the workbook as *Sales Data Revised*.

Exercise 2

1. Open the *Sales Data Revised* workbook that you created in Exercise 1.

2. Using the embedded chart on the West Coast tab, find two other types of charts that present the data in a clear manner.

3. Find two types of charts that make it more difficult to understand the data.

4. Using Microsoft Word, write at least two paragraphs describing why certain types of charts worked well to illustrate the data and why others did not. Try to discern from the chart type description what type of information is needed for each type of chart and why your data did or did not work.

5. Save the document as *Chart Types.doc.* and print it.

Exercise 3

1. Open the *Exports by Country* workbook on your Data Disk.

2. Activate cell A2.

3. Create a line with markers chart using the Chart Wizard.

4. Title the chart "Exports by Country."

5. Add "1999" to the Category (X) axis.

6. Create the chart as an object on Sheet1.

7. Preview and print your chart as part of the worksheet (move the chart or change the paper orientation if necessary).

8. Save the workbook as *Exports by Country Chart*.

Exercise 4

1. Open the *Exports by Country Chart* workbook that you created in Exercise 3.

2. Add the following data to row 5: Japan, $6,438,945.00, $2,345,743.00, $5,098,760.00, $3,198,245.00.

3. Select the chart and use the Range Finder to add Japan's data to the chart.

4. Save the workbook as *Exports by Country Chart Revised* and print the worksheet.

Exercise 5

1. Open the *Expenses* workbook on your Data Disk.

2. Activate cell A2.

3. Create a Bar of Pie type chart using the Chart Wizard (in the Pie chart type category). This type of chart uses a selected number of values from the bottom of a list of values to create a "breakout" section. In this case, the breakout section is the category Taxes.

4. Title the chart "Expenses."

5. Show the percentage data labels.

6. Create the chart as an embedded chart.

7. Save the workbook as *Expenses Chart* and print worksheet.

Exercise 6

1. Open the *Computer Comparison* workbook on your Data Disk.

2. Create a new chart, using the Line – Column on 2 Axes custom type of chart. (*Hint:* Click the Custom Types tab in step 1 of the Chart Wizard.)

3. Title the chart Computer Price/Speed Comparison.

4. Title the *x*-axis "System."

5. Title the *y*-axis "Price."

6. Title the secondary *y*-axis "Speed."

7. Create the chart as a new sheet.

8. Save the workbook as *Computer Comparison Chart* and print the chart sheet.

Exercise 7

1. Open the *Computer Comparison Chart* that you created in Exercise 6.

2. Show the data table on the chart.

3. Click the PII-450 data point to select it (select the individual point, not the series). Drag the data point handle at the top-middle of the data point down until the value reads $3,110.00.

4. Modify the value of the PII-400a data point to become $2,700.00 by dragging the data point handle.

5. Print the chart and save the workbook as *Computer Comparison Chart Revised*.

Exercise 8

1. Open the *Class Attendance* workbook located on your Data Disk.

2. Create a new chart with the Chart Wizard.

3. Use the Custom Types tab to select the Colored Lines chart type.

chapter five

4. Title the chart "Class Attendance."

5. Put the chart on a new sheet called "Attendance Chart."

6. Change the area fill of the Plot Area and the Chart Area to Automatic (white).

7. Print the chart and save your workbook as *Class Attendance with Chart.*

Case Projects

Project 1

As the entertainment editor for a local newspaper, you publish a weekly chart of the top five films based on their box office revenues for the week. Use the Web toolbar to search the Internet for information on the top five movies from the last week. Create a worksheet listing each of the titles and showing how much each film grossed in the last week. Add another column to show total revenues to date for each film. Create a chart that best illustrates the data. Save the workbook as *Box Office.*

Project 2

Use the Office Assistant to find out how to add a text box to a chart. Create a Word document and use your own words to describe step by step how to accomplish this task. Save the document as *Adding a Text Box to a Chart.doc.*

Project 3

As the owner of a mall-based cookie store, you want to track your cookie sales by type and month to determine which cookies are best-sellers and what the best time of the year is for cookie sales. Create a worksheet with 10 types of cookies (examples: chocolate chip, oatmeal, walnut, peanut butter). Include fictitious data for cookie sales for each type of cookie during the past 12 months. Create charts showing overall cookie sales by month and overall cookie sales by type. Save the workbook as *Cookie Sales.*

Project 4

Use the Web toolbar to search the Internet for different types of charts. Look for charts showing sales volume, stock prices, or percentages of sales by category. Print Web pages containing at least three different chart types.

Project 5

Stock price charts are usually displayed using a high-low-close style chart, which requires three columns of data. Use the Web toolbar to search the Internet for stock prices for three companies whose products you use. Locate price histories for the last five days for each stock, including the high, low, and closing prices for each day. Create a High Low Close chart (stock category) for each company, showing the price plotted against the date. Save the workbook as *High Low Close.*

Project 6

Create a worksheet showing one month's expenses for at least 10 expense categories in your household (estimate your family's expenses or supply fictitious data). Create a three-dimensional pie chart, and separate the largest expense from the pie. Use data labels to display the percentage of each expense. Save the workbook as *Family Expenses.*

Project 7

As the weather editor of a local newspaper, your job is to create a chart of the 5-day forecasts for your city. Using the Internet, locate a site that provides a 5-day forecast for your area. Enter the data on a new worksheet and create a chart showing the high and low temperatures for each day. Save the workbook as *Temperature Forecast.*

Project 8

You are interested in finding out how the government spends its budget. Using the Internet, find a site that shows where the government spends taxes. Create a new workbook and pie chart showing the information you find. Include at least 5 categories. Print the chart and save your workbook as *Government Spending.*

Integrating Excel with Office Applications and the Internet

Chapter Overview

Y ou can create reports in Word using Excel data or enhance PowerPoint presentations with Excel data and charts. In addition, you can create Access tables from existing Excel lists or query Access databases from Excel to analyze data. You can paste or link workbook data to documents created in other programs. You also can embed workbooks within other documents to share Excel's functionality with other programs.

Case profile

You are responsible not only for gathering data produced by the various departments of Sweet Tooth, but also for distributing the data to company officers and department managers. For example, you periodically write memos to regional managers, distribute reports to management, and prepare presentations for potential investors. By integrating Excel-based data into other Office documents, you can save both yourself and your co-workers a lot of time and ensure accurate data.

LEARNING OBJECTIVES

► Integrate Excel with Word and PowerPoint
► Integrate Excel with Access
► Import data from other applications
► Send a workbook via e-mail
► Integrate Excel with the Internet

EX.a Integrating Excel with Word and PowerPoint

There are several ways to integrate Excel data with other types of files, such as Word documents and PowerPoint presentations. First, you can insert an Excel file (the **source file**) in a Word document or PowerPoint presentation (the **target file**). Second, you can embed an Excel object in a Word document or PowerPoint presentation. Third, you can create a link between an Excel workbook and a Word document or PowerPoint presentation.

When you insert Excel data in a Word document, you place the data in a Word table that can be edited using Word's Table editing commands. When you **insert** Excel data in a PowerPoint presentation, the data is inserted as graphic object, similar to a picture of the data, which cannot be edited. All links to the original data are lost. Thus, if you modify the data in the target file, the original Excel workbook will not be updated. Likewise, if you update the Excel workbook, the target file will not be updated. Because you can use the Copy and Paste commands to insert Excel data into the target file, this method is very fast.

Embedding an Excel file in a target file creates a link between the target application and Excel. When you double-click an embedded worksheet to edit it, the target application's menu bar and toolbars are replaced with the Excel menu bar and toolbars. Using an embedded worksheet is like opening a window in the target application to the Excel application. Although you can use the familiar Excel menu bar and toolbars to edit the data, you are not actually altering the original data. That is, your changes are not reflected in the original Excel workbook. When you do not need to maintain a link to the original data, but do want access to Excel's features to format and edit data, use this method.

When you **link** an Excel worksheet to a target file, you create a reference to the original Excel worksheet. As with embedded files, double-clicking a linked file to edit the data opens the original file. Because the workbook is linked to the target file, any changes you make in Excel will be reflected in your target file. Linking files saves hard drive space because you do not create a second copy of the data in the target file. If having up-to-date data in the target file is essential, linking is your best option.

Embedding Excel Data in a Word Document

You need to send a memo to the management personnel at Sweet Tooth showing the preliminary sales totals for 1999. You wrote the memo in Word, and you collected the data in Excel. You want to embed the Excel data, so the managers can change the data if necessary. To embed Excel data in a Word document:

Step 1	*Start*	Word
Step 2	*Open*	the *Memo to East Division Manager.doc* file on your Data Disk
Step 3	*Save*	the Word document as *Memo to East Division Manager with Embedded Data.doc*
Step 4	*Key*	your name, replacing *Your Name* on the From line
Step 5	*Press*	the CTRL + END keys to move to the end of the document
Step 6	*Start*	Excel
Step 7	*Open*	the *Mountain Region Sales* workbook on your Data Disk
Step 8	*Click*	the East Division worksheet tab
Step 9	*Select*	cells A1:F9
Step 10	*Click*	the Copy button ⧉ on the Standard toolbar
Step 11	*Click*	the Word taskbar button
Step 12	*Click*	Edit
Step 13	*Click*	Paste Special

The Paste Special dialog box opens in Word.

Step 14	*Click*	Microsoft Excel Worksheet Object in the As: list
Step 15	*Verify*	that the Paste: option button is selected
Step 16	*Click*	OK

The worksheet is embedded in the document as an object. You can drag the object in Word to reposition it, just as you would manipulate drawing objects in Excel. To move the embedded object:

Step 1	*Drag*	the embedded worksheet object below the last line of the memo and center it on the page

integration

When a worksheet is embedded in the target file, you must change it from within the Word target file. To edit the embedded Excel object in the Word document:

| Step 1 | **Double-click** | the embedded worksheet object |

Your screen should look similar to Figure EX-1.

FIGURE EX-1
Embedded
Worksheet Object

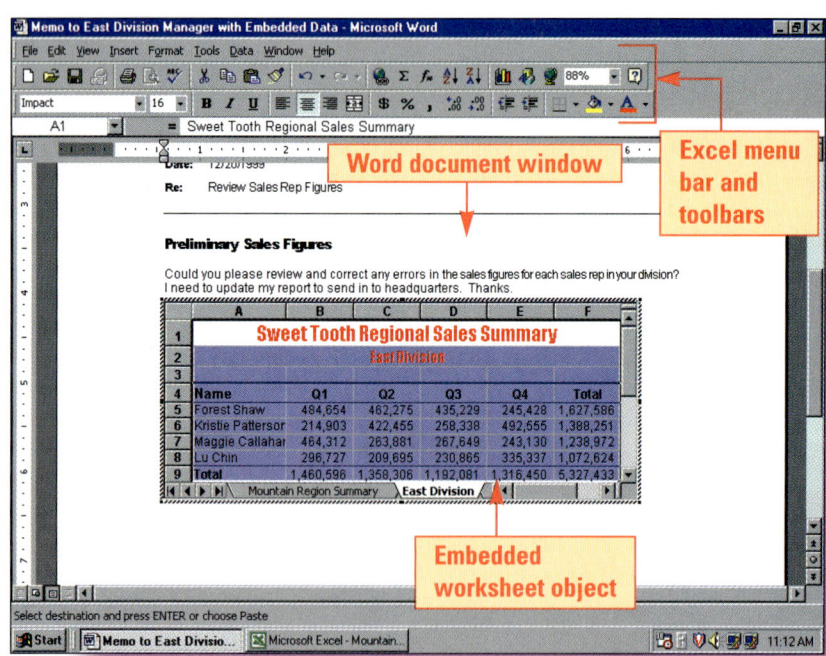

Step 2	**Select**	the range B5:F9
Step 3	**Click**	the Currency Style button $ on the Formatting toolbar
Step 4	**Resize**	columns B:F to fit
Step 5	**Activate**	cell A1
Step 6	**Click**	anywhere in the Word document to deselect the object
Step 7	**Drag**	the embedded worksheet object so that it is centered horizontally on the page
Step 8	**Deselect**	the embedded worksheet object by clicking elsewhere in the Word document

Your document should look similar to Figure EX-2.

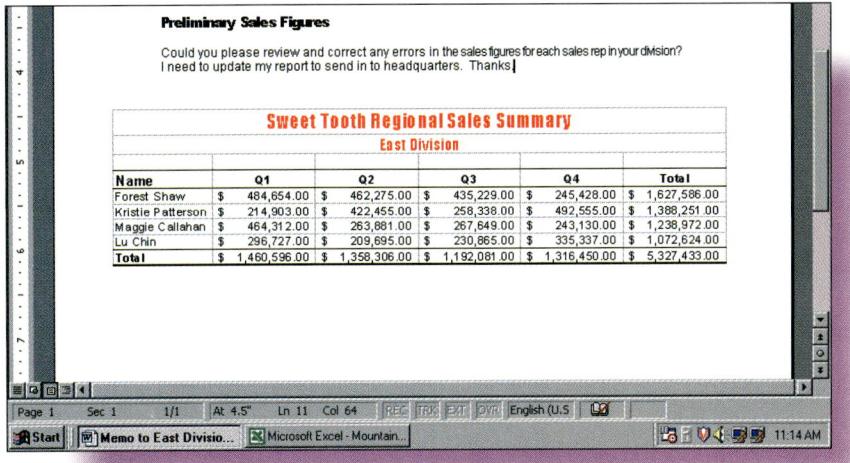

FIGURE EX-2
Embedded Worksheet
Object after Formatting

Step 9	**Save & Close**	the Word document
Step 10	**Exit**	Word
Step 11	**Close**	the *Mountain Region Sales* workbook

Linking an Excel Chart to a PowerPoint Presentation

You are working on a PowerPoint presentation showing sales data for the South Region. You want to include a chart showing this year's data in the presentation. You know that the chart will be updated later, so you decide to link it to the presentation. You will then be able to update the chart right before your presentation. To add a link to the data:

Step 1	**Open**	the *South Division Summary* workbook on your Data Disk (in Excel)
Step 2	**Save**	the workbook as *South Division Summary Revised*
Step 3	**Click**	the Summary Chart worksheet tab
Step 4	**Start**	PowerPoint
Step 5	**Open**	the *South Summary.ppt* file on your Data Disk
Step 6	**Click**	the Excel taskbar button
Step 7	**Click**	the Copy button 🗐 on the Standard toolbar

Step 8	*Click*	the PowerPoint taskbar button
Step 9	*Drag*	the scroll bar down to move to slide 2 in the presentation
Step 10	*Click*	<u>E</u>dit
Step 11	*Click*	Paste <u>S</u>pecial
Step 12	*Click*	the Paste <u>l</u>ink option button

The dialog box on your screen should look similar to Figure EX-3.

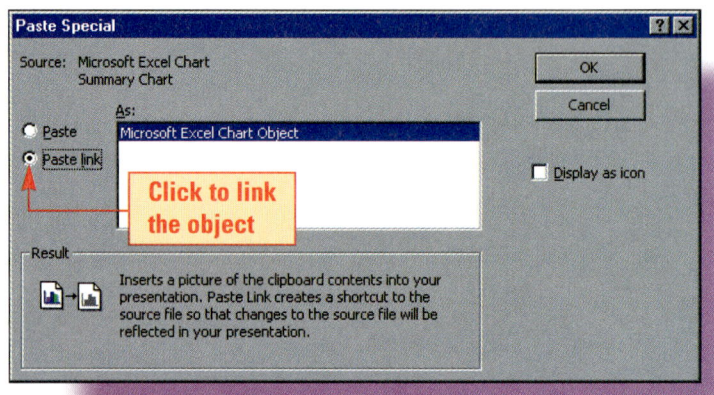

Step 13	*Click*	OK

The chart is now linked to the PowerPoint presentation, but you need to resize it so it fits on the page. To resize the chart object:

Step 1	*Press & Hold*	the CTRL key

When you press and hold the CTRL key while you resize an object, the object resizes proportionally toward or from the center of the object.

Step 2	*Drag*	a corner resize handle until the object fits nicely in the slide
Step 3	*Move*	the object so it is visually centered in the slide
Step 4	*Click*	anywhere in the PowerPoint window to deselect the object
Step 5	*Save*	the presentation as *South Summary Presentation.ppt*

M O U S E   T I P

Right-drag a selection from Excel to Word to create a linked object.

Your screen should look similar to Figure EX-4.

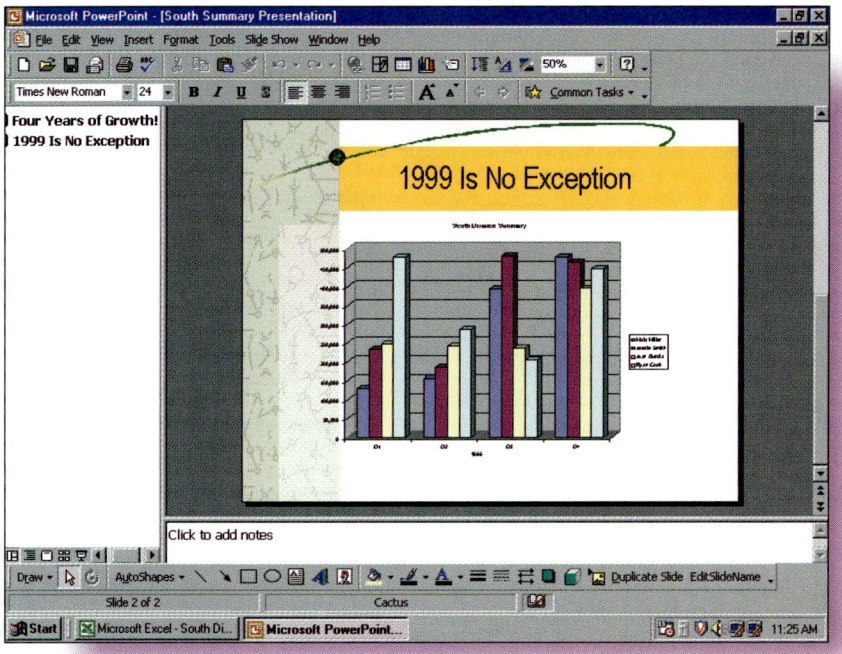

FIGURE EX-4
Adding Linked Excel Data
to a PowerPoint slide

The chart is now linked to the PowerPoint presentation. When an Excel chart is linked to a target file, double-clicking the Excel object takes you directly to Excel. As you edit the linked data, the target file updates automatically. To modify the chart object:

Step 1	**Double-click**	the linked chart object

Excel becomes the active program, and the workbook containing the chart object appears in the active window.

Step 2	**Maximize**	the Excel workbook window, if necessary
Step 3	**Right-click**	the Windows taskbar
Step 4	**Click**	Tile Windows Vertically so you can see both program windows at the same time
Step 5	**Click**	in the Excel window to make it active

Your screen should look similar to Figure EX-5.

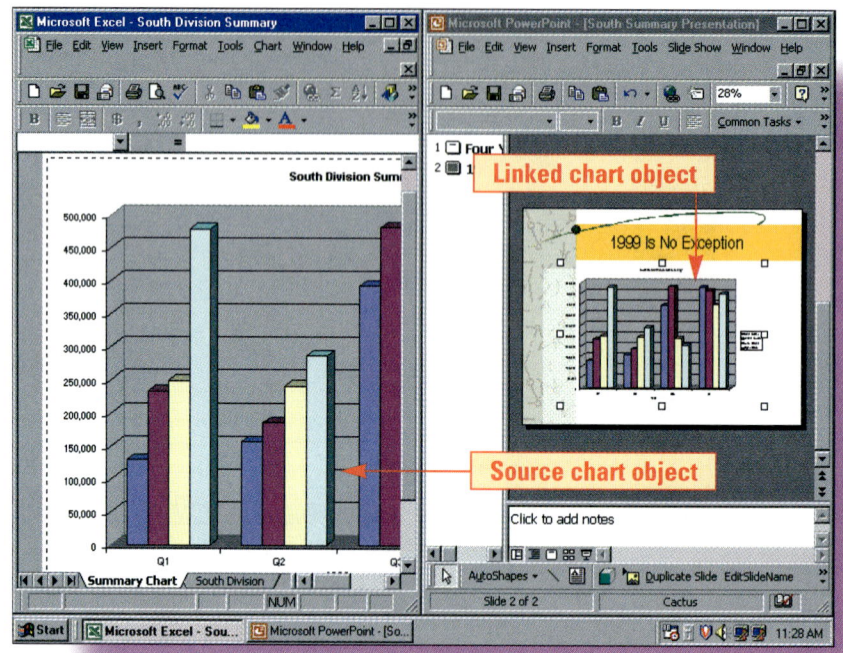

Step 6	*Select*	the Chart Title object
Step 7	*Press*	the DELETE key to delete the Chart Title object

Notice that the linked chart is automatically adjusted in the presentation.

Step 8	*Maximize*	the PowerPoint program window
Step 9	*Save & Close*	the PowerPoint presentation
Step 10	*Exit*	PowerPoint
Step 11	*Maximize*	the Excel program window
Step 12	*Save & Close*	the workbook

EX.b Integrating Excel with Access

Although Excel can store a large volume of data in list form, a database application—such as Access—is better suited to holding large amounts of this type of data. As your Excel lists grow in size, you can export them to create Access tables.

Exporting Excel Data to an Access Database

You can use existing lists of Excel data to build data tables in Access. The *Sales Rep Data* workbook contains a variety of information about the sales for each of Sweet Tooth's divisions. You think it would be a good idea to store the data in a database rather than in Excel. Before you import Excel-based data into Access, however, you should prepare the information. To prepare the Excel data:

Step 1	*Open*	the *Sales Rep Data* workbook on your Data Disk
Step 2	*Save*	the workbook as *Sales Rep Data to Import*

You should delete any worksheet titles and blank rows that appear above the data to be imported into Access.

Step 3	*Delete*	rows 1–4
Step 4	*Verify*	that the column headings appear in the first row of the worksheet you'll be importing

The column headings become the field names in the database.

Step 5	*Activate*	cell A1
Step 6	*Save & Close*	the workbook

Now, you're ready to start Access and create a new database. To create a new database:

Step 1	*Start*	Access
Step 2	*Click*	the <u>B</u>lank Access database option button in the Access startup dialog box

integration

Step 3	*Click*	OK
Step 4	*Select*	the folder containing your Data Files
Step 5	*Drag*	to select the name in the File name: box
Step 6	*Key*	Sales Rep Data in the File name: box
Step 7	*Click*	Create

Once the database has been created, you can import data from an Excel file. To import data:

Step 1	*Click*	File
Step 2	*Point to*	Get External Data
Step 3	*Click*	Import
Step 4	*Click*	the Files of type: list arrow in the Import dialog box
Step 5	*Click*	Microsoft Excel
Step 6	*Click*	Sales Rep Data to Import
Step 7	*Click*	Import

The Import Spreadsheet Wizard opens. The first row of data in the workbook contains the column headings.

| Step 8 | *Click* | the First Row Contains Column Headings check box |

Notice, in the bottom half of the dialog box, that the column headings from the worksheet become the field headings for the new Access table. Below those headings, you see how the data will be divided into records (horizontally) and fields (vertically).

Step 9	*Click*	Next >
Step 10	*Click*	Next > to accept the default of creating the database in new table
Step 11	*Click*	Next > to accept the default and let Access index the table

When you are working with a database, a primary key is used to uniquely identify each record in a table and to speed up data retrieval in large databases. Access adds a primary key by default in Step 4 of the Wizard.

Step 12	*Click*	Next >
Step 13	*Key*	Sales Report Data in the Import to Table: box to name the new Access table
Step 14	*Click*	Finish
Step 15	*Click*	OK to close the alert box that appears

The new table appears in the Database window.

Step 16	*Double-click*	the Sales Report Data table icon

Your screen should look similar to Figure EX-6.

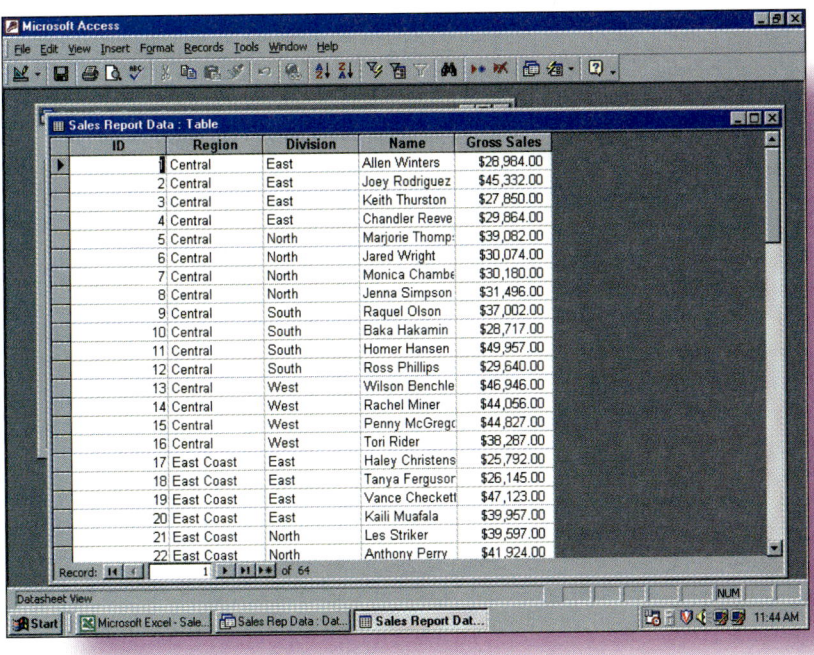

FIGURE EX-6
Access Table Created
Using an Excel List

Step 17	*Close*	Access

Querying Data from an Access Database

A query is a method of extracting information from a database. You can use Excel to query data stored in Access and search for records meeting certain criteria. Then, you can import only those records that meet your criteria into Excel so as to create charts, develop PivotTable

integration

reports, or perform statistical analysis. To query a database, you use Microsoft Query in Excel. To query the database:

Step 1	*Start*	a new workbook in Excel
Step 2	*Click*	Data
Step 3	*Point to*	Get External Data

notes You might need to install Microsoft Query. If an alert box appears, insert the CD and click Yes to install it. If you are working in a lab or on a network, see your instructor.

Step 4	*Click*	New Database Query
Step 5	*Click*	MS Access Database* in the Choose Data Source dialog box
Step 6	*Verify*	that the Use the Query Wizard to create/edit queries check box has a check mark in it
Step 7	*Click*	OK
Step 8	*Click*	Sales Rep Data.mdb in the Database Name list in the Select Database dialog box

This file is the Access database that you created in the previous activity.

Step 9	*Click*	OK

Once you have selected a database source, the Query Wizard starts. In Step 1 of the wizard, you select which columns you want included in your query. If you omit a column, the data in that column will not be extracted from the database. To add columns to your query:

Step 1	*Click*	the + next to Sales Report Data to see which columns are available in your table, Sales Report Data
Step 2	*Verify*	that Sales Report Data is selected
Step 3	*Click*	the > button to add the entire table to the Columns in your query: box
Step 4	*Click*	Next >

QUICK TIP

For more information about using Microsoft Query, click the question mark icon in the Microsoft Query dialog box, then click Help with this feature.

Step 2 of the Query Wizard enables you to set query filters. Filters allow you to view only records meeting criteria you define. For this query, you want to extract only the records of sales representatives who work in the West Coast Region whose gross sales exceed $35,000. To set query filters:

Step 1	*Click*	Gross Sales in the <u>C</u>olumn to filter: list
Step 2	*Click*	the list arrow in the active box
Step 3	*Click*	is greater than from the list of operators
Step 4	*Key*	35000 in the value box on the right
Step 5	*Verify*	that the And option button is selected

At this point, your query will extract all records for which the value in the Gross Sales column is greater than $35,000. See Figure EX-7.

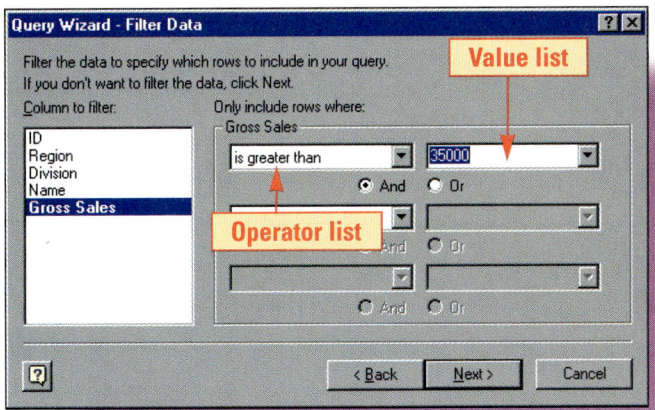

FIGURE EX-7
Step 2 of the Query Wizard

Step 6	*Click*	Region in the <u>C</u>olumn to filter: list
Step 7	*Click*	equals from the operator list
Step 8	*Click*	the value list arrow
Step 9	*Click*	West Coast

Because the And option button was selected before you chose this second filter, the query will extract all records where the value in the Gross Sales column is greater than $35,000 *and* where the region equals West Coast.

| Step 10 | *Click* | <u>N</u>ext > |

integration

The third step of the Query Wizard allows you to define a sort order for the records. To set the sort order:

Step 1	*Click*	the Sort by list arrow
Step 2	*Click*	Gross Sales
Step 3	*Click*	the Descending option button
Step 4	*Click*	Next >

The final step of the Query Wizard allows you to specify where the data should appear. You want to create a new list in Excel. To specify the output option of your query results:

| Step 1 | *Verify* | that the Return Data to Microsoft Excel option button is selected |
| Step 2 | *Click* | Finish |

The Returning External Data to Microsoft Excel dialog box opens. You need to select a location where the data will be placed. Cell A1 (the default) will work just fine.

| Step 3 | *Click* | OK |
| Step 4 | *Save* | the workbook as *Database Query* |

The query returns the results shown in Figure EX-8.

FIGURE EX-8
Results of Database Query

Only Gross Sales over $35,000 are displayed, sorted in descending order

External Data toolbar

| Step 5 | *Close* | the workbook |

EX.c Importing Data from Other Applications

A commonly used method of exchanging data involves **comma-separated**, or **tab-delimited**, text files. These files can be created in any text editor and use commas or tabs to separate columns of data. You can import such a file into an open workbook, or you can create a new workbook using the text file. You have located an old document containing financial data dating from early in Sweet Tooth's history. This file uses tabs to separate information into columns. To import data from a delimited file into Excel:

Step 1	*Start*	a new workbook
Step 2	*Click*	Data
Step 3	*Point to*	Get External Data
Step 4	*Click*	Import Text File

The Import Text File dialog box opens. Note that the Files of type: box at the bottom of the dialog box specifies Text Files.

Step 5	*Select*	*Monthly Cash Flow* from the Data Disk
Step 6	*Click*	Import

Step 1 of the Text Import Wizard appears. This wizard walks you through three steps to help you import and properly separate the text file into columns of data. Because Sweet Tooth's file is delimited, you can leave the settings at their defaults.

Step 7	*Click*	Next > to go to Step 2
Step 8	*Click*	Next > to accept the default choice of tabs as delimiters
Step 9	*Click*	Finish to accept the default settings for specifying how columns of data are formatted
Step 10	*Click*	OK in the Import Data dialog box

Once you have imported the data, you can format and rearrange the data as necessary. Because Sweet Tooth's file is a plain text file, it cannot

carry formulas with it; thus all totals and subtotals are included as values only. Upon reviewing the information, you notice that the totals in the workbook are not correct. You decide to correct the totals by replacing them with functions. To replace values with functions:

Step 1	**Activate**	cell B10
Step 2	**Click**	the AutoSum button ∑ on the Standard toolbar
Step 3	**Press**	the ENTER key
Step 4	**Repeat**	steps 1–3 to sum the total expenses in cells B14:B29 in cell B30
Step 5	**Enter**	=b10-b30 in cell B33
Step 6	**Save**	the workbook as *Old Monthly Cash Flow*
Step 7	**Close**	the workbook

EX.d Sending a Workbook via E-mail

notes The steps in this section describe how to send workbooks via e-mail using Microsoft Outlook as the mail client. Depending on your particular mail client, the process you follow may differ somewhat.

Using Excel's built-in e-mail capabilities, you can quickly send a worksheet or an entire workbook to a colleague. You can transmit a single worksheet as an HTML formatted mail message—an option that allows the recipient to see all the formatting of the original message. The recipient can select the data in his or her message and drag it into Excel. When you need to send an entire workbook, you can transmit it as an attachment. Attachments accompany a regular e-mail message and allow you to send any type of document or program.

When several colleagues need to review a workbook in a certain order, you can set up a routing slip to control the order of delivery. The routing slip accompanies the workbook transmission and contains the e-mail addresses and order in which you'd like the workbook to be reviewed. As each person finishes with the workbook, he or she can send it to the next person on the list.

Sending a Worksheet as HTML Mail

HTML mail allows you to send a Web page as the body of an e-mail message. Microsoft Outlook can receive and display HTML mail. To test this method, you send the Mountain Region Summary worksheet in the *Mountain Region Sales* workbook to yourself. To send a worksheet as part of a message:

Step 1	*Open*	the *Mountain Region Sales* workbook on your Data Disk
Step 2	*Click*	the E-mail button 📧 on the Standard toolbar

A dialog box opens, asking whether you want to send the entire workbook as an attachment or only the current worksheet as the message body. You want to send the current worksheet as the message body.

Step 3	*Click*	the Send the current sheet as the message body option button
Step 4	*Click*	OK

A messaging toolbar appears above the worksheet, as shown in Figure EX-9.

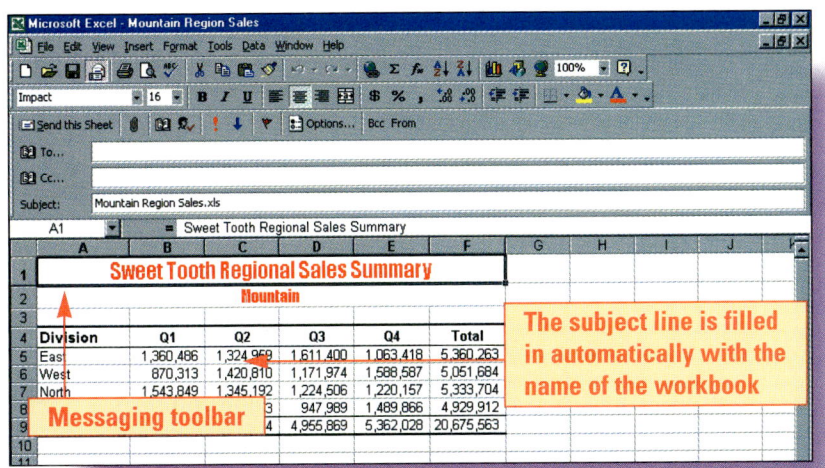

Step 5	*Enter*	your own e-mail address in the To box
Step 6	*Click*	Send this Sheet

FIGURE EX-9
Sending a Worksheet as Part of a Message

integration

The message is sent to your e-mail program's Outbox. You need to start your e-mail program, connect to your ISP, and send the message. After a few minutes, use your e-mail program to check for new messages.

QUICK TIP

If you want to use the Address Book to fill in e-mail addresses, click the To button or the Address Book button on the messaging toolbar. You can also use the shortcut keys, CTRL + SHIFT + B. Change your mind about sending a worksheet? To turn off the messaging toolbar without sending the message, click the E-mail button on the Standard toolbar again.

| Step 7 | **Send** | the e-mail message |
| Step 8 | **Download** | the new message |

If your e-mail program can display HTML mail, your message should look similar to Figure EX-10.

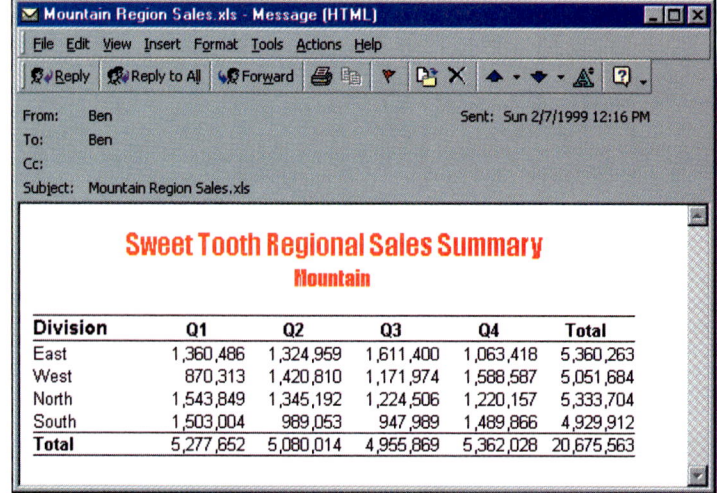

FIGURE EX-10
Viewing HTML Mail

| Step 9 | **Close** | the e-mail message |
| Step 10 | **Click** | the Excel taskbar button, if necessary |

Routing a Workbook

To successfully complete this activity, you will need the e-mail addresses of two classmates. To route a workbook:

Step 1	**Click**	File
Step 2	**Point to**	Send to
Step 3	**Click**	Routing Recipient

The Routing Slip dialog box opens, as shown in Figure EX-11.

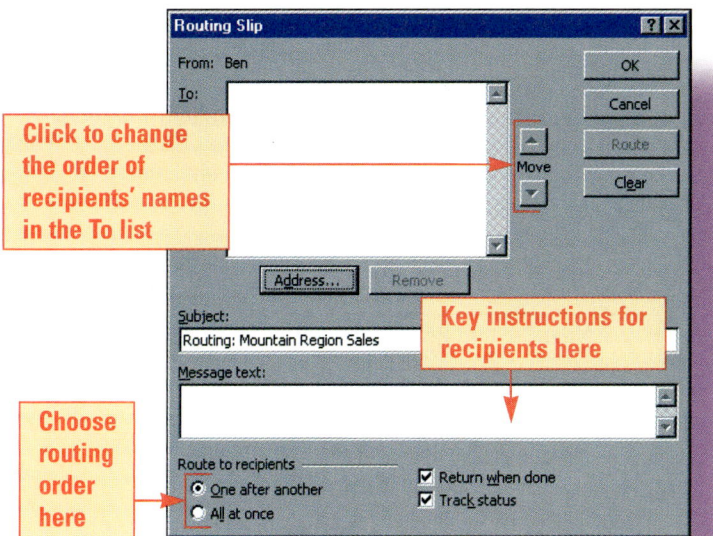

FIGURE EX-11
Routing Slip Dialog Box

| Step 4 | *Click* | A*d*dress |

The Address Book opens, allowing you to select the recipients to whom you want to send the workbook.

Step 5	*Scroll*	the Name list until you find the first person whose address should be added to the recipient list
Step 6	*Double-click*	the name to add it to the *M*essage Recipients: list
Step 7	*Repeat*	Steps 5 and 6 to add the second person's address
Step 8	*Click*	OK

The Routing Slip dialog box appears again. You want to route the workbook to the recipients in the order shown, so leave the settings at their defaults.

| Step 9 | *Click* | *R*oute |
| Step 10 | *Save* | the workbook as *Mountain Region Sales Final* and close it |

The e-mail message and attached workbook are sent to your e-mail client's Outbox. You may need to send the message by clicking the Send button in your e-mail program. After each recipient modifies the workbook, he or she can send the revised workbook to the next recipient.

CAUTION TIP

If you have not added your classmates' addresses to the Address Book, you won't be able to select their names until you do so. Click the Ne*w* Contact button, then fill in the First and Last name boxes, along with the E-mail address.

To send a workbook to the next recipient on a routing slip:

Step 1	**Open**	the e-mail message containing the routed workbook
Step 2	**Open**	the attached workbook from your e-mail message
Step 3	**Click**	File
Step 4	**Point to**	Send to
Step 5	**Click**	Next Routing Recipient

A dialog box informs you that the document has a routing slip. You want to send the workbook using the routing slip, so leave the default setting intact.

Step 6	**Click**	OK
Step 7	**Close**	the workbook in Excel without saving changes
Step 8	**Close**	the e-mail message
Step 9	**Send**	the message from your e-mail program and download new messages

When the last person on the list routes the workbook, it returns to the person who originated the routing slip, along with a message informing the sender that the document has completed its routing and is being returned. You can then open this workbook and save it as a new workbook or replace the original workbook with the final version.

Step 10	**Close**	the e-mail program

EX.e Integrating Excel with the Internet

As business becomes increasingly Web-centered, you undoubtedly will gain a greater appreciation of Excel's wide variety of tools, which enable you to easily publish your workbooks to the Internet. When you save workbooks as Web pages, you can save either individual sheets or entire workbooks. Interactive Web pages allow users to modify data, sort lists, add subtotals, and update charts on the Web page itself. You can also use Excel to open and edit existing Web pages.

Saving Excel Workbooks as Web Pages

Sometimes, you want users to be able to view data, but not to interactively change the data. Saving a workbook as a Web page is nearly as simple as saving any workbook. A few additional options exist when you save Web pages, however. When you **publish** a workbook (or Web page) to a Web server, any hyperlinks in the document are automatically adjusted to match the file structure on the Web server. For Sweet Tooth, you want to publish the data from the *South Division Summary* workbook, including the chart. To save your workbook as a Web page:

Step 1	*Open*	the *South Division Summary* workbook on your Data Disk
Step 2	*Click*	File
Step 3	*Click*	Save as Web Page
Step 4	*Key*	South Division Summary Web Page in the File name: box
Step 5	*Change*	the Save in: drive and directory to your Data Files folder

When you save a workbook or worksheet as a Web page, the Save As dialog box includes a few additional options.

Step 6	*Click*	Save to save the workbook as a Web page
Step 7	*Close*	the workbook

Now try viewing your Web page. To view your Web page:

Step 1	*Open*	your Internet browser
Step 2	*Click*	File
Step 3	*Click*	Open
Step 4	*Click*	Browse
Step 5	*Locate*	the folder where you are storing your Data Files
Step 6	*Click*	South Division Summary Web Page
Step 7	*Click*	Open
Step 8	*Click*	OK

MENU TIP

 You can preview any workbook as a Web page by clicking the File menu, then Web page preview. Your browser will open, along with an HTML preview version of your workbook.

QUICK TIP

If you have access to a Web server, you can click Publish and immediately publish your workbook to the server.

integration

Your Web browser opens, with the South Division Summary page displayed. At the bottom of the Web page, you notice hyperlink "tabs" that enable you to navigate between worksheets.

To navigate the Web page:

Step 1	*Click*	the Summary Chart tab

Your screen should look similar to Figure EX-12.

FIGURE EX-12
Workbook Saved as
Web Page

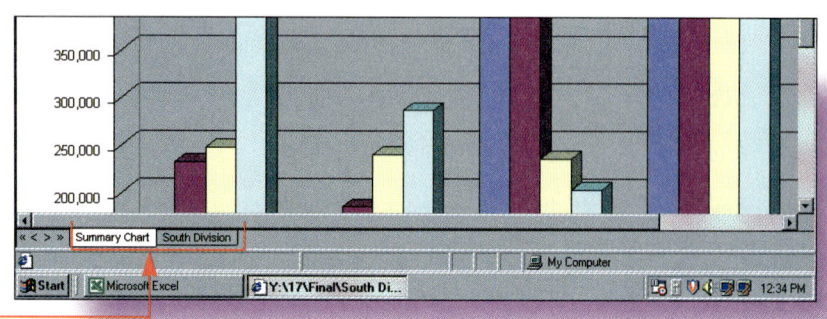

Hyperlink tabs

Step 2	*Click*	the Excel taskbar button

Creating an Interactive Web Page

When you saved the *South Division Summary* workbook as a Web page, the chart and data pages presented static images of the data. Sometimes, however, you want to encourage users to interact with the data. Interactive Web pages enable users to change data, update charts, and rearrange PivotCharts.

To add interactivity to a Web page:

Step 1	*Open*	the *Sweet Tooth Sales to Stores* workbook on your Data Disk
Step 2	*Click*	File
Step 3	*Click*	Save as Web Page
Step 4	*Change*	the Save in: folder to your Data Files folder

CAUTION TIP

When you save a workbook as a Web page, a new folder is created with "_files" added to the end of the filename. If you copy the Web page file to another disk or folder, this folder must be copied with it. If you do not copy the folder to the same disk or folder as the Web page, the Web page will not function correctly.

When you save an entire workbook, you cannot add interactivity. Instead, you save the worksheet or chart which you want to be interactive.

Step 5	*Click*	the Selection: Chart option button

This option button changes to reflect the top worksheet.

Step 6	*Click*	the Add interactivity check box
Step 7	*Click*	Change Title
Step 8	*Key*	Sweet Tooth Sales to Stores

This title will appear centered in your Web page above the PivotChart.

Step 9	*Click*	OK
Step 10	*Drag*	to select the text in the File name: box
Step 11	*Key*	Sales to Stores Interactive Web Page in the File name: box
Step 12	*Click*	Save

Now you can switch to your browser and open the new Web page to test it.

To open the Web page and modify the PivotChart:

Step 1	*Click*	the browser taskbar button
Step 2	*Open*	the *Sales to Stores Interactive Web Page* file in your Data Files folder
Step 3	*Scroll*	to the bottom of the Web page

Your screen should look similar to Figure EX-13. You can modify the table in the Web page by changing filter options on the existing field button.

integration

FIGURE EX-13
An Interactive PivotTable
Web Page

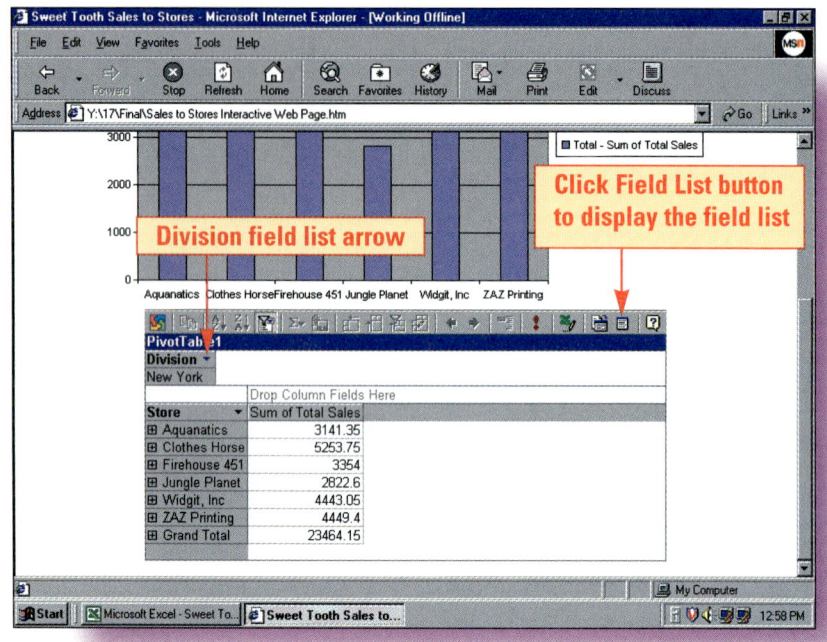

MOUSE TIP

 You can modify the table in the Web page by dragging new field buttons onto the chart from the PivotTable Field List.

QUICK TIP

There are two ways to insert HTML data from an interactive Web page. You can either use the Copy and Paste buttons on the toolbar directly above the table or click the Export to Excel button on that toolbar.

Step 4	*Click*	the field list arrow on the Division button
Step 5	*Click*	the check box next to (All)
Step 6	*Click*	OK

Notice that the chart is updated to include sales to all regions.

Step 7	*Click*	the Excel taskbar button
Step 8	*Close*	the workbook without saving any changes

Importing a Table from a Web Page

notes The following steps can be carried out only with Microsoft Internet Explorer 4.01 or higher. If you do not have Internet Explorer 4.01 or later installed on your computer, read through this section, but you may not be able to follow all of the steps on your computer.

You can import data from any table published on a Web page. This option can prove very useful when you need to track types of data that are frequently displayed in tables, such as stock tables. The Central Region manager has published her region's sales summary as a Web page. You can drag this table from the Web page to create a new

workbook using the same data. To open your Web browser and the
Central Region manager's Web page:

Step 1	*Start*	a new workbook in Excel
Step 2	*Tile*	the Excel and browser windows so that you can see them both at the same time
Step 3	*Open*	the *Central Region Sales.htm* file in your Internet browser

Your screen should look similar to Figure EX-14.

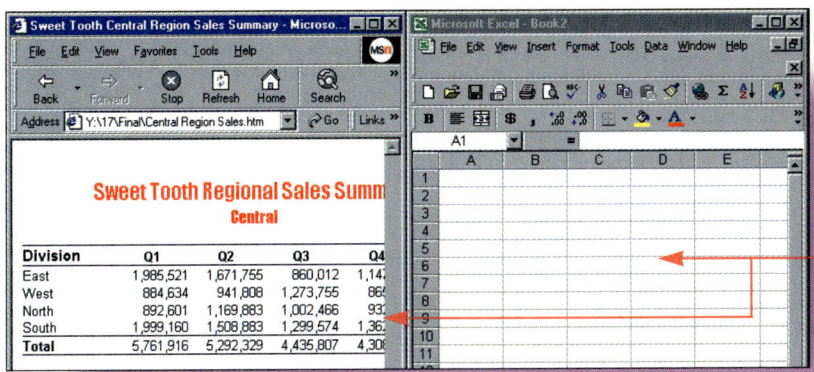

FIGURE EX-14
Web Page with an
Excel Table

To copy the data to Excel:

Step 1	*Select*	the table in the browser by dragging across the data, starting from the left of the title and moving to the right of the bottom corner of the table
Step 2	*Drag*	the selected table from your browser to Excel
Step 3	*Drop*	the cells into cell A1 of your workbook
Step 4	*Activate*	cell B9 to see that the formula remained intact
Step 5	*Save*	the workbook as *Central Region Sales Download* and close it
Step 6	*Right-click*	the Windows taskbar
Step 7	*Click*	Undo Tile to restore Excel and the browser to full screen size
Step 8	*Close*	the Internet browser

   Because formulas remain intact throughout the copying process,
this process can be a very effective method of distributing data to a
wide range of people on a company intranet or on the Internet.

integration

Summary

▶ Paste Excel data into a Word document to use Word's table tools.

▶ Embed Excel data to use Excel's functionality without providing for data to be updated from the source. Link Excel documents when data must be kept up-to-date.

▶ Embed or link charts and data to PowerPoint slides to enhance presentations.

▶ Use Excel lists to create tables in Access. Query Access databases from Excel to create charts, reports, and statistical analysis.

▶ Import data from different types of files using the Import Text Wizard.

▶ Send worksheets or workbooks to others without leaving Excel. E-mail worksheets as HTML mail, or send workbooks as e-mail attachments. Route workbooks to several colleagues when others should review a workbook and then return it to you.

▶ Save Excel workbooks, worksheets, and charts as Web pages. Add interactivity to enable users to manipulate data and modify charts.

Commands Review

Action	Menu Bar	Shortcut Menu	Toolbar	Keyboard
Insert a copy of Excel data in a Word document	Insert, File			ALT + I, L
Place Excel data in a Word document as a Word table	Edit, Copy Edit, Paste	Right-click selected data, Copy Right-click insertion point, Paste	📋 📋	ALT + E, C ALT + E, P CTRL + C CTRL + V
Embed Excel data in a Word document or PowerPoint slide	Insert, Object Edit, Copy Edit, Paste Special, Paste		📋	ALT + I, O ALT + E, C ALT + E, S, P
Link Excel data in a Word document or PowerPoint slide	Edit, Copy Edit, Paste Special, Paste link	Right-click Excel range, Copy	📋	ALT + E, C ALT + E, S ALT + L
Send worksheet as e-mail message	File, Send To, Mail Recipient		📧	ALT + F, D, M
Send workbook as e-mail attachment	File, Send To, Mail Recipient (as Attachment)			ALT + F, D, A
Route a workbook	File, Send To, Routing Recipient			ALT + F, D, R
Route a workbook to next recipient	File, Send To, Next Routing Recipient			ALT + F, D, N
Preview Excel worksheet as a Web page	File, Web Page Preview			ALT + F, B
Publish Excel worksheet or chart	File, Save as Web Page			ALT + F, G

Concepts Review

Circle the correct answer.

1. To embed worksheet data in a Word document:
[a] use Copy and Paste.
[b] use Copy and Paste Special.
[c] press the CTRL key and drag a selection from Excel to Word.
[d] both b and c.

2. Integrating Excel with other applications:
[a] is difficult and creates outdated copies of data.
[b] is unnecessary because Excel can format a worksheet any way you want.
[c] increases your productivity and enhances your options for presenting data.
[d] none of the above.

3. Embedding an Excel file in Word or PowerPoint:
[a] creates a link to the Excel application and the source data.
[b] creates a link to the Excel application but not the source data.
[c] makes a copy of the Excel data using a Word table structure.
[d] makes a picture object of the data that can be only resized or moved.

4. When creating a Word document with integrated Excel data that might change later, you should use:
[a] embedded data.
[b] linked data.
[c] inserted data.
[d] none of the above.

5. If you need to keep a "snapshot" of Excel data in another document at a given time, you should:
[a] use embedded data.
[b] use linked data.
[c] use a screenshot.
[d] insert the data using the Copy and Paste commands.

6. Text files can use which of the following characters as delimiters?
[a] comma
[b] tab
[c] semicolon
[d] all of the above

7. When Excel lists become very large, a better option may be to:
[a] remove infrequently used records.
[b] create a second workbook and move half the records there.
[c] convert the worksheet to an Access database.
[d] condense the data by abbreviating names and other information.

8. You can output the results of a query to:
[a] the Microsoft Query window.
[b] an Excel worksheet.
[c] the Excel Query dialog box.
[d] all of the above.

9. Routing a workbook is a good choice when you need to:
[a] send a workbook to several colleagues and have it returned to you.
[b] send a workbook as the body of a message.
[c] save a workbook as a Web page.
[d] send a workbook to a colleague but don't need it returned.

10. Which application is best suited to storing large lists of data?
[a] Excel
[b] Word
[c] PowerPoint
[d] Access

Circle **T** if the statement is true or **F** if the statement is false.

T F 1. Inserting and embedding data create copies of the data that are not linked to the source data.

T F 2. Linking Excel data to a Word document requires more disk space than embedding because it creates an additional copy of the Excel workbook.

T F 3. You cannot create a simultaneous link to the same data in both a Word document and a PowerPoint presentation.

T F 4. The Paste Special dialog box can be used to embed or link data.

T F 5. Right-click and drag from Excel to a Word document to create a linked object.

T F 6. When editing embedded or linked Excel data in a Word document, you can access the Excel menu and toolbars.

T F 7. Sending a workbook as an e-mail attachment and routing a workbook are identical operations.

T F 8. A routing slip contains the e-mail addresses and order in which a workbook is sent to others.

T F 9. Interactive Web pages enable users to interact with the Web page's data.

T F 10. Learning to use the right software for the job can save time and effort.

Skills Review

Exercise 1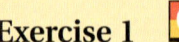

1. Open a new, blank worksheet.

2. Use Microsoft Query (<u>D</u>ata, Get External <u>D</u>ata, <u>N</u>ew Database Query) to query the *Excel List.mdb* database on your Data Disk.

3. Create a query to extract records from the Mountain or Central regions where the gross sales exceed $40,000.

4. Sort the results by gross sales in descending order.

5. Output the results to Excel.

6. Create a chart on a new sheet listing the top 10 sales representatives and their gross sales totals.

7. Add a title to your chart that describes its contents.

8. Print the chart.

9. Save the workbook as *Extract 1*.

Exercise 2

1. Open the *Extract 1* workbook that you created in the Exercise 1.

2. Save the workbook as *Extract 1 Modified*.

3. Open the *Top 10 Sales Representatives.ppt* presentation on your Data Disk using PowerPoint.

4. Save the presentation as *Top 15.ppt*.

5. Link the Top 10 Chart to the first slide in the presentation by using Copy and Paste Special, then selecting Paste <u>l</u>ink.

6. Resize and reposition the chart as necessary.

7. Click the Excel application button on the taskbar.

8. Modify the Chart Source Data to include the top 15 representatives.

9. Rename the tab as Top 15.

10. Remove the chart title.

11. Click the PowerPoint application button on the taskbar.

12. Rename the Slide title as "Top 15 Sales Representatives."

13. Print the slide from PowerPoint.

14. Close the PowerPoint application.

15. Close the workbook.

Exercise 3

1. Open the *Warehouse Inventory* workbook on your Data Disk.

2. Save the workbook as *Warehouse Inventory Modified*.

3. Sort the list by Part No.

4. Select the range A4:F16 and click the Copy button on the Standard toolbar.

5. Open the Word application.

6. Open the *Letter to Warehouse Division Manager.doc* on your Data Disk.

7. Save the Word document as *Letter with Data.doc*.

8. Insert a blank line between the first and second paragraphs of the letter.

9. Use Paste Special from the Edit menu to embed the data.

10. Reposition the embedded object as necessary.

11. Double-click the embedded object to make the following modifications:

    a. Change the price of item 1020 to $29.95.

    b. Change the quantity of item 3001 to 500.

    c. Center column E.

    d. Turn off display of gridlines using the Options dialog box from the Tools menu.

12. Print and save the letter.

integration

Exercise 4

1. Open the *Letter with Data.doc* that you created in Exercise 4, and delete the embedded object.

2. In the Excel file *Warehouse Inventory Modified*, copy the range A4:F16.

3. In Word, use Paste Special to create a linked object in the document.

4. Double-click the link object to edit the data as follows:

    a. Center column E.

    b. Change the price of item 1020 to $35.95.

    c. Change the quantity of item 3001 to 750.

    d. Select the range A5:A16 and left-justify the range.

5. Save the workbook.

6. Save the Word document as *Letter with Linked Data.doc* and print it.

7. Close the workbook and the Word document.

Exercise 5

1. Open the *Work Files Manager* workbook on your Data Disk.

2. Add hyperlinks to each of the bevel objects pointing to the corresponding files on your Data Disk.

3. Save the file as *Work Files Manager Revised*.

4. Save the file as a Web page by clicking Save as Web Page on the File menu. In the Save As dialog box, do the following:

    a. Change the Web page title to Work Files Manager.

    b. Change the filename to *Work Files Manager*.

    c. Click the Save button.

5. Open your Internet browser.

6. Open the *Work Files Manager.htm* file that you just saved by clicking the File menu. Select Open, then click the Browse button and locate your file.

7. Test the hyperlinks, then print the Web page and close your browser and any files you opened.

Exercise 6

1. Use the *Month Calendar* template on your Data Disk to create a new calendar workbook. (*Hint:* In the Open dialog box, select All Microsoft Excel files in the Files of type: box.)

2. Enter the correct dates for the current month.

3. Modify the calendar title in cell A1 to display the current month.

4. Modify the cell shading to correspond to the current month.

5. Select the calendar area.

6. Save the calendar as a Web page with interactivity. Name the Web page *Calendar Web Page.htm*.

7. Print the workbook, then close it.

Exercise 7

1. Open the *Calendar Web Page.htm* file in your browser.

2. Add at least five appointments to the calendar.

3. Click the Export to Excel button in the browser to create a copy of the appointments.

4. Save the workbook as an Excel workbook named *Calendar Export* and print it.

5. In the browser window, click the Copy button on the toolbar directly above the table.

6. In a new Excel workbook, click the Paste button.

7. Save the workbook as *Calendar Copy* and print it.

8. Close the browser.

9. In Excel, click the Open button, select the HTML file *Calendar Web Page*, click the list arrow next to Open, then click Open in Microsoft Excel.

10. Save the workbook as an Excel file named *Final Calendar* and print it. (*Hint:* In the Save As dialog box, click the Save as type: list arrow and select Microsoft Excel Workbook.)

11. Close all open workbooks.

Exercise 8

1. Open the *Extract 1* workbook that you created in Exercise 1.

2. Send the chart as the body of an e-mail message to a classmate.

3. You should receive a similar message from a classmate. Print the e-mail message if your e-mail program is capable of displaying HTML mail.

4. Close the workbook without saving changes.

Case Projects

Project 1

As a mortgage officer, you want to provide the best possible service to your clients. One tool that you find helpful is a mortgage loan calculator, which calculates the monthly payment for a loan at a given percentage. (*Hint:* Use Excel Help to find out how to use the PMT functions.) Use Excel to create an interactive Web page where visitors to your site can input a loan amount, term in months, and interest rate and then calculate a monthly payment and total interest. Save the workbook as *MLC* and the Web page as *MLC.htm*.

Project 2

You are a busy stockbroker. In an effort to drum up investment business, you decide to send a letter to your clients showing the recent results of several stocks that have been performing well lately. Use the Internet to research two or three companies that might pique your clients' interest. Create a workbook to record high/low/close prices for each stock over the last week. Save the workbook as *Stock Prices*. Create a chart for each stock and link the charts to your letter. Print the letter and save the document as *Stock Letter*.

integration

Project 3

You are the assistant to the president of a large advertising company. One of your responsibilities is to prepare a monthly report showing the amounts collected from your five largest clients. Create a workbook with fictitious data for 10 clients over the last three months. Sort the data by totals for the quarter to find your five largest clients. Create a chart of the data for these clients. Save the workbook as *Client Data.* Working in PowerPoint, create a new slide show. Link the chart from your workbook to the first slide. Link the data, including all 10 clients, to the second slide. Save the presentation as *Clients.ppt.*

Project 4

You are the personnel director for a large firm. You have been keeping a list of employee data, including first and last names, ages, phone extensions, and departments in an Excel workbook. Because the list keeps growing larger, you decide to maintain this information in an Access database. Create a workbook containing data for 20 fictitious employees. Save the workbook as *Personnel Data.* In Access, create a new, blank database and import the data from this newly created workbook.

Project 5

Use the Internet to locate a table of data displaying current stock prices for Microsoft (stock symbol: MSFT). Select the table in your browser and drag it into a new Excel workbook. Save the workbook as *Imported Stock Price.*

Project 6

As an investment advisor for a small mutual fund that caters to first-time investors, you want to help your clients see how ups and downs in the stock market have affected their investments. Create a worksheet with an initial investment of 250 shares purchased at a price of $40 per share. Create a formula to calculate the value of the investment. Save the workbook as *Investment.* Next, save the workbook as an interactive Web page called *Investment Interactive.* Test your Web page in a browser by changing the price of the shares (the calculated value of the investment should change).

Project 7

As a travel broker, you want to encourage your existing clients to travel more often. This month, you are featuring a special on travel to Europe. Create an advertisement in Excel using travel-oriented clip art objects. Use the Internet to look up the current exchange rate between U.S. dollars and the euro. Include this information as part of your advertisement. Save the worksheet as a Web page (not interactive) called *Travel to Europe.*

Project 8

You and a colleague work together to record NFL football scores for the local newspaper. Prepare a workbook including two team names, column labels for four quarters, plus a total column. Add a formula in the total column that will sum the total number of points scored by each team. Save the workbook as *NFL Score.* Route the workbook to your colleague, who will then fill in the score (using fictitious data or by looking up the score of a recent NFL game on the Internet) and return the workbook to you. Save the final workbook as *NFL Score Final.*

PowerPoint 2000 ◼

Quick Start for PowerPoint

Chapter Overview

This chapter introduces you to the components of your working environment—the PowerPoint 2000 window. You navigate through a presentation and learn about the various views of PowerPoint. Then you create a new presentation using a design template that consists of a title slide and a bullet slide. You save, check spelling, change the design template, print, and finally close this simple presentation.

LEARNING OBJECTIVES

▶ Start PowerPoint
▶ Explore the PowerPoint window
▶ Navigate through a presentation
▶ Navigate among the PowerPoint views
▶ Close a presentation
▶ Apply a design template
▶ Save a presentation
▶ Check spelling
▶ Change the presentation design
▶ Print a presentation
▶ Exit PowerPoint

Case profile

Teddy Toys, a toy manufacturing company located in Boise, Idaho, manufactures toys for all ages, from infants to grandparents, for distribution internationally as well as within the United States. Although it manufactures a wide range of toys, Teddy Toys is proudest of its line of quality teddy bears.

You are the administrative assistant to Olaf Lerek, the Sales Manager at Teddy Toys. Mr. Lerek has asked you to prepare a presentation that will be given to the regional sales managers in the next couple of weeks.

chapter one

notes This text assumes that you have little or no knowledge of the PowerPoint application. However, it is assumed that you have read Office Chapters 1–4 of this book and that you are familiar with Windows 95 or Windows 98 concepts.

1.a Starting PowerPoint

When you open the PowerPoint application, you immediately have the choice of whether to work with an existing presentation or to create a new one. To open the PowerPoint application:

Step 1	*Click*	the Start button 🏁Start on the taskbar
Step 2	*Point to*	Programs
Step 3	*Click*	Microsoft PowerPoint

The application opens with the PowerPoint dialog box displayed (see Figure 1-1). You can create a new presentation using the <u>A</u>utoContent Wizard, a Design <u>T</u>emplate, or a <u>B</u>lank presentation, or you can <u>O</u>pen an existing presentation.

> **QUICK TIP**
>
> You can open PowerPoint by clicking the New Office Document on the Start menu to start a new presentation or by clicking the Open Office Document command on this menu to open an existing presentation.

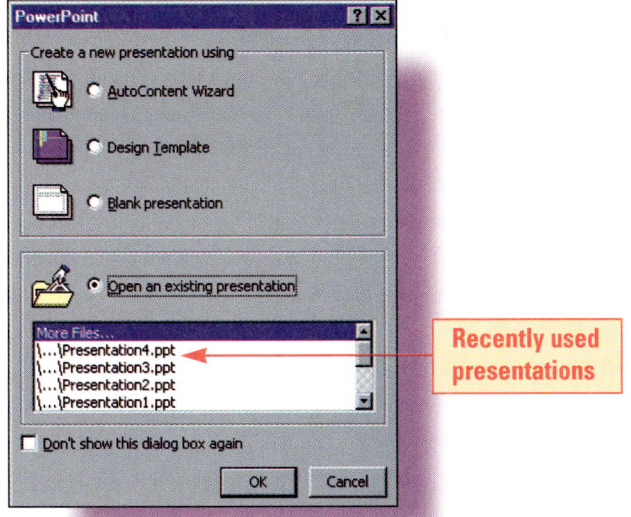

FIGURE 1-1
PowerPoint Dialog Box

chapter
one

To open a predesigned presentation:

Step 1	*Click*	Design Template
Step 2	*Click*	OK
Step 3	*Click*	the Presentations tab in the New Presentation dialog box
Step 4	*Double-click*	the Recommending A Strategy text or icon

The *Recommending A Strategy* presentation opens in Normal view (see Figure 1-2).

FIGURE 1-2
Normal View

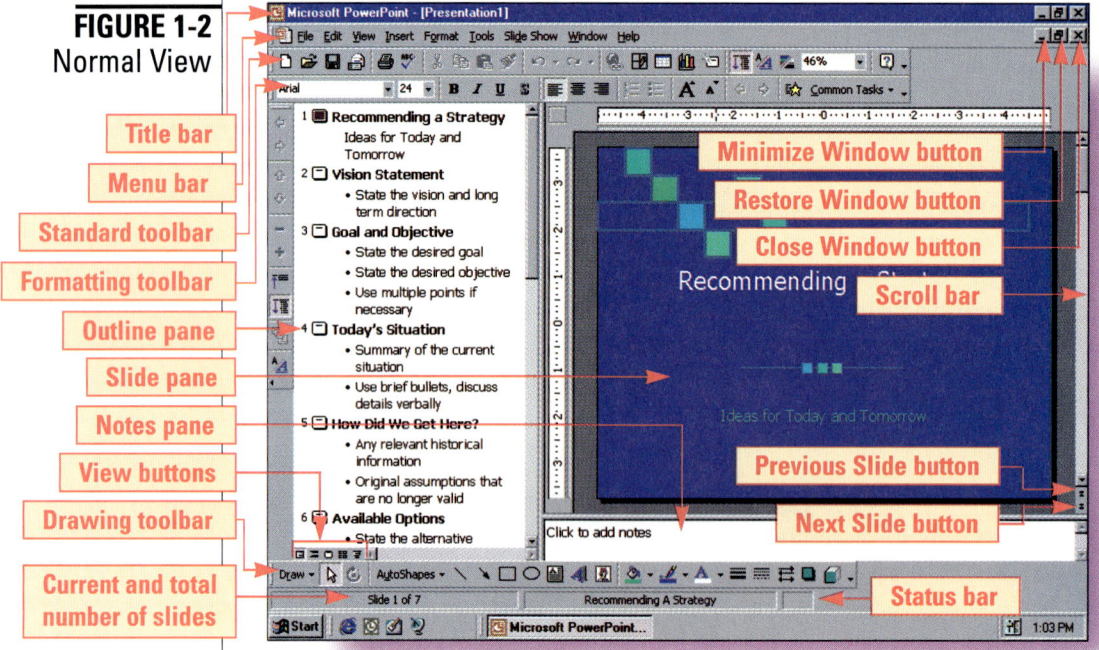

1.b Exploring the PowerPoint Window

At the top of the window is the Microsoft PowerPoint application **title bar**, which indicates the application you are using and the name of the presentation file currently on the screen. Once you save a presentation file, the actual filename replaces the word "Presentation1" in the title bar. At the extreme left of the title bar is the application Control-menu icon, and at the extreme right are the Minimize, Maximize or Restore, and Close buttons for the PowerPoint application window.

Office 2000 features personalized menus and toolbars, which "learn" the commands you use most often. This means that when you first install Office 2000, only the most frequently used commands appear immediately on a short version of the menus and the remaining commands appear after a brief pause. Commands that you select move to the short menu, while those you don't use appear only on the full menu.

The **menu bar**, located below the title bar, contains all the commands you use to work on your presentation, organized into menus.

At the extreme left of the menu bar is the Document Control-menu icon, and at the extreme right are the Minimize, Maximize or Restore, and Close buttons for the document window.

Below the menu bar is the **Standard toolbar**, which contains buttons for easy access to the most commonly used commands of the application. If you do not know what a toolbar button does, simply point to it; a yellow rectangular box called a **ScreenTip** appears with the name of the button.

notes

The Standard and Formatting toolbars appear on the same row when you first install Office 2000. When they appear in this position, only the most commonly used buttons of each toolbar are visible. All the other default buttons appear on the More Buttons drop-down lists. As you use buttons from the More Buttons drop-down list, they move to the visible buttons on the toolbar, while the buttons you don't use move into the More Buttons drop-down list. Unless otherwise noted, the illustrations in this book show the full menus and the Formatting toolbar on its own line below the Standard toolbar.

The **Formatting toolbar**, which contains buttons and list boxes for common formatting commands, can be displayed below the Standard toolbar (as shown in Figure 1-2), or share one row with the Standard toolbar. This toolbar contains several buttons that act like toggle keys; that is, the same button turns on and off a format, such as italics.

The **vertical scroll bar** appears at the right side of the PowerPoint window when you have two or more slides in a presentation and enables you to move through the slides. The vertical scroll bar contains an up scroll arrow, a down scroll arrow, and a scroll box. Clicking activates the scroll arrows. To use the scroll box, you drag it up or down. As you drag, a rectangular box appears indicating the number of the different slides and their titles. You can also click the Previous Slide and Next Slide buttons that appear below the vertical scroll bar to scroll up or down one slide at a time. At the bottom of the screen is the **horizontal scroll bar** with scroll arrows and a scroll box that you use to scroll left and right across the window.

Located directly to the left of the horizontal scroll bar are five **view buttons**: Normal view, Outline view, Slide view, Slide Sorter view, and

---

QUICK TIP

You can customize toolbars and menu options by right-clicking any toolbar and selecting Customize. You can easily add or remove buttons from any toolbar by clicking the Add or Remove buttons on the More Buttons drop-down list, and then clicking the buttons to add or remove.

You can drag the Formatting toolbar below the Standard toolbar, or right-click any toolbar, click Customize on the shortcut menu, and remove the check mark in the Standard and Formatting toolbars share one row check box.

chapter one

Slide Show. Normal view is the PowerPoint default view. It combines three views of your work: an outline pane (where text is displayed in outline format) at the left, a slide pane (where text is displayed on the slide) at the right, and a notes pane (a text area for speaker notes) at the bottom directly below the slide. Switching between views is accomplished by clicking the appropriate view button or by accessing the View menu.

At the bottom of the window is the **status bar** that, depending on the view, contains the current slide number and the total number of slides (Slide 1 of 7); the current presentation design template (*Recommending A Strategy*); the current view; and the Spelling Status button (book icon with a check or x) when PowerPoint is or has completed spell checking your presentation.

Just above the status bar is the **Drawing toolbar**, which contains buttons and list boxes you can use to create and manipulate text and shapes.

The **slide pane** is the working area of the slide for creating and editing slides.

Placeholders are objects on the slide for text, charts, tables, organization charts, clip art, or other objects for the slide. They indicate what information is to be keyed in that location on the slide. For example, when you create a presentation, the title slide contains two placeholders, the "Click to add title" and "Click to add subtitle" placeholders. You do not have to key data in every placeholder on a slide because they do not print or appear on the actual slide. If you want to delete a placeholder, click the fuzzy border and press the DELETE key.

The **Office Assistant**, a Help feature that you can ask questions of, appears automatically when you launch PowerPoint unless you hide it or turn it off. The default Office Assistant animated character is "Clippit." In this book, the Office Assistant is hidden unless you need it for a specific activity. As you view various slides in a presentation, a small light bulb displays with Office Assistant suggestions for clip art images and formatting features. You can click the light bulb, read the suggestion, and then close the Office Assistant. To hide the Office Assistant, if necessary:

Step 1	*Right-click*	the Office Assistant
Step 2	*Click*	Hide

The Office Assistant may pop up at various times indicating presentation design tips as well as software shortcuts. If that happens, just hide the Office Assistant using the same method as described above.

QUICK TIP

To display the Office Assistant, you can click the Microsoft PowerPoint Help button on the Standard toolbar or select the Show the Office Assistant command on the Help menu.

1.c Navigating through a Presentation

To view the slides in a presentation in Normal view or in Slide view, you can click the Previous Slide and Next Slide buttons, drag the scroll box, or press the PAGE UP and PAGE DOWN keys.

You can also check the status bar to tell which slide you are viewing, and how many slides are in your presentation. To view slides in Normal or Slide view:

Step 1	*Press*	the HOME key to display Slide 1, if necessary
Step 2	*Click*	the Next Slide button ⬇ below the vertical scroll bar to view Slide 2
Step 3	*Press*	the PAGE DOWN key to view Slide 3
Step 4	*Drag*	the scroll box on the vertical scroll bar to the right of the slide down to view Slide: 6 of 7
Step 5	*Press*	the HOME key to return to the first slide in the presentation
Step 6	*Press*	the END key to go to the last slide in the presentation

QUICK TIP

When you drag the scroll box up or down the vertical scroll bar, a ScreenTip displays the slide number and the title of the slide.

1.d Navigating Among the PowerPoint Views

You can view a presentation using six different views: Normal view, Outline view, Slide view, Slide Sorter view, Notes Page view, and Slide Show. The default view for a presentation is **Normal view**, where you can view one slide at a time as well as see the outline pane and the notes pane below the slide pane. Normal view is good for creating a presentation because you can see the actual slide as you create it. Notice that the Normal View button appears pressed because that is the current view. To switch to a different PowerPoint view:

| Step 1 | *Click* | the Outline View button ▤ located to the left of the horizontal scroll bar |

Outline view displays the title and main text of all the slides in a presentation in outline format without backgrounds, colors, graphics, text size, or styles (see Figure 1-3). This view is good for quickly

chapter
one

organizing and putting down your ideas. It is also a good view in which to edit slide text because you can view and work with several slides on the screen at the same time.

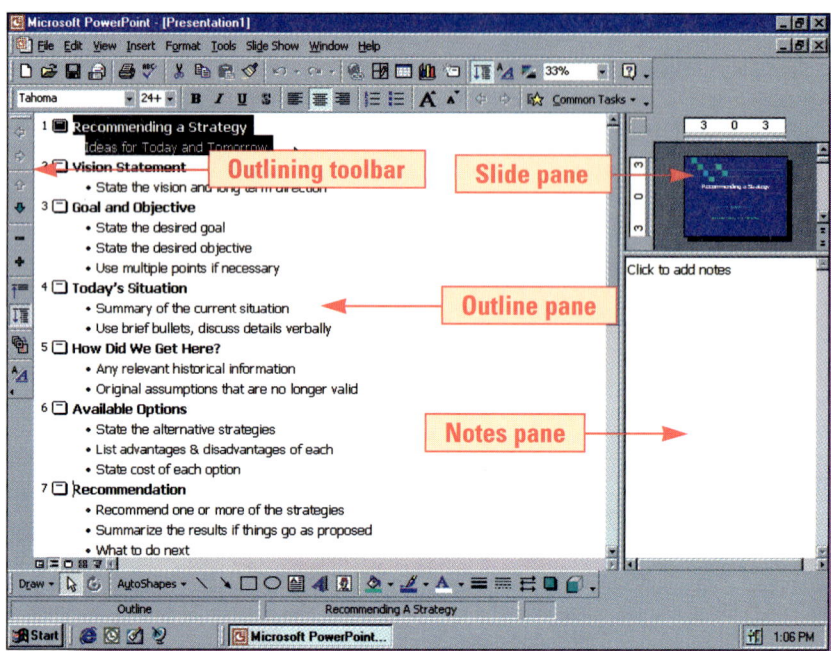

FIGURE 1-3
Outline View

Step 2	*Drag*	the scroll box on the vertical bar at the right of the outline pane to the very top of the scroll bar, then release the mouse button to see the Slide 1 icon
Step 3	*Click*	the Slide 1 icon to select the slide
Step 4	*Right-click*	any toolbar
Step 5	*Click*	the Outlining toolbar to display it at the left, if necessary
Step 6	*Click*	the Slide View button located to the left of the horizontal scroll bar

In **Slide view**, you view the slide in the slide pane and the slide icons display in the outline pane at the left (see Figure 1-4). Slide view is good for creating a presentation because you can see the actual slide in a larger view than in Normal view.

QUICK TIP

You can adjust the width of the outline pane by dragging the border between it and the slide pane. You can also adjust the height of the notes pane window by dragging the border between the slide pane and the notes pane.

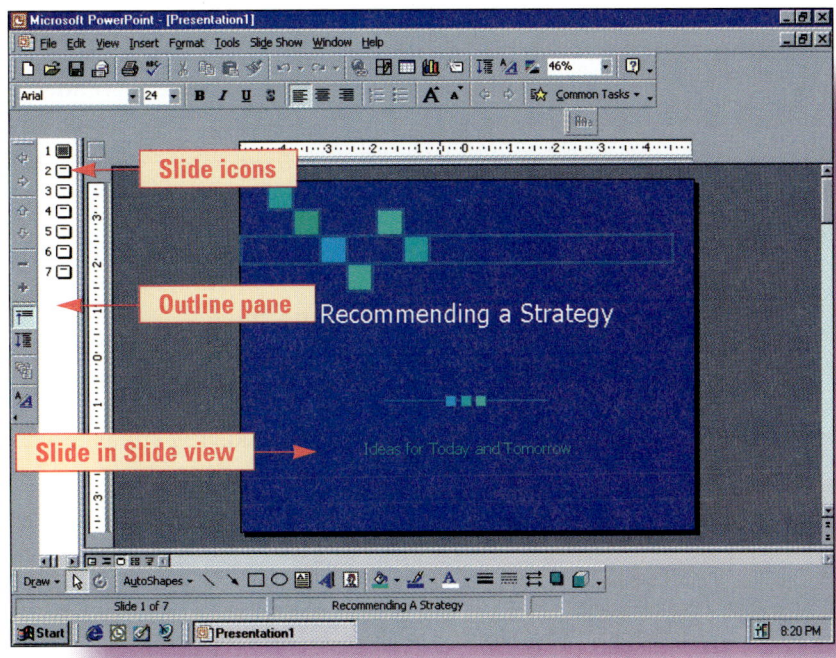

FIGURE 1-4
Slide View

| Step 7 | *Click* | the Slide Sorter View button located to the left of the horizontal scroll bar |

Slide Sorter view displays miniature representations of all the slides in a presentation on screen at one time (see Figure 1-5). This view is excellent

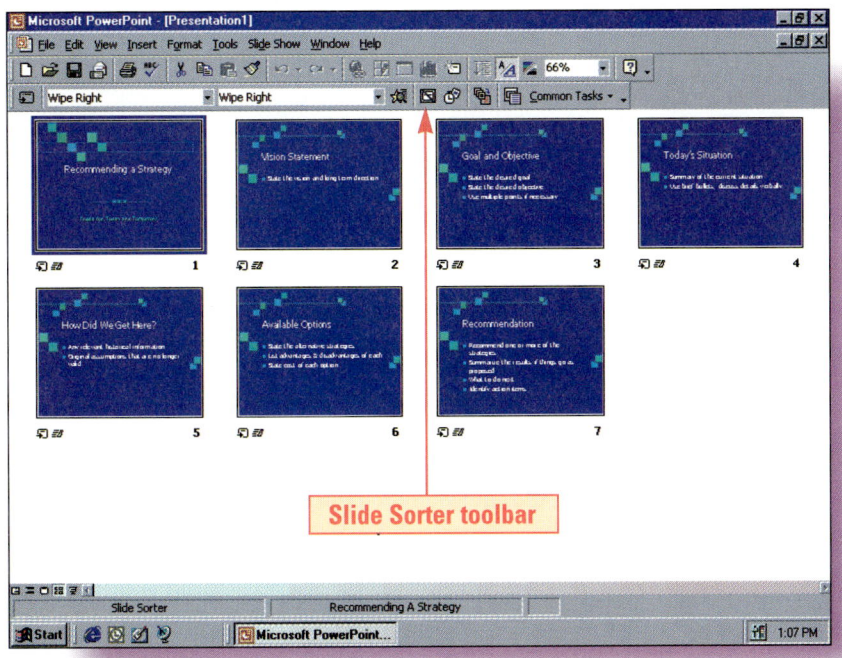

FIGURE 1-5
Slide Sorter View

chapter
one

MOUSE TIP

Double-clicking any slide in Slide Sorter view quickly returns you to the previous view.

for rearranging, copying, or deleting slides as well as for changing the way slides appear on the screen and the speed at which they appear during a visual display of the presentation on the computer screen.

Step 8	*Click*	<u>V</u>iew
Step 9	*Click*	Notes <u>P</u>age

Notes Page view displays a miniature version of the current slide with a notes pane for keying speaker notes that can be printed and used by the presenter during a presentation (see Figure 1-6). A notes pane is provided in both Normal view and Outline view for keying speaker notes. There is no Notes Page View button. To access the notes page, you must use the Notes <u>P</u>age command on the <u>V</u>iew menu.

FIGURE 1-6
Notes Page View

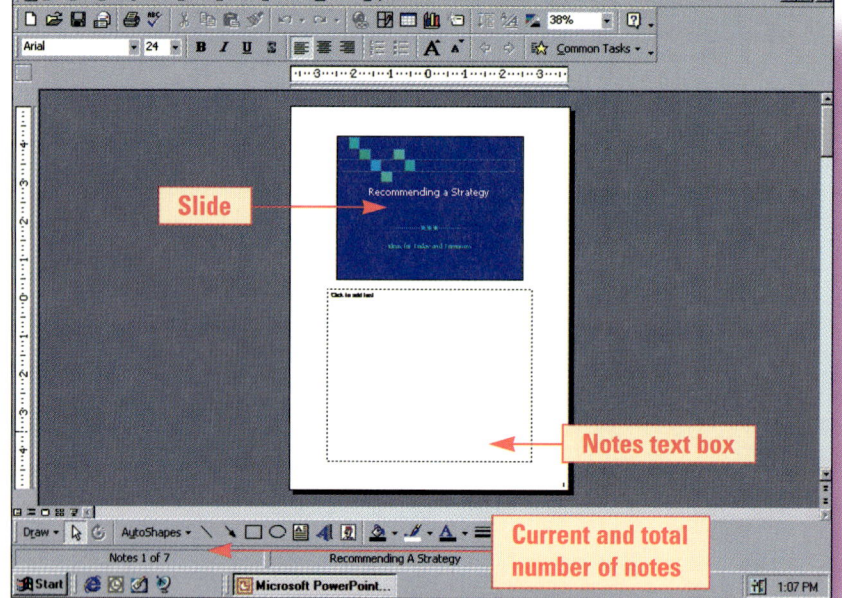

QUICK TIP

The HOME key selects the first slide and the END key selects the last slide in Slide Sorter view.
   You can navigate in Notes Page view and Slide Show view using the PAGE UP, PAGE DOWN, HOME, and END keys.
   You can exit a slide show at any time by pressing the ESCAPE key or right-clicking and then clicking End <u>S</u>how.

Step 10	*Click*	the Next Slide button below the vertical scroll bar to view a different notes page
Step 11	*Click*	the Zoom list arrow on the Standard toolbar
Step 12	*Click*	66% to zoom in to read the speaker notes area

Slide Show displays all the slides in a presentation sized to fill your screen one after another at the speed you choose. The concept is similar to projecting your own slides, assembled in a slide carrousel, on a screen and showing the next slide with the simple click of a button. A slide show begins with the current slide when you click the Slide Show button. To display the Slide Show:

Step 1	*Display*	the first slide (Recommending A Strategy), if necessary
Step 2	*Click*	the Slide Show button located to the left of the horizontal scroll bar
Step 3	*Click*	the left mouse button to progress through the slide show
Step 4	*Click*	the left mouse button until you return to your previous view

1.e Closing a Presentation

PowerPoint enables you to have as many presentations open as your computer resources can handle. However, it is a good idea to close any presentations you are finished with, in order to free computer memory and allow the computer to run more efficiently. To close a presentation:

Step 1	*Click*	the document Close Window button ☒ on the menu bar
Step 2	*Click*	No if you are prompted to save the *Recommending A Strategy* presentation

1.f Applying a Design Template

notes

The presentation design templates used in this book include the new PowerPoint design templates. If the designs do not appear immediately, you need to install them from the Office 2000 CD-ROM before continuing this chapter.

PowerPoint provides many templates of presentation designs to help you in setting up a particular, consistent look for a presentation. **Design templates**, like blueprints, contain a master design that determines the layout of the elements of the slide, a color scheme that coordinates the colors on the slide so they complement each other, appropriate typefaces and fonts that work with the "look" of the presentation, and graphical

chapter
one

QUICK TIP

If you click the <u>N</u>ew command on the <u>F</u>ile menu, the New Presentation dialog box opens, providing you with options for creating a blank presentation or creating a presentation using the AutoContent Wizard.

If you click the New button on the Standard toolbar, you create a new, blank presentation.

You can also key the title in the title placeholder by simply keying before clicking the title placeholder. You can move from the title placeholder to the subtitle placeholder by using the keyboard shortcut, CTRL + ENTER. If you press the CTRL + ENTER keys in the last text box on a slide, you add a new bulleted list slide.

elements to enhance the presentation. Good design is vital to good presentations because the layout, focus, balance, consistency, typeface, and color create appeal and readability that aid in comprehension and retention. Design creates first impressions, gets you to read, buy, or learn, and sets the tone. It also establishes the credibility of the presentation's message. You can create a presentation using a design template or you can apply a design template to an existing presentation. To create a new presentation using a design template:

Step 1	*Click*	<u>F</u>ile
Step 2	*Click*	<u>N</u>ew
Step 3	*Click*	the Design Templates tab in the New Presentation dialog box
Step 4	*Click*	each presentation design in the Design Templates list box to preview the design
Step 5	*Double-click*	the High Voltage design template

The New Slide dialog box shows 24 AutoLayouts in the Choose an AutoLayout: box. **AutoLayouts** are predesigned slide layouts that contain placement for title, text, charts, objects, clip art, and media clips. Instead of designing each slide manually, you can simply choose an AutoLayout that fits your needs. Because you are creating a new presentation and the first slide in a presentation is usually a title slide, PowerPoint automatically selects the Title Slide AutoLayout. Notice the selection border around it and the name "Title Slide" in the lower-right corner of the dialog box. To use the Title Slide AutoLayout:

Step 1	*Double-click*	the Title Slide AutoLayout

A title slide appears in the PowerPoint window with a title placeholder, a subtitle placeholder, and the selected presentation design.

The **title slide**, usually the first slide in a presentation, introduces the topic of the presentation. The goal of a title slide is to grab the audience's attention, set the tone, and prepare the audience for what is to follow. Title slides can also be used to differentiate between sections of a presentation. To enter text on a title slide:

Step 1	*Click*	the "Click to add title" placeholder
Step 2	*Key*	Teddy Toys

Step 3	*Click*	the "Click to add subtitle" placeholder
Step 4	*Key*	Introducing Baby Teddy
Step 5	*Click*	outside the slide area to deselect the placeholder
Step 6	*Switch*	to Slide Show to view the title slide on a full screen
Step 7	*Click*	to return to Normal view

Bullet slides are used to group related topics or items together, list items, emphasize important information, or summarize key points. In the Teddy Toys presentation, for example, you can use a bullet slide to list the sales meeting agenda. **Bullets** are symbols that guide the reader's eye to the start of each item in a list, helping to emphasize important material. To add a new bullet slide:

| Step 1 | *Click* | the New Slide button on the Standard toolbar |

The New Slide dialog box displays the 24 AutoLayouts. PowerPoint assumes the second slide in a presentation is a bullet slide; therefore, the Bulleted List AutoLayout in the second row and second column is automatically selected.

Step 2	*Double-click*	the Bulleted List AutoLayout
Step 3	*Click*	the "Click to add title" placeholder
Step 4	*Key*	Agenda
Step 5	*Click*	the "Click to add text" placeholder
Step 6	*Key*	Highlight current budget
Step 7	*Press*	the ENTER key
Step 8	*Key*	Discuss existing product line
Step 9	*Press*	the ENTER key
Step 10	*Key*	the remaining bullets, including the intentional error: Introduce new product Compare cost vs. price Indicate existing competition Discuss marketing strategies
Step 11	*Click*	outside the slide area and compare your slide to Figure 1-7

chapter
one

FIGURE 1-7
Agenda Bullet Slide

1.g Saving a Presentation

The first time you save a presentation, you can use the Save or the Save As command on the File menu. Both commands open the Save As dialog box. After you have saved your presentation, use the Save command to save the presentation with the same name to the same location, or use the Save As command to give the same presentation a different name or to specify a new disk drive and folder location. Be sure to check with your instructor if you do not know on which disk drive and in which folder to save your presentations. To save the *Teddy Toys* presentation:

| Step 1 | **Click** | the Save button 🖫 on the Standard toolbar |

In the Save As dialog box, the File name: text box suggests a filename based on the first text that appears in the presentation. You can use this name or key a different name of up to 255 characters, including the drive and path. Characters can include letters, numbers, spaces, and some special characters in any combination. Special characters that cannot be used include the following: / \ : ; | ? * > < " "

Step 2	*Key*	Teddy Toys in the File <u>n</u>ame: text box, if necessary
Step 3	*Verify*	that Presentation appears in the Save as <u>t</u>ype: text box
Step 4	*Switch*	to the appropriate disk drive and folder, if necessary
Step 5	*Click*	<u>S</u>ave in the Save As dialog box

Your presentation is saved and the filename, *Teddy Toys*, appears in the title bar. PowerPoint adds a .ppt extension to the presentation filename. This extension may also appear in the title bar. The *Teddy Toys* presentation is used throughout the PowerPoint unit to introduce new slide types and concepts.

1.h Checking Spelling

After you create or edit a presentation, you should save the presentation, check spelling in the presentation, and then resave the presentation with the corrections. Even after you spell check a presentation, it is still necessary to proofread it because the spell checker does not correct grammatical errors, the use of the wrong word (for example, *from* instead of *form*), or know the spelling of proper names.

PowerPoint actively checks your spelling as you key text, while the Spelling Status button in the status bar indicates that action. If you make an error as you key, PowerPoint underscores the error with a wavy red line once the SPACEBAR is pressed, and a red x replaces the red check mark on the Spelling Status button. To correct an error, you can either manually correct the error by selecting and keying the correct spelling; by clicking the right mouse button on the error and selecting the correct spelling; or by double-clicking the Spelling Status button and selecting the correct spelling. You can also click the Spelling button on the Standard toolbar and respond to the suggestions in the Spelling dialog box. The Spelling button method spell checks the entire presentation, regardless of the slide currently in view. To check the spelling of a presentation and save the changes:

| Step 1 | *Click* | the Spelling button on the Standard toolbar (see Figure 1-8) |

chapter
one

FIGURE 1-8
Spelling Dialog Box

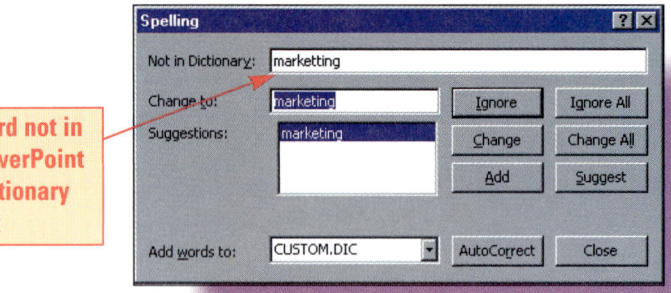

Word not in PowerPoint Dictionary box

Click Ignore if the spelling is correct in the Not in Dictionary: text box, or select the correct word in the Suggestions: list box and click Change. If the spell checker stops at a word that is spelled incorrectly, but offers no suggestions for replacement, key the correct word in the Change to: text box and then click the Change button.

Step 2	*Correct*	the text as needed
Step 3	*Click*	OK when PowerPoint has completed spell checking the entire presentation
Step 4	*Click*	the Save button 🖫 on the Standard toolbar to save your changes to the presentation

1.i Changing the Presentation Design

After you have created a presentation with a design template, you have the option of changing that design template to fit the needs of the presentation. To change a design template:

Step 1	*Double-click*	High Voltage in the status bar
Step 2	*Click*	each presentation design template to view the designs
Step 3	*Double-click*	the Gesture design template
Step 4	*View*	Slides 1 and 2 and notice the changes in the slides
Step 5	*Save*	the *Teddy Toys* presentation

1.j Printing a Presentation

PowerPoint provides different options for printing a presentation. At this time, you will print the entire presentation as slides. To print the presentation:

Step 1	*Click*	the Print button 🖨 on the Standard toolbar to print a hard copy of the slides

1.k Exiting PowerPoint

When you have completed all work in PowerPoint, you should exit the application. Any open documents close when you exit PowerPoint. If you haven't saved, you are prompted to save your changes. To exit PowerPoint and close any open documents:

Step 1	*Click*	the application Close button ⊠ on the PowerPoint title bar

Because you didn't make any changes since you last saved *Teddy Toys*, the presentation closes, the PowerPoint application exits, and the Windows desktop appears.

MOUSE TIP

You can close PowerPoint by right-clicking the Microsoft PowerPoint application button on the taskbar and clicking the Close command.

MENU TIP

You can close PowerPoint by clicking on the Exit command of the File menu.

chapter
one

Summary

▶ The PowerPoint default window includes the menu bar, Standard toolbar, Formatting toolbar, View buttons, scroll bars, Drawing toolbar, status bar, and slide area.

▶ The Standard toolbar and Formatting toolbar buttons are a faster means of accessing commands than the menu bar.

▶ PowerPoint provides six viewing options in which you can view your presentation: Normal view, Slide view, Outline view, Slide Sorter view, Notes Page view, and Slide Show. Normal view offers three views of a presentation by combining an outline pane, a slide pane, and a notes pane.

▶ Presentation design templates enable you to enhance your presentation by including a professionally designed background, color scheme, font appearance, and graphic elements.

▶ PowerPoint provides 24 AutoLayouts for help in creating different slide layouts, such as title slides and bulleted lists.

▶ For the first slide of a new presentation, PowerPoint selects the Title Slide AutoLayout in the New Slide dialog box.

▶ Title slides are used as the first page or section divider pages within a presentation.

▶ For the second slide of a presentation, PowerPoint selects the Bulleted List slide AutoLayout in the New Slide dialog box.

▶ Bullet slides include a title and a list of numbered or bulleted items. Bullets are symbols used to emphasize text that is listed.

▶ After creating a presentation, you should save it for future use.

▶ You can use long filenames (up to 255 characters) when saving in PowerPoint.

▶ The Spelling feature immediately displays errors as you key text, and enables you to spell check an entire presentation for typographical errors.

▶ Proofreading in an essential part of preparing any presentation, as spell checking does not find all types of errors.

▶ Closing a presentation frees computer resources and enables the computer to run more efficiently.

▶ When you finish working in PowerPoint, you should exit the application.

Commands Review

Action	Menu Bar	Shortcut Menu	Toolbar	Keyboard
Create a new presentation	File, New			CTRL + N ALF + F, N
View the next slide			or Drag the scroll box down one slide	PAGE DOWN
View the previous slide			or Drag the scroll box up one slide	PAGE UP
Display the first slide				HOME
Display the last slide				END
Display Normal view	View, Normal			ALT + V, N
Display Outline view				
Display Slide view				
Display Slide Sorter view	View, Slide Sorter			ALT + V, D
Display Notes Page view	View, Notes Page			ALT + V, P
Display Slide Show	View, Slide Show Slide Show, View Show			ALT + V, W ALT + D, V F5
Add a new slide	Insert, New Slide			CTRL + M ALT + I, N ALT + C, N
Apply a design template	Format, Apply Design Template	Right-click, Apply Design Template		ALT + O, Y
Save a presentation	File, Save File, Save As			CTRL + S ALT + F, S ALT + F, A F12
Check the spelling in a presentation	Tools, Spelling	Right-click red wavy line	or double-click the Spelling Status icon in the status bar	F7 ALT + T, S
Print a presentation	File, Print			CTRL + P ALT + F, P
Close a presentation	File, Close			CTRL + F4 ALT + F, C
Exit PowerPoint	File, Exit	Right-click the PowerPoint button on the taskbar, click Close		ALT + F, X ALT + F4

chapter one

Concepts Review

Circle the correct answer.

1. Any and *every* command can be found on the:
[a] menu bar.
[b] Standard toolbar.
[c] Formatting toolbar.
[d] Drawing toolbar.

2. The PowerPoint window displays which of the following toolbars by default?
[a] Outlining toolbar, Standard toolbar, and Clipboard toolbar
[b] Standard toolbar, Formatting toolbar, and Drawing toolbar
[c] Picture toolbar, Formatting toolbar, Drawing toolbar
[d] Standard toolbar, Formatting toolbar, and Drawing + toolbar

3. Which of the following commands does *not* navigate the user through a PowerPoint presentation in Slide view?
[a] PAGE UP and PAGE DOWN keys
[b] dragging the scroll box
[c] Previous Slide and Next Slide buttons
[d] left mouse button

4. Which of the following is a combination view consisting of an outline pane, a slide pane, and a notes pane?
[a] Slide Sorter view
[b] Notes Page view
[c] Normal view
[d] Slide Show

5. Presentation designs regulate the formatting and layout for the slide and are commonly called:
[a] blueprints.
[b] placeholders.

[c] design templates.
[d] design plates.

6. You can create a new presentation by doing any of the following *except*:
[a] pressing the Ctrl + N keys.
[b] clicking File, Open.
[c] clicking File, New.
[d] clicking the New button on the Standard toolbar.

7. Objects on a slide that hold text are called:
[a] textholders.
[b] AutoLayouts.
[c] object holders.
[d] placeholders.

8. The type of slide that is used to introduce a topic and set the tone for a presentation is called a:
[a] title slide.
[b] bullet slide.
[c] graph slide.
[d] table slide.

9. What type of symbols are used to identify items in a list?
[a] graphics
[b] bullets
[c] markers
[d] icons

10. To exit the PowerPoint application, you can:
[a] double-click the document Control-menu icon.
[b] click the application Close button.
[c] click the document Close button.
[d] click the application Minimize button.

Circle **T** if the statement is true or **F** is the statement is false.

T   F   1. You can create a presentation from within PowerPoint or use New Office Document command at the top of the Start menu.

T   F   2. The title bar of PowerPoint contains the name of the application—Microsoft PowerPoint—as well as the name of the active presentation.

T   F   3. In order to begin a new presentation, you must close all current presentations.

T   F   4. When you add a new slide, PowerPoint provides 24 AutoLayout designs from which to choose.

T   F   5. A title slide may be used only as the first slide in any presentation.

T   F   6. A bullet slide should include as many bullets as necessary to fill the slide.

T   F   7. After initially saving a presentation, you should use the Save command to give your presentation a new name.

T   F   8. As you work in PowerPoint, you should save periodically to avoid losing your work.

T   F   9. *Midwest Sales Report** is a valid filename for saving a PowerPoint presentation.

T   F   10. Clicking the Print button automatically prints the presentation.

 **notes**   In subsequent chapters, you build on the presentations you create below. Therefore, it is advisable to complete all exercises and case projects, and to use the filenames suggested, before going on to the next chapter. It is a good idea to save three presentations per one disk so that you do not run out of disk space.

Skills Review

Exercise 1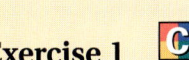

1. Create a new presentation using the Global design template.

2. Use the Title Slide AutoLayout for the first slide. The title should read: *PowerPoint*. The subtitle should display your name.

3. Add a new slide using the Bulleted List AutoLayout. The bullet slide title should read: *PowerPoint Defined*. The following bullet should read: *PowerPoint is an easy to use presentation graphics application that allows you to create slides that entertain, motivate, convey, persuade, sell, or inform.*

4. Save the presentation as *PowerPoint*.

5. Spell check, proofread, and resave the presentation, and then print and close it.

Exercise 2

1. Create a new, blank presentation.

2. Use the Title Slide AutoLayout for the first slide. The title should read: *Why Microsoft Office Professional?* and the subtitle should read: *Are You Ready?*.

3. Apply the Expedition design template to the presentation.

4. Add a new slide using the Bulleted List AutoLayout. The bullet slide title should read: *What is Office Professional?* Key the following as separate bullets: *Word, Excel, PowerPoint, Access*.

5. Save the presentation as *Office*.

6. Spell check, proofread, and resave the presentation, and then print and close it.

chapter one

Exercise 3

1. Create a new presentation using the Checkers design template.

2. Use the Title Slide AutoLayout for the first slide. The title should read: *Creating a Presentation* and subtitle should read: *Your Name*.

3. Add a new slide using the Bulleted List AutoLayout. The bullet slide title should read: *The First Step*. Key the following as separate bullets: *What is my message?, Who is my audience?, Where will my message appear?*

4. Save the presentation as *Design*.

5. Spell check, proofread, and resave the presentation, and then print and close it.

Exercise 4

1. Create a new, blank presentation.

2. Use the Title Slide AutoLayout for the first slide. The title should read: *Precision Builders* and the subtitle should read: *Builders of Distinction*.

3. Apply the Blueprint design template to the presentation.

4. Add a new slide using the Bulleted List AutoLayout. The bullet slide title should read: *Why Precision Builders?*. The following bullet items should read: *Quality craftsmanship, Quality materials, Dedicated personnel*, and *Excellent reputation*.

5. Save the presentation as *Precision Builders*.

6. Spell check, proofread, and resave the presentation, and then print and close it.

Exercise 5

1. Create a new presentation consisting of a title slide and a bullet slide.

2. Apply the Nature design template.

3. Add a title slide with the title *S & L Nature Tours* and the subtitle *Enjoying the Outdoors while Promoting Good Health*.

4. Add a bullet slide with the title *National Park Tours* and the following bullets: *Glacier National Park, Yellowstone National Park, Rocky Mountains National Park*, and *Teton National Park*.

5. Save as the presentation as *Nature Tours*.

6. Spell check, proofread, and resave the presentation, and then print and close it.

Exercise 6

1. Create a new presentation consisting of a title slide and a bullet slide.

2. Apply the Sunny Days design template.

3. Add a title slide with the title *Health in the New Millennium* and the subtitle *Are You Ready to Reduce Stress in Your Life?*

4. Add a bullet slide with the title *Good Health Helps Everyone*. Add the following bullets: *Eat a balanced diet, Drink plenty of water, Exercise regularly, Visit your doctor periodically, Reduce the level of stress*, and *Enjoy life*.

5. Save as the presentation as *A Healthier You*.

6. Spell check, proofread, and resave the presentation, and then print and close it.

Exercise 7

1. Create a new presentation consisting of a title slide and a bullet slide.

2. Apply the Factory design template.

3. Add a title slide with the title *Buying a Computer* and the subtitle *A Guide to Selecting the Perfect Computer for Your Needs*.

4. Add a bullet slide with the title *Getting Started*.

5. Add the following bullets: *What do I need to do on the computer?, How much can I afford?, Where should I purchase the computer?,* and *Where can I find information about computers?.*

6. Save the presentation as *Buying A Computer*.

7. Spell check, proofread, and resave the presentation, and then print and close it.

Exercise 8

1. Create a new presentation consisting of a title slide and a bullet slide.

2. Apply the Strategic design template.

3. Add a title slide with the title *Leisure Travel* and the subtitle *You Deserve a Great Vacation*.

4. Add a bullet slide with the title *Vacation Packages for Everyone*. Add the following bullets: *Spring Rafting Package, Summer Hiking Package, Fall Get-A-Way Package, Winter Ski Package, Canada's Splendor Package,* and *Land Down Under Package*.

5. Save as the presentation as *Leisure Travel*.

6. Spell check, proofread, and resave the presentation, and then print and close it.

Case Projects

Project 1

You have been asked to explain to your fellow assistants how to create a presentation by starting with a template. Using PowerPoint online <u>Help</u>, review information on creating presentations. Print the "Create a presentation based on a design template" topic.

Project 2

You work in the Human Resources Department of Communicate Corporation. You have been selected to give a presentation to train employees on proper telephone usage. Apply a presentation design template of your choice to create a title slide introducing the topic and a bullet slide defining the subject matter and topics to be covered. Save the presentation as *Communicate*. Spell check and proofread the presentation, and then print it.

Project 3

You work for Souner & Associates, a software training company. You are going to give a sales presentation to a group of office managers that contains information about why they should hire your organization. Apply a presentation design template of your choice to create a title slide introducing your company and a bullet slide displaying training classes offered. Spell check the presentation, and then save it as *Souner*. Print the presentation.

Project 4

Create a realistic presentation about the company you work for or an organization with which you are familiar. Choose an occasion on which it might be appropriate to create a PowerPoint presentation

chapter one

for this company or organization. Consider what your message will be, who your audience will be, and what medium you will use to present your topic. Apply a presentation design template of your choice and begin with a title slide and a bullet slide. Use your company or organization name and any other information that pertains to the presentation. Save the presentation as *My Presentation*. Spell check and then print the presentation.

Project 5

You have just accepted a full-time summer job at your local zoo. One of your job responsibilities is to create a presentation that entices grammar school children to visit the zoo during the summer as well as the regular school season. Decide what areas of the zoo would be of interest and possibly any special attractions. Apply a presentation design template of your choice and begin with a title and a bullet slide. Save the presentation as *Zoo*. Print the presentation.

Project 6

Your employer has asked whether or not you think your department should upgrade from your existing PowerPoint software to PowerPoint 2000. Access your Internet service provider (ISP) and visit the Microsoft PowerPoint Web page at *http://www.microsoft.com/powerpoint*. Search

for new features in PowerPoint 2000. Use the presentation design of your choice to create a PowerPoint bullet slide itemizing some of the new features you found. Print the slide and close the presentation without saving it.

Project 7

As a consumer education instructor, part of your curriculum is to educate students on how to purchase a new car. Decide how you plan to introduce this topic to a class of 15- and 16-year olds. Visit the Internet to find out current information on the best selling new cars this past year. Save the presentation as *Cars*, and print it.

Project 8

You are a teaching assistant at Millennium University. Your lead professor is teaching an Introduction to the Internet class for college freshmen. You and another teaching assistant (choose a member of your PowerPoint class to work with) must gather the information and create a PowerPoint presentation for the professor to use in his classes. Decide on the topics to be covered in this eight-week course. Visit the Internet to research new Internet topics that you feel should be covered. Download and use a presentation design template that you find on the Internet. Save the presentation as *Internet*, and print it.

Editing and Formatting Slides

Chapter Overview

I n this chapter you learn about opening a presentation, adding a slide, working with second-level bullets, using AutoCorrect, moving slides, editing and formatting text, using the slide master, and printing an individual slide.

Case profile

Today you are asked to continue working on the *Teddy Toys* presentation. Mr. Lerek would like you to summarize the points to be discussed about the current budget so the sales managers have a strong understanding of Teddy Toy's fiscal position as it attempts to enter a new market. In addition, you need to create a slide to summarize the existing product line of teddys so the managers understand how the new product fits in the Teddy Toys family.

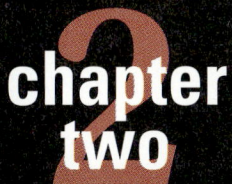

chapter
two

2.a Opening a Presentation and Adding a Bullet Slide

When you add a slide to a presentation, the slide is inserted *after* the currently selected slide. (You learn how to rearrange the slides later in this chapter.) To open an existing presentation and add a bullet slide:

MENU TIP

You can open a presentation by clicking the Open command on the File menu.

Step 1	**Click**	the Open button ⬜ on the Standard toolbar
Step 2	**Display**	the folder or drive containing your Data Files
Step 3	**Double-click**	the *Teddy Toys* presentation
Step 4	**Display**	the last slide in the presentation, if necessary
Step 5	**Click**	the New Slide button ⬜ on the Standard toolbar
Step 6	**Double-click**	the Bulleted List AutoLayout

2.b Working with Second-Level Bullets

PowerPoint has five possible bullet levels, each with a bullet symbol, an indent from the previous bullet level, and a smaller text size. First-level or major bullets introduce an idea. Second-level or minor bullets support or provide additional information about the first-level bullet. Third-, fourth-, and fifth-level bullets provide additional information about each previous bullet level. You should avoid using multiple bullet levels because each subsequent level displays a smaller text size than the previous level and is more difficult to read.

When you create a new supporting bullet level, you demote the bullet by moving the selected paragraph to the next (lower) bullet level. **Demoting** moves the bullet down one level to the right. When you want to create a higher bullet level, you promote the bullet by moving the selected paragraph to the previous (higher) bullet level. **Promoting** moves the bullet up one level to the left. To add first- and second-level bullets, and move a bullet from one level to another:

Step 1	*Click*	the "Click to add title" layout placeholder
Step 2	*Key*	Current Budget
Step 3	*Click*	the "Click to add text" layout placeholder
Step 4	*Key*	Revenues
Step 5	*Press*	the ENTER key
Step 6	*Press*	the TAB key to demote to the second-level bullet position
Step 7	*Key*	Sales
Step 8	*Press*	the ENTER key
Step 9	*Key*	Investments
Step 10	*Press*	the ENTER key
Step 11	*Press & Hold*	the SHIFT key
Step 12	*Press*	the TAB key to return to the first-level bullet position

> **MOUSE TIP**
>
> You can also demote bullet text down a level by clicking the Demote button on the Formatting toolbar or the Outlining toolbar. You can promote bullet text up a level by clicking the Promote button on the Formatting toolbar or the Outlining toolbar.

Using the SHIFT + TAB keys or clicking the Promote button moves a bullet from its existing level to the next level higher. Once you change a bullet level, the new level remains as the current level upon pressing the ENTER key until you press the TAB key or the SHIFT + TAB keys or click the Demote or Promote button on the Formatting or Outlining toolbar.

Step 13	*Key*	Expenses
Step 14	*Press*	the ENTER key
Step 15	*Press*	the TAB key
Step 16	*Key*	the following second-level bullets under Expenses: Salaries Research Manufacturing
Step 17	*Save*	the *Teddy Toys* presentation and compare your slide to Figure 2-1

chapter
two

FIGURE 2-1
Current Budget Slide

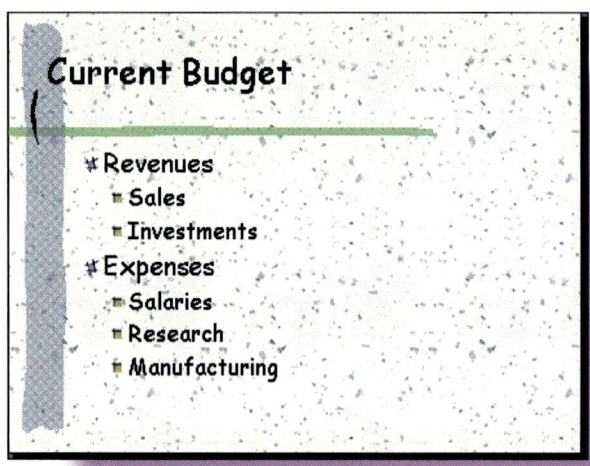

2.c Using AutoCorrect

AutoCorrect is an Office 2000 feature that automatically corrects common keying errors. As soon as you press the SPACEBAR, ENTER key, TAB key, or key any punctuation mark after a word, AutoCorrect reviews and corrects the word if necessary. You can also use AutoCorrect to convert keying shortcuts (such as your initials) to longer words (your complete name).

You can add your own AutoCorrect entries, as a way of customizing AutoCorrect, to save time if you repeatedly key the same information. You can add words you commonly misspell or shortcut keystrokes you want changed to complete text entries. You open the AutoCorrect dialog box by clicking AutoCorrect on the Tools menu. To add an AutoCorrect entry:

QUICK TIP

If you add an AutoCorrect entry in PowerPoint 2000, that entry becomes available in other Office applications.

Step 1	*Click*	Tools
Step 2	*Click*	AutoCorrect (see Figure 2-2)
Step 3	*Click*	in the Replace: text box
Step 4	*Key*	te
Step 5	*Press*	the TAB key
Step 6	*Key*	Teddy in the With: text box
Step 7	*Click*	Add
Step 8	*Click*	OK

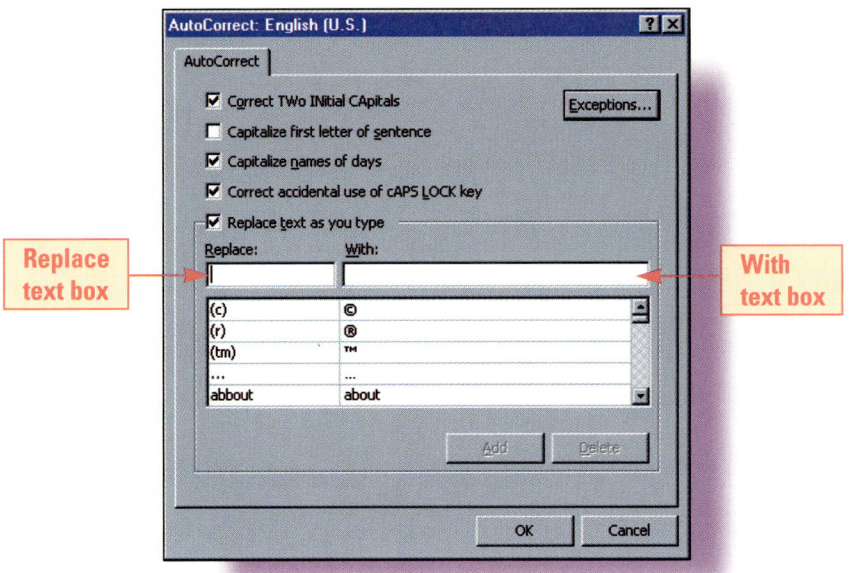

FIGURE 2-2
AutoCorrect Dialog Box

Replace text box

With text box

> ### QUICK TIP
>
> If you enter an AutoCorrect entry in lowercase letters when adding it to PowerPoint, AutoCorrect inserts it in initial capitals if you key the shortcut in initial capitals or all capital letters if you key the shortcut in all capitals.

To test your AutoCorrect entries:

Step 1	*Display*	the last slide in the presentation, if necessary
Step 2	*Click*	the New Slide button ⌧ on the Standard toolbar
Step 3	*Double-click*	the Bulleted List AutoLayout
Step 4	*Click*	the "Click to add title" layout placeholder
Step 5	*Key*	Existing Product Line
Step 6	*Click*	the "Click to add text" layout placeholder
Step 7	*Key*	The te Family
Step 8	*Press*	the ENTER key
Step 9	*Press*	the TAB key
Step 10	*Key*	Papa te
Step 11	*Press*	the ENTER key
Step 12	*Key*	Mama te
Step 13	*Press*	the ENTER key
Step 14	*Press & Hold*	the SHIFT key
Step 15	*Press*	the TAB key to create a first-level bullet
Step 16	*Key*	The Action te
Step 17	*Press*	the SPACEBAR to activate AutoCorrect

chapter two

Step 18	*Press*	the BACKSPACE key to delete the blank space after Teddy
Step 19	*Key*	s
Step 20	*Press*	the ENTER key
Step 21	*Press*	the TAB key
Step 22	*Key*	the following second-level bullets under The Action Teddys: Racing te Superbear te Ice Skating te Rock & Roll te (press the SPACEBAR to activate AutoCorrect)
Step 23	*Save*	the *Teddy Toys* presentation

2.d Working in Outline View

Outline view is useful for creating, editing, and adding slides. You may even find that creating slides in Outline view is easier than in Slide view because you are only looking at the text of the slides in the presentation. Editing is also faster because you do not have to wait for the screen to redraw. To add a slide in Outline view:

Step 1	*Click*	the Outline View button ▤ located to the left of the horizontal scroll bar
Step 2	*Click*	after the last bullet on the last slide ("Rock & Roll Teddy")
Step 3	*Click*	the New Slide button ▤ on the Standard toolbar
Step 4	*Double-click*	the Bulleted List AutoLayout

A new slide icon, preceded by a number is displayed on the screen with the insertion point waiting for your text. When keying a slide in Outline view, the first line is the title and all succeeding lines are subtitles or bullets.

Step 5	*Key*	Introducing Baby te
Step 6	*Press*	the ENTER key to insert the "Baby Teddy" entry and a new slide icon
Step 7	*Press*	the TAB key to demote this from a new slide to a bullet point

| Step 8 | *Key* | the following bullets:
Great new addition to the family
Potential for a teen bear
Targeted for the infant market
Safest & softest te available |

Do not press the ENTER key after keying the last bullet. Doing so would result in an extra bullet appearing on your slide.

| Step 9 | *Save* | the *Teddy Toys* presentation |

Moving Bullets in Outline View

You may often need to rearrange bullets after keying them so that they follow a more logical sequencing of topics. Moving bullets is easy in Outline view. If necessary, right-click any toolbar and click Outlining to display the Outlining toolbar. To move a bullet:

| Step 1 | *Click* | the third bullet item ("Targeted for the infant market") |

| Step 2 | *Click* | the Move Up button 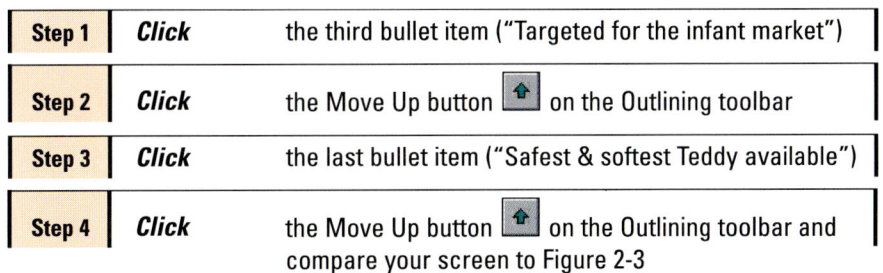 on the Outlining toolbar |

| Step 3 | *Click* | the last bullet item ("Safest & softest Teddy available") |

| Step 4 | *Click* | the Move Up button on the Outlining toolbar and compare your screen to Figure 2-3 |

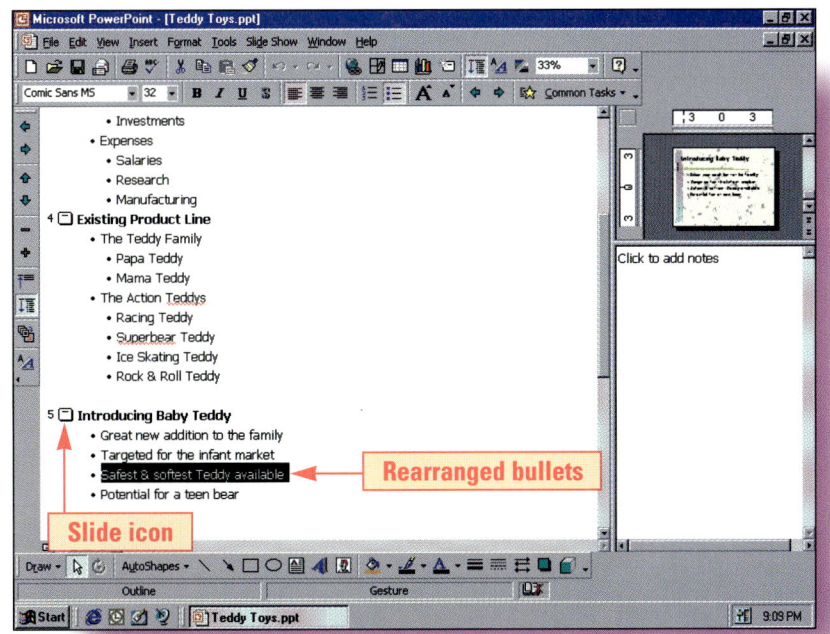

FIGURE 2-3
Introducing Baby Teddy
Slide with Rearranged
Bullets

chapter
two

2.e Moving a Slide in Outline View

In Outline view you can also move an entire slide. First, you select the slide by clicking the four-headed arrow on the slide icon preceding the slide to be moved. Second, you move the slide by dragging it or clicking the Move Up or Move Down buttons on the Outlining toolbar until the slide is where you want it. To move a slide:

Step 1	*Click*	the slide icon to the left of Introducing Baby Teddy
Step 2	*Drag*	to move the slide between the first and second slides (a horizontal line representing the slide appears as you move)
Step 3	*Click*	the Undo button ⤺ on the Standard toolbar to undo this action

2.f Editing and Formatting Slides

After applying a presentation design, or at any time, you may make changes to the look of the slide. You can change the spacing between lines and paragraphs, alignment of text, indents, and type of bullets. Although you can edit and format a slide in Outline view, Slide view allows you to see all editing and formatting changes as they will actually appear on the slide while you work. To add text to an existing slide:

Step 1	*Click*	the Slide View button 🔲
Step 2	*Display*	the first slide, if necessary
Step 3	*Click*	at the end of the "Introducing Baby Teddy" subtitle

A box with eight sizing handles appears around the subtitle text box, indicating that the text box is selected, and the insertion point is positioned just to the right of the text (see Figure 2-4).

MOUSE TIP

You can move a bullet by selecting the entire bullet and dragging it to a new position. To select an entire bullet, point to the bullet before the bullet text you want to move. When the I-beam pointer changes to a four-headed arrow, click the mouse button to select it. Drag the selected bullet to its new position.

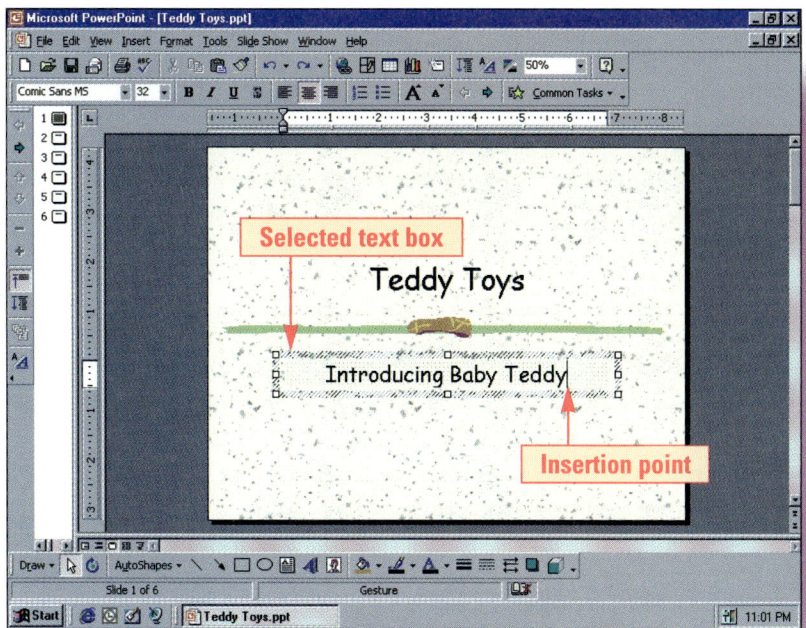

FIGURE 2-4
Selected Text Box

> **QUICK TIP**
>
> The Undo feature enables you to undo your last action. If you decide you did not want to undo what you just did, click the Redo button. The Redo button reverses the Undo.

You can select individual lines of text or you can select an entire text box to apply any editing or formatting changes. To select individual lines of text or individual characters, you drag the mouse pointer; the text you selected is then highlighted. To select an entire text box, you hold down the SHIFT key and click the text box, or you can click in the text box to select it and then click a text box border.

Step 4	*Press*	the ENTER key
Step 5	*Key*	Our Newest Addition
Step 6	*Drag*	to select "Our Newest Addition"
Step 7	*Click*	the Decrease Font Size button on the Formatting toolbar

By clicking the Decrease Font Size button, you reduce the size of the text to the next size smaller in the Font Size box.

Changing Text Alignment

Alignment adjusts the horizontal position of text on a slide. For example, the title and subtitle text boxes on the Gesture design template use center alignment. Four types of alignment options—left, center, right, and justify—are available. For quick alignment change, you can

chapter two

click the Align Left, Center, or Align Right button on the Formatting toolbar. To change the text alignment:

Step 1	*Click*	the *Teddy Toys* title text box
Step 2	*Click*	the Align Left button ▤ on the Formatting toolbar
Step 3	*Click*	outside the text box to deselect it

Changing alignment affects the paragraph in which the insertion point is located. To change the alignment of multiple lines in a text box, you select the entire text box. To select a text box without positioning the insertion point inside it, you use the SHIFT key. To select the subtitle text box and change alignment:

Step 1	*Press & Hold*	the SHIFT key
Step 2	*Click*	the subtitle text box

The text box is selected, but you do not see a flashing insertion point. When you change the alignment, both lines of the subtitle change.

Step 3	*Click*	the Align Left button ▤ on the Formatting toolbar

Changing Tabs

To create a slightly different look to the *Teddy Toys* title slide, you decide to set a tab to indent the second line of the subtitle, "Our Newest Addition," to the right .5". Just as in Word, there are four types of tabs: left, center, right, and decimal. Left tabs align text at the left, center tabs align text at a center point, right tabs align text at the right, and decimal tabs align text at the decimal points.

In order to work with tabs, the ruler should be displayed on the PowerPoint application window. If the ruler is not displayed, click Ruler on the View menu. For your reference, the ruler, tab symbol button, and a tab marker are displayed in Figure 2-5. Before you can add tabs to text in a slide, the insertion point must be flashing in the text box. Before inserting a tab, you need to change to the tab style you want. You can delete a tab by dragging the tab marker down slightly off the ruler. To change and set a tab on a slide:

Step 1	*Click*	immediately to the left of "Our Newest Addition"
Step 2	*Click*	the Tab button ⬛ at the far left of the horizontal ruler to display a Center Tab symbol
Step 3	*Click*	the Tab button ⬛ to display a Right Tab symbol ⬛
Step 4	*Click*	the ruler at the 5" position

A Right Tab marker now appears at 5" on the ruler, indicating that you have set a right tab at this position.

Step 5	*Press*	the TAB key

Our Newest Addition now ends at the 5" mark. To delete a tab and set another tab:

Step 1	*Drag*	the Right Tab marker ⬛ down below the ruler
Step 2	*Click*	the Tab button at the far left of the horizontal ruler until the Left Tab symbol ⬛ is displayed
Step 3	*Click*	the ruler at 2"

A Left Tab symbol now appears at 2" on the ruler and Our Newest Addition has shifted to a new position. You decide that a tab at 2" is not far enough to the right for the look you want. To move a tab:

Step 1	*Drag*	the Left Tab symbol ⬛ to the 2.5" mark on the ruler

The Left Tab symbol now appears at the 2.5" mark, and Our Newest Addition has again shifted to a new position (see Figure 2-5).

chapter
two

FIGURE 2-5
Title Slide with
Tabbed Text

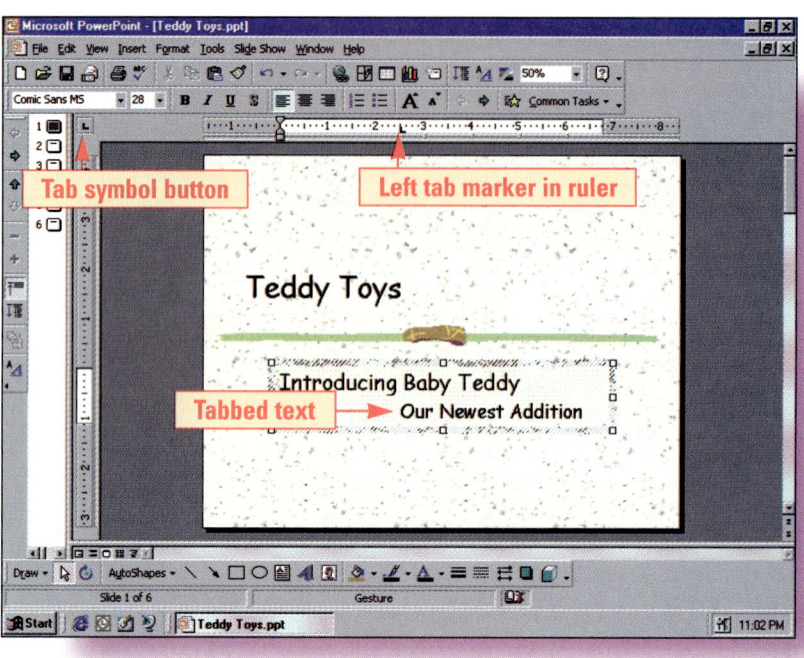

Changing Line Spacing

Depending on the number of lines on a slide, you may wish to either increase or decrease the line spacing in order to fit more lines on a slide, make the lines stand out more, or fill more of the slide. **Line spacing** is the space between lines of text on a slide. **Paragraph spacing** refers to the spacing between paragraphs. Changes to the line spacing on a slide affect the amount of white space between the lines of a paragraph. **White space** is the empty space on a slide between lines or surrounding lines of text and is intended to aid the readability of the text. To change the line spacing of bulleted text on a slide:

Step 1	*Display*	the Agenda slide
Step 2	*Press & Hold*	the SHIFT key
Step 3	*Click*	anywhere in the bullet text box to select the entire bullet text box
Step 4	*Click*	Format
Step 5	*Click*	Line Spacing

The Line Spacing dialog box opens, with options for changing the line spacing and spacing before and after paragraphs. Line spacing increases or decreases the amount of space between all lines of text. The Before and After paragraph spacing options increase or decrease the amount of space before or after paragraphs only, not between the lines within a paragraph.

Step 6	*Drag*	the Line Spacing dialog box to the right so you can see the bullets on the Agenda slide.
Step 7	*Key*	1.2 in the Line spacing box
Step 8	*Click*	Preview to view the changes
Step 9	*Click*	OK
Step 10	*Display*	the Introducing Baby Teddy slide
Step 11	*Press & Hold*	the SHIFT key
Step 12	*Click*	anywhere in the bullet text box to select the entire bullet text box
Step 13	*Open*	the Line Spacing dialog box
Step 14	*Key*	1.4 in the Line spacing box
Step 15	*Click*	Preview to view the changes
Step 16	*Click*	OK

Changing Bullet Symbols

A **bullet symbol** is a design element that sets off each bullet point in a list. PowerPoint enables you to use symbols, pictures, font characters, numbers, and letters as bullet symbols. You can keep the bullet symbol styles determined by the presentation design, or change their color and size, or even select a different bullet symbol. The Formatting toolbar provides a quick method for displaying or hiding bullet symbols and numbers. The Format menu provides additional symbols and bullet customization. To change the bullets symbols on a slide:

Step 1	*Display*	the Agenda slide
Step 2	*Select*	the entire bullet text box
Step 3	*Click*	the Numbering button [icon] on the Formatting toolbar
Step 4	*Display*	the Introducing Baby Teddy slide
Step 5	*Select*	the entire bullet text box
Step 6	*Click*	Format
Step 7	*Click*	Bullets and Numbering
Step 8	*Click*	the Numbered tab in the Bullets and Numbering dialog box, if necessary

chapter
two

Step 9	**Double-click**	the first example in row 2 to display capital letters A. B. C.
Step 10	**Save**	the *Teddy Toys* presentation

If the insertion point is positioned in one bullet line, then the bullet changes on that line only.

2.g Formatting the Slide Master

The **slide master** controls the formatting, color, and graphic elements for the slides in a presentation, including the bullets. Making changes to the slide master enables you to make changes to all slides (except title slides) in a presentation automatically, instead of manually changing each one. The design template selected determines the slide master formats. For now, you use the slide master to make some simple formatting changes. To change bullets on the slide master:

Step 1	**Point**	to the Slide View button ⬚ located to the left of the horizontal scroll bar
Step 2	**Press & Hold**	the SHIFT key until the ScreenTip displays Slide Master View
Step 3	**Click**	the Slide Master View button ⬚

The Slide Master template displays placeholders for the title, bullet, date, footer, and slide number areas. It displays existing formats in terms of font, point size, alignment, color scheme, graphic elements, and bullet symbols.

Step 4	**Right-click**	in the first-level bullet text
Step 5	**Click**	Bullets and Numbering
Step 6	**Click**	the Bulleted tab, if necessary
Step 7	**Click**	Picture

Step 8	*Click*	the bullet example that is a green shaded square (scroll through the list, if necessary)
Step 9	*Click*	the Insert clip button from the shortcut menu
Step 10	*Right-click*	in the second-level bullet text
Step 11	*Click*	Bullets and Numbering
Step 12	*Click*	Character
Step 13	*Click*	the Wingdings font in the Bullets from: list box
Step 14	*Click*	the second bullet in row 4 (diamond shape)
Step 15	*Click*	the bright gold color in the Color: list box (ScreenTip displays Follow Accent and Followed Hyperlink Scheme Color)
Step 16	*Click*	OK
Step 17	*Save*	the *Teddy Toys* presentation

Changing Indents

Indents determine the distance of text from the margins on the slide. Indents can affect first lines of text, succeeding lines of text, or both. In order to change the indent positions for your bullet items, the rulers should be displayed on your screen. If the rulers are not displayed on your screen, you need to display them using the Ruler command on the View menu. The ruler displays five indent markers, one for each of the five levels of bullets beginning with the first-level bullet marker on the far left. The top triangle indents the bullet symbol; the bottom triangle indents the bullet text; and the rectangular box indents both the bullet and the text. To change the bullet indents on the slide master:

Step 1	*Click*	anywhere in the bullet text box
Step 2	*Drag*	the rectangular box of the first-level indent marker to indent the bullet and the text to the right until the marker is resting on the 1" mark on the ruler

This indents the first-level bullet and its text. Notice that the other bullet levels have also moved to the right (see Figure 2-6).

Step 3	*Drag*	the top triangle of the first-level indent marker (the bullet marker) to the left until the marker is resting on the .5" mark on the ruler, to move only the first-level bullet without its text

chapter
two

FIGURE 2-6
Slide Master with Indent
Markers

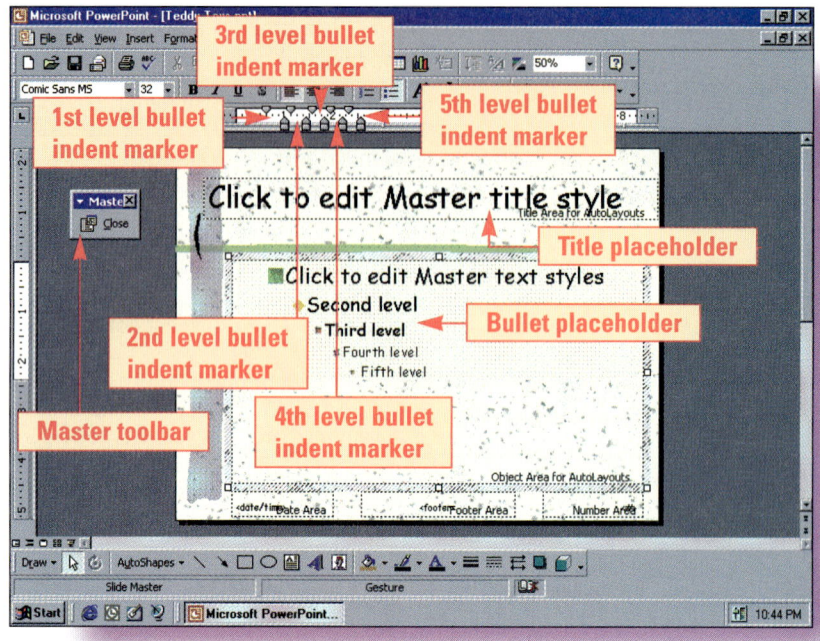

FIGURE 2-6
Slide Master with Indent
Markers

Step 4	*Drag*	the rectangular box of the second-level indent marker to indent the bullet and the text to the right until the marker is resting on the two marks to the left of the 2" mark on the ruler
Step 5	*Drag*	the top triangle of the second-level indent marker (the bullet marker) to the left until the marker is resting two marks to the right of the 1" mark on the ruler
Step 6	*Click*	the Slide Show button located to the left of the horizontal scroll bar to run a slide show to view the bullet changes

Notice that the bullet symbols changed on the slides that used the default bullets. When you change bullets on an individual slide, you override the slide master. You can reapply the slide master formatting to any slide. To reapply the current master styles:

Step 1	*Click*	the Slide View button located to the left of the horizontal scroll bar to accept your changes and close the slide master
Step 2	*Display*	the Agenda slide
Step 3	*Click*	the Slide Layout command on the Common Tasks button on the Formatting toolbar
Step 4	*Double-click*	the Bulleted List AutoLayout to reapply the current master styles

| Step 5 | *Click* | the Undo button on the Standard toolbar to undo this action |

You can change the bullet indent on the numbered and lettered bullet slides to allow more space between the bullet and its text.

Step 6	*Display*	the Agenda slide, if necessary
Step 7	*Click*	anywhere in the bullet text box
Step 8	*Drag*	the bottom triangle of the indent marker to move the text one mark to the right of the 1" mark on the ruler

Only the text indents; the bullet remains at its original position.

Step 9	*Display*	the Introducing Baby Teddy slide
Step 10	*Click*	anywhere in the bullet text box
Step 11	*Drag*	the bottom triangle of the indent marker to move the text one mark to the right of the 1" mark on the ruler

Only the text indents; the bullet remains at its original position.

2.h Printing an Individual Slide

PowerPoint provides different options for printing a presentation. Previously, you accepted the Print button default of printing the entire presentation as slides. If you want to print only a single slide, you can use the Print command on the File menu. To print an individual slide:

Step 1	*Display*	the Current Budget slide, if necessary
Step 2	*Click*	File
Step 3	*Click*	Print to open the Print dialog box
Step 4	*Click*	the Current slide option
Step 5	*Click*	OK
Step 6	*Save*	and close the *Teddy Toys* presentation

chapter
two

Summary

▶ PowerPoint enables you to add slides at any point in the presentation.

▶ First-level bullets introduce a topic and second-level bullets provide additional information regarding first-level bullets.

▶ AutoCorrect automatically corrects common typing errors and can be customized to save time for repeated text.

▶ Outline view is an easy view in which to create, edit, and add slides.

▶ Changes may be made to any presentation design in order to personalize the look of the presentation.

▶ Alignment and indents change the position of text within a text box.

▶ Left, Center, Right, and Justify are four types of alignment for positioning text.

▶ You can set, change, and move tabs using the ruler and the tab symbols.

▶ Increasing or decreasing line spacing changes the appearance of slides.

▶ White space is the empty space on a slide that aids readability.

▶ The slide master controls settings for the formatting, color, and graphic elements for the slides of a presentation.

▶ Indent markers are used to indent bullets from the left edge of the text box.

▶ You can reapply the formatting of the slide master to any slide by reapplying the current master styles of the slide layout.

▶ Print an entire presentation by clicking the Print button on the Standard toolbar.

▶ Print a single slide or selected slides by clicking Print on the File menu.

Commands Review

Action	Menu Bar	Shortcut Menu	Toolbar	Keyboard
Open an existing presentation	File, Open		📂	CTRL + O ALT + F, O
Create an AutoCorrect entry	Tools, AutoCorrect			ALT + T, A
Create a next-level bullet			➡	TAB
Return to a previous-level bullet			⬅	SHIFT + TAB
Use Outline view	View, Outline		▤	ALT + V, O
Change tabs			└ ┴ ┘ ┷	
Change line spacing on a slide	Format, Line Spacing			ALT + O, S
Display the ruler	View, Ruler			ALT + V, R
Print an individual slide	File, Print			CTRL + P ALT + F, P
Undo a previous action	Edit, Undo		↩	CTRL + Z ALT + E, U
Access the slide master	View, Master, Slide Master		SHIFT + ▫	ALT + V, M, S
Reapply the slide master	Format, Slide Layout	Right-click, Slide Layout		ALT + O, L
Change indents			⧗	

Concepts Review

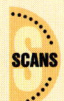

Circle the correct answer.

1. **To add a slide to an existing presentation, click:**
   [a] File, New.
   [b] File, Open.
   [c] Insert, New Slide.
   [d] File, Add a New Slide.

2. **To change the bullet back to a previous level, press the:**
   [a] TAB key.
   [b] ENTER key.
   [c] SHIFT key.
   [d] SHIFT + TAB keys.

3. **AutoCorrect automatically corrects:**
   [a] common typing errors.
   [b] all errors.
   [c] all grammar errors.
   [d] word tense errors.

4. **Bullets order can be changed in Outline view by:**
   [a] clicking the Move Up or Move Down buttons.
   [b] dragging the tab marker to its new location.
   [c] dragging the indent markers to their new location.
   [d] clicking the Collapse or Expand buttons.

5. **You can tell that a text box is selected when:**
   [a] a dotted border appears surrounding the text.
   [b] eight small sizing handles appear surrounding the text.
   [c] the text box is shaded.
   [d] a solid black border surrounds the text.

chapter two

6. Line spacing is the amount of white space:
[a] between lines of text.
[b] before and after paragraphs.
[c] between the characters of a line.
[d] between words of a line.

7. Alignment refers to the:
[a] length of the line.
[b] horizontal position of a line on the page.
[c] vertical space between the lines of text.
[d] size of the characters in a line.

8. Which of the following is *not* used to position text on a slide?
[a] tabs
[b] alignment
[c] line spacing
[d] font color

9. If you want all the slides in the presentation to be formatted with the same *new* bullet symbol, use:
[a] a presentation design template.
[b] the slide master.
[c] the add a slide option.
[d] the slide layout option.

10. Reapplying the current master styles to a slide:
[a] changes the formatting on all slides.
[b] reverts formatting changes to the styles on the slide master.
[c] adds an identical slide.
[d] removes any inserted or drawn objects on a slide.

Circle **T** if the statement is true or **F** is the statement is false.

T F   1. The Common Tasks button on the Formatting toolbar allows you to quickly add a new slide.

T F   2. Second-level bullets are the exact same size as first-level bullets.

T F   3. You cannot add your own entries to the PowerPoint AutoCorrect feature.

T F   4. Bullets can be moved only by clicking the Move Up or Move Down buttons in Outline view.

T F   5. When applying a particular presentation design, you must apply this design to each slide individually.

T F   6. You can set left, right, center, decimal, and dot leader tabs using the ruler.

T F   7. Setting and changing tabs is accomplished with a command from the Format menu.

T F   8. Increasing or decreasing line spacing aids in readability.

T F   9. The Slide Master template displays placeholders for title and text.

T F   10. PowerPoint does not allow you to print an individual slide.

Skills Review

Exercise 1

1. Open the *PowerPoint* presentation.

2. Use the Outline view to add a bullet slide to the end of the presentation.

3. Add an AutoCorrect entry for the word "slide" using sl.

4. Add an AutoCorrect entry for the word "view" using vi.

5. Use the new AutoCorrect entries when you key the following slide. The title should read: *The Views of PowerPoint* and the bullets should read: *Normal View, Slide View, Slide Sorter View, Outline View, Notes Page View*, and *Slide Show*.

6. Move the Outline View bullet up two levels so that it appears under the Normal View bullet.

7. Use the slide master and drag the rectangular box to indent the first-level bullet to the 1" mark on the ruler.

8. Use the slide master and drag the top triangle (bullet marker) to indent the bullet to the .5" mark on the ruler.

9. Save, spell check, and proofread the presentation, then resave if necessary.

10. Print the new slide only, and then close the presentation.

Exercise 2

1. Open the *Office* presentation.

2. Display the *What is Office Professional?* slide.

3. Edit the bullet slide in Outline view by adding the following second-level bullets under each of the first-level bullets: Under the first-level bullet "Word" add the second-level bullet *word processing*; under the first-level bullet "Excel" add the second-level bullet *worksheets*; under the first-level bullet "PowerPoint" add the second-level bullet *presentations*; under the first-level bullet "Access" add the second-level bullet *databases*.

4. In Slide view, drag the rectangular box to indent the second-level bullets to the 1" mark on the ruler.

5. In Outline view, add a bullet slide.

6. Use the Symbol command on the Insert menu to insert the trademark symbol in the fourth bullet. The title should read: *Why Use Office Professional?*. The bullets should read: *Collaboration on HTML-based documents, Sharing of information via the Internet, Integration of office documents via Web browsers, IntelliSense™ technology enhancements*, and *Professional-looking documents*.

7. Using the slide master, change the bullet symbol of the first-level bullet using a Picture bullet.

8. If necessary, indent the bullet or the text to increase the space between the bullet and the text.

9. Using the slide master, change the bullet symbol for the second-level bullet using a Character bullet from the Webdings font list.

10. View the slides and make any other necessary indent changes.

11. Using the line spacing feature, change the paragraph spacing on *Why Use Office Professional?* to .75 lines before the paragraph.

12. Using the Outline view, move a slide.

13. Save the presentation.

14. Save, spell check, and proofread the presentation, then resave if necessary.

15. Print the new slides only, and then close the presentation.

Exercise 3

1. Open the *Design* presentation.

2. Add a bullet slide at the end of the presentation. Key the following title: *Design Tips for Bullet Slides* and key the following bullet items: *Use six or fewer topics per slide, Use six to eight words per topic, Avoid ALL CAPS*, and *Use parallel phrasing*.

3. Change the line spacing of the bullets to 1.5.

4. Using the Outline view, move the Avoid ALL CAPS bullet to the end of the bullet list.

5. Change the bullet symbol using a character from the Wingdings font list.

chapter two

6. Save, spell check, and proofread the presentation, then resave if necessary.

7. Print the new slide only, and then close the presentation.

Exercise 4

1. Open the *Precision Builders* presentation.

2. Add a bullet slide at the end of the presentation.

3. Add an AutoCorrect entry for Precision Builders using pb.

4. Use the new AutoCorrect entry when you key the following slide. The title should read: *Our Motto* and the bullet should read: *Precision Builders wants to work with you to build the home of your dreams at a price that will not shatter your dreams.*

5. Change the line spacing to 1.5 lines.

6. Display the Precision Builders title slide, and set a tab at the 2" mark on the ruler for the subtitle, Builders of Distinction.

7. Change the alignment of the title to center and then to align right.

8. Reapply the current master styles to the Our Motto slide.

9. Save, spell check, and proofread the presentation, then resave if necessary.

10. Print the new slides only, and then close the presentation.

Exercise 5

1. Open the *Nature Tours* presentation.

2. Add a bullet slide at the end of the presentation. The title should read: *Available Tours*. The first-level bullet should read: *Each tour is available at beginning, intermediate, and expert levels*. The second-level bullets should read: *Hiking, Biking, Rafting*, and *Horseback riding*.

3. Change the indent for the second-level bullets by moving to the right approximately .5".

4. Save, spell check, and proofread the presentation, then resave if necessary.

5. Print the new slide only, and then close the presentation.

Exercise 6

1. Open the *A Healthier You* presentation.

2. Using the Outline view, add a bullet slide at the end of the presentation. The title should read: *Balanced Diet at a Glance* and the bullets should read: *Carbohydrates, Proteins, Fats, Minerals, Vitamins*, and *Fiber*.

3. Using the Outline view, move the Fats bullet to the end of the bullet list.

4. Change the paragraph spacing to increase the spacing before the paragraphs.

5. Using the slide master, increase the indent between the first- and second-level bullets symbols and text.

6. Display the Good Health Helps Everyone slide.

7. Add the following first-level bullet as the first bullet: *Basic common sense rules*.

8. Demote the remaining bullets to second-level bullets.

9. Save, spell check, and proofread the presentation, then resave if necessary.

10. Print the new slide only, and then close the presentation.

Exercise 7

1. Open the *Buying A Computer* presentation.

2. Add an AutoCorrect entry for the word "computer."

3. Add a bullet slide at the end of the presentation. The title should read: *Reasons to Buy a Computer* and the bullets should read: *Accessing the Internet, Keying term papers or reports, Playing computer games, Sending e-mail to family and friends, Working at home.*

4. Change the line spacing on the slide master.

5. Change the bullet indents, if necessary.

6. Rearrange the order of the bullets in order of your priority.

7. Change the bullet symbols to numbering.

8. Display the Getting Started slide. Add the following first-level bullet as the first bullet: *Ask yourself the following:.*

9. Demote the remaining bullets to second-level bullets.

10. Save, spell check, and proofread the presentation, then resave if necessary.

11. Print the new slides only, and then close the presentation.

Exercise 8

1. Open the *Leisure Travel* presentation.

2. Add a bullet slide to the presentation. The title should read: *Leave Everything to Us.* The first-level bullet should read: *We do all the work.* The second-level bullets should read: *Travel arrangements, Hotel accommodations, Restaurant reservations, Golf tee times, Sight-seeing tours.* Add another first-level bullet that reads: *You will be pampered and relaxed.*

3. Make changes to the bullets, line spacing, and alignment to one or more slides in the presentation.

4. Save the presentation and print the slides with changes only.

5. Close the presentation.

Case Projects

Project 1

An administrative assistant in the next department has asked you how to remove the bullets in front of the bullet text. Using PowerPoint online <u>H</u>elp, review information on removing bullets or numbering from a slide. Create a simple bullet slide to summarize the information you find so your co-worker can refer to it again. Print the bullet slide, remembering to spell check and proofread your work first.

Project 2

You have been asked to add a bullet slide to your *Communicate* presentation. This bullet slide should provide information about the first bullet on the previous bullet slide. Make any formatting decisions with regard to alignment, line spacing, indents, and bullet symbols. Save the presentation and print the new slide.

chapter two

Project 3

As you work toward your goal of selling your Souner & Associates training program to prospective clients, you need to begin "selling them" early in the presentation. Add a bullet slide detailing what your organization can provide. Make any formatting decisions with regard to alignment, line spacing, indents, and bullet symbols. If possible, make some of the changes to the slide master. Save the *Souner* presentation and print the new slide.

Project 4

As this is the project on which you are working independently, all decisions are entirely up to you. You should edit your previous slides and add another slide to your presentation. Keep in mind your message, audience, and medium as you work. Make any formatting decisions with regard to alignment, line spacing, indents, and bullet symbols. If possible, make some of the changes to the slide master. It may be necessary to change your presentation design template to set the tone of your topic. Save *My Presentation* and print the new slide.

Project 5

Open the *Zoo* presentation and create a bullet slide that can be added to the presentation concerning possible zoo events, occasions, important dates, or animal facts. Make any formatting decisions with regard to alignment, line spacing, indents, and bullet symbols. If possible, make some of the changes to the slide master. Save and print the new slide.

Project 6

You cannot find an appropriate design template for your presentation. So, you decide to access your Internet service provider (ISP) and visit the Microsoft Home Page at *http://www.microsoft.com* to search for information on downloading new presentation design templates and downloading new Office Assistants. Print the Web pages.

Project 7

As you continue building your *Cars* presentation, add a bullet slide on how to purchase a new car. The slide should summarize the locations to use for finding out as much as you can about your particular car choice. Visit the Internet to find out current information about the car you plan to buy. Make any formatting decisions with regard to alignment, line spacing, indents, and bullet symbols. If possible, make some of the changes to the slide master. Save *Cars* and print the new slide.

Project 8

You and your partner continue to work on your *Internet* presentation. Add another bullet slide at the end of the presentation that highlights one of the topics you chose earlier. Visit the Internet for your research. Make any formatting decisions with regard to alignment, line spacing, indents, and bullet symbols. If possible, make some of the changes to the slide master. Save and print the new slide.

Using Clip Art and WordArt

Chapter Overview

I n this chapter you add clip art images and WordArt to enhance slides in your presentation. Clip art is a collection of professionally designed images that are available to enhance the slides in your presentation. WordArt adds interesting special effects to text, such as unusual alignment, stretching, and 3-D effects.

Case profile

Mr. Lerek has sent you to a workshop on creating effective presentations. At that workshop, you learn that adding images to slides in a presentation supports the text or data on the slide. In addition, you learn that images should be added only if they add value to the message, that images should not overwhelm the message. You decide to add images and WordArt to your *Teddy Toys* presentation.

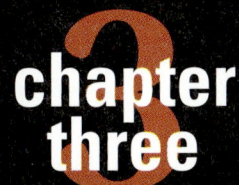

chapter three

3.a Using the Microsoft Clip Gallery

DESIGN TIP

Although graphical images add to a presentation, remember to be selective and allow the images to enhance your presentation, not overtake your message.

notes To view the full Microsoft Clip Gallery images, you must access the Office 2000 CD-ROM. If you do not have access to the full Clip Gallery, you can access the following image files from the Data Disk to continue working on the *Teddy Toys* presentation: *bd07153, pe01686, pe02043, pe02622, pe03166,* and *pe02002.* In addition, you need the files *Tedbear, Light,* and *Toybskt* from the Data Disk. If your Data Files are located on a network drive, check with your instructor to determine what drive and folder to open in order to access the clip art images.

The **Microsoft Clip Gallery** contains a wide variety of pictures, photographs, sounds, and video clips for enhancement of your presentations, or as a means of conveying an idea through the use of clip art images only. The Clip Gallery also enables you to import clips from other sources as well as search the Web for **online clips**.

Adding Clip Images

Clip images can be added to slides from the Microsoft Clip Gallery, a disk, a hard drive folder, a CD-ROM, or the Internet. Images in the Clip Gallery are arranged by category so they are easy to access. You can browse the Clip Gallery, selecting a category related to your presentation and scrolling through a selected list of images; or you can search for an image by keying a description in the Search for clips: text box and then choosing from the matches found. To add an image by browsing the Clip Gallery:

MENU TIP

Once you open a presentation, you can access the Microsoft Clip Gallery by clicking Picture on the Insert menu and then clicking Clip Art on the submenu, or by clicking Object on the Insert menu and then clicking Microsoft Clip Gallery in the Object type: list.

Step 1	*Open*	the *Teddy Toys* presentation and display the last slide in the presentation
Step 2	*Click*	the New Slide button 🗗 on the Standard toolbar
Step 3	*Double-click*	the Blank AutoLayout to display a new blank slide
Step 4	*Click*	the Insert Clip Art button 🖼 on the Drawing toolbar

The Insert ClipArt dialog box opens (see Figure 3-1).

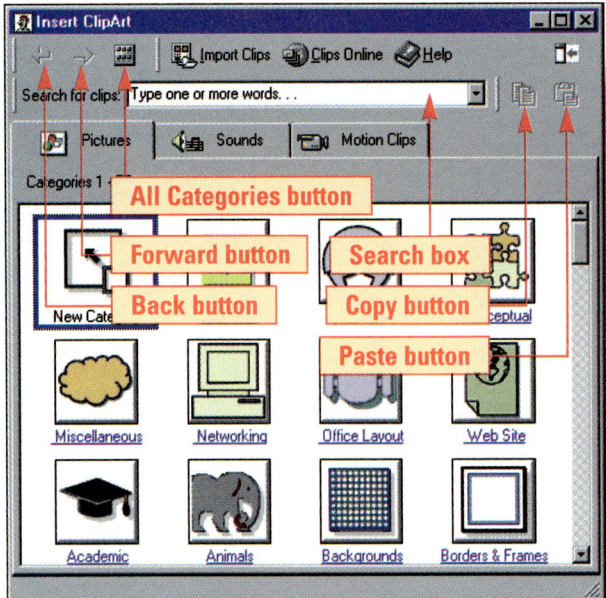

FIGURE 3-1
Insert ClipArt Dialog Box

Q U I C K   T I P

If the Office Assistant is open, it displays an AutoClipArt message indicating that there are appropriate media clips that can be added to your particular slides. You can ask the Assistant to help you find the appropriate images or you can use the Clip Gallery to find images on your own.

You can also add a Clip Art and Text AutoLayout slide from the New Slide dialog box to add images.

notes Depending on your installation of Microsoft Office, the Microsoft Clip Gallery may display different categories and clip art images than displayed in this text. If you don't see an image shown here, click the Keep Looking button or insert the image from the Data Disk using the Picture, From File command on the Insert menu.

Step 5	*Scroll*	down to the People category and click the People button
Step 6	*Scroll*	through the People category
Step 7	*Click*	the seniors image (elderly couple on a picnic; *pe02622* on the Data Disk)
Step 8	*Click*	the Insert clip button
Step 9	*Close*	the Insert ClipArt dialog box and compare your screen to Figure 3-2

chapter
three

FIGURE 3-2
Slide with Seniors Image

The clip art image is automatically aligned at the center of the slide
and selected so that you can work with it. When an image is selected,
eight sizing handles surround it, and the Picture toolbar is displayed.
If the Picture toolbar is not displayed, right-click any toolbar and click
the Picture toolbar. If the toolbar is in the way of the image, drag its
title bar to move it out of the way. To add images using the Search for
clips: box:

Step 1	*Click*	the Insert Clip Art button 🖼 on the Drawing toolbar
Step 2	*Click*	in the Search for clips: text box
Step 3	*Key*	desk and press the ENTER key
Step 4	*Click*	the image of the man at the desk (ScreenTip displays: sadness; *bd07153* on the Data Disk)
Step 5	*Click*	the Insert clip button
Step 6	*Key*	baseball in the Search for clips: text box and press the ENTER key
Step 7	*Click*	the baseball player image (ScreenTip displays: baseball; *pe01686* on the Data Disk)
Step 8	*Click*	the Insert clip button
Step 9	*Minimize*	the Insert ClipArt dialog box

Moving, Resizing, and Deleting an Image

Images are objects that can be resized, edited, moved, and copied. Because an image is automatically placed at the center of the slide when it is inserted, it is easy to manipulate. You can **move** an image by pointing to the center of the image (the mouse pointer changes to a four-directional arrow ⁜) and dragging. You can **resize** (change the shape of) an image by dragging any sizing handle (pointer becomes a double-headed arrow ↖). If you drag a middle handle, you resize only in one direction, changing the proportions of the image. If you drag a corner handle, you maintain the image's original proportions. To move the seniors image:

Step 1	*Click*	the baseball player image to select it, if necessary, to display the selection handles
Step 2	*Point to*	the middle of the image
Step 3	*Drag*	the baseball image to the upper-right corner of the slide

To resize an image:

Step 1	*Click*	the man at the desk image to select it, if necessary
Step 2	*Point to*	the lower-right corner sizing handle until the mouse point becomes an angled double-headed arrow ↘
Step 3	*Drag*	the sizing handle down and to the right approximately 1"
Step 4	*Click*	the Undo button ⟲ on the Standard toolbar to resize the image to its previous size
Step 5	*Drag*	the man at the desk image to the lower-right corner of the slide
Step 6	*Resize*	the man at the desk image and the baseball image so they are approximately the same size as the seniors image

Sometimes, you may want to resize while keeping the center of an image in its original location. To resize from the center of the image:

Step 1	*Click*	the seniors image to select it
Step 2	*Press & Hold*	the CTRL key
Step 3	*Drag*	the lower-right corner sizing handle of the seniors image down and to the right approximately 1"
Step 4	*Release*	the mouse button before releasing the CTRL key

chapter
three

| Step 5 | *Click* | the Undo button on the Standard toolbar |
| Step 6 | *Drag* | the seniors image to the lower-left corner of the slide |

If you find that your choice of clip art does not really "fit" your presentation, delete it. To delete a clip art image:

Step 1	*Click*	the seniors image to select it, if necessary
Step 2	*Press*	the DELETE key
Step 3	*Click*	the Undo button on the Standard toolbar

3.b Editing Clip Art Images

The goal of using clip art images is to customize the images to fit your presentation design, slides, and words. Suppose you want to use a clip art image, but the colors within the image clash with those colors used on the presentation design? Or, suppose you want to use part of the clip art image, not the entire image; or the image directs the eye away from the words you want to reinforce, instead of toward them. To remedy such situations, you can edit by recoloring, cropping, or flipping the clip art image.

Recoloring and Cropping an Image

When a clip art image is placed on a slide using the Clip Gallery, the image is inserted as a metafile. **Metafiles** are images that can be converted into drawing objects, which can then be extensively edited. If you choose not to convert a metafile into a drawing object, you can do basic editing to the image such as recoloring or cropping the image. **Recoloring** an image changes the original colors. **Cropping** an image trims or cuts part of an image or object so that you can use only part of it. You decide to recolor parts of an image on a slide to match the color scheme of your design template. To recolor an image:

| Step 1 | *Select* | the man at the desk image |
| Step 2 | *Click* | the Recolor Picture button on the Picture toolbar to open the Recolor Picture dialog box (see Figure 3-3) |

FIGURE 3-3
Recolor Picture Dialog Box

MOUSE TIP

You can recolor a picture by right-clicking the object, clicking Format Picture, clicking the Picture tab, and then clicking the Recolor button.

Step 3	*Drag*	the Recolor Picture dialog box so that you can see the image you are recoloring, if necessary
Step 4	*Click*	the bright orange color list arrow in the New: list box
Step 5	*Click*	the black color (ScreenTip displays: Follow Text and Lines Scheme Color) to recolor the man's hair
Step 6	*Click*	the blue-gray color list arrow in the New: list box
Step 7	*Click*	the pale green color (ScreenTip displays: Follow Accent Scheme Color) to recolor the phone
Step 8	*Click*	Preview to see the changes on the slide
Step 9	*Click*	the brown color list arrow in the New: list box
Step 10	*Click*	the burgundy (deep red) color (ScreenTip displays: Follow Shadows Scheme Color) to recolor the desk
Step 11	*Change*	the white color in the New: list box (scroll to view the white color) to purple (ScreenTip displays: Follow Accent and Hyperlink Scheme Color)

CAUTION TIP

The recolor option is only available for Microsoft Clip Gallery images. The recolor option is not available if a Clip Gallery image has been converted into a Microsoft Office drawing.

If you change your mind and want to use the default color, remove the check mark from the check box in the Original: column.

| Step 12 | *Remove* | the check mark from the white color check box in the Original: column |
| Step 13 | *Click* | OK |

**chapter
three**

Cropping an image enables you to trim or cut off a portion of that image so that you can use only part of it. You decide to add another image to this slide and crop the image. To crop an image:

Step 1	*Display*	the Microsoft Clip Gallery
Step 2	*Insert*	the graduations image (two graduates; *pe03166* on the Data Disk) from the Academic category
Step 3	*Minimize*	the Insert ClipArt dialog box
Step 4	*Click*	the Crop button ⊞ on the Picture toolbar
Step 5	*Move*	the mouse pointer to the bottom-middle handle of the graduations image
Step 6	*Drag*	the bottom-middle handle up so that only the faces of the graduates are displayed
Step 7	*Release*	the mouse button
Step 8	*Click*	outside the image area and compare your slide to Figure 3-4

FIGURE 3-4
Slide with Cropped Image

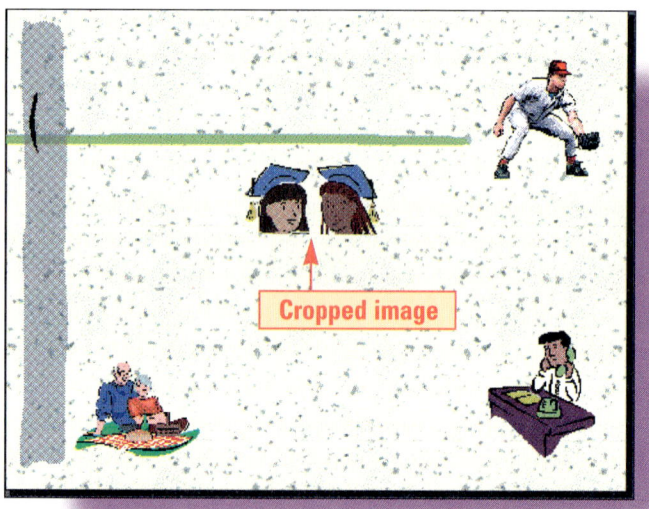

Cropped image

Step 9	*Select*	the graduations image, if necessary
Step 10	*Click*	the Crop button ⊞ on the Picture toolbar
Step 11	*Drag*	the bottom-middle handle down so that the entire graduations image displays
Step 12	*Click*	the Crop button to deselect it

Step 13	*Resize*	the graduations image so it is approximately the same size as the seniors image
Step 14	*Move*	the graduations image to the bottom center of the slide
Step 15	*Save*	the *Teddy Toys* presentation

Flipping and Rotating an Image

You can **flip** an object to change its vertical or horizontal direction. You can also **rotate** an object to change its angle. When you flip or rotate, you are actually manipulating objects. A **drawing object** consists of several objects grouped together to create the image. You can flip or rotate one or all the objects in an image, but in order to use these features, the image must be recognized as a drawing object. When you import an image into PowerPoint—for example, when you insert a clip art image—the image is not a drawing object but simply an imported picture. In order to convert the image into a **Microsoft Office drawing object**, you must first ungroup and then group the image. After an image has been converted into a drawing object, you can then ungroup various parts of that image and recolor or delete parts as desired. To ungroup and group an image:

Step 1	*Insert*	the children image (child on scooter; *pe02043* on the Data Disk) from the Home & Family category in the Microsoft Clip Gallery
Step 2	*Minimize*	the Insert ClipArt dialog box
Step 3	*Click*	the D<u>r</u>aw button Draw ▾ on the Drawing toolbar
Step 4	*Click*	<u>U</u>ngroup

A PowerPoint warning question displays indicating that this is an imported picture, not a group, and asks whether you want to convert it to a Microsoft Office drawing.

| Step 5 | *Click* | <u>Y</u>es to convert the picture to a Microsoft Office drawing |

The child on the scooter image is now ungrouped into many separate objects. Do not click outside the group of selected objects at this point.

| Step 6 | *Click* | the D<u>r</u>aw button Draw ▾ on the Drawing toolbar |

DESIGN TIP

Images should not be facing off the page, because they draw attention away from your message. Try to rotate or flip an image so that it points or leads the eye to the text message.

QUICK TIP

After an image has been converted to a Microsoft Office drawing, you must use the SHIFT key when you drag to resize if you want to maintain the proportions of the image.

chapter
three

Step 7	*Click*	Group to make the child on the scooter image a PowerPoint drawing
Step 8	*Press & Hold*	the SHIFT key so you can maintain the image's proportions
Step 9	*Drag*	a corner handle to resize the image approximately the same as the other images
Step 10	*Move*	the child image to the upper-left corner of the slide

When viewing a presentation, the eye goes to the top of the slide first, then works from left to the right and down in a Z pattern. When an image points off the slide, the eye follows the direction of the image off the slide. To avoid having the audience work to bring their eyes back to the rest of the slide once they have been guided off, it is best to flip the image so that it points into the slide. To flip and rotate an image:

Step 1	*Select*	the child image, if necessary
Step 2	*Click*	the Draw button [Draw ▾] on the Drawing toolbar
Step 3	*Click*	Rotate or Flip
Step 4	*Click*	Flip Horizontal
Step 5	*Click*	the Free Rotate button [⟳] on the Drawing toolbar
Step 6	*Drag*	the lower-right green corner handle to rotate the image up and to the right slightly to rotate or tilt the image
Step 7	*Click*	outside the image

Looking at the slide, you realize that the baseball player is also pointing off the slide. You need to convert that image to an Office drawing so that you can flip the image to face into the slide. To flip an image:

Step 1	*Ungroup*	the baseball player
Step 2	*Group*	the baseball player
Step 3	*Flip*	the baseball player horizontally
Step 4	*Save*	the *Teddy Toys* presentation

3.c Inserting Images from Another Source

You can insert images on a slide from other folders on your computer's hard drive, data disks, a network server, or the Internet. Mr. Lerek has two images available on disk he would like you to add to the *Teddy Toys* presentation. To add an image from another source:

Step 1	**Add**	a new slide with the blank AutoLayout at the end of the presentation
Step 2	**Display**	the Picture toolbar, if necessary
Step 3	**Click**	the Insert Picture from File button on the Picture toolbar
Step 4	**Click**	the Look in: list arrow and click the appropriate drive or folder
Step 5	**Click**	the *Toybskt* image (basket of toys) and click Insert
Step 6	**Click**	the Insert Picture from File button on the Picture toolbar
Step 7	**Switch**	to the appropriate drive or folder
Step 8	**Double-click**	the *Light* image (light bulb)
Step 9	**Move**	the light bulb image to the upper-right corner of the slide
Step 10	**Resize**	the basket of toys image to approximately 3.2" high and the light bulb image to approximately 1.25" high

3.d Adding an Image to the Slide Master

Consistency throughout a presentation creates a sense of unity, a feeling among the audience that the slides belong together and work to reinforce the intended goal of the presentation. You decide to use your company logo image (a teddy bear) on all slides, in the same location, and of the same size to maintain consistency to the look of your presentation. To accomplish this, you simply add the image to

QUICK TIP

You can add a scanned image that has been saved to disk to a PowerPoint slide by clicking the Insert Picture From File button on the Picture toolbar.

MENU TIP

You can also add an image by clicking the Picture command on the Insert menu, then clicking From File.

chapter
three

the slide master. The slide master controls the font, size, color, style, and alignment for the titles and main text on your slides. It also determines the location of the placeholders, background colors, and objects. If you add an image to the slide master, the image appears on all slides in a presentation except for the title slides (there is a separate title master for the title slides in a presentation). To add an image to the slide master:

Step 1	*Press & Hold*	the SHIFT key
Step 2	*Point*	to the Slide View button ▣ located to the left of the horizontal scroll bar
Step 3	*Click*	when the button displays Slide Master View
Step 4	*Click*	the Insert Picture from File button 🖼 on the Picture toolbar
Step 5	*Insert*	the *Tedbear* image (teddy bear) from the Data Disk
Step 6	*Resize*	the teddy bear image until it is approximately 1.5" high
Step 7	*Flip*	the teddy bear image so it faces to the left
Step 8	*Move*	the teddy bear image to the lower-right corner of the slide master
Step 9	*View*	the slide show to verify that the teddy bear image does not overlap any other text boxes on the slides
Step 10	*Resize*	or move the teddy bear image as needed
Step 11	*Click*	the Slide View button ▣ located to the left of the horizontal scroll bar to return to Slide view
Step 12	*Save*	the *Teddy Toys* presentation

You notice that the slide containing all the people clip images does not require the teddy bear image at the bottom. PowerPoint provides an option that enables you to omit or hide a background graphic on an individual slide. When you hide a background graphic on an individual slide, all graphics from the design template are also hidden. To hide a background image on a slide:

Step 1	*Display*	the slide with the people clip images
Step 2	*Right-click*	in a blank area on the slide

CAUTION TIP

If you click the Apply to All button in the Background dialog box, the background graphics would be hidden on all the slides in the presentation.

MENU TIP

You can hide a background graphic by clicking the Background command on the Format menu.

Step 3	*Click*	Back__g__round
Step 4	*Click*	the Omit background graphics from master check box in the Background dialog box
Step 5	*Click*	__A__pply

3.e Using the Clipboard Toolbar

The slide master makes it easy to add the same image to many slides in the presentation. At times, however, you may want to copy an image from one slide and place it on another slide. The **Clipboard toolbar** enables you to copy up to 12 objects so you can paste them to different locations. You decide to copy the teddy bear image from the slide master and paste it on the first slide. To copy and paste an image:

Step 1	*Switch*	to Slide Master view
Step 2	*Select*	the teddy bear image
Step 3	*Click*	the Copy button 🖻 on the Standard toolbar

The Clipboard toolbar displays with options to copy, paste, paste all, clear the Clipboard, and close the Clipboard. The Clipboard displays icons indicating what has been copied to the Clipboard. The ScreenTip indicates the text or image that has been copied. If the Clipboard toolbar does not display, right-click any toolbar and then click Clipboard.

Step 4	*Switch*	to Slide view
Step 5	*Display*	the slide with the people clip images, if necessary
Step 6	*Select*	the seniors image
Step 7	*Click*	the Copy button 🖻 on the Clipboard toolbar
Step 8	*Select*	the child on the scooter
Step 9	*Click*	the Copy button 🖻 on the Clipboard toolbar and compare your Clipboard toolbar to Figure 3-5

MENU TIP

You can also copy an image by clicking the Copy command on the Edit menu. You can also paste an image by clicking the Paste command on the Edit menu.

QUICK TIP

You can copy an image by using the keyboard shortcut CTRL + C. You can paste an image by using the keyboard shortcut CTRL + V.

chapter
three

FIGURE 3-5
Clipboard Toolbar

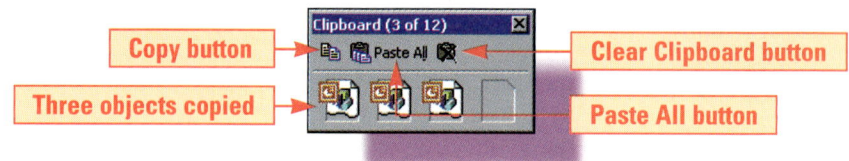

Step 10	*Display*	the Teddy Toys title slide
Step 11	*Click*	the first item (Picture 1) on the Clipboard toolbar
Step 12	*Resize*	the teddy bear image until it is approximately 2.5" high
Step 13	*Move*	the teddy bear image to the upper-right corner of the slide
Step 14	*Click*	the Clear Clipboard button 🗙 on the Clipboard toolbar to clear any copied images
Step 15	*Close*	the Clipboard toolbar

3.f Adding WordArt to a Slide

WordArt enables you to enhance a string of text by using the Insert WordArt button on the Drawing toolbar. **WordArt** enhances text by shadowing, skewing, rotating, and stretching, as well as applying a predefined shape to the text. To create an artistic representation of text, you decide to add WordArt to the last slide in the *Teddy Toys* presentation. To insert WordArt:

| Step 1 | *Display* | the last slide in the presentation |
| Step 2 | *Click* | the Insert WordArt button ▲ on the Drawing toolbar |

The WordArt Gallery dialog box opens, displaying 30 WordArt styles.

| Step 3 | *Double-click* | the yellow and orange WordArt style in the third row, first column |
| Step 4 | *Key* | We Welcome New Ideas in the WordArt Text dialog box (see Figure 3-6) |

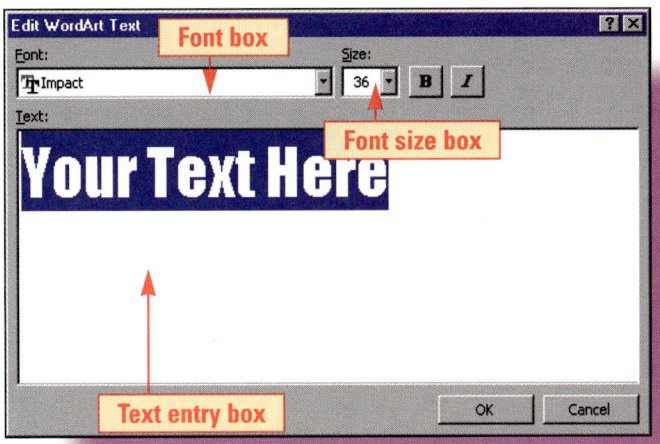

FIGURE 3-6
Edit WordArt Text
Dialog Box

| Step 5 | *Click* | OK |
| Step 6 | *Drag* | the WordArt object just above the basket of toys image |

Editing a WordArt Object

WordArt objects can be resized and moved just like other objects. You can edit and format WordArt text using the WordArt toolbar, which opens when a WordArt object is selected. To edit the WordArt object:

Step 1	*Double-click*	the WordArt object
Step 2	*Click*	the Size: list arrow
Step 3	*Click*	40
Step 4	*Click*	OK

To change the colors of the WordArt object:

Step 1	*Click*	the Format WordArt button on the WordArt toolbar
Step 2	*Click*	the Colors and Lines tab, if necessary
Step 3	*Click*	the Fill Color: list arrow
Step 4	*Click*	the purple color (ScreenTip displays: Follow Accent and Hyperlink Scheme Color)
Step 5	*Verify*	that the Line Color: list box displays No Line
Step 6	*Click*	OK

MOUSE TIP

You can right-click any toolbar and click WordArt to display the WordArt toolbar.

You can access the Edit WordArt Text dialog box by right-clicking the WordArt object and clicking Edit Text, or by clicking the Edit Text button on the WordArt toolbar.

You can also change the color of the WordArt object by right-clicking the WordArt object and clicking Format WordArt.

MENU TIP

You can also change the color of the selected WordArt object by clicking the WordArt command on the Format menu.

chapter
three

Changing the shape of a WordArt object adds interest to the artistic text. In addition, you can create different moods simply by changing the shape of the WordArt object. To change the WordArt shape:

| Step 1 | *Select* | the WordArt object, if necessary |
| Step 2 | *Click* | the WordArt Shape button [Abc] on the WordArt toolbar (see Figure 3-7) |

FIGURE 3-7
WordArt Shapes

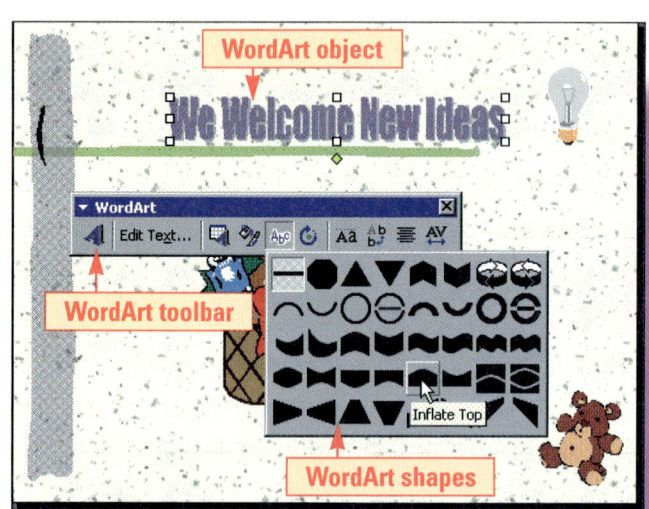

Step 3	*Click*	the Inflate Top shape in the fourth row, fifth column
Step 4	*View*	the slide show
Step 5	*Save*	and close the *Teddy Toys* presentation

The WordArt and images you added to the *Teddy Toys* presentation make it much more interesting and effective.

Summary

▶ The Microsoft Clip Gallery contains a wide variety of pictures, photographs, sounds, and video clips, organized by category.

▶ Images are objects that can be moved, resized, deleted, recolored, cropped, and copied.

▶ Images can be converted into Microsoft Office drawing objects that can be moved, resized, deleted, colored, flipped, rotated, and copied.

▶ Limit the number of clip images per slide in order to eliminate the possibility of the audience being distracted.

▶ When you resize by dragging the corner handles of an image, the image maintains its original proportions.

▶ When you resize by dragging the middle handles of an image, you distort the image's original proportions.

▶ After an image has been ungrouped and grouped, you must use the SHIFT key when resizing to maintain proportions.

▶ Images can be added from other folders, clip art packages, and the Internet.

▶ Images that are placed on the slide master can be hidden on individual slides.

▶ Clip art images can be added to any slide in a presentation, as well as the slide master.

▶ The Clipboard toolbar allows you to copy up to 12 objects so you can quickly paste the objects on the slides.

▶ WordArt is used to shape, skew, and change the appearance of a string of text.

chapter three

Commands Review

Action	Menu Bar	Shortcut Menu	Toolbar	Keyboard
Insert an image from the Clip Gallery	Insert, Picture, Clip Art Insert, Object, Microsoft Clip Gallery			ALT + I, P, C ALT + I, O
Insert an image from another source	Insert, Picture, From File			ALT + I, P, F
Move a selected image			Drag the middle of the image	
Resize a selected image			Drag a sizing handle	
Delete a selected image				DELETE
Recolor a selected image	Format, Picture, Picture, Recolor	Right-click image, Format Picture, Picture, Recolor		ALT + O, I, E
Crop a selected image	Format, Picture, Picture	Right-click image, Format Picture, Picture		ALT + O, I
Rotate an Office drawing image	Draw button on Drawing toolbar, Rotate or Flip	Right-click image, Format Picture, Position		ALT + R, P
Flip an Office drawing image	Draw button on Drawing toolbar, Rotate or Flip			ALT + R, P
Copy an image	Edit, Copy; Edit, Paste	Right-click image, Copy Right-click image, Paste		ALT + E, C ALT + E, P CTRL + C CTRL + V
Insert a WordArt image	Insert, Picture, WordArt			ALT + I, P, W
Edit a selected WordArt image	Edit, Text	Right-click image, Edit Text	Edit Text...	ALT + E, X
Change the WordArt shape				

Concepts Review

Circle the correct answer.

1. **The Microsoft Clip Gallery allows you to:**
   [a] add slides to a presentation.
   [b] add picture, sound, and motion clips to a slide.
   [c] spell check your presentation.
   [d] add WordArt images to a slide.

2. **When an image is selected, it displays:**
   [a] six boxes.
   [b] eight sizing handles.
   [c] six middle handles.
   [d] two corner handles.

3. **When you want to resize an image from the center and keep it proportioned, press the:**
   [a] SHIFT key.
   [b] CTRL key.
   [c] ALT key.
   [d] SPACEBAR.

4. **After moving a clip art image to a particular location on the slide, you can immediately reverse the action by doing all of the following *except*:**
   [a] clicking the Redo button.
   [b] clicking the Undo button.
   [c] clicking the Undo Move Object command on the Edit menu.
   [d] pressing the CTRL + Z keys.

5. **A good design practice when adding clip art images to your slides is to:**
   [a] add as many clip art images as you desire.
   [b] resize the image so it takes up as much space as your text.
   [c] be sure to place at least one clip art image per slide.
   [d] add clip art sparingly and only if it relates to your topic.

6. **In order to delete an image, you must first:**
   [a] move the image to a new location.
   [b] resize the image.
   [c] select the image.
   [d] double-click the image.

7. **What term describes dragging a handle of an image?**
   [a] copying
   [b] selecting
   [c] resizing
   [d] moving

8. **What term describes the separation of a clip art image into different parts so that it becomes a Microsoft Office drawing?**
   [a] grouping
   [b] ungrouping
   [c] regrouping
   [d] embedding

9. **What is the term for changing the direction in which a clip art image faces?**
   [a] crop
   [b] flip
   [c] group
   [d] align

10. **You to copy and paste more than one object with the:**
    [a] Drawing toolbar.
    [b] Clipboard toolbar.
    [c] Formatting toolbar.
    [d] Copy and Paste toolbar.

chapter three

Circle **T** if the statement is true or **F** is the statement is false.

T F 1. Clip art and WordArt should be used only to enhance the goal of a presentation.

T F 2. Images in the Microsoft Clip Gallery are arranged by category so they are easy to access.

T F 3. The Picture toolbar may appear when you insert an image from the Microsoft Clip Gallery.

T F 4. Selecting the image and dragging it to a new location is the same as moving an image.

T F 5. To resize an image from the center while maintaining its original proportions, you should press the ALT key when you drag to resize.

T F 6. Once an image is added to a slide, you cannot remove it.

T F 7. By design, images should face off the slide, away from the text.

T F 8. The slide master enables you to create consistency in your presentation by adding images so they appear on all slides in your presentation, except the title slide.

T F 9. The Clipboard toolbar allows you to copy and paste up to 200 objects.

T F 10. WordArt contains only five styles to display your text.

Skills Review

Exercise 1

1. Open the *PowerPoint* presentation, and display a slide that could benefit from clip art images.

2. Access the Microsoft Clip Gallery and select a category that pertains to the topic of the slide.

3. Add a clip art image to the slide, and then resize and move the image as needed.

4. If necessary, flip the image so it faces the text.

5. Add a blank slide at the end of the presentation for a WordArt object.

6. Use the WordArt style in the fourth row, third column.

7. Add the following text: *PowerPoint*

8. Change the WordArt font to Impact and the Font size to 48.

9. Resize the WordArt object to approximately 3.5" high and 6.5" wide.

10. View the slide show.

11. Save the presentation, print the slides with images and WordArt only, and then close the presentation.

Exercise 2

1. Open the *Office* presentation.
2. Use the Search for clips feature to find an image for one of your bullet slides. Make sure the clip art image enhances and complements the text on the slide.
3. Recolor the clip art image to match the design template, if necessary.
4. Add a blank slide at the end of the presentation for a WordArt object.
5. Use the first WordArt style in the first row, first column. Add the following text: *Office 2000 Is Here!*
6. Change the WordArt font to Times New Roman, Bold and the font size to 60.
7. Change the shape of the WordArt object to Can Down.
8. Change the WordArt fill color to Tan (Follow Accent Scheme Color) and the WordArt line color to Brown (Follow Title Text Scheme Color). Resize the WordArt object as needed.
9. Add an image from the People or the People at Work category.
10. View the slide show.
11. Save the presentation, print only the slides containing images and WordArt, and then close the presentation.

Exercise 3

1. Open the *Design* presentation.
2. Add a blank slide at the end of the presentation for a WordArt object.
3. Use the WordArt style in the second row, fourth column.
4. Add the following text: *Design and You*
5. Change the WordArt font to Impact and the font size to 60, and then resize the WordArt object as needed.
6. Display a bullet slide, and then use the Search for clips feature to find the image relating to the topic of the slide.
7. Resize and move the image as needed.
8. Flip the image so it faces the text, and then rotate the image to find a more eye-catching angle.
9. Add the compasses image from the Navigation Controls category to the slide master.
10. Recolor the image. Resize the image and place it in the lower-right corner.
11. Omit the background graphics from one slide only.
12. Save the presentation, print only the slides containing images and WordArt, and then close the presentation.

Exercise 4

1. Open the *Precision Builders* presentation.
2. Add the industry image (worker with tools; *pe02002*) from the Data Disk to a slide of your choice.
3. Resize the image and place it attractively on the slide.

chapter three

4. Add a blank slide at the end of the presentation for a WordArt object.

5. Use the WordArt style in the third row, fifth column.

6. Add the following text: *Your Dreamhouse*

7. Change the WordArt font to Comic Sans and the font size to 60.

8. Resize the WordArt object as needed.

9. Place the WordArt object within the 90° angle design on the left of the slide.

10. Save the presentation, print only the slides containing images and WordArt, and then close the presentation.

Exercise 5

1. Open the *Nature Tours* presentation.

2. Add an appropriate clip art image to one of the slides.

3. Resize, move, rotate or flip the image as needed.

4. Add a clip art image to the slide master. Resize, move, rotate or flip the image as needed.

5. Add a blank slide at the end of the presentation for the following WordArt object: *Are You Ready for a Great Tour?*

6. Change the WordArt font, size, and colors to match the design template.

7. Resize the WordArt object as needed.

8. Save the presentation, print only the slides containing images and WordArt, and then close the presentation.

Exercise 6

1. Open the *A Healthier You* presentation.

2. Use the Search feature to add an appropriate clip art image to one of the slides.

3. Resize, move, recolor, crop, rotate, or flip the image as needed.

4. Add a blank slide at the end of the presentation for the following WordArt object: *A Healthy Body is a Happy Body*

5. Change the WordArt font, size, and colors to match the design template.

6. Resize the WordArt object as needed.

7. Save the presentation, print only the slides containing images and WordArt, and then close the presentation.

Exercise 7

1. Open the *Buying A Computer* presentation.

2. Add a computer clip art image or an appropriate image to a slide of your choice.

3. Add a clip art image from the People category to a different slide of your choice.

4. Resize, move, recolor, crop, rotate, or flip the images as appropriate.

5. Add a blank slide at the end of the presentation for the following WordArt object: *E-mail at Last!*

6. Change the WordArt font, size, and colors to match the design template.

7. Resize the WordArt object as needed.

8. Save the presentation, print only the slides containing images and WordArt, and then close the presentation.

Exercise 8

1. Open the *Leisure Tours* presentation.

2. Add a blank slide at the end of the presentation for the following WordArt object: *Make the World Your Playground*

3. Change the WordArt font, size, and colors to match the design template. Resize the WordArt object as needed.

4. Use the Search for clips feature to find an image relating to world travel and add this image to the WordArt slide.

5. Add images that convey the message on one of the bullet slides.

6. Modify and move the images as appropriate.

7. Save the presentation, print only the slides containing images and WordArt, and then close the presentation.

Case Projects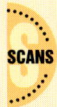

Project 1

You have been asked by an assistant in the manufacturing department to explain how to use the Clips Online button that appears in the Insert ClipArt dialog box. Access online Help to find out how to connect to the Clip Gallery Live Web site where you can preview and download additional clips. Download a few clips so you can explain the button correctly to the other assistant. Print the help topic.

Project 2

You decide to find and add Microsoft Clip Gallery images to your *Communicate* presentation. Use the Search for clips feature and be selective with the clip art images. Resize and move the images as needed. Recolor or crop as needed. Add a WordArt slide at the end of the presentation. View the slide show and save the presentation. Print the slides with WordArt or clip art images only.

Project 3

As you look over your *Souner* presentation, you feel you need to incorporate an image of cooperation between clients and your company, so you decide to add an appropriate clip art image to one of the existing slides. The image you portray should be positive and encourage the spirit of teamwork. You also decide to add a new slide at the end of the presentation consisting of a WordArt object. Be as creative as possible. View the slide show and save the presentation. Print the slides with WordArt or clip images only.

Project 4

You determine that there are several options you can pursue to enhance your independent presentation, *My Presentation*. You can let the software help you find appropriate images by using the Search for clips feature, you can ask co-workers if they have clip art images you can add, or you can create a WordArt object. Decide what option(s) to pursue and make whatever editing changes necessary to enhance your selection(s). Save and print the presentation.

chapter three

Project 5

Since you work for a zoo, your *Zoo* presentation should definitely include appropriate clip art images on several of the slides. Remember that the audience of this presentation is children. Be selective and remember not to overload the slides with clip art images. Make all decisions regarding placement, size, color, and rotation of the images. Add an image to the slide master. Save and print the new slides.

Project 6

You are taking a class at the local community college and are assigned to a group that will be conducting a class discussion on multiculturalism in the workplace. Access the PowerPoint home page through online <u>H</u>elp, Office on the <u>W</u>eb. Search for clip art images that best illustrate the term multicultural. Download at least one clip art image and add the clip art images to a PowerPoint slide. Print the slide containing the clip art images.

Project 7

You want to dress up your *Cars* presentation by adding clip art images to a slide or slides of the presentation. Use the <u>C</u>lips Online feature in the Clip Gallery to download clip art images from the Internet. Make all formatting decisions regarding the images. If possible, make changes to the slide master. Add WordArt to a new slide or an existing slide. Save the presentation and print only the slides with WordArt or clip art images.

Project 8

You and your partner want to use the most recent and high-tech images available for your presentation. Visit the Internet and download clip art images that relate to your *Internet* presentation. The two of you also investigate bringing in clip art images from others sources such as different clip art software and scanned images. Make all formatting decisions regarding the images. If possible, make changes to the slide master. Add WordArt to a new slide or an existing slide. Save the presentation and print only the slides with WordArt or clip art images.

Using Drawing Tools and AutoShapes

Chapter Overview

This chapter presents various techniques for adding shapes, such as a square, circle, rectangle, or line, to a slide. You also learn to use the AutoShapes tool to quickly draw common shapes. By using the drawing tools, you can grab the audience's attention, control the focus of the audience on a word or point, and enhance interest.

LEARNING OBJECTIVES

- ▶ Add shapes
- ▶ Use the AutoShapes tool
- ▶ Edit and format shapes
- ▶ Use the Format Painter
- ▶ Work with multiple objects
- ▶ Add text

Case profile

Reading through the material you received when you attended the workshop on design, you notice that several example slides used shapes and lines to control eye movement and add visual interest to the slide. These elements helped the audience to arrive quickly at the main point of the slide, instead of scanning needlessly. Looking at your *Teddy Toys* presentation, you determine that visual stimulation will help your sales managers follow the presentation and remember the important points.

chapter four

notes In this chapter the terms object and shape may be used interchangeably. The term *shape* usually refers to a drawing shape such as a rectangle, oval, square, circle, or an AutoShape. *Objects* are clip art images, text boxes, AutoShapes, and drawing shapes.

4.a Adding Shapes

Shapes are objects added to a slide for visual stimulation, direction, and retention of ideas. PowerPoint lets you easily add text to shapes and format shapes by changing fill and line colors, text wrap, and rotating.

Drawing Simple Objects

You can easily add simple shapes, such as rectangles, squares, ovals, circles, lines, and arrows, to slides. After drawing shapes have been added, you can move, copy, format, resize, and delete them. It is a good idea to display the ruler and the guides to assist you in placing and drawing your shapes. The horizontal and vertical guides divide the slide area into four equal parts, making it easy to align or draw shapes to a given dimension. To add a blank slide and display the ruler and guides:

Step 1	*Open*	the *Teddy Toys* presentation
Step 2	*Add*	a blank slide (using the Blank AutoLayout) to the end of the presentation
Step 3	*Click*	View
Step 4	*Click*	Ruler
Step 5	*Click*	View
Step 6	*Click*	Guides

When you use drawing tools to draw, you click a tool, and then drag the mouse to create the desired shape. If you click a tool and then click the slide, you create a small proportionally shaped object where you clicked. If you double-click a tool, you can continue to draw using that tool until you click it again or click the Select Objects tool. To draw a rectangle on a slide:

Step 1	*Click*	the Rectangle button  on the Drawing toolbar

Step 2	*Position*	the mouse pointer at the center of the slide (intersection of guides)
Step 3	*Drag*	down and to the right until you reach the 2" mark on the vertical ruler and the 3" mark on the horizontal ruler
Step 4	*Release*	the mouse button

The rectangle is filled with a color and is selected displaying the eight sizing handles.

| Step 5 | *Drag* | the center of the rectangle to the upper-right corner of the slide |

You can draw a perfectly shaped object, such as a square or a circle, using the SHIFT key and the proper drawing tool. To draw a square:

Step 1	*Click*	the Rectangle button ▣ on the Drawing toolbar
Step 2	*Press & Hold*	the SHIFT key
Step 3	*Drag*	from the center of the slide to draw a 2" square
Step 4	*Release*	the mouse button before you release the SHIFT key
Step 5	*Drag*	the square to the upper-left corner of the slide

You use similar steps to draw an oval and a circle. To draw an oval and a perfect circle:

Step 1	*Click*	the Oval button ◉ on the Drawing toolbar
Step 2	*Drag*	from the center of the slide down and to the right until you reach the 2" mark on the vertical ruler and the 3" mark on the horizontal ruler
Step 3	*Drag*	the oval to the lower-left corner of the slide
Step 4	*Click*	the Oval button ◯ on the Drawing toolbar
Step 5	*Press & Hold*	the SHIFT key
Step 6	*Drag*	from the center of the slide to draw a 2" circle
Step 7	*Release*	the mouse button before you release the SHIFT key
Step 8	*Drag*	the circle to the lower-right corner of the slide
Step 9	*Click*	outside the circle to deselect it, and then compare your slide to Figure 4-1

DESIGN TIP

The color of a drawing shape is dependent on the color scheme of the Presentation design template.

QUICK TIP

If you make an error while drawing, simply click the Undo button on the Standard toolbar, choose the appropriate drawing tool, and start over.

chapter
four

FIGURE 4-1
Slide with Drawing Shapes

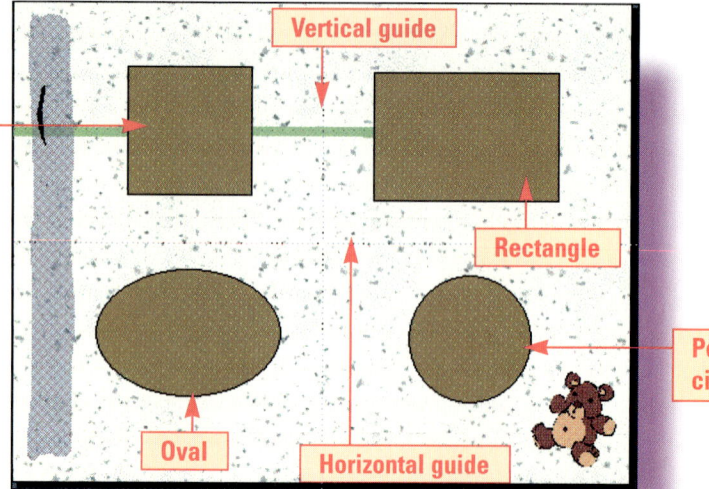

You can also include lines and arrows on a slide to enhance or guide the eye. To draw a perfectly straight line or straight arrow, use the SHIFT key. To draw a line and an arrow:

Step 1	*Click*	the Line button ▨ on the Drawing toolbar
Step 2	*Press & Hold*	the SHIFT key
Step 3	*Drag*	to the right from the center of the slide to draw a straight line to the 3" mark on the horizontal ruler
Step 4	*Release*	the mouse button before you release the SHIFT key
Step 5	*Drag*	the line up and to the right just below the rectangle
Step 6	*Click*	the Arrow button ▨ on the Drawing toolbar
Step 7	*Press & Hold*	the SHIFT key
Step 8	*Drag*	from the center of the slide to draw a straight arrow to the 3" mark on the horizontal ruler
Step 9	*Release*	the mouse button before you release the SHIFT key
Step 10	*Drag*	the line up and to the left just below the square
Step 11	*Deselect*	the arrow
Step 12	*Save*	the *Teddy Toys* presentation

4.b Using the AutoShapes Tool

The AutoShapes tool helps you draw common shapes with great ease. **AutoShapes** are ready-made shapes—squares, rectangles, hearts, stars, callouts, and so on. You simply select the type of shape you want to draw and drag to create it. You decide to add a heart-shaped AutoShape to a slide in the *Teddy Toys* presentation. To add the heart AutoShape to the slide:

Step 1	*Display*	the slide with the people clip images
Step 2	*Click*	the AutoShapes button AutoShapes ▾ on the Drawing toolbar
Step 3	*Click*	Basic Shapes
Step 4	*Click*	the Heart AutoShape
Step 5	*Position*	the mouse pointer to the center of the slide (intersection of guides)
Step 6	*Press & Hold*	the CTRL + SHIFT keys
Step 7	*Drag*	to draw the heart from the center of the slide approximately to the 1.5" mark on the horizontal ruler
Step 8	*Drag*	the heart shape up so that it does not cover any images on the slide

4.c Editing and Formatting Shapes

You can edit and format AutoShapes by resizing and rotating, changing the fill and line options, adding 3-D effects, adding text to shapes, and duplicating shapes. To size and scale an object:

| Step 1 | *Display* | the slide with the drawing shapes |
| Step 2 | *Drag* | the lower-right corner handle of the square horizontally to the right of the 0 mark on the horizontal ruler |

chapter four

Notice that the square has now changed to a rectangle because the proportions were not maintained.

Step 3	*Click*	the Undo button 🔙 on the Standard toolbar
Step 4	*Press & Hold*	the SHIFT key
Step 5	*Drag*	the same corner handle of the square to the right of the 0 mark on the horizontal ruler

Notice that the square has maintained its proportions and is now a larger size square.

| Step 6 | *Click* | the Undo button 🔙 on the Standard toolbar |

You can change fill and line options of shapes and AutoShapes to improve their appearance. Drawing shapes and basic AutoShapes automatically use the colors from the design template. AutoShapes from the More AutoShapes dialog box, however, do not use the design template colors. You can change the **fill color** of shapes and AutoShapes to solid colors, gradients, textures, and patterns. You can even fill a shape with a picture. PowerPoint provides 24 preset gradients to help you if you want to use a specific look instead of creating your own gradients. **Gradients** are shaded variations of a color or combination of colors. To change the fill options:

Step 1	*Click*	the square shape to select it
Step 2	*Click*	the Fill Color list arrow 🎨▾ on the Drawing toolbar
Step 3	*Click*	More Fill Colors
Step 4	*Click*	the Standard tab in the Colors dialog box, if necessary
Step 5	*Click*	the bright yellow color in the third row from the bottom
Step 6	*Click*	OK to fill the square with a solid yellow color
Step 7	*Click*	the circle shape to select it
Step 8	*Click*	the Fill Color list arrow 🎨▾ on the Drawing toolbar
Step 9	*Click*	Fill Effects to open the Fill Effects dialog box (see Figure 4-2)

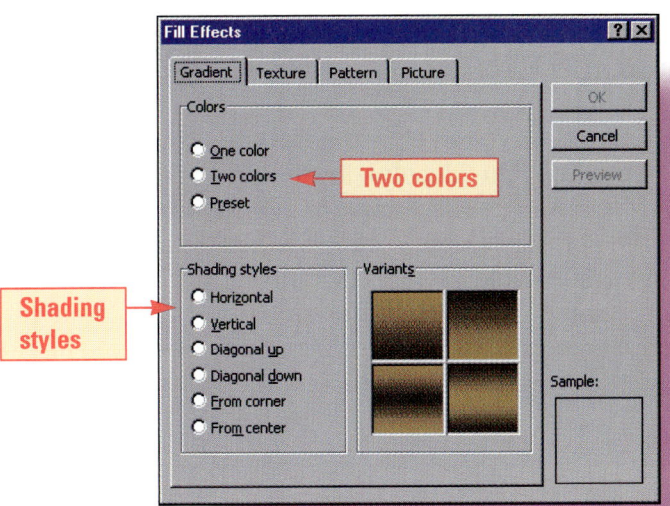

FIGURE 4-2
Fill Effects Dialog Box

> ### QUICK TIP
>
> To change line options, including line color, thickness, and arrowhead direction, select the object and then use the Line Color list arrow, Line Style button, and Arrow Style button on the Drawing toolbar to make your changes.

Step 10	*Click*	the Two colors option button in the Colors box
Step 11	*Click*	the Color 1: list arrow
Step 12	*Click*	the purple color (ScreenTip displays: Follow Accent and Hyperlink Scheme Color)
Step 13	*Click*	the From center option button in the Shading styles box
Step 14	*Click*	the rightmost Variants example
Step 15	*Click*	OK to shade the circle in two colors from the inside out

The Drawing toolbar makes it easy to add shadow and 3-D effects to images. When objects appear three-dimensional (**3-D**), they are raised instead of flat. To add 3-D effects and change the color:

Step 1	*Display*	the slide with the people clip images and heart AutoShape
Step 2	*Select*	the heart shape
Step 3	*Click*	the Fill Color list arrow on the Drawing toolbar
Step 4	*Click*	More Fill Colors
Step 5	*Click*	the Standard tab, if necessary
Step 6	*Click*	the bright red color in the second row from the bottom
Step 7	*Click*	OK
Step 8	*Click*	the 3-D button on the Drawing toolbar
Step 9	*Click*	the first example (ScreenTip displays: 3-D Style 1)

> ### DESIGN TIP
>
> Be sure not to overdo the shadow or 3-D effects. The AutoShape object is the important element—not the effects.

chapter
four

4.d Using the Format Painter

The **Format Painter** allows you to copy the attributes of objects and text boxes. You can copy the fill color, line color, line thickness, font, font size, font style, 3-D effects, etc. from one shape to another. You decide to use the Format Painter to copy the attributes of the formatted shapes to other shapes. If you click the Format Painter button one time, you can paint the attributes one time. If you double-click the Format Painter button, you can paint and paint until you click the Format Painter button again. To use the Format Painter:

Step 1	*Select*	the heart shape
Step 2	*Click*	the Format Painter button 🖌 on the Standard toolbar
Step 3	*Display*	the slide with drawing shapes
Step 4	*Click*	the oval shape to copy the attributes from the heart shape
Step 5	*Click*	the purple circle
Step 6	*Double-click*	the Format Painter button
Step 7	*Click*	the yellow square and then click the rectangle to copy the attributes from the purple circle to both the square and the rectangle
Step 8	*Click*	the Format Painter button 🖌 to turn it off

4.e Working with Multiple Objects

When working with multiple objects on a slide, you often need to select more than one object at a time to delete, duplicate, move, arrange, or align them attractively. To select and delete multiple objects:

Step 1	*Display*	the slide with drawing shapes, if necessary
Step 2	*Select*	the rectangle shape, if necessary
Step 3	*Press & Hold*	the SHIFT key
Step 4	*Click*	the square shape

Step 5	*Press & Hold*	the SHIFT key and click each remaining object on the slide
Step 6	*Press*	the DELETE key to delete all selected objects
Step 7	*Click*	the Undo button  on the Standard toolbar to undo the deletion
Step 8	*Press & Hold*	the SHIFT key
Step 9	*Click*	the circle and the square to deselect the two objects
Step 10	*Press*	the DELETE key to delete the other objects, leaving the square and circle on the slide

Duplicating Objects

You can easily **duplicate** or make a copy of an object and paste it on the same slide or a different slide. The Duplicate command on the Edit menu makes an exact duplication of the object and places it slightly down and to the right of the original object. To duplicate an object:

Step 1	*Select*	the square shape
Step 2	*Press & Hold*	the right mouse button
Step 3	*Drag*	the square to the upper-right corner of the slide
Step 4	*Release*	the mouse button
Step 5	*Click*	Copy Here on the shortcut menu
Step 6	*Display*	the slide containing the heart shape
Step 7	*Right-click*	the heart shape
Step 8	*Click*	Copy
Step 9	*Display*	the slide with the drawing shapes
Step 10	*Right-click*	the slide area
Step 11	*Click*	Paste

Aligning Objects

Even with the help of the guides, it can be difficult to align two or more objects by dragging them separately. PowerPoint enables you to **align** objects on the same line at the left, right, center, top, bottom, or middle. When objects are aligned, it is easier for the audience to follow

chapter
four

the directional flow of the slide. You can also distribute the shapes so that the space between the shapes is even. To align objects:

Step 1	*Delete*	the square on the right
Step 2	*Select*	the square shape and change the fill to yellow
Step 3	*Select*	the circle first, then the heart shape
Step 4	*Click*	the Draw button [Draw ▾] on the Drawing toolbar
Step 5	*Click*	Align or Distribute
Step 6	*Click*	Align Right to right-align the heart and the circle
Step 7	*Click*	the Undo button [↶] on the Standard toolbar
Step 8	*Select*	all three objects
Step 9	*Click*	the Draw button [Draw ▾] on the Drawing toolbar
Step 10	*Click*	Align or Distribute
Step 11	*Click*	Align Center to vertically align all three shapes at their center points
Step 12	*Click*	the Draw button [Draw ▾] on the Drawing toolbar
Step 13	*Click*	Align or Distribute, and then click Align Middle

All three objects are now perfectly centered on top of one another. The **order**, or layering position, of the objects is determined by the order that the objects were drawn or copied onto the slide. Each time an object is added to a slide, that object is placed on an invisible plane. If three objects are added to the slide, there are three planes, each succeeding one placed atop the previous one. PowerPoint provides options for sending objects to the back, to the front, backward one layer, or forward one layer. To change the order of objects:

Step 1	*Click*	outside the objects to deselect them
Step 2	*Select*	the heart shape
Step 3	*Click*	the Draw button [Draw ▾] on the Drawing toolbar
Step 4	*Click*	Order

Step 5	*Click*	Send to Ba<u>c</u>k to send the heart shape behind the square and the circle
Step 6	*Right-click*	the heart shape, which is still selected
Step 7	*Click*	O<u>r</u>der and then click Bring <u>F</u>orward

Notice that the heart is now between the circle and the square (see Figure 4-3). When you bring an object forward, you move it up a layer.

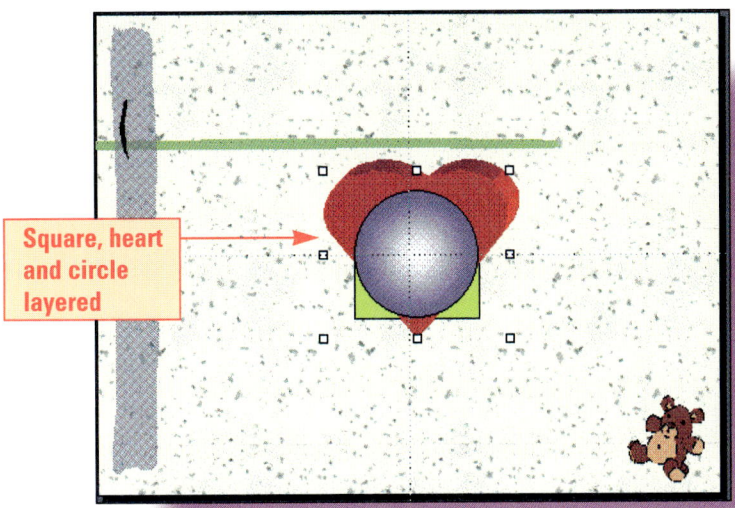

Square, heart and circle layered

FIGURE 4-3
Layered Objects

Step 8	*Select*	the square
Step 9	*Press & Hold*	the CTRL + SHIFT keys
Step 10	*Drag*	the right corner handle of the square to resize it to the 2.5" mark on the horizontal ruler
Step 11	*Select*	the circle
Step 12	*Press & Hold*	the CTRL + SHIFT keys
Step 13	*Drag*	the right corner handle of the circle to resize it to the .5" mark on the horizontal ruler
Step 14	*Click*	outside to deselect the object

Your slide should look similar to Figure 4-4, with the square in the back, the heart shape in the middle, and the circle on the top layer.

chapter
four

FIGURE 4-4
Resized Layered Objects

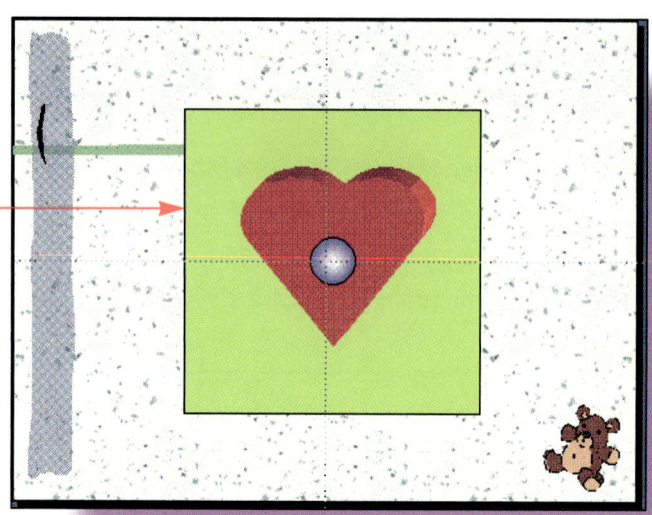

Square, heart, circle resized and layered

Step 15	*Save*	the *Teddy Toys* presentation

4.f Adding Text

Just as you can add text to a slide and format it, you can add text to a shape or an AutoShape. You can add text to a shape or an AutoShape by selecting the shape and then typing the text. The text within a shape can be edited and formatted to add interest to the shape. To add text to a slide without using a placeholder, you use the Text Box tool. The **Text Box** tool draws a text box wherever you click or drag in the active window that contains text. To add text to an AutoShape:

Step 1	*Display*	the slide with the people clip images and heart shape
Step 2	*Select*	the heart shape
Step 3	*Key*	Gifts for all ages
Step 4	*Click*	outside to deselect the heart

The font, size, and color of text can be changed to enhance the AutoShape. To format the text:

Step 1	*Select*	the heart shape
Step 2	*Click*	the Font Color list arrow ▲▾ on the Drawing toolbar

CAUTION TIP

When selecting a shape that contains text, be sure to click when you see the four-directional arrow. If you select a shape when the text cursor is present, you are only placing the cursor in that text area.

MENU TIP

You can format an object by clicking the AutoShape command on the Format menu.

| Step 3 | *Click* | the white color (ScreenTip displays: Follow Background Scheme Color) |
| Step 4 | *Click* | the Increase Font Size button on the Formatting toolbar until the Font Size box displays 36 |

MOUSE TIP

You can format an object by double-clicking the object. Be careful not to double-click in the text area or you select the text and not the object.

The text is too wide for the shape. You can adjust the shape to fit the size of the text, or you can wrap the text to fit inside the shape. To wrap the text within the shape:

Step 1	*Double-click*	the heart shape
Step 2	*Click*	the Text Box tab
Step 3	*Click*	the Word wrap text in AutoShape check box
Step 4	*Click*	OK
Step 5	*Click*	outside to deselect the heart, then compare your slide to Figure 4-5

FIGURE 4-5
Slide with Wrapped Text in AutoShape

QUICK TIP

You can format an object by right-clicking the object, and then clicking Format AutoShape.

Using the Text Box Tool

You can add additional text objects to a slide without keying text into a layout placeholder. You can move, resize, edit, and format text boxes to help convey the message of your slide. To add a text box to your slide:

| Step 1 | *Display* | the slide with the basket of toys (We Welcome New Ideas) |

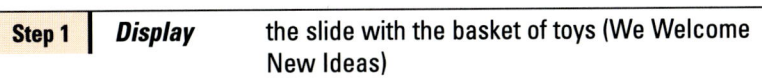

chapter
four

FIGURE 4-6
Slide with Text Box

Step 2	*Click*	the Text Box button on the Drawing toolbar
Step 3	*Position*	the mouse pointer on the vertical guide just below the basket of toys image
Step 4	*Click*	the vertical guide
Step 5	*Click*	the Center button on the Formatting toolbar
Step 6	*Key*	Toys With Heart
Step 7	*Click*	the border of the text box to select the entire text box
Step 8	*Click*	the Increase Font Size button on the Formatting toolbar until the Font Size box reads 32
Step 9	*Click*	the Font Color list arrow on the Drawing toolbar
Step 10	*Click*	the dark gold color (ScreenTip displays: Follow Fills Scheme Color) and compare your slide to Figure 4-6

Step 11	*Display*	the slide with the drawing shapes
Step 12	*Click*	Edit
Step 13	*Click*	Delete Slide to delete the practice slide because you don't need it for the presentation
Step 14	*Save*	and close the *Teddy Toys* presentation

The practice you gained with the drawing tools will help you enhance any presentation.

Summary

▶ Drawing shapes can enhance a slide presentation.

▶ The ruler and guides help you place and position objects on slides.

▶ AutoShapes is a tool that provides many common shapes that you can create for use in a slide.

▶ 3-D effects may be added to drawing and AutoShape objects.

▶ Using the SHIFT key in combination with drawing tools lets you draw straight lines, circles, and squares.

▶ The fill and line colors of drawing shapes may be changed.

▶ The Format Painter feature allows you to copy the attributes of one object onto another object.

▶ Multiple drawing shapes can be deleted from a slide.

▶ Drawing shapes can be duplicated quickly.

▶ Objects can be aligned at the top, middle, bottom, left, center, or right.

▶ The order of objects can be rearranged so that one object appears behind or in front of another object.

▶ The Text Box tool allows you to add text to any location on the slide.

chapter four

Commands Review

Action	Menu Bar	Shortcut Menu	Toolbar	Keyboard
Display ruler	View, Ruler			ALT + V, R
Display guides	View, Guides			ALT + V, G CTRL + G
Draw a rectangle			▭	
Draw a square			▭ + SHIFT	
Draw an oval			⬭	
Draw a circle			⬭ + SHIFT	
Draw a line			╲	
Draw a straight line			╲ + SHIFT	
Draw an arrow			↘	
Draw a straight arrow			↘ + SHIFT	
Add AutoShapes	Insert, Picture, AutoShapes		AutoShapes ▾	ALT + I, P, A
Select all objects	Edit, Select All		SHIFT + click each object, or draw a marquee box around all objects	CTRL + A
Change fill and line colors	Format, Colors and Lines, or Format, AutoShape	Right-click object, Format AutoShape	Double-click object	ALT + O, N ALT + O, O
Duplicate objects	Edit, Duplicate Edit, Copy, then Edit, Paste	Right-click object, Copy, then right-click, Paste	Right-drag, then Copy Here CTRL + drag the left mouse	ALT + E, I ALT + E, C, then ALT + E, P CTRL+ D
Align selected objects	Draw, Align or Distribute			ALT + R, A
Order selected objects	Draw, Order	Right-click, Order		ALT + R, R
Add text to selected drawings and AutoShapes				Key text in selected object
Insert a text box	Insert, Text Box		📝	ALT + I, X

Concepts Review

Circle the correct answer.

1. Rulers and guides:
   [a] help place objects on the slide.
   [b] print on the slide.
   [c] cannot be turned on or turned off.
   [d] automatically appear when drawing shapes.

2. When you want to draw a perfect shape, use the mouse and the:
   [a] SHIFT key.
   [b] CTRL key.
   [c] ALT key.
   [d] SPACEBAR.

3. If you release the mouse button before releasing the SHIFT key when you draw a square, the square will:
   [a] be larger.
   [b] be smaller.
   [c] not be at the center of the slide.
   [d] not be a perfect square.

4. The AutoShapes tool provides you with:
   [a] clip art that is related to your presentation.
   [b] any shape you want to add on a slide.
   [c] commonly found shapes.
   [d] fancy text to place on your slide.

5. Which option changes the fill color of an object back to the default color?
   [a] fill colors
   [b] patterns
   [c] Automatic fill
   [d] template

6. Special effects that can be applied to drawing shapes include which of the following *except*:
   [a] 3-D shadows.
   [b] rotating.
   [c] gradient fills.
   [d] copying.

7. When selecting multiple objects to be deleted, which command selects all objects at one time?
   [a] ALT + A
   [b] SHIFT + ENTER
   [c] CTRL + A
   [d] CTRL + SHIFT

8. To place one object on top of another object, use the:
   [a] Align and Distribute feature.
   [b] Order feature.
   [c] Duplicate feature.
   [d] Rotate or Flip feature.

9. Which of the following is not an advantage in using the text box tool?
   [a] You can create text anywhere on the slide.
   [b] You can move the text box after you have keyed the text.
   [c] You can format the text size and style easily.
   [d] You can only have one text box on a slide.

10. To add text to a slide without using the standard placeholders, use the:
   [a] AutoShapes tool.
   [b] Drawing tool.
   [c] Line tool.
   [d] Text Box tool.

chapter four

Circle **T** if the statement is true or **F** if the statement is false.

T   F   1. Guides are nonprinting lines to help you place and position objects on a slide.

T   F   2. After drawing a perfect shape, you must release the mouse after releasing any other keys.

T   F   3. PowerPoint limits you to six colors for fill and line color changes.

T   F   4. Shadows and 3-D effects can be added to enhance the AutoShape object.

T   F   5. A marquee box may be drawn around all objects to encompass them for selecting purposes.

T   F   6. You can duplicate an object by right-dragging the object to a new location on the slide.

T   F   7. You can copy objects by clicking and dragging while holding down the CTRL key.

T   F   8. The Text Box tool enables you to type text anywhere on the slide area.

T   F   9. Gradients require the selection of two or more colors.

T   F   10. PowerPoint allows you to add textures that resemble real-life textures that can be used to fill drawing shapes and AutoShapes.

Skills Review

Exercise 1

1. Open the *PowerPoint* presentation and display the slide master view.

2. Add the 16-Point Star from the Stars and Banners AutoShapes category.

3. Resize the star AutoShape so it is approximately .75" high by .75" wide and move it to the lower-right corner of the slide master.

4. Change the AutoShape fill to the Gold II fill effects from the Preset colors: list and select the From center shading style and the variant on the right. (*Hint*: Click the Fill Color list arrow, click Fill Effects, and then click Gradient tab.)

5. Add the 3-D Style 5 to the AutoShape.

6. Add a blank slide at the end of the presentation.

7. Add the Bevel Shape from the Basic Shapes AutoShapes category (fourth row, third column). Draw or resize the bevel shape so that it is approximately 3" high by 6" wide.

8. Center the shape on the slide.

9. Change the fill color to the light gold color (ScreenTip displays: Follow Accent and Hyperlink Scheme Color).

10. Key the following text: *PowerPoint will help sell your products and ideas.* Change the font to Times New Roman, 44 pt., Bold, and Italic.

11. Format the bevel shape so that the text wraps within the shape.

12. Save the presentation, print the slides with changes only, and then close the presentation.

Exercise 2

1. Open the *Office* presentation and add the Down Ribbon (third row, second column) from the Stars and Banners AutoShapes category to Slide 1.

2. Resize the Down Ribbon to approximately 1" high by 6" wide.

3. Add the following text to the AutoShape: *Software for the Future.* (Press the ENTER key after the word "for" so the text wraps to the next line.) Change the fill color of the ribbon shape to match the color scheme of the slide, and change the font, font color, and font size as appropriate.

4. Select all three objects on the slide and align them at the centers.

5. Add a blank slide at the end of the presentation and omit the background graphics from this slide only.

6. Add two arrows from the Block Arrows AutoShapes category: a Curved Right Arrow, a Curved Left Arrow—each arrow should be 4" high by 1.5" wide, and a Curved Up Arrow, and a Curved Down Arrow—each arrow should be 1.5" high by 4" wide. Change the fill color of one of the arrows using a gradient or a texture fill effect. Then use the Format Painter to apply this fill coloring to the remaining three arrows.

7. Position the arrows around the center section of the slide.

8. Add a text box with the following: *All Roads Lead to Office 2000.* (Press the ENTER key after the word "Lead"). Change the text size to 44 pt and change the text color and font, and position the text box in the center of the slide.

9. Key *Excel* in the Curved Right Arrow, *Word* in the Curved Left Arrow, *PowerPoint* in the Curved Down Arrow, and *Access* in the Curved Up Arrow.

10. Save the presentation, print the slides with changes only, and then close the presentation.

Exercise 3

1. Open the *Design* presentation and add the Up Ribbon AutoShape from the Stars and Banners AutoShapes to Slide 1.

2. Position the ribbon shape on top of your name. Send the ribbon shape to the back so your name appears on top of the shape. Resize and move the shape and text box as needed.

3. Add the 24-Point Star AutoShape from the Stars and Banners AutoShapes category to slide with the WordArt object or any slide. Resize the star shape to approximately 5" high by 5.5" wide. Change the fill color to the black color. (ScreenTip displays: Follow Text and Lines Color Scheme.)

4. Drag the star shape and position it over the word Design of the WordArt object or any text object. Then send the star shape to the back. (Change the text color if you cannot read the text after the star shape is sent behind the text.)

5. Select and group the star shape with the WordArt object or the text object.

6. Add a blank slide at the end of the presentation. Omit the background graphics from this slide only.

7. Draw an oval approximately 2.5" high by 3.5" wide. Then key the following text in the oval shape: *Ovals and Circles Give a Feeling of Indecision.*

chapter four

8. Format the shape to wrap the text.

9. Add the 3-D Style 2 to the oval. Change the fill color to aqua color (ScreenTip displays: Follow Background Scheme Color), and change the font of the text to Tahoma, 24 pt, bold.

10. Draw a rectangle approximately 2.5" high by 3" wide, and key *Rectangles and Squares Relate to Rigidity* in this shape.

11. Add the Isosceles Triangle shape from the Basic Shapes AutoShapes category, resize it to approximately 4" high by 4" wide, and key *Triangles Allow All Ideas to be Considered* in it.

12. Use the Format Painter to copy the attributes of the oval shape to both the rectangle and the triangle shapes.

13. Position all three shapes attractively on the slide.

14. Save the presentation, print the slides with changes only, and close it.

Exercise 4

1. Open the *Precision Builders* presentation.

2. Add the Cloud Callout from the Callouts AutoShapes category to the slide with the WordArt object or any slide.

3. Resize the cloud shape to approximately 5" high by 9.25" wide.

4. Change the color of the cloud shape to the light blue color (ScreenTip displays: Follow Accent and Followed Hyperlink Scheme Color).

5. Send the cloud shape to the back.

6. Readjust the cloud shape so that the WordArt text fits into the cloud.

7. Add a 5-Point Star from the Stars and Banners AutoShapes category.

8. Change the fill color to the bright blue color (ScreenTip displays: Follow Accent and Hyperlink Scheme Color).

9. Add the 3-D Style 1 to the star shape.

10. Resize the star shape to approximately 1.25" high by 1" wide.

11. Make six copies of the star and place them on the slide as you desire.

12. Add a blank slide at the end of the presentation, create a textbox, and key the following: *Decisions Before Building a Home.*

13. Change the font to 36 pt, and center the text within the text box.

14. Add the Flowchart Decision shape from the Flowchart AutoShapes, make three additional copies, and key the following text in the respective shapes: *Location?, Split-level or Ranch?, Number of Bedrooms?, Number of Baths?*

15. Change the font to Tahoma, 20 pt, word wrap the text, and add a shadow effect to one of the shapes.

16. Use the Format Painter and copy the attributes to the other shapes.

17. Save the presentation, print the slide with changes only, and then close the presentation.

Exercise 5

1. Open the *Nature Tours* presentation and add a Title Only slide at the end of the presentation. The title should read *Special Tours*.

2. Using the Basic Shapes AutoShapes category, add the Sun and the Moon shapes to the Title Only slide.

3. Using the Text Box tool, create two separate text boxes. Key *For the Early Risers* in one box and *For the Night Owls* in the other.

4. Format the text boxes in regard to font style, size, and color.

5. Format the shapes in regard to color, size, and placement on the slide.

6. Align the Sun and Moon images and their appropriate text boxes.

7. Group the Sun and its appropriate text box. Repeat for the Moon and its text box.

8. Add an AutoShape from the More AutoShapes dialog box to any slide. Resize, recolor, and/or move the AutoShape.

9. Save the presentation, print the slides with the changes only, and then close the presentation.

Exercise 6

1. Open the *A Healthier You* presentation.

2. Add the Heart AutoShape to the slide master. Resize the Heart AutoShape, change the color of the heart, and use a 3-D effect.

3. Position the heart attractively on the slide master. If necessary, move the text placeholders on the slide master if the text overlaps with the heart shape.

4. Add a blank slide at the end of the presentation. Add an AutoShape of your choice and key *Reduce Your Stress!*.

5. Add at least four copies of another AutoShape to this slide, and key *Relax!* in each of the AutoShapes.

6. Format the color and size of the AutoShapes. Use 3-D styles, if desired.

7. Omit the background graphics from this slide only.

8. Position the shapes attractively on the slide. Format the font, font size, and font color of the text.

9. Save the presentation, print the slides with changes only, and then close the presentation.

chapter four

Exercise 7

1. Open the *Buying A Computer* presentation.

2. Add a Title Only slide at the end of the presentation. Key the following title: *Where to Buy My Computer?*

3. Add various computer and other AutoShapes to this slide indicating at least four different types of places to purchase your computer. (For example: retail store, internet, computer catalog, computer outlet.) Format the AutoShapes with regard to size, color, and 3-D effect.

4. Key each different place in an AutoShape. (Word wrap the text, if necessary.)

5. Use the Straight Arrow Connector from the Connectors AutoShapes category to connect the AutoShapes in the order that you would prefer to begin shopping for your computer. Change the arrow thickness and color, if appropriate.

6. Save the presentation, print the slides with changes only, and then close the presentation.

Exercise 8

1. Open the *Leisure Travel* presentation and add a Title Only slide at the end of the presentation. The title should read *Your Season – Your Choice.*

2. Add an appropriate AutoShape to the center of the slide. Change the color of the shape.

3. Key the following text in the shape: *Anywhere - Anytime.* Wrap the text and format the text as desired.

4. Add an appropriate Star AutoShape, and then make three copies of the star shape.

5. Key the name of one season into each of the star shapes (i.e., *Summer, Fall, Winter,* and *Spring*).

6. Add 3-D effects to the star shapes, and add appropriate fills to each of the star shapes depicting that season.

7. Format the font within the stars as desired.

8. Omit the background graphics from this slide only.

9. Save the presentation, print the slides with changes only, and then close the presentation.

Case Projects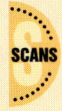

Project 1

You are curious to know if you can simply change an AutoShape from one shape to another without deleting the original shape and then creating the new one. You decide to access the online <u>H</u>elp feature to determine how to add or change an AutoShape. Print the AutoShapes help topic. Print the adjustment handle help topic definition as well.

Project 2

Looking at the *Communicate* presentation, you decide that in addition to using clip images on some of the slides you could also use AutoShapes that resemble the cartoon balloons or a phone or a sound file. Add a blank slide using AutoShapes and text to encourage courteous telephone answering. Add AutoShapes to any slide where you feel the shape enhances the slide message. Change colors and size to fit the presentation. Save the presentation and print the slides with the AutoShapes only.

Project 3

Open the *Souner* presentation and view the presentation, looking for places where you may want to add an AutoShape. When finished, add AutoShapes to a slide or slides to help deliver the theme of the training organization. Add a blank slide at the end of the presentation incorporating AutoShape objects, lines or arrows, or text boxes. Make color, size, and font enhancements. If possible, duplicate an AutoShape object to add

interest to your slide. Align shapes and order shapes as needed. Add 3-D or shadows to the shapes to enhance them. View the slide show. Save the presentation and print the slides with the AutoShapes only.

Project 4

You decide to view your *My Presentation* presentation in order to enhance it by adding AutoShapes. You want to add a text box inside an AutoShape to describe your company's service or product. You can add a new blank slide or enhance an existing slide or slides. Be careful not to let the AutoShape become the dominant part of your presentation. If appropriate, consider adding an AutoShape or text box to the slide master. Save the presentation and print the slides with AutoShapes only.

Project 5

You try to think of creative ways to show the paths to certain areas in the zoo. You decide that using the flowchart symbols and connecting lines would be a great way to help children find the zoo exhibits. Open your *Zoo* presentation and add the appropriate AutoShapes to accomplish the task. Add 3-D and various fill effects to the AutoShapes to help enhance their interest to the children. Change the color and thickness of the arrows. Use the guides to place the shapes. Save the presentation and print the slide with AutoShapes only.

chapter four

Project 6

You want to use clip art, WordArt, and AutoShapes to enhance slides, guide the eye through a slide, and/or bring attention to an idea or concept on a slide. You also want to learn more about design tips that you can apply to your presentations. Access the Internet to search for design tips. Be sure to check out the fonts available for specific moods or tones and additional clip art or images that can be downloaded for future use. Create a presentation consisting of a title slide, a bullet slide with several design tips, a slide illustrating several new fonts, and a slide with clip art or images accessed via the Internet. Include drawing shapes or AutoShapes in your presentation. Print the presentation.

Project 7

You decide to incorporate some drawing shapes in your *Cars* presentation. You want to add shapes to display the different types of places that students can find information about new and used cars.

Add text to some of the AutoShapes, as well as individual text boxes. To create interest on some of your existing slides, add shapes and send them behind some of the text already in your presentation. Resize, color, and align shapes as desired on each slide. If possible, add a shape to the slide master. Save the presentation and print the slides with the AutoShapes only.

Project 8

In your *Internet* presentation, you and your partner discuss how to handle the lecture on search engines. The two of you visit the Internet to find information about the various search engines. You decide to add AutoShapes to show why you would or should use a particular search engine on the Internet. You may need to create a new slide for each search engine you researched. Format your AutoShapes and drawing shapes to fit the design and color scheme of your *Internet* presentation. Save the presentation and print the slides with the AutoShapes only.

Step 8	*Click*	Microsoft PowerPoint
Step 9	*Click*	the Microsoft PowerPoint - [Presentation1] button on the taskbar, if necessary
Step 10	*Save*	the PowerPoint presentation as *Academy Award Winners*

The Movies Outline opens in PowerPoint in Normal view (see Figure PX-5).

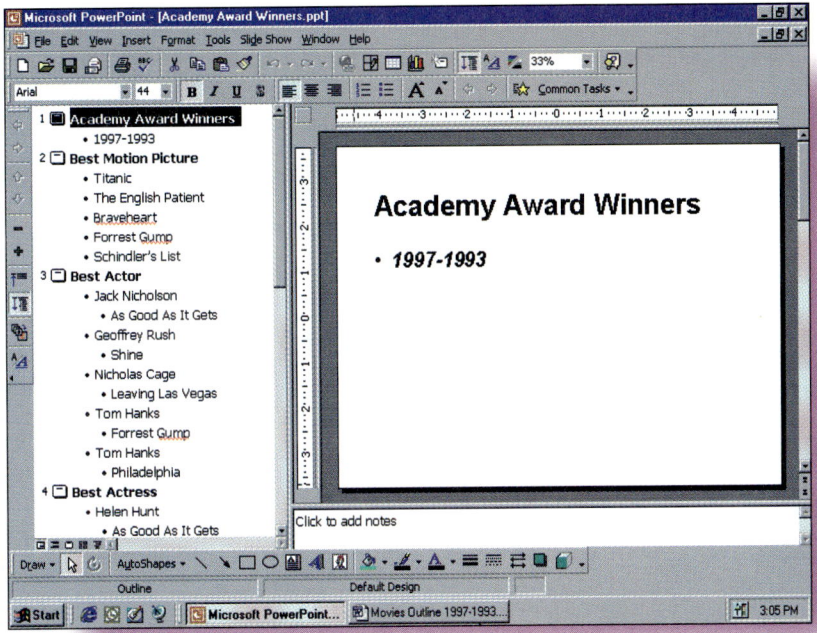

FIGURE PX-5
Academy Award Winners

| Step 11 | *View* | the slide show |

When an outline opens in a PowerPoint presentation, the slides created are bullet slides. The new PowerPoint presentation consists of a bullet slide for each Heading 1 style in the Word outline. Each Heading 1 style becomes the title of a bullet slide. The Heading 2 styles under each Heading 1 style in the Word outline become first-level bullets. The Heading 3 styles under each Heading 2 style in the Word outline become second-level bullets. The Default Design is simple black text on a white background, and some of the bulleted lists are too long to fit the slides.

integration

To format the new presentation:

Step 1	*Click*	the Slide View button ⬚
Step 2	*Double-click*	Default Design on the status bar
Step 3	*Double-click*	the Azure design template
Step 4	*Press & Hold*	the Shift key
Step 5	*Click*	the Slide Master View button ⬚
Step 6	*Click*	in the second-level bullet text on the slide master
Step 7	*Change*	the font to 24 pt
Step 8	*View*	the slide show
Step 9	*Click*	the Slide View button to return to Slide view

Changing the Layout for One or More Slides

You want the first slide (Academy Award Winners) to be a title slide rather than a bullet slide, to introduce the presentation properly. You can change the slide layout of an existing slide or slides by using the Slide Layout dialog box. To change a bullet slide to a title slide:

Step 1	*Display*	the first slide (Academy Award Winners)
Step 2	*Click*	the Common Tasks button Common Tasks ▾ on the Formatting toolbar
Step 3	*Click*	Slide Layout
Step 4	*Double-click*	the Title Slide AutoLayout to apply the master layout style
Step 5	*View*	the slide show from the beginning
Step 6	*Save*	and close the *Academy Award Winners* presentation
Step 7	*Close*	the *Movies Outline 1997-1993* Word document
Step 8	*Close*	the Microsoft Word application

MENU TIP

You can change the slide layout by clicking the Slide Layout command on the Format menu.

MOUSE TIP

You can change the slide layout by right-clicking outside a text box and selecting Slide Layout.

PX.c Inserting Slides from a Word Outline

You can insert a Word outline into an existing PowerPoint presentation. In order to do so, the Word document must be closed, the PowerPoint application must be open, and the existing presentation (or a new presentation, if you plan to add a Word outline to a new presentation) must be open.

Tracy calls and tells you that she researched five additional award-winning years for the presentation and entered the information in a Word outline. You need to open the *Academy Award Winners* PowerPoint presentation and insert the new information in the PowerPoint presentation. To insert slides from a Word outline:

Step 1	**Verify**	that you are in the PowerPoint application
Step 2	**Open**	the *Academy Award Winners* presentation
Step 3	**Display**	the last slide in the presentation
Step 4	**Click**	Insert
Step 5	**Click**	Slides from Outline

The Insert Outline dialog box opens.

Step 6	**Double-click**	the *Movies Outline 1992-1988* Word document
Step 7	**View**	the slide show from the beginning

The *Academy Award Winners* presentation consists of eight slides, with the last four slides inserted from the Word outline and added to the end of the presentation.

Step 8	**Change**	the Academy Award Winners 1992-1988 bullet slide (Slide 5) to a title slide
Step 9	**Save**	the *Academy Award Winners* presentation

integration

PX.d Inserting Slides from one PowerPoint Presentation to Another

Inserting slides from one presentation to another is helpful even if you only use part of the slide that you insert. While the slide, text, and clip art images are added to the existing presentation, the slide design template is not brought into the existing presentation. You can also copy and paste slides from one open presentation to another using Slide Sorter view and the <u>A</u>rrange All command on the <u>W</u>indow menu.

The presentation design template will automatically apply the formatting to the slides inserted into the existing presentation. Mr. Lerek asks you to research five additional award winning years. Tracy offers to help and creates a PowerPoint presentation with the additional information. To insert slides from one presentation to another:

Step 1	*Verify*	that you are in the PowerPoint application
Step 2	*Display*	the last slide in the *Academy Award Winners* presentation
Step 3	*Click*	<u>I</u>nsert
Step 4	*Click*	Slides from <u>F</u>iles to open the Slide Finder dialog box (see Figure PX-6)

FIGURE PX-6
Slide Finder Dialog Box

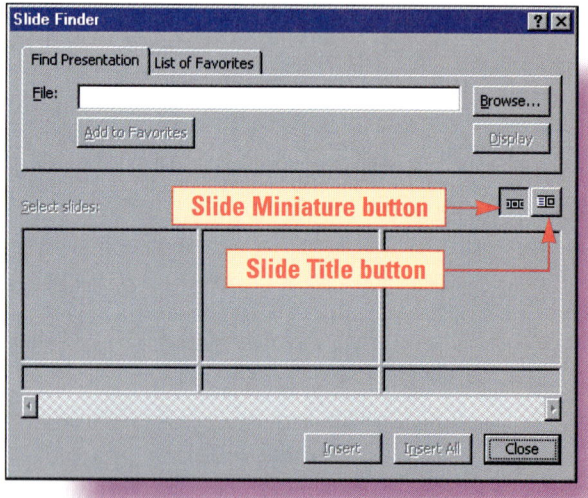

When you insert slides or outlines into a PowerPoint presentation, they are inserted *after* the currently viewed slide. If you want to add slides to the end of the presentation, you must be on the last slide of the presentation before you start inserting slides.

Step 5	*Click*	Browse
Step 6	*Verify*	the location of the *Academy Award Winners 1987-1983* presentation
Step 7	*Double-click*	the *Academy Award Winners 1987-1983* presentation
Step 8	*Click*	Display to view the slides

Figure PX-7 displays a slide miniature of each slide in the presentation in the Select slides: area. You can view all the slides by scrolling through the presentation. The Slide Finder dialog box displays the slides, the text only, or the text with the respective slide. You want to insert all the slides from the *Academy Award Winners 1987-1983* presentation into the *Academy Award Winners* presentation.

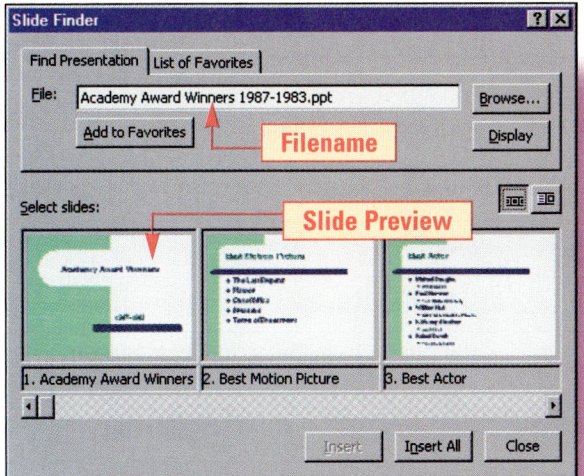

FIGURE PX-7
Slide Finder Dialog Box with Preview

QUICK TIP

You can select an individual slide or slides by clicking each desired slide.

Step 9	*Click*	Insert All to insert all the slides
Step 10	*Click*	Close
Step 11	*View*	the slide show

integration

The *Academy Award Winners* presentation should consist of 12 slides; the four additional slides have been added at the end of the presentation.

Step 12	*Change*	the Academy Award Winners 1987-1983 slide (Slide 9) to a title slide, if necessary
Step 13	*Save*	the *Academy Award Winners* presentation

PX.e Adding a Word Table to a PowerPoint Slide

You can add a Word table into a PowerPoint presentation either by embedding or linking it. Tracy created a table in Word that lists winners in the Best Motion Picture category from 1983 through 1997. You want to add this table to a new slide in the *Academy Award Winners* presentation without linking it to the Word document. To add a Word table to a PowerPoint slide:

Step 1	*Display*	the last slide in the presentation
Step 2	*Add*	a Title Only slide (third row, third column)
Step 3	*Key*	the title: Best Motion Pictures
Step 4	*Click*	Insert
Step 5	*Click*	Object
Step 6	*Click*	the Create from file option button in the Insert Object dialog box
Step 7	*Click*	Browse
Step 8	*Verify*	the location of the *Academy Award Winners Table* Word document
Step 9	*Double-click*	the *Academy Award Winners Table* Word document
Step 10	*Click*	OK

The Word table appears on the PowerPoint slide.

In order to edit an embedded object, you access the source application by double-clicking the object and make the changes using the source application's features. You decide to change the color of the text and then resize the table so that it appears centered on the slide. To edit and resize the embedded table:

Step 1	*Double-click*	the Word table
Step 2	*Drag*	to select the entire table
Step 3	*Click*	the Font Color list arrow ▲▾ on the Formatting toolbar
Step 4	*Click*	Turquoise
Step 5	*Click*	outside the Word table

Compare your slide to Figure PX-8.

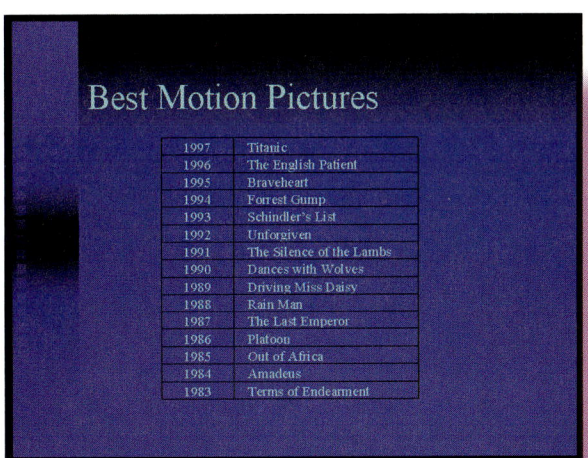

FIGURE PX-8
Slide with Embedded Word Table

| Step 6 | *Drag* | the object to reposition it on the slide |
| Step 7 | *Save* | the *Academy Award Winners* presentation |

Tracy created an Excel worksheet and chart indicating the top moneymaking movies. She wants to integrate the chart into the PowerPoint presentation.

integration

PX.f Embedding an Excel Worksheet in a PowerPoint Slide

When you insert an Excel worksheet or chart into a presentation, you have the option of embedding it or linking it to the PowerPoint presentation. If the Excel object is linked, the PowerPoint presentation automatically updates each time you make changes to the Excel worksheet or chart.

Tracy has researched the opening gross sales for the 1997–1993 Academy Award winning movies. She created a worksheet and a pie chart in Excel. You embed and link these two objects into your PowerPoint presentation. The *Movies Workbook* Excel file is on the Data Disk. To link an Excel worksheet to a PowerPoint slide:

Step 1	*Open*	the *Academy Award Winners* presentation, if necessary
Step 2	*Display*	the last slide in the presentation
Step 3	*Add*	a Title Only slide (third row, third column)
Step 4	*Key*	the title: Opening Weekend Gross Sales
Step 5	*Click*	Insert
Step 6	*Click*	Object

The Insert Object dialog box opens. See Figure PX-9.

QUICK TIP

You can also add or embed a table from Word by copying and pasting it into a PowerPoint slide. If you want to link the Word table to a PowerPoint slide, you must use the Paste link option in the Paste Special dialog box.

FIGURE PX-9
Insert Object Dialog Box

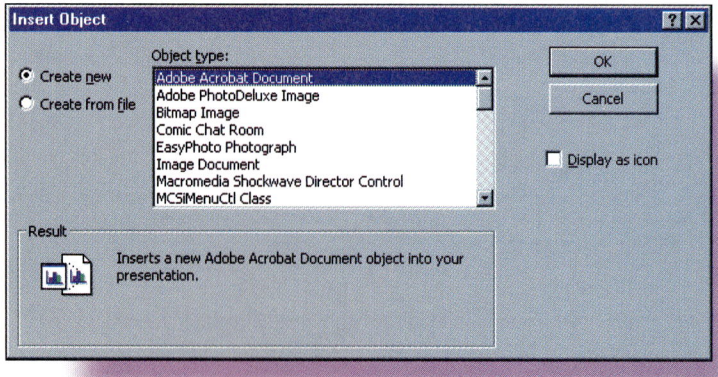

Step 7	*Click*	Create from file
Step 8	*Click*	Browse
Step 9	*Verify*	the location of the *Movies Workbook* Excel file
Step 10	*Double-click*	the *Movies Workbook* Excel file
Step 11	*Click*	OK

A small object appears on the slide. The last active worksheet in the saved Excel file is the part placed in PowerPoint (see Figure PX-10).

FIGURE PX-10
Slide with Embedded Excel Object

You decide to resize the object so that you can read it more easily. You use the same resizing techniques to resize any object in PowerPoint. After resizing the object, you want to edit it so that you can see the worksheet displaying the exact opening weekend sales figures. To resize and edit the embedded object:

Step 1	*Resize*	the Excel object using the CTRL key and a corner handle to resize the object from the center until it is approximately 3.5" high
Step 2	*Double-click*	the Excel object

You now edit in Excel, the source application (see Figure PX-11). In order to view the worksheet data, you may have to click the first sheet tab (Movie Data) in the Excel file so that you can see the text and numbers.

integration

FIGURE PX-11
Excel Application in
PowerPoint

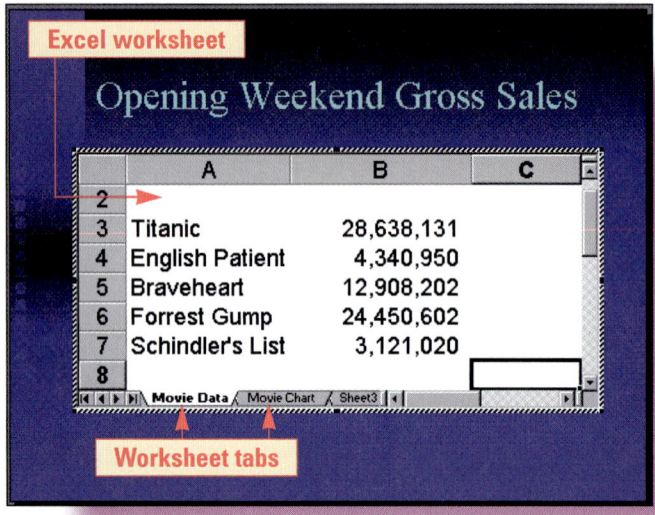

Step 3	*Click*	the Movie Data sheet tab, if necessary
Step 4	*Drag*	to select cells A3 through B7
Step 5	*Click*	the Font Color list arrow 🅰️▾ on the Formatting toolbar
Step 6	*Click*	Yellow
Step 7	*Drag*	to select cells B3 through B7
Step 8	*Right-click*	the selected cells
Step 9	*Click*	Format Cells
Step 10	*Click*	the Number tab, if necessary
Step 11	*Click*	Currency in the Category: list box
Step 12	*Key*	0 in the Decimal places: text box
Step 13	*Click*	$ in the Symbol: list box
Step 14	*Click*	OK
Step 15	*Click*	outside the Excel object

Compare your slide to Figure PX-12.

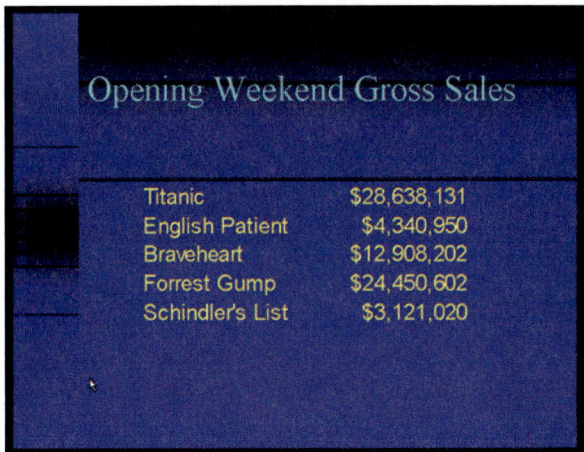

Opening Weekend Gross Sales

Titanic	$28,638,131
English Patient	$4,340,950
Braveheart	$12,908,202
Forrest Gump	$24,450,602
Schindler's List	$3,121,020

FIGURE PX-12
Slide with Completed
Excel Object

Step 16	*Drag*	the object to reposition on slide
Step 17	*Save*	the *Academy Award Winners* presentation

The changes you make affect only the PowerPoint presentation because you did not link the Excel file to the PowerPoint slide.

PX.g Linking an Excel Chart to a PowerPoint Slide

In addition to inserting objects into a PowerPoint slide, you can use the copy and paste special features in PowerPoint. You can use the same process from the steps in the previous section to link an object by simply checking the Link check box in the Insert Object dialog box. However, you decide to copy the chart from Tracy's Excel file and paste it with a link to the PowerPoint slide. You can copy an object from Word or Excel, then use the Paste Special command on the Edit menu to paste the link between the two applications. To link an Excel Chart to a PowerPoint slide:

Step 1	*Display*	the last slide in the presentation
Step 2	*Add*	a Title Only slide
Step 3	*Key*	the title: Opening Weekend Percentages

integration

Step 4	*Click*	the Start button 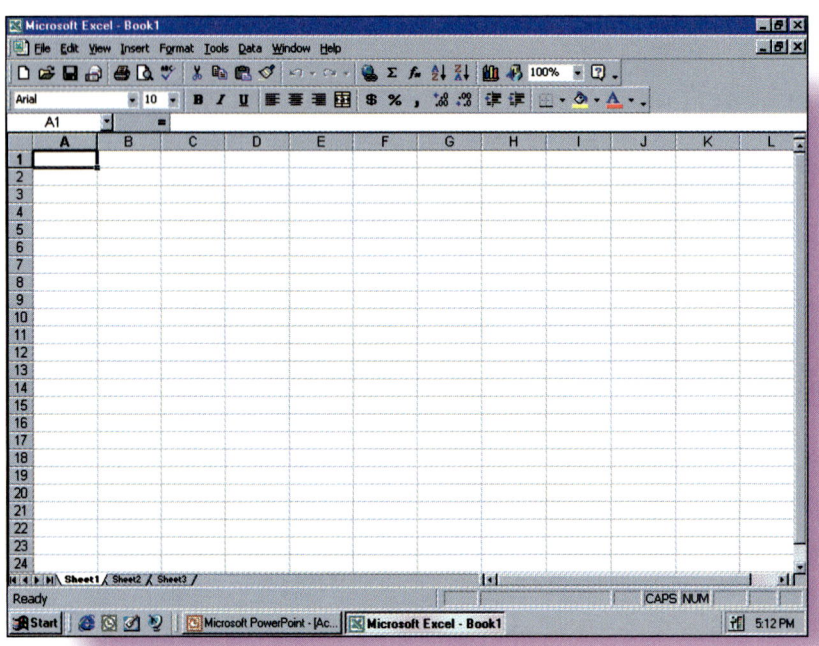 on the taskbar
Step 5	*Point to*	Programs
Step 6	*Click*	Microsoft Excel

The Microsoft Excel application opens. See Figure PX-13.

FIGURE PX-13
Microsoft Excel
Application

Step 7	*Click*	File
Step 8	*Click*	Open
Step 9	*Double-click*	the *Movies Workbook* Excel file
Step 10	*Click*	the Movie Chart sheet tab at the bottom (refer to Figure PX-11)
Step 11	*Click*	the Chart Area (wait until ScreenTip displays: Chart Area) to select the pie chart
Step 12	*Click*	the Copy button on the Standard toolbar
Step 13	*Click*	the Microsoft PowerPoint – *[Academy Award Winners]* button on the taskbar
Step 14	*Click*	Edit
Step 15	*Click*	Paste Special to open the Paste Special dialog box (see Figure PX-14)

M O U S E   T I P

You can copy the chart
in Excel by right-clicking
the chart, then clicking
Copy.

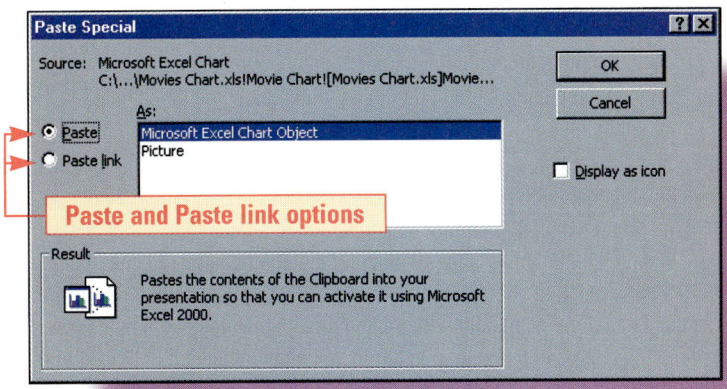

> **MENU TIP**
>
> You can copy the selected chart by clicking the Copy command on the Edit menu.

Step 16	*Click*	Paste link
Step 17	*Click*	OK

You insert the chart as a linked object on the slide. Observe the sizing handles on the object.

Step 18	*Resize*	the pie chart object to approximately 4" high using one of the corner handles
Step 19	*Drag*	the pie object to center it on the slide

Compare your slide to Figure PX-15.

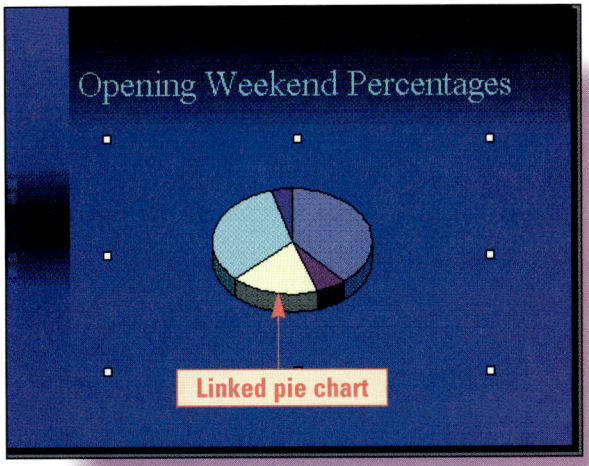

FIGURE PX-15
Slide with Linked
Chart Object

integration

If you want to make changes to the 3-D look or rotate the pie, you make those changes using the Excel features.

To format the linked object:

| **Step 1** | ***Double-click*** the chart object |

When you double-click the linked chart object, the Excel application opens and you edit the original Excel *Movies Workbook* file. You can switch between Excel and PowerPoint using the taskbar, however, you can also tile the two application windows so you can see changes take place immediately.

| **Step 2** | ***Right-click*** | an empty area on the taskbar |
| **Step 3** | ***Click*** | Tile Windows Vertically in order to see the Excel and the PowerPoint application windows side by side |

Compare your screen to Figure PX-16. Excel and PowerPoint windows may be displayed in reverse order.

FIGURE PX-16
Excel and PowerPoint
Tiled

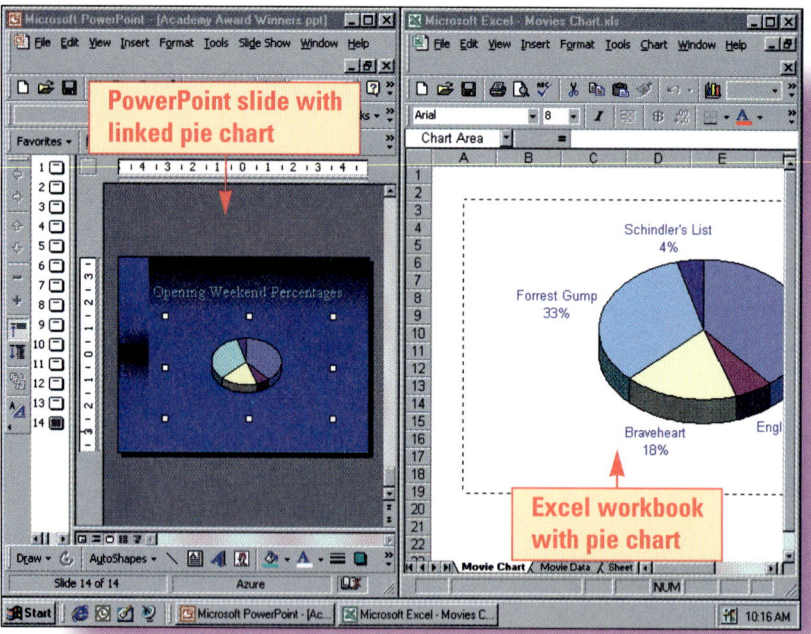

Step 4	*Click*	the Titanic slice in the Excel file twice (do not double-click)
Step 5	*Drag*	the Titanic slice away from the rest of the pie and observe the change in the PowerPoint window
Step 6	*Click*	a data label to select all data labels
Step 7	*Change*	the font color to Turquoise
Step 8	*Save*	and close the *Movies Workbook* Excel file
Step 9	*Close*	the Microsoft Excel application
Step 10	*Maximize*	the *Academy Award Winners* PowerPoint presentation
Step 11	*Save*	and close the *Academy Award Winners* PowerPoint presentation

When you next open the *Academy Award Winners* PowerPoint presentation, any changes made to the *Movies Workbook* Excel file are updated on the PowerPoint slide.

integration

Summary

▶ You can send slides, notes, handouts, or an outline from a PowerPoint presentation (source file) to a Word document (destination file).

▶ You can link or embed an object from another application (source file) into a PowerPoint presentation (destination file).

▶ An embedded object becomes part of the destination file with no links to the source file.

▶ A linked object does not become part of the destination file; it remains linked to the source file.

▶ When you modify an embedded object, the source file does not change.

▶ When you modify a linked object, you actually modify the source file, so the change reflects in both the source file and the destination file.

▶ You can change the slide layout of one or more slides in a presentation.

▶ An outline created in Word and inserted in a PowerPoint presentation opens as bullet slides according to the heading styles.

▶ The Slide Finder allows you to insert slides in a PowerPoint presentation from a different PowerPoint presentation.

▶ You can embed and link a Word table into PowerPoint slides.

▶ You can embed and link Excel worksheet data and charts into PowerPoint slides.

▶ The taskbar allows you to place two or more applications side by side using the Tile commands on the taskbar.

Commands Review

Action	Menu Bar	Shortcut Menu	Toolbar	Keyboard
Send a PowerPoint presentation to Word	File, Send To, Microsoft Word			ALT + F, D, W
Send a Word outline to a PowerPoint presentation	File, Send To, Microsoft PowerPoint			ALT + F, D, P
Insert a Word outline into a PowerPoint presentation	Insert, Slides from Outline			ALT + I, L
Change slide layout	Format, Slide Layout	Right-click, Slide Layout	Common Tasks ▾, Slide Layout	ALT + O, L
Insert slide(s) from one PowerPoint presentation to another	Insert, Slides from Files			ALT + I, F
Embed an object	Insert, Object			ALT + I, O
Copy an object (in source program)	Edit, Copy	Right-click, Copy	▤	ALT + E, C CTRL + C
Paste a link (in destination program)	Edit, Paste Special			ALT + E, S

Concepts Review

Circle the correct answer.

1. **Linking or embedding objects from one application to another is called:**
   [a] copying.
   [b] pasting.
   [c] integrating.
   [d] multiple pasting.

2. **An object placed in a document in another application that retains no ties to the original source file is called a(n):**
   [a] linked object.
   [b] template design.
   [c] graphic image.
   [d] embedded object.

3. **All of the following can be sent from PowerPoint into the Word application *except*:**
   [a] slides.
   [b] handouts.
   [c] notes.
   [d] masters.

4. **When linking or embedding, the original file is called the:**
   [a] destination file.
   [b] source file.
   [c] input file.
   [d] output file.

integration

5. When you insert a Word outline into a PowerPoint slide, you create:
   [a] bullet slides.
   [b] chart slides.
   [c] title slides.
   [d] table slides.

6. When creating a PowerPoint presentation from a Word outline, the title in a PowerPoint slide is created from which heading level in the Word outline?
   [a] Heading 1
   [b] Heading 2
   [c] Subheading 1
   [d] Subheading 2

7. Which of the following is true with regard to linking an Excel chart to a PowerPoint slide?
   [a] If you change the color of the bars in Excel, only the Excel chart changes.
   [b] If you change the color of the bars, only the PowerPoint slide changes.
   [c] If you change the chart type, the chart changes in both Excel and PowerPoint.
   [d] If you change the chart data (values), only the Excel chart changes.

8. When copying an object from one application to another, you do which of the following in order to link the object?
   [a] Edit, Link
   [b] Edit, Embed
   [c] Edit, Paste
   [d] Edit, Paste Special

9. Which of the following is *not* true about linked objects?
   [a] You must save the Excel worksheet changes in order to update the PowerPoint slides.
   [b] You do not have to save the Excel worksheet changes in order to update the PowerPoint slides.
   [c] You must save the Word outline changes in order to update the PowerPoint slides.
   [d] You must save the PowerPoint presentation with the linked objects.

10. Which of the following taskbar commands can you use to view two or more applications side by side?
   [a] Tile All Windows
   [b] Tile Windows Vertically
   [c] Cascade Windows
   [d] Minimize All Windows

Circle **T** if the statement is true or **F** is the statement is false.

T **F**   1. You can edit an embedded chart by double-clicking it.

T **F**   2. The source file is the original file from which an object is embedded and linked.

T **F**   3. Linking allows you to make simultaneous changes to separate files in separate software applications.

T **F**   4. If you create five top-level headings in a Word outline, you get one title slide with four separate bullets.

T **F**   5. In order to insert an existing object into a PowerPoint slide, you must first start the application that contains the object you want to insert.

T **F**   6. Embedding and linking achieve exactly the same result when inserting an object from another application into a PowerPoint slide.

T F   7. The Slide Finder dialog box enables you to copy one or more slides from one PowerPoint presentation to another.

T F   8. You cannot insert a Word table into a PowerPoint slide.

T F   9. When you can change the font and alignment of a linked object in the source file, you also make those changes to the destination file.

T F   10. It is impossible to see formatting changes between linked objects at the exact same time.

 **notes** You use the following additional data files from the Data Disk for the exercises at the end of this chapter: *PowerPoint Integrated, Office Integrated, Design Integrated, Office Workbook, Planning a Presentation, Precision Builders Outline, Precision Builders Integrated, Nature Tours Integrated, A Healthier You Integrated, A Healthier You Workbook, Computer Reference Manuals Outline, Leisure Travel Integrated, Leisure Travel Workbook, Communicate Integrated, Communicate Workbook, Souner Integrated, Souner Outline, My Presentation Integrated, Zoo Integrated, Zoo PowerPoint Presentation, Cars Integrated, Cars Workbook,* and *Internet Integrated.*

Skills Review

Exercise 1

1. Open the *PowerPoint Integrated* presentation.

2. Send the *PowerPoint Integrated* presentation to Word, choosing the Blank lines next to the slides layout option.

3. Save the Word document as *PowerPoint Integrated*.

4. Print and close the Word document.

5. Send the *PowerPoint Integrated* presentation to Word as an Outline only.

6. Save the Word outline document as *PowerPoint Outline*. (Remember to change the type of document to a Word Document in the Save as type: list box.)

7. Print and close the Word outline document.

8. Close the *PowerPoint Integrated* presentation.

Exercise 2

1. Open the *Office Integrated* presentation.

2. Add a Title Only slide at the end of the presentation.

integration

3. Add the following title: *Office Users By Department*

4. Insert an Excel chart using the *Office Workbook* file from the Data Disk.

5. Embed the chart without linking it in the PowerPoint presentation, on the Office Users By Department slide.

6. Resize and reposition the chart, if necessary.

7. Change the font size, color, style, etc. so the chart is easy to read in PowerPoint.

8. Using Chart Options from the Chart menu, add titles to the axes to further aid readability of the chart.

9. Reposition and format the legend as desired.

10. Print the new slide only.

11. Save and close the *Office Integrated* presentation.

Exercise 3

1. Open the *Design Integrated* presentation.

2. Display the second slide in the presentation.

3. Use the Slide Finder to insert all the slides from the *Planning a Presentation* presentation from the Data Disk.

4. Make any necessary changes to the newly added slides in order to aid readability.

5. Print the presentation as a four-slide per page handout.

6. Save and close the *Design Integrated* presentation.

Exercise 4

1. Open the *Precision Builders Outline* document in the Word application.

2. Send the *Precision Builders Outline* document to PowerPoint.

3. Save the new PowerPoint presentation as *Precision Builders PowerPoint Outline*.

4. Close the *Precision Builders PowerPoint Outline* presentation.

5. Open the *Precision Builders Integrated* presentation in PowerPoint.

6. Insert the slides from the *Precision Builders PowerPoint Outline* presentation at the end of the *Precision Builders Integrated* presentation.

7. Print the newly added bullet slides.

8. Save and close the *Precision Builders Integrated* presentation.

Exercise 5

1. Open the *Nature Tours Integrated* presentation.

2. Send the *Nature Tours Integrated* presentation to Word as an Outline only.

3. Save the Word document as *Nature Tours Outline.* (Remember to save as a Word Document.)

4. Send the *Nature Tours Integrated* presentation as a linked object to Word with Notes next to the slides.

5. Add a clip art image to one of the slides in the PowerPoint application.

6. Save and close the *Nature Tours Integrated* presentation.

7. Save the Word document with the linked PowerPoint slide as *Nature Tours Linked.*

8. Print the Word outline and the linked Word document.

9. Save and close the Word document.

Exercise 6

1. Open the *A Healthier You Integrated* presentation.

2. Add a Title Only slide at the end of the presentation with the following title: *Daily Water Sources*

3. Open the *A Healthier You Workbook* file in Excel.

4. Copy the Excel worksheet and use the Paste Special feature to link to the new PowerPoint slide.

5. Resize and reposition the Excel worksheet, if necessary.

6. Change the font size, color, style, etc. to enhance the look of the chart.

7. Add borders to the Excel worksheet.

8. Remove the gridlines under <u>T</u>ools, <u>O</u>ptions, View in Excel.

9. Print the slide with the linked Excel chart.

10. Save and close the *A Healthier You Workbook* file.

11. Save and close the *A Healthier You Integrated* presentation.

integration

Exercise 7

1. Create a new presentation in PowerPoint with a design template of your choice.

2. Insert the slides from the *Computer Reference Manuals Outline*.

3. Delete the first blank title slide.

4. Change the first slide to a Title slide.

5. Make adjustments to font size, color, style, and placement on slides.

6. Save the new presentation as *Computer Reference Manuals* presentation.

7. Print the new presentation as a four-slide per page handout.

8. Insert "The Internet and Your Kids" slide in the *Buying A Computer Integrated* presentation after Slide 3 (Reasons to Buy a Computer).

9. Reapply the slide master to this slide so that it matches the remaining slides in the *Buying A Computer* presentation.

10. Print the new slide in the *Buying A Computer Integrated* presentation.

11. Close all files.

Exercise 8

1. Open the *Leisure Travel Integrated* presentation.

2. Add a Title Only slide at the end of the presentation with the following title: *Current Bookings*

3. Insert an Excel chart with a link from the *Leisure Travel Workbook* file.

4. Tile the windows so that you can see both applications open at the same time.

5. Change the color of the slices to match the *Leisure Travel Integrated* presentation design.

6. Change the font size, color, style, etc. to enhance the readability of the chart.

7. Resize and reposition the pie chart so it is placed attractively on the slide.

8. Print the new slide.

9. Save and close the *Leisure Travel Integrated* presentation.

10. Save and close the *Leisure Travel Workbook* file.

Case Projects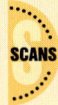

Project 1

You understand how to link and embed objects in PowerPoint. However, you want to explain these concepts to your fellow students. Use the online Help to research information on linking and embedding objects. Print all the help topics including information on using linked objects and embedded objects to share information between Office products. Include all the links.

Project 2

One of the administrative assistants at Communicate Corporation, the company where you work, created an Excel workbook that contains a column chart comparing last year's typical calls with this year's typical calls. Open the *Communicate Integrated* presentation. You want to copy and paste a link between the Excel chart from the *Communicate Workbook* file and a slide in your *Communicate Integrated* presentation. Add a Title Only slide at the end of the presentation with a title suggesting this comparison. Use the *Communicate Workbook* file from the Data Disk and be sure you link the chart when you paste it from Excel into PowerPoint. Make any formatting changes to the chart to fit your presentation design. Remember that all changes made in the *Communicate Workbook* file automatically update the chart slide in the *Communicate Integrated* PowerPoint presentation. Print the new slide. Save and close both files.

Project 3

At Souner & Associates, the software training company where you work, your employer finds an outline created in Word from a previous employee. The outline contains helpful information that your employer would like to include in the *Souner Integrated* PowerPoint presentation. Open the *Souner Integrated* presentation. He asks you to insert the outline document from Word into the *Souner Integrated* presentation. The outline, *Souner Outline,* is on the Data Disk. Decide where the slide belongs in the presentation. Make any changes to the slide as desired. Print the new slide only. Save and close the *Souner Integrated* presentation.

Project 4

You plan to travel over the weekend and you want to review one of your presentations, called *My Presentation Integrated.* You plan to make some changes to the content of the presentation, but not to the background, colors, or clip art images. Open the *My Presentation Integrated* presentation. You decide to send the presentation to Word as an outline and as a Word document with blank lines next to the slides. In this way, you can make your own handwritten notes over the weekend. Link the slides to the original PowerPoint presentation. Save the Word outline as *My Presentation Integrated Outline* and it. Save the linked Word document as *My Presentation Integrated Slides* and print it. Close the Word documents and the presentation.

integration

Project 5

At your summer job at the local zoo, you make considerable progress in creating a presentation that motivates children to visit the zoo. One of the other summer employees also works on slides for the children's presentation. After reviewing her slides, you decide to incorporate them into your presentation. Open the *Zoo Integrated* presentation. Insert the slides from the *Zoo PowerPoint Presentation* that is on the Data Disk. Decide on the order of the new slides in the presentation. Make any changes to the presentation to maintain a consistent look. Print the presentation as a nine-slide per page handout. Save and close the *Zoo Integrated* presentation.

Project 6

You find linking and embedding objects in PowerPoint very exciting. Visit the Internet at the Microsoft Web site and search for recent articles on OLE (Object Linking and Embedding). Print at least three current articles and include a summary indicating how you could use linking or embedding in your next PowerPoint presentation.

Project 7

One of the greatest challenges in your job as a consumer education instructor is coming up with facts your teenage students can relate to in learning to shop smarter. Luckily, one of your outstanding students completed an independent project on buying a car; this information fits perfectly in the upcoming lecture you plan to give on this topic. Your student created a worksheet and a chart in Excel that shows the current market share of popular vehicles. You want to add this information to the presentation on buying a car, which you plan to use in your lecture. Open the *Cars Integrated* presentation. You decide to copy the Excel chart from the *Cars Workbook* file on the Data Disk and paste it without links on a new slide in the *Cars Integrated* presentation. Make any changes to the chart in the *Cars Integrated* presentation with regard to data labels, rotating slices, tilting the pie, etc. Save the *Cars Workbook* file. Save the *Cars Integrated* presentation and print the new slide. Close both documents.

Project 8

As a teaching assistant at Millennium University, you are always on hand to help your lead professor maintain and supplement his teaching resources, so students get the best education possible. Your professor decides to manually enter some notes for his lecture on the Internet, which he plans to present during his Introduction to the Internet class for college freshman. He asks you and a fellow teaching assistant to work together to send the *Internet Integrated* PowerPoint presentation to Word as a document with blank lines below the slides so he can write his notes during his upcoming plane trip to the West Coast. Open the *Internet Integrated* presentation. You and your partner decide to link the slides to the Word document and save it for future semesters. Save the Word document as *Internet Integrated Notes* and print it. Save and close both documents.

Microsoft
Access 2000

Introduction to Access

Chapter Overview

In this chapter, you explore the format and design of Access. You learn about the purpose of this database application, become familiar with its menus and toolbars, and view some of its objects, including a table, form, query, report, and data access page. You also learn how to use online Help.

Case profile

You work for Dynamic Inc., an import/export company that has been in business for the past three years. The company imports and exports household and personal items. As the Information Services Manager, you are responsible for creating and managing one of the company's databases, which needs to include accurate information about its products, customers, orders, and personnel. You use Microsoft Access 2000 to create and maintain this database. You decide to view one of Dynamic's existing Access databases, *mdbImporters,* so you can better understand how to use its powerful features.

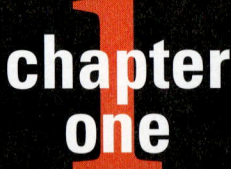

chapter one 1

 **notes** This text assumes that you have little or no knowledge of Access. It also assumes that you have read Office Chapters 1–4 of this book and that you are familiar with Windows 95 or Windows 98 concepts.

1.a Defining Access

In its simplest form, Access is a database application. A **database** is a collection of records and files organized for a particular purpose. For example, you could use a database to store information about your friends and family, including their addresses and phone numbers. Access, however, is more powerful than a simple database because it uses a **relational database management model**, which means you can relate each piece of information to other pieces of information by joining them. For example, suppose you have a database table that lists customers and their addresses. In another table, you have information about the orders that these customers place with your company. You can join the two tables by using a relationship. This way you don't have to reenter customers' information every time they place an order. You see how to take advantage of Access's power in the following pages.

You are now ready for your tour of Access.

1.b Opening the Access Application

Before you can work with Access, you must open the application. When you start Access, you see a dialog box asking if you want to create a new database or open an existing one. For your tour, open the existing database called *mdbImporters*.

To start Access and open an Access database:

Step 1	*Click*	the Start button 🏁 Start on the taskbar
Step 2	*Point to*	Programs
Step 3	*Click*	Microsoft Access

The Microsoft Access application and dialog box open and, as with other Office applications, the Office Assistant may appear. The Microsoft Access dialog box allows you to open an existing database, create a new blank database, or create a database by using a Database Wizard. See Figure 1-1.

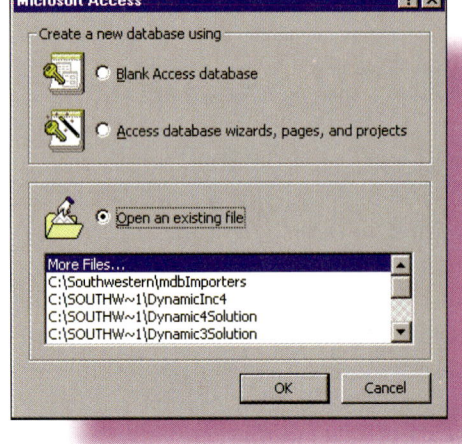

To become familiar with the Access window, open the sample database, *mdbImporters*. The Microsoft Access dialog box lists existing databases. If you want to open a database that is not on the list, click the More Files option. You can then locate a database on your hard drive or network.

Step 4	***Click***	More Files
Step 5	***Click***	OK
Step 6	***Change***	the Look in: list box to the drive that contains your Data Disk
Step 7	***Click***	the *mdbImporters* database in the Open dialog box
Step 8	***Click***	Open

Your screen should look similar to Figure 1-2.

QUICK TIP

Mastering Access 2000 uses the Leszynski naming convention (LNC) for databases and database objects. The following prefixes indicate the kind of database object you're working with:

dap: data access page
frm: form
mcr: macro
mdb: database
qry: query
rpt: report
tbl: table

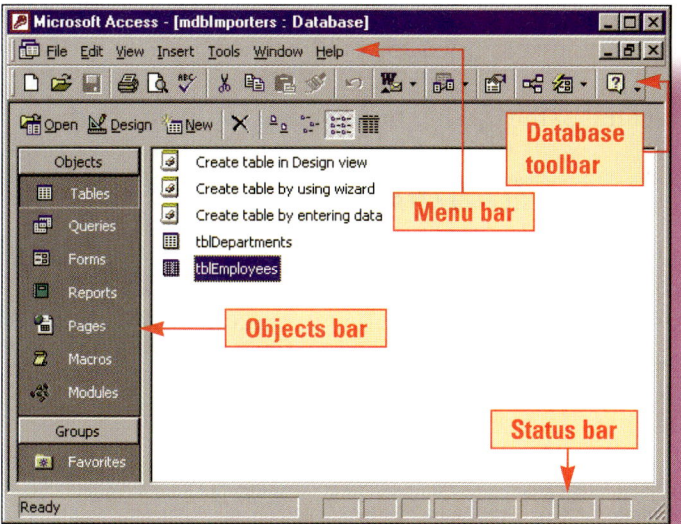

FIGURE 1-2
mdblmporters Database

You are now ready to tour the Access window.

1.c Viewing the Access Window

notes

Office 2000 features personalized menus and toolbars, which "learn" the commands you use most often. This means that when you first install Office 2000, only the most frequently used commands immediately appear on a short version of the menus and the remaining commands appear after a brief pause. Commands that you select move to the short menu, while those you don't use appear only on the full menu.

The Standard and Formatting toolbars appear on the same row when you first install Office 2000. When they appear in this position, you can see only the most commonly used buttons of each toolbar. All the other default buttons appear on the More Buttons drop-down lists. As you use buttons from the More Buttons drop-down list, they move to the visible buttons on the toolbar, while the buttons you don't use move into the More Buttons drop-down list. If you arrange the Formatting toolbar below the Standard toolbar, you can see all the buttons. Unless otherwise noted, the illustrations in this book show the full menus and the Formatting toolbar on its own line below the Standard toolbar.

chapter
one

When you look at Figure 1-2, some components of the Access window may seem familiar to you, because they are similar to other Office applications. However, other components are unique to Access, such as some of the toolbar buttons and menu options.

Database Toolbar

The default Access toolbar, the Database toolbar, appears below the menu bar. The Database toolbar changes according to the type of information you are showing on your screen. When you first start Access, you see the features that are common to all Office applications, such as the Save button. You also see many of the Access database tools, such as the Relationships button.

Status Bar

The **status bar** is an area of the Access screen that indicates the condition of the open database, such as READY. Other areas of the status bar indicate such features as NUM LOCK or CAPS LOCK.

Access Database Views

Access lets you view the information in your database from different perspectives. These **views** let you work with your database in different ways. **Datasheet view** displays records in a row-and-column format, similar to a table, and allows you to see many records at the same time. **Design view** lets you design and modify your database, such as its tables, queries, forms, reports, and macros. **Form view** displays records in a layout you design to make data entry easy. **SQL view** shows the SQL programming for the limiting factors of a query. **Print Preview** shows how your report looks when it is printed. **Layout Preview** shows a small portion of your data in a report before printing.

Menu Bar

The **menu bar** offers options that make using Access easier and more efficient. For example, the File menu includes the **Get External Data** command, which allows you to either import or link to an Excel spreadsheet or other database program. This feature expands the scope of the database by allowing you to access databases located on other computers in your network. Using the Edit menu, you can create a shortcut. A **shortcut** is a path to a resource on your network or local computer. This makes finding your work easier.

Many options on the Tools menu are unique to the Access application. **Relationships** shows the current relationships in the database and lets you create and edit them. **Analyze** allows you to run a diagnostic tool to locate potential problems in your database. **Security** helps you set a password and permissions for your database.

> ### Quick tip
>
> To customize your toolbars, click the View menu, point to Toolbars, and then click Customize. You can then choose the types of toolbars you want Access to display when you open the program.

The Window menu allows you to change the way you view the items on your screen. It also lets you hide a database window without closing it.

Finally, the Help menu provides ways to get help in Access. Getting help in Access is critical to learning how to use its powerful features. You can either use the Help menu or the Office Assistant.

1.d Getting Help

You can use the extensive online Help in Access to find a wealth of help topics. Many topics guide you step-by-step through a procedure; others provide quick answers or definitions.

Using the Help Menu

To find a help topic, you click Help on the menu bar and then click Microsoft Access Help. You can then click the Contents tab, click a Help book icon, and then click a page icon to open the topic. You can also click the Index tab and then type the topic you want to find. Or, when you're working with a dialog box, you can get context-sensitive help by pressing the F1 key or by clicking the Help button. Finally, you can also get context-sensitive help on menu options. Highlight an option and then press the F1 key to see a related help topic.

Using the Office Assistant

The **Office Assistant**, an animated character you can use to search for online Help topics, may appear automatically when you work in Access unless you hide it or turn it off. In the illustrations in this book, the Office Assistant is hidden. To hide the Office Assistant, if necessary:

Step 1	*Right-click*	the Office Assistant
Step 2	*Click*	Hide

After you hide the Office Assistant multiple times, you may see a dialog box that asks if you want to turn off the Office Assistant. If you do turn off the Office Assistant, you can turn it back on by clicking the Show the Office Assistant command on the Help menu.

Now that you are more familiar with the Access window, you are ready to view the database objects.

QUICK TIP

When you're working anywhere in Access, including a wizard, dialog box, or toolbar, press the Shift + F1 keys to switch to the Help pointer. You can then click on any item, such as a button or field, to see a quick explanation.

MOUSE TIP

You can change the Office Assistant by right-clicking the Office Assistant icon and then clicking Choose Assistant. Under the Gallery tab, choose the Assistant that appeals to you.

chapter
one

1.e Identifying Access Objects

Access uses **objects**, which are the components of the database. They relate to the data stored in the database. The most frequently used objects are the table, form, query, report, and data access page. More advanced Access objects include macros and modules.

Tables

Tables are at the heart of every database; when you create a database, you most often start by creating tables. **Tables** store the information in records and fields. **Records** are database entries (such as information about a customer), which are stored in rows. **Fields** are categories of information (such as first name, last name, and phone number), which are stored in columns.

Each table contains information about a specific topic. For example, tblEmployees contains Importers' personnel information. When you open your database, the tables are shown by default.

To open the *mdbImporters'* tblEmployees table by using the Objects bar:

| Step 1 | *Click* | Tables 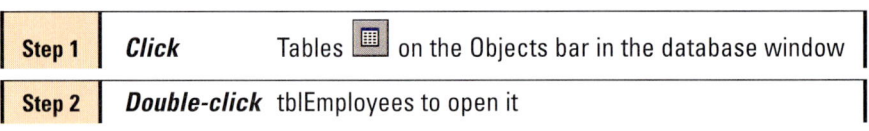 on the Objects bar in the database window |
| Step 2 | *Double-click* | tblEmployees to open it |

Your screen should look similar to Figure 1-3.

FIGURE 1-3
tblEmployees Table

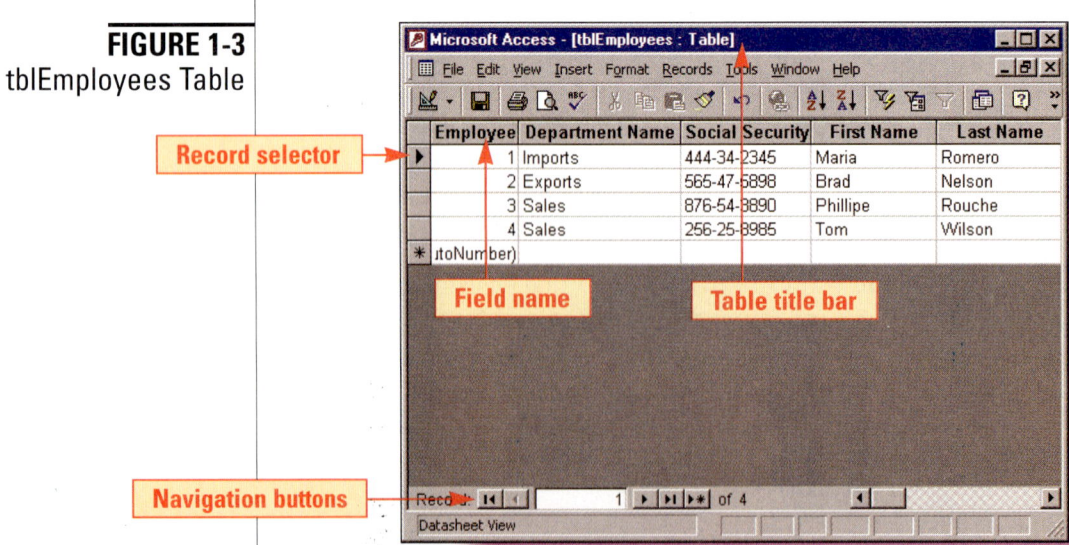

Figure 1-3 shows the parts of an Access table. Notice that the Database toolbar is now the **Table Datasheet toolbar**, which contains tools for working with the Access table. The status bar also shows that you are in Datasheet view. The **record selector** allows you to select or highlight an entire record in a table. Record selector symbols include a triangle, which points to the current record; an asterisk, which shows a new blank record; a drawing pen, which tells you that you are editing a record; and a null symbol, which indicates the record is locked and cannot be changed.

Tour **navigation buttons** allow you to move from one record to the next. The middle two buttons move one record at a time in the direction of each arrow. The first button on the left moves to the first record in the table. The fourth button on the right moves the insertion point to the last record. The **New Record button** adds a new, blank record to the table. The **Specific Record box** indicates the number value of the current record as related to the rest of the records in the table. Finally, the **horizontal scroll bar** allows you to view the rest of the fields. These navigational tools work the same for all database objects.

After you have examined the table, you should close it before viewing other Access objects.

To close the tblEmployees table:

| Step 1 | *Click* | the Close button ⊠ on the table |

Once you create a table, you often create a form next.

Forms

A **form** is a convenient way to enter or find information in tables. Although you can enter information directly into a table, it is easier to use a form. The form displays a blank template that you tab through as you enter data. Each box is labeled so that you know the type of information you are entering. You can also use forms to search or review your data.

One advantage of forms is that they are easily changed. You can add graphics or rearrange the fields to make them more helpful and appealing for the person entering the data. Further, Access links the form information to the tables you used when creating the form. Whenever you use the form to enter data, it places the data in the table to which it is linked.

QUICK TIP

When you open an object you may also see part of the database window in the screen. Although Access does not allow you to open more than one database at a time, you can open more than one object (table, query, form, report, etc.). This is beneficial when you want to compare information in different Access objects.

QUICK TIP

You can use a single form to enter data into several tables at once.

To look at the parts of an Access form:

| Step 1 | *Click* | Forms  on the Objects bar in the database window |
| Step 2 | *Double-click* | frmEmployees |

The status bar tells you that you are in Form view, that is, that the active window contains a form. Your screen should look similar to Figure 1-4.

FIGURE 1-4
frmEmployees Form

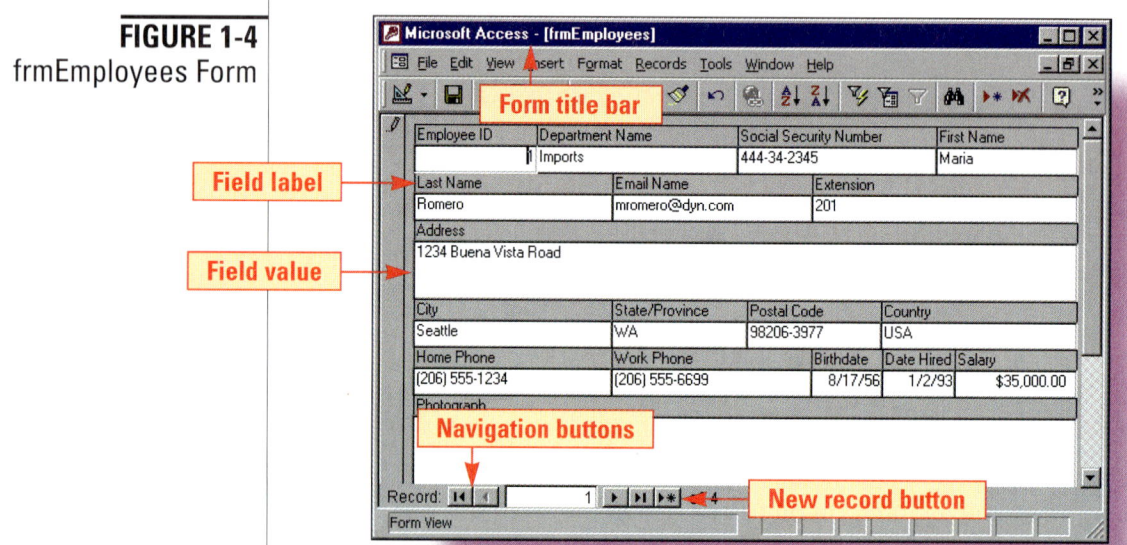

The field names on a form are called **labels**. These are the same fields found in the tables used to generate the form. A **value** is the data that is entered and contained in a single field in a single record. For example, an employee's last name, such as Romero, is a value.

After you finish looking at the layout of the form, you need to close it. To close the frmEmployees form:

| Step 1 | *Click* | the Close button  on the frmEmployees title bar |

After creating a form, you use it to enter data into one or more Access tables. Once you enter the data, you can then locate specific data by using queries.

Queries

One of the most powerful features of Access is the **query**, which allows you to ask questions of your information. Access then uses your questions to generate a subset of the data in your database. The data may be drawn from multiple tables. Start by opening the query.

Opening a Query in Design View

If you double-click a query object to open it, you open the results of the query. Because you want to look first at the design of a query, you must click the Design button in the database window.

To open an Access query:

Step 1	*Click*	Queries 🔲 on the Objects bar in the database window
Step 2	*Click*	qryEmployees
Step 3	*Click*	Design 🖉 on the Objects bar

Your screen should look similar to Figure 1-5.

MOUSE TIP

To open a query quickly in Design view, highlight the object name, right-click, and then click Design view.

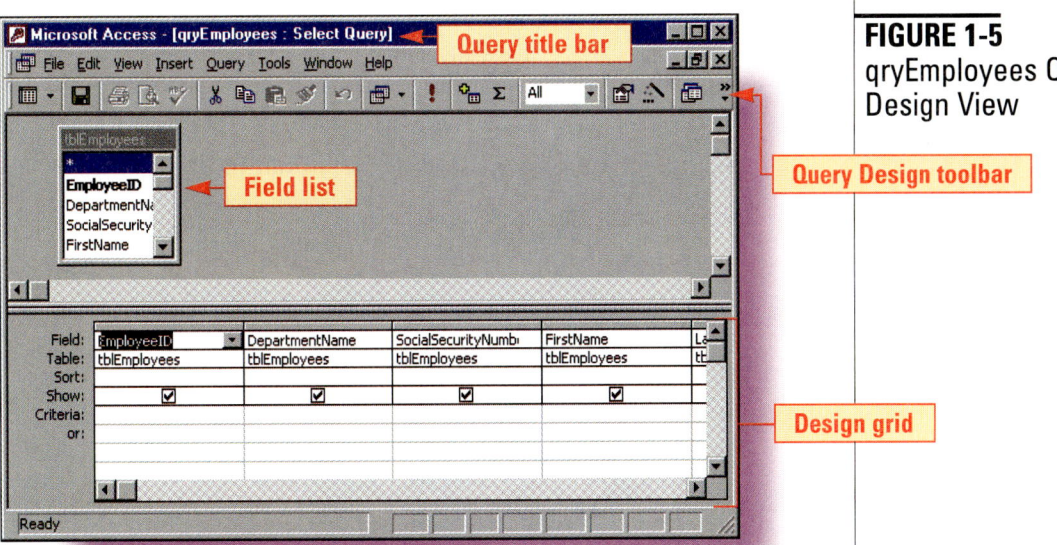

FIGURE 1-5
qryEmployees Query in Design View

Figure 1-5 shows the parts of a query. Notice that the current toolbar is now the Query Design toolbar, which contains tools that you use only for an Access query.

The query title bar indicates the name (here, qryEmployees) and type of query (here, Select Query). The default query type is the **select query**, which you use when you want to view a set of records for examination or modification. The **field list** contains all the fields from

**chapter
one**

MOUSE TIP

When the query is open in Design view, the option showing in the View button on the Query Design toolbar is the Datasheet View icon . Conversely, when the query is open in Datasheet view, the Design View icon shows on the View button.

the table or query being used in the query. In designing your query, you may choose fields from different tables and use as many fields in your query as you wish.

The **design grid** resembles a table and contains the criteria used in the query. The **Field: row** is the top row of the design grid and contains fields used in the query. The **Table: row** indicates the name of the tables that your query is based on. The **Sort: row** indicates the sort order of a particular field. The **Show: check box** indicates the field is shown in query results. If you remove the check mark from the Show check box for a field, that field does not appear in the query results. This is useful if you want to query on a certain field but do not want that field to be shown in the results. The **Criteria: row** is used to determine which records appear in the query results. This is a limiting feature such as "France" or "<25." Finally, the **or: row** is used in sorting the information similar to the Criteria: row.

You can see the results of a query by switching to Datasheet view.

Switching Between Object Views

You can easily switch views of any object by clicking the appropriate View button on the Query Design toolbar. You can also switch views by clicking <u>V</u>iew on the menu bar.

To see the query results by switching views:

| Step 1 | *Click* | the View button 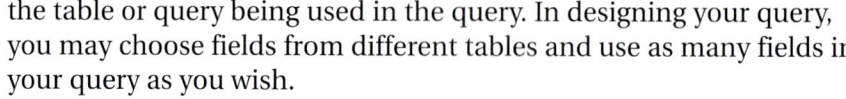 on the Query Design toolbar |

The results of the query should look similar to Figure 1-6.

FIGURE 1-6
Results of qryEmployees

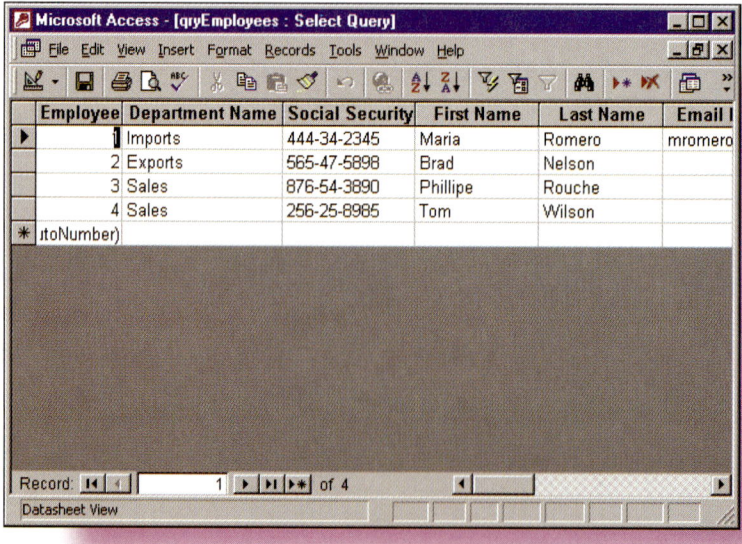

The employees are listed in numerical order according to their employee ID number. You can also resort the data by using any other field, such as the Last Name field. Sorting information allows you to view the same information from a different perspective.

To sort on the Last Name field:

| Step 1 | *Click* | the Last Name field to highlight the entire column |
| Step 2 | *Click* | the Sort Ascending button  on the Query Datasheet toolbar |

After looking at the sort, you need to close the query.

| Step 3 | *Click* | the Close button ☒ on the query title bar |

You do not want to save changes.

| Step 4 | *Click* | <u>N</u>o |

After a query has been performed, you then typically print a report.

Reports

A **report** is an organized presentation, designed to be printed, of the information in your tables or queries. You can create a report from a single table or from a query of two or more tables. A report can also process data and can automatically calculate and show subtotals and totals. Finally, inserting graphic elements and using formatting techniques often improve the readability and attractiveness of reports.

To open the rptEmployees report:

| Step 1 | *Click* | Reports ▣ on the Objects bar in the database window |
| Step 2 | *Double-click* | rptEmployees |

Your screen should look similar to Figure 1-7.

chapter
one

FIGURE 1-7
rptEmployees Report

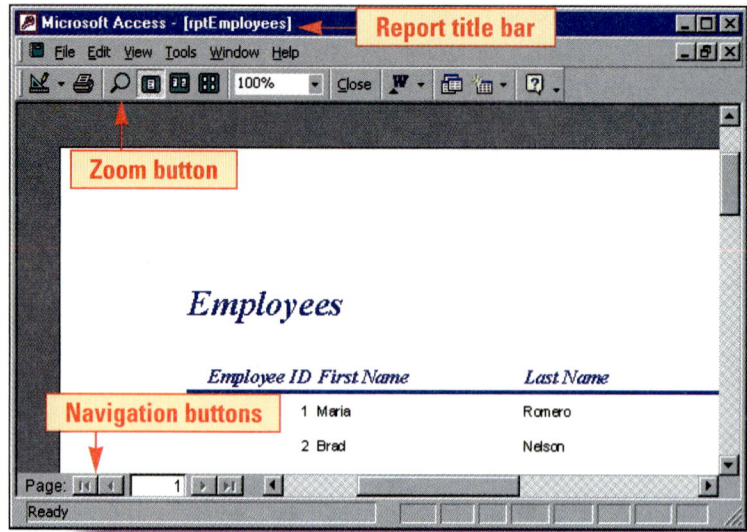

Figure 1-7 identifies the parts of a report. The Database toolbar is now the Print Preview toolbar and contains tools used by Access reports. For example, the **Zoom** button allows you to magnify a particular area of the report. Notice the report is in Print Preview, which allows you to see what the report looks like when it is printed. This saves you time and paper, as you can determine what needs to be modified before you print.

After you look at the report, you need to close it.

To close the rptEmployees report:

Step 1	*Click*	the Close button  on the report title bar

The final Access object you tour is the data access page.

Data Access Pages

A **data access page (DAP)** allows you to extend the database by creating HyperText Markup Language (HTML) pages quickly and easily. HTML pages are written for use on an intranet or the Internet, and let you share information with others in any location.

Data access pages are stored as an HTML file, not a database file. This allows others who do not have Access installed on their computers to browse the information. A DAP can be mailed to your co-workers using **Outlook**, which is Microsoft's e-mail application. Access and Outlook are completely compatible, which is not always true with other e-mail applications.

DAPs are more than Internet packaging for Access; they are a new way to interact with Access data. People with whom you share your data can view, sort, and print the data, even if they do not have Access loaded on their computers.

You open the DAP created for *mdbImporters*.

To open a DAP:

Step 1	*Click*	Pages 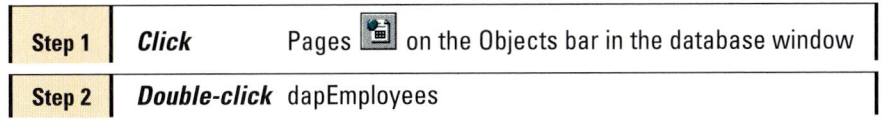 on the Objects bar in the database window
Step 2	*Double-click*	dapEmployees

Your screen should look similar to Figure 1-8.

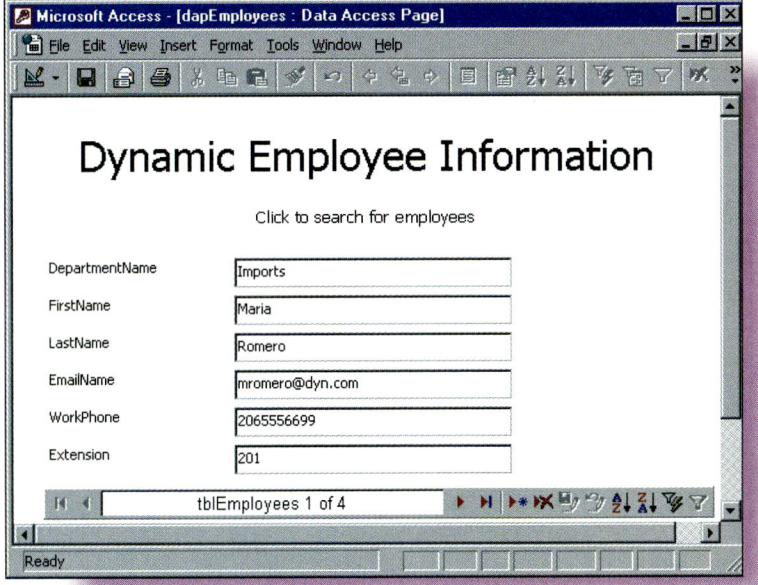

FIGURE 1-8
dapEmployees Data
Access Page in
Preview Mode

> **CAUTION TIP**
>
> Because of the way Access stores data access pages, you may see some error messages when you try to open a DAP. Click OK to respond to the message boxes until you see the Data Link Connection dialog box. In the select or enter a database name: text box, enter or select the location and name of the *mbdImporters* database.

Figure 1-8 shows the components of a DAP. Notice that there are no tools available at this time. This is because you are in **Preview mode**, which lets you browse records but not enter information or make changes. The DAP's navigation bar allows you to view the records included in the DAP. To modify a DAP, first switch from Preview mode to Design view.

Step 3	*Switch*	to Design view

Your screen should look similar to Figure 1-9.

chapter
one

FIGURE 1-9
dapEmployees Data
Access Page in
Design View

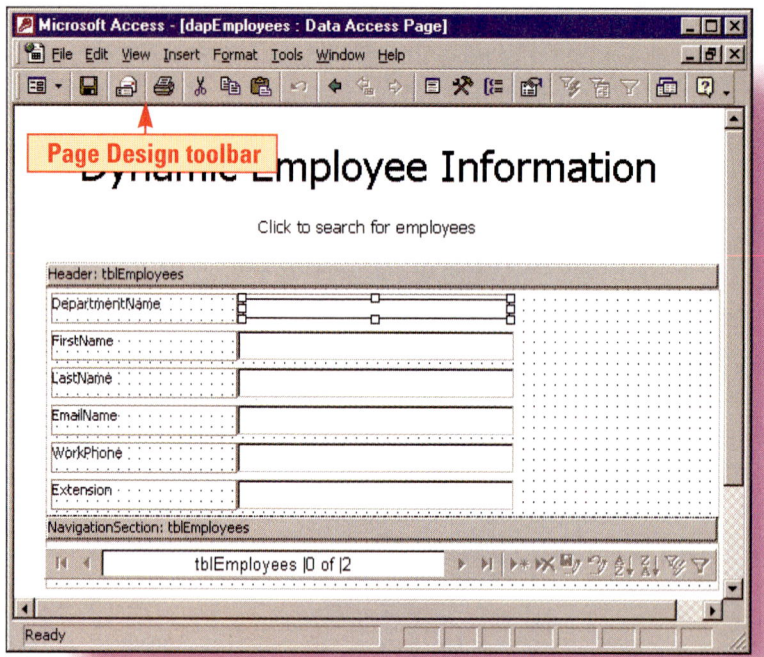

In Design view, you can create and edit a DAP using the Web Editing toolbar. The **Web Editing toolbar** includes tools for modifying the text, background, and placement of objects on the DAP. The **Page Design toolbar** allows you to add, delete, group, and sort the fields that you chose for your HTML file. Finally, the **Toolbox** has the tools you need to build the fields for the HTML page.

After you finish looking at the dapEmployees DAP, you should close it. To close the dapEmployees DAP:

Step 1	*Click*	the Close button  on the dapEmployees DAP

Macros

An Access **macro** is a set of one or more actions that perform a particular operation, such as opening a form or printing a report. A **macro group** is a collection of related macros stored together under a single macro name.

Modules

Modules are programs written in the Visual Basic language. Office applications use Visual Basic (VB) 6. With Visual Basic you can program all aspects of your Access database, including your own tables, forms, reports, and queries. Although this is a challenge at first, modules can provide incredible functionality to your database. For example, you can use a module to check the accuracy of the typed information in your database, or to check for redundant data.

You are now familiar with the Access objects. Next, you exit the application.

1.f Exiting Access

Access automatically saves changes whenever you exit the application. However, if you made changes to the *design* of any database objects since you last saved them, Access asks if you want to save these changes before quitting. When saving your database, Access automatically compresses it, saving space on your hard drive and making it easier to transfer the file to other locations on your network.

To exit Access:

Step 1	*Click*	File
Step 2	*Click*	Exit

The Access application and the *mdbImporters* database close. Because you did not make any changes to the database, Access did not prompt you to save changes.

chapter
one

Summary

▶ A database is a collection of related information. An example of a database is a list of customers and their contact information.

▶ Access includes many views. The most common are Design view and Datasheet view. Design view is where you create the look of the database. Datasheet view is where you view your data.

▶ The menus provide you with many useful tools and options in creating and viewing your database.

▶ Access uses objects such as tables, queries, forms, reports, and data access pages. These objects all relate to the data that is stored in the database.

▶ An Access table contains data in columns (fields) and rows (records) called a datasheet. A field in a database contains the same type of information, such as customers' phone numbers. A record in a database contains all of the fields for one item, such as for one customer.

▶ Use Access forms to enter, update, search, or review data in tables.

▶ An Access query allows you to ask questions about your data. A query shows you specific data that you want to work with.

▶ Create Access reports to share database information in printed form.

▶ A data access page (DAP) allows you to create an interactive HTML page using the information stored in your Access database. This tool allows you to share your database with others who may not have Access installed on their computers.

▶ Macros and modules are advanced Access features that allow you to customize the database and automate tasks that you perform on a regular basis.

▶ When you exit Access, your changes are automatically saved. You should always exit Access before turning off your computer.

Commands Review

Action	Menu Bar	Shortcut Menu	Toolbar	Keyboard
Open an existing database	File, Open Database			CTRL + O ALT + F, O
Open an object	View, Database Objects	Right-click object	Select object, click	ALT + V
Get help	Help			F1
Close an object	File, Close	Right-click object, click Close	on the object's title bar	ALT + F, C
Exit Access	File, Exit	Right-click the application button on the taskbar, click Close		ALT + F4 ALT + F, X

Concepts Review

Circle the correct answer.

1. A database is a:
[a] tool for editing documents.
[b] way to automate common tasks.
[c] collection of related information.
[d] link to the World Wide Web.

2. Access 2000 has special menus and toolbars that:
[a] learn what you do.
[b] are the same for all objects.
[c] are exactly the same as the toolbars in other Office products.
[d] never change.

3. In Datasheet view, you can:
[a] design tables and forms.
[b] view data in rows and columns.
[c] preview your printed reports.
[d] customize the Database toolbar.

4. Which of the following is not an Access database object?
[a] table
[b] form
[c] query
[d] datasheet

5. A category of information, such as last names or phone numbers, is called a:
[a] field.
[b] record.
[c] form.
[d] module.

6. Which record selector symbol points to the current record in a table?
[a] drawing pen
[b] asterisk
[c] null symbol
[d] triangle

chapter one

7. To enter, update, search, or review data quickly, use a:
[a] form.
[b] table.
[c] data access page.
[d] query.

8. You can switch between Design view and Datasheet view by clicking the:
[a] Queries object tab.
[b] Switch command on the View menu.
[c] View button, and then clicking a view option.
[d] select query title bar.

9. A data access page lets you:
[a] access a database.
[b] create a Web site using your database.
[c] write an HTML page.
[d] select a page to print.

10. Modules are:
[a] a selection of commands used to automate repetitive tasks.
[b] programs written in Visual Basic.
[c] object tabs.
[d] a group of records.

Circle **T** if the statement is true or **F** is the statement is false.

T   F   1. An example of a database is a list of customers and their addresses and phone numbers.

T   F   2. You can open more than one database file at a time in Access.

T   F   3. You cannot hide or change the Office Assistant.

T   F   4. Access automatically opens a blank database when you start the program.

T   F   5. Tables store information in rows of records and columns of fields.

T   F   6. Layout Preview shows a small portion of data in a report before printing.

T   F   7. You can use the magnifier to zoom a particular area in Design view.

T   F   8. You can use a query to ask for help from the Office Assistant.

T   F   9. A macro forces you to perform one task at a time.

T   F   10. If you create a data access page, you can share your database with others, even if they don't use Access 2000.

Skills Review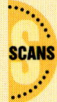

Exercise 1

1. Start Access and open the *mdbImporters* database.

2. Change the Office Assistant.

3. Save and close the database.

Exercise 2

1. If necessary, open the *mdbImporters* database.

2. Open the tblEmployees table.

3. Move to the last record in the table.

4. Scroll to see all the fields in the record, including the last field.

5. Close the table.

Exercise 3

1. If necessary, open the *mdbImporters* database.

2. Open the frmEmployees form.

3. Click the first field—EmployeeID—and then press the TAB key to move to the next field.

4. Press the TAB key until you select the Address field.

5. Close the form.

Exercise 4

1. If necessary, open the *mdbImporters* database.

2. Open qryEmployees in Design view.

3. In the list of fields, click DepartmentName.

4. In the design grid, review the criteria for this query: the fields and tables used, sort order, and whether to show the field in the query results.

5. Switch to Datasheet view to see the query results.

Exercise 5

1. If necessary, open the *mdbImporters* database.

2. Open qryEmployees in Design view.

3. Sort the list in ascending order by the first name of the employee.

4. Switch to Datasheet view to see the query results.

5. Close the Query window.

chapter one

Exercise 6

1. If necessary, open the *mdbImporters* database.

2. Open the rptEmployees report.

3. Preview the report.

4. Click the Print button in the Print Preview toolbar to print the report.

5. Close the report.

Exercise 7

1. If necessary, open the *mdbImporters* database.

2. Open the dapEmployees data access page.

3. Scroll to see all the employee records.

4. Switch to Design view and then click and delete a field name and value, such as the Extension field.

5. Close the data access page.

Exercise 8

1. If necessary, open the *mdbImporters* database.

2. Open any database object, such as a table, form, or report.

3. Get help on any part or feature of Access.

4. Close the object, and then exit Access.

Case Projects

Project 1

Your supervisor at Dynamic, Inc., asks you to write an introduction to Access databases, using *mdbImporters* as an example. People recently hired by Dynamic plan to use your introduction to learn the basics about Access databases. In a Word document, write two to three paragraphs defining terms every Access user should know. Explain the purpose of and provide an example for each term. Save and print the document.

Project 2

Create a new document for the Dynamic Employee Handbook that contains one to two paragraphs about getting help while working in Access, including using the online Help, the F1 key, and the SHIFT + F1 context-sensitive Help pointer. Use Word to create, save, and print the document.

Project 3

To increase efficiency, your supervisor at Dynamic asks you to create a chart of Microsoft Office shortcuts. Working with a coworker, use the Office Assistant to review the shortcut keys every Office application uses. In Word, create a table showing each shortcut command and the action it performs. Save and print the document.

Project 4

Dynamic is organizing a meeting for people new to Access. Your supervisor asks you to present solutions to common questions people have about Access and its features. Connect to the Internet and, using the Microsoft on the Web command on the Access Help menu, link to the Frequently Asked Questions page and research questions about Access and its features. Print at least two Web pages.

Project 5

You decide to create a notebook for your department that outlines the features of Access. Create a new document for your notebook that identifies one Access toolbar and lists the name and purpose of each button on the toolbar. (*Hint:* Use the What's This? command on the Help menu to get online Help for the buttons.) Use Word to create, save, and print the document.

Project 6

You decide to include information about the Access views in your Access notebook. Write two paragraphs explaining the purpose and features of two views. Use Word to create, save, and print the document.

Project 7

Your supervisor at Dynamic asks you to show several new employees how to open a database. Using the tools on the Help menu, research how to do this. In Word, create a new document with one to two short paragraphs describing how to open an existing database in Access. Save and print the document. Then demonstrate to your coworkers how to open a database in Access.

Project 8

Connect to your ISP and load the home page for a search engine. Search for companies on the Web who are similar to Dynamic, Inc. Print at least three Web pages for similar companies. Close the browser and disconnect from your ISP.

chapter one

Designing and Creating a Database

Chapter Overview

I n this chapter, you plan a database for Dynamic, Inc. by learning and applying principles of effective database design. You then create the database by adding tables. You also learn how to modify a database table by changing field layouts, deleting field names, and rearranging fields. Finally, you print a database table.

LEARNING OBJECTIVES

► Plan a new database
► Create a database
► Save a database
► Create a table by using the Table Wizard
► Create a table in Design view
► Modify tables using Design view
► Print a table

Case profile

The owner of Dynamic, Inc., Maria Moreno, asks you to design and create an Access 2000 database that tracks products and orders for the company as well as maintains current employee information.

chapter two

2.a Planning a New Database

Before you create a database, take some time to plan it. A good database design is the most important step in creating a database that does what you want it to do. When planning a database, follow the general steps listed below.

Determining Appropriate Data Inputs and Outputs for your Database

Start by describing the inputs and outputs of your database, that is, the data that will be entered into it and the information that it will provide. Talk to the people who will use your database and find out what they expect from the database. What are the subjects your database covers? These subjects become tables. What facts do you store about each subject? These facts become fields in the tables.

To determine the purpose of the Dynamic database, you talk with department managers to determine the kind of information they want to include and how they and their staff want to work with the database.

Once you determine what your database will include and how it will be used, your next step is to list the tables you need.

Changing Table Structures

List the subjects or types of information your database will cover, such as customer, product, and employee information. You'll store each type of information in a table. Be sure each table is dedicated to only one subject and that you don't duplicate information within a table or between tables.

Deciding What Tables Are Necessary

If you store each type of information in a separate table, you only have to go to one place to add or update the information. You also avoid duplicating records and entering the same information more than once. For example, store customer information in one table and the customer orders in another table. This way, if a customer changes an order, you modify only the order information, not the customer information.

Maria asks you to include three types of information for the Dynamic database: product, order, and employee information. Though Dynamic has hundreds of products, ranging from clothing to gifts, they fit into only a few categories. It simplifies data entry and tracking to also maintain information about product categories. For the Dynamic database, you need four tables: one listing employee information (tblEmployees), one containing product categories (tblCategories), one tracking products in each category (tblProducts), and one tracking customer orders (tblOrders).

After you determine the tables you need, your next step is to decide which fields to include in each table.

Determining Essential Fields

Each table contains facts about the same subject; each field in a table contains specific facts about that subject. When determining the fields for each table, keep the following four principles in mind: (1) relate each field to the subject of the table, (2) omit any calculated data, (3) include all of the information you need, and (4) store information in small bits (e.g., "last name" and "first name").

For the tblEmployees table, Maria asks you to include the following information about each employee: their ID number, first and last name, address, including city and state, and home phone number.

After planning and consideration, you determine the necessary fields for the four tables, as shown in Table 2-1.

TABLE 2-1
Planned Dynamic Database
Tables and Fields

Required Tables	Necessary Fields
Employees	Employee ID, Department ID, Last Name, First Name, Address, City, State, Postal Code, Home Phone
Categories	Category ID, Category Name
Products	Product ID, Product Name, Product Description, Per Unit Cost
Customer Orders	Order ID, Customer ID, Order Date, Name, Address, City, State, Phone Number, Shipping Date

After you plan and review your database, you can begin to create it. You can create one by starting with a blank database or using a wizard.

2.b Creating a Database

The **Database Wizard** guides you step-by-step through the process of creating a database. Access includes a number of sample databases, such as those for contact, order, or personal information. If you create a database of similar information, you can use the wizard to choose a sample database. Access then creates all the necessary tables and fields (as well as forms and reports) for that type of database. You can change the information to suit your needs. The Database Wizard saves you time when creating common types of databases.

If the database you want to create is not similar to one of the sample databases, you can start with a blank database. You have more flexibility when you start with a blank database.

To learn all the steps of creating a database, you start with a blank one. You use a wizard later in this chapter when creating tables.

To open the Access application and the Access dialog box:

Step 1	*Click*	the Start button 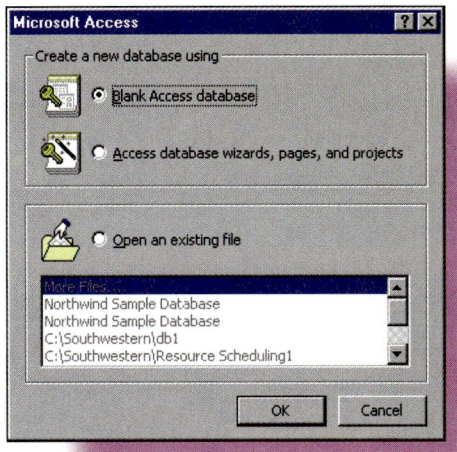 on the taskbar
Step 2	*Point*	to Programs
Step 3	*Click*	Microsoft Access
Step 4	*Click*	the Blank Access database option button

Your screen should look similar to Figure 2-1.

FIGURE 2-1
New Database Dialog Box

Step 5	*Click*	OK

Now save the database you just created.

2.c Saving a Database

Whenever you create a new database file, Access requires you to name and save the file before continuing. Access gives your database a temporary name, such as "db1," which you see in the File name: text box. Accept or switch to the location where you want to store your file (a floppy disk or a folder on your hard disk or network server), and then type the filename you want to use. A filename can have up to 255 characters including the disk drive reference and path, and can contain letters, numbers, spaces, and some special characters in any combination.

chapter
two

CAUTION TIP

Filenames cannot include the following special characters: the forward slash (/), the backward slash (\), the colon (:), the semicolon (;), the pipe symbol (|), the question mark (?), the less than symbol (<), the greater than symbol (>), the asterisk (*), the quotation mark ("), and the period (.).

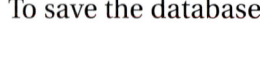

Be sure to check with your instructor if you do not know which disk drive and folder to use to save your documents.

To save the database:

Step 1	*Click*	the Save in: list arrow
Step 2	*Switch*	to the appropriate disk drive and folder
Step 3	*Key*	*mdbDynamicInc2* in the File name: text box
Step 4	*Click*	Create

The *mdbDynamicInc2* database window opens. Your screen should look similar to Figure 2-2.

FIGURE 2-2
mdbDynamicInc2
Database Window

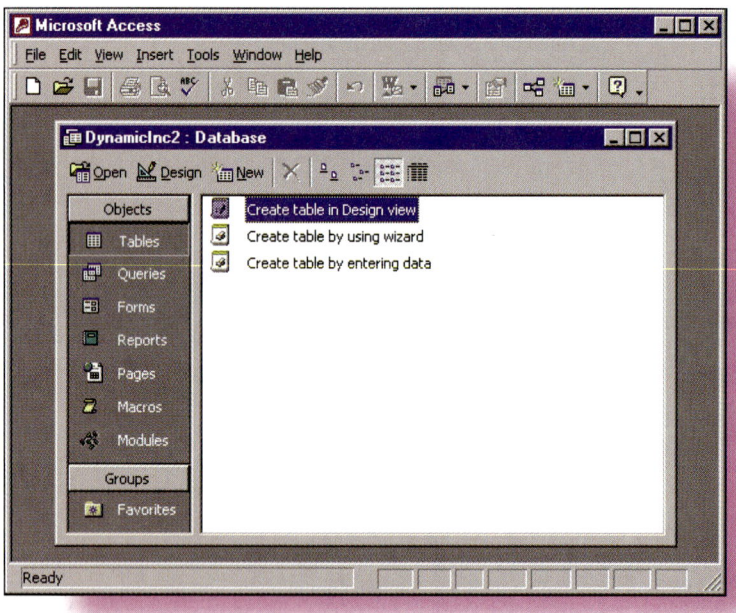

You are ready to create the first table.

QUICK TIP

Once you create and save a database, you should also take advantage of the Create Replica menu command, which you can use to quickly back up your database. Click the Tools menu, point to Replication, and then click Create Replica. You can then use the backup copy to restore data that may get lost, for example, due to a power surge.

2.d Creating a Table by Using the Table Wizard

Access provides three options for creating tables: You can open a blank empty table and then enter the data, use the Table Wizard, or create one in Design view. The **Table Wizard** allows you to create a table by choosing from a list of commonly used table templates. For your database, you create tables using both the Table Wizard and Design view.

You create your first table, the tblEmployees table, using the Table Wizard, because it is similar to one of the wizard's templates.

To create the tblEmployees table using the wizard:

Step 1	**Double-click** the Create table by using wizard option

Your screen should look similar to Figure 2-3.

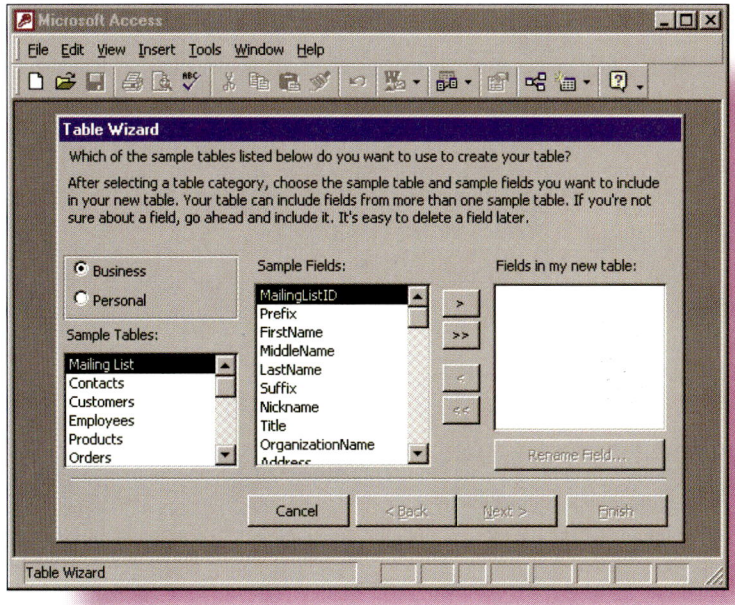

FIGURE 2-3
Table Wizard

Step 2	**Click**	Employees in the Sample Tables: list

Access displays the selected table templates fields in the Sample Fields: list.

Step 3	**Click**	LastName

chapter
two

QUICK TIP

To move the entire contents of the selected Sample Table to your table, click the >> button.

If you see a field similar to one you want but it has a different name, add it to your list. Then select the field in your database field list, click the Rename Field button, type a new name in the Rename field: text box, and then click OK.

Step 4	***Click***	the > button to move the selected field to the Fields in my new table: list

Refer to Table 2-1 for the fields you need in your tblEmployees table.

Step 5	***Repeat***	Steps 3 and 4 until you choose all of the field names you need to include in the tblEmployees table
Step 6	***Click***	Next >

Access asks you to name the table. The default name is tblEmployees, which is the name you also want to use. Access also asks if you want a primary key. A **primary key** is the designated field that uniquely identifies the record (you learn more about the primary key later in this chapter). For now, choose Yes, which is already selected as the default. You are ready to continue.

Step 7	***Click***	Next >

Access now asks if you want to enter data into the table. To keep it simple, have Access design a form for you.

Step 8	***Click***	the Enter data into the table using a form the wizard creates for me option button
Step 9	***Click***	Finish

Your screen should look similar to Figure 2-4.

FIGURE 2-4
frmEmployees Form

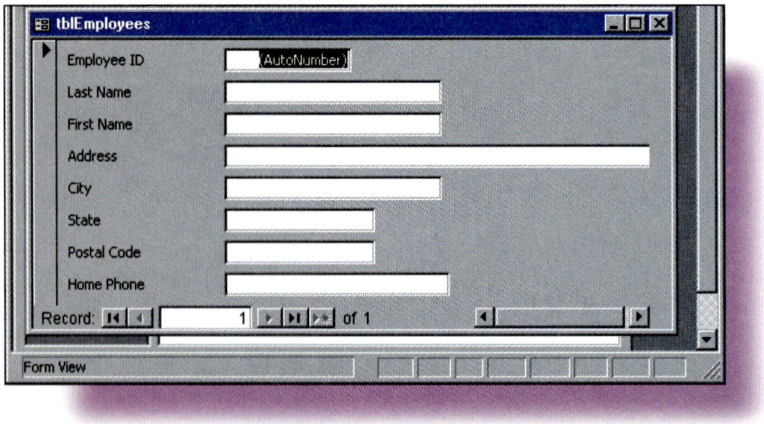

Access displays the form it created for the tblEmployees table. Because you want to create the other database tables before entering records, close the form now.

| Step 10 | *Click* | the Close button  on the frmEmployees form title bar |

A dialog box opens and asks if you would like to save the changes to the form.

Step 11	*Click*	Yes
Step 12	*Key*	frmEmployees in the Form Name: text box in the Save As dialog box
Step 13	*Click*	OK

If you click Forms on the Objects bar, you now see that the frmEmployees form is included in the list of forms for this database.

Using the Table Wizard allows you to quickly create tables of common information. For unique or very simple tables, however, such as the tblProduct Categories table in the *mdbDynamicInc2* database, use Design view.

2.e Creating a Table in Design View

Design view gives you complete control over the contents of your tables. You add fields and assign a data type to each. A **data type** determines what kind of information each field can contain, such as a number or a date, and helps guide you when entering data. You can then set properties for each field—the characteristics of a field, such as the number of characters it can contain or whether the field is required. You can also set a primary key to use when sorting records. For example, if you make the Last Name field the primary key, Access sorts the table alphabetically according to last name. Finally, you can customize the design of your table, such as changing the column widths so you can see necessary information.

Using Multiple Data Types

As mentioned above, you select a data type for each field to determine the kind of information the field contains. For example, if

chapter two

you select Currency as the data type, Access formats that field to include a dollar sign and a decimal point. Most databases contain multiple data types; the more specific you are when selecting a data type for a field, the more likely your database will include the correct inputs. You can select the following data types.

Text

Use the **Text data type,** the default in Access, to enter the following in a field: text; numbers that do not require any calculations, such as phone numbers or zip codes; or a combination of text, numbers, and symbols. A text field can contain up to 255 characters per record.

Memo

Use the **Memo data type** to enter lengthy text or combinations of text and numbers or symbols. Memo fields can contain up to 65,535 characters per record. You can also use returns or tabs within a memo data type.

Number

Use the **Number data type** to include simple numbers, such as those that identify a record, and numeric data in mathematical calculations. By entering a simple formula, the calculations become part of the data. Do not use this data type for phone numbers, Social Security numbers, and so forth that are not used in calculations; instead, use the text data type.

Date/Time

Use the **Date/Time data type** to include the date and time values for the year 100 through the year 9999. The date and time data type is useful for calendar or clock data. It also lets you calculate seconds, minutes, hours, days, months, and years. For example, use a date/time field to find the difference between two dates.

Currency

Use the **Currency data type** to insert the currency symbol and calculate numeric data with one to four decimal places. This data is accurate to 15 digits on the left of the decimal point and up to 4 digits on the right of the decimal point. Currency has the accuracy of integers, but with a fixed number of decimal places.

AutoNumber

The **AutoNumber data type** is a unique number Access automatically inserts each time you add a new record to a table. These numbers follow a consecutive number sequence, such as 1, 2, 3, and so on. You cannot change or update an AutoNumber field. Access uses the AutoNumber

---

QUICK TIP

You can further optimize data type usage by specifying what type of number should be entered. For example, for the Category ID field, enter an integer (int).

data type to generate the primary key value. You can only include one field using the AutoNumber data type in a table.

Yes/No

The **Yes/No data type** can contain only information that uses one of three values: Yes/No, True/False, On/Off. Use a yes/no data type, for example, to flag accounts paid or unpaid, active or inactive, or orders filled or not filled.

OLE Object

The **OLE Object data type** contains an object (Excel spreadsheet, Word document, or graphic image) that is linked or embedded into an Access table. A linked object is one where the source is not a part of the Access database. An embedded object is placed in the database as part of the data.

Hyperlink

The **Hyperlink data type** stores a path and filename to a Web page URL on your computer, another computer, or a Web address. This provides a link to a customer's home page, or to a file on the Intranet that will provide additional information about a product or service. When you enter or select the hyperlink, you "jump" to the associated location.

Lookup Wizard

Use the **Lookup Wizard data type** to choose a value from another table or from a list of values by using a list box or combo box. This is a useful tool for an order form—you can then select a product from a list, or type the first few letters of the product and insert the complete name in the field. When you select the Lookup Wizard data type, you start the Lookup Wizard, which guides you through the steps of creating the list or combo box.

Now that you are familiar with the data types, you can begin to create your second table.

To create tblCategories in the *mdbDynamicInc2* database:

Step 1	*Click*	Tables on the Objects bar in the database window
Step 2	*Double-click*	Create table in Design view

Your screen should look similar to Figure 2-5.

chapter two

FIGURE 2-5
New Table in Design View

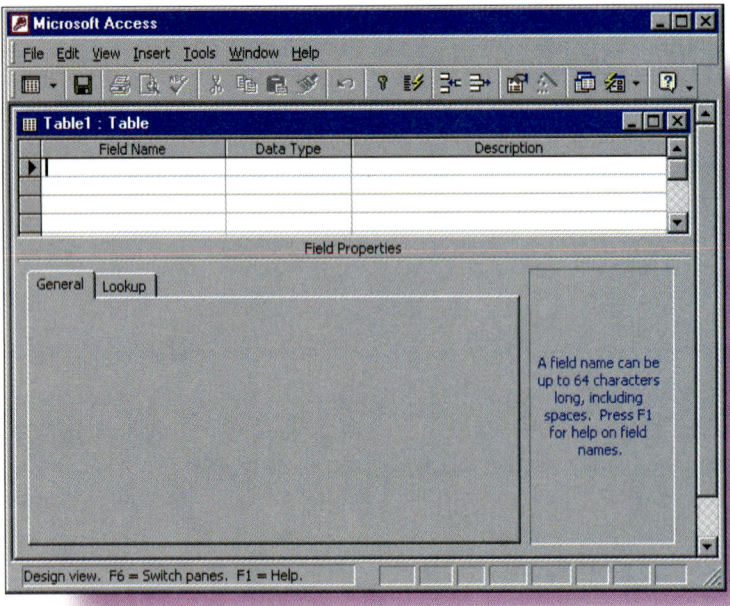

You are now ready to add fields to your table.

Using Design View to Add Fields

The Design View window contains two panes, field name at the top and field properties at the bottom. You add field names and data type information in the top pane and then set individual field properties in the bottom pane (you learn about field properties later in this chapter). The Help box in the lower-right corner of the window displays help text for the column where your insertion point is located.

You are now ready to add fields to your new table. You can move the insertion point from column to column in the top pane using the TAB key or arrow keys.

To begin adding fields to the table:

Step 1	*Verify*	the insertion point is in the top field name box in the Field Name column
Step 2	*Key*	Category ID
Step 3	*Press*	the TAB key to move the insertion point to the Data Type column

The Text data type (the default) appears in the Data Type column. You can select a different data type from a list box by clicking the Data Type list arrow. Because the Category ID field will contain simple numbers to identify each record, change the data type to Number.

| Step 4 | *Click* | the list arrow |

The contents of the Help box now define the term "data type."

| Step 5 | *Click* | Number |
| Step 6 | *Repeat* | Steps 1–3 to key in the second field name of Category Name with data type Text |

This completes the field names for the tblCategories table; your screen should look similar to Figure 2-6.

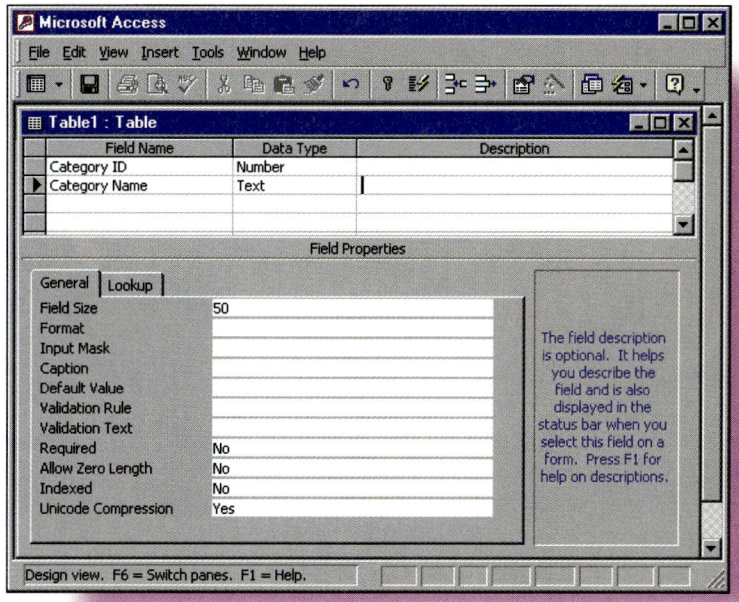

FIGURE 2-6
tblCategories Table in Design View

You created a simple table in Design view using the field name pane to enter fields. If you need to change the information, you can also do so in Design view. For example, you can change the properties of the Category ID field so it only contains certain kinds of information.

Modifying Field Properties

Field properties are characteristics of a field, such as their length or format. Selecting properties for your fields ensures the information in your records is consistent—every state field, for example, contains two uppercase characters. The General tab in Design view groups the

chapter two

field properties you can modify when you enter a new field in a table, as follows:

The **Field Size property** indicates the maximum number of characters someone can enter in this field. Although the default size is 50 characters, a Text field can have a maximum number of 255 characters.

The **Format property** indicates how you want the information to appear. For example, if a field should contain all uppercase text, as in a state abbreviation, choose All Uppercase for this field property.

The **Input Mask property** defines a standard pattern for the appearance of all data entered in this field. For example, if the field is a Social Security number, you can have Access insert the hyphens in the correct places (e.g., 123-45-6789), which makes it easier to enter accurate data.

The **Caption property** appears as the column header in the table and overrides the field name you entered in the field name pane. For example, if you enter the caption "Category Number," the caption appears on the table, form, or report instead of the field name strCategory ID.

The **Default Value property** is information Access automatically enters in the field when you add a new record. For example, if you almost always enter "50" in the Price field, you could enter "50" as the Default Value property. Access then inserts 50 in the Price field of every new record. You can enter a value other than 50 if necessary.

A **Validation Rule** is an expression that limits what information you can enter into a field. An **expression** is a set of specific instructions. Access only accepts information that fulfills the expression requirements. For example, if a salary cannot be greater than $50.00 per hour, Access will not allow you to key $60.00. The **Validation Text property** is the error message you display when an entry breaks the validation rule.

The **Required property** indicates whether you must complete the field for all records. If the field is required, change this property to Yes; Access does not save the record until information is entered in this field.

In contrast to the Required property, the **Allow Zero Length property**, when set to Yes, tells Access that it is acceptable if no value is entered in this field. You can use this option in only Text, Memo, or Hyperlink data types.

The **Indexed property** creates an index for the primary key. For example, if you search for a specific product category in the tblCategories table, you can create an index to speed up sorting and searching. Keep in mind, however, if a table contains several indexes, it may slow data entry.

The **Unicode Compression property** tells Access to compress the Unicode file format, which lets you code data so it can be used in the world's major languages. A Unicode file format makes it easier for multinational organizations to share documents, because it prevents font compatibility issues.

QUICK TIP

Define data validation criteria when creating a database table. For example, you can set the criteria for seven digits to be entered for the Phone Number field. You can then set validation text that indicates how to correct the mistake. For example, if someone entered only six digits for a phone number, you could display an error message that reads "A phone number must contain seven digits."

Review the current properties of the Category ID field: the default size is Long Integer, the Required property box indicates that the field can remain blank, and the Indexed property box indicates duplicate Category ID numbers can exist in the table.

You can modify these properties to prevent data entry errors and to maintain consistency among records. Change the field size to two characters, make it a required field so all records have a Category ID, and make sure no other records have the same ID. These changes create **data integrity**, which is a set of rules to ensure the information in your database is accurate.

To change the field properties, move the insertion point into the field properties pane by clicking in the pane. You can also move from one pane to another by pressing the F6 key. To move from one property box to another, press the UP ARROW, DOWN ARROW, TAB, or SHIFT + TAB keys. As you move the insertion point to a different property box, the Help box displays text for the property.

To modify the Category ID field properties:

Step 1	*Click*	in the Category ID field
Step 2	*Press*	the F6 key to move the insertion point to the field properties pane

The Field Size property box is selected. Notice the new help text in the Help box.

Step 3	*Click*	the list arrow
Step 4	*Select*	Double from the drop-down list
Step 5	*Move*	the insertion point to the Required property box
Step 6	*Click*	the Required list arrow
Step 7	*Click*	Yes
Step 8	*Move*	the insertion point to the Indexed property box
Step 9	*Click*	the Indexed property box list arrow
Step 10	*Click*	Yes (No Duplicates)

You changed the field properties for the Category ID field. You can also include a description for this field.

To add a description:

Step 1	*Move*	the insertion point to the Description box

The text in the Help box now defines a field description. The **field description** is optional information for a text field. Field descriptions appear on the status bar when you select the field to enter data in a form or table.

Step 2	*Key*	Enter the number of the product category
Step 3	*Repeat*	Steps 1 and 2 to include the field description "Enter the name of the product category" in the Description box for the Category Name field

Once you enter all the fields in a table, you can set a primary key.

Setting Primary Keys

Recall that a primary key is a field you designate to uniquely identify a record. Primary keys prevent the duplication of an entry in that field. When you open a table that has a primary key field, records are sorted by the field in ascending order. **Ascending order** lists the data from A–Z or from 1–100. **Descending order** lists the data from Z–A or from 100–1.

Every table must have at least one field that is used as the primary key. Select the field you want to use as the primary key—it should be one with no duplicates, such as the Category ID field.

To select a field as a primary key:

Step 1	*Click*	in the Category ID field
Step 2	*Right-click*	to open the shortcut menu
Step 3	*Click*	Primary Key

Your screen should look similar to Figure 2-7.

FIGURE 2-7
tblCategories Primary Key

Primary key

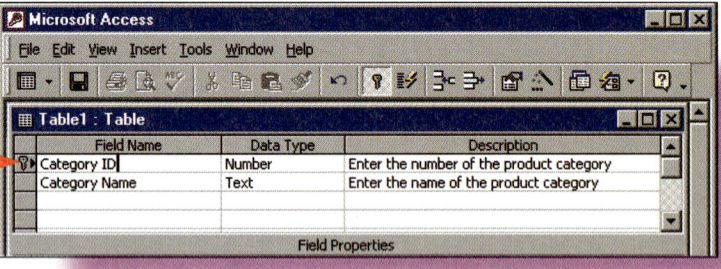

After you complete the table, you should close it.

| Step 4 | *Click* | the Close button ⊠ on the table title bar |

Access asks if you want to save the table.

Step 5	*Click*	Yes
Step 6	*Key*	tblCategories
Step 7	*Click*	OK

Your table is now closed and saved.

You create the tblProducts table and the tblOrders table in the Skills Review exercises at the end of the chapter.

To open tblCategories in Datasheet view:

| Step 1 | *Double-click* | tblCategories |

Looking at the table, you notice you need to add more space for the fields. You can allow for more space by increasing the column width.

Changing Column Widths

Access uses the same column width for every field you enter in a table. But often, as in the tblCategories table, one or more columns are too narrow to display the entire field name. This text is not lost, just hidden. If you widen the column, you can see the full field name.

To change column width:

| Step 1 | *Point to* | the right edge of the Category Name in the field labels row, so that the mouse pointer changes to a double-headed arrow |

This allows you to adjust the width of the column in the table.

| Step 2 | *Drag* | the mouse pointer to the right until you can see the entire field label, Category Name |
| Step 3 | *Repeat* | Steps 1 and 2 to increase the width of the other column if necessary so that you can read all the field labels |

Your screen should now look similar to Figure 2-8.

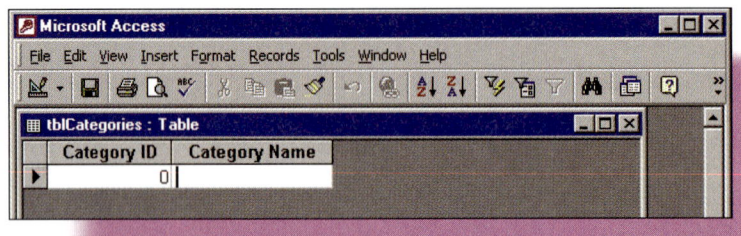

| Step 4 | *Click* | the Close button on the table title bar |

You are now prompted to save your changes.

| Step 5 | *Click* | Yes |

You have created two tables for your database. You should review your work to see if you need to make any modifications.

2.f Modifying Tables Using Design View

Once you create a table, you should carefully review it to ensure you designed it accurately. If you need to make changes, modifying a table (using Design view) is easy as long as you haven't entered any data yet. Once you start entering data, modifying a table design becomes increasingly more difficult.

When you review your tables and fields for *mdbDynamicInc2's* database, you notice you need a field for employees' Social Security numbers. This is important data as employees cannot be paid without it. You add this field to the tblEmployees table now.

Adding Fields

Even after you save a table, you can still enter new fields anywhere in the table by inserting a row where you want the field.

To add the Social Security field:

Step 1	*Open*	the tblEmployees table

When you open the table, you see it in Datasheet view. Switch to Design view to modify the table.

Step 2	*Switch*	to Design view
Step 3	*Click*	in the first blank row in the Field Name column
Step 4	*Key*	SS Number
Step 5	*Press*	the TAB key to move to the Data Type column

You do not need to change the default Text data type, but because all Social Security numbers follow the same pattern (000-00-0000), you choose the Input Mask property for this field. To set the Input Mask property, you use the Input Mask Wizard.

Using the Input Mask Wizard

Recall that the Input Mask field property sets the display format and limits the type of data that can be entered, making data entry faster and more precise. The **Input Mask Wizard** guides you through the tasks of creating an input mask.

To use the Input Mask Wizard:

Step 1	*Click*	in the Input Mask field property box

You should now see an ellipsis icon at the right side of the box.

Step 2	*Click*	the ellipsis icon

Access reminds you to save your table and then starts the Input Mask Wizard. Your screen should look similar to Figure 2-9.

QUICK TIP

 Once you create an input mask, you can also modify it. Click the ellipsis icon in the Input Mask property box to open and modify the input mask.

chapter
two

FIGURE 2-9
Input Mask Wizard

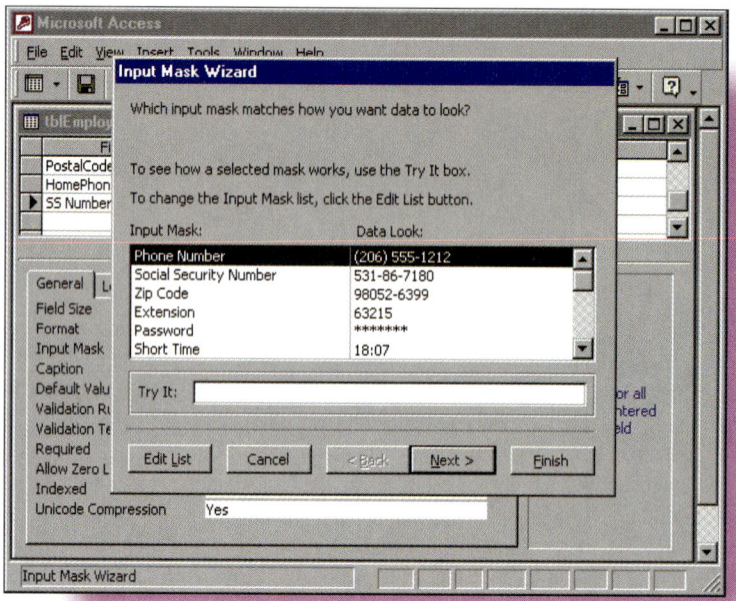

Step 3	*Click*	Social Security Number
Step 4	*Click*	Next >

Access shows you the input mask for Social Security numbers and asks what placeholder you want to use. For a Social Security number, you want to use a hyphen (-) to separate the numbers.

Step 5	*Click*	in the Placeholder character: field and select the – placeholder option from the menu
Step 6	*Click*	in the Try It: box to make sure this is the option you want
Step 7	*Click*	Next >

Access asks how you want to save the data. You can save the data with or without the placeholders.

Step 8	*Click*	the With the symbols in the mask, like this: option
Step 9	*Click*	Finish
Step 10	*Switch*	to Datasheet view to review your changes (Access lets you save your changes before switching)

Reviewing the table, you realize you don't need the Department ID field. You delete it from the tblEmployees table.

Deleting Fields

Though it's easy to delete a field, be careful before you do so. If you delete the field and any information stored in it, you cannot reverse your action with the Undo command.

To delete the Department ID field:

Step 1	*Switch*	to Design view
Step 2	*Click*	the box to the left of the Department ID row

This highlights the entire row. Your screen should look similar to Figure 2-10.

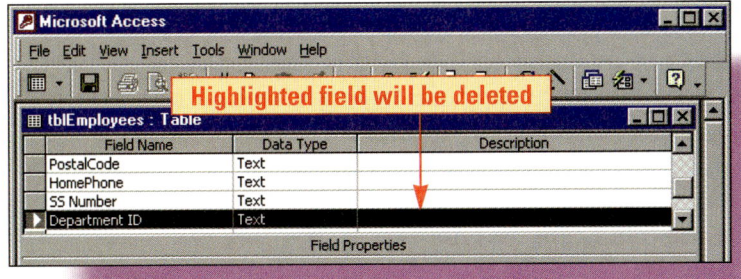

Step 3	*Click*	Edit
Step 4	*Click*	Delete

You see a warning explaining that you are about to delete the field and all of its indexes and a question asking if you want to proceed.

Step 5	*Click*	Yes

The field is deleted.

Looking at the tblEmployees table, you notice that the fields are not in a user-friendly order. You can rearrange the fields to make data entry more efficient.

FIGURE 2-10
Deleting a Field

chapter
two

Rearranging Fields

After you add fields, you can rearrange them so they appear in a logical order. For the tblEmployees table, it might make sense to move the LastName field after the FirstName field.

To rearrange a field:

Step 1	*Verify*	that tblEmployees is open in Design view
Step 2	*Click*	in the box to the left of the row that contains the LastName field information
Step 3	*Click*	and drag the LastName field after the FirstName field

After you finish modifying the tblEmployees table, you can print it.

2.g Printing a Table

A printed copy of a table, with or without data, can be useful. For example, you can print a copy of a table to check its structure and field order before entering data, or you can verify data in a table.

Maria wants to see the fields you created for the tblEmployees table. You print a copy for her.

To print the tblEmployees table:

Step 1	*Switch*	to Datasheet view

Access reminds you to save the table first.

Step 2	*Click*	the Print Preview button ⬛ on the Standard toolbar

You see a preview of the datasheet on your screen. The mouse pointer appears as a magnifying glass. You can use the magnifying glass to zoom in to see the data.

| Step 3 | *Move* | the zoom pointer over the data and click to enlarge your view |

You are satisfied with how the table appears. You are ready to print.

| Step 4 | *Click* | the Print button 🖨 on the Standard toolbar |

After the table prints, close the table.

| Step 5 | *Close* | the tblEmployees table |

Save your changes.

| Step 6 | *Exit* | Access |

The *mdbDynamicInc2* database now contains two tables: the tblEmployees table and the tblCategories table.

M ENU TIP

You can print by selecting the Print command from the File menu. You then see the Print dialog box, which offers a variety of print options, such as number of copies.

chapter
two

Summary

▶ When designing a database, determine the fields you need to include in a table, what type of information appears in each field, and how to arrange the fields in each record.

▶ Access offers field data types to help make tables unique and descriptive.

▶ Each field in a table has properties such as the field size or format. You can control data entry by choosing appropriate properties for each field. For example, you can require that fields contain data, and that the data is unique to that record.

▶ You create table fields and modify properties in Design view. Enter data in a table in Datasheet view.

▶ Set a primary key in a table that Access can use to identify each unique record.

▶ Select and size columns in Datasheet view to view all of your data without wasting screen space.

▶ After you create a table and enter data, you can still modify the table by adding new fields or changing the name of existing fields.

Commands Review

Action	Menu Bar	Shortcut Menu	Toolbar	Keyboard
Create a new table	File, New		⊞ or ⊞ ▾	ALT + F, N CTRL + N
Open a table	File, Open	Right-click table name, click Open	⊞	ALT + F, O
Switch between panes in Design view			Click in the pane	F6
Select a field property			Click in the field properties pane	UP or DOWN ARROW, TAB or SHIFT + TAB
Set a primary key	Edit, Primary Key	Right-click field, click Primary Key		ALT + E, K
Resize columns in a table	Format, Column Width	Right-click column	Drag column boundary	ALT + O ALT + F, M
Delete a field	Edit, Delete	Right-click a field, click Delete Rows		DELETE
Close and save a table			✕	
Print a table	File, Print	Right-click a table, click Print	⊟	ALT + F, P CTRL + P

Concepts Review

Circle the correct answer.

1. **Which of the following is not a data type?**
   [a] text
   [b] currency
   [c] date/time
   [d] HTML

2. **To move the insertion point in Design view, you can press the:**
   [a] TAB key.
   [b] F1 key.
   [c] BACKSPACE key.
   [d] SHIFT + ESCAPE keys.

3. **You can change a field's properties in:**
   [a] Datasheet view.
   [b] the table pane.
   [c] the query pane.
   [d] Design view.

4. **Which key can you press in Design view to get online Help for a field property?**
   [a] F6
   [b] SHIFT + F6
   [c] F1
   [d] ENTER

5. **The Input Mask field property controls the:**
   [a] number of characters in a field.
   [b] default value of a field.
   [c] label for a field that you see on a report.
   [d] pattern for how data appears in a field.

6. **You can delete a field:**
   [a] in Design view.
   [b] by dragging it out of Datasheet view.
   [c] by highlighting the field text and pressing the DELETE key.
   [d] only after creating a new table.

chapter two

7. Printed tables allow you to:
- [a] check your responses to the Table Wizard.
- [b] see the fields and the information they contain.
- [c] preview how a report will look.
- [d] list the field data types.

8. The first step in designing your database is determining the:
- [a] data type for each field.
- [b] purpose of the database.
- [c] field properties you will use.
- [d] fields you need.

9. A database wizard is a:
- [a] magician who does your work for you.
- [b] tool that guides you through the steps of creating a database.
- [c] way to modify the tables in a database after you have entered data.
- [d] shortcut for saving data.

10. A primary key:
- [a] defines a special table in the database.
- [b] is the default value of a field.
- [c] is always chosen for you.
- [d] uniquely defines a record.

Circle **T** if the statement is true or **F** is the statement is false.

T   F   1. An employee identification number must be a Number field.

T   F   2. After entering field names and modifying properties, you should set a primary key for a table.

T   F   3. The default size for a Text field is 30 characters.

T   F   4. You cannot change the position of a field in a table once you have saved the table.

T   F   5. If a field's Required property is set to "Yes," you can skip that field when entering data.

T   F   6. The Counter data type automatically displays a unique identifying number for a record.

T   F   7. You must use a Number field for integers or decimal numbers that can be values in calculations.

T   F   8. You cannot add a new field to a table once it has been saved.

T   F   9. You can change the appearance of a table after you create one.

T   F   10. A table is the framework for storing data in a database.

Skills Review

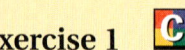

Exercise 1

1. Open the *mdbDynamicInc2* database created in this chapter.

2. Use the Table Wizard to create a new table based on the Orders sample table.

3. Refer to Table 2-1 for a list of fields you need for the customer orders table. Add these seven fields to the new table.

4. Name the new table tblOrders.

5. Let Access select a primary key.

6. Let Access design a form for entering data into the tblOrders table.

7. Close and save the form for the tblOrders table.

Exercise 2

1. If necessary, open the *mdbDynamicInc2* database.

2. Create a new table in Design view.

3. Add the following fields to the table: Product ID, product name, product description, and per unit cost.

4. Assign the appropriate data type to each field: Product ID (number), product name (text), product description (text), and per unit cost (number).

5. Set the Product ID field as the primary key.

6. Save the table with the name tblProducts. Close the table.

Exercise 3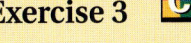

1. If necessary, open the *mdbDynamicInc2* database.

2. Use the Table Wizard to create a new table based on the Contacts sample table.

3. From the list of Contacts sample fields, use only those for contact ID, first and last name, address, and city. Rename the ContactID field to ClientID.

4. Set ClientID as the primary key.

5. In Datasheet view, enter the following information in the appropriate fields:
Antonio Fuentes, Mataderos 2312, Mexico D.F.
Thomas Tolliver, 120 Hanover Square, London
Rene Phillipe, 2743 Toulouse Street, Montreal

6. Print the new tblClients table.

7. Save and close the tblClients table.

Exercise 4

1. If necessary, open the *mdbDynamicInc2* database.

2. Open the tblClients table in Design view.

3. Add a new 15-character Text field named Sales Rep.

4. Position the Sales Rep field after the ClientID field.

5. In Datasheet view, add the following sales representatives for each record:
Record 1   *Wilson*
Record 2   *Howard*
Record 3   *Nguyen*
Record 4   *Dominguez*

6. Resize all the column widths to accommodate the longest entry in each column.

7. Print the tblClients table.

8. Save and close the tblClients table.

chapter two

Exercise 5

1. If necessary, open the *mdbDynamicInc2* database.

2. Open the tblEmployees table in Design view.

3. Change the caption of the Postal Code field to Zip Code.

4. Save the tblEmployees table.

5. Change to Datasheet view.

6. Resize the Address and Last Name columns.

7. Print the tblEmployees table.

8. Save and close the tblEmployees table.

Exercise 6

1. If necessary, open the *mdbDynamicInc2* database.

2. Open the table you created in Exercise 1 (tblOrders).

3. Assign an appropriate data type to the OrderID field.

4. Assign data types to at least two of the other fields.

5. Save and close the tblOrders table.

Exercise 7

1. If necessary, open the *mdbDynamicInc2* database.

2. Open the table you created in Exercise 6 (tblOrders).

3. Change the properties of the CustomerID field so that it can contain only two characters, must be completed for all records, and that duplicates are not allowed.

4. Change the properties of at least two of the other fields.

5. Save and close the tblOrders table.

Exercise 8

1. If necessary, open the *mdbDynamicInc2* database.

2. Open the tblEmployees table.

3. Delete the Home Phone field.

4. Add a new field called Primary Phone.

5. Use the Input Mask Wizard to set the standard pattern for this field as (xxx) xxx-xxxx where x is a number.

6. Save and close the tblEmployees table.

Case Projects

Project 1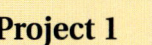

Using the Microsoft on the <u>W</u>eb command on the Help menu, open the Microsoft home page and then link to pages that provide basic information about Access databases. Print at least two of the Web pages.

Project 2

Connect to your ISP and load the home page for a search engine. Search for companies on the Web who export products from the United States to other countries. Research the types of products they export, who their customers are, and how they ship and deliver the products. Print the relevant Web pages. Use this information for Projects 3–8.

Project 3

Maria asks you to create a database called *mdbExporters* for Dynamic, Inc. This database includes information about the Dynamic's export customers and the types of products they export. You need to design four new tables for this database. You create these tables in Projects 4–7.

Project 4

Use the Table Wizard to create the first table that contains Customer information. Dynamic exports products to companies, not individuals. Include fields for the company ID, name, address, phone number, and postal code information of the Dynamic customers. Add two other appropriate fields, such as Country and E-mail address.

Project 5

Create the second table that contains Export Product information. Include any fields for identifying the products Dynamic exports, such as product ID, price, and description.

Project 6

Create the third table that contains Subcontractor information. Dynamic works with other companies around the United States to provide packaging, shipping, and customs services. The company gives preference to long-term suppliers who provide discounted rates or special terms for large orders. Include a field to identify these special suppliers.

Project 7

Create the fourth table by using the Lookup Wizard to create a list of possible choices for the Region Description field. Then modify the Lookup field to add other regions Dynamic may use in the future: Australia and Eastern Europe.

Project 8

Maria wants to make it easy for users to enter valid data. Define data validation criteria for at least one field in a table in *mdbExporters*. Open the table in Design view and click the field. Click the Validation Rule box, and then type the rule. For example, to validate a field containing a state abbreviation, type =2 to make sure users enter 2 characters. Click the Validation Text box, and then type a message, such as *You must key two characters.*

chapter two

Entering and Editing Data into Tables

Chapter Overview

I n this chapter you enter, modify, and edit data into tables. You also insert pictures into data fields.

▶ Enter records using a datasheet
▶ Navigate through records
▶ Modify data in a table
▶ Add pictures to records

Case profile

Maria Moreno, the owner of Dynamic, Inc., approves the design of the tables in the database you created for her. She gives you the go-ahead to begin the next phase: entering the data into the database.

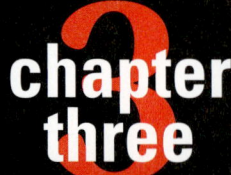

chapter
three

3.a Entering Records Using a Datasheet

Once you design your database, create its tables, and define the tables' fields, you're ready to enter records. Recall that a record is a row in your table and contains specific information about the table's subject. You can enter values for each record directly in the table datasheet, that is, in the columns of your table. A **value** is the data in each field of the record. For example, Moreno would be the value of the Last Name field for Maria Moreno. A **cell** is where the column and row meet, similar to a cell in a spreadsheet.

Start by entering data in the tblCategories table. To enter data into the table:

Step 1	*Start*	Microsoft Access
Step 2	*Open*	*mdbDynamicInc3* located on the DataDisk
Step 3	*Click*	Tables 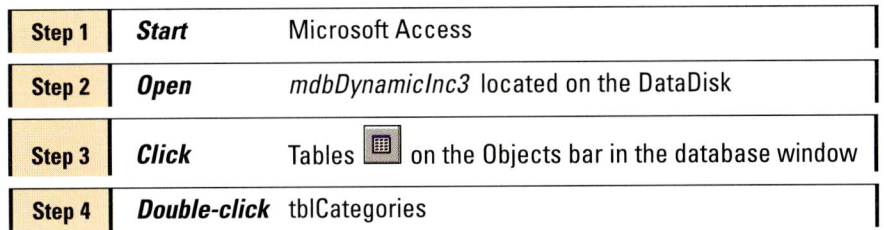 on the Objects bar in the database window
Step 4	*Double-click*	tblCategories

Notice this table contains only two fields, and one contains an AutoNumber data type. You will enter data only in the Category Name field. The six categories of Dynamic's import and export products are: Machinery, Clothing, Housewares, Automotive, Toys, and Electronics. You enter these categories now.

Step 5	*Click*	in the first row of the Category Name field
Step 6	*Key*	Machinery

Your screen should look similar to Figure 3-1.

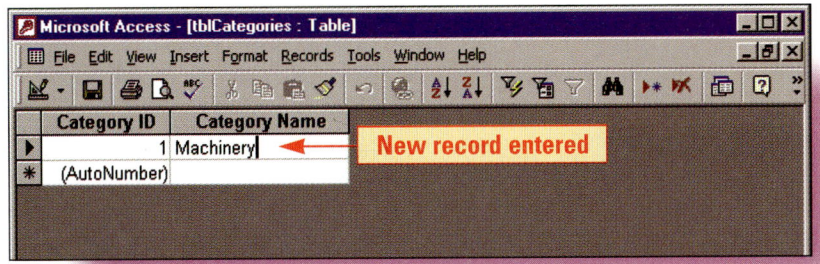

QUICK TIP

Entering records directly into a table is a good choice when you only have to enter one or two records. If you have several records to enter, use a form instead. Remember that if you use the Table Wizard, you can also let Access automatically create a form for you.

CAUTION TIP

If you set up a field automatically listing the record number, such as a Customer ID field, make sure you start entering data in the second field.

FIGURE 3-1
tblCategories Table with One Record Entered

chapter three

QUICK TIP

You can insert the current date by pressing the CTRL + ; (semicolon) keys and insert the current time by pressing the CTRL + : (colon) keys. If you have a default value set for the field, you can enter it by pressing the CTRL + ALT + SPACEBAR keys. To repeat the same value from the same field in the previous record, press the CTRL + ' (apostrophe) keys.

Step 7	Press	the TAB key twice to move to the second row of the Category Name field
Step 8	Key	Clothing
Step 9	Repeat	Steps 7 and 8 to enter the remaining four categories
Step 10	Close	the tblCategories table

You now enter data into the tblDepartment table. Dynamic has six departments: Administration, Accounting, Sales, Imports, Exports, and Customer Service. To enter information in the tblDepartment table:

Step 1	Double-click	tblDepartment to open it
Step 2	Click	in the first row of the Department Name field
Step 3	Key	Administration
Step 4	Press	the TAB key twice
Step 5	Repeat	Steps 3 and 4 to enter the remaining five departments

Your screen should look similar to Figure 3-2.

FIGURE 3-2
tblDepartment Table

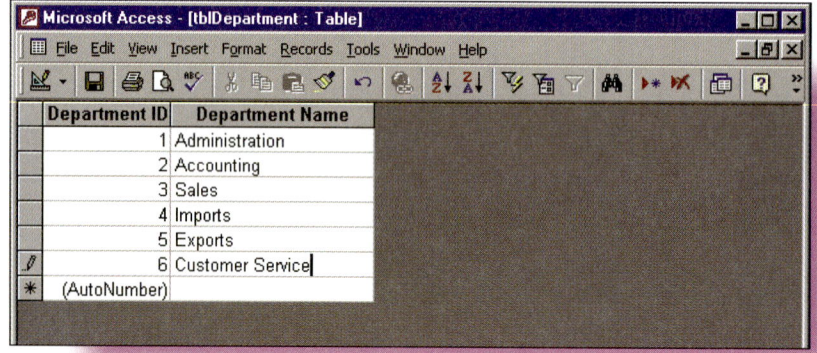

| Step 6 | Close | the tblDepartment table, making sure that you save your changes |

After you entered several records, you want to know how to navigate through the datasheet more easily. You learn some shortcuts next.

3.b Navigating Through Records

Using the TAB key to move around in an Access table as you enter records is often the most efficient method. That way you do not have to move your hand from the keyboard to use the mouse. Table 3-1 lists the keys you can use to move around a table.

To Move to the	Press
Next field	TAB
Previous field	SHIFT + TAB
Last field of a record	END
First field in a record	HOME
Same field in the next record	DOWN ARROW
Same field in the previous record	UP ARROW
Same field in the last record	CTRL + DOWN ARROW
Same field in the first record	CTRL + UP ARROW
Last field in the last record	CTRL + END
First field in the first record	CTRL + HOME

TABLE 3-1
Shortcut
Navigational Keys

Your assistant Chang entered additional records into the *mdbDynamicInc3* database. You decide to review his work. If you need to make corrections, you can easily modify the data.

3.c Modifying Data in a Table

Access allows you to edit table data easily. You can correct text, add and copy data, and delete information as necessary. Your first modification is to correct text.

Correcting Data in a Table

When you review the tblEmployees table in *mdbDynamicInc3*, you notice that Jan Sinclair's last name is incorrectly listed as Bouchard, her maiden name. Because this data is completely wrong, the most efficient method of correcting it is to reenter the entire field.

M O U S E   T I P

After you enter data, you might find using the mouse more effective for navigating a table. You can click directly in any cell at any time to move the insertion point.

**chapter
three**

To replace data by reentering it:

Step 1	*Open*	the tblEmployees table
Step 2	*Click*	in the cell with the last name Bouchard
Step 3	*Point*	to the left edge of the field so that the mouse pointer becomes a cross
Step 4	*Click*	to select the entire contents of the cell
Step 5	*Key*	Sinclair

The new data then replaces the old data that was in the cell. Your screen should look similar to Figure 3-3.

FIGURE 3-3
Modified
tblEmployees Table

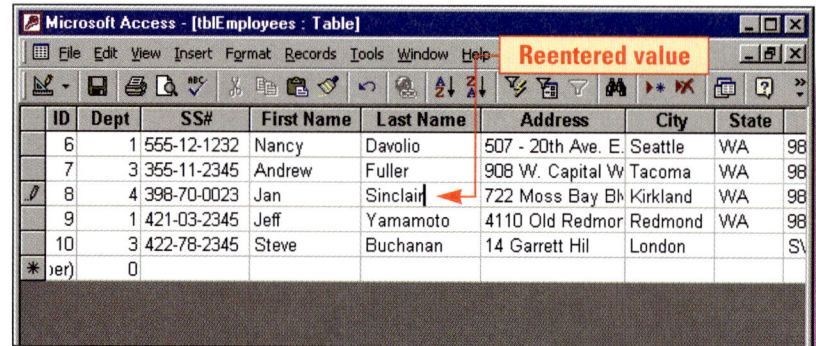

If the modification you need to make involves minor editing changes, you don't have to retype completely the information in a field. For example, Steve Buchanan's e-mail address changed to sBuchanan@dyn.com. You can edit the text of his current e-mail address.

To edit a cell's contents:

Step 1	*Click*	in the cell containing Steve Buchanan's e-mail address
Step 2	*Move*	the insertion point to where you want to make the change
Step 3	*Press*	the BACKSPACE key to remove the word "rio"

Step 4	*Key*	dyn
Step 5	*Close*	the table, making sure you save your changes

You can use the mouse to click in the appropriate place within a cell, or you can use the keyboard commands shown in Table 3-2.

To Move	Press
One character to the right	RIGHT ARROW
One character to the left	LEFT ARROW
One word to the right	CTRL + RIGHT ARROW
One word to the left	CTRL + LEFT ARROW
To the end of the line	END
To the end of the field	CTRL + END
To the beginning of the line	HOME
To the beginning of the field	CTRL + HOME

TABLE 3-2
Shortcut Keys for Editing Data

If you have data in one field that you want to use in another, you can copy the data.

Copying Data into a Table

Cut, Copy, and Paste are commands that you can use with all Windows programs. In Access, you can use these commands to move data within records.

The tblCustomers table includes an Address field. As your assistant Chang begins to enter data, he discovers he needs a second field to enter complete address information. You can save time by copying a field and all of its attributes instead of creating a new field from scratch. To add a second address field, copy the Address field and rename it Address 2.

To copy and paste a field within a table:

Step 1	*Open*	the tblCustomers table
Step 2	*Switch*	to Design view

Your next step is to determine where to locate the new field. It makes sense to place the Address 2 field immediately after the Address field. To do this, you need to insert a new row. By default, the Insert Rows command inserts a blank row before the selected field, so you need to select the City field.

MENU TIP

To select all the records in a table, click Edit and then click Select All Records.

CAUTION TIP

If you select several records, only the first record will have the triangle symbol next to it, even though they are all selected.

chapter
three

To insert a new row:

Step 1	*Click*	in the City field
Step 2	*Click*	Insert
Step 3	*Click*	Rows

This inserts a new row after the Address field. Your screen should now look like Figure 3-4.

FIGURE 3-4
New Row in tblCustomers

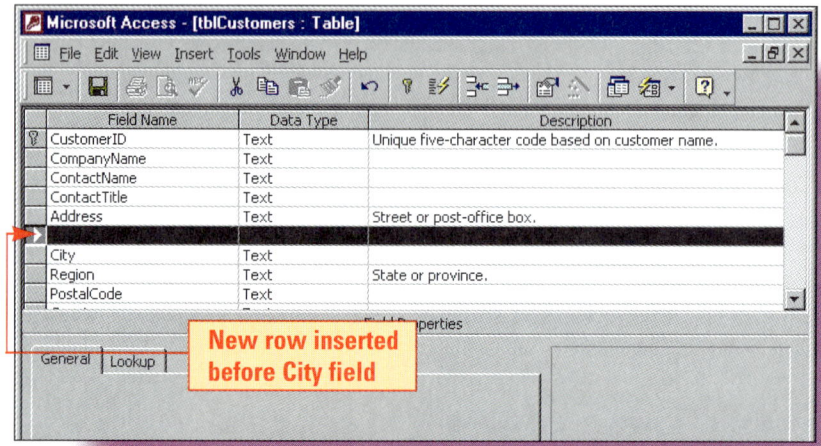

You are ready to copy and paste the duplicate billing address field into the blank row.

Step 4	*Click*	to select the Address field

Your screen should look like Figure 3-5.

FIGURE 3-5
Address Field Selected
for Copying

MOUSE TIP

To copy and paste an object, right-click and then use the commands on the shortcut menu.

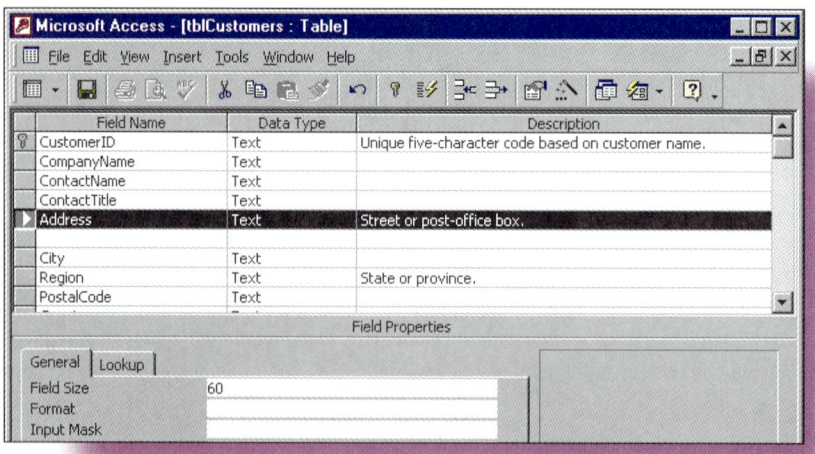

Step 5	*Click*	the Copy button on the Table Design toolbar
Step 6	*Click*	in the blank field name
Step 7	*Click*	the Paste button 📋 on the Table Design toolbar

You must now rename the field.

Step 8	*Click*	the new field
Step 9	*Key*	2 at the end of the field name

It should now read Address2.

Step 10	*Close*	the tblCustomers table, saving your changes

MENU TIP

You can also use the Cut, Copy, and Paste commands on the Edit menu.

QUICK TIP

If the Clipboard toolbar is floating in the middle of your screen, remember you can dock it, as you would any other toolbar.

You can use the same copy-and-paste process when copying records, cells, or text. You can also move and copy entire objects between databases.

In addition to using cut-and-paste or copy-and-paste to modify a database, you can use the Clipboard toolbar. The **Clipboard toolbar**, which is available in all Office applications, stores up to 12 text or other selections that you cut or copy. You can then choose the item you want to paste into an object. If you try to store more than 12 items on the Clipboard, you can either delete the first item or keep the original 12 without adding the new 13th item. The contents of the Clipboard are available to all Office applications until you close them.

To view the Clipboard toolbar, you simply click the View menu, point to Toolbars, and then click Clipboard. The Clipboard toolbar appears on your screen, as shown in Figure 3-6.

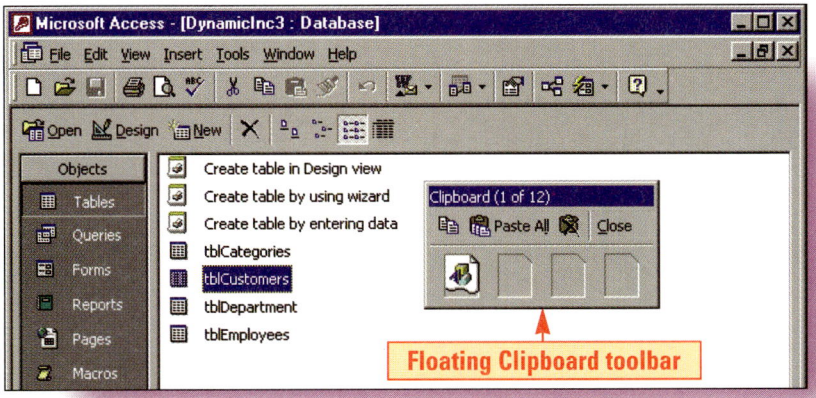

Floating Clipboard toolbar

FIGURE 3-6
Clipboard Toolbar

chapter
three

If you make a mistake entering or editing data, you can reverse or undo a change that you made to a record in Datasheet or Form view.

Undoing a Change

To undo changes, you click the Undo button on the Standard toolbar. This restores your most recent change. If you already saved changes to the current record, or moved to another record, you can still undo the last change.

Deleting Records from a Table

When you want to delete data, consider whether you need to remove only part of a record or the entire record. To delete selected parts of the record, use the Delete command on the Edit menu. To delete the entire record, use the Delete Record command.

In the tblEmployees table, delete the record of Andrew Fuller, who left the company last week.

To delete a record from a table:

Step 1	*Open*	tblEmployees
Step 2	*Click*	in the record selection area of Andrew Fuller's record
Step 3	*Click*	Edit
Step 4	*Click*	Delete Record

A dialog box asks if you want to delete this record, and reminds you that if you delete this record you will not be able to retrieve it.

Step 5	*Click*	Yes

Your last task in modifying your database is adding photographs of Dynamic's employees.

3.d Adding Pictures to Records

Access lets you add pictures and clip art to records. Each image is saved as an **OLE object**, which means it was created in another program but appears as a separate object in Access. There are two types of OLE objects, linked and embedded. A **linked object** is not saved as part of the Access database, but includes a reference to the location of the file so Access can find it. An **embedded object**, however, is stored as part of your Access database.

Link an object if want to keep the database small, the object being linked is still under construction, you are sure that a server containing the file is stable, or you will not be sending the file via e-mail. (A linked file expects the server to be in a specific location, and if you e-mail the file, that location is not available to the end user.)

Embed an object if you have enough room for a large database, you do not need to keep the file as a separate document, or you will be sending the document via e-mail or disk.

To add photographs to a record, they must first be saved as bitmap images. You can do this by using **Microsoft's Photo Editor**. This is a simple image program that ships with Office 2000, and is fully integrated into the Office suite. You do not need additional hardware or software.

You already received the bitmap image containing the photograph of Catherine Moore, the Executive Vice President of Dynamic. You are ready to add it to the tblEmployees table.

To add a picture to a table record:

Step 1	*Open*	the tblEmployees table, if necessary
Step 2	*Click*	in the Photograph cell of Catherine Moore's record
Step 3	*Click*	Insert
Step 4	*Click*	Object

The Insert Object dialog box opens, as shown in Figure 3-7.

chapter
three

FIGURE 3-7
Insert Object Dialog Box

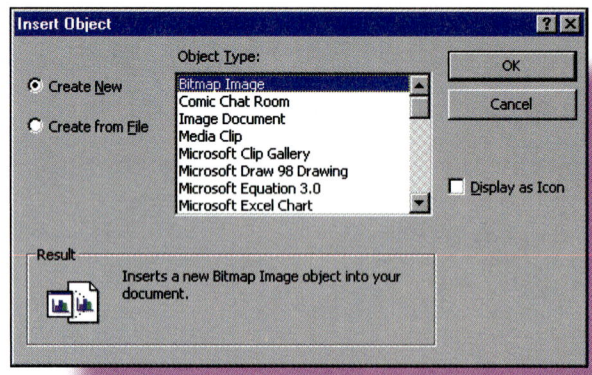

FIGURE 3-7
Insert Object Dialog Box

Step 5	*Click*	Bitmap Image, if necessary
Step 6	*Click*	the Create from File option button
Step 7	*Click*	Browse to see the images available
Step 8	*Click*	*Moore.bmp* located on the Data Disk
Step 9	*Click*	OK
Step 10	*Click*	OK in the dialog box

The image is now embedded in the Access database. When you look at the Datasheet view of the table, the Photograph cell lets you know you have a bitmap image for this record, as shown in Figure 3-8.

FIGURE 3-8
Datasheet View of
Photograph Cell

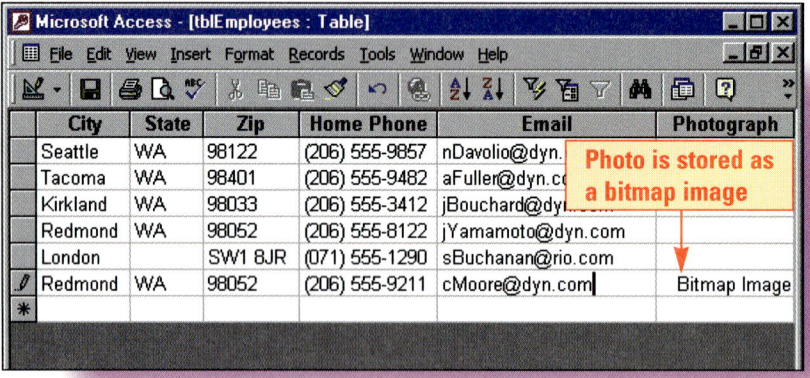

You can view the photograph only in Form view of the tblEmployees table. To do so, you first need to close the table.

Step 11	*Close*	the tblEmployees table, saving your changes

The tblEmployees table has an associated frmEmployees form. You need to open that form to view the photograph.

To view the image in the frmEmployees form:

Step 1	*Click*	Forms on the Objects bar in the database window
Step 2	*Double-click*	frmEmployees
Step 3	*Select*	Catherine Moore's record by pressing the PAGE DOWN key until you see the appropriate record

After you view the record and see the photo, close the form and exit Access.

Step 4	*Close*	the frmEmployees form
Step 5	*Exit*	Access

As you can see, you can enter photographs in a database table just as easily as you enter text.

chapter three

Summary

▶ A cell is the intersection between a row and a column.

▶ To navigate through records, you can use the mouse, the TAB key, and a variety of other keys.

▶ To replace text in a cell, click in the cell and rekey the information.

▶ You can copy a field and its attributes and then paste it to save time when creating new fields.

▶ The Office Clipboard stores up to 12 items you cut or copied and can paste into your current file.

▶ You can undo many mistakes made when entering data.

▶ The Delete command deletes the item you are working with; the Delete Record command deletes the entire record.

▶ To insert a picture in a table, use the Object command on the Insert menu. You can only view the picture on the screen, however, in Form view.

Commands Review

Action	Menu Bar	Shortcut Menu	Toolbar	Keyboard
Enter the current date				CTRL + ;
Enter the current time				CTRL + :
Repeat the same value				CTRL + '
Enter the default values set for the field				CTRL + ALT + SPACEBAR
Go to the next field				TAB
Go to the previous field				SHIFT + TAB
Go to the last field of a record				END
Go to the first field in a record				HOME
Go to the same field in the next record				DOWN ARROW
Go to the same field in the previous record				UP ARROW
Go to the same field in the last record				CTRL + DOWN ARROW
Go to the same field in the first record				CTRL + UP ARROW
Go to the last field in the last record				CTRL + END
Go to the first field in the first record				CTRL + HOME
Move one character to the right				RIGHT ARROW
Move one character to the left				LEFT ARROW
Move one word to the right				CTRL + RIGHT ARROW
Move one word to the left				CTRL + LEFT ARROW
To the end of the line				END
Go to the end of the field				CTRL + END
Go to the beginning of the line				HOME
Go to the beginning of the field				CTRL + HOME
Undo a change	Edit, Undo		↺	ESC CTRL + Z ALT + E, U
Delete a record	Edit, Delete Record	Delete		DELETE ALT + E, R

chapter three

Concepts Review

Circle the correct answer.

1. When you enter records, you enter data in the form of:
[a] cells.
[b] values.
[c] pictures.
[d] linked objects.

2. To enter the current date, press the:
[a] CTRL + D keys.
[b] CTRL + ' keys.
[c] CTRL + ; keys.
[d] CTRL + : keys.

3. To enter the current time, press the:
[a] CTRL + T keys.
[b] CTRL + ' keys.
[c] CTRL + ; keys.
[d] CTRL + : keys.

4. Besides using a table to enter data, you can use a(n):
[a] datasheet.
[b] Clipboard.
[c] embedded object.
[d] form.

5. To enter data into the table:
[a] press the TAB key.
[b] press the INSERT key.
[c] click in the cell and type.
[d] press the ENTER key.

6. One way to create a new field is to:
[a] insert a blank row and then copy information from another field.
[b] press the CTRL + HOME keys.
[c] undo a deleted field.
[d] press the SHIFT key to select more than one record.

7. You can use the Clipboard to:
[a] take notes while entering data.
[b] store and paste multiple items.
[c] delete data from a table.
[d] undo a change you made to a record.

8. To work with an entire record, click or press the:
[a] DELETE key.
[b] gray box to the left of the record.
[c] CTRL + END keys.
[d] LEFT ARROW key.

9. If you select several records in a table, a triangle marks:
[a] all the selected records.
[b] the first and last records.
[c] the first record.
[d] the last record.

10. When you add a picture to a record, Access saves the image as a:
[a] photograph.
[b] form or table.
[c] linked or embedded object.
[d] hypertext link.

Circle **T** if the statement is true or **F** if the statement is false.

T   F   1. You can only enter data in a table.

T   F   2. You can enter data by keying text.

T   F   3. Once you enter data in a field and save a table, you cannot edit the data.

T   F   4. To delete a record, you must delete each field one at a time.

T   F   5. You can use the Cut, Copy, and Paste commands to move data within records.

T   F   6. You can select a record by clicking in the record selection area.

T F   7. To add a picture to table, you must link the picture.

T F   8. An OLE object can be either embedded or linked.

T F   9. To view a picture that is placed in a table, you must be in Datasheet view.

T F   10. You can reverse your last change by using the Redo option.

Skills Review

Exercise 1

1. If necessary, open the *mdbDynamicInc3* database.

2. Open the tblRegions table.

3. Enter the following region names: *Mexico, Canada, Northern Europe, Southern Europe, Asia.*

4. Save and close the table.

Exercise 2

1. If necessary, open the *mdbDynamicInc3* database.

2. Open the frmOrders form.

3. Enter two new records of information based on the ones already in the frmOrders form. Use the keyboard shortcut to enter the Order Date.

4. Save and close the form.

Exercise 3

1. If necessary, open the *mdbDynamicInc3* database.

2. Open the tblRegions table.

3. Edit the region names to match the following: *Mexico, Canada, N. Europe, S. Europe, Asia.*

4. Save and close the table.

Exercise 4

1. If necessary, open the *mdbDynamicInc3* database.

2. Open the tblOrders table.

3. Insert a new field called *BillAddress* after the Ship Address field. Copy, paste, and edit information from the Ship Address field in the new field.

4. Save and close the tblOrders table.

Exercise 5

1. If necessary, open the *mdbDynamicInc3* database.

2. Open the tblCategories table.

3. Copy the text in the Category Name field of each record, and then close the tblCategories table.

4. Open the tblProducts table.

chapter three

5. Add two new records based on the others in tblProducts. Copy one item from the Clipboard to the Category Name field in the two different records.

6. Save and close the tblProducts table.

Exercise 6

1. If necessary, open the *mdbDynamicInc3* database.

2. Open the tblProducts table.

3. Change Housewares in the Category Name field to *Kitchen Supplies*.

4. Undo the change.

5. Delete the record for the Swedish building set.

6. Save and close the tblProducts table.

Exercise 7

1. If necessary, open the *mdbDynamicInc3* database.

2. Open the tblProducts table.

3. In the Sample field for the Electronic pocket watch, insert the *Sample* clip art image from the Data Disk. Add it as an embedded object.

4. View the image in the frmEmployees form.

5. Save and close the tblProducts table.

Exercise 8

1. If necessary, open the *mdbDynamicInc3* database.

2. Use the Table Wizard to create a new table based on the Contacts sample. Use five or six of the suggested fields.

3. Name the new table tblContacts.

4. Let Access create a form based on the new table.

5. Enter three records using the form.

6. Save the form as frmContacts and close it.

Case Projects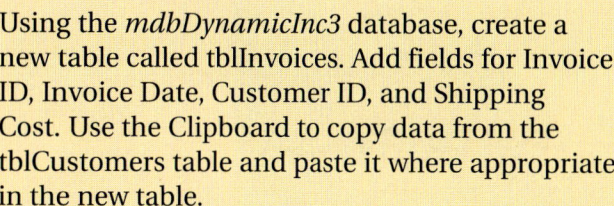

Project 1

Using the *mdbDynamicInc3* database, enter information for two new customers in the tblCustomers table. Use a keyboard shortcut to enter some data. For example, press the CTRL + ' (apostrophe) keys to insert the same state for both customers.

Project 2

Using the *mdbDynamicInc3* database, enter information for two new employees in the frmEmployees form. Use keyboard shortcuts to navigate the form.

Project 3

Using the *mdbDynamicInc3* database, edit all of the department names in the tblDepartment table. Use keyboard shortcuts to navigate the table.

Project 4

Using the *mdbDynamicInc3* database, open the tblOrders table and add two new fields for phone numbers. Create the first and enter data for two or three records. Then create a field for a second phone number, such as for a fax machine or mobile phone. Copy data from the first Phone Number field and modify it.

Project 5

Using the *mdbDynamicInc3* database, create a new table called tblInvoices. Add fields for Invoice ID, Invoice Date, Customer ID, and Shipping Cost. Use the Clipboard to copy data from the tblCustomers table and paste it where appropriate in the new table.

Project 6

Using the *mdbDynamicInc3* database, open the frmEmployees form. Edit some of the data, but undo all of your changes. Delete one record.

Project 7

Connect to your ISP and load the home page for a search engine. Search for an online computer dictionary or encyclopedia and look up information on at least three terms defined in this chapter, such as value, OLE, Clipboard, and embedded object. Print the explanations.

Project 8

Connect to your ISP and load the home page for a search engine. Search for a site offering copyright-free clip art. Download one small bitmap file. Add it to an appropriate table in *mdbDynamicInc3*.

chapter three

Designing and Using Basic Forms

Chapter Overview

In this chapter, you explore how to design and create forms using the Form Wizard. You learn why forms are useful, what they look like, and how to use them. You also modify your form designs.

LEARNING OBJECTIVES

► **Understand forms**
► **Create a form with the Form Wizard**
► **Create a custom form**
► **Modify a form design**
► **Use the Control toolbox to add and modify controls**
► **Modify format properties**
► **Print a form**

Case profile

You designed and created an Access database for Dynamic, Inc. Now, Kang Leing, the warehouse manager, and Natasha Diggins, the personnel manager, ask you to make it easy for their department personnel to use the database. Because forms simplify data entry and viewing, you can create several Access forms to meet their needs. Create a form Natasha's staff can use to efficiently enter new employee information. Then create a form Kang's warehouse staff can use to enter and track the company products.

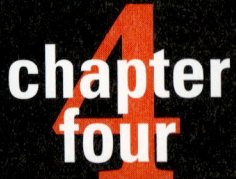

chapter four

4.a Understanding Forms

Most people prefer to use forms when they enter or view information in a database. Like paper-based forms, electronic Access forms can be visually appealing and can guide users through the process of entering data. Use Access forms to accomplish the following tasks.

Enter and view data. The most common use of forms is to enter and view data in records. Well-designed forms make it easy to enter data by using clear field labels and including only the necessary fields. They also make it easy to view data by arranging fields in appealing, logical ways.

Automate your tasks. Forms can work with Access programming features, such as macros or Visual Basic, to automate certain actions. With macros and Visual Basic, you can open other forms, run queries, and restrict the data you display. You can also use macros or modules in forms to provide data values, which let you perform calculations quickly and accurately.

Provide instructions. You can include instructions, tips, notes, and other information on your forms to provide information about how to use Access or special features of your database.

Print information. You can use forms to increase your flexibility when printing information. For example, you can design an order form that has two sets of headers and footers: one for entering data and the other for printing a customer invoice based on the order information.

You are ready to create your first form. Start with the form for Natasha's Personnel department.

4.b Creating a Form with the Form Wizard

From your discussions with Natasha, you understand she wants a form so her staff can efficiently enter, update, and maintain information for new employees. With that in mind, you list the fields you want to include in the form, such as name, address, home phone, and Social Security number.

Now that you know the purpose and content of the form, you are ready to create it. You create the form using the Form Wizard. Like other Access wizards, the **Form Wizard** guides you through the steps of creating a form. You can use it to create a simple form that includes all the fields from a related table, or you can select the fields to include in a form. Although the Form Wizard saves you time, it limits your design decisions.

Using the Form Wizard

As you step through a Form Wizard, you locate and select the information to include in the form, and then Access creates the form for you. Your first step is to start the Form Wizard.

To start the Form Wizard:

Step 1	*Open*	the *mdbDynamicInc4* database
Step 2	*Click*	Forms ⊞ on the Objects bar in the database window
Step 3	*Double-click*	Create form by using wizard

The dialog box on your screen should look similar to Figure 4-1.

FIGURE 4-1
Form Wizard

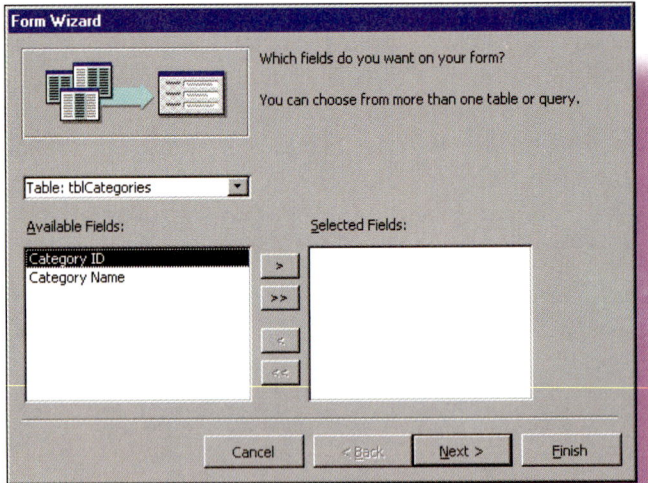

The Form Wizard can create a simple columnar form that contains all of the fields in the tblEmployees table. You can also select only some fields from the tblEmployees table. For your form, you use all the fields, except for the Photograph field. Natasha's department is not sure they want to include photographs at this time.

Step 4	*Click*	Table: tblEmployees in the Table/Queries list box

In the Available Fields: list box, you see the fields you can use, as shown in Figure 4-2.

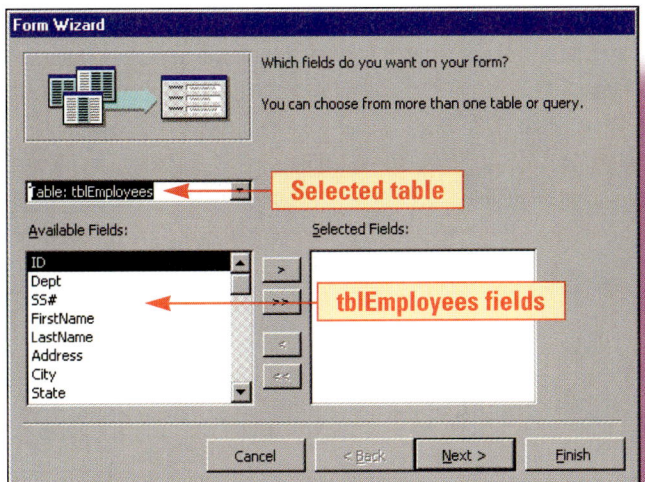

FIGURE 4-2
Available Fields from the
tblEmployees Table

The most efficient way to choose all the fields except the Photograph field is to select all the fields at once, and then move the Photograph field back to the Available Fields: list box.

Step 5	*Click*	>>
Step 6	*Click*	Photograph in the Selected Fields: list box
Step 7	*Click*	<
Step 8	*Click*	Next >

The dialog box on your screen should look similar to Figure 4-3.

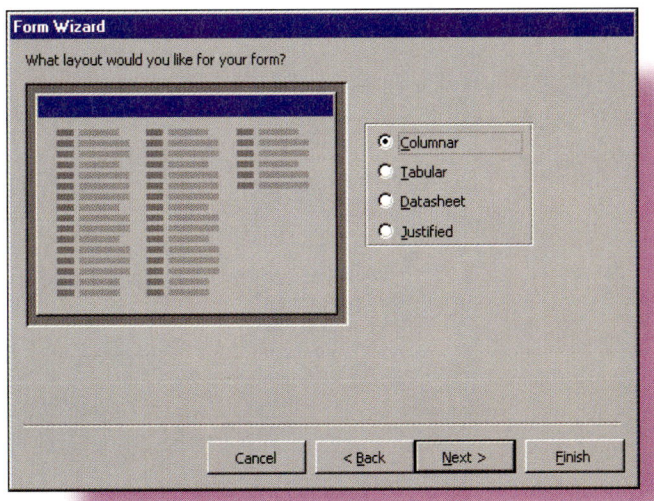

FIGURE 4-3
Form Layout Options

Use this dialog box to choose a layout for the form. Choose a columnar, tabular, datasheet, or justified layout. Click an option to see a sketch of that layout. For Natasha's form, use the columnar layout, which is the default.

To continue using the Form Wizard:

Step 1	*Click*	the Columnar option button, if necessary
Step 2	*Click*	Next >

Use the next dialog box to select the background design of your form. Click an option to see a sample of the background. For example, selecting the International style inserts a background graphic of a globe in your form. Because you want to keep Natasha's form as simple as possible, choose the Standard style, which is the default.

Step 3	*Click*	Standard, if necessary
Step 4	*Click*	Next >

The last Form Wizard dialog box asks you for a form title, and whether you want to open the form at this time or modify it.

Step 5	*Key*	frmEmployees as the name of the form

The dialog box on your screen should look similar to Figure 4-4.

FIGURE 4-4
Completing the
Form Wizard

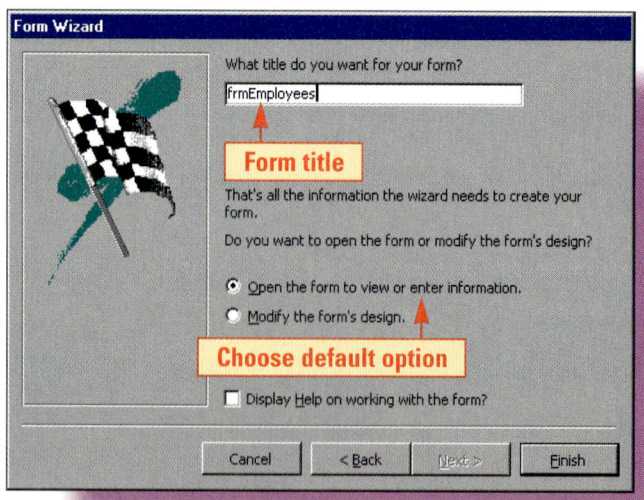

Step 6	*Click*	Finish

Your screen should look similar to Figure 4-5.

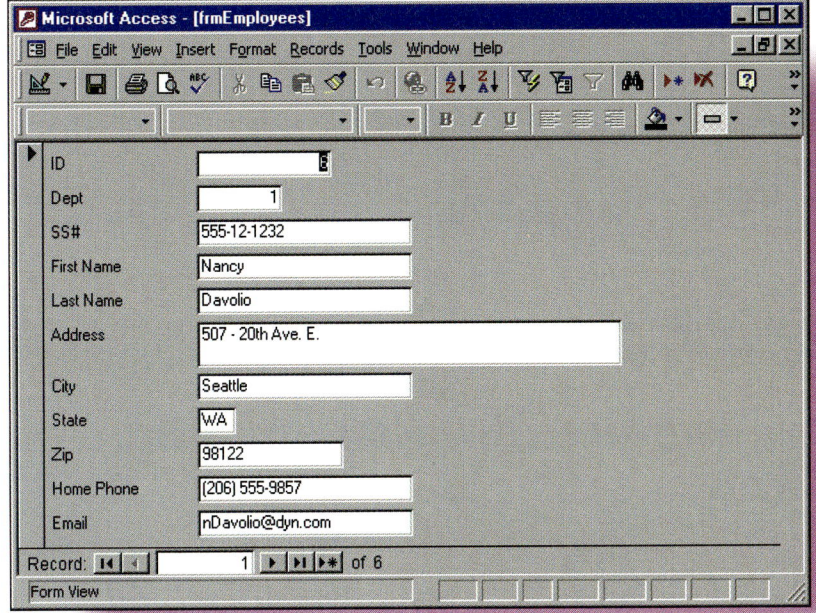

FIGURE 4-5
frmEmployees Form

You used the Form Wizard to create the frmEmployees form. To make sure that it serves Natasha's purposes, use the form to enter data.

Entering Records Using a Form

One purpose of creating forms is to make data entry more efficient. A form is often created to "mask" the datasheet. Some datasheets are overwhelming, especially to novice users, and the mask provides a user-friendly interface for data entry.

To enter data into a form:

Step 1	*Click*	the New Record button on the Form View toolbar
Step 2	*Press*	the TAB key to accept the ID field (AutoNumber)
Step 3	*Key*	2 in the Dept field
Step 4	*Press*	the TAB key
Step 5	*Key*	the information shown in Table 4-1 to complete the record

chapter
four

TABLE 4-1
Information to Enter in
frmEmployees

Field	Data	Field	Data
Social Security Number	546-58-2139	State	WA
First Name	Marcia	Zip Code	98056
Last Name	Wilson	Home Phone	(425) 555-6897
Address	315 Garden Ave N	Email Name	mwilson@dyn.com
City	Bellevue		

Access automatically saves the data after you enter it.

Step 6	*Click*	the First Record navigation button to go to the first record

Now make sure that Natasha's department can easily modify records using the form.

Modifying an Existing Record Using a Form

To modify a record in a form, first locate the record. You can do so using the Find command, or you can scroll through the records using the navigation buttons. Then edit the record as you would edit any other item: Click in the field containing the value you want to change, and then use standard editing commands to modify the value. As a test, find and modify Marcia Wilson's record.

To find and modify a record in the Form window:

Step 1	*Click*	Edit
Step 2	*Click*	Find

The dialog box on your screen should look similar to Figure 4-6.

FIGURE 4-6
Find and Replace
Dialog Box

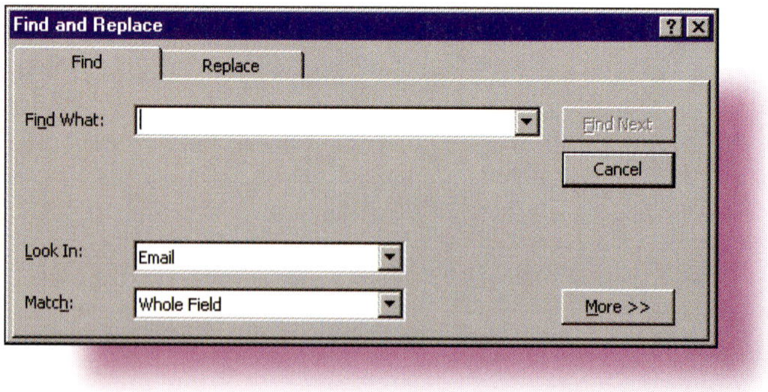

Step 3	*Key*	Marcia in the Fi<u>n</u>d What: text box
Step 4	*Click*	frmEmployees in the <u>L</u>ook In: text box
Step 5	*Click*	<u>F</u>ind Next
Step 6	*Close*	the Find and Replace dialog box

You now see Marcia's record. Change her address to 351 Garden Ave. S.

| Step 7 | *Click* | in the Address field |
| Step 8 | *Change* | the field to 351 Garden Ave S. |

You completed the frmEmployees form for Natasha's department. You can now close the form.

| Step 9 | *Close* | frmEmployees |

You are ready to create another form, this one for Kang's department. To fit his needs, you create a custom form.

4.c Creating a Custom Form

You can use the Form Wizard to create more complex and custom forms, such as those that allow you to enter information from several tables at once. For Kang's department, this is useful because his staff needs to enter information about both products and suppliers, as shown in Table 4-2.

tblProducts Fields	tblSuppliers Fields
Product ID, Category Name, ProductDescription, and SupplierID	SupplierName, Address, City, State, Zip Code

TABLE 4-2
Fields Needed for Kang's Custom Form

Create a custom form that includes parts of the tblProducts and tblSuppliers tables.
To create a custom form:

| Step 1 | *Click* | Forms  on the Objects bar in the database window |

chapter
four

Step 2	*Double-click*	Create form by using wizard
Step 3	*Click*	Table: tblProducts in the Tables/Queries list box
Step 4	*Move*	ProductID, Category Name, ProductDescription, and SupplierID to the Selected Fields: list box
Step 5	*Click*	Table: tblSuppliers table in the Tables/Queries list box
Step 6	*Move*	SupplierName, Address, City, State, and Zip Code to the Selected Fields: list box
Step 7	*Click*	Next >

This dialog box asks how you want to view your data. Because Kang's department works primarily with suppliers, tblSuppliers is the "parent" category for this form.

| Step 8 | *Click* | by tblSuppliers |

The dialog box on your screen should look similar to Figure 4-7.

FIGURE 4-7
Creating a Custom Form

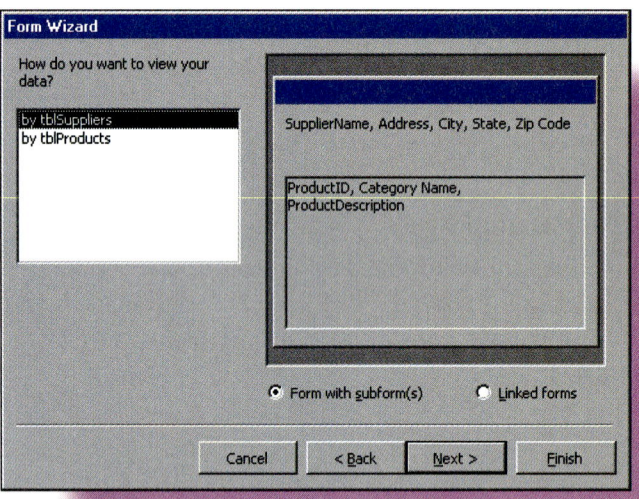

The dialog box indicates you are creating a form with a subform, which occurs when you use more than one table to create a form.

| Step 9 | *Click* | Next > |

The rest of the Form Wizard dialog boxes are similar to those you used when creating the frmEmployees form.

To complete your custom form using the Form Wizard:

Step 1	*Click*	Datasheet if necessary to accept the default layout for the form
Step 2	*Click*	<u>N</u>ext >

The next dialog box concerns the style of the form. You can choose a more decorative background for this form.

Step 3	*Click*	Sumi Painting
Step 4	*Click*	<u>N</u>ext >
Step 5	*Key*	frmSuppliers and frmProducts Subform as the title

Accept the defaults in the next dialog box, because you want frmSuppliers to be the form with the product information as a subform. You also want to open the form after Access creates it.

Step 6	*Click*	<u>F</u>inish

When the form opens, your screen should look similar to Figure 4-8.

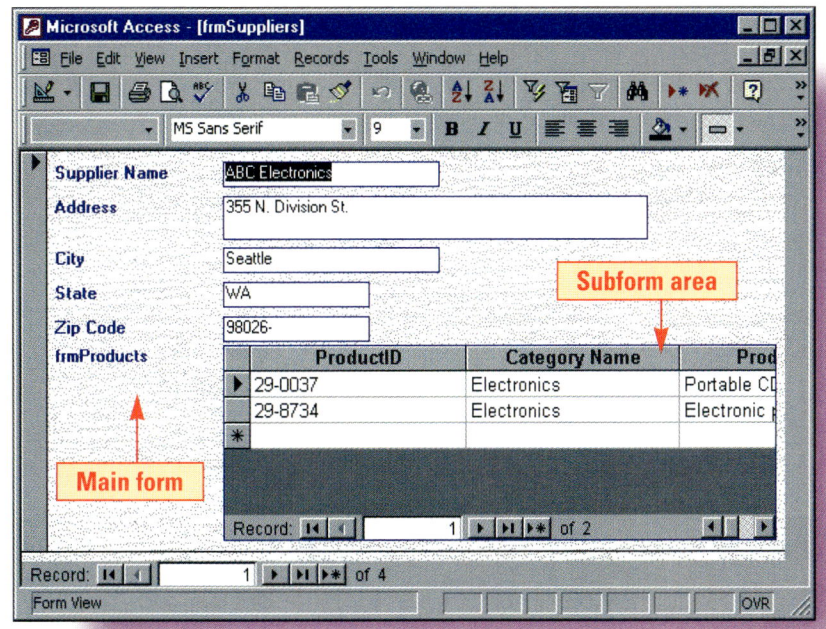

FIGURE 4-8
frmSuppliers Form with frmProducts Subform

Now that you created the form using the Form Wizard, you can modify it as necessary using Design view.

4.d Modifying a Form Design

After you create a form, you can modify its design without affecting its data. For the frmSuppliers form, you decide to rearrange the fields on the form, as well as move and enlarge the frmProducts subform.

Rearranging Fields and Moving the Subform

After you use the Form Wizard to create a form, you may often find that you want to modify the appearance of the form on the screen. In this case, you want to move some of fields as well as the subform. To redesign frmSuppliers and move fields:

Step 1	*Switch*	to Design view

Your screen should look similar to Figure 4-9.

QUICK TIP

You can modify any form properties by right-clicking the appropriate object, and then clicking Properties on the shortcut menu.

FIGURE 4-9
frmSuppliers in
Design View

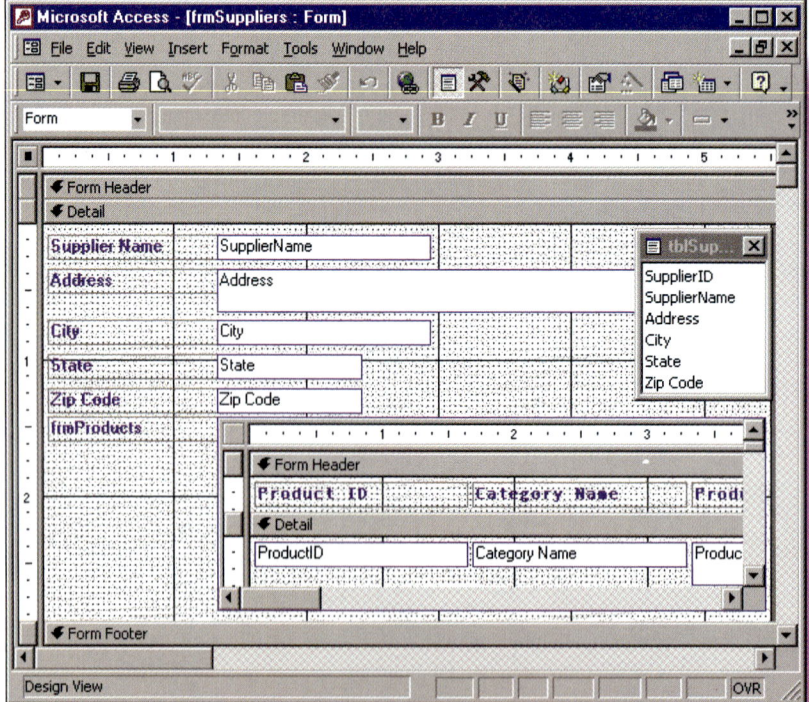

| Step 2 | *Click* | anywhere in the Zip Code field to select it |

You see **selection handles** around the form. They indicate you can move the field around the form.

| Step 3 | *Point to* | the Zip Code field's outline until the pointer becomes a hand |
| Step 4 | *Move* | the Zip Code field about .25" lower than its current position |

Your next task is to move the frmProducts subform below the frmProducts field label and then enlarge it, so that users can see the fields more clearly.

To move the frmProducts subform and enlarge it:

Step 1	*Click*	the frmProducts subform to select it
Step 2	*Point to*	the upper-left corner selection handle until the mouse becomes a pointing hand
Step 3	*Move*	the subform so that it is positioned directly below the frmProducts field label

Your screen should now look similar to Figure 4-10.

QUICK TIP

You can select several fields by holding down the SHIFT key and clicking each field.

CAUTION TIP

Be careful when you position your mouse over a selected field. If you click on a selection handle, the mouse pointer changes to a pointing hand, which lets you move only the field box, or the label, whichever one is selected.

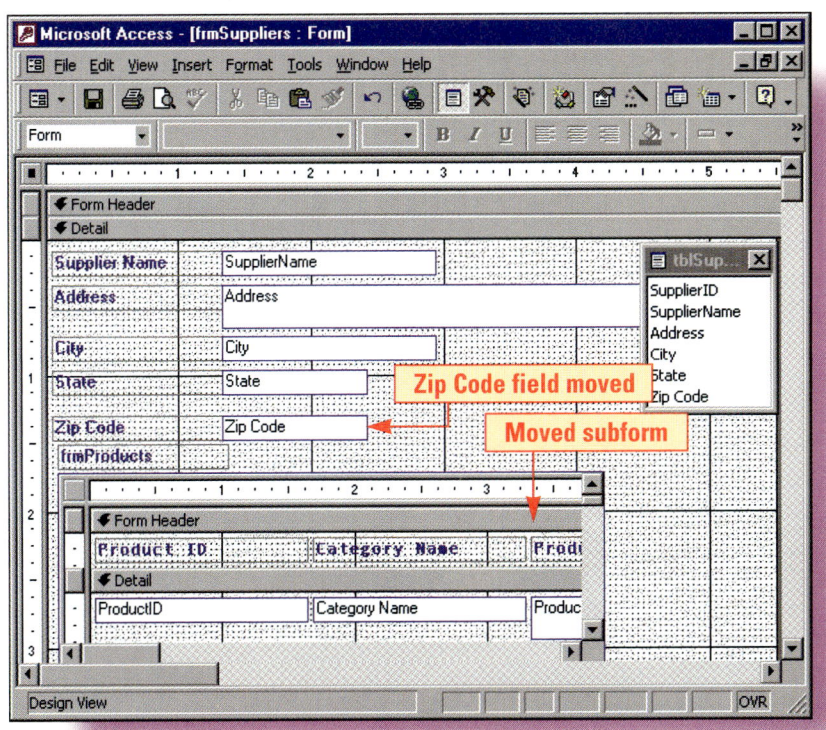

FIGURE 4-10
Modified frmSuppliers/Products Form

chapter
four

MOUSE TIP

If you move more than one field, you can position the mouse on any of the selected fields.

| Step 4 | *Point to* | the left center selection handle on frmProducts |

The mouse pointer becomes a double arrow.

| Step 5 | *Drag* | the subform so that the width fills the form page |

Your screen should look similar to Figure 4-11.

FIGURE 4-11
Enlarged Subform Area

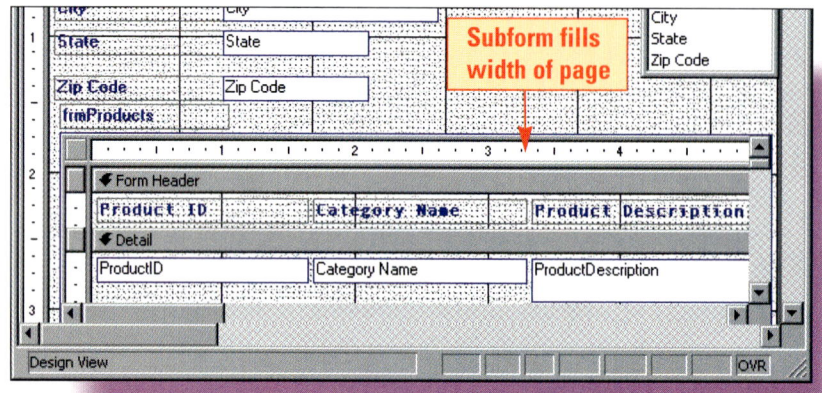

| Step 6 | *Close* | frmSuppliers, saving your changes |

Now that you modified Kang's form, you decide to modify Natasha's form by adding a field.

Adding Fields

You can also use Design view to add (and delete) fields in your form. Natasha's Personnel department is ready to add a photograph of each employee to their record. You now need to add the field to the form.

To add a field to the frmEmployees form:

QUICK TIP

To select a block of fields to add, click the first one you want, press and hold the SHIFT key and then click the last one. To select non-adjacent fields, hold down the CTRL key and then click each one you want. To select all of the fields in the field list, double-click the field list title bar.

Step 1	*Open*	frmEmployees in Design view
Step 2	*Click*	View
Step 3	*Click*	Field List
Step 4	*Click*	Photograph
Step 5	*Click*	in the Detail area of the form

Your screen should look similar to Figure 4-12.

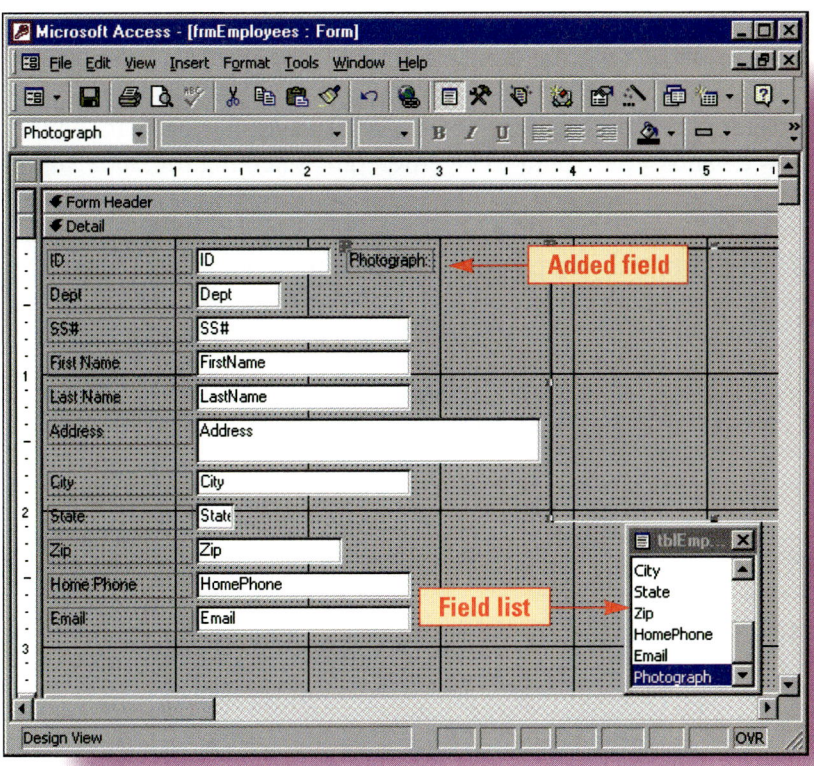

FIGURE 4-12
Adding a Field

MENU TIP

If you find it difficult to align the fields, click Format, and then click Snap to Grid.

QUICK TIP

 You can use **calculated controls** in your Access form, which allow you to perform calculations on your data. For example, you can calculate and display the total price of fields that show individual prices.

| Step 6 | *Move* | the field below the Address field |
| Step 7 | *Close* | the form, saving your changes |

Now that you added the fields, you can add form controls.

4.e Using the Control Toolbox to Add and Modify Controls

The data in a form is contained in **controls**, such as a text box. Other controls include option buttons, check boxes, toggle buttons, and option groups, which are similar to the controls you find on standard Office dialog boxes.

Use option buttons, check boxes, toggle buttons, and option groups when you display information that can have two or three valid choices. For example, if you have a Yes or No choice, use a check box. If the user checks the box, the answer is yes; an unchecked box means no. Option groups provide controls for more than two choices. If options are grouped, then users can select only one option.

chapter
four

Use a **list box** when you want to list values from which users can select. A **combo box** is a list box with drop-down options. Use a combo box when you are trying to conserve space on the form.

You decide to create a combo box for the frmEmployees form, which will allow a valid department to be entered by selecting the department name or typing the first few letters of the department. This speeds up data entry. To create a combo box, use the **Combo Box Wizard**, which guides you through the steps of creating a combo box.

To create a combo box entry:

Step 1	*Open*	the frmEmployees form
Step 2	*Switch*	to Design view
Step 3	*Click*	the Dept field
Step 4	*Press*	the DELETE key
Step 5	*Click*	the Combo Box button 📇 on the toolbox
Step 6	*Click*	the blank space for the department name box

The Combo Box Wizard dialog box on your screen should look similar to Figure 4-13.

MENU TIP

To display the toolbox, click <u>V</u>iew on the menu bar, and then click <u>T</u>oolbox.

FIGURE 4-13
Combo Box Wizard

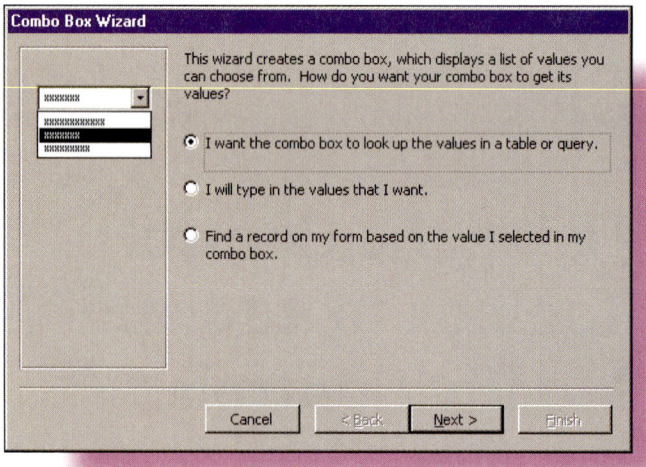

You are now ready to use the Combo Box Wizard to complete your combo box.

To use the Combo Box Wizard:

Step 1	*Click*	the I want the combo box to look up values in a table or a query option button, if necessary
Step 2	*Click*	Next >
Step 3	*Click*	the Tables option button, if necessary, to select it
Step 4	*Click*	tblDepartment from the list box
Step 5	*Click*	Next >
Step 6	*Double-click*	the Department Name field to add it to the Selected Fields: list

The dialog box on your screen should look similar to Figure 4-14.

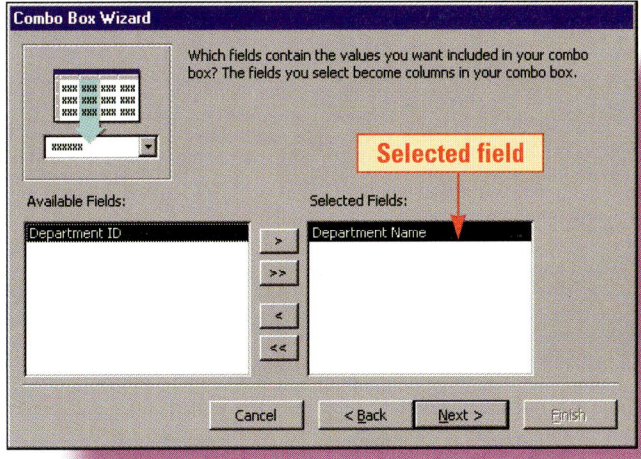

FIGURE 4-14
Selected Field for
Combo Box

Step 7	*Click*	Next >

As you complete the Combo Box Wizard, you can have the combo box adjust its width to accommodate the text it contains. You decide to do this, as it gives you more flexibility when displaying records.

chapter
four

To complete the Combo Box Wizard:

Step 1	**Double-click**	the right border of the column header
Step 2	**Click**	Next >
Step 3	**Click**	the Store that value in this field option button
Step 4	**Select**	Dept from the list in the combo box
Step 5	**Click**	Next >
Step 6	**Key**	Department Name as the label for the combo box
Step 7	**Click**	Finish

Now reposition the combo box on the form.

You do not need the combo box label in Design view, so you delete it.

Step 8	**Click**	the new label in Design view
Step 9	**Press**	the DELETE key
Step 10	**Move**	the new combo box into the position shown in Figure 4-15

FIGURE 4-15
Combo Box Position

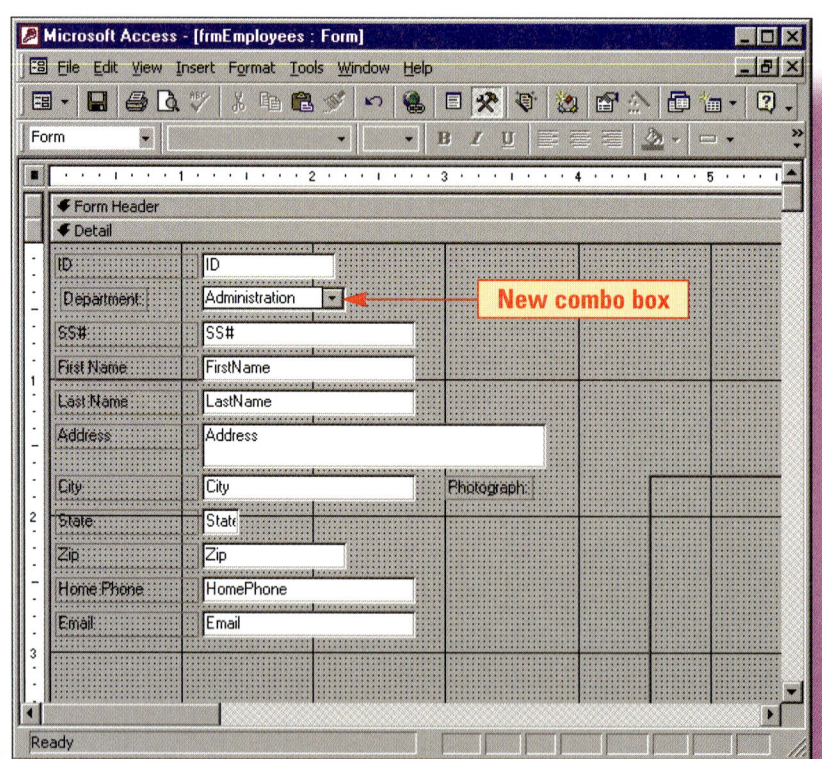

When you show the form to Natasha, she tests it by entering data. She notices that she skips around the form instead of moving from one field to another in logical order. You can change the **tab order** of the form to define which field becomes active when the user presses the TAB key.

To change the tab order of a form:

Step 1	*Click*	View
Step 2	*Click*	Tab Order
Step 3	*Click*	the gray selection box next to the First Name field
Step 4	*Press & Hold*	the SHIFT key while you click the gray selection box to select the Last Name field
Step 5	*Drag*	the First Name and Last Name fields before the Social Security field
Step 6	*Click*	OK

QUICK TIP

Move the fields that are not often used to the end of the tab order list to make data entry easier.

You decide to enhance frmEmployees further by modifying some of its format properties.

4.f Modifying Format Properties

You can enhance a form's design by modifying format properties, such as the form's font, style, font size, and color. You decide to enhance Natasha's form by setting a theme, modifying the form's header, and inserting a picture.

To select a theme for the frmEmployees form:

Step 1	*Verify*	frmEmployees is open in Design view
Step 2	*Click*	Format
Step 3	*Click*	AutoFormat

MOUSE TIP

You can also select the AutoFormat button on the Design View toolbar.

One principle of good design is to be consistent. Use the same format for each record and for each form in a database. Because you used Sumi Painting as a background for the frmSuppliers form, you should use it as the format for the frmEmployees form.

| Step 4 | *Click* | Sumi Painting |
| Step 5 | *Click* | OK |

Now that you applied a theme to the form, you are ready to create a header and add a picture to it.

Using Form Sections

Recall that a form consists of three sections: Form Header, Detail, and Form Footer. The **Form Header** appears at the top of the form page, whereas the **Form Footer** appears at the bottom of the form page. You are already familiar with working with the Detail area. For the frmEmployees form, you decide to add a header with the form's title, to let the Personnel staff know they are entering data into the correct form.

To add a header to a form:

| Step 1 | *Verify* | that frmEmployees is open in Design view |
| Step 2 | *Point to* | the line between the Form Header and Detail sections of the form |

The mouse pointer becomes a double-headed arrow.

Step 3	*Drag*	the arrow down about .5"
Step 4	*Click*	the Text Box button [ab|] on the toolbox
Step 5	*Drag*	in the Form Header section from the first vertical line to the edge of the form to create a text box approximately 4 inches wide and almost .5 inches tall
Step 6	*Key*	Dynamic Inc. Employees
Step 7	*Click*	the text box to select it
Step 8	*Change*	the font size to 18, in the font of your choice
Step 9	*Click*	the text box

You decide to insert a graphic in the Form Header section as well.

Inserting a Graphic on a Form

Inserting a graphic in a form often improves its appearance and makes it look more user-friendly. To insert a graphic, you use the Image tool in the toolbox.

To insert a graphic using the Control toolbox:

Step 1	*Click*	the Image button 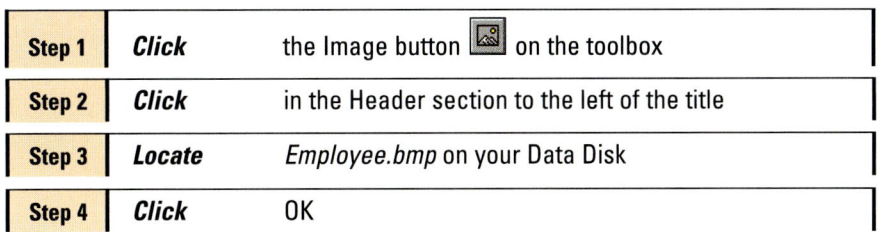 on the toolbox
Step 2	*Click*	in the Header section to the left of the title
Step 3	*Locate*	*Employee.bmp* on your Data Disk
Step 4	*Click*	OK

The image now appears on the form.

| Step 5 | *Resize* | the image as necessary to fit within the header |

Your screen should now look similar to Figure 4-16.

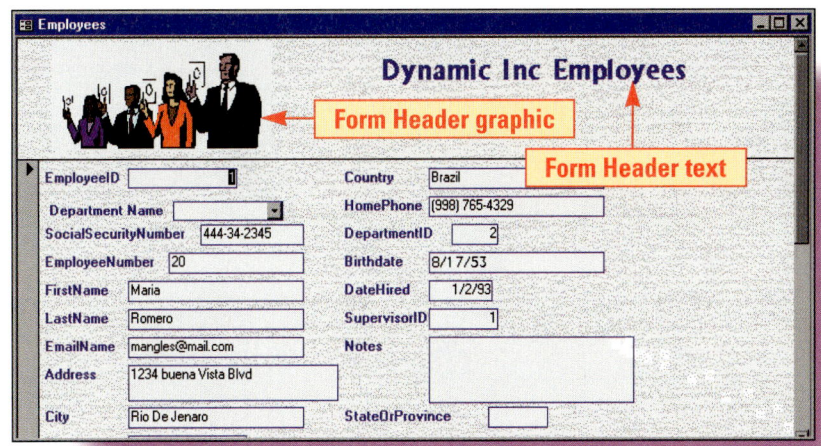

FIGURE 4-16
frmEmployees with Form Header

You completed the form for Natasha's group.

chapter four

4.g Printing a Form

Natasha wants a copy of the frmEmployees form to show to her department when she explains how to use it for data entry. You print the form for her.

To print the frmEmployees form:

Step 1	*Verify*	the frmEmployees form is open in Design view
Step 2	*Click*	File
Step 3	*Click*	Print Preview

You can now review the form. When you are satisfied, you can print from the Print Preview window.

Step 4	*Click*	the Print button on the Print Preview toolbar
Step 5	*Close*	frmEmployees, saving your changes
Step 6	*Exit*	Access

You may also want to print other forms. An order form, for example, may contain all the information that you want to send when you ship the order to your customer. Therefore, you can also print the form to use as a shipping invoice.

Summary

► Create an Access form to enter and view data in records, control application flow, automate your application, provide instructions, and print a version of the record and its data.

► Use the Form Wizard to create a simple form that contains all the fields in the related table or only selected fields. You can also use Design view to create a custom form to modify an existing form.

► Create a custom form when you need a form different from those offered by the Form Wizard or when you want to use information from more than one table.

► After you create a form, test it by using it to enter data and create records. Press the TAB key to move from one field to another. Click in a field and key in the data. To modify an existing record, first click the navigation buttons or the Find button to locate it. Then click in a field and key the modified data.

► Use Design view to modify a form's design without changing your data. You can add, delete, rearrange fields, add controls, insert pictures, change the background color, and choose a theme to improve the appearance and usefulness of your form.

► Form controls let you select options, as you do on a standard Windows dialog box. You can include text boxes, option buttons, check boxes, toggle buttons, option groups, list boxes, and combo boxes. Use a list box when you want to list all the valid values for a field. Use a combo box, which is like a list box with drop-down options, when you want to conserve space. Access includes a Combo Box Wizard to guide you through the steps of creating a combo box.

► One principle in good design is to be consistent. You can keep the design of all the forms in your database consistent by setting a theme.

► Add a header to a form to let users know the topic of the form. You can include text and graphics in the form's header.

► If a form contains information you want to print, as with an order form, you can print the form and specify its printed layout.

chapter four

Commands Review

Action	Menu Bar	Shortcut Menu	Toolbar	Keyboard
When entering or editing form data:				
Open a combo box or a drop-down list		Right-click the box or list and select <u>O</u>pen	Click the list or drop-down arrow	F4 or ALT + DOWN ARROW
Move up or down one line			Click the line	UP or DOWN ARROW
Move to the previous or next page			Click the scroll arrows	PAGEUP or PAGEDOWN
Move to the next field			Click the next field	TAB
Find a record	Edit, <u>F</u>ind Edit, <u>G</u>o To	Right-click a record and select <u>F</u>ind		CTRL + F ALT + E, F ALT + E, E
When designing a form:				
Select a field			Click to see selection handles	TAB
Select more than one field			SHIFT + click to select adjacent fields; CTRL + click to select non-adjacent fields; double-click field list title bar to select all fields	SHIFT + ARROW or CTRL + ARROW

Concepts Review

SCANS

Circle the correct answer.

1. A form should:
 [a] be visually appealing and guide users through the process of entering data.
 [b] automate queries.
 [c] help to create a paperless office.
 [d] use macros to display images.

2. One of the purposes of a form is to:
 [a] print the complete contents of a database.
 [b] enter and view data.
 [c] create special wizards.
 [d] design a layout for your tables.

3. The form acts like a _____ to hide the database from the user.
 [a] tool
 [b] mask
 [c] creator
 [d] wizard

4. Editing records in a form is the _____ editing records in a table.
 [a] same as
 [b] opposite of
 [c] result of
 [d] only way of

5. To modify a form:
- [a] you must be in Datasheet view.
- [b] you must be in Design view.
- [c] use the Form Wizard.
- [d] you need to know advanced Access techniques.

6. When you want to create a simple form using all the fields in the related table use:
- [a] Design view.
- [b] the Form Wizard.
- [c] the Table Wizard.
- [d] Datasheet view.

7. Create a custom form when you want to:
- [a] add a visually appealing background.
- [b] use information from more than one table.
- [c] add a photograph to a record.
- [d] detach a form from a table.

8. Adding a title to a form:
- [a] lets you use information from more than one table.
- [b] lets you list valid options for a field.
- [c] tells the user the subject of the form.
- [d] is part of data entry.

9. Creating controls:
- [a] helps users know the purpose of a form.
- [b] lets users select a valid option from a list.
- [c] restricts field length.
- [d] provides instructions for printing the form.

10. You can enhance the design of a form by:
- [a] modifying it in Datasheet view.
- [b] choosing a theme.
- [c] entering all the required data.
- [d] creating a custom form.

Circle **T** if the statement is true or **F** if the statement is false.

T   F   1. A control determines the format of a form.

T   F   2. You can print a form, but not the data included in it.

T   F   3. You can change the tab order of a form so users can move logically from one field to another.

T   F   4. You can only create a form using the Form Wizard.

T   F   5. You can create forms that will allow you to enter information from several different tables.

T   F   6. Forms simplify data entry.

T   F   7. To find a record you want to edit, you can use the Locate command.

T   F   8. You cannot delete or move fields once you finish designing a form.

T   F   9. The Combo Box Wizard guides you through the steps of including a dialog box in your form.

T   F   10. One principle in good design is to use a lot of formatting features.

chapter four

Skills Review

Exercise 1

1. If necessary, open the *mdbDynamic4Inc* database.

2. Use the Form Wizard to create a new form based on the tblRegions table.

3. Name the new form frmRegions.

4. Close and save the frmRegions form.

Exercise 2

1. If necessary, open the *mdbDynamic4Inc* database.

2. Use the Form Wizard to create a new form based on the tblCustomers table. Use only the following fields in the form: Customer ID, Company Name, Address, City, Country, and Phone Number.

3. Choose the justified layout for the form.

4. Name the new form frmCustomers.

5. Save and close the frmCustomers form.

Exercise 3

1. If necessary, open the *mdbDynamic4Inc* database.

2. Open the frmCustomers form you created in Exercise 2.

3. Enter the following information in new records in the form:

CANAD, Canadian Products, 12 N. Ontario, Ontario, Canada

MEXIC, Mexican Goods, Pampas 900, Mexico City, Mexico

JAPAN, Japanese Gifts, 67 Kyoto, Tokyo, Japan

4. Print the frmCustomers form with the data.

5. Save and close the frmCustomers form.

Exercise 4

1. If necessary, open the *mdbDynamic4Inc* database.

2. Open the frmCustomers form you created in Exercise 2.

3. In Design view, rearrange the fields in the form. For example, move the Address field below the Customer ID and Company Name.

4. Add a new field for Phone Number.

5. Print the frmCustomers form.

6. Save and close the frmCustomers form.

Exercise 5

1. If necessary, open the *mdbDynamic4Inc* database.

2. Open the frmCustomers form you created in Exercise 2.

3. In Design view, add a combo box to the list. Save your form design.

4. Test the form by entering data in the records using the combo box.

5. Close the frmCustomers form.

Exercise 6

1. If necessary, open the *mdbDynamic4Inc* database.

2. Open the frmCustomers form you created in Exercise 5.

3. Change the tab order of the form.

4. Test the tab order in the form.

5. Save and close the frmCustomers form.

Exercise 7

1. If necessary, open the *mdbDynamic4Inc* database.

2. Open the frmCustomers form you created in Exercise 6.

3. Choose a theme for the form's design.

4. Save and close the frmCustomers form.

Exercise 8

1. If necessary, open the *mdbDynamic4Inc* database.

2. Open the frmCustomers form you created in Exercise 7.

3. Add a header to the form.

4. Test the form by adding one record of information.

5. Save and close the frmCustomers form.

chapter four

Case Projects

Project 1

Using the Microsoft on the Web command on the Help menu, open the Microsoft home page and then link to pages that provide basic information about Access forms. Print at least two of the Web pages.

Project 2

Connect to your ISP and load the home page for a search engine. Search for sites that provide principles for good design of paper-based publications, such as a newsletter, or electronic publications, such as a Web page. Print at least two of the Web pages. Use this information for Projects 3–8.

Project 3

Maria Moreno, the owner of Dynamic, Inc., asks you to create four forms for the other tables in *mdbDynamic4Inc*. Start by creating a simple form for the tblDepartment table. Choose a theme for the form. Modify and enhance the form to conform to the principles of good design.

Project 4

Use the Form Wizard to create the second form based on the tblProducts table. Use the same theme for the frmProducts form as you did for the frmDepartment form. Add a control that lists the values from the tblSuppliers table.

Project 5

Create the third form based on the tblOrders table. Use the same design as you did for the other forms. Rearrange the fields on the form. Check the tab order so users can complete the fields in logical order. Add a calculated control to calculate the total price of the orders. See online Help for instructions on adding a calculated control to a form.

Project 6

In Design view, create the fourth form based on the tblSuppliers table. Use the same design as you did for the other forms. Add other fields, such as phone and fax number. If necessary, use online Help for instructions on creating a form in Design view.

Project 7

Open one of the forms you created in Projects 3–6. Test the form design by entering data. Modify the design to make data entry easier.

Project 8

Open one of the forms you created in Projects 3–6. Test the form design by entering data. Enhance the design by adding a graphic (search the Office Clip Art folder, if necessary), adding a header, or changing the font styles of the field labels.

Integrating Access with Other Office Applications and the Internet

I

Chapter Overview

In this chapter, you learn to use an Access database with other Office 2000 applications. You export an Access table to a Word document, import an Excel spreadsheet, and link an Excel spreadsheet. You also create hyperlinks to connect to the Internet and visit Web sites or send e-mail messages.

LEARNING OBJECTIVES

► Export database objects
► Export database records to Excel
► Use Excel data with Access
► Integrate Access with the Internet

Case profile

Managers at Dynamic, Inc., realize it is more efficient if they use information they create in other Office applications, such as Word and Excel, with the Access database information. For example, Kay Wong, the marketing manager, wants to create a product catalog listing the information from an Access table. Maria Moreno, the owner of Dynamic, wants to use information from Excel spreadsheets to create new Access tables. Maria also wants you to make it easy to send e-mail messages from Access.

integration

AX.a Exporting Database Objects

You may find it helpful to use information from your Access database in other Office 2000 applications. Using Office 2000, you do not need to re-enter the information. Instead, you can simply export the database object(s) to the appropriate Office application.

For example, Kay began creating a catalog of Dynamic's products and prices using Microsoft Word, but asks you to complete it by supplying the most current information. You realize that this information is already contained in the Access database, so you decide to export the data from an Access table to the Word document.

Exporting an Access Table to a Word Document

Word's **Mail Merge Helper** dialog box guides you through the steps of merging Access data into a Word document. First, you specify the main document—the Word document that will contain the Access data. Next, you identify the data source—the Access table containing the data you want to include in the Word document. You can merge selected fields and records, or all of them. If necessary, you can return to the main document and enter or edit text and fields. The main document can include text that doesn't change when you merge, as well as merge fields for information that comes from Access. For example, Kay's document includes text identifying the document as the Dynamic Product Catalog, and fields for the product information and prices.

When you're ready to merge, Word finds the table, records, and fields you specified, and merges that information into the main document. Figure AX-1 shows how the Access table, Word main document, and merged document relate.

FIGURE AX-1
Merging Access Data with
a Word Document

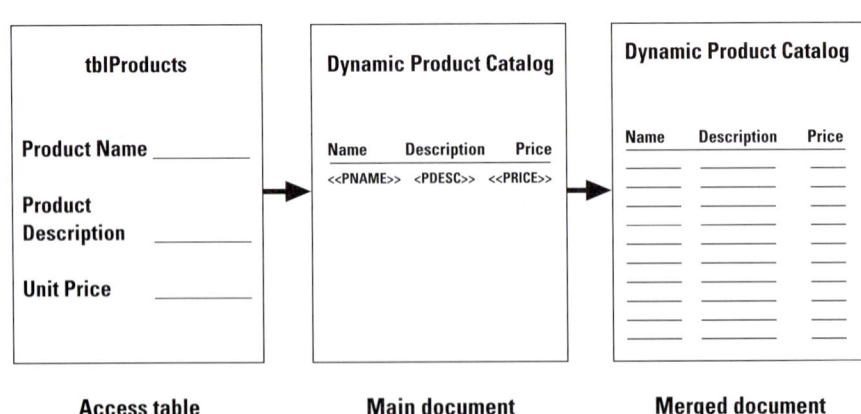

Access table   Main document   Merged document

Now that you understand the process, you are ready to start the Mail Merge Helper.

Starting the Mail Merge Helper

To start the Mail Merge Helper, you first open the Word document with which you merge the Access data.

To start the Mail Merge Helper:

Step 1	*Start*	Microsoft Word 2000
Step 2	*Open*	the *Catalog* Word document located on your Data Disk
Step 3	*Click*	Tools
Step 4	*Click*	Mail Merge

The Mail Merge Helper dialog box on your screen should look similar to Figure AX-2.

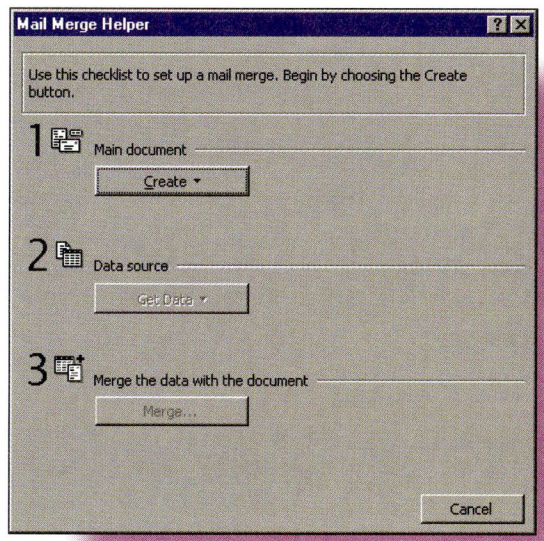

FIGURE AX-2
Mail Merge Helper Dialog Box

The Mail Merge Helper dialog box includes three sections where you need to provide information: Main document, Data source, and Merge the data with the document. You first need to complete the Main document section.

Selecting the Main Document

The **main document** is the document you edit or create that stays the same each time you merge. In this case, the *Catalog* document you opened is the main document.

integration

To select the main document:

| Step 1 | *Click* | Create in the Main document section |
| Step 2 | *Click* | Catalog as the type of main document you are creating |

A dialog box opens and asks if you want to use the open document or create a new one. Use the active document.

| Step 3 | *Click* | Active Window |

The next step is to specify a data source by choosing the Get Data button.

Selecting the Data Source

The **data source** is the document or object containing the information you merge into the Word document. For the product catalog, this is the Access table containing product information.

To select the data source:

| Step 1 | *Click* | Get Data in the Data source section |
| Step 2 | *Click* | Open Data Source |

The Open Data Source dialog box on your screen should look similar to Figure AX-3.

FIGURE AX-3
Open Data Source
Dialog Box

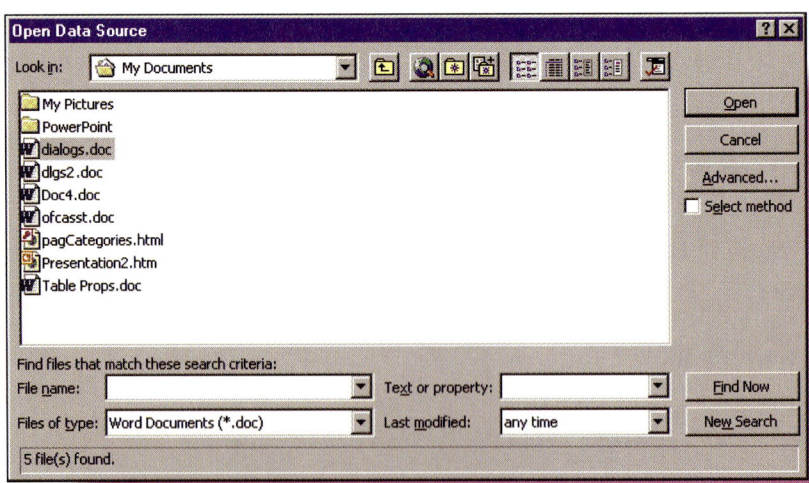

You need to locate the Dynamic database. To do that, change the file type in the Files of type: list box to MS Access Databases and change the Look in: list box as necessary to locate your Data Disk.

Step 3	**Locate**	*mdbDynamicInt* database on your Data Disk
Step 4	**Double-click**	*mdbDynamicInt* database to open it
Step 5	**Double-click**	tblProducts

You are now ready to set up the main document for merging.

Setting Up the Main Document for Merging

After you select the data source, a dialog box asks if you want to edit the main document. You can do so to enter and edit text and merge fields. In Kay's document, you include four fields for merging: ProductID, Category_Name, ProductDescription, and Unit_Price.

To set up the main document:

| Step 1 | **Click** | Edit Main Document |

Your screen should look similar to Figure AX-4.

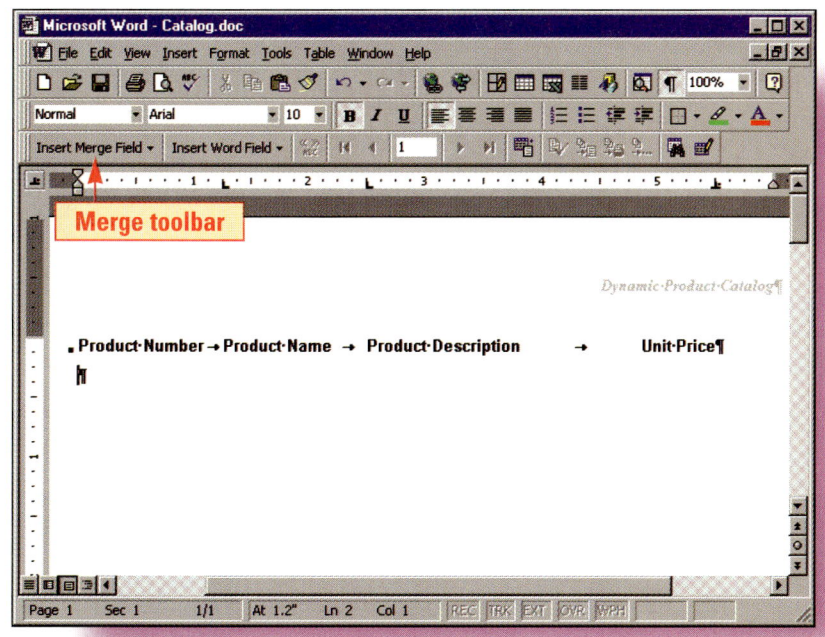

FIGURE AX-4
Word Main Document

integration

Notice the **Merge toolbar** at the top of the screen, which lets you perform your merging tasks.

Step 2	*Click*	in the *Catalog* document below the Product Number column heading
Step 3	*Click*	the Insert Merge Field button on the Merge toolbar
Step 4	*Select*	the ProductID field
Step 5	*Press*	the TAB key
Step 6	*Repeat*	Steps 3–5 to insert the Category_Name, ProductDescription, and Unit_Price fields

Your screen should look similar to Figure AX-5.

FIGURE AX-5
Main Document with
Access Fields

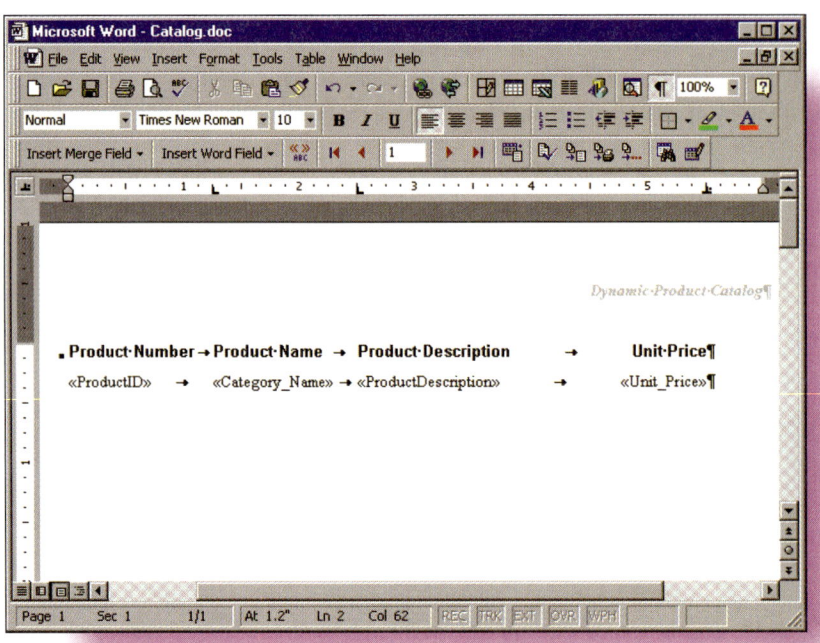

QUICK TIP

You can also start the merge process within Access. In the Database window, click the name of the table or query you want to export. Click the Tools menu, point to Office Links, and then click Merge it with MS Word. Follow the instructions in the Mail Merge Wizard to complete merging.

All the fields you selected for merging are shown within << >> characters, which means the data source supplies the information. Now you're ready to insert the data into these fields.

Merging the Data

After you select and set up the main document, you're ready to merge information from the data source, such as an Access table, into the document. When you merge, you replace the fields (the <<*text*>> items) with the corresponding data from each record you select in the data source. For the product catalog, merge the ProductID, Category_Name, ProductDescription, and Unit_Price records from the tblProducts table into the appropriate fields in the *Catalog* document.

To merge the data:

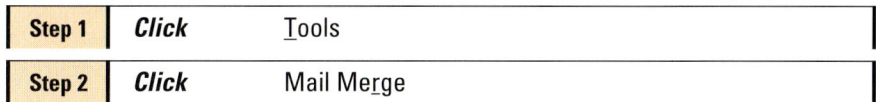

Step 1	*Click*	<u>T</u>ools

Step 2	*Click*	Mail Me<u>r</u>ge

The Merge button is now available in the Merge the data with the document section of the Mail Merge Helper dialog box.

Step 3	*Click*	Merge

The Merge dialog box on your screen should look similar to Figure AX-6.

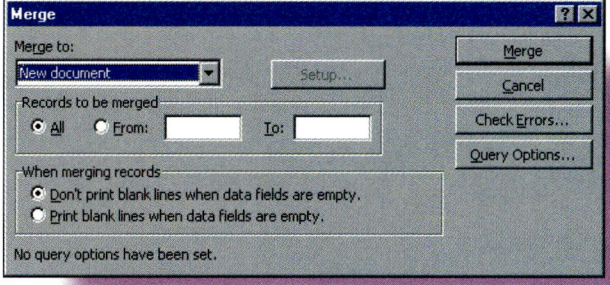

FIGURE AX-6
Merge Dialog Box

Use this dialog box to select the document you want to merge into, and to select the records you want. If you want to create address labels or envelopes, click the <u>P</u>rint blank lines when data fields are empty option button. For the Dynamic product catalog, you accept the default choices: active document, all records, and do not print blank lines. You are ready to merge.

integration

Step 4	*Click*	<u>M</u>erge

The Mail Merge Helper inserts the data from the fields in the tblProducts table into the *Catalog* document. Your screen should look similar to Figure AX-7.

FIGURE AX-7
Merged Document

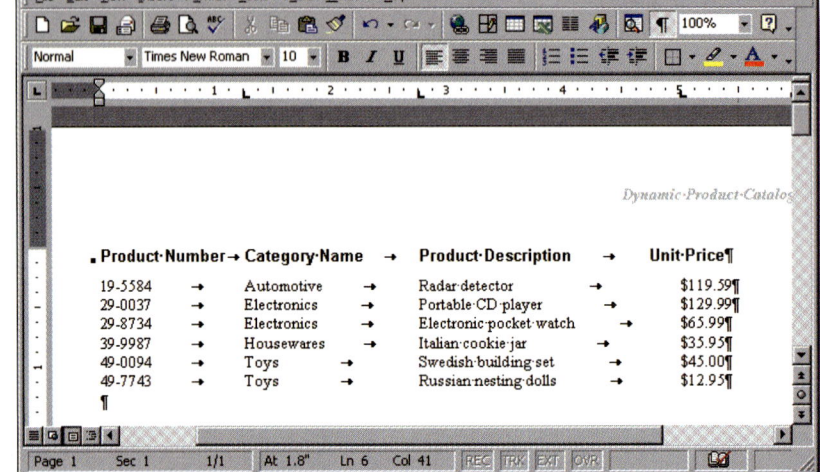

You need to save your work.

Saving the Merged Document

After you merge, you want to save the new document you created that contains the actual data, not the fields. In this case, you want to save the merged *Catalog* document, which lists Dynamic's products and prices.

To save a merged document:

Step 1	*Click*	<u>F</u>ile
Step 2	*Click*	Save <u>A</u>s
Step 3	*Save*	the document as *Dynamic Catalog*
Step 4	*Exit*	Word

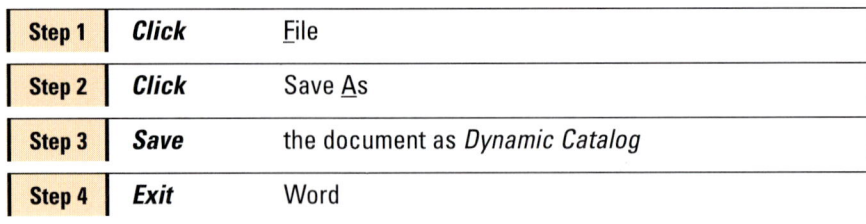

You can also merge Access information into other Office applications, such as Excel.

QUICK TIP

You can also use the Merge toolbar to perform other merging tasks. Use the Merge tools to check for errors, merge to a new document, merge to a printer, or merge with the current settings.

AX.b Exporting Database Records to Excel

If you want to use your Access data in Excel or another spreadsheet program, you can export your Access records. You can export a datasheet with or without formatting, such as fonts and colors. Exporting data without formatting speeds up the export process. You can also save the formatted output of a datasheet, form, or report as an Excel file. If you want to immediately work with the exported information, you can export records by loading them directly into Excel.

Maria wants to export tblProducts so she can work with unit price information in Excel. You can export all the records in the table to an Excel file.

To export records to an Excel file:

Step 1	*Open*	*mdbDynamicInt*
Step 2	*Click*	Tables 🔳 on the Objects bar in the Database window
Step 3	*Click*	tblProducts
Step 4	*Click*	File
Step 5	*Click*	Export

You see the Export Table To dialog box, where you can select the name, location, and type of file you want to export. You can save the exported file in the default location, which should be your Data Disk.

Step 6	*Click*	the File name: text box
Step 7	*Key*	tblProducts
Step 8	*Click*	the Save as type: list arrow
Step 9	*Click*	Microsoft Excel 97-2000 (*.xls)
Step 10	*Click*	the Save formatted check box

CAUTION TIP

You can export to an existing spreadsheet file if you like. However, if you export to an Excel version earlier than 5.0, Access deletes and replaces the data in the existing spreadsheet. If you export to an Excel version 5.0 or later, Access copies the data to the next available worksheet.

integration

This saves the field widths in tblProducts. If tblProducts also contained fonts, colors, or data from Lookup fields, checking the Save formatted check box would also save that formatting. The Export Table To dialog box on your screen should look similar to Figure AX-8.

FIGURE AX-8
Export Table To Dialog Box

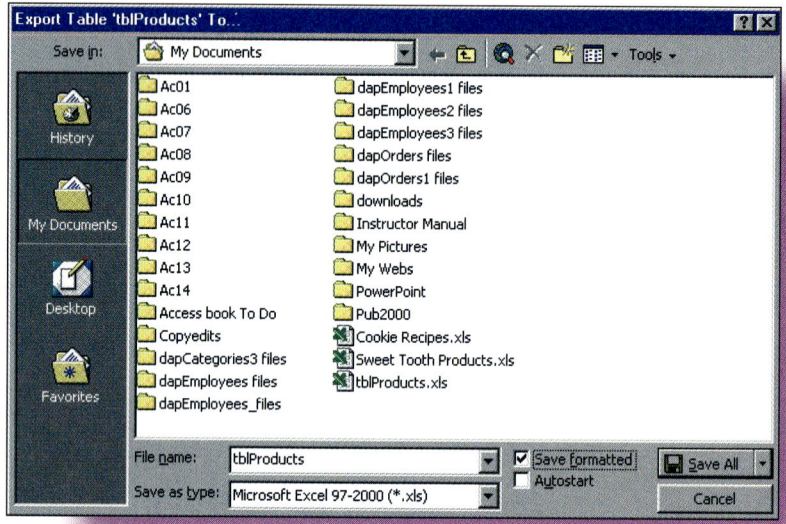

Step 11	*Click*	Save All

Access creates the spreadsheet file containing the records from tblProducts, and puts the field names in the first row of the spreadsheet.

Now Maria wants to select only a few records from tblProducts and load them directly into an Excel spreadsheet. You can do this by using an Office Links command.

To export selected records and open an Excel file:

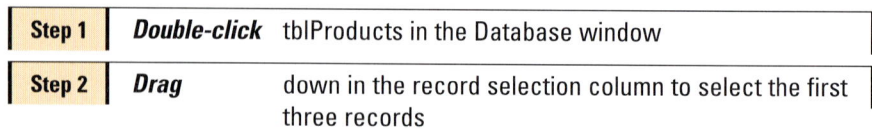

Step 1	*Double-click*	tblProducts in the Database window
Step 2	*Drag*	down in the record selection column to select the first three records

Your screen should look similar to Figure AX-9.

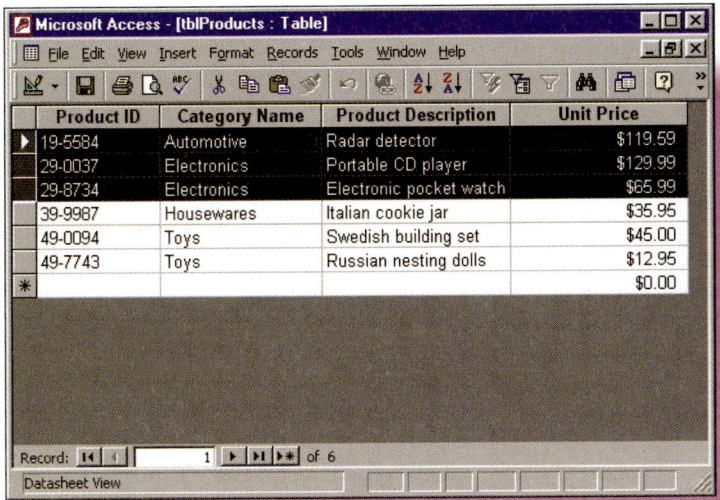

Step 3	*Click*	Tools

Step 4	*Click*	Office Links

Step 5	*Click*	Analyze It With MS Excel

Access saves the records as an Excel file in the default database folder, and then Excel automatically starts and opens the file.

Step 6	*Exit*	Excel

You can also share other Office application data with Access by importing or linking.

AX.c Using Excel Data with Access

If you work with Microsoft Excel, you can easily include spreadsheets in your Access database by importing or linking the Excel data. When you import, you take information from an Excel spreadsheet and copy it into an Access table. The Excel data becomes part of your Access database—you can change the imported data without affecting the original file. When you link, you insert an object in your database that names an Excel spreadsheet and its location. You insert a reference to the Excel file so Access can display the information in the spreadsheet. The major advantage of linking is that if you change the original Excel file, the Access database reflects those changes, and vice versa—if you change the linked data, you change the original file.

In general, link Excel data when you expect that data to change. Import when you simply want to insert a copy of Excel data in your database without changing it. The Table AX-1 lists considerations for deciding when to import and when to link Excel data.

TABLE AX-1
Importing or Linking Excel Data

	When Importing Excel Data	When Linking Excel Data
Disk storage required	You copy information from an Excel spreadsheet into your database, which requires extra disk storage space.	You insert an object in your database that references an Excel spreadsheet. Because you are inserting a link, and not the data itself, you do not need extra disk space.
Original file status	You do not need an up-to-date copy of the original Excel file.	Access must be able to find the file so it can display up-to-date information.
Data format	You convert the Excel data to Access format.	The Excel data remains in its original format, but acts like an Access database.
Properties and structure	You can change all properties and structure.	You can change some properties, but not the structure.
Performance	Access performs at normal speed.	Access performs more slowly.
Deletions	You delete the data when you delete the object, such as a table, containing it.	You delete the data, but not the data from the original file.
Data type translations	You translate some data types from Excel to Access.	Access does not translate linked data types.

Importing Data to a New Table

Dynamic recently purchased a small candy factory. Ben Mayer, the sales manager for the Sweet Tooth Candy Company, created an Excel spreadsheet listing their product types. Maria, Dynamic's owner, asked you to add the product type information to your database. To do this, you decide to import the information into your Access database because the product types do not frequently change.

To begin importing Excel data into Access:

Step 1	**Verify**	*mdbDynamicInt* is open
Step 2	**Click**	<u>F</u>ile
Step 3	**Click**	<u>G</u>et External Data
Step 4	**Click**	<u>I</u>mport

The Import dialog box on your screen should look similar to Figure AX-10.

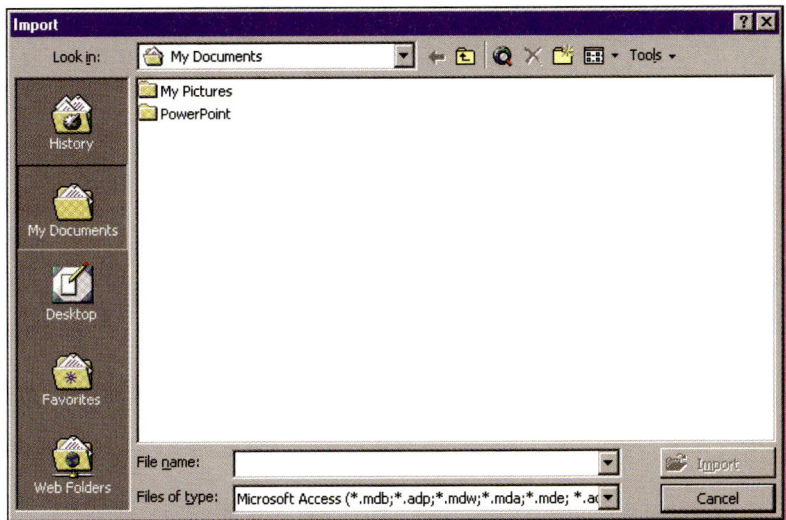

FIGURE AX-10
Import Dialog Box

You do not see any Excel files listed in the dialog box because you need to change the Files of <u>t</u>ype: list box to read Microsoft Excel.

Step 5	**Click**	Microsoft Excel in the Files of <u>t</u>ype: list
Step 6	**Double-click**	*Sweet Tooth Products* to open the Excel file

The Import Spreadsheet Wizard dialog box on your screen should look similar to Figure AX-11.

integration

FIGURE AX-11
Import Spreadsheet
Wizard Dialog Box

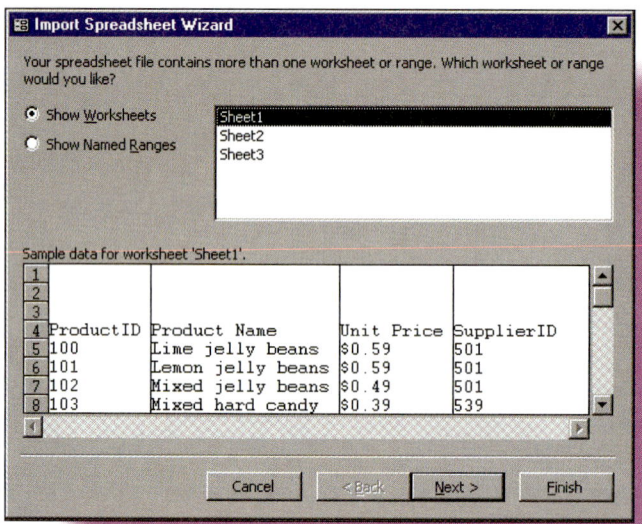

The **Import Spreadsheet Wizard** guides you in both selecting the information to import from the Excel file and determining how you want it to appear in your Access database.

The first dialog box in the wizard asks which worksheet or ranges you want to use and previews the data.

To begin the Import Spreadsheet Wizard:

| Step 1 | *Click* | Next > |

This dialog box asks you if the first row contains the column headings. In the preview, you see that there are no headings, so do not click the box.

| Step 2 | *Click* | Next > |

You can now import the information into a new table.

| Step 3 | *Click* | Next > |

Your screen should look similar to Figure AX-12.

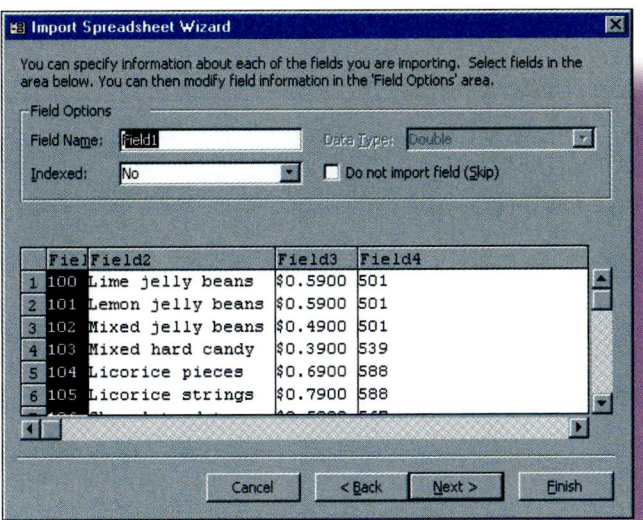

You can now select the fields you want to import. (When you import an Excel spreadsheet where the column headings are in the first row, Access automatically selects the appropriate fields.) Select the first three fields for Product ID, Product Name, and Unit Price fields to import, but skip the last field for Supplier ID.

Step 4	*Click*	Field1
Step 5	*Key*	Product ID in the Field Name: box
Step 6	*Repeat*	Steps 4 and 5 to name Fields2 and 3 Product Name and Unit Price, respectively

Now indicate that you don't want to import the Supplier ID field.

Step 7	*Click*	Field4
Step 8	*Click*	the Do not import field (Skip) check box

Your screen should look similar to Figure AX-13.

integration

FIGURE AX-13
Fields to Import

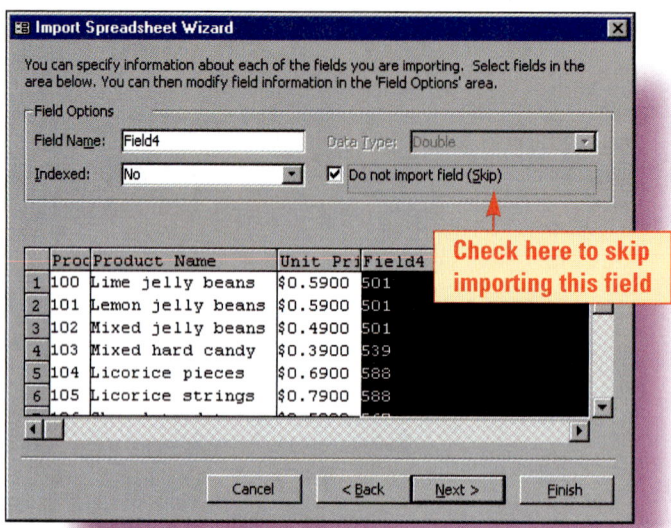

Check here to skip importing this field

Step 9	*Click*	Next >

Access asks if you want to select the primary key. Choose Product ID as the primary key, otherwise Access will add an ID field to use as the primary key.

Step 10	*Click*	Choose my own primary key

Access shows the first field, Product ID, as the primary key. You can now complete the Import Spreadsheet Wizard.

To complete the Import Spreadsheet Wizard:

Step 1	*Click*	Next >

Although Access usually gives the table the same name as the original table, you can change the name if necessary.

Step 2	*Key*	tblSweetProducts
Step 3	*Click*	Finish

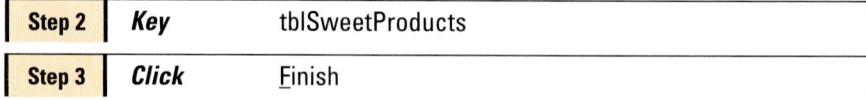

Step 4	*Click*	OK

Access imports the data, which may take some time depending on the size of the Excel spreadsheet and the processing speed of your machine. Once you import the table, it becomes an Access object. You can then use Access commands to change the table. Open the table to check it.

Step 5	*Double-click*	tblSweetProducts

You can now modify the data or the table design as you would any Access table. For example, you could resize the Product Name field to see all the complete entries.

When you finish working with the table, you are ready to close it.

Step 6	*Close*	tblSweetProducts

When you import data, any changes you make to the table do not affect the original Excel spreadsheet. When you link data, however, any changes you make are also reflected in the original file.

Linking to Existing Data

Ben Mayer's Excel spreadsheet lists the sales representatives and their commission rates. Maria asks you to also add this information to your database. Because this information periodically changes, link the data. That way, any changes in the original Excel spreadsheet are reflected in your database. You use the Link Spreadsheet Wizard, which is similar to the Import Spreadsheet Wizard.

To link an Excel table to an Access database:

Step 1	*Click*	File
Step 2	*Click*	Get External Data
Step 3	*Click*	Link Tables

integration

The Link dialog box opens. You need to change the file type.

Step 4	*Click*	Microsoft Excel from the Files of type: list

Step 5	*Double-click*	*Sweet Tooth Sales*

Access now starts the Link Spreadsheet Wizard.
To use the Link Spreadsheet Wizard:

Step 1	*Click*	Next >

This dialog box asks if the first row contains the column headings. In this spreadsheet, the first row does contain the column headings.

Step 2	*Click*	the First Row Contains Column Headings check box

Step 3	*Click*	Next >

Step 4	*Click*	Next >

Access asks if you want to link the information into a new table, which you do.

Step 5	*Click*	Next >

Access asks if you want to select the primary key. Recall that the primary key is a unique identifier for each record. In this case, let Access select the primary key for you. You can now complete the Link Spreadsheet Wizard.
To complete the Link Spreadsheet Wizard:

Step 1	*Click*	Next >

Although Access usually gives the table the same name as the original table, you can change the name if necessary.

Step 2	*Key*	tblSweetSales

Step 3	*Click*	<u>F</u>inish

Now you can open the new table.

Step 4	*Click*	OK

Step 5	*Double-click*	tblSweetSales

Your screen should look similar to Figure AX-14.

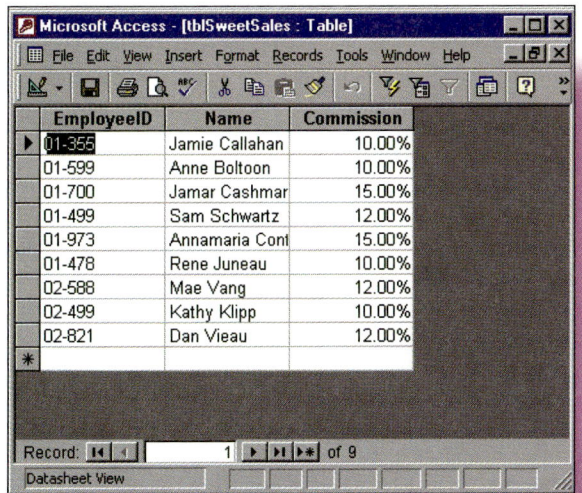

FIGURE AX-14
Table with Linked Data

The Link Spreadsheet Wizard creates the tblSweetSales table with a link to the *Sweet Tooth Sales* Excel spreadsheet. When you work with the linked table, you change the data in both the Access tblSweetSales table and the original *Sweet Tooth Sales* spreadsheet.

You are ready to close the table.

Step 6	*Close*	the table

integration

Your final task is to enable Dynamic's database users to connect easily to the Internet.

AX.d Integrating Access with the Internet

You can integrate your Access database with the Internet to connect to sites on the World Wide Web as well as to send e-mail messages. Maria Moreno wants you to add a field to the new tblSweetProducts table so she can instantly connect to the Sweet Tooth Web site and other related Web sites. She also wants you to add a button to the frmEmployees form to include the employee's e-mail address. You can create a command button Maria can click to create an e-mail message.

Creating and Adding Hyperlinks

If your users have access to the Internet, they can visit Web sites from within an Access database. To do this, you simply add a **hyperlink field**, a field containing a Web address, to a table. You can insert a hyperlink to connect to the Sweet Tooth Web site so Maria can visit the site while she's working with the tblSweetProducts table.

To add a field with a hyperlink:

Step 1	*Click*	Tables on the Objects bar
Step 2	*Double-click*	tblSweetProducts
Step 3	*Switch*	to Design view
Step 4	*Key*	Web Site in the first blank field
Step 5	*Click*	the Data Type column list arrow
Step 6	*Click*	Hyperlink

Your screen should look similar to Figure AX-15.

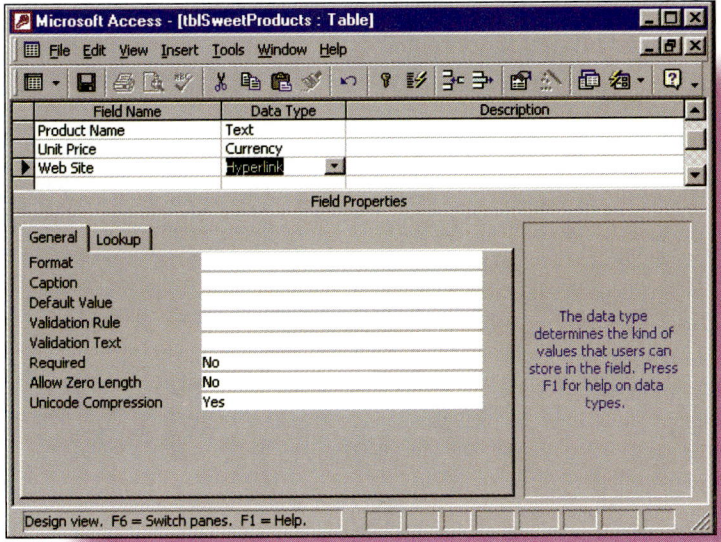

Step 7	*Click*	the Save button 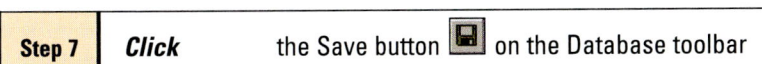 on the Database toolbar

You can now enter Web addresses in the tblSweetProducts table. To enter a Web address:

Step 1	*Switch*	to Datasheet view
Step 2	*Key*	www.sweettooth.com in the Web Site field

Your screen should look similar to Figure AX-16.

FIGURE AX-16
Adding a Web Address
to a Table

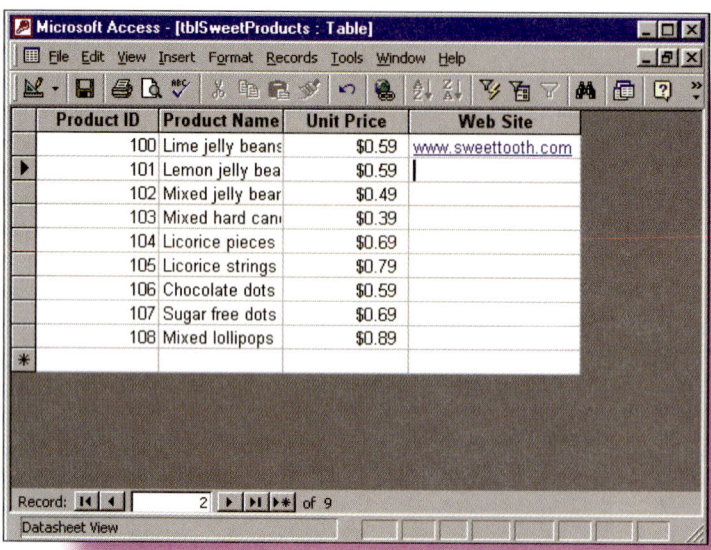

| Step 3 | *Close* | the table, saving your changes |

Now that you created a hyperlink, you are ready to create a command button.

Creating E-Mail Messages from Within Access

If your users have access to the Internet, they can send e-mail messages from an Access object, such as a form. You can create a command button on the frmEmployees form. When Maria clicks the button, Access opens her e-mail application and creates a new message, with the address already filled in.

To create a command button to send e-mail messages:

| Step 1 | *Click* | Forms 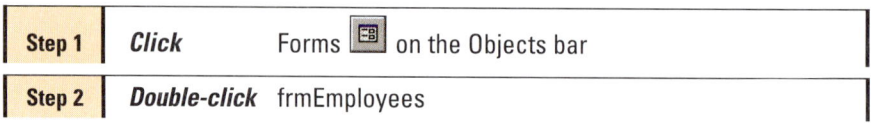 on the Objects bar |

| Step 2 | *Double-click* | frmEmployees |

| Step 3 | **Switch** | to Design view |

Deselect the Control Wizards tool on the toolbox, if necessary.

Step 4	**Verify**	the Control Wizards button ⬚ is not selected
Step 5	**Click**	the Command button ⬚ on the toolbox
Step 6	**Click**	the form where you want to place the command button; in the frmEmployees form, click next to the Employee ID field

Your screen should look similar to Figure AX-17.

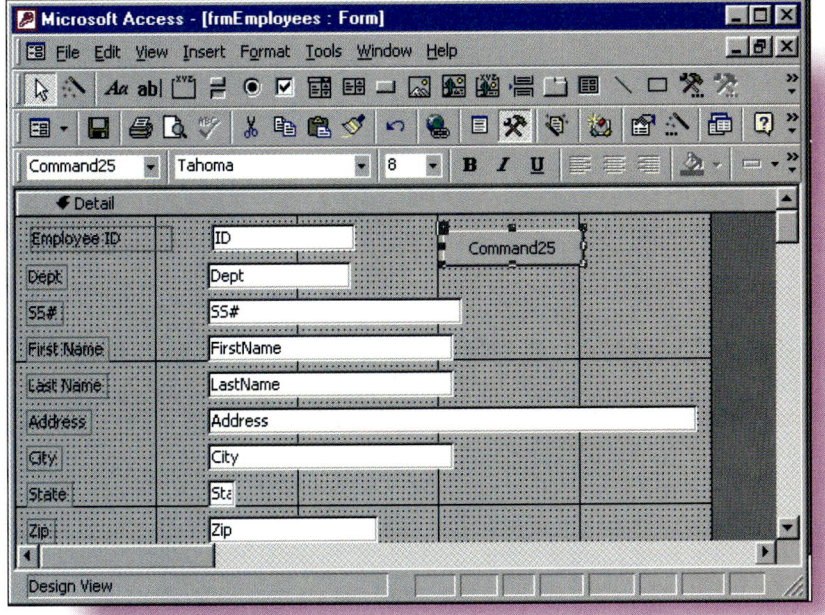

FIGURE AX-17
Adding a Command Button to a Form

integration

Now you're ready to set up the button so you can click it to send e-mail messages. Make sure the command button is selected before continuing.

To set up the command button to send e-mail messages:

| Step 1 | *Click* | the Insert Hyperlink button  on the Form Design toolbar |

The Insert Hyperlink dialog box opens, allowing you to specify the type of hyperlink you want to create. Your screen should look similar to Figure AX-18.

FIGURE AX-18
Insert Hyperlink
Dialog Box

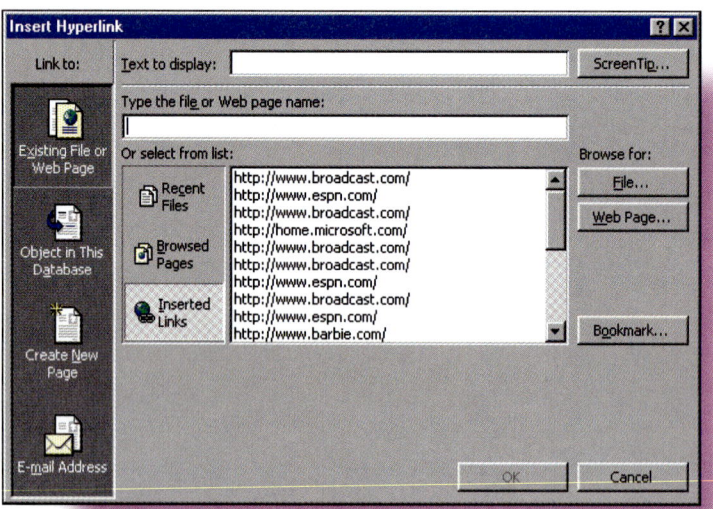

Step 2	*Click*	E-mail Address in the Link to: column on the left of the dialog box
Step 3	*Key*	E-mail Address in the Text to display: box
Step 4	*Key*	kWong@dyn.com in the E-mail address: box

Step 5	*Click*	OK

If necessary, you can reposition the command button on the form. You can now send e-mail messages from the frmEmployees form.

Step 6	*Close*	the form, saving your changes
Step 7	*Exit*	Access

Hyperlinks in Access make it easy for Dynamic managers to connect to the Internet and visit Web sites or send e-mail messages.

integration

Summary

▶ You can merge data from an Access table to a Word document using Word's Mail Merge Helper. Specify the Word document to use as the main document and the Access table to use as the data source. Then enter or edit the text and merge fields in the main document, and merge the records and fields you selected from the Access table into the Word document.

▶ You can include Excel data in an Access table by importing or linking an Excel spreadsheet to a new or existing Access table.

▶ When you import an Excel spreadsheet, you copy the Excel data into an Access table. The Excel data becomes part of your Access database—you can change the imported data without affecting the original file.

▶ When you link an Excel spreadsheet to an Access table, you insert a reference to the Excel file so Access can display the information in the spreadsheet. If you click anywhere in the linked table, you can use Excel commands to enter and edit information.

▶ In general, link Excel data when you expect that data to change. If you change the original spreadsheet, the Access database reflects those changes. If you change the linked table, the Excel spreadsheet reflects those changes.

▶ You can connect to the Internet and the World Wide Web from Access. Add a hyperlink to a table or form so you can click it and use your e-mail application to send e-mail messages, or go to a specified site on the Web.

Commands Review

Action	Menu Bar	Shortcut Menu	Toolbar	Keyboard
Import a table	File, Get External Data, Import	Import		ALT + F, G, I
Link to a table	File, Get External Data, Link to a table	Link Tables		ALT + F, G, L
Export records	File, Export	Export		ALT + F, E
Export records and open Excel	Tools, Office Links		🖹 ▾	ALT + T, L
Insert a hyperlink	Insert, Hyperlink	Hyperlink	🌐	CTRL + K ALT + I, i

Concepts Review

Circle the correct answer.

1. **Which option do you use to merge data between Word and Access?**
   [a] Merge
   [b] Mail Merge
   [c] Import Data
   [d] Get External Data

2. **When merging Access data into a Word document, the data source is:**
   [a] the Word document that will contain the Access data.
   [b] the Access object containing the data you want to merge.
   [c] the document containing the text that doesn't change when you merge.
   [d] a list of fields you can merge.

3. **In a Word document, all the fields you select for merging are shown as:**
   [a] {Field}
   [b] <Field>
   [c] [[Field]]
   [d] <<Field>>

4. **Which one is *not* a wizard used to integrate Access with other Office products?**
   [a] Mail Merge Wizard
   [b] Import Spreadsheet Wizard
   [c] Form Wizard
   [d] Link Spreadsheet Wizard

5. **Merge Access data into Word when you want to:**
   [a] insert a reference to Access within a Word document.
   [b] create Word documents customized with Access information.
   [c] copy an entire Access table into a Word document.
   [d] change fields frequently.

integration

6. Link an Excel spreadsheet to an Access table when you:
[a] expect the Excel spreadsheet data to change.
[b] do not need up-to-date information.
[c] want to convert the spreadsheet to an Access table.
[d] want to merge the Excel data into Access.

7. Import Excel data to Access when you:
[a] expect the Excel spreadsheet data to change.
[b] want a copy of the data in an Access object.
[c] want to use Excel commands to edit the data later.
[d] want to merge the Excel data into Access.

8. Imported data does *not*:
[a] reference an external source.
[b] convert to Access format.
[c] work faster with Access.
[d] allow data type translation.

9. Linked data does *not*:
[a] require extra storage space.
[b] allow you to update information.
[c] work slower with Access.
[d] allow you to change any properties.

10. You can add a hyperlink to an Access object to:
[a] use an Excel spreadsheet in an Access table.
[b] simplify mail merging.
[c] visit a Web site or send an e-mail message.
[d] change the properties of a linked table.

Circle **T** if the statement is true or **F** if the statement is false.

T F 1. Merging data requires the help of a database expert.

T F 2. When you prepare to merge, you can create a main Word document and identify an Access table as a data source.

T F 3. The merge fields you insert in a Word document don't have to match any fields in the Access data source to merge successfully.

T F 4. When you import Excel data, you do not convert it into Access format.

T F 5. Access works fastest with a linked table.

T F 6. You must close Access before visiting sites on the World Wide Web.

T F 7. You can change all the properties of the Excel data you import.

T   F   8. Any changes made to linked data affect the original source.

T   F   9. Importing a table lets you make a copy of the data and turn it into an Access object.

T   F   10. If you need to include up-to-date data that changes frequently, you should import the data.

Skills Review

Exercise 1

1. Open the *PhoneList* Word document on your Data Disk.

2. Merge the tblEmployees table from *mdbDynamicInt* into the Word document. Merge all the fields from all the records.

3. Print the merged document and save it as *PhoneList1*.

4. Close the *PhoneList* document without saving it.

Exercise 2

1. In Word, create a main document to list the address of Dynamic employees. Using *PhoneList* as an example, include column headings for ID, Dept., Name, Address, City, State, and ZIP Code.

2. Use the tblEmployees table from *mdbDynamicInt* as the data source.

3. In the main document, insert fields for each column heading.

4. Merge the data, and then save the document as *AddressList1*.

5. Print and close *AddressList1*.

Exercise 3

1. If necessary, open the *mdbDynamicInt* database.

2. Import the *Sweet Tooth Salary* Excel spreadsheet from the Data Disk. Use Employee ID as the primary key.

3. Save the imported table as tblSalary and then close it.

integration

Exercise 4

1. If necessary, open the *mdbDynamicInt* database.

2. Import the *Sweet Tooth Staff* Excel spreadsheet. Select only the Employee ID, Name, and Total Salary fields to import. Retain their names.

3. Save the imported table as tblStaff, and then open it.

4. Add a new record, as well as a new field for Position.

5. Save and close the tblStaff table.

Exercise 5

1. If necessary, open the *mdbDynamicInt* database.

2. Link the *Sweet Tooth Staff* Excel spreadsheet from the Data Disk. Use all the fields.

3. Save the linked table as tblSweetTooth.

Exercise 6

1. If necessary, open the *mdbDynamicInt* database.

2. Open the tblSweetTooth table you created in Exercise 5.

3. Add a record to the table.

4. Open the table in Design view and try to change a data type. Then add a new field called Position.

5. Save and close the tblSweetTooth table.

Exercise 7

1. If necessary, open the *mdbDynamicInt* database.

2. Open the tblProducts table in Design view.

3. Add a field called Links with a Hyperlink data type. Save the table.

4. In Datasheet view, enter *www.microsoft.com*.

5. Use it to connect to the Microsoft Web site.

Exercise 8

1. If necessary, open the *mdbDynamicInt* database.

2. Open the frmOrders form in Design view.

3. Add a command button to send an e-mail message to *mMoreno@dyn.com*.

4. Save and close the form.

Case Projects

Project 1

Maria Moreno, the owner of Dynamic, Inc., asks you to find out if you can convert an Access 2000 database so someone with a previous version of Access can use it. Search the Access online Help for information on converting an Access 2000 database to a previous version. Use Word to create a document that provides the information. Print and save the document.

Project 2

Maria wants you to find a quick way to use Access tables and queries in an Excel spreadsheet. Open Microsoft Excel and resize Excel and Access so you can see both windows on your desktop. In the Access Database window, click tblProducts and drag it from Access to a blank worksheet in Excel. Do the same for qryProducts. Save and print the new spreadsheets.

Project 3

Maria wants to see the information in the frmChart from *mdbDynamicInt* presented as a bar chart. You can do this by integrating with Microsoft Graph. On the Insert menu, click Chart. Click in the form where you want the chart to appear. Then follow the steps in the Chart Wizard dialog box to insert a bar chart based on the frmChart table.

Project 4

Maria thinks some information in your database is appropriate for the Dynamic Web site. You can publish HTML pages on the World Wide Web. Search the Access online Help for instructions on exporting an Access object as HTML. Then follow those instructions to export the tblProducts table in *mdbDynamicInt* as HTML.

integration

Project 5

Maria asks you to create a supplement to the product catalog that lists the newest products—those offered in the last month. She created a query called qryNewProducts in *mdbDynamicInt* that finds all the new Dynamic products. Search the Word online Help for instructions on using an Access query as a data source for mail merge. Then follow the instructions to merge the records in qryNewProducts to a new Word document that you save as *Catalog Supplement.*

Project 6

Before you created the database for Dynamic, Maria stored important customer information in a text file. Now she wants you to import this text file—*Best Customers*—into the tblCustomers table. Search the Word online Help for instructions on importing a Word text file to Access. Then follow these instructions to import the text in to the tblCustomers table.

Project 7

Using the Microsoft on the Web command on the Help menu, open the Microsoft home page and then link to pages that provide information about data integration topics, such as mail merge, importing and exporting, and linking. Print at least two of the Web pages.

Project 8

Add a control to a form in *mdbDynamicInt* that creates an e-mail message when selected. Send an e-mail message to someone whose e-mail address you know.

Integrating Word and Excel with PowerPoint

Chapter Overview

This chapter shows you how to integrate objects created in other Office programs, such as Word and Excel, into PowerPoint presentations. It also illustrates how to integrate PowerPoint slides into other Office programs.

LEARNING OBJECTIVES

- ▶ Send a PowerPoint presentation to Word
- ▶ Send a Word outline to a PowerPoint presentation
- ▶ Insert slides from a Word outline
- ▶ Insert slides from one PowerPoint presentation to another
- ▶ Add a Word table to a PowerPoint slide
- ▶ Embed an Excel worksheet in a PowerPoint slide
- ▶ Link an Excel chart to a PowerPoint slide

Case profile

Mr. Lerek asks you to send the presentation you created for an upcoming regional sales meeting directly to an outline in Word so that he can include some of the information in a quarterly report. He would also like you to create an entertaining presentation about Academy Award winning movies that he will present during an afternoon break at the sales meeting. His daughter, Tracy, a movie buff, has prepared a Word outline that can be used for that presentation.

integration

notes You use the *Teddy Toys Sample Integrated* presentation, the *Movies Outline 1997-1993* document, the *Movies Outline 1992-1988* document, the *Movies Workbook* file, and the *Academy Award Winners 1987-1983* presentation from the Data Disk for this chapter.

PX.a Sending a PowerPoint Presentation to Word

Integrating is the process of embedding and linking objects from one application to another. You can send slides, notes, handouts, or outlines from a PowerPoint presentation directly to Word, where you can then use the presentation as a Word document. When you send slides from PowerPoint to Word, you actually paste them into a Word document. When you paste a presentation, it is embedded into Word. You also have the option of linking the slides between the Word document and the PowerPoint presentation. It is important to understand the differences between linking and embedding before you integrate your PowerPoint presentation into other applications.

An object created in one application (**source file**) can be inserted or copied into another application (**destination file**). You have the option of embedding or linking the objects between applications. When you **embed** an object, the object becomes a part of the destination file. You edit and format the object using the source application features, but your changes do not affect the source file. There is no connection between the source file and the embedded object, so any changes that are made to the embedded object do not affect the source file, and any modifications that are made to the source file do not affect the embedded object.

When you **link** an object, you are actually creating a dynamic connection between the source file and the destination file. You insert a reference or pointer to the object (rather than the object itself) in the destination file. When you edit a linked object, you work with the source file. You can open a linked object either by opening it from the destination file or by opening the source file from within the source application; when you change the source file, the linked information is updated automatically.

Embedding a PowerPoint Presentation in a Word Document

When you embed or link a PowerPoint presentation in a Word document, the slides are placed in a Word table. This gives you greater versatility in the arrangement of the slides, the placement of the notes lines, and the creation of a Word outline from a PowerPoint presentation. Mr. Lerek wants to have the *Teddy Toys Sample Integrated* presentation sent to Word as an embedded outline because he does not want future changes made to the presentation to affect the Word outline. You want to send your PowerPoint presentation to Word for editing purposes without linking the two files. To send a presentation to Word:

Step 1	**Open**	the *Teddy Toys Sample Integrated* presentation
Step 2	**Save**	the presentation as *Teddy Toys Integrated*
Step 3	**Click**	File
Step 4	**Point to**	Send To
Step 5	**Click**	Microsoft Word

The Write-Up dialog box allows you to place your Notes next to or below slides, to place Blank lines next to or below slides, or to place an Outline only (see Figure PX-1). You can Paste the presentation to embed it into Word, or you can Paste link to link the presentation to the Word document.

CAUTION TIP

When you send a PowerPoint presentation to Word as an outline, Word automatically assigns a temporary filename (such as *ppt2562*), and the PowerPoint presentation is sent to Word as an outline in a rich text format (.rtf). You should change the type of file to a Word document when you save the outline in Word.

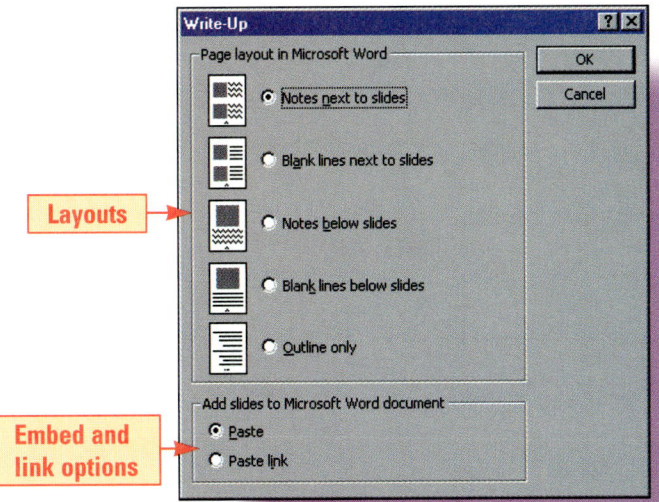

Layouts

Embed and link options

FIGURE PX-1
Write-Up Dialog Box

Step 6	*Click*	Notes next to slides, if necessary

Step 7	*Click*	Paste, if necessary

Step 8	*Click*	OK

Word opens and displays a new document containing your PowerPoint slides in a three-column tabular format. The first column displays the slide number; the second displays a miniature slide; and the third column displays any speaker notes.

Step 9	*Click*	File

Step 10	*Click*	Save As

Step 11	*Key*	Teddy Toys Embedded in the File name: text box

Step 12	*Click*	Save

Compare your Word document to Figure PX-2. Your Teddy Toys Embedded document will not display any speaker notes in the third column as shown in Figure PX-2.

FIGURE PX-2
Embedded PowerPoint
Slides in Word

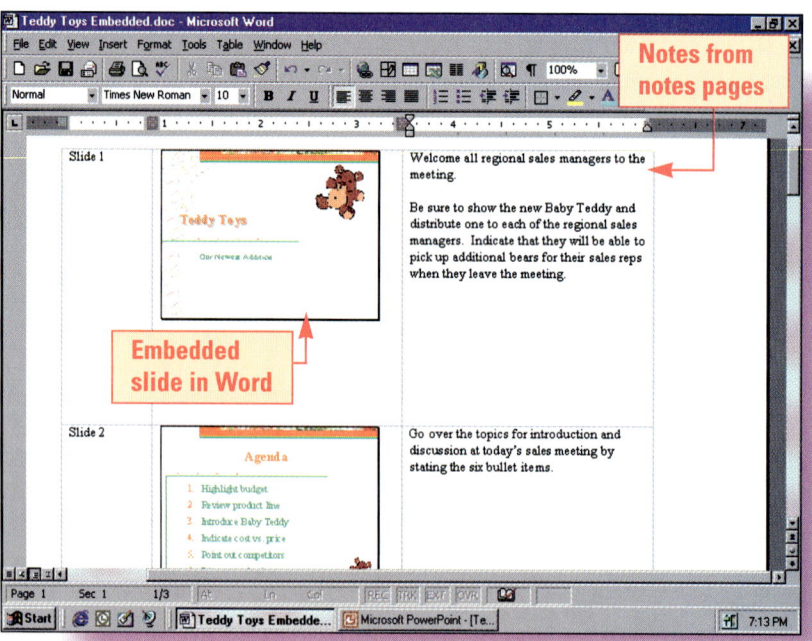

The slides in the Word document are embedded objects; as such, edits made to the objects do not affect the source document. To edit an embedded object, you double-click it. You decide to change the title on the first slide in the Word document to Teddy Toys Embedded. To edit the embedded slide object in Word:

Step 1	*Scroll*	to the first slide object
Step 2	*Double-click*	the slide object

A border appears around the slide object, and you can now edit using the PowerPoint application features.

Step 3	*Click*	directly to the right of Teddy Toys in the title area
Step 4	*Press*	the SPACEBAR
Step 5	*Key*	Embedded
Step 6	*Click*	outside the slide object border
Step 7	*Save*	and close the *Teddy Toys Embedded* Word document
Step 8	*Click*	the Microsoft PowerPoint - [*Teddy Toys Integrated*] button on the taskbar to switch to the PowerPoint application, if necessary
Step 9	*Display*	the first slide

Notice that the title still reads Teddy Toys. This document is not affected by any changes you made to the Word document.

Linking a PowerPoint Presentation to a Word Document

Use linking when you want the information in the destination file to change every time the information in the source file changes. In addition, you should link any time there is limited disk space; a link takes less disk space than an embedded object. Each time you open a PowerPoint presentation containing links, the application asks if you want to update the links. If you click OK, all links to the presentation automatically reestablish upon opening the file.

integration

Mr. Lerek informs you that he plans to update the *Teddy Toys Integrated* presentation each year. If you link the *Teddy Toys Integrated* presentation to a Word outline, the Word outline automatically updates whenever anyone makes changes to the *Teddy Toys Integrated* presentation. To link your *Teddy Toys Integrated* PowerPoint file to a Word document:

Step 1	*Click*	File
Step 2	*Point to*	Send To
Step 3	*Click*	Microsoft Word
Step 4	*Click*	Notes next to slides, if necessary
Step 5	*Click*	Paste link in the Add slides to Microsoft Word document area
Step 6	*Click*	OK
Step 7	*Save*	the Word document as *Teddy Toys Linked*

The PowerPoint slides have been sent to Word in a three-column tabular format again. This time, however, the slide objects directly link to your PowerPoint presentation.

To edit the linked slide object in Word:

Step 1	*Scroll*	to the first slide object
Step 2	*Double-click*	the slide object

You view the source file (*Teddy Toys Integrated* presentation) in the PowerPoint application window; you do not merely access PowerPoint editing features, you actually work in the application.

Step 3	*Edit*	the title in the *Teddy Toys Integrated* PowerPoint presentation to read: Teddy Toys Linked

Compare your slide to Figure PX-3.

Step 4	*Save*	and close the *Teddy Toys Integrated* PowerPoint presentation so that the Word document automatically updates the changes
Step 5	*Click*	the *Teddy Toys Linked* Word document button in the taskbar

Observe that the title changed on the first slide object in the Word document.

Step 6	*Save*	and close the *Teddy Toys Linked* Word document

When you make any changes to the *Teddy Toys Integrated* PowerPoint presentation, those changes are automatically updated when you open the *Teddy Toys Linked* Word document because the slide objects are linked.

PX.b Sending a Word Outline to a PowerPoint Presentation

You can create a presentation by inserting slides from an outline or you can send an outline (from Word) to create slides in a PowerPoint presentation. If you create the Word document with heading styles, PowerPoint uses those styles to create slides. Each paragraph that is formatted with the Heading 1 style becomes the title of a new slide. Each paragraph that is formatted with the Heading 2 style becomes the first-level bullet on a slide. The remaining heading styles follow the same pattern.

You want to use Tracy's Academy Award Winners Word outline to create a PowerPoint presentation. To send a Word outline to a PowerPoint presentation:

Step 1	*Verify*	that the Word application is open on your screen
Step 2	*Click*	File
Step 3	*Click*	Open
Step 4	*Double-click*	the *Movies Outline 1997-1993* document from the Data Disk

Compare your Word outline to Figure PX-4.

FIGURE PX-4
Word Outline

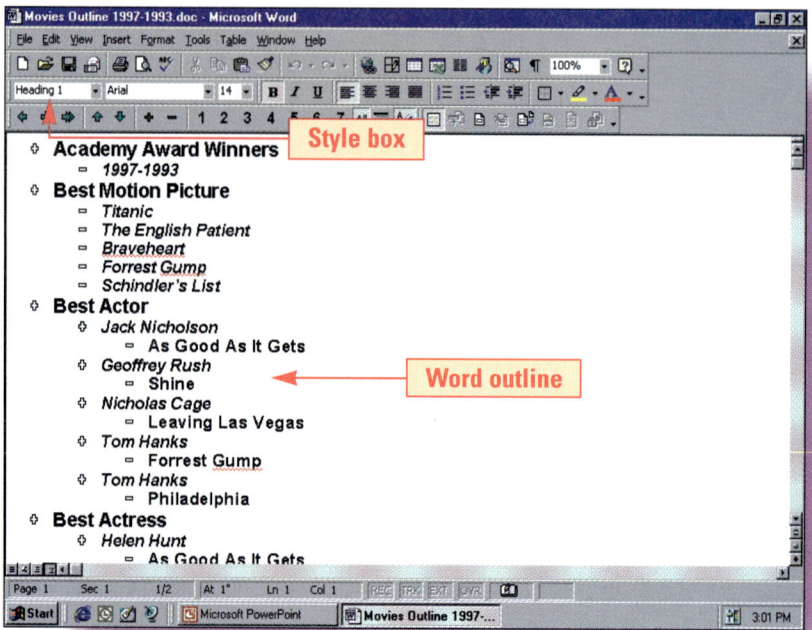

Step 5	*Click*	each line of text in the outline

As you click each line, observe the Style box on the Formatting toolbar, the styles are Heading 1, Heading 2, and Heading 3. Because Tracy used heading styles to create the outline, this should be an easy integration from Word to PowerPoint.

Step 6	*Click*	File
Step 7	*Point to*	Send To

Formatting Tips for Business Documents

MAppendix **Overview**

ost organizations follow specific formatting guidelines when preparing letters, envelopes, memorandums, and other documents to ensure the documents present a professional appearance. In this appendix you learn how to format different size letters, interoffice memos, envelopes, and formal outlines. You also review a list of style guides and learn how to use proofreader's marks.

appendix

C.a Formatting Letters

The quality and professionalism of a company's business correspondence can affect how customers, clients, and others view a company. That correspondence represents the company to those outside it. To ensure a positive and appropriate image, many companies set special standards for margins, typeface, and font size for their business correspondence. These special standards are based on the common letter styles illustrated in this section.

Most companies use special letter paper with the company name and address (and sometimes a company logo or picture) preprinted on the paper. The preprinted portion is called a **letterhead** and the paper is called **letterhead paper**. When you create a letter, the margins vary depending on the style of your letterhead and the length of your letter. Most letterheads use between 1 inch and 2 inches of the page from the top of the sheet. There are two basic business correspondence formats: block format and modified block format. When you create a letter in **block format**, all the text is placed flush against the left margin. This includes the date, the letter address information, the salutation, the body, the complimentary closing, and the signature information. The body of the letter is single spaced with a blank line between paragraphs.[1] Figure C-1 shows a short letter in the block format with standard punctuation.

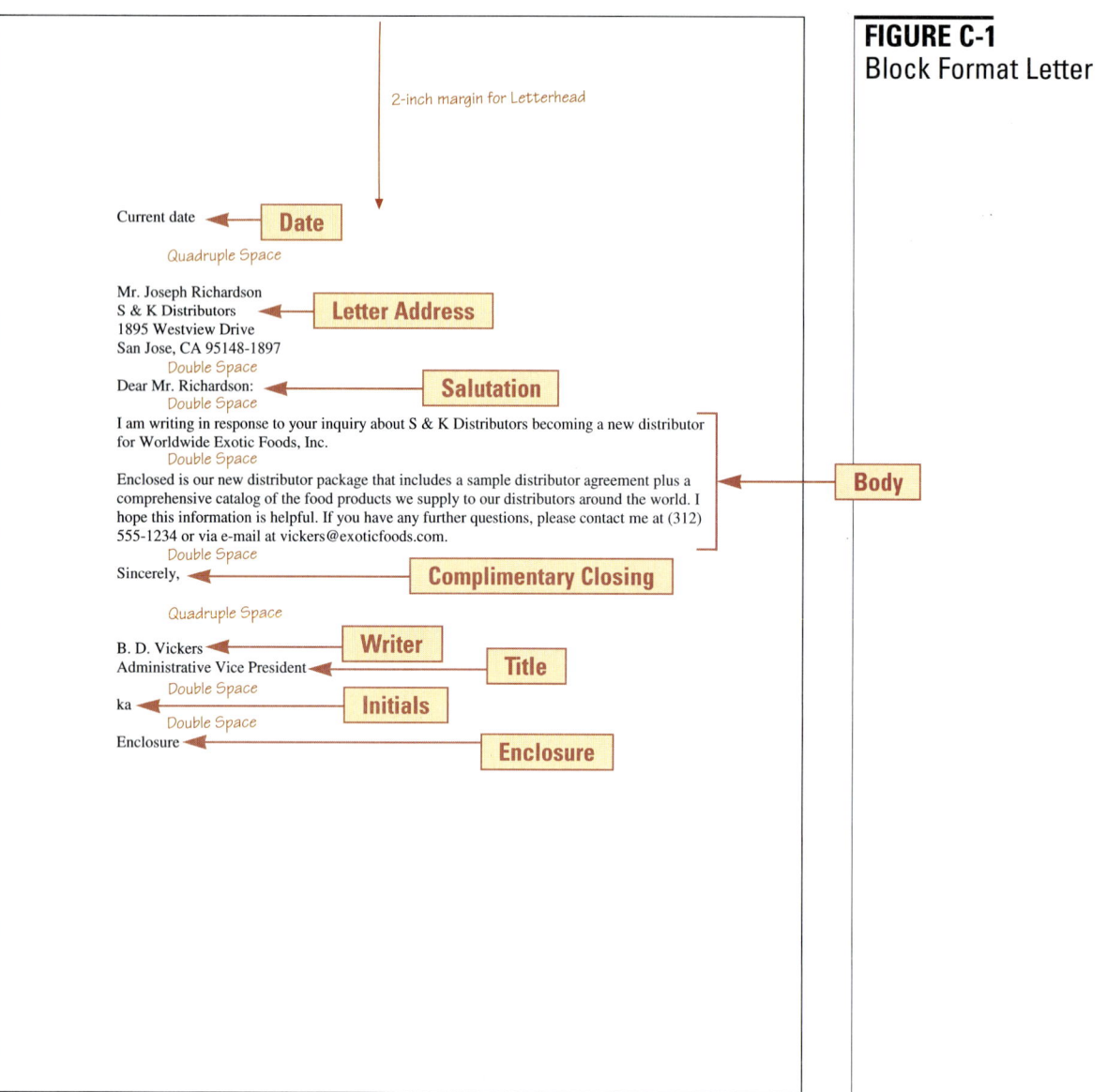

FIGURE C-1
Block Format Letter

QUICK TIP

When you key a letter on plain paper in the modified block format, the return address usually appears near the right margin and above the date, with one blank line between the return address and the date.

In the **modified block format**, the date begins near the center of the page or near the right margin. The closing starts near the center or right margin. Paragraphs can be either flush against the left margin or indented. Figure C-2 shows a short letter in the modified block format with standard punctuation.

Both the block and modified block styles use the same spacing for the non-body portions. Three blank lines separate the date from the addressee information, one blank line separates the addressee information from the salutation, one blank line separates the salutation from the body of the letter, and one blank line separates the body of the letter from the complimentary closing. There are three blank lines between the complimentary closing and the writer's name. If a typist's initials appear below the name, a blank line separates the writer's name from the initials. If an enclosure is noted, the word "Enclosure" appears below the typist's initials with a blank line separating them. Finally, when typing the return address or addressee information, one space separates the state and the postal code (ZIP+4).

FIGURE C-2
Modified Block
Format Letter

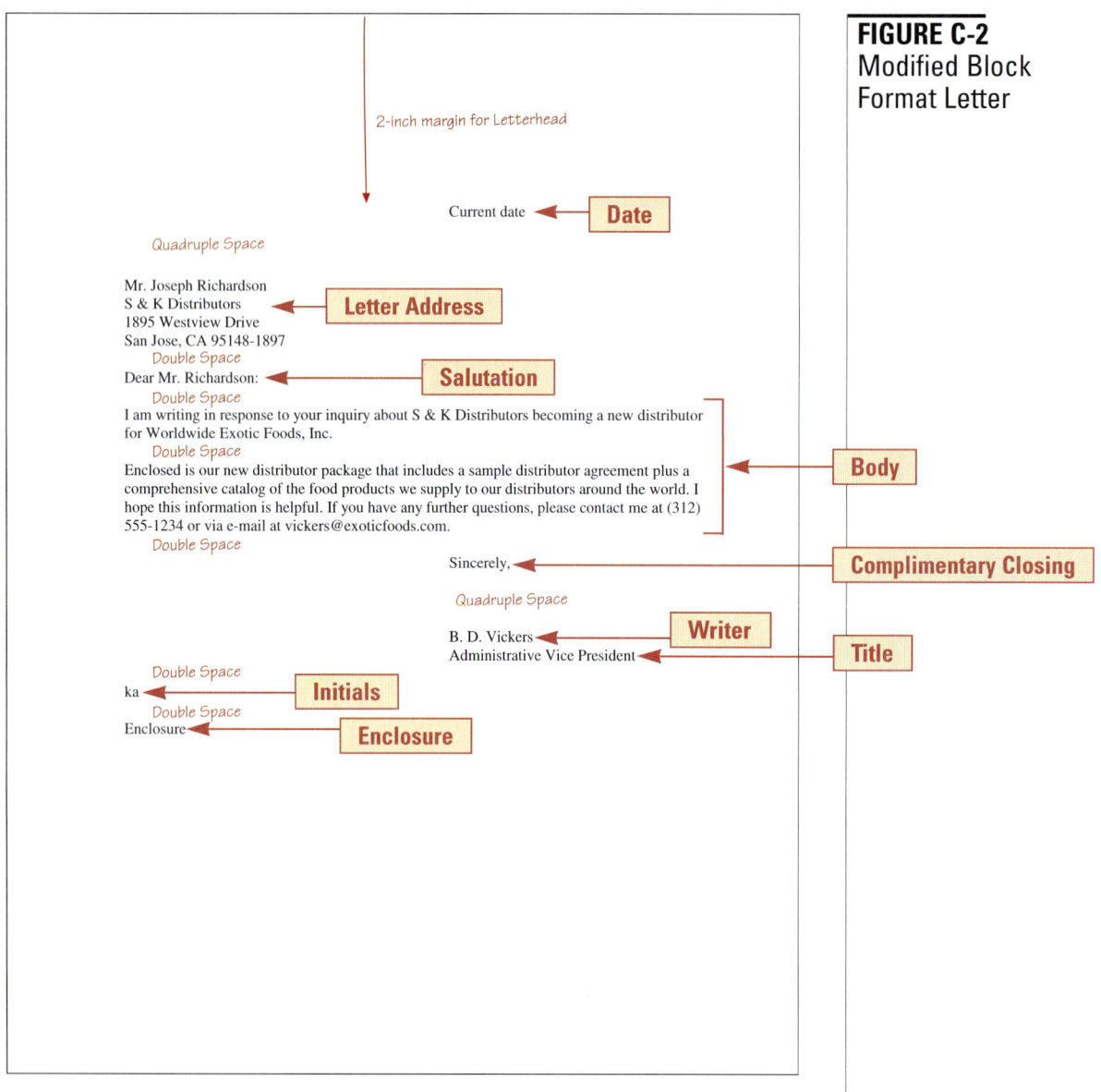

C.b Inserting Mailing Notations

Mailing notations add information to a business letter. For example, the mailing notations CERTIFIED MAIL or SPECIAL DELIVERY indicate how a business letter was sent. The mailing notations CONFIDENTIAL or PERSONAL indicate how the person receiving the letter should handle the letter contents. Mailing notations should be keyed in uppercase characters at the left margin two lines below the date.[2] Figure C-3 shows a mailing notation added to a block format business letter.

Current date
Double Space
CERTIFIED MAIL ◄──── **Mailing Notation**
Double Space
Mr. Joseph Richardson
S & K Distributors
1895 Westview Drive
San Jose, CA 95148-1897

Dear Mr. Richardson:

I am writing in response to your inquiry about S & K Distributors becoming a new distributor for Worldwide Exotic Foods, Inc.

Enclosed is our new distributor package that includes a sample distributor agreement plus a comprehensive catalog of the food products we supply to our distributors around the world. I hope this information is helpful. If you have any further questions, please contact me at (312) 555-1234 or via e-mail at vickers@exoticfoods.com.

Sincerely,

B. D. Vickers
Administrative Vice President

ka

Enclosure

FIGURE C-3
Mailing Notation on Letter

appendix
C

C.c Formatting Envelopes

Two U. S. Postal Service publications, *The Right Way* (Publication 221), and *Postal Addressing Standards* (Publication 28) available from the U. S. Post Office, provide standards for addressing letter envelopes. The U. S. Postal Service uses optical character readers (OCRs) and barcode sorters (BCSs) to increase the speed, efficiency, and accuracy in processing mail. To get a letter delivered more quickly, envelopes should be addressed to take advantage of this automation process.

Table C-1 lists the minimum and maximum size for letters. The post office cannot process letters smaller than the minimum size. Letters larger than the maximum size cannot take advantage of automated processing and must be processed manually.

TABLE C-1
Minimum and Maximum
Letter Dimensions

Dimension	Minimum	Maximum
Height	3½ inches	6⅛ inches
Length	5 inches	11½ inches
Thickness	.007 inch	¼ inch

The delivery address should be placed inside a rectangular area on the envelope that is approximately ⅝ inch from the top and bottom edge of the envelope and ½ inch from the left and right edge of the envelope. This is called the **OCR read area**. All the lines of the delivery address must fit within this area and no lines of the return address should extend into this area. To assure the delivery address is placed in the OCR read area, begin the address approximately ½ inch left of center and on approximately line 14.[3]

The lines of the delivery address should be in this order:

1. any optional nonaddress data, such as advertising or company logos, must be placed above the delivery address
2. any information or attention line
3. the name of the recipient
4. the street address
5. the city, state, and postal code (ZIP+4)

The delivery address should be complete, including apartment or suite numbers and delivery designations, such as RD (road), ST (street), or NW (northwest). Leave the area below and on both sides of the delivery address blank. Use uppercase characters and a sans serif font (such as Arial) for the delivery address. Omit all punctuation except the hyphen in the ZIP+4 code.

Figure C-4 shows a properly formatted business letter envelope.

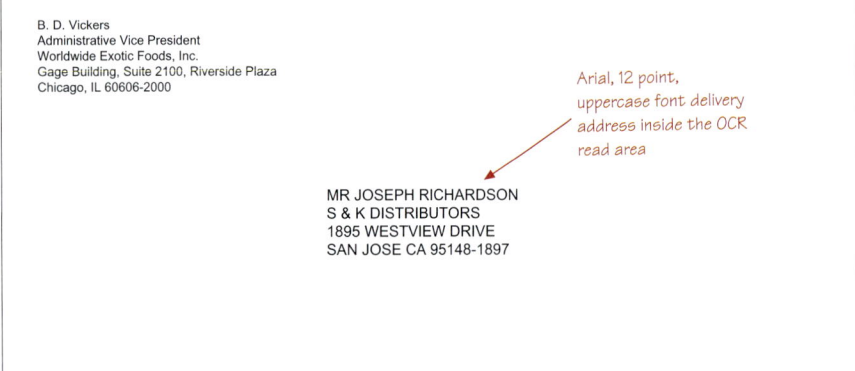

> **QUICK TIP**
>
> Foreign addresses should include the country name in uppercase characters as the last line of the delivery address. The postal code, if any, should appear on the same line as the city.

FIGURE C-4
Business Letter Envelope

appendix
C

C.d Formatting Interoffice Memorandums

Business correspondence that is sent within a company is usually prepared as an **interoffice memorandum**, also called a **memo**, rather than a letter. There are many different interoffice memo styles used in offices today, and word processing applications usually provide several memo templates based on different memo styles. Also, just as with business letters that are sent outside the company, many companies set special standards for margins, typeface, and font size for their interoffice memos.

A basic interoffice memo should include lines for "TO:", "FROM:", "DATE:", and "SUBJECT:" followed by the body text. Memos can be prepared on blank paper or on paper that includes a company name and even a logo. The word MEMORANDUM is often included. Figure C-5 shows a basic interoffice memorandum.

FIGURE C-5
Interoffice Memorandum

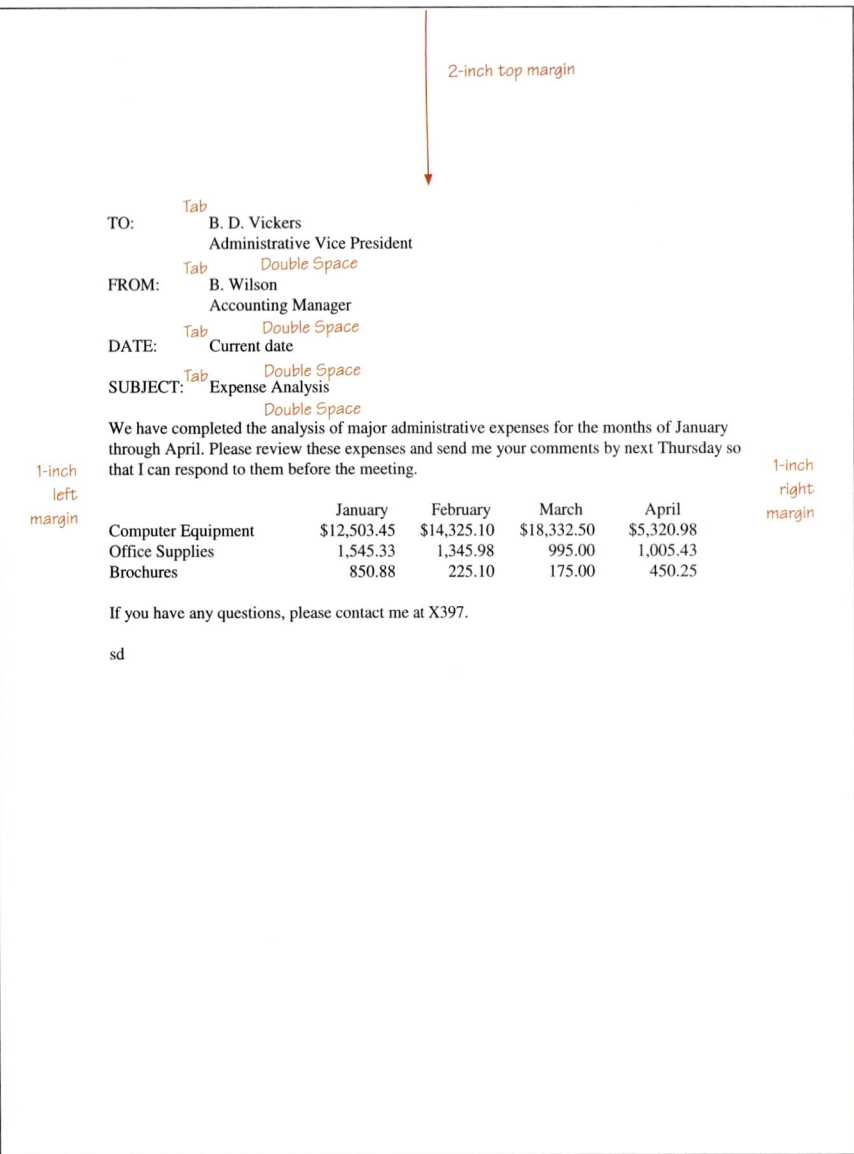

TO: B. D. Vickers
Administrative Vice President

FROM: B. Wilson
Accounting Manager

DATE: Current date

SUBJECT: Expense Analysis

We have completed the analysis of major administrative expenses for the months of January through April. Please review these expenses and send me your comments by next Thursday so that I can respond to them before the meeting.

	January	February	March	April
Computer Equipment	$12,503.45	$14,325.10	$18,332.50	$5,320.98
Office Supplies	1,545.33	1,345.98	995.00	1,005.43
Brochures	850.88	225.10	175.00	450.25

If you have any questions, please contact me at X397.

sd

2-inch top margin

Tab
Double Space
1-inch left margin
1-inch right margin

appendix
C

C.e Formatting Formal Outlines

Companies use outlines to organize data for a variety of purposes, such as reports, meeting agenda, and presentations. Word processing applications usually offer special features to help you create an outline. If you want to follow a formal outline format, you may need to add formatting to outlines created with these special features.

Margins for a short outline of two or three topics should be set at 1½ inches for the top margin and 2 inches for the left and right margins. For a longer outline, use a 2-inch top margin and 1-inch left and right margins.

The outline level-one text should be in uppercase characters. Second-level text should be treated like a title, with the first letter of the main words capitalized. Capitalize only the first letter of the first word at the third level. Double space before and after level one and single space the remaining levels.

Include at least two parts at each level. For example, you must have two level-one entries in an outline (at least I. and II.). If there is a second level following a level-one entry, it must contain at least two entries (at least A. and B.). All numbers must be aligned at the period and all subsequent levels must begin under the text of the preceding level, not under the number.[4]

Figure C-6 shows a formal outline prepared using the Word Outline Numbered list feature with additional formatting to follow a formal outline.

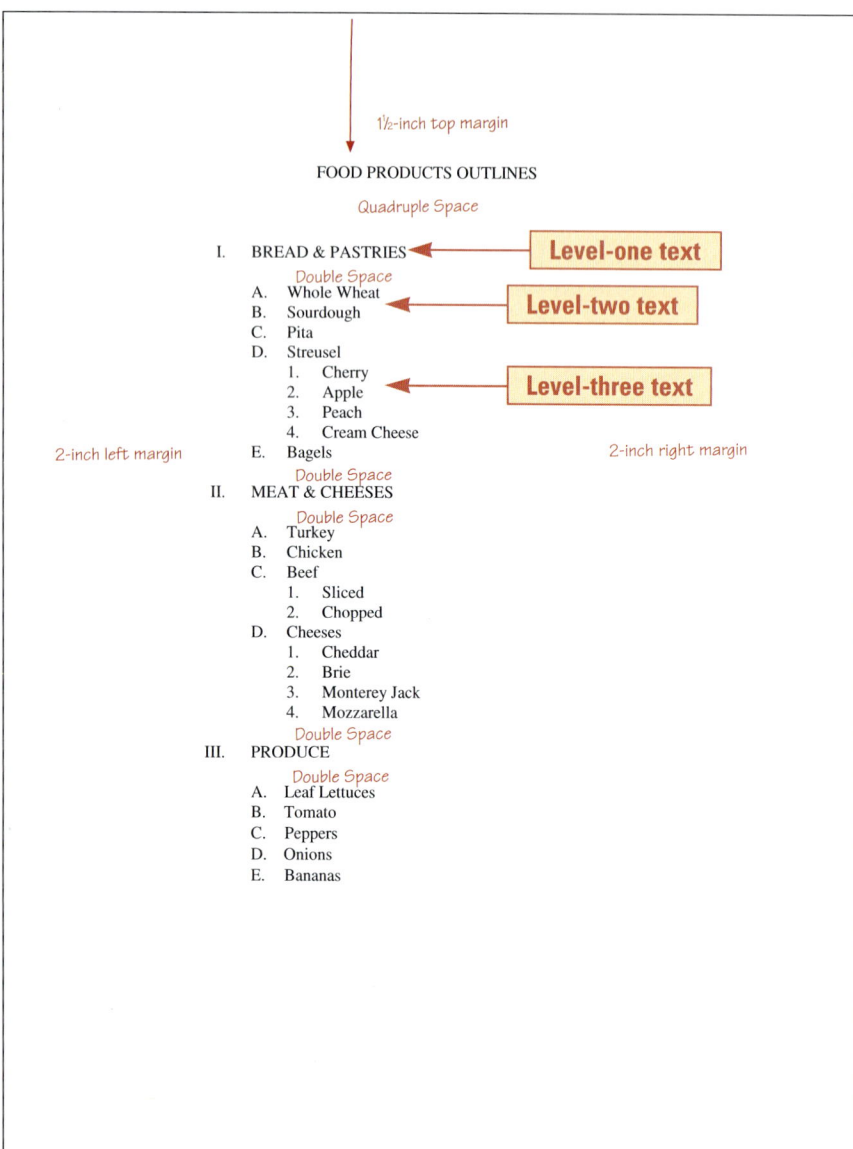

FIGURE C-6
Formal Outline

appendix
C

C.f Using Proofreader's Marks

Standard proofreader's marks enable an editor or proofreader to make corrections or change notations in a document that can be recognized by anyone familiar with the marks. The following list illustrates standard proofreader's marks.

Defined		Examples
Paragraph	¶	¶ Begin a new paragraph at this
Insert a character	∧	point. Ins^e^rt a letter here.
Delete	ℓ	Delete ~~these words.~~ ℓ Disregard
Do not change	stet or ...	the previous correction. To
Transpose	tr	transpose is to around turn.
Move to the left	⊏	[Move this copy to the left.
Move to the right	⊐	Move this copy to the right.]
No paragraph	No ¶	No ¶ Do not begin a new paragraph
Delete and close up		here. Delete the hyphen from
		pre‑empt and close up the space.
Set in caps	Caps or ≡	a sentence begins with a capital
Set in lower case	lc or /	letter. This Word should not
Insert a period	⊙	be capitalized. Insert a period⊙
Quotation marks	⌄" "⌄	"Quotation marks and a comma
Comma	∧	should be placed here he said.
Insert space	#	Space between these#words. An
Apostrophe	∨	apostrophe is whats needed here.
Hyphen	=	Add a hyphen to Kilowatt=hour. Close
Close up	◡	up the extra spa ce.
Use superior figure	∨	Footnote this sentence. Set
Set in italic	ital. or ___	the words, _sine qua non_, in italics.
Move up		This word is too ⌐low.⌐ That word is
Move down		too ⌐high.⌐

C.g Using Style Guides

A **style guide** provides a set of rules for punctuating and formatting text. There are a number of style guides used by writers, editors, business document proofreaders, and publishers. You can purchase style guides at a commercial bookstore, an online bookstore, or a college bookstore. Your local library likely has copies of different style guides and your instructor may have copies of several style guides for reference. Some popular style guides are *The Chicago Manual of Style* (The University of Chicago Press), *The Professional Secretary's Handbook* (Barron's), *The Holt Handbook* (Harcourt Brace College Publishers), and the *MLA Style Manual and Guide to Scholarly Publishing* (The Modern Language Association of America).

appendix
C

Endnotes

[1] Jerry W. Robinson et al., *Keyboarding and Information Processing* (Cincinnati: South-Western Educational Publishing, 1997).

[2] Ibid.

[3] Ibid.

[4] Ibid.

Index

Explanation of Prefixes

AB = Access Beginning
AP = Appendixes
AX = Access Integration
EB = Excel Beginning
EX = Excel Integration
OF = Office
OL = Outlook
PB = PowerPoint Beginning
PX = PowerPoint Integration
WB = Word Beginning
WI = Word Intermediate

Special Characters

* (asterisk), WB 9
\ (backward slash), WB 9
: (colon), WB 9
© (copyright), WI 146
= (equal sign), EB 14
/ (forward slash), WB 9
– (minus sign), AP 14, WI 118
¶ (paragraph mark character), WB 12
| (pipe symbol), WB 9
+ (plus sign), AP 14, WI 118, WI 119
? (question mark), WB 9
" (quotation mark), WB 9
; (semicolon), WB 9
(space between words), WB 12
=SUM(ABOVE), WI 63
(tab character), WB 12
3-D button, WI 43
3-D effects, adding, PB 79
3-D shapes, WI 43, WI 45

A

absolute cell references in formulas, EB 63, EB 64

Access 2000, OF 3, OF 10, OF 17, OF 21, OF 31
creating and adding hyperlinks, AX 20–22
creating e-mail messages from within Access, AX 22–25
database views in, AB 6
defining, AB 3
dialog box of, AB 4
exiting, AB 17, AB 18
exporting Excel data to, EX 9–11
getting help in, AB 7
identifying objects in, AB 8–17
integrating other applications, AX 20–25
introduction to, AB 2–23
opening the application, AB 3–4
querying Excel data from, EX 11–14
using Excel data with, AX 11–19
using the Office Assistant in, AB 7
viewing the window, AB 5–7
active cell, EB 4
editing in, EB 11–12
active desktop, AP 2
Add or Remove buttons, WB 124
adding
Clip Gallery/clip art images, PB 50–52
Command button to a form, AX 23
pictures to records, AB 61–63, AB 64
slides to Outline view, PB 30–31
text to AutoShapes, PB 84–86
Web address to a table, AX 22
WordArt to slides, PB 62–64
Word table to PowerPoint slide, PX 14–15
Address bar, OF 57, AP 5
address book, OL 8, OL 29, OL 30, OL 41, EX 16, EX 18, EX 19
address entered with AutoText, WB 168
Align Left button, WB 131, WB 136
Align Right button, WB 130, WB 136
alignment formats, WB 129–131, WI 74
alignment
of cell content, changing, EB 35–36, EB 45
of objects, PB 81–84
of text, PB 33–34
All Borders command, EB 41
Allow Zero Length property, AB 36
ALT key, EB 4, EB 55, EX 3
AltaVista, OF 60, OF 61

Always create backup copy option, WB 33
America OnLine, OF 55, OF 62
analyze, AB 6
animation effects, WB 87–88, WB 96, WB 97
Application Close button, WB 21
application Control-menu icon, OF 4
applications. *See also specific applications*
closing, OF 16, OF 17
starting, OF 7, OF 17
Apply Design Template, PB 16, PB 19
Apply to All button, PB 60
Appointment Recurrence dialog box, OL 15
appointment scheduling, OL 12, OL 29, OL 30
arguments, EB 16
ARPAnet, OF 51, OF 62
Arrange All command, PX 12
arrow keys, EB 9, EB 104
to move images, PB 54
to move objects, PB 86
arrows, drawing, PB 76
ascending order, AB 38
Attach File button, WB 18
Attendee Availability tab, OF 41. *See also* Outlook Meeting Window
AutoClip Art, PB 51
AutoComplete feature, WB 66–67, WB 68, EB 61
AutoContent wizard, PB 3, PB 12
AutoCorrect dialog box, WB 57–58, WB 76, WB 94
AutoCorrect Exceptions dialog box, WB 60, WB 61
AutoCorrect, PB 28–30
commands review, PB 43
dialog box, PB 28, PB 29
AutoCorrect tool, WB 57, 58–59, WB 68, WB 69, WB 94
AutoFill, EB 30
AutoFit, EB 32–33, EB 45
AutoFormat As You Type feature, WB 76, WB 92, WB 96, WI 98
AutoHide, OF 29
setting exceptions to, WB 60–62

AutoLayouts, PB 12
  bulleted list, PB 13
Automatically add words to list
  option, WB 60
AutoNumber data type, AB 32
AutoRecover feature, WB 33
AutoShape command, PB 84
AutoShapes, PB 77, WI 38, WI 40,
  WI 45
  adding text to, PB 84–86
  commands review, PB 88
  fill colors, changing, PB 78–79
AutoSum button, EB 17, WI 63
AutoText entries, WB 62–66, WB 68,
  WB 69
  address entry, WB 168
  custom, WB 63–65
  deleting, WB 66
  editing, WB 65–66
  inserting, WB 64–65, WB 68, WB 69
  printing, WB 66, WB 69
  standard, WB 62–63
  storing and sharing, WB 65
AutoText toolbar, WB 64
Available Fields: list box, AB 72–73
Avery labels, WB 166, WB 167, WB 170
axes, formatting, EB 103–104

B

Back Button, WB 9
Background command, PB 60
Background dialog box, PB 60
bar code sorter (BCS), AP 24
BCS. *See* bar code sorter
bitmaps, WI 42
Blank presentation, PB 3
block format (block style), WB 29,
  WB 44
Bold button, WB 81, WB 89, WB 97,
  WI 3
boldface, EB 33, EB 35, EB 45
bold style, applying, WB 80–81, WB 96,
  WB 97
bookmark, WI 146, WI 154
Bookmark dialog box, WI 146
Borders and Shading command,
  WI 43, WI 66–67
borders, applying, WI 66–67, WI 69,
  WI 81, WI 82, WI 97
  adding, EB 40–42, EB 45
  dotted, EB 59

Border tab, EB 41, EB 42
Break dialog box, WI 10
Browse option buttons, WI 7
bulleted list
  creating, WB 91–92, WI 144–145
  multilevel, WB 92
Bulleted List AutoLayout, PB 13
bullets, PB 13, WB 91, WB 96, WB 97
  commands review, PB 43
  demoting, PB 26–27
  moving, in Outline view, PB 31,
    PB 32
  promoting, PB 26–27
  second-level, PB 26–28
Bullets and Numbering dialog box,
  WB 91
Bullets button, WB 92, WB 97
bullet slides, PB 13, PX 9
  adding, PB 26
bullet symbols, changing, PB 37–38
business documents, formatting,
  WB 105
button(s), OF 21. *See also individual*
  button names
  adding to toolbar, OF 23, OF 27
  default, OF 23

C

calculated controls, AB 83
calculations in table, WI 62–64
Calendar (Outlook), OL 11–16
caption property, AB 36
case options, WB 90–91, WB 96, WB 97
categories primary key, AB 38
categories table in Design View, AB 35
category axis, EB 103
cell, AB 53, AB 64, WB 169, WI 54,
  WI 56, WI 81, WI 82
  address, WI 64
  erasing boundary of, WI 71
  formats, WI 59, WI 61
  merging, WI 61
  modifying alignment of contents,
    EB 35–36
  selecting, WI 57–59
  splitting, WI 61, WI 62
cell references, EB 4
  absolute, EB 63, EB 64
  adding to formulas, EB 15–16
  commands review, EB 74
  mixed, EB 63, EB 64
  relative, EB 63–64

cells, EB 4
  clearing contents and formatting,
    EB 13
  commands review, EB 22
  deleting, EB 61–62
  editing, EB 11–12
  inserting, EB 61–62
  merging, to create worksheet title,
    EB 29
  range of, EB 9–10
  selecting, EB 9–11
center alignment, WB 129, WB 130
center-aligned tabs, setting,
  WB 110–111, WB 116
Center button, WB 130, WB 136,
  EB 29, EB 35
Change Case
  command, WB 90, WB 97
  dialog box, WB 91
Change Text Direction button, WI 74,
  WI 82
changes, automatically saved, AB 17,
  AB 18
channel. *See* Internet channel
character effects, applying WB 83–88,
  WB 96, WB 97. *See also individual*
  formats: outline, small caps, strikethrough, subscript, superscript
character formats
  multiple, WB 88
  repeating, WB 88–89
  viewing, WB 127
character formatting, WB 80–86
  automatic, WB 76
  removing, WB 91
character spacing, WB 87, WB 127
character style, WI 92, WI 93, WI 107,
  WI 108
charts, OF 3
  Chart wizard for creating,
    EB 88–102
  commands review, EB 108
  components of, EB 102
  embedded, EB 99, EB 106–107
  linking Excel to PowerPoint slide,
    PX 19–23
  linking to PowerPoint presentation,
    EX 5–8
  objects, EB 101, EB 102
  previewing, EB 105–106
  printing, EB 105–106, EB 107
  resizing, EB 106–107, EX 6

sheets, EB 99
titles, changing, EB 103
charts, formatting and modifying, EB 102
   adding data tables, EB 104–105
   axes, EB 103–104
   fonts, changing, EB 103
Chart wizard, EB 88–102
Chart wizard button, EB 99
chat, OF 39, OF 47, OF 53
Check boxes, AB 83, AB 91
circles, drawing, PB 75–76
Clear All command, EB 13
Clear Clipboard button, WB 39
Clear Contents command, EB 13
Clear Formats command, EB 13
clearing contents and of cells, EB 13
click, AP 4, AP 13, OF 8
Click and Type feature, WB 43, WB 115, WI 40, WI 145
clip art, adding to records, AB 61–63
Clip Gallery/clip art images, WI 41
   accessing, PB 50
   adding, PB 50–52
   adding to slide master, PB 59–61
   commands review, PB 66
   copying and pasting, PB 61–62
   deleting, PB 54
   editing, PB 54–58
   flipping and rotating, PB 57–58
   grouping and ungrouping, PB 57–58
   inserting images from other sources, PB 59
   moving, PB 53
   online clips, PB 50
   recoloring and cropping, PB 54–57
   resizing, PB 53–54
clip, WI 39
Clipboard. *See also* Office Clipboard and Windows Clipboard
Clipboard toolbar, AB 59, PB 61–62, WB 38
Clippit the Office Assistant, WB 4
Clips Online button, PB 52
Close button, AP 4, AP 7, EB 20, EB 61, OF 4, PB 4, PB 5, PB 17, PB 40, WB 3, WB 4, WB 11, WB 21
Close command, PB 11, PB 17, PB 19
Close Window button, EB 20, OF 6, WB 4, WB 11, WB 21

closing
   presentations, PB 11
   slide master, PB 40
   workbooks, EB 20, EB 22
collaboration, OF 37, OF 38, OF 39, OF 47
collapsing outlines, EB 70
collating, EB 91
collating option, WB 152
Collect and Paste feature, WB 38, WB 44
color
   default, PB 78
   fill colors of shapes and AutoShapes, changing, PB 78–79
   of a drawing shape, PB 75
   of fonts, changing, EB 34, EB 45
   of WordArt objects, changing, PB 63
   recoloring clip art images, PB 54–57
   shading, adding, EB 40, EB 42–43
column(s), EB 3, WI 54, WI 56, WI 81, WI 82
   adding labels to, EB 30–32
   balancing, WI 35
   capitalization in, EB 16
   changing width of, AB 39–40, WI 37, WI 45, WI 65, WI 66
   creating, WI 33–38, WI 45, WI 46
   deleting, EB 62
   formatting, WI 36–37
   freezing and unfreezing, EB 67–68
   hiding and unhiding, EB 67–68
   inserting, EB 62, WI 60–61
   labels, WI 59
   length, WI 35
   marker, WI 56
   modifying size of, EB 32–33, EB 45
   selecting, EB 10, WI 57–59
   viewing, WI 35, WI 45
column chart, EB 99
column headings, EB 3
Column Width dialog box, EB 32
Columns button, WI 34, WI 45, WI 46
Columns dialog box, WI 36, WI 37, WI 45
Combo Box wizard, AB 84–86, AB 91
Combo boxes, AB 84–86, AB 91
Command button, adding to a form, AX 23
commands, EB 22, EB 45, EB 74, EB 92, EB 108, EX 26, PB 19, PB 25,

PB 43, PB 66, PB 88, OL 30, OF 17, OF 32, OF 47, OF 63, WB 21, WB 44, WB 69, WB 97, WB 116, WB 136, WB 153, WB 170, WI 25, WI 46, WI 82, WI 108, WI130, WI 154. *See also specific command*
comma-separated text files, EX 15
commercial network, OF 55. *See also* America Online, Microsoft Network
Compact and Repair tool. AB 40
conditional formatting, AB 90
conferencing, OF 36
Contact dialog box, OL 17–18
Contact Manager (Outlook), OL 8, OL 16–18, OL 29, OL 30
Contacts folder (Outlook), OL 16
Contents pane, AP 13
Control-menu icon, AP 4, OF 6, PB 4
Control toolbox, using to add and modify controls, AB 83–87
Control wizards button, AX 23
Convert Text to Table dialog box, WI 78
copy and paste, WB 36
Copy button, EB 59, WB 38
Copy command, EB 59, EB 60, PB 61, PB 81
Copy Here command, WB 39
copying
   data into a table, AB 57–60
   data with copy and paste, EB 59–61, EB 74
   data with drag and drop, EB 54–55
   fill handle, EB 30
   Format Painter for, PB 80
   guides, PB 74
   images, PB 61–62
   objects, PB 81
copying worksheets, EB 57–58, EB 74
copyright symbol. *See* special characters section
correcting data in a table, AB 55–57
Create New Folder button, WB 17
Create Replica menu command, AB 28
create table, AB 29
creating
   and adding hyperlinks, AX 20–22
   custom form, AB 77–80, AB 91
   database, AB 26–27
   e-mail messages from within Access, AX 22–25, AX 26

form with Form wizard, AB 71–77
table in Design View, AB 31–40
table using the Table wizard,
  AB 29–31
Criteria: row, AB 12
cropping clip art images, PB 54–57
CTRL + ALT keys, EB 55
CTRL key, EB 57, EX 5, PB 74, PB 76,
  PB 77, PB 82
Currency data type, AB 32
custom form, creating, AB 77–80,
  AB 91
Customize Outline Numbered List
  dialog box, WI 123
customizing toolbars and menus,
  PB 5
cut and paste, EB 58–59, EB 74, WB 36
Cut command, EB 58, EB 59

D

data
  copying and moving, EB 54–55,
    EB 58–61
  copying into a table, AB 57–60
  correcting in a table, AB 55–57
  detail, EB 68
  embedding, in a Word document,
    EX 2–5
  entering and editing into tables,
    AB 52–69, EB 7–9
  exporting, to Access database,
    EX 9–11
  importing from other applications,
    EX 15–16
  labels, EB 102, EB 104
  linking to, AX 17–19
  merging, AX 7–8
  modifying in a table, AB 55–60
  points, EB 102, EB 105
  querying from Access database,
    EX 11–14
  series, EB 102
data access pages (DAP), AB 14–16,
  AB 18
data integrity, AB 37
data source, selecting, AX 4–5
data tables, adding to charts,
  EB 104–105
data types, AB 31–33, AB 46
  AutoNumber, AB 32
  Currency, AB 32
  Date/Time, AB 32

Hyperlink, AB 33
Lookup wizard, AB 33
Memo, AB 32
Number, AB 32
OLE Object, AB 33
Text, AB 32
Yes/No, AB 33
database, OF 3
  changing table structures for,
    AB 25–26
  creating, AB 26–27
  definition of, AB 3, AB 18
  designing and creating, AB 24–51
  inputs and outputs for, AB 25
  linked and embedded objects,
    AB 61
  planning, AB 25–26
  saving, AB 27–28
database objects, exporting, AX 2–8
database records, exporting to Excel,
  AX 9–11
Database toolbar, AB 6, AB 14
Database wizard, AB 4, AB 26
datasheet, using to enter records,
  AB 53–54
datasheet view, AB 6, AB 18, AB 39,
  AB 46
date(s)
  entering, AB 54, EB 7–9
  values of, EB 40
Date and Time dialog box, WB 32
date and time field, inserting, WB 32,
  WB 44, WB 66–67
Date/Time data type, AB 32
Decimal Tab alignment button, WI 65,
  WI 82
decimal tabs, setting, WB 111–112,
  WI 65, WI 81, WI 82
decimals, EB 37–39
Decrease Font Size button, PB 33
Decrease Indent button, WB 132,
  WB 136
default settings, OF 8, OF 25
Default Value property, AB 36
Define Name dialog box, EB 65–66
Delete command, EB 13, EB 56
Delete dialog box, EB 61
DELETE key, EB 13, EB 59, EB 107,
  PB 54
deleting
  cells, EB 61–62
  clip art images, PB 54
  columns, EB 62

commands review, EB 74
fields, AB 43
multiple objects, PB 80–81
named ranges, EB 65–66
records from a table, AB 60
rows, EB 62
worksheets, EB 56, EB 59
delimiters, EX 15
Delivery point barcode, WB 162
Demote button, PB 27
demoting bullets, PB 26–27
descending order, AB 38
design grid, AB 12
Design Templates, PB 3
  applying, PB 11–14
  changing, PB 16
  commands review, PB 19
design view, AB 6, AB 18, AB 71, AB 80,
  AB 82, AB 86–87, AB 90, AB 91
  creating tables in, AB 31–40
  modifying tables with, AB 40–44,
    AB 46
  opening a query in, AB 11–12
  using to add fields, AB 34–35,
    AB 46
designing and creating a database,
  AB 24–51
designing and using basic forms,
  AB 70–96
desktop, AP 1
  icons, WB 10
  shortcuts, creating, AP 16
Desktop toolbar, AP 5
destination file, PX 2, PX 6
detail data, EB 68
dialog box tabs, AP 7
dialog boxes, AP 7, OF 9
  Appointment Recurrence, OL 15
  AutoCorrect Exceptions, WB 60,
    WB 61
  AutoCorrect, PB 28, PB 29,
    WB 57–58, WB 76, WB 94
  Background, PB 60
  Bookmark, WI 146
  Break, WI 10
  Bullets and Numbering, WB 91
  Change Case, WB 91
  Column Width, EB 32
  Columns, WI 36, WI 37, WI 45
  Contact, OL 17–18
  Convert Text to Table, WI 78
  Customize Outline Numbered
    List, WI 123

Date and Time, WB 32
Define Name, EB 65–66
Delete, EB 61
Envelope Options, WB 162
Envelopes and Labels, WB 161, WB 170
Find and Replace, WI 3, WI 5, WI 6, WI 8, WI 9
Font, WB 82
Format AutoShape, WI 41
Format Cells, EB 29, EB 35, EB 36, EB 39, EB 41–42
Format, EB 102, EB 103
Formula, WI 63
Header/Footer, EB 86–87
Hyphenation, WI 20
Import Text File, EX 15
Insert Clip Art, PB 51, PB 52
Insert Object, PX 16
Insert Outline, PX 11
Insert, EB 61
Line Spacing, PB 36
Manual Hyphenation, WI 21
Message (Outlook), OL 10
Modify Style, WI 99–100
More AutoShapes, PB 78
New Slide, PB 12, PB 13
Open, EB 6
Options, EB 8
Organizer, WI 100
Page Number format, WI 15
Page Numbers, WI 14
Page Setup, EB 82–83
Paste Name, EB 67
Paste Special, EX 3, PX 16, PX 21
PowerPoint, PB 3
Print, EB 88, EB 90–91
Recolor Picture, PB 55
Routing Slip, EX 18–19
Row Height, EB 32, EB 33
Save As, EB 18, EB 19, PB 14, WB 91
Series, EB 31
Slide Finder, PX 12–13
Sort, EB 53–54
Spelling, EB 71–72
Subtotal, EB 69
View, EB 68
WordArt Text, PB 62–63
Write–Up, PX 3
directory, OF 53, OF 60
discussion groups, OF 53
discussion items, OF 42, OF 47

disk, reformatting, AP 16
disk drive icon, AP 13
Distribute Columns Evenly button, WI 71
Distribute Rows Evenly button, WI 71
Document Control-menu icon, PB 5
Document Properties, WB 152
document(s)
    closing, WB 11, WB 17
    composing, WB 6–7
    creating, OF 9, WB 17, WB 21
    document, navigating, WB 14, WI 6
    editing, WB 7–8, WB 20, WB 21
    e-mail notice of changes to, OF 46
    Find and Replace options, WI 8–WI 9
    formatting, AP 17–29, WI 3
    opening, WB 11–12, WB 21
    previewing, WB 10–11, WB 21
    printing, WB 10–11, WB 20, WB 21, WB 150–152, WB 153
    removing text from, WB 20, WB 21, WB 40
    replacing formatting, WI 3
    saving in HTML format, WB 9, WI 138–140
    saving, WB 8–9, WB 20, WB 21
    section of, WB 6
    wizard, OF 12, WI 105–106
document view, changing, WB 13
document window, zooming, WB 13, WB 20
documentation worksheet, EB 71
domains, OF 55
double-clicking, EX 7, OF 8, PB 4, PB 10, PB 85
download, OF 51
Drafts folder (Outlook), OL 7
drag and drop, AP 8, EB 54–55, EB 74, WB 39
dragging, AP 4, AP 13, OF 8, PB 7, PB 82
    guides, PB 74
Draw Table button, WI 54, WI 71, WI 73
Draw button, PB 57
Drawing button, WI 38, WI 44
drawing objects, PB 74–76, WI 38, WI 40, WI 42, WI 45, WI 46
    arrows, PB 76
    circles, PB 75–76
    commands review, PB 88

inserting into Web pages, WI 148
    lines, PB 76
    modifying, WI 40–44
    rectangles, PB 74–75
    squares, PB 75
Drawing toolbar, PB 6, PB 57, PB 74, PB 79, WI 38–44, WI 45, WI 46,
Duplicate command, PB 81
duplicating. *See* copying

E

editing
    active cell, EB 11–12
    cell content, EB 11–12
    clip art images, PB 54–58
    Formula Bar for, EB 12
    shapes, PB 77–79
    slides, PB 32–38
    WordArt objects, PB 63–64
electronic bulletin board, OF 53
electronic "mail box", OF 54
electronic signature, OL 11
em dash. *See* special characters
e-mail attachments, OL 9
e-mail button, WB 18, WB 21
e-mail form, OL 8
e-mail message(s), OF 9, OF 40, OF 53, OL 7–11, OL 29, OL 30, WB 18
    attaching document to, OF 40
    creating from within Access, AX 22–25, AX 26
    encryption/decryption, OF 56
    forwarding, OL 9, OL 10–11
    replying to, OL 9–10
    sending workbooks via, EX 16–20
embed, defined, PX 2
embedded charts, EB 99, EB 106–107
embedded object, AB 61
embedding, WB 37
    Excel worksheet in a PowerPoint slide, PX 16–19
    PowerPoint presentation in Word document, PX 3–5
embedding Excel data in a Word document, EX 2–5
en dash. *See* special characters
    shortcut key for, WI 20, WI 33
endnotes, AP 32
end-of-cell marker, WI 56
end-of-file marker, WB 4, WB 5
end-of-row marker, WI 56

Windows Explorer
   opening, AP 12
   options, AP 13–14
wizard, OF 12, WI 105–106, WI 107,
   WI 108
Word 2000 application, OF 3, OF 9,
   OF 17
   adding Word table to PowerPoint
     slide, PX 14–15
   closing, WB 18
   integrating Excel with, EX 2–8
   linking PowerPoint presentation
     to, PX 5–7
   sending PowerPoint presentation
     to, PX 2–7
   sending Word outline to
     PowerPoint presentation, PX 7–10
   setting as e-mail editor, OL 7–8
Word document
   embedding Excel data in, EX 2–5
   embedding PowerPoint presen-
     tation in, PX 3–5
   exporting an Access table to, AX 2
   inserting slides from Word out-
     line, PX 11
   main document, AX 5
   merging Access data with, AX 2
   opening, WB 3
   viewing changes in, PX 5
word processing, OF 3
Word Window, WB 3, WB 4
word wrap, WB 20
WordArt, WI 40, WI 41
   adding to slides, PB 62–64

   commands review, PB 66
   editing objects, PB 63–64
WordArt command, PB 63
WordArt Gallery button, PB 64
WordArt Shape button, PB 64
WordArt Text dialog box, PB 62–63
WordArt toolbar, PB 63
workbook(s), EB 3
   closing, EB 20, EB 22
   commands review, EB 22
   opening, EB 5–6, EB 22
   printing entire, EB 90–91
   publishing, EX 21
   routing, EX 18–20
   saving, EB 18–20, EB 22
   saving as Web pages, EX 21–22
   sending, via e-mail, EX 16–20
workgroup, OF 35, OF 36
worksheet(s), OF 3, OF 17
   check spelling of, EB 71–72
   commands review, EB 74
   components of, EB 3–4
   copying, EB 57–58
   deleting, EB 56, EB 59
   inserting, EB 56–57
   moving, EB 57–58, EB 57–58, EB 74
   navigating, EB 6–7
   previewing and printing, EB 80–92
   renaming, EB 56
   sending, as HTML mail, EX 17–18
worksheets, formatting
   alignment of cell content, EB 35–36
   borders, adding, EB 40–42
   commands review, EB 45

   embedding Excel in a PowerPoint
     slide, PX 16–19
   fonts and font styles, changing,
     EB 33–35
   merging cells to create titles, EB 29
   modifying size of columns and
     rows, EB 32–33
   number formats, EB 37–40
   rotating text and changing
     indents, EB 36–37
   shading, adding, EB 40, EB 42–43
   working with a series to add
     labels, EB
World Wide Web (WWW), AX 26,
   OF 53, OF 62
wrapping text, PB 85
Write-Up dialog box, PX 3
WWW. *See* World Wide Web

X

x-axis, EB 100, EB 103

Y

y-axis, EB 103
Yahoo, OF 60
Yes/No data type, AB 33

Z

z-axis, EB 103
zoom, WB 13, WB 20, WB 21
Zoom button, AB 14

Working with Windows 98

T Appendix Overview

The Windows 98 operating system creates a workspace on your computer screen, called the desktop. The desktop is a graphical environment that contains icons you click with the mouse pointer to access your computer system resources or to perform a task such as opening a software application. This appendix introduces you to the Windows 98 desktop by describing the default desktop icons and showing how to access your computer resources, use menu commands and toolbar buttons to perform a task, and select dialog box options.

LEARNING OBJECTIVES

► Review the Windows 98 desktop
► Access your computer system resources
► Use menu commands and toolbar buttons
► Use the Start menu
► Review dialog box options
► Use Windows 98 shortcuts
► Understand the Recycle Bin
► Shut down Windows 98

appendix

A.a Reviewing the Windows 98 Desktop

Whenever you start your computer, the Windows 98 operating system automatically starts and the Windows 98 desktop appears on your screen. To view the Windows 98 desktop:

| Step 1 | *Turn on* | your computer and monitor |
| Step 2 | *Observe* | the Windows 98 desktop, as shown in Figure A-1 |

FIGURE A-1
Windows 98 Desktop

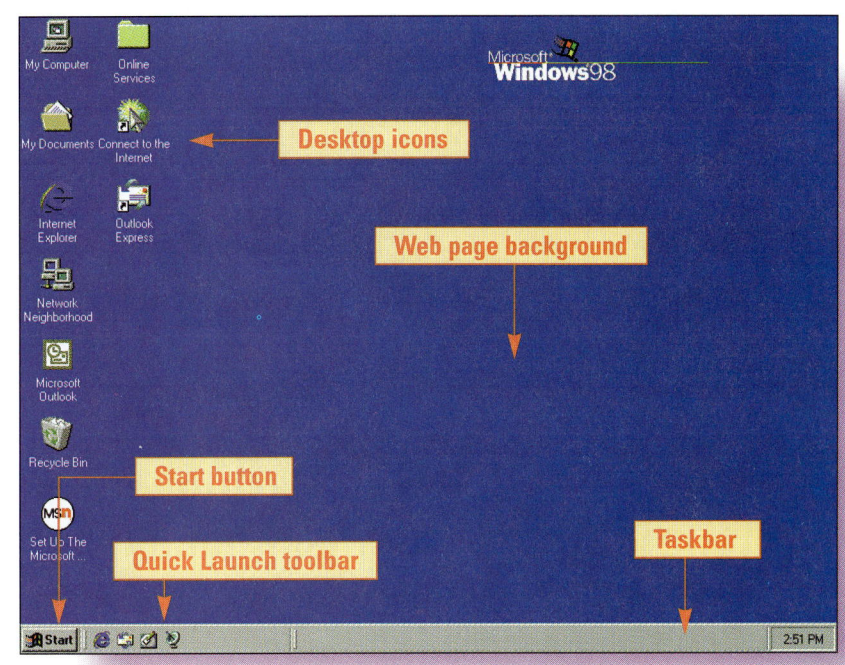

The Windows 98 desktop contains three elements: icons, background, and taskbar. The icons represent Windows objects and shortcuts to opening software applications or performing tasks. Table A-1 describes some of the default icons. By default, the background is Web-page style. The taskbar, at the bottom of the window, contains the Start button and the Quick Launch toolbar. The icon types and arrangement, desktop background, or Quick Launch toolbar on your screen might be different.

The Start button displays the Start menu, which you can use to perform tasks. By default, the taskbar also contains the **Quick Launch toolbar**, which has shortcuts to open Internet Explorer Web browser, Outlook Express e-mail software, and Internet channels, as well as to switch between the desktop and open application windows. You can customize the Quick Launch toolbar to include other toolbars.

Icon	Name	Description
🖥	My Computer	Provides access to computer system resources
📁	My Documents	Stores Office 2000 documents (by default)
e	Internet Explorer	Opens Internet Explorer Web browser
📧	Microsoft Outlook	Opens Outlook 2000 information manager software
🗑	Recycle Bin	Temporarily stores folders and files deleted from the hard drive
🖧	Network Neighborhood	Provides access to computers and printers networked in your workgroup

TABLE A-1
Common Desktop Icons

A.b Accessing Your Computer System Resources

The My Computer window provides access to your computer system resources. To open the My Computer window:

Step 1	*Point to*	the My Computer icon 🖥 on the desktop
Step 2	*Observe*	a brief description of the icon in the ScreenTip
Step 3	*Double-click*	the My Computer icon 🖥 to open the My Computer window shown in Figure A-2

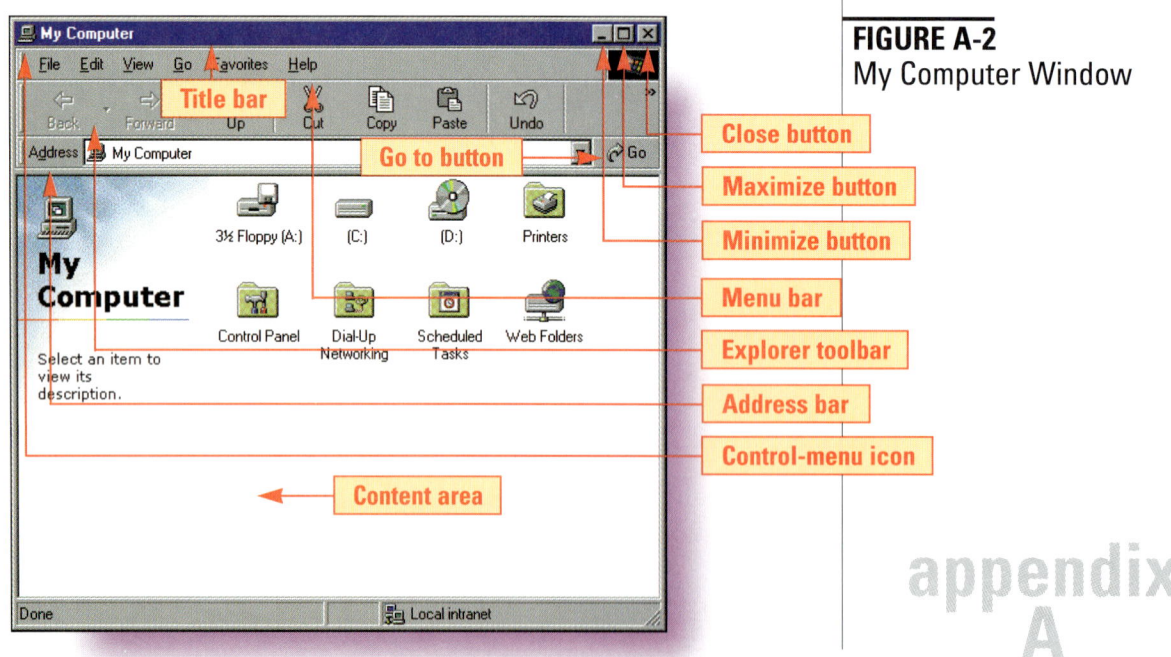

FIGURE A-2
My Computer Window

appendix
A

MOUSE TIP

Point means to place the mouse pointer on the command or item. **Click** means to press the left mouse button and release it. **Right-click** means to press the right mouse button and release it. **Double-click** means to press the left mouse button twice very rapidly. **Drag** means to hold down the left mouse button as you move the mouse pointer. **Right-drag** means to hold down the right mouse button as you move the mouse pointer. **Scroll** means to use the application scroll bar features or the IntelliMouse scrolling wheel.

A window is a rectangular area on your screen in which you view operating system options or a software application, such as Internet Explorer. Windows 98 has some common window elements. The **title bar**, at the top of the window, includes the window's Control-menu icon, the window name, and the Minimize, Restore (or Maximize), and Close buttons. The **Control-menu icon**, in the upper-left corner of the window, accesses the Control menu that contains commands for moving, restoring, sizing, minimizing, maximizing, and closing the window. The **Minimize** button, near the upper-right corner of the window, reduces the window to a taskbar button. The **Maximize** button, to the right of the Minimize button, enlarges the window to fill the entire screen viewing area above the taskbar. If the window is already maximized, the Restore button appears in its place. The **Restore** button reduces the window size. The **Close** button, in the upper-right corner, closes the window. To maximize the My Computer window:

| Step 1 | *Click* | the Maximize button 🔲 on the My Computer window title bar |
| Step 2 | *Observe* | that the My Computer window completely covers the desktop |

When you want to leave a window open, but do not want to see it on the desktop, you can minimize it. To minimize the My Computer window:

| Step 1 | *Click* | the Minimize button ▬ on the My Computer window title bar |
| Step 2 | *Observe* | the My Computer button added to the taskbar |

The minimized window is still open but not occupying space on the desktop. To view the My Computer window and then restore it to a smaller size:

Step 1	*Click*	the My Computer button on the taskbar to view the window
Step 2	*Click*	the Restore button 🗗 on the My Computer title bar
Step 3	*Observe*	that the My Computer window is reduced to a smaller window on the desktop

You can move and size a window with the mouse pointer. To move the My Computer window:

| Step 1 | *Position* | the mouse pointer on the My Computer title bar |

| Step 2 | *Drag* | the window down and to the right approximately ½ inch |
| Step 3 | *Drag* | the window back to the center of the screen |

Several Windows 98 windows—My Computer, My Documents, and Windows Explorer—have the same menu bar and toolbar features. These windows are sometimes called **Explorer-style windows**. When you size an Explorer-style window too small to view all its icons, a vertical or horizontal scroll bar may appear. A scroll bar includes scroll arrows and a scroll box for viewing different parts of the window contents.

To size the My Computer window:

Step 1	*Position*	the mouse pointer on the lower-right corner of the window
Step 2	*Observe*	that the mouse pointer becomes a black, double-headed sizing pointer
Step 3	*Drag*	the lower-right corner boundary diagonally up approximately ½ inch and release the mouse button
Step 4	*Click*	the right scroll arrow on the horizontal scroll bar to view hidden icons
Step 5	*Size*	the window twice as large to remove the horizontal scroll bar

You can open the window associated with any icon in the My Computer window by double-clicking it. Explorer-style windows open in the same window, not separate windows. To open the Control Panel Explorer-style window:

| Step 1 | *Double-click* | the Control Panel icon |
| Step 2 | *Observe* | that the Address bar displays the Control Panel icon and name, and the content area displays the Control Panel icons for accessing computer system resources |

A.c Using Menu Commands and Toolbar Buttons

You can click a menu command or toolbar button to perform specific tasks in a window. The **menu bar** is a special toolbar located below the window title bar that contains the File, Edit, View, Go, Favorites, and Help menus. The **toolbar**, located below the menu bar, contains shortcut "buttons" you click with the mouse pointer to execute a variety of commands. You can use the Back and Forward

---

QUICK TIP

The Explorer-style windows and the Internet Explorer Web browser are really one Explorer feature integrated into Windows 98 that you can use to find information on your hard drive, network, company intranet, or the Web. Explorer-style windows have a Web-browser look and features. You can use Internet Explorer to access local information by keying the path in the Address bar or clicking an item on the Favorites list.

MOUSE TIP

You can display four taskbar toolbars: Quick Launch, Address, Links, and Desktop. The Quick Launch toolbar appears on the taskbar by default. You can also create additional toolbars from other folders or subfolders and you can add folder or file shortcuts to an existing taskbar toolbar. To view other taskbar toolbars, right-click the taskbar, point to Toolbars, and then click the desired toolbar name.

appendix
A

buttons on the Explorer toolbar or the Back or Forward commands on the Go menu to switch between My Computer and the Control Panel. To view My Computer:

Step 1	*Click*	the Back button ⬅ on the Explorer toolbar to view My Computer
Step 2	*Click*	the Forward button ➡ on the Explorer toolbar to view the Control Panel
Step 3	*Click*	Go on the menu bar
Step 4	*Click*	the My Computer command to view My Computer
Step 5	*Click*	the Close button ✖ on the My Computer window title bar

A.d Using the Start Menu

The **Start button** on the taskbar opens the Start menu. You use this menu to access several Windows 98 features and to open software applications, such as Word or Excel. To open the Start menu:

Step 1	*Click*	the Start button 🟦Start on the taskbar to open the Start menu (see Figure A-3)

FIGURE A-3
Start Menu

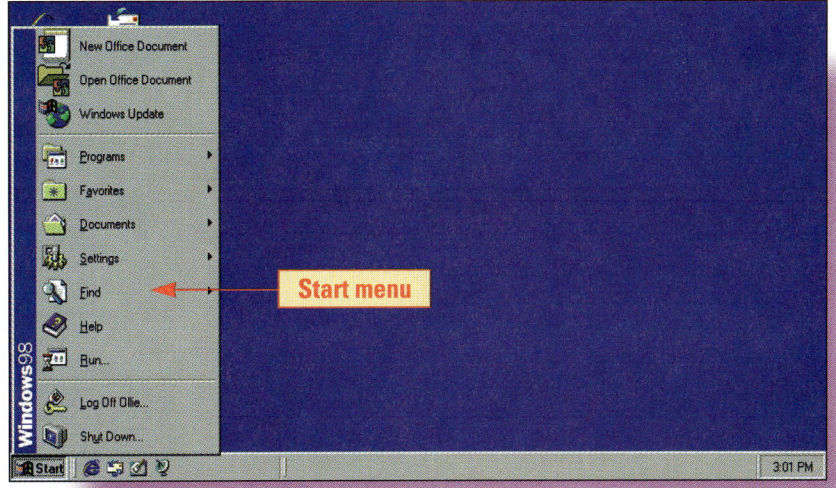

Step 2	*Point to*	Programs to view the software applications installed on your computer
Step 3	*Click*	the desktop outside the Start menu and Programs menu to close them

A.e Reviewing Dialog Box Options

A **dialog box** is a window that contains options you can select, turn on, or turn off to perform a task. To view a dialog box:

Step 1	*Click*	the Start button ![Start] on the taskbar
Step 2	*Point to*	Settings
Step 3	*Point to*	Active Desktop
Step 4	*Click*	Customize my Desktop to open the Display Properties dialog box
Step 5	*Click*	the Effects tab (see Figure A-4)

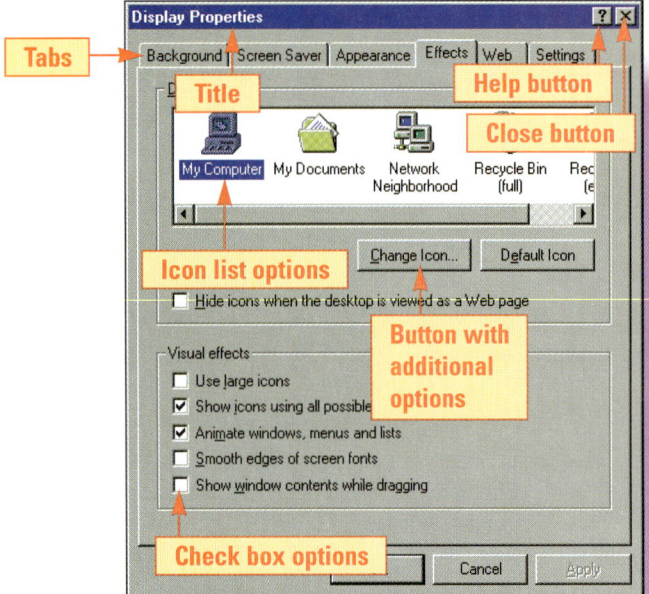

FIGURE A-4
Effects Tab in the Display Properties Dialog Box

Step 6	*Click*	each tab and observe the different options available *(do not change any options unless directed by your instructor)*
Step 7	*Right-click*	each option on each tab and then click What's This? to view its ScreenTip
Step 8	*Click*	Cancel to close the dialog box without changing any options

appendix
A

QUICK TIP

Many of the Windows 98 shortcuts are also available in Windows 95 and NT 4.0 if you have Internet Explorer 4.0 or later and Windows Desktop Update installed.

A.f Using Windows 98 Shortcuts

You can use the drag-and-drop method to reposition or remove Start menu commands. You can also right-drag a Start menu command to the desktop to create a desktop shortcut. To reposition the Windows Update item on the Start menu:

Step 1	*Click*	the Start button **Start** on the taskbar
Step 2	*Point to*	the Windows Update item
Step 3	*Drag*	the Windows Update item to the top of the Start menu

To remove the Windows Update shortcut from the Start menu and create a desktop shortcut:

Step 1	*Drag*	the Windows Update item to the desktop
Step 2	*Observe*	that the desktop shortcut appears after a few seconds
Step 3	*Verify*	that the Windows Update item no longer appears on the Start menu

To add a Windows Update shortcut back to the Start menu and delete the desktop shortcut:

Step 1	*Drag*	the Windows Update shortcut to the Start button **Start** on the taskbar and then back to its original position when the Start menu appears
Step 2	*Close*	the Start menu
Step 3	*Drag*	the Windows Update shortcut on the desktop to the Recycle Bin
Step 4	*Click*	Yes

You can close multiple application windows at one time from the taskbar using the CTRL key and a shortcut menu. To open two applications and then use the taskbar to close them:

| Step 1 | *Open* | the Word and Excel applications (in this order) from the Programs menu on the Start menu |

MOUSE TIP

One way to speed up tasks is to single-click (rather than double-click) a desktop icon just like you single-click a Web page hyperlink. You can create a Web-style, single-click environment by opening the Folder Options dialog box from the View menu in any Windows 98 Explorer-style window or from the Settings command on the Start menu. The Web Style option adds an underline to icon titles, similar to a hyperlink.

Step 2	*Observe*	the Word and Excel buttons on the taskbar (Excel is the selected, active button)
Step 3	*Press & Hold*	the CTRL key
Step 4	*Click*	the Word application taskbar button (the Excel application taskbar button is already selected)
Step 5	*Release*	the CTRL key
Step 6	*Right-click*	the Word or Excel taskbar button
Step 7	*Click*	Close to close both applications

You can use the drag-and-drop method to add a shortcut to the Quick Launch toolbar for folders and documents you have created. To create a new subfolder in the My Documents folder.

Step 1	*Click*	the My Documents icon on the desktop to open the window
Step 2	*Right-click*	the contents area (but not a file or folder)
Step 3	*Point to*	New
Step 4	*Click*	Folder
Step 5	*Key*	Example
Step 6	*Press*	the ENTER key to name the folder
Step 7	*Drag*	the Example folder to the end of the Quick Launch toolbar (a black vertical line indicates the drop position)
Step 8	*Observe*	the new icon on the toolbar
Step 9	*Close*	the My Documents window
Step 10	*Position*	the mouse pointer on the Example folder shortcut on the Quick Launch toolbar and observe the ScreenTip

You remove a shortcut from the Quick Launch toolbar by dragging it to the desktop and deleting it, or dragging it directly to the Recycle Bin. To remove the Example folder shortcut and delete the folder:

Step 1	*Drag*	the Example folder icon to the Recycle Bin
Step 2	*Click*	Yes
Step 3	*Open*	the My Documents window
Step 4	*Delete*	the Example folder icon using the shortcut menu
Step 5	*Close*	the My Documents window

appendix
A

A.g Understanding the Recycle Bin

The **Recycle Bin** is an object that temporarily stores folders, files, and shortcuts you delete from your hard drive. If you accidentally delete an item, you can restore it to its original location on your hard drive if it is still in the Recycle Bin. Because the Recycle Bin takes up disk space you should review and empty it regularly. When you empty the Recycle Bin, its contents are removed from your hard drive and can no longer be restored.

A.h Shutting Down Windows 98

It is very important that you follow the proper procedures for shutting down the Windows 98 operating system when you are finished, to allow the operating system to complete its internal "housekeeping" properly. To shut down Windows 98 correctly:

| Step 1 | *Click* | the Start button ![Start] on the taskbar |
| Step 2 | *Click* | Shut Down to open the Shut Down Windows dialog box shown in Figure A-5 |

FIGURE A-5
Shut Down Windows
Dialog Box

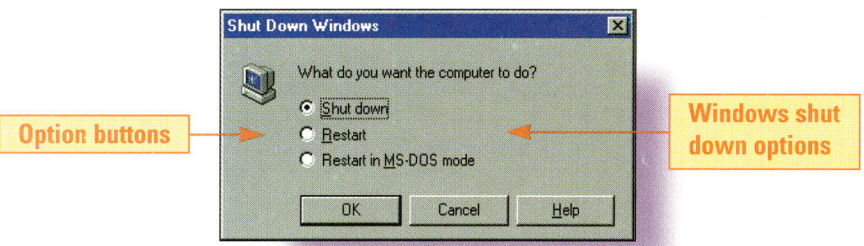

You can shut down completely, restart, and restart in MS-DOS mode from this dialog box. You want to shut down completely.

| Step 3 | *Click* | the Shut down option button to select it, if necessary |
| Step 4 | *Click* | OK |

Managing Your Folders and Files Using Windows Explorer

W Appendix Overview

Windows Explorer provides tools for managing your folders and files. This appendix introduces the Windows Explorer options of expanding and collapsing the folder view, creating new folders, renaming folders and files, deleting folders and files, and creating desktop shortcuts.

LEARNING OBJECTIVES

▶ Open Windows Explorer
▶ Review Windows Explorer options
▶ Create a new folder
▶ Move and copy folders and files
▶ Rename folders and files
▶ Create desktop shortcuts
▶ Delete folders and files

appendix

notes The default Windows 98 Custom folder options are used in the hands-on activities and figures. If you are using the Windows 95 operating system, your instructor will modify the hands-on activities and your screen will look different.

B.a Opening Windows Explorer

You can open Windows Explorer from the <u>P</u>rograms command on the Start menu or from a shortcut menu. To open Windows Explorer using a shortcut menu:

Step 1	*Right-Click*	the Start button **Start** on the taskbar
Step 2	*Click*	<u>E</u>xplore
Step 3	*Maximize*	the Windows Explorer window, if necessary (see Figure B-1)

FIGURE B-1
Windows Explorer
Window

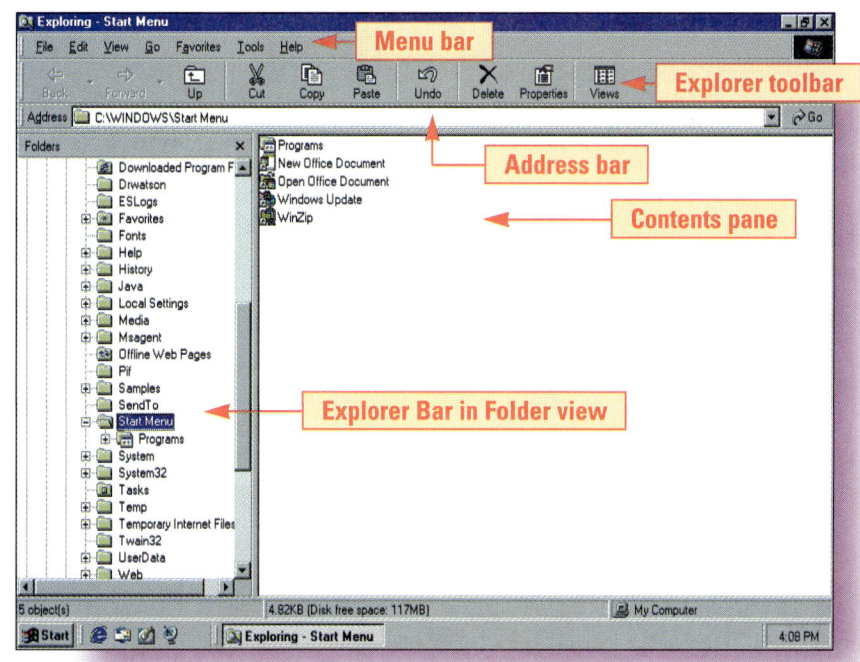

The window below the menu bar, toolbar, and Address bar is divided into two panes: The **Explorer Bar** on the left shows the computer's organizational structure, including all desktop objects, My Computer objects, and the disk drive folders. The **Contents pane** on the right shows all subfolders and files for the folder selected in the Explorer Bar. The panes are divided by a **separator bar** that you drag left or right to resize the panes.

B.b Reviewing Windows Explorer Options

You can view disk drive icons, folders, and files (called **objects**) for your computer by selecting an item from the Address bar list or by clicking an object in the Explorer Bar. To view all your computer's disk drives and system folders:

Step 1	*Click*	the Address bar list arrow
Step 2	*Click*	My Computer to view a list of disk drives and system folders in the Contents pane
Step 3	*Click*	the (C:) disk drive object in the Explorer Bar to view a list of folders (stored on the C:\ drive) in the Contents pane

You can expand or collapse the view of folders and other objects in the Explorer Bar. To collapse the view of the C:\ drive in the Explorer Bar:

Step 1	*Click*	the minus sign (–) to the left of the (C:) disk drive object in the Explorer Bar
Step 2	*Observe*	that the C:\ drive folders list is hidden and the minus sign becomes a plus sign (+)
Step 3	*Click*	the plus sign (+) to the left of the (C:) disk drive object in the Explorer Bar
Step 4	*Observe*	that the list of folders stored on the C:\ drive is again visible

You can view a folder's contents by clicking the folder in the Explorer Bar or double-clicking the folder in the Contents pane. To view the contents of the folder that contains the Data Files:

Step 1	*Click*	the disk drive in the Explorer Bar where the Data Files are stored

appendix
B

Step 2	Double-click	the Data Files folder in the Contents pane (scroll, if necessary) to view a list of Data Files and folders

You can resize and reposition folders and files in the Contents pane and add more details about the file size, type, and date modified. To change the size and position of the Data Files and folders:

Step 1	Click	the Views button list arrow ▦▾ on the Explorer toolbar
Step 2	Click	Large Icons to view horizontal rows of larger folder and file icons in the Contents pane
Step 3	Click	Small Icons on the Views button list to view horizontal rows of smaller folder and file icons in the Contents pane
Step 4	Click	Details on the Views button list to view a vertical list of folders and files names, sizes, types, and dates modified
Step 5	Click	List on the Views button list to view a simple list of the files and folders

B.c Creating a New Folder

You can create a new folder for an object in the Explorer Bar or the Contents pane. To add a folder to the My Documents folder in the C:\ drive folder list:

Step 1	Click	the My Documents folder in the Explorer Bar to select it (scroll, if necessary)
Step 2	Click	File
Step 3	Point to	New
Step 4	Click	Folder
Step 5	Observe	the newly created folder object in the Contents pane with the selected temporary name New Folder

To name the folder and refresh the Explorer Bar view:

Step 1	Key	Practice Folder
Step 2	Press	the ENTER key
Step 3	Observe	the new folder name in the Contents pane
Step 4	Click	View

Step 5	*Click*	Refresh
Step 6	*Observe*	that the My Documents folder has a plus sign, indicating that the folder list can be expanded

B.d Moving and Copying Folders and Files

You select folders and files by clicking them. You can then copy or move them with the Cut, Copy and Paste commands on the Edit menu or shortcut menu, the Copy and Paste buttons on the Explorer toolbar, or with the drag-and-drop or right-drag mouse methods. To copy a file from the Data Files folder to the Practice Folder using the right-drag method:

Step 1	*View*	the list of Data Files in the Contents pane
Step 2	*Right-drag*	any file to the My Documents folder in the Explorer Bar and pause until the My Documents folder expands to show the subfolders
Step 3	*Continue*	to right-drag the file to the Practice Folder subfolder under the My Documents folder in the Explorer Bar
Step 4	*Click*	Copy Here on the shortcut menu
Step 5	*Click*	the Practice Folder in the Explorer Bar to view the copied file's icon and filename in the Contents pane

B.e Renaming Folders and Files

Sometimes you want to change an existing file or folder name to a more descriptive name. To rename the copied file in the Practice Folder:

Step 1	*Verify*	the icon and filename for the copied file appears in the Contents pane
Step 2	*Right-click*	the copied file in the Contents pane
Step 3	*Click*	Rename
Step 4	*Key*	Renamed File
Step 5	*Click*	the Contents area (not the filename) to accept the new filename

---

MOUSE TIP

You can use the SHIFT + Click method to select adjacent multiple folders and files in the Contents pane by clicking the first item to select it, holding down the SHIFT key, and then clicking the last item. You can use the CTRL + Click method to select nonadjacent files and folders in the Contents pane by clicking the first item, holding down the CTRL key, and then clicking each additional item.

MENU TIP

You can quickly copy a file to a disk from a hard disk or network drive, create a desktop shortcut, or send the file as an attachment to an e-mail message by right-clicking the file, pointing to Send To, and clicking the appropriate command.

appendix B

QUICK TIP

To erase all the files stored on a disk, you can reformat it. Insert a used disk in drive A, right-click the drive A icon in the Explorer Bar, and click For_mat. Specify the disk's capacity. Select the _Full option to erase all files and check the disk for bad sectors. Click the _Start button.

B.f Creating Desktop Shortcuts

You can add a shortcut for folders and files to the Windows desktop by restoring the Windows Explorer window to a smaller window and right-dragging a folder or file icon to the desktop. You can also right-drag a folder or file icon to the Desktop icon in the Explorer Bar inside the Windows Explorer window. To create a desktop shortcut to the Practice Folder using the Desktop icon:

Step 1	*Expand*	the My Documents folder in the Explorer Bar, if necessary, to view the Practice Folder subfolder
Step 2	*Right-drag*	the Practice Folder to the Desktop icon at the top of the Explorer Bar
Step 3	*Click*	Create _Shortcut(s) Here
Step 4	*Minimize*	the Windows Explorer window to view the new shortcut on the desktop
Step 5	*Drag*	the Shortcut to Practice Folder desktop shortcut to the Recycle Bin to delete it
Step 6	*Click*	_Yes
Step 7	*Click*	the Exploring-Practice Folder taskbar button to maximize the Windows Explorer window

MOUSE TIP

You can delete a file or folder by dragging or right-dragging it to the Recycle Bin object on the desktop or the Recycle Bin object in the Explorer Bar. If you hold down the SHIFT key while dragging the file or folder to the Recycle Bin, Windows deletes the file or folder without placing it in the Recycle Bin.

B.g Deleting Folders and Files

When necessary, you can delete a folder and its contents or a file by selecting it and then clicking the _Delete command on the _File menu or shortcut menu, or pressing the DELETE key. You can also delete multiple selected folders and files at one time. To delete the Practice Folder and its contents:

Step 1	*Click*	the Practice Folder in the Explorer Bar to select it, if necessary
Step 2	*Press*	the DELETE key
Step 3	*Click*	_Yes to send the folder and its contents to the Recycle Bin